PHL
D1576678

To illustrate the monuments

John Piper
Pentre Ifan

To illustrate the monuments

*

Essays on archaeology presented to Stuart Piggott

CBE, B.Litt, D.Litt, DHL, FBA, FSA, FRSE
Abercromby Professor of Prehistoric Archaeology
in the University of Edinburgh

on the occasion of
his sixty-fifth birthday

Edited by
J. V. S. Megaw

THAMES AND HUDSON
LONDON

Printed in Great Britain
at the Alden Press, Oxford

Contents

Editorial Preface

In 1723 at the Fountain Tavern in London's Strand, William Stukeley was addressing the 'pretorium' of the Society of Roman Knights, an antiquarian club for the study of Roman Britain which he had founded with some friends in the previous year. 'The business of this Society', said Stukeley, 'is to search for and illustrate the Roman monuments in the Britannic Isles . . . we are . . . to be the Secretarys, the interpreters and preservers of the memorials of our ancestors.' Those who wish to learn more about the Society of Roman Knights must turn to Stuart Piggott's own study of William Stukeley, and although his self-chosen nick-name is selected from the works of Kenneth Grahame and bears no relation to the Asterix-like Chyndonax and Cartismandua chosen by Stukeley and his wife, this eighteenth-century archaeological manifesto seems to me admirably to sum up Stuart Piggott's own major contributions to his subject, both as lecturer and researcher. As he himself has said, although he has done his fair share of field work and excavation, his prime concern has been to produce works of synthesis and interpretation. Eschewing temporal or spatial boundaries Stuart Piggott has regarded the world of archaeology as an oyster to be savoured whole and not simply to be subjected to the minutiae of macrofaunal and calorific analyses. At a time when the discipline of prehistory seems to be indulging in the dubious pleasures of agonizing self-dissection, Stuart Piggott both innovates and conserves his interests. As is to be expected of one who has studied the elusive world of the ancient Celts, his views may from time to time change shape and meaning, but they never lose sight of the essentially human and humane origins of his chosen discipline.

In 1968 a number of Stuart Piggott's former pupils and colleagues returned the compliment of his dedication to them of his *Ancient Europe from the beginnings of agriculture to classical antiquity* by assembling a first collection of essays under the title of *Studies in Ancient Europe*.

The present volume extends its horizon beyond Europe to the Americas where he received his first doctorate. There are also contributions on Asia where archaeology and Stuart Piggott paradoxically gained so much by the fortunes of war. Since he is not only an antiquary living in Sir Walter Scott's own city, but a poet and a painter, it seemed only proper to include birthday tributes to celebrate these aspects also of Stuart Piggott's talents. As a twice-dubbed knight of Mark Twain and one who is immortalized elsewhere as

'Piggott the taxi-driver', it seems also fitting to include here a long overdue summary of the role of the archaeologist in fiction. Only evidence of Stuart Piggott, the star of television, is missing although his producer is not.

It has been remarked that *Festschriften* such as this are nowadays an expensive anachronism. Since the present volume is primarily intended to give pleasure to a single and singular individual, friend, colleague and teacher, I am particularly grateful to all those who have so readily and wholeheartedly assisted in the realization of what has truly been a labour of love. My own friends and former colleagues at Thames and Hudson have generously aided every stage of the planning and have, of course, assumed responsibility for the production of this project. It is a matter of deep regret to us all that two of the contributors have not lived to see its completion.

It seems a far cry from the seventeen-year-old Reading Museum assistant to the internationally renowned professor completing his third decade of occupancy of the Abercromby Chair; no single volume can adequately reflect every aspect of the past and present of either the man or his work. None the less, we all hope that when Stuart Piggott leafs through these pages he will feel ready to partake unhesitatingly of the champion's portion of meat and wine which is so justly his.

Leicester, 28 May 1975 VINCENT MEGAW

Drawing by Brian Hope-Taylor

Stuart, I sit here in a grateful haze
Recalling those spontaneous Berkshire days
In straw-thatched,
                    chalk-built,
                                        pre-War
                                                            Uffington
Before the March of Progress had begun,
When all the world seemed waiting to be won,
When evening air with mignonette was scented,
And 'picture-windows' had not been invented,
When shooting foxes still was thought unsporting,
And White Horse Hill was still the place for courting,
When church was still the usual place for marriages
And carriage-lamps were only used for carriages.

How pleased your parents were in their retirement
The garden and yourself their chief requirement.
Your father, now his teaching days were over,
Back in his native Berkshire lived in clover.
Your cheerful mother loyally concealed
Her inward hankering for Petersfield.
For Hampshire Downs were the first Downs you saw
And Heywood Sumner taught you there to draw.

Under great elms which rustled overhead
By stile and foot-bridge village pathways led
To cottage gardens heavy with the flower
Of fruit and vegetables towards your tower
St Mary, Uffington, famed now as then
The perfect Parker's Glossary specimen
Of purest Early English, tall and pale,
—To tourists Cathedral of the Vale
To us the church. I'm glad that I survive
To greet you, Stuart, now you're sixty-five.

John Betjeman

NOTE Following current convention, uncorrected (i.e. non-calibrated) radiocarbon dates are indicated with lower-case letters thus: 1125 bc. BP designates 'before the present' or before AD 1950.

1

LILI KAELAS

Cultural Heritage, Archaeological Museums, and Public Opinion[1]

1 Translated by Birgitta Frykman

In Scandinavian countries, and particularly in Sweden, the duties of archaeological museums are undergoing a transformation. The discipline of archaeology is likewise being transformed from – in some respects – previous exclusiveness to social orientation and utility. It has, in other words, followed and adapted itself to the development of society.

Much of the change is due to an unprecedented concern about environment. A general interest in the problems of pollution, mismanagement of land and other resources, and disturbances in the ecological balance has been awakened, and public attention is increasingly being focused on the man-made environment. The general public has become aware of the fact that our physical surroundings are largely a cultural product and that this is true of agricultural landscapes and forests no less than cities and industrial landscapes. The man in the street has discovered the values of existing milieus – the heritage of a remote or more recent past. This discovery has created an active interest in the care and protection of the familiar surroundings when bulldozers threaten to destroy them. During the last decade the attitudes and actions of politicians in dealing with the planning and preservation of existing environments have been influenced by public opinion and pressure groups. Political and administrative decisions have been taken with regard to public opinion in order to secure and guarantee the economic means necessary for the practical protection of our cultural heritage.

Needless to say, this development has influenced archaeological museums and their activities.[2] Only ten to fifteen years ago Swedish archaeologists employed in museums could choose their subject of research freely. Though this freedom still exists, it is no longer unconditional. Society's demand for museum services, including the preservation of ancient man-made environments, has influenced the choice of research topics. Museums today are less focused on isolated study of artifacts and more directed towards environmental problems than previously.

The recent government statement expressed in the 'Culture Proposition' of 1974, to the effect that the preservation of cultural heritage is one of the most important goals of the total cultural policy,[3] is a challenge to the museums. It implies planning and management of the cultural heritage of the country in the same way as is done when natural and other resources are exploited. To achieve the intended result in practical work, this new approach presupposes that the work for the protection of the cultural heritage is linked not only to special archaeological and historical institutes and museums but also to communal, regional and provincial authorities. This kind of collaboration offers the only chance for museums and institutes to be consulted at an early enough stage when the preservation of complete environments is involved.

What influence will this new cultural policy have on the current work of archaeological museums? Before describing the practical work, some intro-

---

[2] In Scandinavian countries archaeological museums are often called either 'historical' or 'national' museums. The first-mentioned title is also used for historical museums proper, that is, museums with collections of furniture and period objects from upper- (and occasionally middle-) class urban or country homes as well as folk-life collections, usually dating from the sixteenth century, or in rare cases, from the Middle Ages to the present day. A 'national' museum in Sweden, on the other hand, corresponds to an art gallery in international terminology. In Denmark, however, the National Museum, Copenhagen, houses prehistoric, historical, ethnological and ethnographical collections. Thus, the name 'Historical Museum' does not always describe the real field of work of the museum in question.

[3] The Australian Federal Government's statement (also in 1974) on the National Heritage demonstrates a very similar growing awareness in the Antipodes. *Ed.*

ductory words need to be said about monuments and the man-made landscape, in what I hope will be an acceptable illustration of my respect for Stuart Piggott.

The physical environment is first of all a product of the combined effects on the landscape by man, tradition and innovation, which have caused a large variety of types and patterns. Depending on man's relation to his environment, the quality of his impact varies in strength and character. This has been, and still is, dependent on the technological level of the socio-economic systems for the provision of food and other necessities in the society in question. In the remote past the impact on nature was limited to the spade in man's hand. Over the last century these limits have been diminishing and are now entirely removed. Due to this development, conflicts between modern exploitation and ancient landscapes, including old town centres and similar sites, arise almost daily in industrialized countries. This is the case in Sweden as well. Since we are aware that modern society must have its chance just as the old environment must, a clash between them can be prevented only when we are prepared to act in time. This requires collaboration with the authorities responsible for the planning and management of our physical environment.

The first condition for such collaboration is that the specialized authorities, including for instance archaeological museums, should have a thorough knowledge of old environments not only as regards the region in question but in a larger area. Consequently the central authority should possess a general plan for the whole country, especially as the current interest in different parts of the cultural landscape varies with the demands from the living environment. By and large the ancient landscapes can be divided into two categories: fossil landscapes and those in continuous use. In Sweden the fossil ones are mainly prehistoric, although fossil industrial sites are frequent too. Fossil urban sites are rare in Sweden. As all ancient sites cannot be preserved, the selection for preservation must be carefully prepared. It cannot be done at random but requires systematic action. For this purpose a survey of existing material is needed. The surveys of prehistoric monuments in Sweden cover almost the whole country. All the monuments have been recorded according to the same system. Besides a classification according to the type and the number of visible graves, the collected information includes geographical and topographical information, morphological characteristics, and descriptions of the present state of the setting of the monument. It also lists previous records and investigations as well as folklore and other traditions relating to the monument and/or its topographical setting. As the same system has been applied throughout the country, the surveys are of an equivalent standard and fully compatible, and constitute an excellent basis for further research, not least with regard to selection for preservation.

As regards buildings, the situation is not so uniformly satisfactory. Systematic surveys do not exist for all types of buildings. Most surveys have so far been carried out along individual lines and are selective. This is a handicap, especially when the material has to be classified and evaluated. There are gaps in the inventories particularly for less outstanding buildings. There is a considerable lack in the inventories of crofters' cottages and other simple local house types in the countryside and, in towns and urban districts, of ordinary buildings such as apartment houses, one-family houses, small shops, and kiosks.

Both the classification and evaluation of sites should be made with regard to the country as a whole, as well as to the area and region in question. This implies evaluation on at least two if not three different levels. Up to the present time evaluation has been based on the cultural and historical value of the site. In the last few years a new concept is, however, gaining ground. The sites are evaluated – sometimes mainly on the ground just mentioned – according to their rôle in the environment in question. A new national economic map which shows prehistoric and historic monuments (including prehistoric and historic habitation sites invisible above the ground but known through excavations, finds, or written records) offers a good aid for the study of the relationship between the monuments and their settings, especially as regards cultivated fields, forests, and farmsteads, as well as other settlements.

As a rule traditional attitudes have determined the selection of objects to be preserved and conserved. The unique or most impressive monuments have come to predominate. There are, however, now no objections to giving high priority to the biggest or most remarkable monuments of the country, such as the so-called 'royal mounds', the largest grave-fields with up to a thousand graves, and the comparatively rare megalithic tombs, rock-carvings and rock-paintings, pictorial stones, rune stones, forts or remains of medieval forts and castles, medieval churches, monuments commemorating social functions and important events in the country's history.

1 Björkö, an island in Lake Mälaren, Adelsö parish, Uppland: the town area, the so-called 'black earth', can be seen in the foreground; the fort lies to the north of the road.

2 Björkö, an island in Lake Mälaren: gravefield of about 2000 mounds, the so-called '*Hemlanden*'. All the prehistoric remains and their environment (the largest part of the island) are under permanent protection. The town area, the fort and the large gravefield belong to the Viking Age and constitute one of the most important records for the history of the country.

All these categories are not only comparatively rare but also original historical records.

The fossil urban site on the island of Björkö in Lake Mälaren can be mentioned as an example of the class of outstanding monuments. Together with a hill-fort, and a grave-field having more than 2000 mounds, this site is dated to the Viking period and must of course be regarded as one of the most important historical records in the country. Consequently the whole area – in practice the whole island – should be preserved forever. This was realized as early as 1912 and preservation work began when the State bought some 150 hectares of land. At that time the area was to a large extent tree-covered or otherwise in a state less favourable for the preservation of monuments. The large-scale restoration of agricultural and pastoral landscape – the traditional surroundings of this type of monument – began comparatively late, in the early 1930s. Today the entire area has been restored to the traditional type of landscape of the eighteenth and nineteenth centuries AD (*Ills. 1, 2*).

High priority must also be given in the future to comparatively rare monuments such as megalithic tombs, rock-carvings, rune stones, and 'stone ships' (*Ills. 3, 4*). Besides the rare and impressive monuments (*Ill. 5*) there are numerous less outstanding ones (*Ills. 6, 7*). These 'ordinary' monuments also record the past of the country and, for the study of its history, are no less important than the first category. Their frequency alone indicates that they are the memorials of the majority of the past population. Thus the country cannot afford to lose all such sites. How to make an adequate selection of both categories is a difficult problem and one of the most crucial in our practical work. To secure an adequate quantity for preservation, our evaluations must be made according to a scale quite different from those previously employed. The new approach to this problem claims that the guiding criteria for selection must be dependent on the frequency, age, and historical content of these ordinary monuments in the area of their occurrence.

From the above it can be concluded that the two categories of monuments – what have been termed here the outstanding ones and the ordinary ones – must be evaluated separately and not according to the same scale and criteria as have been used up to now (Janson 1974). Otherwise we risk the loss of a great many records relating to the settlement history and the social development of the majority of the population.

Although a new attitude towards the evaluation

3 Among the more remarkable Iron Age monuments are cemeteries with mounds and so-called 'stone ships'. Today most of them are protected, including the big 'stone ship' next to Anund's Mound near Västerås, Badelunda parish, Västmanland.

4 The 'stone ship' at Blomsholm, Skee parish, Bohuslän, is the second largest in Sweden. Thanks to the surrounding farmland, which is still being cultivated, its impressive monumentality can be fully appreciated.

5 Monumental coastal cairns dating to the Bronze Age line the shores and are clearly visible from the sea. The open country around them, which is part of the area subject to preservation, is a prerequisite for an understanding of the aims of the cairn builders. Näskroken, Örmanäs village, Örmvalla parish, Halland.

6 Less impressive cairns than those at Näskroken also exist. There is a group of one medium-sized and several small and almost insignificant ones at Fåglevik, Björlanda beach, Gothenburg.

7 On the west coast of Sweden gravefields are usually very modest in size and appearance. In view of their frequency, however, they must also be included in the selection of remains and environments for preservation. In the foreground can be seen the gravefield at Kalshed, Säve, Gothenburg, comprising six graves. Almost all of them are insignificant and practically invisible to the untrained eye.

8 Preservation of an area with prehistoric remains at Karla Högar, Västerbitterna parish, Västergötland, has been possible through the application of the Nature Preservation Law. The black lines mark the different groups of monuments on the ridge. To protect the whole ridge, quarrying for gravel has been stopped in the area between the prehistoric sites following the withholding of permission by the county administration, based on the Nature Protection Law. The landowner was compensated for his economic losses out of public funds.

of the ordinary monuments is gaining ground, application in practice still has its problems. In Sweden the preservation of the cultural heritage is considered a public matter which should not be dependent on the undertakings of individual citizens. Consequently it is based on laws and regulations (Kaelas 1972). Among these the Swedish Ancient Monuments Act of 1942 is the only one that provides unconditional protection of all ancient monuments. But this law in itself is unsatisfactory in some respects, for instance in cases of a conflict of interest between the desires to exploit the ground and to preserve the ancient monuments. According to the law, permission to remove an ancient monument must be granted if the obstructions and disadvantages caused by it are unreasonable in relation to its importance. The wording of the law implies an estimation of what is reasonable. In reality it often proves difficult to decide what is reasonable, when both cultural and economic values are set against each other and when the ancient monument does not appear very spectacular on the surface. From the cultural point of view a successful result is thus dependent on a consistent line of action in cultural politics to prevent chance decisions. The prerequisites, then, include a high level of preparedness on the research side, so that facts in support of the interests of historical preservation can rapidly be brought to light.

In truth, the problems are even greater when one is forced to apply the Ancient Monuments Act for the protection of the environment where relatively large areas are concerned. As a typical instance of such problems and the possibilities of solving them, a specific case of the need for protection can be mentioned. In the southern, western and central parts of Sweden the landscape is characterized by undulating plains and moraine ridges. From the agricultural point of view such areas are not particularly fertile, but they are rich in visible prehistoric monuments. In prehistoric times these natural obstacles were suitable for Iron Age settlement with an economy based on the extensive use of the damp clay plains. Today the moraines are extensively exploited for gravel and sand. The monuments on the moraine ridges can be preserved through the Ancient Monuments Act, but the law can only protect the environment of the monument to a certain extent. On the ridges there is, however, often more than one group of graves, each of which certainly corresponds to one of the contemporary settlements. The groups of graves often lie so far apart that the intervening ground is too extensive to be included in the area which can be protected

by the Ancient Monuments Act. On the other hand, from an absolute point of view the ridge with the groups of barrows forms a unity with the surrounding agricultural landscape. A division resulting from the exploitation of the ground between the grave groups would not only destroy the unity but would also make the comprehensive experience of the growth and development of settlement meaningless. Collaborations with, and application of, the Nature Protection Law has therefore taken place in several cases. A typical example (*Ill. 8*) is a moraine ridge with Iron Age barrows in the south of Sweden in the parish of Västerbitterna, Västergötland county. Through the Ancient Monuments Act it proved possible to preserve both the three groups of graves and their immediate surroundings. But the areas between the groups were planned to be quarried for gravel, and the distance between the groups was too wide to be included as a whole in the environment of the monument. To have done so would not have been 'reasonable' according to the Ancient Monuments Act. To preserve the whole ridge the Nature Protection Law was applied by adducing the beauty of the scenery. Permission to use the ground as a gravel pit was not granted but the landowner was compensated by the government for loss of income.

9 Stensjö village, Oskarshamn, Småland, is an example of a whole area being preserved through private donation. The village developed in the eighteenth century and now comprises some 520 hectares, including 20 hectares of in-fields and 47 hectares of grassland and pastures. The small stony in-fields are older than the village itself. The road through the village was built in the 1920s. The original thoroughfare cut across the west edge of the village (not visible here). The village was bought in 1960 and restored in 1960–69. It is now owned by the Swedish Royal Academy of Letters.

10 Stensjö village. Detail of a farm.

Problems of this kind are often brought to extremes in cases involving the preservation of extensive cultural landscapes containing remains from historic as well as prehistoric times. Such sites illustrate the relation between the ecology and prehistoric man, but are also visible examples of development from the Late Iron Age through medieval settlement down to modern times. These areas are usually found in rural districts or in previously rural parts which have now been incorporated into towns. They include different traces and types of settlement, and here the preservation of practically every feature is important for the understanding of the development of settlement. In addition, some parts are of great importance for the type of environment, such as groups of buildings in relation to each other, or former roads and the topography of the rest of the area. With the present legislation, the difficulties are most apparent when it comes to the protection of total environments. This is particularly true of that part of the environment which contains nothing more spectacular than the ordinary run of buildings. It has often proved difficult to convince authorities and politicians of the value and importance of seemingly common features, for instance in a village the area around a railway station or a suburb. In recent years a certain change of attitude has occurred, not least as a result of public opinion. In some cases it has been possible to arrive at an understanding of the importance of also protecting the commonplace buildings as interesting both in themselves, and as a complement to the so-called culturally and historically important buildings in order to gain a full picture of the historical and social development of a local community (*Ills. 12, 13*). But if such an environment cannot be saved on the basis of argument, there is at present no law which makes it possible to create a cultural reserve approximately corresponding to the national parks envisaged by the Nature Protection Law.

In some instances it has been feasible to save a uniform and comparatively well-preserved rural milieu through the acquisition of the whole area. This can be exemplified by the village of Stensjö, Oskarshamn (*Ills. 9–11*), occupying an area of some 520 hectares. This village was saved for posterity through a private donation and is now owned by the Swedish Royal Academy of Letters (*Kungl. Vitterhetsakademien*). The village originally developed during the eighteenth century. Farming ceased in 1945 and the village was almost totally derelict when it was bought in 1960. Several houses had been pulled down, fields and pastures were overgrown. Today the fields are cultivated and the pastures grazed as in former times.

Evidently the saving of a total settlement and its surroundings through purchase, and its subsequent regeneration through a source of livelihood carried out according to old methods, is exceptional. It presupposes that the owners want to sell instead of changing their source of livelihood to something more profitable, as for instance forestry, and the possibilities of such a purchase are usually dependent on donations made specially for the purpose. On the other hand, there are alternative ways of saving a total environment. This presupposes a new line of action in cultural politics, but above all a change of attitude amongst the authorities responsible for the protection of the cultural heritage, to which museums also belong. Up to now officialdom has as a rule used prohibitions to enact its interests. This is of course necessary in some cases and will remain so in the future. But for those who serve as consultants on cultural matters to local planning authorities, the normal procedure ought to be to work along the lines of specific positive suggestions rather than prohibitions, and to give advice as to how the area or the buildings could find new and economically justifiable uses when their present functions cannot be continued.

In the case of prehistoric monuments the areas to be preserved can be regarded as public domain – which in fact they are. Such areas could be formed in cooperation with representatives of, among others, those whose duty it is to preserve history and nature. In order to preserve old buildings it is necessary to find new usages when the old functions have ceased. It can be difficult to find such alternatives if preparatory work has not been done. No matter how favourable the attitude to preservation, it is clear that the problems cannot be satisfactorily solved through a purely 'museological' attitude that buildings should be left standing but remain unused except as museums. We must never forget that preservation and protection also have important economic aspects. The goal of preservation should include keeping the surroundings populated and alive, either as recreational areas or as other public

11 Stensjö village. Part of restored outhouses.

12 Ålem, Pataholm. A densely built-up area which is going to be preserved.

13 Ålem, Pataholm. Detail of the same urban environment.

places within which ancient monuments are sited, or else steps should be taken to ensure that those areas are allowed to live on as urban environments with new functions. There is a wide range of variation from a fossil to a living environment, and the persons responsible must be prepared to suggest uses. Only then can we feel confident and assured that preservation and protection are carried out in an unartificial way.

The reasons for preserving urban environments with a predominance of dwelling-houses are not only historical, but also concern housing policies and public economy. Many people prefer to live in old, centrally positioned residential areas rather than moving to modern suburbs. This is true not only of historically interesting environments, architecturally laid out, but also of more ordinary dwellings such as for instance industrial or artisans' housing. This has also been emphasized in a new report on clearing policies (Sanering 1971–3; 1974). In practice the new attitude to town centres and town districts has influenced building developers to start the reconstruction of old residential houses.

The changed attitude to environmental problems presupposes an adequate education on the part of the staff of museums and institutes for the preservation of the cultural heritage. So far, such personnel (not least in the archaeological museums, in which I have gained my own personal experience and which take a central place in this paper) have obtained their professional training and skill through practical work. This is particularly true of duties which involve planning and cooperation with planning authorities (Kaelas 1972). University undergraduate teaching for archaeologists – prehistorians, medieval archaeologists and the like – still entails learning little more than the rudiments of the subject of archaeology. Archaeological teaching on an advanced or postgraduate level has concentrated on the training of scholars in specialized fields. A formal education for museum staff or other similar professions within the cultural sphere does not exist. In Sweden during the last few years a number of courses in museum technique – given in alternate years by different universities – have provided information about the type of work rather than practical skill, although the latter has also been introduced in a few instances. The duration of such courses, one term, has also been too short. This is also true of environmental courses where cultural and historical aspects have been dealt with.

In view of the fact that many other subjects in the humanities have a practical professional education on top of, or parallel with, theoretical teaching, it is only natural that the same should apply to archaeologists. One of the reasons for the difficulties which arise in the maintenance of preservation interests in a wide sense of the word, that is, active work in the fields of cultural and historical preservation, lies in the lack of suitably trained staff. It does not really help to have the laws and regulations if one does not have trained professionals who can put such laws into practice. The question of education is the key to the solution of the problems as regards preservation of our cultural heritage with which the modern development of society confronts museums and other institutes. A change in the present educational system cannot, however, become useful if it is not worked out in active cooperation with the employers. And realistic professional training must be located where the work is – take for instance the training of medical doctors, which nobody would dream of placing outside hospitals. For this to come true, it is necessary to maintain a dialogue between the universities and the active institutes dealing with cultural and historical matters. Even those who are already working in museums need further education in their subject, not least at a theoretical level. Concentrated training and concrete orientation in new methods would certainly result in a new outlook on the tasks. Without adequately trained staff it is going to be difficult to maintain cultural and historical interests as an important part of modern politics. Herein lies society's challenge to both the universities and the museums.

Bibliography

JANSON, Sverker 1974 Kulturvård och samhällsbildning, *Nordiska Museets handlinger* 83, 202–95.

KAELAS, Lili 1972 Museum – Man – Environment, *Helinium* XII, 116–38.

SANERING 1971–3 Betänkande avgivet av saneringsutredning (= Government Committee Report on Slum Clearance). *SOU* (= Swedish Government Official Report) I–III.

SANERING I GÖTEBORG Göteborgs saneringsberedning 1974 (= Report on the Gothenburg Slum Clearance). *Göteborgs kommunfullmäktiges handlingar* (= The Proceedings of the Gothenburg City Council) 356A, 356B.

2

STEWART F. SANDERSON

Druids-As-Wished-For

To MANY of his friends it seems particularly fitting that Stuart Piggott should have written a book on Druids (Piggott 1968, 2nd edn 1975). Those who are not themselves archaeologists are naturally content to recognize that his professional reputation is securely based on other foundations – his early work at Avebury, his interpretation of European Neolithic cultures, the illuminating and superbly delivered Rhind lectures which looked afresh at problems in the prehistory and history of ancient Europe.

Yet one must equally recognize the particular symmetry of the progression which led him eventually to choose, or perhaps to be gently induced to choose, to take up the theme of the Druids in his admirable study; for his earliest scholarly publications (Piggott 1928, 1929) were not only in the field of folklore, but indeed appeared in the journal of that name (and are cited somewhat bewilderingly as PigF and PigL in the arcane cryptographical referencing of Cawte, Helm and Peacock's *English Ritual Drama*). Avebury and Stonehenge, however, were soon to exert greater attraction than the texts of Berkshire mummers' plays, and archaeology's consequent gain was folklore's loss. But happily not a total loss. Folklore, as part of the history of human experience and ideas, was bound to remain one of the interests of a mind well furnished with the productions of at least four centuries of English literature and the writings of seventeenth- and eighteenth-century antiquarians in particular; and the path leading to his examination of Druids as facts and fictions is surely signposted by his affection for the writings and the personality of dear, curious, garrulous old John Aubrey, and by his biographical study of William Stukeley (Piggott 1950), who descried archetypal sylvan groves in the forms of Gothic architecture and restored Stonehenge and Avebury to the British Druids as temples of their pagan religion.

In marrying together the evidence of archaeology, literature, and folklore, Stuart Piggott has illustrated the monuments in question, and the attitudes of successive generations towards them, with a style of wit and urbanity which has itself become a kind of folkloristic stereotype, identified in popular tradition (and even, surprisingly, by some academics) as characteristic of learned but not unworldly dons in Senior Common Rooms. Folklore beliefs and verifiable facts, however, are more often at variance than otherwise: *O si sic omnes!* we may well murmur when comparing a genuine example of the stereotype with realities of a more common order. But that is by the way. Among the most fascinating parts of his book, for students of folklore and anthropological theory, are his lucid treatment of the problem of 'hard and soft primitivism' (Piggott 1968, especially 91–103) and the excursus in his Epilogue on Druids as fact and symbol, passages which well repay repeated reading and thought. So too does the chapter on 'Druids in Decline', whose exemplification splendidly illuminates the concept of Druids-as-wished-for, and hardly better than in his all too brief reference to the Druid's Temple constructed by William Danby of Swinton Hall (Piggott 1968, 174) (*Ill. 1*). This is listed with two other sites associated in Yorkshire tradition with Druids, the Rishworth Rocking Stone and the Idol Rock at Brimham. Mention might also be made – as was made in *Sybil* (1845, 248–9) by Disraeli who visited the place in 1844 – of the so-called Druid's Altar which towers above the Aire Valley near Bingley: there are in fact two large weathered rocks here, one the altar for the sacrificial victims, the other (of course) a platform for the priests. Some further information on William Danby's Temple and its place in Yorkshire folk tradition may, one hopes, be acceptable in this volume as a tribute from a folklorist to an archaeologist of polymathic temper, coupled as it is (and as readers who persist will discover) with a firm invitation to him to visit the site on the first convenient and suitably warm summer's day.

Field archaeologists are no doubt accustomed to having their monuments located by reference to the Ordnance Survey's National Grid, but one may perhaps be allowed in this instance to describe the Druid's Temple more prosaically as being situated

1 Drawing by Barbara Jones of the Megalithic Folly at Ilton, West Riding, Yorkshire.

in the parish of Ilton-cum-Pott. It stands about one mile east and slightly north of the village of Ilton, and a mile and a half south of Healey, on the 900 foot contour line. The one-inch O. S. map shows it as being just on the edge of a wood called the Druid's Plantation, a happy instance of the persistence of an orally transmitted place-name tradition, now a century and a half old, in the official world of Government agencies; for the woods around here were felled in the First World War and the Forestry Commission is now restoring the area to the boskiness which characterized it when William Danby conceived the notion of building his Druid's Temple in the third decade of the nineteenth century.

Born in 1752, William Danby was a descendant of those Danbys who became Lords of Masham in the reign of Henry VIII. On succeeding to the family seat, Swinton Hall, he set about improving his property with energy, according to the romantic taste of his times, and as it turned out in a spirit of responsibility which one is bound to recognize as showing a well-developed social conscience – if one must use the jargon of later generations who do not always speak kindly or gratefully of the power and privilege of landlords such as he, though they appreciate the cultural heritage which power and privilege have handed on. Over a period of years Danby rebuilt the Hall itself, adding a fine library and a museum with a collection of minerals, and laying out pleasure-grounds in the vicinity of the house. Here in 1829 he entertained Robert Southey, who described him as being 'the most interesting person whom I saw during this expedition' (Southey 1850, 78) and commented in particular on his amiable and happy disposition.

Of his literary work we need say nothing here, though he published philosophical essays and a volume of poetry, and translated Cicero. But his literary imagination deserves our attention, for it is a type and paradigm of that literary and antiquarian romanticism, founded on a sound bottom of Classical learning, which begat one of the kinds of Druids-as-wished-for which Stuart Piggott has described. And it was an imagination tempered with practical humanitarianism. Having obtained permission to enclose parts of the surrounding moorland, William Danby proceeded to improve and embellish the landscape, just as he had his pleasure-grounds, with various works, one of whose purposes was to relieve unemployment amongst the labouring class in the parish.

So it was that in the 1820s he set in hand the construction of the Druid's Temple, paying his workmen at the rate of one shilling per day and so guaranteeing at least a continuing livelihood as the Temple and its outlying structures were built according to his elaborate plan. These latter units, trilithons it seems at a distance in the woods, were conceived as some sort of sentry-boxes to shelter lookouts and guards while within the sacred temenos the priests would conduct their religious ceremonies.

Local rumour had it that Danby called on the services of an expert on druidical buildings to supervise the design of his temple reconstruction. The likelihood is, however, that he consulted the architect Richard Lugar, a specialist in castellated Gothic, who was employed in the remodelling and extension of Swinton Hall between 1821 and 1824 (Pevsner 1966, 47 and 363).

The main part of the temple, suitably decked with trilithons, was elliptical in shape, and measured close on 100 feet in length by about 50 feet in breadth at the widest point. The tallest stones were about 10 feet high. Two flat slabs served as altar stones, one a few yards from the entrance at the east of the structure, the other at the western end, where a small chamber was hollowed out in the hillside and later reported to harbour a rare species of luminous moss. According to local tradition Danby advertised for a hermit to occupy the chamber and offered a reasonable wage to the incumbent, but failed even in the famine years of the 1820s to secure a tenant for his sylvan fane. Tradition may however have confused this chamber with other grottoes constructed on the estate, including one he built with a stone seat (Pevsner 1966, 364) in the woodlands above a gorge on the River Burn a year before his death. On this he affixed a plaque with the inscription 'This seat, overlooking some of the beautiful works of the Creator, was built with a grateful mind by William Danby, Esq., A.D. 1832.'

In his Pindaric ode, *The Bard* (1757), Thomas Gray projects another image of the Druid, foretelling the doom of Edward's line and lamenting Cadwallo, Urien and Mordred, 'dear lost companions of my tuneful art.' And yet, he says,

They do not sleep.
On yonder cliffs, a griesly band,
I see them sit, they linger yet. . . .

William Danby, one may legitimately presume, was familiar with this poem and the romantic vision it enshrines; and it is not beyond the bounds of fair conjecture to wonder what he would have thought about the bands who in later days have lingered pleasurably on the steep banks of the temple he constructed. These include in recent years the annual open-air rally of Ilton Methodist Chapel, complete with tea-urns, chairs and tables, whose tuneful art has been expressed in community hymn-singing. And in an idle moment Stuart Piggott himself has been heard to express a tentative desire to visit the Druid's Temple and inspect the remains of Danby's magnificently conceived and executed folly.

Druids-as-follies. . . . It seems as valid an attitude as any; and what better function can a folly have than to serve as the pretext for a light-hearted excursion and a luncheon *al fresco*? The invitation is open to him; all it requires is resolute acceptance and a little planning. Not Methodist hymn-singing on this occasion, perhaps: it would be best to avoid the first Monday in August. But on a sunny day in May before the University examinations are on us, or else in July when term is over, a picnic in the Druid's Temple, seasoned no doubt with scholarly discourse and sociable gossip, might well approximate to Druids-as-wished-for by Stuart Piggott himself. The shade of William Danby, that amiable and happy man, would probably approve.

And then there is the matter of the picnic-hamper. York ham, surely, and a plump-breasted chicken apt for the sacrificial knife, not of obsidian or ritual silver, but Sheffield carbide steel. Wensleydale cheese in these parts, of course, blue if one can be found; and to drink what more appropriate than the excellent local ale from the Masham brewery, Theakston's Old Peculiar? On the other hand, one should maybe think of wine. The Château du Chayne of Bergerac, paronomastically subtitled Vin des Druides, seems altogether too recondite a choice. There must be something less obscurely obvious, yet wholly appropriate for such an occasion. Yes, of course: Vin Fou, surely, is the drink for picnics in follies.

Bibliography

CAWTE, E. C., HELM, Alex and PEACOCK, N. 1967 *English Ritual Drama: A Geographical Index*, London.

GRAY, Thomas 1757 *Odes*, Strawberry Hill.

DISRAELI, Benjamin 1845 *Sybil, or The Two Nations*, London.

PEVSNER, Nikolaus 1966 *The Buildings of England: Yorkshire; The North Riding*, Harmondsworth.

PIGGOTT, Stuart 1928 Berkshire Mummers' Plays and other Folk Lore, *Folk-Lore* XXIX, 271–9.

1929 Mummers' Plays from Berkshire, Derbyshire, Cumberland, and Isle of Man, *Folk-Lore* XL, 262–73.

1950 *William Stukeley: An Eighteenth-Century Antiquary*, Oxford.

1968, 2nd ed. 1975 *The Druids*, London.

SOUTHEY, The Rev. Charles Cuthbert (ed.) 1850 *The Life and Correspondence of Robert Southey* VI, London.

3

SETON LLOYD

Illustrating Monuments: Drawn Reconstructions of Architecture

In reading the quotation which provides a title for the present volume, I was reminded that Stuart Piggott, to whom this contribution is dedicated in friendship and respect, has a subsidiary but practical interest in all forms of draftsmanship and typography (Piggott 1965). I was accordingly tempted to take the phrase more literally than was perhaps intended, and to choose as my subject some technical aspects of graphic illustration, as applied to archaeological reconstruction, of which my own experience might lead to some useful reflections.

In the first place then, one must consider in general terms the function and usefulness of perspective reconstructions, as a supplement to the bare pictorial recording of archaeological evidence, in the form of ground-plans, drawings of objects and so forth. At the same time one must remember that the status of such devices, in the canonical prescription governing the shape of archaeological reports, has been in the past to some extent controversial. Theoretically, they could be accepted as a convenient expedient for the clarification of well-authenticated conclusions; yet it could also be seen that some latitude had usually to be allowed for the draftsman's natural tendency to exercise his imagination, and it was this factor which at times caused the practice to be frowned upon. As a result, authors of excavation reports tended to be inhibited by the realization that any attempt to reconstruct the architectural or environmental setting of a hypothetical situation in antiquity might prove as distasteful to the purists among their colleagues as an historical novel is to some historians.

In the realm of architecture, the most obvious examples of reconstructions based on inadequate information, and misunderstanding of archaeological evidence, are of course to be found in the almost ludicrous 'artist's impressions' commissioned by the early excavators of the nineteenth century. One remembers immediately the elaborately fanciful drawings published by Layard or Place, to suggest the original appearance of Assyrian palaces (Layard 1853, frontispiece): pictures conceived in an imagination limited by the known conventions of classical design, paying little attention to the logical interpretation of the surviving ruins. But in Mesopotamia, one also sees how in due course these mistakes and misapprehensions began to be rectified, for instance by the German excavators at Babylon. Deprived of large-scale discoveries in the realm of removable antiquities, they were free to concentrate on a more disciplined study of architectural remains, setting themselves a high standard of ethical validity in such reconstructions as their conclusions seemed to justify. At Babylon, the evidence was fortunately so detailed and unequivocal that valid inferences could often be made, to the exclusion of mere conjecture (Andrae 1938). These German reconstructions, first in the form of line drawings and later of three-dimensional models, were an innovation with far-reaching results. They added a new page of information, intelligibly presented, to standard histories of architecture, and this development was in tune with the drastic change which was then beginning to take place in the public attitude to archaeology. Antiquarian research might remain a narrow specialization with its own disciplinary regulations, but a second and increasingly important obligation consisted now in the presentation and diffusion of its results for educational purposes. 'Popularization' has ceased to be a pejorative concept.

It was of course, as has been implied above, primarily in the realm of architecture that the function of draftsmanship in the presentation of archaeological discoveries at once became apparent. In those early days, styles of drawing and techniques of reproduction were naturally of a sort which today would be regarded as unsuitable or even primitive. Since the instructional value of visual presentation has more recently come to be increasingly appreciated, new skills have been brought to the aid of illustration and standards of draftsmanship have been improved and diversified. It is on this subject that I now propose to comment and, as one of the few archaeologists who is also a qualified architect, my position in doing so is perhaps sufficiently singular to warrant a reversion to the first person.

At Tell el-Amarna in 1929, I was the first of three graduates from the Architectural Association in London enlisted to assist in recording the buildings during the Egypt Exploration Society's excavations. I was astonished and attracted by the fine detail and symmetry of the great XVIII Dynasty mansions in the North Suburb, with their gardens and ornamental shrines, and I enjoyed recording their reconstructed plans for publication (Frankfort and Pendlebury 1933, e.g. Pl. XII-XIII). The contemporary draftsmanship style taught at the 'A. A.' pleased the late H. Frankfort, who was then field-director, and the same formula was adopted in subsequent seasons by my successors, Hilary Waddington and Ralph Lavers (Frankfort and Pendlebury 1933, Pl. XIV-XV) and in later reports of the expedition (*Journ. Egyptian Arch.* XIII-XX). I successfully applied the current technique of pencil drawing rendered in watercolour to the restored section of a particular house (Frankfort and Pendlebury 1933, Pl. XVI); but faced with a request to produce a perspective reconstruction of a picturesque group of merchants' houses overlooking a wādi, I lost heart and enlisted the aid of my then partner, E. B. O'Rorke (*Journ. Egyptian Arch.* XVII, Pl. VII). This watercolour is in a sense historical, since O'Rorke afterwards became a Royal Academician. In 1930, I also made a full set of working drawings for a scale-model of the same house, to which reference will presently be made. I mention these details because I consider that the introduction to archaeological expeditions at this time of field assistants with architectural qualifications marked a commendable revival of the German initiative in this field.

And here it should be admitted that, where the actual quality of draftsmanship is concerned, I am myself by no means uncritical of the style adopted by Andrae, Koldewey and their assistants. After regarding with admiration their Babylonian scale-models, now in the Vorderasiatisches Museum in East Berlin, I turn always with less enthusiasm to the perspective reconstructions of buildings, for instance in Andrae's *Das Wiedererstandene aus Assur* (1938), lamenting always the absence of a tree or human figure to break the uncongenial monotony of their punctilious discretion, and I hope to show how the austerity of their presentation has more recently been improved upon.

Meanwhile, it would be fair by contrast to consider what was being done by excavators of nationalities other than German, during the early decades of the present century. And here I am reminded of a sentence in the first edition of a book on the preparation of archaeological reports: 'A good reconstruction is usually beyond the artistic competence of the excavator, unless he is particularly talented in this direction, and a competent local (*sic*) artist is often called in to undertake this work' (Grinsell *et al.* 1966). One agrees; but it would perhaps be invidious to cite specific cases in which this might profitably have been done. An exception might be made regarding a well-known reconstruction of the platform temple at Al 'Ubaid, carrying the signature of the excavator, who was in fact a Licentiate of the Royal Institute of British Architects. It is not a good drawing (Woolley, Pl. XXXVIII).

At Tell Asmar in 1931, I experimented (once more for the approval of Frankfort) with the presentation of a complicated plan in what is now called 'axonometric projection' – a device by which the plan is set at an angle and the walls projected vertically to a uniform height. With or without shading on appropriate wall-faces, this can create a visual clarification for those who have difficulty in understanding an ordinary ground-plan, and it has been used in every conceivable context since that time. The first drawing of this sort, of the Gimilsin temple complex at Eshnunna, appears as Pl. I in *Chicago Oriental Institute Publications* XLII, and it is a great deal better than my first line-drawing reconstruction of the same subject, forming the frontispiece of the same volume, in which the tentative reconstruction of the parapet design is conjectural. It would in fact, as one now knows, have been possible to combine these two forms of presentation in a single drawing, by what has been called the 'cut-away' device, by which a section of the building in perspective is removed to expose another section in axonometric projection. This has been done by a modern draftsman, whose work I shall presently have reason to mention.

Later in the 1930s, Frankfort's Diyala and Khorsabad expeditions were well served by two American architects, Hamilton Darby and Harold Hill, both graduates of Harvard, who devised new techniques for presenting reconstruction of the major building complexes. They used a device – unfamiliar to me at that time – of shading a pencil drawing with rubbed graphite. To cite one example, Hill's drawing of the great Ishtar-Kititum temple at Ischali must be considered superlatively effective (Frankfort 1954, Pl. 55). A slightly different technique was used by C. B. Altman, in his equally impressive panorama of Sargon II's palace and citadel at Khorsabad (Loud 1938). It should at this point be noted that the two drawings just mentioned are of the sort which can only be reproduced by halftone or lithographic methods. Since occasionally considerations of economy restricted one to the use of line-blocks, we were also at that time experimenting with devices such as stippling or blockmaker's tints, which make this form of reproduction practicable, but which in more recent years have been largely superseded by the invention of 'dry transfer' transparencies, such as 'Letratone'. This brings one to a subject worthy of special consideration: namely the subsequent reproduction – often in a different medium – of drawings originally published in archaeological reports. At the time we are considering, many of these were of subjects sufficiently important to require secondary reproduction in later years, to illustrate more general books on regional archaeology or historical architecture. Needless to say, the varying methods by which this has been done are of special interest to the original draftsmen, and it occurred to me that something might be gained by analyzing an arbitrarily chosen group of examples.

ANALYSIS

I have taken six illustrated books, including four for which I have myself supplied all or part of the text, and two more which contain one or more adaptations of my own drawings. I have then listed a dozen architectural subjects which have usually needed to be represented in any serious summary of Near Eastern archaeology or early history of architecture, and examined the comparative merits of the various pictorial devices, techniques of draftsmanship and reproduction used by their publishers, ranking these as either grades A, B or C. The books chosen are as follows:

AANE 1965 *Art of the Ancient Near East*, London.
DAWN 1961 *Dawn of Civilization*, London.
WA 1963 *World Architecture: an Illustrated History*, London.
AMP 1967 *Architettura Mediterranea Preromana*, Milan.
AOM Strommenger, Eva 1967 *The Art of Mesopotamia*, London.
BF Fletcher, Bannister 1975 *A History of Architecture*, 18th edn rev. by J. C. Palmes, London.
SL = Seton Lloyd

The subjects may be dealt with under geographical headings:

MESOPOTAMIA

1 *Tell Hassuna*
Reconstruction of a prehistoric farmhouse. Original drawing by SL in *Journal of Near Eastern Studies* IV, No. 4, Fig. 36. In *AANE* (257, No. 216), it is very well redrawn by Martin Weaver, slightly enlarged, with black shadows giving greater contrast (*Grade A*). In *WA* (16, No. 4), it is badly redrawn by the same draftsman with changed figures (*Grade B*), and in *AMP* (12, No. 11), standardized in a poor line drawing without shadows (*Grade C*).

2 *Tepe Gawra*
Reconstruction of Al 'Ubaid period 'acropolis'. *AANE* (258, No. 217), has a very successful ink drawing rendered in watercolour by Martin Weaver, 'after Herget' (*Grade A*). In *AMP* (13, Fig. 15), the same drawing is again standardized in line without shadows (*Grade C*).

1 Eridu: reconstruction of the Protoliterate temple. Original watercolour by Seton Lloyd.

3 *Eridu* (*Ill. 1*)
Reconstruction of the late Protoliterate period temple. Original drawing by SL in ink, rendered in watercolour, for the Iraq Museum. *AANE* (259, No. 218), has it finely redrawn in ink with black shadows (*Grade A*). *DAWN* (67, No. 3), has a halftone of another redrawing in ink with colour washes (*Grade A*). *WA* (17, No. 10), has a less good line drawing with changed figures, and *AMP* (15, No. 23), the usual poor simplification (*Grades B and C*).
Note: No evidence was found for the summit temple in this picture; it is based on parallels at Uruk and 'Uqair.

4 Khafaje

Reconstruction of the 'Oval Temple'. Original drawing by Darby (cf. Delougaz 1940, frontispiece). He appears to have used a very effective American technique, with pencil lines and rubbed graphite shading. *WA* (20, No. 23 and *BF*, 57A), have small halftones of the original. *DAWN* (93, Fig. 13), has a very fine miniature redrawing of the original in line (*Grade A*). *AMP* (16, No. 24), a less good simplification in line (*Grade C*).

5 Ischali (Ill. 2)

Reconstruction of the Ishtar-Kititum temple. Original drawing by the late Harold Hill for the Oriental Institute, Chicago, first published by Frankfort (1945). An outstanding drawing of the pencil and graphite technique. *BF* (57B), and *AMP* (24), each have halftone reproductions of the original, the latter occupying a whole page. *AANE* (266, No. 231), and *WA* (20, No. 21), both have redrawings in line, the first good and the second less so (*Grades A and B*). See also work of W. Suddaby (p. 34).

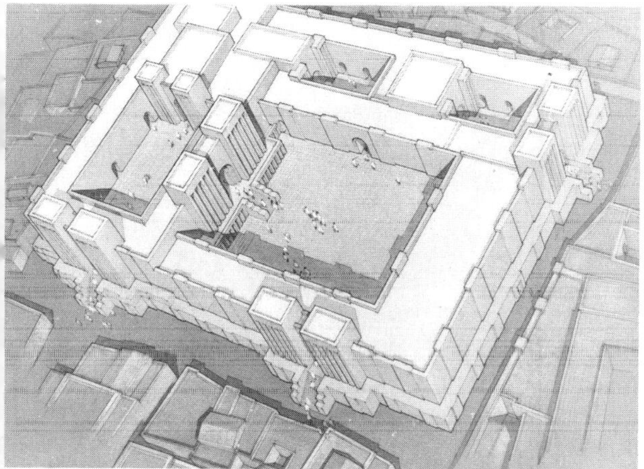

2 Ischali: reconstruction of the Ishtar-Kititum temple. Original watercolour by William Suddaby.

6 Tell Asmar (Ill. 3)

Reconstruction of the Gimilsin temple. Original drawing by SL for the Oriental Institute, Chicago, (Frankfort *et al.* 1940, frontispiece). A line drawing in perspective, with a then-original suggestion for the upper terminal treatment of the towers, buttresses and recesses, not now generally acceptable. *AOM* (411, Nos. 28, 29), gives a line-block reduced from the original, and, below it, my own axonometric plan. *WA* (18, No. 12), has a small, neat redrawing of the original (*Grade A*), and *AMP* (22, Fig. 37), both perspective and axonometric, rather bleakly redrawn in line. See also work of R. Leacroft (p. 34).

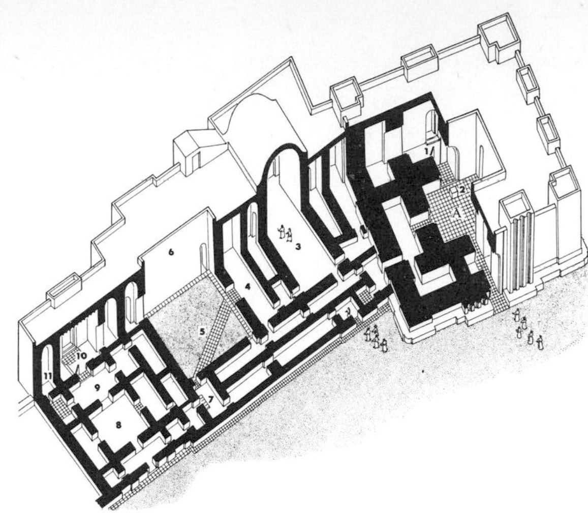

3 Tell Asmar: temple of Gimilsin, a deified king of Ur, and palace of the governors of Eshnunna. Reconstruction drawing by Richard Leacroft. Reproduced courtesy Brockhampton Press Ltd.

A Temple: 1 Sanctuary
2 Altar
B Palace: 3 Great hall (vaulted roof uncertain)
4 Throne room
5 Courtyard
6 Private court
7 Ablutions
8 Palace chapel
9 Ante-chamber
10 Sanctuary
11 Toilet

7 Ur

Various reconstructions of the Ur-nammu ziggurat. Two originals are both from Woolley (1939, frontispiece and folding Pl. 86). One is a rather pretentious pen drawing, looking at the right-hand side of the central stairway, from which a procession is emerging. The second is a very finely drawn bird's-eye view, which has never been improved on. (Now in the British Museum.) *AOM* (409, No. 25 and 407, No. 22), has reduced line-blocks of both. *WA* (19, No. 18), uses a tiny but clever redrawing of the first (*Grade A*). *DAWN* (78, No. 42), has a curious rendering in colour by Ian Mackenzie-Kerr, looking from the left-hand side of the stairway, apparently by moonlight (*Grade B*). *BF* (54B), has the usual good simplified reduction of the original bird's-eye view (*Grade A*).

8 *Khorsabad*
Reconstruction of Sargon II's palace complex. Original, a very fine pen and wash perspective by C. B. Altman, published in Loud (1938). *AM* (445, No. 51), has wisely shown a halftone of the original. *WA* (22, No. 25), has a small competent line reduction of the original, with contrasting black shadows (*Grade B*). *AANE* (274, No. 243), has the same type of redrawing, but larger and with more detail (*Grade A*). *AMP* (40, No. 72), has the usual redrawing in line without shadows (*Grade C*). *BF* (64A), has a standardized line drawing from Victor Place's original, dating of course from before the citadel was excavated.

EGYPT

9 *Sakkara*
Reconstruction of the entrance colonnade to the Step Pyramid. The original is a very sensitive watercolour drawing by J.-P. Lauer, (1934, Pl. XLV). *WA* (28, No. 37), has a satisfying line drawing of this, and *AANE* (260, No. 220), for once, a rather less good one in a 'fussy' technique (*Grades A and B*). *BF* (18C), sensibly gives a halftone of the original.

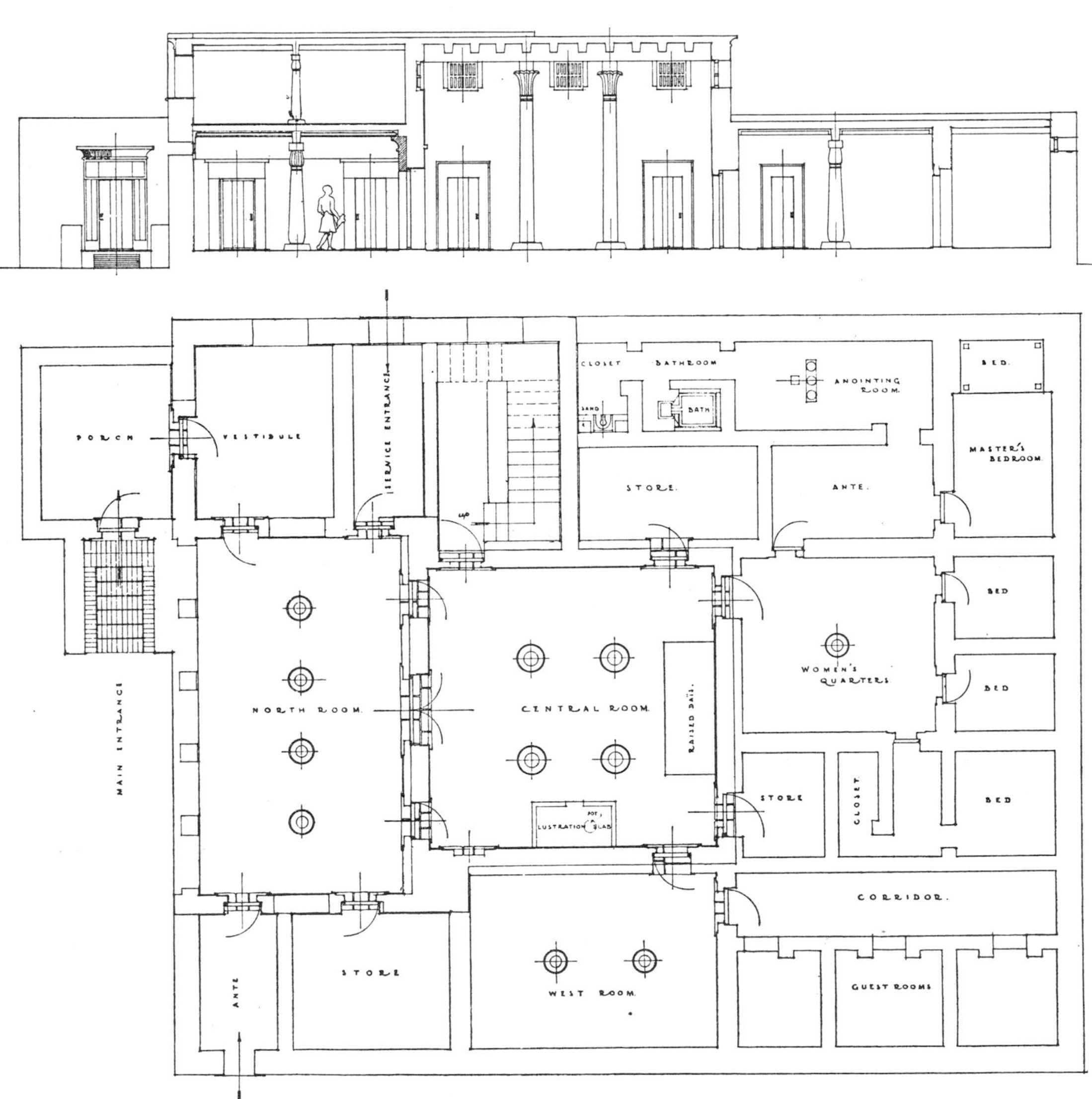

4 Tell el-Amarna: working drawing by Seton Lloyd of a house from which a model was made.

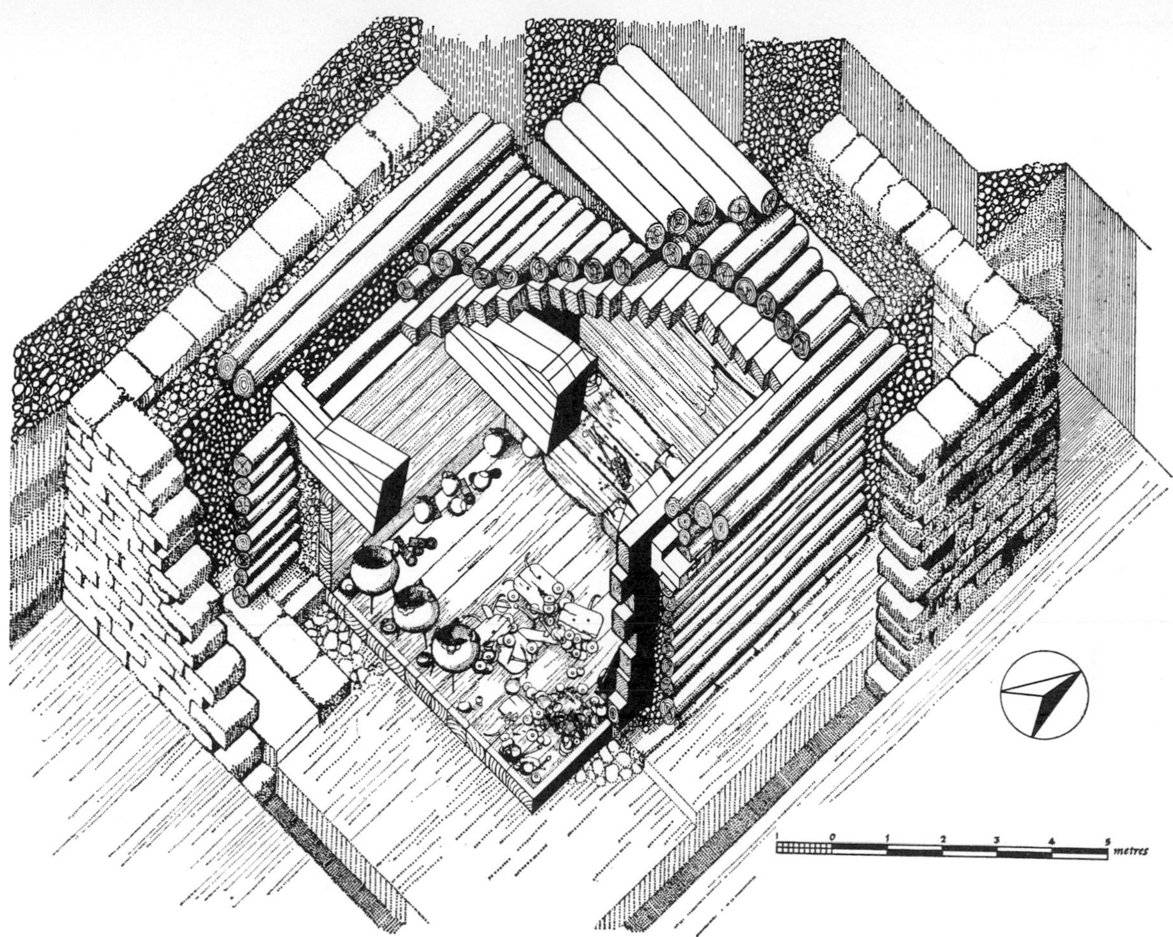

5 Gordion: 'Tomb of Midas'. Reconstruction of burial chamber. Drawn by M.E. Weaver. Based on information supplied by Professor R.S. Young.

10 *Karnak*
Reconstruction of the temple of Khons. *BF* (31E), is the first example cited in this list of an isometric perspective in line, 'cut away' to show half the plan in axonometric projection. The vertical and horizontal sectional parts are filled in in black for clarity. An exemplary treatment (*Grade A*). *WA* (32, No. 54), has a smaller reproduction of the same drawing.

11 *Karnak*
Explanatory diagram of roof construction in the Great Temple of Ammon. This drawing, in *BF* (32B), is an extremely useful type of isometric presentation, redrawn in *WA* (35, No. 66). Similar diagrams showing, for example, the construction of a Greek Doric temple (*BF* 205), may be compared.

12 *Tell el-Amarna* (*Ill. 4*)
Reconstruction of a private dwelling-house. The original of this was a model made from working drawings by SL for the Egypt Exploration Society. *WA* (34, No. 63), shows a photograph of it in halftone; early editions of *BF* have the same with the rooms numbered. Clearly, a model of this sort is the best device of all for reconstruction; but in *AANE* (273, No. 220), where a halftone would be out of place, a neat line drawing of it is made to a smaller scale. Another example is the model of the 'Uqair temple, now in the Iraq Museum (Lloyd 1943), a photograph of which is usually preferred to a drawn reconstruction.

ANATOLIA

A few outstanding reconstructions in the Anatolian field should be added.

1 *Çatal Hüyük*
Reconstructed interiors of private houses and shrines in the Neolithic township. These line drawings in perspective (Mellaart 1967, *passim*), reach a very high standard indeed.

2 *Mersin*
Reconstruction of the prehistoric fortress. Original drawing in line by SL in Garstang (1953, 132, Fig. 80a), is nicely redrawn to a smaller scale in *DAWN* (185, Fig. 1).

3 *Beycesultan*
Reconstruction of the 'Burnt Palace'. Original drawing in line by SL (Lloyd 1965, Fig. 413), again, beautifully redrawn in *DAWN*, (119, Fig. 12), with an equally good restoration of detail (Fig. 13).

4 *Gordion* (*Ill. 5*)
Reconstruction of burial chamber in the 'Tomb of Midas'. Perhaps the best reconstruction of this sort that one has seen (Martin Weaver, 'from information supplied by Professor R. S. Young', in *DAWN* 193, Fig. 16).

Some conclusions to be drawn from this selective review are the following. First that, in the rare cases where a reliable scale-model is available, a photograph of it is probably the simplest and best form of illustration; similarly, that an existing colour reconstruction often merits a monochrome reproduction in halftone. Second that, if requirements of space or the aesthetics of book production necessitate redrawing and stylistic standardization, a properly qualified draftsman, using up-to-date techniques, can frequently improve on the original. (Here a passing tribute is due to the publishers of the present volume for their appreciation of architectural qualifications.) Thirdly that standardized redrawings in line can suffer severely from oversimplification, if all forms of shading are eliminated.

Finally, I might add to my comparative schedule three examples of individual presentation techniques which deserve special praise. Where exploitation of 'cut-away' and axonometric techniques are concerned, in line-block perspectives, I would invite attention to Richard Leacroft's drawings (*Ill. 3*), head of the School of Architecture at the Leicester Polytechnic, in his recently published books on aspects of architectural history. Less well known in this country is the name of a prolific draftsman and artist, Mahmut Akok, whose large-scale reconstructions, depending exclusively on the deft handling of pen and ink, continually appear as striking features of Turkish publications. In a different category are the colour-frame 'strips' for projection, created by Visual Publications Ltd for educational purposes. Included among them are simplified architectural reconstructions in colour by William Suddaby, whose adaptations – sometimes of subjects mentioned in this article (*Ill. 2*) – seem to me in every way exemplary. The importance, then, of the graphic devices here discussed, as assets to the presentation of archaeological reports and the illustration of more comprehensive studies, can hardly remain in doubt. Provided the draftsman's imagination is restrained by the requirements of demonstrable validity, there should be no objection to them on the grounds of professional ethics.

Bibliography

Andrae, W. 1938 *Das Wiedererstendene Assur*, Leipzig.

Delougaz, P. 1940 The Temple Oval at Khafajah, *Oriental Institute Publications* LIII, Chicago.

Frankfort, H. and Pendlebury, J. D. S. 1933 The City of Akhenaten II: The north suburb and the desert altars. *Egypt Exploration Soc. Memoir* 40, London.

Frankfort, H. *et al.* 1940 The Gimilsin Temple and the Palace of the Rulers of Tell Asmar. *Oriental Institute Publications* XLIII, Chicago.

Frankfort, H. 1954 *The Art and Architecture of the Ancient Orient, Pelican History of Art*, Harmondsworth.

Garstang, J. 1953 *Prehistoric Mersin: Yümük Tepe in Southern Turkey*, Oxford.

Lauer, J.-P. 1934 *La Pyramide à dégrès*, Paris.

Layard, A. H. 1853 *Nineveh and Babylon*, London.

Leacroft, H. and R. 1974 *The Buildings of Ancient Mesopotamia*, Leicester.

Lloyd, S. 1943 Tell 'Uqair. *Journal of Near Eastern Studies* II: 2.

Lloyd, S. and Mellaart, J. 1965 *Beycesultan II: Middle Bronze Age architecture and pottery*. Occ. Publ. British Inst. Archaeol. Ankara no. 8.

Loud, G. and Altman, C.B. 1938 Khorsabad II, the citadel and town. *Oriental Institute Publications* XL, Chicago.

Mellaart, J. 1967 *Çatal Hüyük, a neolithic town in Anatolia*, London.

Piggott, S. 1965 'Archaeological Draughtsmanship: Principles and Practice', *Antiquity* XXXIX, 165–76.

Woolley, C. L. 1939 *Ur Excavations* V, *The Ziggurat and its surroundings*, London.

4

GLYN DANIEL

Stone, Bronze and Iron

When, in 1943, I published *The Three Ages: an Essay on Archaeological Method*, I began by quoting the views of two distinguished archaeologists on the concept of the three technological ages of man: Déchelette who described it as 'the basis of prehistory' (1908, 11) and Macalister who called it 'the corner stone of modern archaeology' (1921, 11). Recently David L. Clarke, in his *Analytical Archaeology*, writes 'The "three-age system" represents the development of the essential basis of modern analytical archaeology' (1968, 11). It was indeed when Christian Jurgensen Thomsen organized the collections in the Danish National Museum on the basis of ages of stone, bronze, and iron, and showed this organized museum to the public in 1819, that the world saw the first archaeological model of the ancient past of man. This replaced the mythological and literary models of the past based on guesswork, eponymous heroes, the Bible, and Classical writers which had passed for prehistory for so long (Piggott 1959; Daniel 1971). To some it is still a surprise that the three-age system was devised in Scandinavia and not in Italy, France or Britain. It is also still a matter of speculation as to the origins of Thomsen's ideas and to what extent he was in any way affected in his thinking by Classical writers or by sixteenth-, seventeenth- and eighteenth-century writers in Italy, France and Britain. Thirty years ago it seemed to me that he was little influenced by these. How does it look now?

The recognition of the existence of a stone age in the past of man demanded, first, an appreciative acceptance that there was some truth in what some Classical writers had said about the technological evolution of man; second, the acceptance that stone objects like Palaeolithic handaxes, Neolithic polished axeheads, arrowheads of the Neolithic and Early Bronze Ages, were artifacts made and fashioned by man, and not *lusus naturae*, thunderbolts, or things made by elves and fairies; and in the third place, the observation of living societies in a stone state of technology, and the extrapolation of this stage into the past of European man.

The passage in the *De Rerum Natura* of Lucretius is often quoted. Here he describes how man first used nails and teeth, then stones and wood and fire, then copper, and how still later iron gained in popularity. His dates were 98 to 55 BC, but in the ninth century BC Hesiod expressed ideas similar to those of Lucretius and, in his *Works and Days* (1.150), refers to a period when bronze had not been superseded by iron. Virgil describes the heroes of the *Aeneid*, and certain ancient peoples of Italy, as equipped with bronze arms; and Pausanias, writing about AD 170, declares that in Homeric times all weapons were of bronze. It has been argued that the scheme set out by Lucretius was a general one based entirely on abstract speculation, and that his ages should be set alongside the other ages postulated by the Greeks, such as the Age of Reason, the Golden Age and the Heroic Age. But there probably did survive in Greece from Mycenaean times a memory of the Bronze Age, even if the ages of stone and wood were intelligent speculations. Certainly in ancient China there was a memory of the three-age technological succession of man, but these Chinese ideas were unknown to the Greeks and to the European antiquaries of the eighteenth and early nineteenth centuries (Sikes 1914).

The discovery of America at the end of the fifteenth century posed many problems to philosophers and historians: the first was the relation of the Americas to the rest of the world – how had man got there, and what was his relation to the men of the Old World; and second, the observation of people who knew not the use of metal – here were people living in a stone age. If such stone-age people existed in America, could there not have been similar people, not knowing the use of metal, living in the past in ancient Europe? These were ideas discussed by Peter Martyr – Pietro Martire d'Anghiera, whose books were published between 1504 and 1530 and by Ferrante Imperato in his *Dell'Historia Naturale* of 1599 (Hodgen 1964).

The renaissance of learning brought to the minds of sixteenth- and seventeenth-century scholars what had been said by Hesiod, Lucretius, Virgil and Pausanias, and some people began to question whether what we now know to be stone artifacts were of celestial origin. Agricola (1490–1555) was one of these, but the most serious and influential was Michele Mercati (1541–93) who has been enthusiastically described as 'the archaeological counterpart of Cardano in mathematics, Vesalius in anatomy, Galileo in the physical sciences and Copernicus in astronomy' (Clarke 1968, 9). Mercati was appointed Superintendent of the Vatican Botanical Gardens by Pope Pius V and was retained in that office by his successors Gregory XIII and Sixtus V. He had become an institution: he collected fossils, minerals and artifacts and wrote about them in his *Metallotheca* which remained in manuscript in the Vatican Library until its publication in 1717. In this work he illustrated stone artifacts and said that they were weapons of war which were used before metal was known. Until his time stone artifacts had been called *ceraunia* and thought to be non-human: Mercati said that they were human, and in coming to this revolutionary point of view he drew on Classical writers and the Bible, but was also impressed by the collection of native American Indian artifacts which were being accumulated in the Vatican as presents from Italian, Spanish and Portuguese explorers.

But though unpublished until the early eighteenth century, Mercati's views were apparently widely known and discussed in the late sixteenth and early seventeenth centuries in Italy and in France. Ulisse Aldrovandi (1522–1605), one of the universal and multi-faceted polymaths characteristic of the Renaissance, who was in charge of the museum and botanical garden in the University of Bologna and then became professor of the history of 'simples', argued very cogently in his *Museum Metallicum* (1648) for a stone age. Seven years later, in 1655, Isaac de la Peyrère of Bordeaux published in Amsterdam and London his *A Theological System upon that Pre-supposition that Men were before Adam*. His theological views, and particularly his theory of pre-Adamites, were fiercely criticized: he and his book were seized by the Inquisition, the book publicly burnt in Paris, and the author forced to recant. Among other wise things, he had said that the 'thunderbolts' were in fact the artifacts of a primitive and ancient pre-Adamitic race of human beings, and here he was right (Casson 1939, 114–18).

In the year following the publication of de la Peyrère's book, Sir William Dugdale (1605–86) in his *The Antiquities of Warwickshire* (1656, 778) describes and illustrates a stone axe and refers to the finding of several of them 'curiously wrought by grinding or some such way . . . being at first so made by the native Britans . . . were made use of for weapons, inasmuch as they had not then attained to the knowledge of working iron or brass to such uses.' Dr Robert Plot (1640–96), the first Keeper of the Ashmolean, published his *History of Staffordshire* in the year of Dugdale's death, and in it he had no doubt of the true nature of stone implements. He described an axe of speckled flint with a ground edge, saying that either the Britons, or Romans, or both made use of such axes, and says 'how they might be fastened to a helve may be seen in the Museum Ashmoleanum, where there are several Indian ones of this kind fitted up in the same order as when formerly used'. Plot, writing of the use of iron by the ancient Britons in Caesar's time, said 'we have reason to believe that, for the most part at least, they sharpen'd their warlike instruments rather with stones than metall, especiall in the more northerly and inland countries, where they sometimes meet with flints in shape of arrow-heads, whereof I had one sent me by the learned and ingenious Charles Cotton Esq., found not far from his pleasant mansion at Beresford, exactly in the form of a bearded arrow, jagg'd at each side, with a larger stemm in the middle, whereby I suppose it was fixt to the wood. . . . These they find in Scotland in much greater plenty, especially in the prefectury of Aberdeen, which, as the learned Sir Robert Sibbald informs us, they there call elf-arrows . . . imagining they drop from the clouds not being to be found upon a diligent search, but now and then by chance in the high beaten roads.' (Plot 1686, 396–7). Plot also published engravings of two flint implements.

Sir Robert Sibbald, to whom Plot refers, declares that these flint arrowheads or elf-stones were in fact man-made and he had no doubt of this (1684, 49). Plot's assistant and successor at the Ashmolean was Edward Lhuyd, an assiduous collector of fossils and artifacts. Lhuyd had discussed with Plot the nature of British stone implements and studied together the ethnographical collections in the Ashmolean. Lhuyd wrote on 17 December 1699, during his Scottish travels, to Dr Richard Richardson about stone implements as follows: 'But what we were most diverted with, was their variety of Amulets, many of which, if not all, were certainly used by the Druids, and so have been handed down from parents to children ever since. Some of these may be render'd in English . . . Elf-arrow . . . as to this *elf-stricking*, their opinion is, that the fairies (having not much power themselves to hurt animal bodies) do sometimes carry away men in the air, and, furnishing them with bows and arrows, employ them to shoot men, cattle, etc. I doubt not but you have often seen these Arrow-heads they ascribe to elfs or fairies; they are just the same chip'd flints the natives of New England head their arrows with at this day: and there are several stone hatchets found in this kingdom, not unlike those of the Americans . . . they were not invented for charms, but were once used in shooting here, as they are still in America. The most curious, as well as the vulgar throughout this country, are satisfied they often drop out of the air, being shot by fairies, and relate many instances of it, but for my part I must crave leave to suspend my faith, untill I see one of them descend' (Gunther 1945, 425).

The views of Plot and Lhuyd, the one definitely for stone artifacts, the other definitely against elf-arrows, were by no means widely accepted. Martin Lister, Fellow of St John's College, Cambridge, corresponded with Robert Plot and was a close friend of Lhuyd, but insisted that what we know now as unmistakable and genuine flint implements were the products of nature without any human intervention whatsoever.

In 1685 a megalithic tomb was discovered and excavated at Cocherel near Dreux in the valley of the Eure in north France; it was a good example of what we should now call the Paris Basin type of *allée couverte*. We have an account of the excavation, dated 11 July 1685, by Olivier Estienne: it was published in 1722 in Le Brasseur's *Histoire Civile et Ecclésiastique du Comté d'Evreux* in which he describes the finding of polished axes, including one of jade, but all said to have been placed under the heads of the twenty skeletons inhumed in the tomb. Estienne thought the remains were those of pagan Gauls; the absence of writing and the presence of stone axes were, he said, sure proof of superstition and idolatry. Le Brasseur's book contained a note by the Abbé of Cocherel, who had decided the bodies were those of Huns who had come to France with Attila: he noted that the stone implements were like those used by American Indians and suggested that the Scythians were possible links between America and the tomb builders of Cocherel. Another account of this very early excavation of a megalithic tomb is given by Dom Bernard de Montfaucon in his *L'Antiquité expliquée et representée en figures* (Paris 1719; English translation by David Humphreys, 1722); and he concludes very percipiently and correctly, that the tomb was built by 'some barbarous nation, that knew not yet the Use either of Iron or any other metal.' Here is one of the first examples of the ascription of prehistoric monuments, as distinct from stone axes and arrowheads, to a stone age.

In France in the eighteenth century, particularly after the publication of Mercati's *Metallotheca* in 1717, many scholars spoke of a stone age. In 1721 Antione de Jussieu read a paper to the Académie des Sciences denying the celestial origin of stone implements and comparing them again with those found in North America. In 1724 there appeared Père Lafitau's *Mœurs des Sauvages Amériquains Comparées aux Mœurs des Premiers Temps*: he presses the ethnographical comparison, saying 'I was not content with knowing the nature of the savages and with learning of their customs and practices. I sought to find in these practices and customs vestiges of the most *remote* antiquity' (Hodgen 1964, 348–9; Harris 1968, 17, 388). In 1734 Mahudel read a paper to the Académie des Inscriptions in Paris in which he said that man had existed for a long time in different countries, using implements of stone and with no knowledge of metal. Mahudel quoted Mercati and set out clearly the idea of three successive technological ages in the past of man. His paper entitled 'Les Monuments les plus anciens de l'Industrie des Hommes, et des Arts reconnus dans les Pierres de Foudre' was published in the *Memoires* of the Académie in 1740 (Laming 1952, 18–19, Pl. 1).

In the same year, 1734, Montfaucon read a paper to the same Académie reiterating what Mahudel had said, making more precise his own previous observations about Cocherel, and arguing for a three-age system of stone, bronze and iron. Later in the same century Eccard, Goguet and Legrand d'Aussy repeated the conclusions of Mahudel and Montfaucon. Antoin Yves Goguet (1716–58) published, in 1758, a book translated into English three years later under the title, *The origin of laws, arts and sciences and their progress among the most ancient nations*. He was much concerned with the value of ethnographical parallelism for the study of ancient Europe, and regarded the account of American Indians as extremely valuable and relevant. He argued that we could judge the state of the ancient world 'by the condition of the greatest part of the New World when it was first discovered'. To quote him further 'the use of bronze preceded that of iron . . . formerly stones, flint pebbles, bones, horn, fish-bones, shells, reeds and thorns were used for everything for which civilised peoples use metal today. Primitive peoples give us a faithful picture of ancient societies' (Cheynier 1936, 10–14).

It cannot be denied, then, that in the eighteenth

century some scholars were prepared to argue for the three-age system in France; and in England a few were prepared to take the views of Plot and Dugdale and argue for a stone age. In 1765 Lyttleton, Bishop of Carlisle, wrote a paper which was read to the Society of Antiquaries of London in 1776 and published in the second volume of *Archaeologia* in 1773. His paper was based on a stone battle-axe found in a barrow near Carlisle; he compares it with other objects of the same form and says, 'There is not the least doubt of these stone instruments having been fabricated in the earliest times, and by barbarous people, before the use of iron or other metals was known.' He repeats the ethnographical parallel saying, 'When Mexico was first discovered by the Spaniards, the use of iron was unknown among the inhabitants.' Bishop Lyttleton had read Aldrovandi, Sibbald, Montfaucon, Plot and Dugdale, and his conclusions, arising directly from Dugdale, are remarkable and worth quoting *in extenso*.

'I entirely agree with Dugdale', writes Bishop Lyttleton, 'that they were British instruments of war, and used by them, before they had the art of making arms of brass or iron; but I go farther, and am persuaded that when they fabricated these stone weapons they had no knowledge at all of these metals; and that must have been at a very early period indeed, as in Julius Caesar's time they had abundance of *scythed* chariots, which probably were introduced here by the Phoenicians some ages before. . . . How low an idea soever some people may entertain of the Antient Britons, they can hardly be thought so barbarous and ignorant as to have made their battle-axes and spear-heads of stone, and this with great labour and difficulty in the execution, when, at the same time, they were mechanics sufficient to make iron scythes. . . . On the whole, I am of the opinion that these stone axes are by far the most antient remains existing at this day of our British ancestors, and probably coeval with the first inhabitants of this island' (Lyttleton 1773, 118–22).

In the same volume of *Archaeologia* that contained Lyttleton's paper was one by Samuel Pegge entitled 'Observations on Stone Hammers'. Pegge did not dispute with Montfaucon, Lyttleton and others that the objects being discussed were stone implements made and fashioned by the ancient Britons: he merely disputed that they were weapons of war, and argued 'the conclusion then must be, that these perforated stones were not originally applied to any warlike purpose, but rather to some domestic service, either as a hammer, or beetle, for common use, or . . . for the flaying of larger beasts in sacrifice' (Pegge 1773, 127).

Yet the excitement of war and the martial image of the prehistoric past survived. Twenty years after Bishop Lyttleton's paper a gentleman farmer of East Anglia, by name John Frere (1740–1807), wrote a letter to the Secretary of the Society of Antiquaries of London which is one of the most quoted documents in the history of archaeology. Written in 1797, it was published in the twelfth volume of *Archaeologia*: he says, 'I take the liberty to request you to lay before the Society some flints found in the parish of Hoxne, in the county of Suffolk, which, if not particularly objects of curiosity in themselves, must, I think, be considered in that light from the situation in which they were found. They are, I think, evidently weapons of war, fabricated and used by a people who had not the use of metals. They lay in great numbers at the depth of about twelve feet in a stratified soil. . . . The situation in which these weapons were found may tempt us to refer them to a very remote period indeed, even beyond that of the present world' (Frere 1800, 204–5).

Frere's words and conclusions attracted little attention and there was no widespread discussion of Bishop Lyttleton's paper. It is easy to list writers in England and France who, in the seventeenth and eighteenth centuries, believed that stone implements were human artifacts and that there was a time in man's past when he used only stone implements; and to make a shorter list of those who thought that a period when 'brass' or bronze implements were used existed between the stone age and the historical time when man was iron-using: and this has often been done (Evans 1897; MacCurdy 1924; Macalister 1921, 1–15; Clarke 1968, 4–11). It is less easy to know to what extent these oft-quoted writers from Mercati to Frere were individualists, were original and thoughtful scholars but did not much affect or reflect the general thought of archaeologists and antiquaries. One can be sure that in England, despite Plot, Dugdale, Lyttleton and Frere, no specific concept of three technological ages emerged, and that Colt Hoare, after ten years of digging barrows in Wiltshire, was forced to confess 'total ignorance as to the authors of these sepulchral memorials: we have evidence of the very high antiquity of our Wiltshire barrows, but none respecting the tribes to whom they appertained that can rest on solid foundations.'

We can agree with D. L. Clarke that Mercati's

work was 'widely disseminated and appreciated' (1968, 8) but we must not exaggerate the effect such dissemination had on antiquarian thought, and in the application of his ideas to the problems of classifying antiquities in collections and understanding artifacts found in excavations. It remains true that the majority of antiquaries in the eighteenth century still saw no way to the past except through Classical writers. Our own great antiquaries, John Aubrey and William Stukeley, had no concept of a three-age system or indeed of a stone age. But it is without any doubt true that the idea existed and, in retrospect, we ask why it was that this idea became the firm basis of man's ancient history and prehistory, and transformed antiquarianism into archaeology, in Denmark and not in the country of Mercati, Mahudel and Lyttleton.

Clarke, in an excellent summary of the development of the three-age system, thinks that the full implications and explicit formulation of the three-age system in Denmark rather than France or Italy was due to 'a curious but not inexplicable chance', and describes Italian Renaissance learning reaching Denmark from the secondary centre of France in the seventeenth and eighteenth centuries (Clarke 1968, 8–9). But Olaf Worm was uncertain about the artifactual nature of prehistoric stone implements, although he recognized a flint harpoon for what it was when discovered embedded in a marine animal in Greenland, and realized that the inhabitants of North America used flint and stone implements. When the Museum Wormianum, transferred to be a Royal Collection, was opened to the public of Copenhagen in 1680, there was no arrangement of artifacts to indicate the technological development of man, as there was not in the Ashmolean which opened three years later.

But a hundred years later Danish historians were setting out the three-age concept. P. F. Suhm in his *History of Denmark, Norway and Holstein* (1776) stated that in those areas tools and weapons were first of stone, then of copper and then of iron; and Skuli Thorlacius in his *Concerning Thor and his Hammer, and the earliest weapons that are related to it, and also the so-called Battle-Hammers, Sacrificing Knives and Thunder-Wedges, which are found in Burial Mounds* (1802) refers throughout to three successive ages of stone, copper and iron. L. S. Vedel Simonsen repeated this concept in his writings and the clearest statement is in his *Udsigt over Nationalhistoriens aeldste og maerkeligste Perioder* (1813–16) in which he wrote, 'At first the tools and weapons of the earliest inhabitants of Scandinavia were made of stone or wood. Then the Scandinavians learnt to work copper and then to smelt and harden it . . . and then latterly to work iron. From this point of view the development of their culture can be divided into a Stone Age, a Copper Age and an Iron Age. These three ages cannot be separated from each other by exact limits for they encroach on each other. Without any doubt the use of stone implements continued among the more impoverished groups after the introduction of copper, and similarly objects of copper were used after the introduction of iron . . . artifacts of wood have naturally decomposed, those of iron are rusted in the ground: it is those of stone and copper which are the best preserved' (Daniel 1967, 90).

It is again easy to quote these and a few other Scandinavian writers, but this was not the general way of thinking at the turn of the eighteenth and nineteenth centuries in Denmark, any more than it was in England or France. Rasmus Nyerup (1759–1829), Professor of History in the University of Copenhagen, who became first secretary of the Danish Royal Commission for the Preservation and Collection of National Antiquities, wrote despairingly in 1806 in his *Oversyn over Faedrelandets Mindesmaerker fra Oldtider*: 'everything which has come down to us from heathendom is wrapped in a thick fog: it belongs to a space of time which we cannot measure. We know that it is older than Christendom, but whether by a couple of years or a couple of centuries, or even by more than a millennium, we can do no more than guess' (Daniel 1950, 1975; Klindt-Jensen 1975).

It is a matter for discussion whether the total ignorance and fog of Cunnington and Nyerup or the three ages of Vedel Simonsen were most representative of general antiquarian thought in the second half of the eighteenth century; it is also a matter of discussion to what extent, if any, Thomsen and Worsaae were affected by Mercati or, for that matter, Lucretius. The formulation of the three-age system in Denmark is explicable in terms of one man – Christian Thomsen. D. L. Clarke writes, 'Whether Mercati's renaissance idea reached Thomsen through a knowledge of the French works of Montfaucon, Mahudel, Goguet and their many contemporaries, or whether they came from the same source via the assimilations of Skuli Thorlacius, Vedel Simonsen and others, remains unknown . . . the diffusion of ideas is a most complex business' (1968, 10). This is so, and I do not pretend that my interpretation of the development of Thomsen's ideas is necessarily the right one: it is however the view of most Scandinavian scholars who have written on this subject. Thomsen was aware of the ideas of Mercati and Mahudel, and he may well have thought back to Lucretius, but these ideas did not affect him in any very significant way. His object was to arrange the materials in the new museum in some order and there were various orders that he could adopt; indeed for a while he adopted a classification according to material, i.e. stone, pottery, metal, and there was also the suggestion of a classification according to purpose. It is to the genius of this one person that, considering all possibilities, he decided to select a three-age system: it was convenient, and there was no other way of fitting a stone age into man's past and the ethnographical parallels seemed to demand this. In 1819 Thomsen was not giving a practical demonstration of Mercati's theories; he was applying to his own collections a way of ordering the material remains of the past, which his predecessor Nyerup had certainly not thought of as a possibility, and which no one in any museum in the world had done before (Hermansen 1935; Daniel 1943, 1967).

Worsaae in Denmark and others in Switzerland and elsewhere were able to demonstrate stratigraphically the truth of Thomsen's museum arrangement. And Worsaae himself was very clear about the origin of the Danish three-age system: 'This division of the ancient times in Denmark into three periods', he wrote, 'is solely and entirely founded on the accordant testimony of antiquities and barrows for the ancient traditions do not mention that there was a time when, for want of iron, weapons and edged tools were made of bronze.' Worsaae admits that, 'it is stated by Homer, Hesiod and other authors that the Greeks in the most ancient time, before they had knowledge of iron, used bronze, which was also the case with the Romans.' But he does not regard this as evidence of the three ages in Greece itself, let alone in Denmark.

Worsaae, in his *Danmarks Oldtid oplyst ved Oldsager og Gravhoje* (1843), a remarkable book translated into English in 1849, explains how he was moved to accept the three-age system and how Thomsen explained it to him. He was sure that all the pre-Christian antiquities of Denmark could not possibly belong to one period and, as Ole Klindt-Jensen recounts elsewhere (1975, 68–75), was aware of the use of ethnographic parallels. Worsaae had read how stone implements were at the present day used by Pacific islanders, and, knowing that the Goths made no such use of stone implements, concluded that there must have been a stone age. 'As soon as it was pointed out that the whole of these antiquities could by no means be referred to one and the same period, people began to see more clearly the difference between them' (Worsaae 1849, 76, 124–6).

The Italian Renaissance scholars were engaged in general philosophical speculations about the past of man, and so were their successors in seventeenth- and eighteenth-century France, England and Denmark. And there were other comparable philosophical speculations during these centuries, such as those of Montboddo and the Scottish primitivists, of Governor Pownall (Orme 1974), and of Sven Nilsson (1868). None of them managed to penetrate the fog and total ignorance until a museum curator arranged his artifacts according to the three-age system. It was Thomsen, more than anyone else, who produced the revolution in antiquarian thought that, together with the revolution in geological thought of Lyell's uniformitarianism, and the acceptance of the antiquity of man, gave birth to the scientific discipline of archaeology between 1819 and 1859. Worsaae was not exaggerating when he referred to the Danish three-age system as 'the first clear ray . . . shed across the Universal prehistoric gloom of the north and the world in general.'

Bibliography

CASSON, S. 1939 *The Discovery of Man: the Story of the Inquiry into Human Origins*, London.

CHEYNIER, A. 1936 *Jouannet, grandpère de la Préhistoire*, Brive.

CLARKE, D. L. 1968 *Analytical Archaeology*, London.

DANIEL, G. E. 1943 *The Three Ages: An Essay on Archaeological Method*, Cambridge.

1950 *A Hundred Years of Archaeology*, London.

1960 *The Prehistoric Chamber Tombs of France*, London.

1967 *The Origins and Growth of Archaeology*, Harmondsworth.

1971 From Worsaae to Childe; the models of prehistory, *Proc. Prehist. Soc.* XXXVIII, 140–53.

1975 *A Hundred and Fifty Years of Archaeology*, London.

DÉCHELETTE, J. 1908 *Manuel d'archéologie préhistorique*, I, Paris.

EVANS, Sir John 1897 *The Ancient Stone Implements, Weapons and Ornaments of Great Britain*, London. (2nd revised ed., first published 1872).

FRERE, J. 1800 Account of Flint Weapons discovered at *Hoxne* in *Suffolk*, *Archaeologia* XIII, 204–5.

GUNTHER, R. T. 1945 *Life and Letters of Edward Lhuyd*, Oxford. (Vol. XIV of *Early Science in Oxford*, ed. Gunther).

HARRIS, Marvin 1968 *The Rise of Anthropological Theory: a History of Theories of Culture*, New York.

HERMANSEN, V. 1935 C. J. Thomsen's Første Museumsordning, *Aarbøger for Nordisk Oldkyndighed og Historie*, 99–122.

HODGEN, M. T. 1964 *Early Anthropology in the Sixteenth and Seventeenth Centuries*, Philadelphia.

KLINDT-JENSEN, O. 1975 *A History of Scandinavian Archaeology*, London.

LAMING, A. 1952 La découverte du passé, in *La Découverte du Passé*, ed. Laming, Paris, 11–31.

LYTTLETON, C. 1773 Observations on Stone Hatchets, *Archaeologia* II, 118–23.

MACALISTER, R. A. S. 1921 *A Textbook of European Archaeology. I. The Palaeolithic Period*, Cambridge.

MACCURDY, G. C. 1924 *Human Origins*, New York.

NILSSON, S. 1868 *The Primitive Inhabitants of Scandinavia*, London. (Edited from the Swedish by John Lubbock.)

ORME, B. 1974 Governor Pownall, *Antiquity* XLVIII, 116–25.

PEGGE, S. 1773 Observations on Stone Hammers, *Archaeologia* II, 124–8.

PIGGOTT, S. 1959 *Approach to Archaeology*, London.

PLOT, R. 1686 *Natural History of Staffordshire*, London.

SIBBALD, Sir Robert 1684 *Scotia Illustrata*.

SIKES, E. E. 1914 *The Anthropology of the Greeks*, Cambridge.

WORSAAE, J. J. A. 1849 *The Primeval Antiquities of Denmark*, London. (Translated from the Danish by W. J. Thoms.)

5

OLE KLINDT-JENSEN

The Influence of Ethnography on Early Scandinavian Archaeology

It is interesting to note that scholars even in Classical times have found resemblances between primitive foreign peoples and traits in the culture of their own forefathers (Klindt-Jensen 1950, 29). This strange analogy was studied again when European explorers brought home objects no less than tales from America, the South Pacific and Asia (Orme 1973, 487). Independently several antiquarians realized that implements and ornaments from these exotic continents could be compared with antiquities found in the soil of their own country and – so it seemed – could explain the latter's use. The idea was also apparent to scholars who actually studied ethnography from the eighteenth century onwards. They tried to see primitive peoples as part of universal human history. The titles of two books give an indication of the idea: *Mœurs des Sauvages Amériquains, Comparées aux Mœurs des Premiers Temps* by J. T. Lafitau, published in Paris in 1724, and Jens Kraft's *Brief Account of the Principal Institutions, Customs, and Ideas of the Savage Peoples Illustrating the Human Origin and Evolution Generally* – to translate the Danish title of this work which appeared in 1760. Lafitau, a former French missionary in Canada, was the first to study Indians as cultural and social beings, and looked in the Bible and Classical literature for comparative early material; the Danish teacher, Kraft, inspired by this famous predecessor, widened the outlook and gave a description of institutions, behaviour, economic life and so on which is considered to be the first scholarly study of our times. But even though it was translated into German and Dutch it was almost unnoticed by contemporary and later scholars (Birket-Smith 1960, 5). This is all the more astonishing as antiquaries of the time were becoming involved in ethnographic parallels.

Kraft was fully aware of the importance of comparing antiquities and foreign aboriginal implements and expressed his view as follows: 'Tools of wood and in particular of stone were the essential riches which man knew on the first stage of mundane society. The great number of such stones which we in our times still dig up from the soil, and which the easier use of iron has later made despicable, proves that they have been used all over the world and even among ourselves' (Kraft 1760, 9). His conception of the evolution of man's economic and social life from hunting savages to the distinct and partly contemporary stages – cattle-breeding tribes, semi-agriculturalists, peasants and so forth – was given in a careful and competent way taking into consideration different development in different areas (Kraft 1760, 156).

The first Scandinavian antiquary to use ethnographic parallels was the Swedish professor of sciences at the University of Lund, Kilian Stobaeus. He published two flint daggers found in Scania and added some reflections on the objects, which were accurately illustrated. But most remarkable in this study of 1738, *Ceraunii betulique lapides*, was his observation that such flint implements were the very oldest in the country and should be compared with stone objects used by primitive peoples, which he knew from collections like the Royal Danish Kunstkammer, specimens which were known also by antiquaries like Ole Worm (Rydbeck 1943, 3).

Stobaeus influenced his successors in Lund, above all Sven Nilsson, also a professor in science with wide knowledge in archaeology and ethnography. He visited foreign collections such as those of the British Museum and had in mind a new method which he called 'comparative ethnography'. His studies on the history of hunting and fishing in Scandinavia (1834) and on the indigenous peoples of Scandinavia were later widely known through John Lubbock's translation of the second edition of 1865 which in English was called *The Primitive Inhabitants of Scandinavia* (1868). In these publications Nilsson put parallel antiquities and ethnographic objects side by side and gave a detailed description of the ethnographic background of the latter. His constant emphasis on implements belonging to hunting and fishing may have irritated C. J. Thomsen who was prepared to accept ethnographic parallels, but who looked for other forms of use as weapons (Hindenburg 1859, 62).[1] In show-cases of the Royal Museum

1 Two polished stone axes from Brazil sent to the Royal Society of Northern Antiquaries by P.W. Lund.

of Northern Antiquities, Thomsen put South Pacific hafted stone axes beside the Danish flint axes to give an idea of what the original prehistoric method of hafting might have been.

Among the objects illustrated by Nilsson was a bone implement which he had seen in a private collection owned by a young man living in Copenhagen, J. J. A. Worsaae. Nilsson and Worsaae met later from time to time and exchanged views – they were not always of the same opinion – but the young man gladly admitted that the Swedish scholar had devised an interpretation of the Stone Age which his Danish colleagues had not yet realized fully and which offered him fascinating insights (Worsaae 1934, 61; Klindt-Jensen 1975).

Nilsson saw the development of early society in Scandinavia as an evolution of the economic bases of life. He does not seem to have known Kraft, but had borrowed the model from eighteenth-century ethnographers in France, amongst others who again were influenced by the Classical model of Lucretius (Harris 1868, 35 ff.). This was the simple scheme which led from hunting and fishing through nomadism and cattle breeding to agriculture and so on. Nilsson concentrated on the first stage, studying contemporary hunting and fishing tribes.

One of Nilsson's informants was a Danish scientist, P. W. Lund, who worked with astonishing results in Brazil. He not only collected animal bones and other items of interest, but as a member of the Royal Society of Northern Antiquaries he sent home to the Society in Copenhagen polished stone axes which he compared with Danish antiquities (*Ill. 1*); moreover, he referred these axes to the contemporary primitive peoples' everyday life in Brazil. The secretary of the Copenhagen society, Rafn, who realized the importance of these observations, had the letter 'On the Stone Axes of the South American Savages' printed in the *Annaler for nordisk Oldkyndighed* (1838–39). The paper is indeed a vivid record of tribes living in some sort of Stone Age.

Lund was a wealthy young man, who had to go to a warm climate to be cured of a serious disease and – at any rate for a time – to give up a very promising scientific career (*Ill. 2*). As Brazil seemed to offer the best conditions for his complaint, he chose this vast country as resort; but soon he was trying to widen his knowledge of natural sciences and began a travelling life which, after a visit home, ended in Lagoa Santa, a charming little village several hundred kilometres north of Rio de Janeiro. He happened to meet with a Norwegian adventurer who told Lund that in this area there were a great many caves with animal bones. They became partners – the wealthy young and acute scholar and the dissipated traveller – and stayed for the rest of their lives in Lagoa Santa, where Lund established an active research institution, at times assisted by colleagues from Copenhagen who came to visit and work with him. Lund himself investigated more than 800 caves, where he found bones of extinct animals. In one of these were also human skeletons. He did not hesitate to point out that this must be evidence of aboriginal people from a remote past.

From 1835 to 1844 Lund worked energetically on these problems and, since he found a polished axe in one of the caves, he realized their importance for the dating of such objects. After this early hectic activity he relaxed and lived rather passively, but in uninterrupted contact with the Copenhagen scholars. When the so-called Kitchen-midden Commission discussed Worsaae's interpretation of shell mounds as remains of human activity Lund was asked to give his opinion. On 11 March 1852, Lund answered and not only gave his support to the observation but added that along the whole east coast of Brazil shell mounds could be seen, and the natives 'are of the same opinion as the one you have

[1] Hindenburg is supposed to have incorporated Thomsen's views in his survey.

2 P.W. Lund (1801–80).

arrived at by your investigation, which therefore would give confirmation' (Petersen 1939, 204).

Lund's description of primitive economy and industry had further influence on archaeological studies. Details were used by Worsaae (*Ill. 3*) in his excellent little book, *Danmarks Oldtid* (1843), translated six years later into English: *The Primeval Antiquities of Denmark*. The author does not explicitly mention Lund, but it is obvious from such specific references as the following:

The most ancient inhabitants, or as we may term them, the aborigines, would have made but little progress, had they attempted to fell a large and full-grown tree, with nothing more than so imperfect an instrument as the stone hatchet. They doubtless pursued the same method as the savages of our own day, who when about to fell a tree with stone hatchets, avail themselves also of the assistance of fire, in the following manner. In the first place some of the bark is peeled off, by means of the hatchet, from the tree which is to be felled. In the opening thus made coals are placed, which are fanned till they are all consumed. By this means a portion of the trunk is charred, which is then hewn away with the hatchet, and fresh coals are continually added until the tree is burned through. In our peat bogs old trunks of trees have been found which appear to have been thus felled by stone hatchets with the aid of fire.

It can scarcely be doubted that their boats must have been of a very simple kind. From several relics which have been dug up, we may conclude that the aborigines in the usual manner of savage nations, charred the stem of the tree at the root and the sumit only, and then hollowed it out by means of fire till it acquired its equilibrium on the water. To this use the instruments which have been termed hollow chisels, were most probably destined (Worsaae 1843, 13).

When he wrote this Worsaae was a young man of 22 years, and it is easy for us now with our deeper knowledge to point out that the parallels he chose – and which were first put forward by Lund – do not in fact fit well. The method of felling trees by use of hot coals is rather peculiar. It is not known in the primitive technology of the Waiwai of northern Brazil. The building of boats in Brazil was done by hollowing a tree firstly by axes or adzes, and then the hollowed tree was opened out by putting the

3 J.J.A. Worsaae (1821–85).

tree over a fire and using the heat – not the charcoal – for bending out the sides (Yde 1965, 239). A related procedure is still known in Finland for making dug-out canoes, and it would be more reasonable to parallel this technique rather than the one mentioned by Worsaae which for many years was repeated in archaeological literature (cf. for example Horn 1874, Fig. opp. p. 168; Dreyer 1899, Fig. 25).

Some years later an amateur archaeologist, N. F. B. Sehested, made practical experiments with different types of flint axes and proved that these implements were as a matter of fact quite efficient. It was possible without much difficulty to use them as carpenters' axes (Sehested 1884).

Even if Worsaae, in the case I have just quoted, did not choose the best analogies, his idea of interpretation was right, and his study was a step forward in relation to contemporary studies. Also his conception of economic and social development was of basic value. He did not stop with Nilsson's hunting and fishing stage, but pointed out that the next stage, agriculture, was well documented in the finds of the Bronze Age (Worsaae 1843, 98).

Worsaae's interest for the modern student of ethnography is partly due to his use of the material for comparative studies. When in 1865 he became Thomsen's successor as director of the museum in the Palace of the Prince, where Danish prehistory, foreign antiquities, ethnography and other collections were combined, he rearranged this heterogeneous material into some unifying categories. Foreign antiquities were in fact placed in show-cases at the beginning of the exhibition of ethnography (Worsaae 1872, Preface). He wanted to show to the public comparative material explaining and illustrating conditions in the prehistoric past of Denmark. In this way it may indeed be claimed that Worsaae put the Royal Museum of Northern Antiquities into the proper world perspective.

Bibliography

Birket-Smith, K. 1960 Jens Kraft: a pioneer of ethnology in Denmark, *Folk* 2, 5.

Dreyer, W. 1899 *Nordens Oldtid*, 'Frem', Copenhagen.

HARRIS, M. 1968 *The rise of anthropological theory*, London.

HINDENBURG, T. 1859 *Bidrag til den danske Archaeologis Historie*, Copenhagen.

HORN, Fr. W. 1874 *Mennesket i den forhistoriske Tid*, Copenhagen.

KLINDT-JENSEN, O. 1950 *Foreign influences in Denmark's Early Iron Age* = *Acta Archaeologia* (Copenhagen) XX, 1949.

1975 *A History of Scandinavian Archaeology*, London.

KRAFT, J. 1760 *Kort Fortaelning af de Vilde Folks fornemmeste Indretninger, Skikke og Meninger*. . ., Copenhagen.

LAFITAU, J.T. 1724 *Mœurs des sauvages Amériquains, Comparées aux Mœurs des Premiers Temps*, Paris.

ORME, Bryony, 1973 Archaeology and ethnography, in *The explanation of culture change: models in prehistory*, ed. A. C. Renfrew, London, 481.

PETERSEN, C. S. 1939 *Stenalder–Broncealder–Jernalder*, Copenhagen.

RYDBECK, O. 1943 Den arkeologiska forskningen och historiska museet vid Lunds universitet under tvåhundra år, 1735–1937, *Meddelanden fran Lunds Universitets Historiska Museum*, 165.

SEHESTED, N. F. B. 1884 Praktiske Forsøg, *Archaeologiske Undersøgelser 1878–81*.

STOBAEUS, K. 1738 *Ceraunii betulique lapides*, Lund.

WORSAAE, J. J. A. 1843 *Danmarks Oldtid*, Copenhagen.

1872 *Kort Veiledning i det Kgl. ethnografiske Museum*, Copenhagen.

1934 *En Oldgrandskers Erindringer*, ed. V. Hermansen, Copenhagen.

YDE, J. 1965 *Material Culture of the Waiwai*, Copenhagen.

6

PAUL JOHNSTONE

Shipwrights and Wheelwrights in the Ancient World

I HAD the pleasure, early in the 1960s, of having two small models made for a television programme in which Stuart Piggott was taking part. These were of an early waggon and cart from Lchashen. They both survive until today and, I understand, still make their appearance in appropriate lectures.

These were a small incidental reflection of Professor Piggott's long-lasting interest in early wheels and wheeled vehicles, which has been expressed in a number of papers (Piggott 1957; 1962; 1968; 1974). Some years before the models were made, I was involved with both Stuart Piggott and Richard Atkinson in another television project to do with early water as well as land transport. This was the experimental moving of a copy of a Stonehenge bluestone. I think that at that time few people would have thought there was much to be gained by any relative study of early wheels and water transport. However, the situation has changed very considerably in recent years.

In the 1950s it was possible for a reputable archaeologist and fellow contributor to this Festschrift, when translating the *Epic of Gilgamesh*, to describe Ziusudra's building of the Sumerian Ark as a process of 'laying the keel and ribs, then making fast the planking'. At that time, this implication that the Ark was built skeleton- rather than shell-fashion would hardly have attracted a moment's attention. But by 1971, it was possible to list no less than twenty Classical wrecks that had been found with mortise-and-tenon fastened shell-construction (Casson 1971, 214–16). Admittedly some of these vessels, the County Hall ship, Nero's great barges from Lake Nemi, and the so-called 'Caesar's galley' from Marseille, had been available as evidence for this type of construction before 1939, and there was also, as Basch has observantly pointed out, the Roman vessel from Golo in Corsica whose similar build had been accurately recorded as long ago as AD 1777 by M. Jacotin and published by Admiral Paris in 'Souvenirs de Marine Conservés' in 1892 (Basch 1973, 329) (*Ill. 1*). However, it was the numerous and largely underwater finds of the 1950s and 1960s that really enabled Peter Throckmorton to declare that 'all Roman ships found to date in the Mediterranean were carvel-built by the shell-first method and were tenoned' (Throckmorton 1973, 246).

To these Classical wrecks, one can now add the Cheops ship, found in pieces in a pit near the great Pyramid at Gizeh in 1952 and finally restored and published in 1971 (Abubakr *et al.* 1971). Though with planks lashed to each other, this 5000-year-old vessel is still built shell-fashion, with round pegs inserted edgeways between strakes for additional strength.

Unless there was a type of vessel of which we have as yet no knowledge, and this is not impossible, it seems likely that shell-building was the standard technique in the early Eastern Mediterranean for anything other than reed – or papyrus – bundle craft, dug-outs or simple sewn boats. Thus it would be something of a surprise if Ziusudra had used a skeleton-technique to build his Ark.

Though these underwater finds and the restoration of the Cheops ship have greatly clarified our knowledge of the early shipwright's art, they compete poorly in sheer numbers, especially in the early period, with wheels surviving from antiquity – over fifty in Europe and Western Asia, from the middle of the third millennium to the second half of the second millennium BC (Piggott 1965, 266). It is therefore suggested here that some use can be made of comparisons between the surviving examples of these two different but related crafts. This is particularly so, now we know that the fastening of planks by mortises and tenons was such an integral part both of early Mediterranean ships and of tripartite wheels. Moreover, as a method it seems to have had an obsessive attraction for both shipwright and wheelwright alike. The waggon from Barrow 11 at Lchashen had no less than 12,000 mortises (Piggott 1968, 289), while Basch has described the use of mortises in the Nemi ships as 'almost manic' (Basch 1972, 24).

There are certain technological affinities between dug-outs and solid disc wheels in their use of solid wood, and between tripartite wheels with external struts and boats with planks joined by floor-timbers. But the next stage of development in both wheel and boat is perhaps the most interesting of all, as far as parallels are concerned. This is the removal of the external cross-piece or strut and the fastening of the timber parts to each other by pegs or tenons set into the thickness of the component parts. The wheels from Trialeti seem to suggest that this had occurred in Transcaucasia before the end of the third millennium bc (Piggott 1968, 285) (*Ill. 2*).

As far as boats and ships are concerned, Basch has conveniently summarized the five main methods, other than lashing, of assembling planking carvel-fashion, that is, set edge to edge (Basch 1973, 337) (*Ill. 3*). They are:

(a) with vertical pegs or tenons in mortises in the thickness of the planks, the tenons usually being secured in Classical times by circular dowels through them at right-angles
(b) with oblique tree-nails
(c) with dovetail clamps let into the surface of the adjoining planks
(d) with oblique nails, which are often a replacement for earlier oblique or vertical tenons
(e) with metal clamps, their pointed and bent-over ends hammered into the adjoining strakes

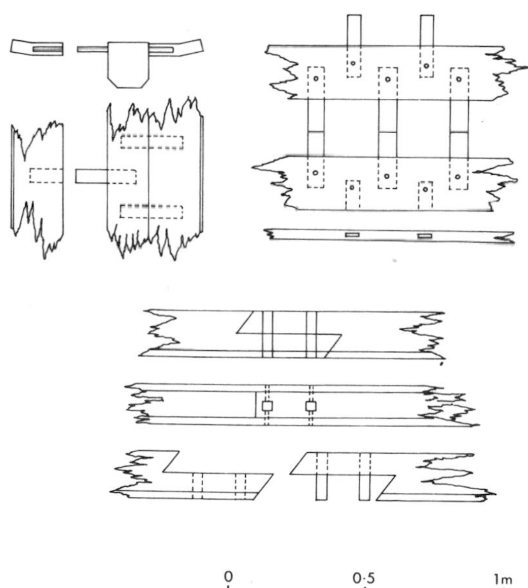

1 Details of the Golo ship as recorded by M. Jacotin in 1777, showing the mortise-and-tenon construction with the dowels piercing the tenons at right-angles (after Basch).

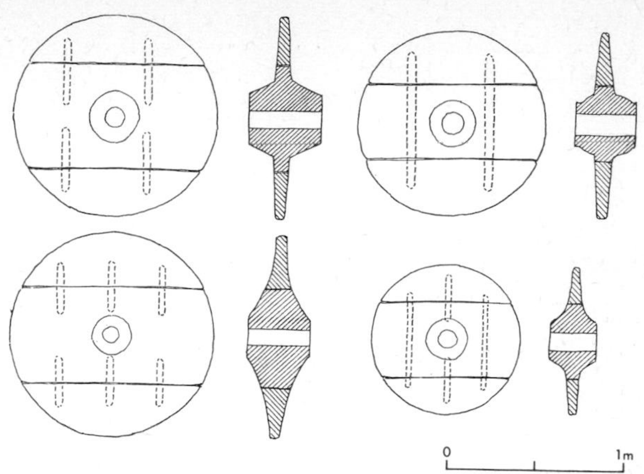

2 Mortise-and-tenon fastened tripartite wheels from Trialeti (above), and (below) from Lchashen and Nergetashen (after Piggott).

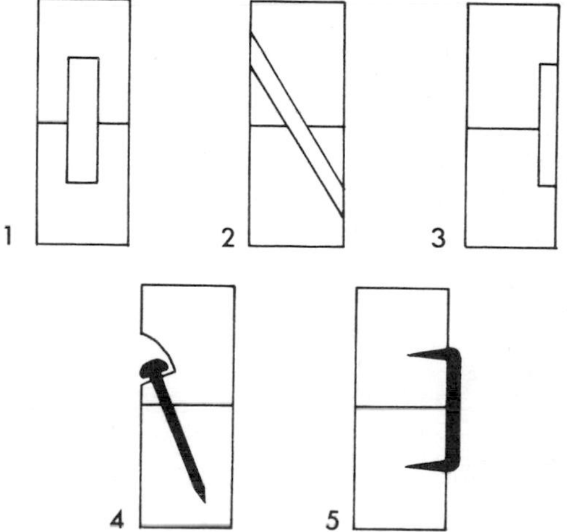

3 The five main methods of fastening planking edge to edge, carvel fashion, other than by lashing (after Basch).

Tripartite wheels seem generally to confine themselves to (a) though without dowels at right-angles through the tenons. Nevertheless, this does seem to suggest some ideas, other than just the similarity of two different crafts working with much the same material for different ends. The importance of the mortise-and-tenon method to Classical shipbuilding, the lateness of the first true example – fourth century BC – and the early and widespread use of the same practice in wheel construction makes these ideas the more worth considering.

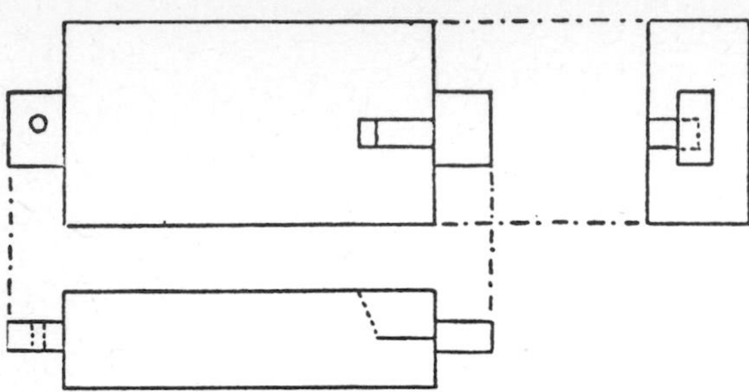

4 Rectangular block of wood with tenons pierced to take dowels at right-angles. From Tomb 3504 at Sakkara (after Emery).

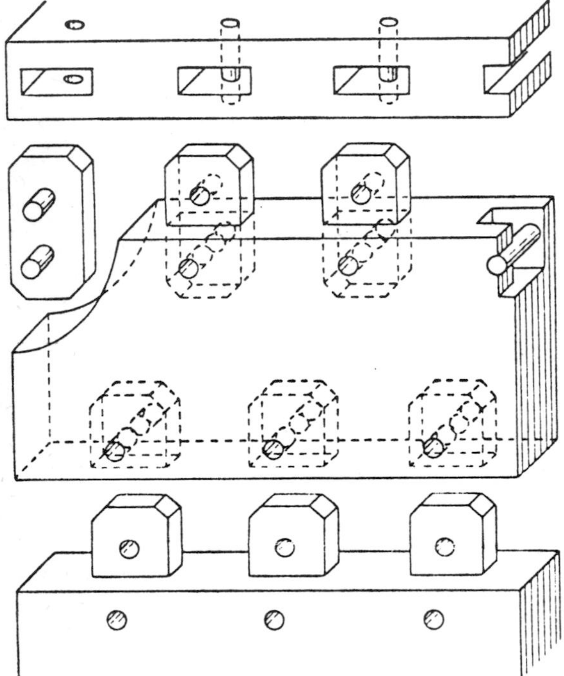

5 Diagram of the mortise-and-tenon construction of the Vechten ship, found near Utrecht in 1888 (after Ellmers).

One point is the geographical area where this technique was used. Another is the technological capacity which made this particular practice possible. Finally there is the question why this particular method seems non-existent in early indigenous West European vessels.

To begin with the geographical factor, Piggott has pointed out that the areas where tripartite wheels have been found in archaeological contexts virtually coincides with the area where copper and bronze gouges have appeared (Piggott 1968, 305). This is scarcely surprising. As Deshayes writes of gouges making mortises, 'le gouge creuse facilement les rainures dans le bois, – en coupant les ligaments lateraux de chaque fibre' (Deshayes 1960, 109). Piggott's description of mortises on ancient wheels being cut with a narrow metal gouge and finished by reaming out (Piggott 1968, 270) also compares with Casson's translation of τέτρηνεν δ'ἄρα πάντα in the *Odyssey* when Odysseus is building a boat to leave the island of Ogyia and 'bores' all his planks to make slots for the tenons (Casson 1971, 218).

If one looks at these tools on Deshayes' distribution maps, at least three points emerge. Firstly there is the existence of a copper gouge at Harappa, which fits rather pleasingly with the model wheel found at Chanhu-daro by Mackay (1943, 165 and Pl. LVIII: 8). This was painted to appear tripartite. Our knowledge of Harappan ships is limited to a few sketchy illustrations, but here is the suggestion that some may have been craft with mortise-and-tenon fastened planks. The Indian sub-continent of course has an immense variety of surviving primitive craft, but it is at least worth noting that the Calcutta *manche* was reported in the nineteenth century to have tenon-fastened planks (Paris 1841, 20).

Another area where there is a strong concentration of both early tripartite wheels and chisels and gouges is Transcaucasia. Not many early wrecks have as yet been reported from the Black Sea, and one, from near Donuzlav, dated to the fourth century BC, has no mention of mortises and tenons in its publication (Blavatsky *et al.* 1973). This, however, was an amphora-carrying vessel and had lead-sheathing fastened with bronze nails, like the more or less contemporary Kyrenia ship, so it does not seem unreasonable to suppose that it was mortise-and-tenon fastened in the same way as the Cypriot vessel.

Then, as with the Calcutta *manches*, Basch has suggested that it is possible to see in the form of a nineteenth-century coaster from Ineboli, the ancient town of Abonuiteichos on the northern Anatolian coast, what he calls a 'wooden coelacanth'. Though now having strakes joined by nails inserted obliquely through grooves, it was, he believes, in its original version assembled with mortises-and-tenons and was a survivor of Classical shipbuilding practice (Basch 1973, 308).

The wheel came late to Egypt. Nor does that country seem to have had much use for gouges in its early days. On the other hand, as Aldred has pointed out, the introduction of copper tools in themselves did much for the technique of joining timber, from the fifth millennium bc on (Aldred 1954, 683). In fact, one useful point of our knowledge that early wheels with their planks secured by mortise-and-tenon existed from Lchashen and Trialeti to Kish and Ur and on to Harappa is that it decreases the temptation to see in Egypt the solitary origin of the mortise-and-tenon method of Classical shipbuilding. For if one looks at the piece of wood found by Emery at Sakkara in Tomb 3504, the Tomb of Uadji, third king of the First Dynasty, with its tenons at either end pierced with holes at right-angles for retaining dowels (Emery 1954, 53) (*Ill. 4*), it is so like the construction of a Roman ship that it would be very easy, with the ghost of Elliot Smith at one's shoulder, to say that here must be the origin of the whole practice.

But as well as remembering the broader picture given by wheels, it is also worth recalling a comment by Petrie:

> The heavy strong chisel came in with the free supply of copper in the First Dynasty; it was set in a wooden handle and struck by a mallet to cut the mortice holes in beams for boats and house building.... The connecting of boards was by slots and flat tongues down to the Sixth Dynasty; in the decay of work which followed, the easier method of boring round holes and inserting pegs of wood was adopted.
>
> Slots and tongues were again revived and are found in coffins down to the Greek period (Petrie 1940, 122–3).

So this raises the intriguing possibility that the properly admired Cheops and Dahshur vessels, with their round peg fastenings, could even have been reversions from earlier flat-tenon-fastened vessels!

There is one final point about the distribution of copper gouges. As Deshayes notes, one of the surprising aspects is their absence from the Aegean and none are known from the Creto-Mycenaean world, the westernmost example being from Troy (Deshayes 1960, 110). It looks as if an arc of mainland from Egypt to Phoenicia and on to Transcaucasia is the most likely area of origin for this type of shipbuilding. Crete, despite its maritime seals, may not have contributed at first, though perhaps with the appearance of the four-spoked chariot wheel in the middle of the second millennium bc, like the one on the amygdaloid sard bead seal from Knossos (Mylonas 1951, 135), the position could have changed. Certainly the part of an Egyptian spoked chariot wheel found in the tomb of Amenophis III, dating to about a quarter of a century before Tutankh-amun, has an extremely elaborate mortise-and-tenon join between flange and nave (Western 1973, 92, Fig. 2).

In Western Europe the position is less clear. There are four main examples of mortise-and-tenon fastened craft from that area. One is the Vechten ship found near Utrecht in 1888 (Ellmers 1973, 293–4) (*Ill. 5*). Next is the County Hall ship found in 1910 and currently being republished by Peter Marsden (Marsden 1972, 116). From Zwammerdam in the Netherlands, where a now filled-in branch of the old Rhine ran in front of the Roman frontier fort of Nigrum Pullum, have come a piece of decking, a large steering oar, and a river barge (de Weerd 1973; 1974) (*Ill. 6*). Finally there is a description dating back to AD 1809, of a vessel found in the Somme Valley, surrounded by various Roman coins and pottery, and with a peach-stone which could only have been put there by colonists from Italy, who introduced the fruit to Gaul. This craft seems to have been built in the traditional Classical fashion (Traullé 1809, 8). All these are in provincial Roman contexts and could therefore be the result of intrusive influence.

Wheels are not as helpful here either. According to Anati, the two-wheeled spoked chariot is found in the Camonica Valley and probably at Mont Bego in the fifteenth century bc. By the late thirteenth or twelfth century it had reached Kivik in Sweden, and by the tenth century it had arrived in central Scandinavia, the Île de France and Los Buitros in Spain (Anati 1960, 62–3; Breuil 1935, 63). These fairly early dates are not too relevant to our argument in view of Eogan's statement that the metal gouge did not reach Western Europe until the tenth century bc (Eogan 1960, 99). According to Kossack also, board felloes of any type were unknown in Central Europe before the seventh century (Kossack 1971, 147). These were immediately preceded by solid cast-bronze wheels. Other wooden wheels, like the Mercurago one which definitely has mortises and tenons, and the Sassari model, which seems to be a copy of it (Déchelette 1924, II, 289–90), are in a Mediterranean context.

Nevertheless, mortises and tenons must have been used in early Western Europe. The lintels at Stonehenge are too well known to need further comment. A specific wooden example is the piece of timber, probably once the upright of a building, with a tenon on the end, from the site of Storrs Moss in Lancashire. Professor Powell dates this to about

6 A Roman river barge during excavation at Zwammerdam in Holland. Though the bottom is built carvel-fashion, the two strakes of the sides overlap. The mast-step is on the right. It has no mortise-and-tenon fastening.

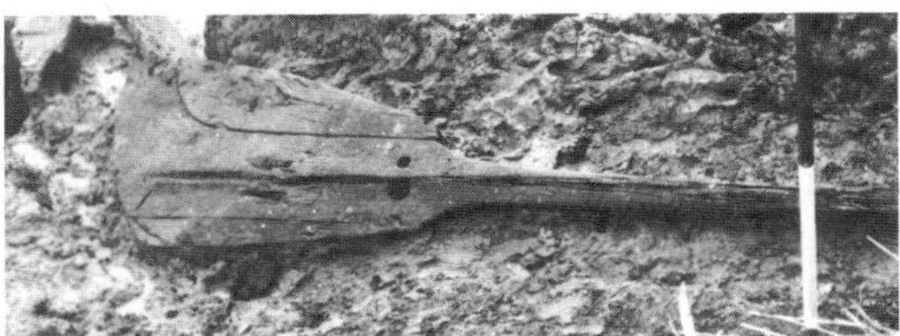

7 A large steering oar found at Zwammerdam, with its parts secured by mortise-and-tenon. The white marks on the oar show the position of the dowels.

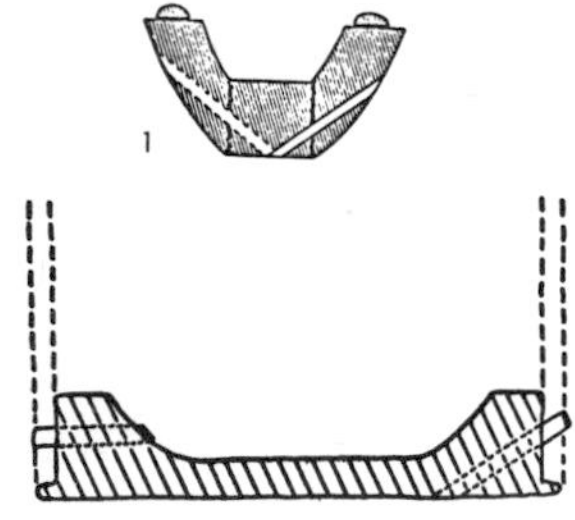

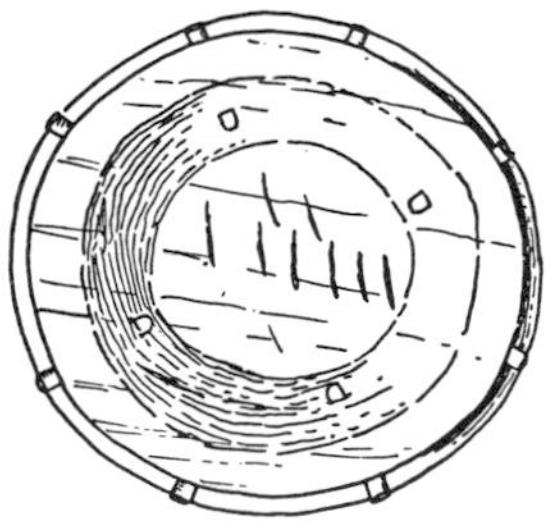

8 1, The bottom of one of the Dahshur ships (after Reisner); 2, base of a wooden container with wooden pegs for securing its side walls, from a Late Bronze Age settlement at Zurich-Alpenquai (after Clark).

4000 bc (Powell *et al.* 1971, 124). There must surely have been many more similar pieces in the timber-built villages of the early forest-exploiters of temperate Europe (cf. Zürn 1965).

Why do the shipwrights of the early West appear not to have used this technique? There is a possible answer in van der Waals' well-known study of early disc wheels from Holland, including a discussion of the mortise-and-tenon fastened tripartite wheels from Ezinge which he suggests date from about 400 BC. These show time and again, he notes, missing or broken pegs which must have caused the wheels to collapse (van der Waals 1964, 123). So neither the local technology nor the local conditions enabled this method to maintain the strength it achieved in the East. The Atlantic, with its rougher seas, stronger tides, and lack of harbours, must have had much the same equivalent relationship to the Mediterranean. Without the same long tradition of skilled carpentry behind them, the shipwrights of the West, like the wheelwrights, must have found this elaborate method impractical. This was all the more so because they had a simpler, cruder, but effective alternative.

In 1969, Ellmers postulated a new category of ancient shipbuilding, the so-called 'Celtic' tradition, which was neither shell- nor skeleton-built (Ellmers 1969). To begin with, this view was based largely on theory and the Roman-period ship from Blackfriars, found in 1958, with its then unique form of construction. Within the next four years, numerous finds of wrecks, notably some of the great Roman river barges from Zwammerdam (*Ill. 6*) and Yverdon and Bevaix in Switzerland (de Weerd *et al.* 1973; 1974; Egloff 1972; 1973), strongly confirmed this hypothesis. There obviously was an indigenous school of early Western European shipbuilding marked by flat bottoms, hard chines, L-shaped floor timbers, caulked seams, and nails hammered in from the outside and with the ends bent back again.

The caulking is interesting, because the cabinet-work tightness of the joins given to Classical wrecks by the mortise-and-tenon method seems to have made it unnecessary in their case. There was a guild of caulkers (*stuppatores*) in Rome but they must have operated in a small way, because Strabo's surprise at the seaweed caulking of Venetic ships is obvious, as was Pliny's at the sticky pounded concoction of reeds used for the same purpose in the Low Countries (Casson 1971, 209–10). This latter point is the more relevant because reeds were found to have been used as caulking in some of the Zwammerdam wrecks (de Weerd 1973, 394).

But there must presumably have been a stage before these craft when the metal, used so generously to provide, for instance, the Bevaix barge, dated to the first century AD, with no less than 4000 nails, was not available. It is suggested here that this lavish use of metal came in with what Sir Cyril Fox called the Celtic passion for smelting, and that was used before in place of nails was basically the wooden peg. Pegs had been used as tenons in all the tripartite wheels from Transcaucasia to Ezinge and Blair Drummond in Scotland (Piggott 1957). It was used in the Cheops and Dahshur ships, and in a late Bronze Age bucket from Zurich-Alpenquai (Clark 1952, 212) (*Ill. 8*). Add a head, and a peg becomes a tree-nail. These were used on the Viking ships from Roskilde, Askekarr, Hedeby, Eltang and other vessels (Crumlin-Pedersen 1967, 168). Perhaps the most striking western contemporary example is the Portugeuse fishing boat, the *saveiro* or *xavega* (*Ill. 9*). As long ago as 1952, Lethbridge suggested that this crescent-shaped vessel might be a Bronze Age survival (Lethbridge 1952, 118). Watching it on the stocks, it is possible to see in it the various features of the 'Celtic' school of shipbuilding, flat bottom, hard chine, caulked seams, two-part U-frames, with the futtock scarfed to the L-piece at the chine alternately on each side (*Ill. 9*); but instead of iron nails it has wooden tree-nails, 1600 to a boat on average (*Ill. 10*). It is also built by laying down the flat central plank and the two outside planks of the bottom first, then adding the L-shaped internal members next on alternate sides (*Ill. 9*). After that, the strakes of the sides are tree-nailed on, always horizontally, and the upright pieces of the internal members, or futtocks, are scarfed and tree-nailed onto the L-pieces, to make U-shaped frames; finally, the rest of the flat bottom is filled in. So a method that is neither truly skeleton- nor shell-fashion is used, and may well be how the Blackfriars, Zwammerdam, Yverdon, Bevaix and Venetic craft were built.

If, therefore, there was such a tradition of sea-going in the West which antedated the arrival of either mortise-and-tenon fastened ships or tripartite wheels, and proved successful in the difficult conditions of the Atlantic, then perhaps after the simple lashed-planked craft with cross-members like Ferriby and Brigg (Wright *et al.* 1947), craft were used whose planks were attached to internal frames by hammered-in wooden pegs or tree-nails, until these were eventually replaced in some cases by iron nails. Thus if, one day, a pre-Iron Age 'Celtic' ship is found, perhaps it too will have in it that essential of the tripartite wheel, the round peg or dowel or tree-nail, not inserted between the thickness of the planks, but hammered through them at right-angles into frames. Or did wooden tree-nails just replace iron nails in the post-Roman economic decline? That is still an unanswered question.

9 A Portuguese *saveiro* or *xavega* being built at Pardilho, May 1974. The L-pieces of the U-frames have been attached by tree-nails on alternate sides of the three main bottom planks.

10 The *saveiro*-builder's tree-nails – from the slab of pine wood he starts with to the finished article – and the tools he uses.

Bibliography

ABUBAKR, A. M. and AHMED, Y. M. 1971 The Funerary Boats of Khufu, *Beiträge zur Ägyptischen Bauforschung und Altertumskunde* 11, 1–16.

ALDRED, C. 1954 Fine Wood-working, in *A History*

of Technology 1, ed. C. Singer, E. J. Holmyard and A. R. Hall, Oxford, 684–703.

ANATI, E. 1964 *Camonica Valley*, London.

BLAVATSKY, V. C. and PETERS, B. G. 1973 A Wreck of the Late Fourth or Early Third Century B.C. near Donuzlav, *International Journal of Nautical Archaeology* 2, 25–32. (Translated by D. Blackman.)

BASCH, L. 1972 Ancient Wrecks and the Archaeology of Ships, *International Journal of Nautical Archaeology* 1, 1–58.

1973 The Golo Wreck and Sidelights on other Ancient Ships Culled from Admiral Paris, 'Souvenirs de marine conservés', *International Journal of Nautical Archaeology* 2, 239–44.

BREUIL, H. 1933 *Les Peintures Rupestres Schématique de la Péninsule Ibérique* II, Paris.

CASSON, L. 1971 *Ships and Seamanship in The Ancient World*, Princeton.

CLARK, J. G. D. 1952 *Pre-Historic Europe: The Economic Basis*, London.

CRUMLIN-PEDERSEN, O. and OLSEN, O. 1967 The Skuldelev Ships. *Acta Archaeologica* XXXVIII, 73–124.

DÉCHELETTE, J. 1910 *Manuel d'Archéologie* II, Part 1, Paris.

DESHAYES, J. 1960 *Les Outils de Bronze de L'Indus au Danube*, Paris.

EGLOFF, M. 1972 *Du Lac de Neuchâtel considerée comme un musée d'antiquités*, Neuchâtel.

1973 Épave gallo-romaine dans le lac de Neuchâtel, *Avis de Neuchâtel*, 4 August 1973.

ELLMERS, D. 1969 *Keltischer Schiffbau. Jahrbuch d. Röm.-Germ. Zentralsmuseum Mainz* 16, 73–122.

1972 *Fruhmittelalterliche Handelschiffahrt in Mittel- und Nordeuropa*, Neumünster.

EMERY, W. B. 1952 *Great Tombs of the First Dynasty* II, Oxford.

EOGAN, G. 1966 Some notes on the origin and diffusion of the Bronze Socketed Gouge, *Ulster Journal of Archaeology* XXIX, 97–102.

KOSSACK, G. 1971 The construction of the felloe in Iron Age spoked wheels, in *The European Community in Later Prehistory*, ed. J. Boardman, M. A. Brown and T. G. E. Powell, London, 143–63.

LETHBRIDGE, T. C. 1952 *Boats and Boatmen*, Cambridge.

MACKAY, E. H. J. 1943 Chanhu-Daro Excavations, 1935–1936, *American Oriental Series* 20, New Haven.

MYLONAS, G. E. 1951 The Figured Mycenaean Stelae. *American Journal of Archaeology* 54, 121–47.

MARSDEN, P. 1972 Ships of the Roman Period and after in Britain, in *A History of Seafaring*, ed. G. F. Bass, London, 113–32.

PARIS, F. E. 1841 *Essai sur la Construction navale des Peuples extra-Européens*, Paris.

1892 *Souvenirs de marine conservés* V, Paris.

PETRIE, F. W. M. 1940 *The Wisdom of the Egyptians*, London.

PIGGOTT, S. 1957 A Tripartite Disc Wheel from Blair Drummond, Perthshire, *Proc. Soc. Ant. Scot.* XC, 238–41.

1962 Heads and Hoofs, *Antiquity* XXXVI, 110–18.

1968 The Earliest Wheeled Vehicles and the Caucasian Evidence, *Proc. Prehist. Soc.* XXXIV, 266–318.

1974 Chariots in the Caucasus and China, *Antiquity* XLVIII, 16–24.

POWELL, T. G. E., OLDFIELD, F. and CORCORAN, J. X. W. P. 1971 Excavation in Zone VII Peat at Storrs Moss, Lancashire, England 1965–67, *Proc. Prehist. Soc.* XXXVIII, 112–37.

THROCKMORTON, P. J. 1973 The Roman Wreck at Pantano Longarini, *International Journal of Nautical Archaeology* 2, 243–66.

TRAULLÉ, M. 1809 *Lettre addressée à M. Mongez, Membre de l'Institut*, Paris.

VAN DER WAALS, J. D. 1964 Neolithic disc wheels in the Netherlands, *Palaeohistoria* X, 103–46.

WEERD, de. M. D. and HAALEBOS, J. D. 1973 Scheppen voor Het opscheppen, *Spiegel Historiael* 8 ste Jaargang No. 7/8, 386–97.

WESTERN, A. C. 1973 A wheel hub from the tomb of Amenophis III, *Journal of Egyptian Archaeology* 59, 91–4.

WRIGHT, E. V. and WRIGHT, C. W. 1947 The North Ferriby Boats, *Mariner's Mirror* XXXIII, 235–55.

ZÜRN, H. 1965 Das Jugsteinzeitliche Dorf Ehrenstein (Kries Ulm). Veröffentlichingen des staatlichen Amtes für Denkmalplege Stuttgart, *Vor-und Frühgeschichte* 10–11.

Acknowledgments

I am grateful to Cyril Aldred, Reynold Higgins, and Professor T. G. E. Powell for advice, to Dr D. Ellmers for the Traullé quotation, to Professor Willem Glasbergen and Mr M. D. de Weerd of the Instituut Voor Prae- en Protohistorie, Rijksuniversiteit, Amsterdam, for permission to publish photographs of the Zwammerdam site, and to Major David Goddard, Director of the Exeter Maritime Museum, and Mrs Valerie Fenwick for the use of photographs taken by them.

7

A. M. SNODGRASS

Conserving Societies and Independent Development

A GOOD synthesis, even when its author is trying to be purely descriptive, will inevitably exert an influence for years afterwards on its field of study. Whether it was Stuart Piggott's intention or not, ancient Europe has never been the same since *Ancient Europe*. What were modestly described as 'some general observations on the wider problems of prehistory' grew, in the event, into something more. A recurrent theme of the book was the antithesis between conserving and innovating societies; indeed, this was really the model which the book adopted for the study of the remoter European past, from the Neolithic era to the Roman Empire. As a model, it has the obvious virtues of serviceability and familiarity – familiarity in the most direct sense that we can see the antithesis still operating with our own eyes, if we visit certain areas of even the 'innovating' Western world. 'It is important in a small community that people should not be markedly different in their way of life, yet there can be no evolution without differentiation of behaviour. The initial attempts at being different are the dangerous ones, and therefore we like privacy for experiment so that we shall not be different in the beginning.' These words were written by an observer of a Celtic social system, not two thousand years ago but twenty (Fraser Darling 1955, 304). They will be recognized as giving a valid contemporary picture of a West Highland township by anyone fortunate enough to be familiar with such communities. They are indeed communities of conservators, and the attitudes described above – the author was writing in the specific context of agricultural technology – are applicable to a wide range of activity, and surely inherited from their own distant past. But we, with the privileged status of contemporary observers, can also note other attributes of these communities. They are not conservators in everything. Consider, for example, how utterly we should be misled in this instance if we equated material conservatism with conservatism in politics, or with backwardness in literacy. 'One would not,' wrote the late Gavin Maxwell of his West Highland neighbour, 'expect him to be able to quote the greater part of the *Golden Treasury*, to have read most of the classics, to have voluble and well-informed views on politics national and international, or to be a subscriber to the *New Statesman*. Yet these were the facts . . .' (Maxwell 1960, 31) – and they are not at all untypical. They may be connected with another good conserving quality: 'The Highlander, like many primitive peoples, valued leisure more than economic gain, for himself if not for his wife' (Mitchison 1962, 104). But it will be clear that communities of conservers are complex things, which may hold surprises for the unwary. What, if anything, can this teach us about the remote past?

The prime lesson of the last few years in archaeology would appear to be that the conserving communities of the past have even greater surprises to spring upon us. We must not exaggerate the impact of this discovery. The physical evidence for some of the spectacular achievements of early conserving cultures has been in front of us all along, in the form of monumental constructions that extend through space and time from Maes Howe to Zimbabwe, and of superbly designed artifacts. The attempts to explain these attainments uniformly as the results of cultural diffusion from innovating societies have long ago begun to look a little lame, where they have not broken down entirely. The antithesis between conserving and innovating societies did not in any sense depend on a naïvely diffusionist interpretation of the more striking individual products of the conserving societies. What it did perhaps to some extent depend on was a view of the comparative *chronology* of the innovating and conserving areas, which allowed a margin of temporal priority to the innovators in the development of most of the more permanently significant and useful arts, such as wheeled transport, writing, metallurgy or monumental architecture in its most generalized sense (compare Piggott 1965, 44 on early metallurgy, 92 on wheeled vehicles; but contrast 35 on the domestication of the dog). But this assumption was not in any way the cornerstone of the dichotomy between conservators and innovators. True, the inherent characteristics of an innovating society are such that it could be expected, more often than not, to see the possibilities of a new technique earlier than would a conserving society; but any simplistic picture of a series of innovations being passed on, by a sort of conveyor-belt of historical necessity, from innovators to conservers across large geographical distances, must at once be modified by other considerations: the appropriateness of the ideas to new and quite different environments; the relative importance of a given problem to two diverse economies; and the overriding aims of two different societies, not excluding the social inhibitions suggested in the first quotation above referring to the West Highlands. The whole relationship between the two kinds of society is too complex to depend on the simple issue of temporal priority. I shall be arguing in this paper that the revised view of the relative chronologies of some 'conserving' and 'innovating' cultures within Europe and the Near East, which has won wide acceptance in the last few years, may indeed be open to more doubts than is often now suggested; but that even if it is not, this will not to any serious degree affect the validity of the original antithesis between these two kinds of society.

To take first the chronological adjustments which have resulted in this new view of the comparative dating of some European and Mediterranean cultures, it is important to remember that they are essentially chronological adjustments and nothing more. The end results of these adjustments may include complete and very valuable reappraisals of cultures, and especially of 'barbarian' or 'conserving' cultures; but the fact remains that these reinterpretations have their origin in purely chronological deductions, and the question arises how far their validity depends on the soundness of those deductions.

The technique of calibrating radiocarbon dates against dendrochronological dates has, I think, been rather unevenly applied to different types of archaeological culture. Recently I considered elsewhere (1976, 39 ff.) one limited sector in which the chronological revision has been applied – that of barbarian Europe and the Aegean in the middle and later part of the second millennium BC. It seemed to me that a fundamental error of method had been made in the way in which historical dates had been brought into chronological comparisons between cultures. To confront radiocarbon dates on one side of a comparison with historical dates on the other (when radiocarbon dates were available for both), and then to adopt one of the proposed calibrations for the former, appeared (and still appears) to me to represent a gratuitous confusion of categories. I fully acknowledge that this methodological flaw, if such it is, affects only a limited range of cultural comparisons; and that elsewhere, if only of necessity, the proper course of comparing radiocarbon dates with radiocarbon dates has more often been followed. But the particular span of time and space that I considered does encompass the cultures of Wessex and Mycenae, which Professor Renfrew for one has repeatedly singled out as an emphatic example of the revolution in approach to prehistory (e.g. 1968; 1969, 39; 1970, 199). Historical dates have in fact a proper application to questions of this kind: namely, to serve as a check on the reliability of radiocarbon dates, whether calibrated or uncalibrated, within *one and the same* culture – that is, the one from which the historical dates themselves also come. Indeed, a brief application of that method was what aroused the suspicions of others (e.g. McKerrell 1972) about the validity of the calibrations so far proposed for certain areas. On present evidence there are, over much of the second millennium BC, major and unsettling anomalies which have beset the experiments so far made in the calibration of radiocarbon dates, in those areas – such as Egypt and the Aegean in the later, and much of Europe in the earlier Bronze Age – where some sort of independent check exists. Such independent checks will ideally take the form of a historical chronology which is, so to speak, indigenous to the area in question. But where, as in the majority of cases, this is absent, the traditional course is to replace it by the evidence of intrusive objects and features, which may link one culture with another without implying any kind of substantial diffusionist influence.

Here we strike at the heart of the recent controversy; for it is the rejection of this traditional course, and the denial of these intrusive features, which has been the most conspicuous feature in the early stages of the reinterpretation of some 'conserving' cultures. The reason is obvious: compatible chronologies for two different cultures need entail no links between them, but totally *incompatible* chronologies necessarily exclude the possibility of such cultural links, except through major time-lags in one direction. This is why so much energy is devoted to the process of uprooting, one by one, the often tiny pieces of evidence on which the traditional picture of contact between 'innovating' and 'conserving' cultures has so largely rested. At its best, this extirpation is achieved by scrutinizing the alleged archaeological contexts of the intrusive finds, and showing them to be only very loosely datable in the sequence of the 'host' culture, or even to be modern imports; this aspect of the method is often convincing enough. But sometimes the evidence stubbornly resists this procedure; the 'intrusive' objects are too firmly rooted in their contexts. Here one feels that, to be fully consistent, the process should be extended to cover, not merely a number of such residual instances singly, but the whole principle and method which underlies them all: the largely visual processes of typological recognition, comparison and distinction. If so many archaeologists, in the years before the late 1960s, detected so many intrusive features and inferred cultural contacts from them, in cases where such contacts are now held to be chronologically impossible, then surely the logical conclusion is that they were using a fundamentally unsound method. It could perhaps be argued that they were to some extent conditioned by their own preconception that such links *were* chronologically possible and even historically likely, and that they 'saw' the resemblances which they wanted to see.

Personally, however, I cannot find this explanation satisfactory in every case. There is a hard core of instances where the 'intrusive' features remain obstinately intrusive; where their resemblances to the products of other cultures, sometimes quite distant, refuse to fade away; and where their archaeological context is unimpeachable. In European prehistory, the sword from Ørskovhede, supported by its associated bronzes, would serve as a case in point (Randsborg 1967). In these instances, the proponents of the revised chronologies must in the last resort devise a new rationale, a new way of looking at these 'resemblances' in terms of coincidence or determinism or some other concept. But there is an alternative, which is to stand firm on the traditional methods of visual differentiation, and to say 'Not proven' to many of the claims for chronological revision. This is the course that I prefer to follow at present. Radiocarbon dates are, after all, extremely imprecise things (as would be more apparent if we stated them in terms of two standard deviations instead of one); and calibration, besides its other effects, serves to widen their margin of uncertainty. On the other side, I would not claim that a good archaeologist's eye cannot deceive him; indeed the visual aptitude of our profession has not always held high repute. To quote Osbert Lancaster's words of some years ago, 'The average archaeologist . . . being almost invariably totally deficient in visual sense, is about as safe a person to have around a well-conducted city as a bomber-pilot or a by-pass builder' (1947, 49). It may be that we have, along with the by-pass builders if not the bomber-pilots, improved a little in this respect over the last generation. What I would reject utterly is any suggestion that, instead of improving our visual sensitivity, we should as far as possible abstain from using it in our work. The visual process is an important adjunct to the progress of the whole discipline of archaeology, and an absolutely central factor in certain areas of it; this is one of the attributes which distinguish it fundamentally from many of the social sciences to which some are currently assimilating it.

This last stage in the argument applies, it is true, to only one narrow aspect of the wider question originally posed: in cases where the proposed revision in relative chronology, for whatever reason, is not accepted, how much of the proposed reappraisal of 'conserving' cultures lapses with it? My suspicion is that the removal or modification of the chronological argument would change the picture of 'independent development' in a few other ways besides the merely chronological. It becomes very much harder to argue that this or that practice is not *in fact* affected by the operation of external factors, when these factors could have been present, and when there may even be other circumstantial evidence for their presence. And a society which finds its own way to a new technique, with all external inspiration excluded, is in a rather different position from one which has access, even by the most indirect hearsay and at a remote distance, to the advances already made by another society. Most obviously, it may then follow quite different paths in the relevant technological processes. But, again, there are other aspects of the picture which remain unaffected; and these should perhaps account for the greater part of the study of any culture, though they have not often done so in the past. The whole social and economic organization of a society, in so far as we are able to recover it, is unlikely to be much affected by such considerations, since a society does not normally model its social system or its economic structure on outside models. The study of these and other important matters can often be pursued in disregard of such questions as the presence or absence of intrusive artifacts, and indeed of relative and absolute chronology.

But this raises in one's mind the perhaps slightly mischievous question: in that case, why has the study of such aspects been so largely promoted in recent years by recourse to the chronological argument? At times it is as if we are being told, 'This "backward" culture is not after all contemporary with that "precocious" culture, but antedates it; therefore it can owe nothing to it in terms of diffusion; therefore let us study those aspects of the "backward" culture which are in any case unlikely to be affected by diffusion.' As a sequence of logical thought, it leaves something to be desired, and suggests a residual fear of the ogre of diffusionism. But does this seriously matter? As long as the resultant studies bring genuine benefit to the subject, it does not make much difference in the long run what occasioned their undertaking. And, better still, the validity of the studies will not be much impaired if the chronological premisses should have to be considerably modified – as I believe they will in many cases.

Let me bring this discussion to an overdue conclusion by reverting to an earlier point in the argument (p. 59). I made the assertion that even the complete acceptance of the proposed revision in comparative chronologies would not destroy the value of the antithesis between conserving and innovating societies. This implies that even a society which achieves major technological advances unaided may nevertheless belong securely to the conserving type. This is not as paradoxical as it may appear, if we accept that the decisive criterion for an innovating culture is not the mere independent *invention* of new techniques and types; it is the ability to *sustain* technological progress, together with social and economic advance. A good illustration of this was given by Renfrew in his notable paper on the autonomy of the South-eastern European copper age. The smiths of the Balkan area, he argued, must have developed the basic techniques of copper smelting and working independently, but a delay of perhaps fifteen hundred years then apparently ensued before they were able to advance on this by producing a workable bronze alloy (Renfrew 1969, 29, 36). The implication was perhaps that this later step might still have to be attributed to external inspiration; but irrespective of that, the pattern and speed of development, after the first remarkable achievements, does not fulfil the criteria of an innovating society. From the same cultural area, if not necessarily from so early an epoch (see most recently Whipp and Hood 1973), comes that remarkably isolated phenomenon, the Tartaria tablets, which give a nice illustration of the kind of surprise which a conserving society can occasionally spring.

At the opposite extreme, I suppose that the first instance of an innovating society that springs to mind is that of Classical Greece – or rather, of the many communities which made up the Greek world. Certainly they illustrate very clearly the aptitude for sustained development which is the truest test of such a society, although there was much diversity of progress even within Greece. If not a line of Greek literature had survived, the permanently innovative character of Greek civilization would still be clear from its material culture. Yet it also provides a warning against using definitive criteria, for innovating as for conserving societies, that are too narrow. It has been well observed (Cook 1961, 132) that in the purely technological field, over an eight-hundred-year period covering the whole climax of Classical civilization, between about 1000 and 200 BC, the Greeks achieved no invention more remarkable than that of the catapult, or of the modifications of the borrowed Phoenician alphabet. The Greeks' aptitude for innovation very often went hand in hand with their propensity for borrowing from others, which should warn us that innovation is not synonymous with inventiveness.

In my view, as I hope I have made clear, the antithesis between conserving and innovating societies remains not merely useful, but highly illuminating as an archaeological concept. I hope that it will be explored further by those more competent to do so than I. We must only remember to be as broad and imaginative in our application of these categories as their original proponent has always been.

Bibliography

COOK, R. M.. 1961 *The Greeks till Alexander*, London.

DARLING, F. Fraser 1955 *West Highland Survey: an Essay in Human Ecology*, Oxford.

LANCASTER, O. 1947 *Classical Landscape with Figures*, London.

MCKERRELL, H. 1972 On the origins of British faience beads and some aspects of the Wessex-Mycenae relationship, *Proc. Prehist. Soc.* 38, 286–301.

MAXWELL, G. 1960 *Ring of Bright Water*, London.

MITCHISON, R. 1962 *Agricultural Sir John*, London.

Piggott, S. 1965 *Ancient Europe from the beginnings of agriculture to classical antiquity*, Edinburgh.
1970 New configurations in Old World archaeology, *World Archaeology* 2, 199–211.
Randsborg, K. 1967 'Aegean' bronzes in a grave in Jutland, *Acta Archaeologica* (Copenhagen) 38, 1–27.
Renfrew, A. C. 1968 Wessex without Mycenae, *Ann. Brit. School at Athens* 63, 277–85.
1969 The autonomy of the South East European copper age, *Proc. Prehist. Soc.* 35, 12–47.
Snodgrass, A. M. 1976 An outsider's view of radiocarbon calibration, in *Radiocarbon: Calibration and Prehistory*, ed. T. Watkins, Edinburgh, 39–46.
Whipp, D. and Hood, M. S. F. 1973 The Tartaria tablets, *Antiquity* XLVII, 147–9.

8

HERMANN BEHRENS

East or West? The Beaker Cultures of Europe Re-examined[1]

[1] Translated by S. J. Shennan

I HOPE Stuart Piggott will forgive my heading this contribution with parts of the titles of two of his own articles, among many of his works which I as a Central European archaeologist have found especially useful in my comparative studies. In this short paper I wish to voice some general thoughts on a problem which has already concerned European prehistoric research for decades; a problem on which Piggott too has expressed his opinions. I am speaking of the 'Beaker Cultures' and I use the term generically to describe all those Late Neolithic, or Eneolithic, cultures which figure in archaeological classifications as the Corded Ware Culture(s), the Battle-axe Culture(s), the Single Grave Culture(s), the Bell Beaker culture(s), and finally, as the Beaker Culture(s) in British terminology.

Although prehistory today, as a result of growing international contacts, is endeavouring to survey large-scale interactions, we must still remember that all the prehistoric research of previous decades and centuries began as the result of national and even regional studies. Even in the past, however, archaeologists working on related traits and trait complexes began to direct their interest beyond the boundaries of their own area to similar phenomena elsewhere. An example relevant to this topic is the work of Götze (1891), whose study of the Saale Corded Ware (*Ills. 1–6*) drew attention to the related pottery in the rest of Central Europe, and, indeed, in Northern, Western, and Eastern Europe as well. Another example is Abercromby (1912), who cited all sorts of continental parallels in his work on the British Beakers, including Corded Ware and Single Grave Beakers, not to mention Bell Beakers, from many different countries.

In what follows, I wish to treat the Beaker Cultures not only as a problem of archaeological taxonomy but to throw light on other aspects, in order to arrive at definite conclusions. From the temporal point of view, the historical process goes on continuously, without a break; considered spatially, it proceeds on a pattern of world-wide connections. It follows that exact boundaries in space and time for the phenomenon of the Beaker Cultures can never be established. All archaeological attempts to define chronological and spatial boundaries for the Beaker Cultures are thus somewhat artificial, or at least slightly unrealistic. Such division, nevertheless, is important for scientific understanding, as a means of creating order. Leo Klejn (1969) in a short article on 'The Problem of the Taxonomy of the Battle-axe Culture Group' (another name for the Beaker Cultures) has shown that the boundaries of this culture area, and its definition, vary from worker to worker as a result of different classificatory criteria; but, he argues, it is only at a superficial level that these differences of opinion stem from the differing views of individual researchers. In fact, they reflect the objective historical situation: that the chronological limits and the areal extent of the Beaker Cultures can never be defined with mathematical precision. If one is aware of this, then all the feuding over whose opinions about the extent of the Beaker Cultures are right or wrong becomes superfluous.

It must of course be borne in mind that the question of establishing boundaries is connected with the ideas a given researcher has about the contents of those groups whose boundaries he is trying to determine. Klejn has also drawn attention to the fact that various scholars, starting from different criteria of classification, have arrived at different assemblages for the Beaker Cultures they have isolated. Here too, differences of opinion may easily be regarded as exclusively of a subjective nature. The elements gathered together by people to form a culture complex do not constitute any closed unity in their distribution, 'as the combination of elements in the individual participant cultures does not cover the whole distribution area. Neither cord decoration, nor Beakers, nor Battle-axes are found in every group' (Junghans, Sangmeister and Schröder 1960, 31). For this practical reason, and also because of the subjectivity involved in the definition of the cultures, I conclude again that there is confirmation for the historical view that the Beaker Cultures cannot be exactly defined on the basis of their contents and that all the attempts at grouping are only significant as arrangements of the find material. If one restricts oneself to this limited objective and regards the Beaker Cultures solely as a pattern of archaeological classification, 'if one allows a certain shifting in the combination of elements from Russia to Holland, then one can outline an extensive cultural sphere for which none of the names so far proposed is completely valid' (Junghans, Sangmeister and Schröder 1960, 31).

Taken as a whole, then, the Beaker Cultures are not really an historical problem, but a problem of archaeological classification, and therefore, in the absolute sense, an academic problem. Nevertheless, we still have a genuine historical question to answer when considering the Beaker Cultures as a unity: how are we to explain the connections which have led scholars to regard the Beaker Cultures as such a unity? In previous decades it was believed that specific historical facts, such as ethnic grouping or a linguistic unit (like the Indo-European language family) could be seen behind the cultural similarities; on this basis it was possible to explain common cultural features even without any special ethnic or political relations, as a result of general contact between human groups. The historical problem of the Beaker Cultures is a problem of cultural dynamics: where and how did the individual cultural elements originate? How and where did they spread? How did such complex structures, or groupings, of cultural elements arise? Finally, how and why did the Beaker Cultures come to an end? Here lies the real field of activity for archaeological research: much effort has already been devoted to this, but a lot more is necessary. The varied cultural mosaic with which the European Beaker Cultures present us cannot be analyzed here in all its detail, but some remarks must be made on the main elements which have given rise to the nomenclature of this large culture group. We can speak with most confidence, perhaps, about battle-axes, suggesting that they are to be derived from predecessors in South-east Europe or the Near East. As regards cord decoration, this appears before the Beaker Cultures, both in Central Europe (Jażdżewski 1936) and in Western Europe (Piggott 1961) as well as in the south-east (Roman 1974), and it is consequently not possible at the moment to come to any definite conclusions about the origin of this element of the Beaker Cultures. Finally we come to the beaker element itself of the Beaker Cultures: as a ceramic form this too is present earlier than the actual Beaker Cultures, in the TRB Culture. As a generalized form in certain regions of the Beaker Cultures, for example in Central Europe (*Ills. 1, 5*), it could be of local origin; but elsewhere, for example in Britain, it is regarded as intrusive (Piggott 1964; most recently Clarke 1970). We must add to this the fact that the beakers of our Beaker Cultures (in the sense used in this paper) perhaps constitute not a single problem but two different ones, if for instance we contrast the Bell Beaker with the beakers of the Corded Ware or Single Grave Cultures.

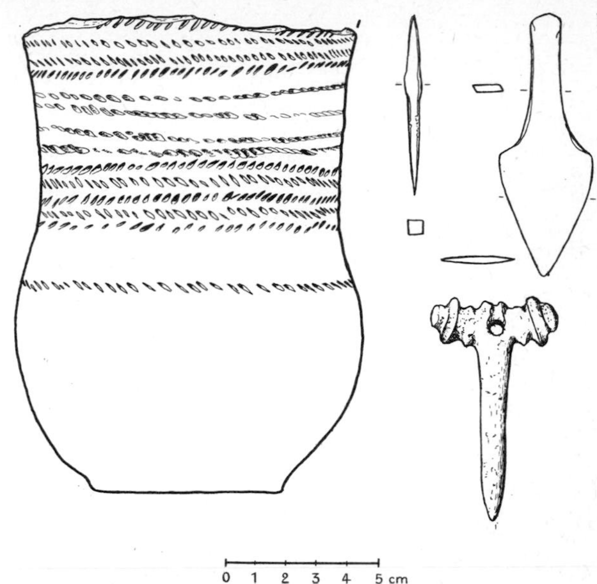

1 Bleckendorf, Bez. Halle (Saale). Grave finds of the Saale Corded Ware Culture. The types illustrated are of 'international' form.

But enough of these general reflections on archaeological problems. I certainly do not wish to call into question with my critical observations the basic methods of scientific research, analysis and synthesis. Nevertheless, history always has both a chronological and a spatial dimension, and this should not be forgotten in a truly historical evaluation of the material basis for archaeological research.

I now want to approach the problem of the Beaker Cultures from two other aspects. On the basis of their economic relations, I assume that the local settlement community formed the basic socio-economic unit in the Neolithic; for in almost the whole distribution area of the European Beaker Cultures, agriculture and stock-rearing formed the economic basis. In favourable ecological and

2, 3 Dölauer Heide, Halle (Saale). Interior of a megalithic tomb of the Saale Corded Ware Culture, with a detail, left, showing incised decoration.

climatic conditions, which allowed complex systems of mixed farming, most of the local settlement communities must have been largely in a position of economic self-sufficiency. But although there was no compulsion towards integration at a higher organizational level from the economic point of view, one may assume that at the time of the Beaker Cultures, especially with the increasing cultural influence from the area of early states in the Eastern Mediterranean, a greater or lesser number of local settlement communities had united into tribal units, capable of communal efforts such as the construction of impressive funerary monuments (*Ills. 2–4*). In the absence of definite figures, one must not set too high estimates of the size of the territory and the population which formed the basis for an ethnic or political unit, since means of communication were limited in the Neolithic (such as drum signals or individual messengers). In any case, in view of the low socio-economic level which may be assumed for the Neolithic, I think we can exclude any idea that the whole distribution area of the European Beaker Cultures was under the sovereignty of a single state.

The second problem is whether the distribution area of the Late Neolithic or Eneolithic European Beaker Cultures can be identified with the presumed homeland of the Indo-European language family. In order to answer this question adequately, extensive comparative research would have to be undertaken for which there is no space here. I will

4, 5 Above, Göhlitzsch, Bez. Halle (Saale). Decorated slab from a megalithic tomb of the Saale Corded Ware Culture; below, Dölauer Heide, Halle (Saale). Pottery from a cist grave of the Saale Corded Ware Culture.

6 Stedten, Bez. Halle (Saale). Wooden bowls from a cist grave of the Saale Corded Ware Culture.

only quote Piggott (1965, 80) who has stated that on the whole philologists are agreed that an area west of the Urals and north of the Black Sea, between the Carpathians and the Caucasus, is most likely to be the homeland of the undivided Indo-European language family in the third millennium BC. On this basis there exists only a negligible possibility of overlap in the distribution areas of the Beaker Cultures and the primary Indo-European languages. Again, Piggott (1965, 84ff.) discusses the question of whether the presumed east-west spread of the bearers of the Beaker Cultures from an *Urheimat* in the south Russian steppes could have been at the same time a spread of Indo-European languages. Indeed, 'this is a question difficult to answer, and we must temporarily postpone asking it' (Piggott 1965, 85).

Even if our comments are considered brief and critical, they permit a realization that the problems of the European Beaker Cultures consist of the problems of the individual cultures, as they existed between 2500 and 1500 bc in the various regions of Western, Central, Northern and Eastern Europe. Investigating the many different aspects of these individual cultures, both archaeologically and historically, remains a perennially topical task of European research on the Neolithic, which Stuart Piggott has served well for forty-five years.

Bibliography

ABERCROMBY, J. 1912 *A study of the Bronze Age pottery of Great Britain and Ireland and its associated grave-goods*, 2 vols, Oxford.

CLARKE, David L. 1970 *Beaker pottery of Great Britain and Ireland*, 2 vols, Cambridge.

GÖTZE, A. 1891 *Die Gefässformen und Ornamente der neolithischen schnurverzierten Keramik im Flussgebiet der Saale*, Jena.

JAŻDŻEWSKI, K. 1936 *Kultura puharów lejkowatych w Polsce zachodniej i środkowej*, Poznań.

JUNGHANS, S., SANGMEISTER, E. and SCHRÖDER, M. 1960 *Metallanalysen kupferzeitlicher und frühbronzezeitlicher Bodenfunde aus Europa = SAM 2*, Berlin.

KLEJN, Leo S. 1969 Zum Problem der Aussonderung und Gliederung des Streitaxtkulturkreises, *Veröffentlichungen des Landesmuseums für Vorgeschichte Halle* XXIV, 209–14.

PIGGOTT, S. 1954 *The Neolithic cultures of the British Isles*, Cambridge.

1955 Windmill Hill – East or West? *Proc. Prehist. Soc.* XXI, 96–101.

1961 The British Neolithic cultures in their continental setting, in *L'Europe à la fin de l'âge de la pierre*, ed. J. Böhm and S. J. De Laet, Prague, 557–74.

1963 Abercromby and after: the Beaker cultures of Britain re-examined, in *Culture and environment: essays in honour of Sir Cyril Fox*, ed. I. Foster and L. Alcock, London, 53–91.

1965 *Ancient Europe from the beginnings of agriculture to classical antiquity*, Edinburgh.

ROMAN, P. 1974 Das Problem der 'schnurverzierten' Keramik in Südosteuropa, *Jahresschrift mitteldt. Vorgesch.* LVIII, 157–74.

9

IDA BOGNÁR-KUTZIÁN

On the Origins of Early Copper-Processing in Europe

In his comprehensive book on the prehistory of Europe, Professor Stuart Piggott makes a concise analysis and a pertinent assessment of the importance of the discovery and utilization of metals, and of copper metallurgy: 'the recognition of the fact that metallic copper could be artificially produced from an ore which in no way resembled the end product, crucial to real metallurgy, involved an increase in man's understanding of nature. It meant a realization that a sort of transmutation of one natural substance into another was within man's power, a step in understanding beyond the simpler process of fire-hardening clay into pottery' (Piggott 1965, 71–3). He defines the Iberian Peninsula and South-eastern Europe as centres of copper metallurgy on our continent where the impetus for evolving the new technology had come from the south, brought by Anatolian or Aegean prospectors or metal smiths. As to the Iberian Peninsula his arguments are conclusive, but the provenance of metallurgy in the South-east European centre has remained an unsolved issue.

The debate is not of recent origin. The theory of local evolution had a particularly large number of adherents in the years between the two World Wars, such as Schuchardt, Schmidt (1924, 56; 1932, 119), Wilke (1923, 53) and Fimmen (1924, 72, 101). Reinecke and Witter's statements were criticized by Nestor twenty years ago (1955, 61–3). As to the Hungarian prehistorians let me mention first Tompa's similar approach (1929, 7; 1937, 56). His contemporary, Hillebrand (1931, 248, 250) presumes that the tribes in Hungary adopted the Copper Age culture gradually, through trade carried on with Aegean cultures.

Among the prehistorians assuming local origin, Renfrew (1969; 1973) adopted the most unequivocal stand on the independence of metallurgy in South-eastern Europe. His research was focused mainly on the origin of real metallurgy. I shall now try to approach this problem of great historical and cultural importance, tracing it from the first appearance of this new knowledge in Europe down to the evolution of metallurgy.

The region to be examined covers the Carpathian Basin, Romanian and Soviet Moldavia and the northern parts of the Balkans (*Ill. 1*). The period extends from the Early Neolithic to the end of the Early Copper Age, in radiocarbon dating from about the middle of the fifth to the last third of the fourth millennium bc. My relative datings are based on the horizons established earlier for the region outlined above (1972, 207–11).

Thus the first question is when the first copper object appears in the region examined. The earliest object is a copper awl found at Balomir (Transylvania) deriving from the very end of the Körös (Criş, Early Neolithic) Culture (Vlassa 1967, 407, 423, Fig. 6). No other copper awl of an identical, earlier or directly subsequent age is known from this region. Its early appearance is surprising, and so are its size (length 14.3 cm) and its massive character. It is made of native copper.

Another awl, the one from Neszmély, Hungary, belonging to the Zseliz (Zeliezovce) group, crops up after a very long interval, in the Middle Neolithic (Bognár-Kutzián 1963, 333–4, 485 ff., 499, 536). This is again an isolated find in the Carpathian Basin. From Romania we know about ornaments: beads from the Cernica cemetery of Boian I-II (Cantacuzino and Morintz 1963, 72–5, Fig. 28:18, 19), one from the Cernavoda cemetery of the Hamangia Culture (Berciu 1967, 53) and about bracelets from Agigea (Slobozianu 1959, 751, Fig. 2:1). The spiral bracelet from Hódmezővásárhely-Kopáncs-Kökénydomb, a Tisza Culture settlement, can be dated at the turn of the Middle and the Late Neolithic (Bognár-Kutzián 1963, 332–3, 336).

The most noteworthy find of the Late Neolithic is the Mlynarce chisel (Novotny 1958, 28). It belongs to the Lužianky group of the Early Lengyel Culture (Lengyel I). In addition to this chisel, the sphere of tools comprises hooks, while that of the ornaments is enriched by rings, pins and a small plate pendant. At Zengővárkony, of the Early Lengyel Culture, an awl was found in the settlement, and beads, rings and bracelets in the graves (Dombay 1960, 76, 86, 88, 123, 125, 134, 136–8 and Pls. V: 2,

XXXIV: 18, 19, XLI: 10, XLII: 6–8, LXIV: 11–20, LXV: 18–20, LXXI: 9, LXXIII: 2–4, LXXIV: 6–9, 11, 13). The bracelets are made of flat plates, from wire of a round or flattened cross-section, and are bent into spirals or their terminals overlap.

Copper objects are known from every single Late Neolithic group of eastern Hungary: tube-shaped beads, made of plate, are known from the Csőszhalom tell of the eponymous group (Bognár-Kutzián 1963, 331–3, 336), a deformed bracelet with originally overlapping terminals from the Herpály settlement of the eponymous group (Korek and Patay 1956, 42, Pl. IV: 8), an awl from the Berettyószentmárton settlement of the same group (Bognár-Kutzián 1963, 336–7) and a triangular plate pendant decorated with embossed bead pattern from its Zsáka-Markó settlement (Bognár-Kutzián 1963, 487). Bracelets are known from the Gorzsa site of the Gorzsa group, one with overlapping terminals from the Czukor-major settlement, a spiral-shaped one and an open bracelet hammered flat both from grave 2 (Gazdapusztai 1963, 47, Pl. IV: 1–3). The grave belongs to the last phase of the group. The graves of sites B and C at Tápé-Lebő have yielded a rather high number of disc-shaped beads (Bognár-Kutzián 1963, 331; 1972, 86).

We have beads from the beginning of phase C of Vinča, from the eponymous site (Jovanović 1971a, 107). Awls, disc-shaped beads, a spiral ring and a fragment of a bracelet come from layer III of Gornja Tuzla (Čović 1961, 135, 336, Pl. X: 12–15), from the beginning of the late period of the East Bosnian variant of this culture. It is more difficult to assign the bracelet of quadrangular cross-section and a wire fragment from Velika Gradina to our horizon, because the dating of the younger Vinča Culture is less detailed than here required.

I can quote well-datable finds of the Pre-Cucuteni phase from the Izvoare I settlement, Romanian Moldavia, such as a piece of wire with bent terminal, a fragmentary pendant-like object and one of unknown function (Vulpe 1957, Figs. 72:3 and 85:5, 6). This last object may have been damaged or else may never have assumed its final shape. Among the small copper objects found at the early Tripolje A settlement of Luka-Vrublevetskaya near the Dniester, in the south-south-west part of the Soviet Union, hooks could be observed (Bibikov 1953, Fig. 51).

Among the copper finds at Izvoare II dated in Proto-Cucuteni or Cucuteni A1, A2 there are straight and roll pins, spiral bracelets and a ring without analogues (Vulpe 1957, Figs. 272:1–3, 273:1–5, 274:3–5). An awl of thick, round cross-section and a ring were found by F. László in layer Ia of a similar age at Erősd (Ariușd) (Roska 1942, Fig. 92:2, 3).

The next horizon belongs to the Early Copper Age, when the knowledge of copper metallurgy can no longer be questioned (Charles 1969) and even reaches its first culmination in the second phase, phase B. It is enough here to recall the datable massive copper objects (all discussed in Bognár-Kutzián 1972, 139–44, 197–200, 206). The first copper objects with shaft-holes, the hammer-axes, appear in phase A of the Early Copper Age: this is, at least, what I have inferred from analyzing the environment of find-assemblages in two regions located far from one another.

One of these complexes is the Karbuna hoard determined as Tripolje A, containing 444 copper objects including a hammer-axe and a simple axe or chisel (Sergeev 1963, 137–8, Fig. 2). According to the synchronization generally used nowadays, this would be dated to the Late Neolithic horizon; but for reasons expounded elsewhere (Bognár-Kutzián 1972, 197–8, 217–18), I dated it to phase A, the early horizon of the Early Copper Age. Another is the Hotnica find where hammer-axes were discovered in three houses, one of them in house no. 2 (Angelov 1958, 403, Fig. 7). The radiocarbon dating of this house is Bln-125 3610±100 bc (Kohl and Quitta 1966, 38) which corresponds to Gumelnița A2 and also to Early Copper Age phase A (Bognár-Kutzián 1972, 198, 210–11). The Brodzany chisel (Novotná 1955, 89) found in a pit of a settlement of the eponymous group (Lengyel III) also belongs to this horizon.

A hammer-axe recently found at the Cucuteni settlement comes from phase A3 of the culture (Petrescu-Dîmbovița 1965, 267, Fig. 3). This makes it necessary to consider both horizons A and early B of the Early Copper Age for dating it (Bognár-Kutzián 1972, 208). The hammer-axe found at the Reci settlement and dated to Cucuteni A raises some problems too (Székely 1962, 339, Fig. 4:1; 1964, 288).

The hammer-axes of phase B of the Early Copper Age are as follows: one belonging to the Lucska group of the Tiszapolgár Culture is known from Lucska (Lučky) (Pulszky 1884, 35–7, Fig. 28) and six from the Tibava cemetery (Šiška 1964, Figs. 7:24, 8:19, 10:25, 11:30, 15:27, 17:11). The Csóka (Čoka) settlement lies in the region of the Deszk group and has yielded a hammer-axe later buried there (Bognár-Kutzián 1972, 140, Fig. 26). The most valuable finds of the phase are the three hoards found

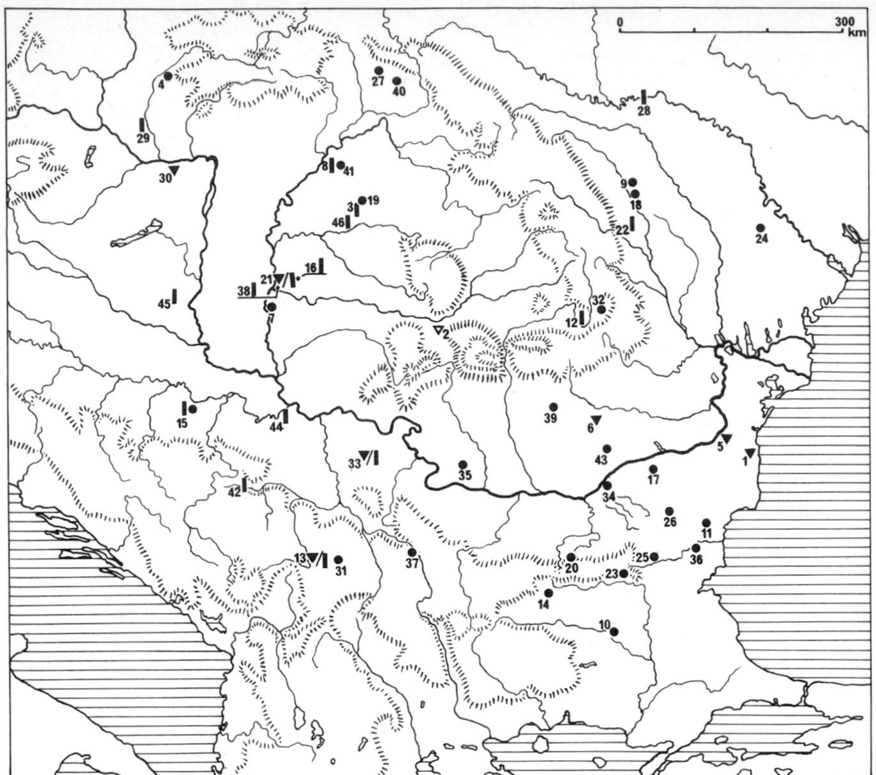

1 Main sites of the earliest copper finds in Europe.

▽ Early Neolithic

▼ Middle Neolithic

▮ Late Neolithic

● Early Copper Age

at the Pločnik settlement (Grbić 1929; Stalio 1964) containing, among other things, four hammer-axes and nineteen chisels or simple axes.

The other important site is the Devnja cemetery which has yielded thirteen copper finds, including six hammer-axes and two chisels or simple axes (and also gold ornaments as in the Tibava cemetery). It is dated Karanovo VI 3 (Todorova-Simeonova 1971, 23–5, Pls. VI:4, VIII:13–17, XIII:25–28, 33–35). Within Karanovo VI, the hammer-axes of the Gjuzeldze-Alan grave (H. and K. Skorpil 1898, 89, 104, Fig. 35), of the Gabarevo settlement (Gaul 1948, Pl. XXXIV: 12, 13) and of the Slivnica hoard (Popov 1921, 21, Fig. 25:1–3) can be dated less precisely.

The hammer-axe from layer IIC of the Vidra tell comes from the late (B1) phase of the Gumelniţa Culture (Rosetti 1934, Fig. 42) and the one from Teiu may be dated similarly or somewhat later (B1 or B2?) (Vulpe 1964, 458, 462). Chisels or simple axes datable in Karanovo VI are known from Ruse (Georgiev and Angelov 1957, Fig. 31), from Kodzadermen, from Devebargan (Gaul 1948, 139, 175, Pl. XXXIV:11) and from Karnobat (*op. cit.* 148, Pl. XXXIV:10). The one from Sava (Mirtchev and Zlatarski 1960, 26, Fig. 4) may be the oldest. The

1 Agigea
2 Balomir
3 Berettyószentmárton
4 Brodzany
5 Cernavoda
6 Cernica
7 Csóka (Čoka)
8 Csőszhalom/Tiszapolgár/
9 Cucuteni
10 Devebargan
11 Devnja
12 Erősd (Ariusd)
13 Fafos
14 Gabarevo
15 Gornja Tuzla
16 Gorzsa-Czukor major/Hódmezővásárhely/
17 Gjuzeldze-Alan
18 Habaşeşti
19 Herpály/Berettyóujfalu/
20 Hotnica
21 Hódmezővásárhely-Kopáncs-Kökénydomb
22 Izvoare
23 Karanovo
24 Karbuna
25 Karnobat
26 Kodzadermen
27 Lucska (Lučky)
28 Luka-Vrublevetzkaja
29 Mlynárce
30 Neszmély
31 Pločnik
32 Reci
33 Rudna Glava
34 Ruse
35 Salcuţa
36 Sava
37 Slivnica
38 Tápé-Lebő B, C
39 Teiu
40 Tibava
41 Tiszapolgár-Hajdunánási ut
42 Velika Gradina
43 Vidra
44 Vinča
45 Zengővárkony
46 Zsáka-Markó

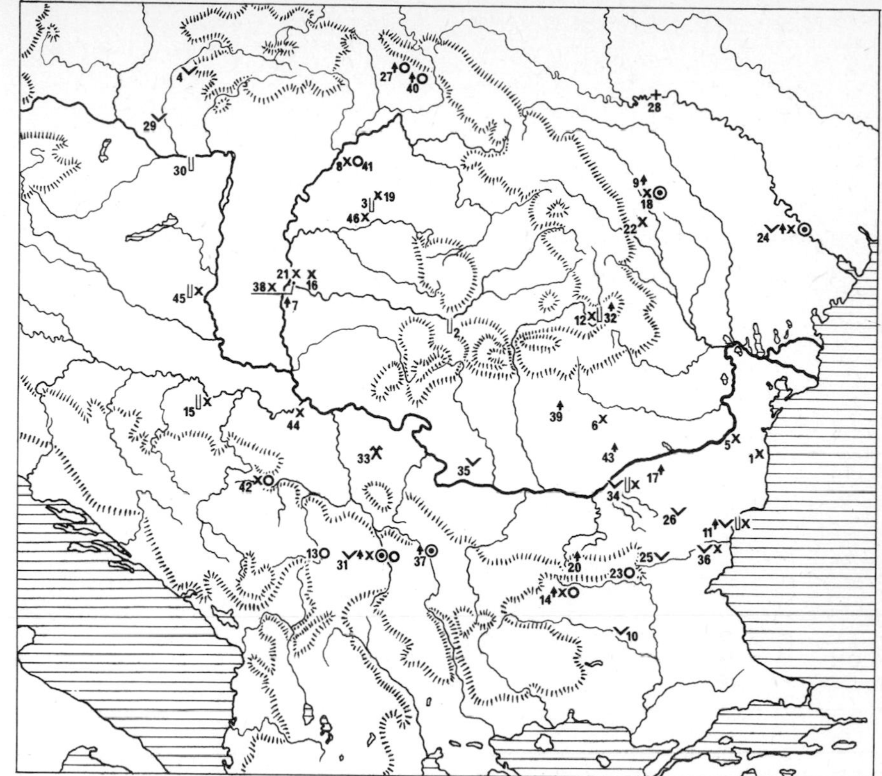

2 Principal copper find types from sites shown in Ill. 1.

awl

hook

chisel or simple axe

hammer-axe

ornament

hoard

mining shaft

traces of copper-processing

Devebargan tell had a Marica Culture (Karanovo V) layer too. The examples recovered from house 1a of the Salcuța site are dated by Berciu (1961, 566–8, Figs. 70:1, 2; 71:1, 2) in Salcuța III.

This sequence of development (*Ill. 2*) which deliberately disregards the copper finds that can only be dated typologically, makes the following conclusions possible concerning the region examined:

a) the earliest copper find is not an ornament but a tool: an awl, and this sole find of the Early Neolithic horizon comes from the Carpathian Basin;

b) the same applies to the subsequent, Middle Neolithic horizon with only the difference that ornaments appear already in the North Balkans;

c) the second type of tool is the chisel, from the early Late Neolithic;

d) the hook appears as the third implement in the younger Late Neolithic;

e) the first copper object with shaft-hole, the hammer-axe, appears at the dawn of the Copper Age;

f) the first hoard is known from this same horizon;

g) the chisels or simple axes survive (together with the hammer-axes and axe-adzes to the end of the Middle Copper Age), and can be traced down to the end of the Copper Age, but never – not even prior to the Copper Age – do they constitute an independent horizon.

Researches carried out by Jovanović on Rudnik-Dnevnikop at Rudna Glava, area of Majdanpek, resulted in conclusions of particular importance. By analyzing seven shafts he learned not only the manner of mining, but also the fact that copper oxide appearing there in veins was mined in the Late Neolithic. The pottery found in shaft No. 7 set the time of exploration in the transitional phase between the early and late periods of the Vinča Culture (Jovanović 1971a; 1971b; 1972). This evidence proves chronological order and establishes that the Vinča Culture maintained close links with the earliest known copper ore mines. Small lumps of crushed ore mixed with remains of charred wood and soot in Fafos I can be dated in the same phase of the Kosovo variant of the culture. At Velika Gradina a piece of amorphous copper comes from the later Vinča Culture, very much like Gornja Tuzla III where, in describing the copper objects mentioned above, Ćović claims to have found traces of copper processing (1961, 135–6). In any case, the other copper finds of the site, the Vinča beads and the Velika Gradina objects may have been manufactured at the time when copper oxide ore was mined in shaft 7 at Rudna Glava. Jovanović calls this horizon the exploratory-classificatory stage of the oldest copper industry and assigns it to the Late Neolithic (1971a, 117).

From the Late Neolithic we have no other finds in support of copper-processing. The earliest hoard of the region is also more likely to have appeared in Early Copper Age A; at any rate this complex of finds is not of an industrial character.

The signs of local copper-processing grow in number during the Early Copper Age but not in proportion to the amount of copper processed. All the three finds of this type in the Carpathian Basin can be dated in phase B of the Tiszapolgár Culture and are limited to the region of the Lucska group. At the eponymous site traces of melted metal were observed in some vessels (Sztáray 1881, 275), a crucible-like vessel covered with blue verdigris and with two small copper crumbs was found in grave 2 at Tiszapolgár–Hajdunánás road (Bognár-Kutzián 1972, 98),[1] and another crucible-like vessel was recovered from grave 17/55 at Tibava (Andel 1958, Pl. 1:7). An ingot in hoard 3 at Pločnik proves that cast copper in a semi-finished state was in circulation at the end of the Vinča–Pločnik period. This is the latest horizon to which the crucible-like small vessels of the Gumelnița Culture found at Gabarevo, Poljanovgrad and Karanovo may belong. At Karanovo the two crucibles were found in a burnt house, and one of them contained malachite ore (Georgiev 1958, 386–7, Figs. 11–13; 1961, 76, Pl. XVI:1–4). Further proof is needed to substantiate Ćović's assumption (1961, 135, Pl. XIII:7) that an object of specific shape was used for casting shaft-holed hammer-axes in Gornja Tuzla II.

In analyzing the diffusion of the Tiszapolgár Culture it became evident that this typical lowland culture, attached to flood areas, created settlements along the foot of the surrounding hills too. I assumed that their purpose was to secure the supply of raw

[1] This is the oldest relic in Hungary proving local copper metallurgy and not – as Kalicz says – the two crucible fragments of the Middle Copper Age from Zalavár–Mekenye. Neither are the two small copper objects found in the pit the first authentic copper finds of Transdanubia: these are the ones from Neszmély and Zengővárkony. (Kalicz 1969, 85, Figs. 1, 2; cf Dombay 1960, and Bognár-Kutzián 1963, 485, 502.)

materials, including copper (1972, 161–2, 173–180, suppl. 2). The discovery of the mines at Rudna Glava seems to confirm my hypothesis.

The finds from South-eastern Europe and from the Carpathian Basin classified above reflect a gradual development. As regards Yugoslavia, Jovanović distinguishes three stages in copper production (1971a, 117–18). Wertime's evolutionary sequence of general validity (1964; 1973) extends from cold-working through annealing and casting native copper to the smelting of ores.

Does gradual development prove the independence of knowledge? In the region or regions of emergence it must have been independent, but borrowing could have been gradual too. If, however, borrowing happened in the earliest stage, further development must have been gradual.

There is no doubt that the raw material did exist in the given region, and we also have evidence of its exploitation. The stone hammer-axes may be prototypes, but can also be interpreted as witnesses of a constant need inherited from the Neolithic. The simple copper axes do not constitute a horizon prior to those of the copper hammer-axes. The proof of advanced pyrotechnology deriving from Karanovo VI – one which real metallurgy cannot dispense with – has become untenable very recently (Kingery and Frierman 1974, 204–5). Certain advances in social and economic life, associated with the availability of raw materials, with demand for shaft-holed massive axes and with an advanced level of pyrotechnology, are preconditions for the adaptation of an external impetus and for local invention alike.

Thus the above data and observations yield no decisive answer to the question. But can it be answered at all? Our actual knowledge hardly admits of an affirmative answer.

In any event, copper was recognized earlier in the Orient. A collation of the significant finds (Renfrew 1969, 35–6; 1973, 478; Wertime 1973, 484–6) reveals that the cold-worked native copper finds of Çatal Hüyük precede the awl from Transylvanian Balomir by two millennia. The smelting of copper ore is contemporaneous or an earlier invention in the Orient, and real metallurgy also seems to be older as indicated by the Can Hasan macehead. The first copper find of our region is an isolated one, followed by authentic proofs of local processing only half a millennium later. Nevertheless, it is clear that neither the import nor the impetus can be attested, nor can we mark their way with the help of connecting stations. We must, however, not forget that the earliest copper find in our region has been known for eight years, and Neolithic copper mines for as little as four years.

There can be hardly any doubt that the population of the North Balkans and of the Carpathian Basin – irrespective of having adopted or invented copper-processing – was familiar with this new substance ever since the Early Neolithic, began to exploit it at the beginning of the Late Neolithic, rose from the stage of hammering to the level of real metallurgy at the dawn of the Early Copper Age and, by then a metallurgical centre, forwarded some products to more remote regions of Europe.

Bibliography

ANDEL, K. 1958 Pohrebisko z doby medenej v Tibave na Vychodnom Slovensku, *Slov. Arch.* VI, 39–49.

ANGELOV, N. 1958 Der Siedlungshügel bei Hotnica, *Studia Detchev*, 403.

BERCIU, D. 1961 *Contribution à l'étude des problèmes de Néolithique à la lumière des nouvelles recherches*, Bucharest.

1967 *Romania*, London.

BIBIKOV, S. N. 1953 Rannetripolskoe poselenie Lukavrublevetskaya na Dnestre, *Materialy i Issledovanija po Arkheologii SSR*, 38.

BOGNÁR-KUTZIÁN, I. 1963 *The Copper Age Cemetery of Tiszapolgár-Basatanya*, Budapest.

1972 *The Early Copper Age Tiszapolgár Culture in the Carpathian Basin*, Budapest.

CANTACUZINO, G. and MORINTZ, S. 1963 Die jungsteinzeitlichen Funde in Cernica, *Dacia* 7, 27–89.

CHARLES, J. A. 1969 A metallurgical examination of South-East European copper axes, *Proc. Prehist. Soc.* XXXV, 40–2.

ĆOVIĆ, B. 1961 Resultate der Sondierungen auf der prähistorischen Siedlung in Gornja Tuzla, *Glasnik* (Sarajevo), 132–9.

DOMBAY, J. 1960 *Die Siedlung und das Gräberfeld in Zengövárkony*, Budapest.

FIMMEN, D. 1924 *Die kretisch-mykenische Kultur*, Leipzig-Berlin.

GAUL, J. H. 1948 *The Neolithic Period in Bulgaria*, Cambridge, Mass.

GAZDAPUSZTAI, G. 1963 Siedlung und Friedhof aus dem Spätneolitikum in Hódmezövásárhely-Gorzsa, in *A Móra Ferenc Muzeum Évkönyve* 46–8.

GEORGIEV, G. I. 1958 Über einige Produktionswerkzeuge aus dem Neolithikum und Aeneolithikum in Bulgarien, *Studia Detchev* 385–7.

1961 Kulturgruppen der Jungstein- und der Kupferzeit in der Ebene von Thrazien, *L'Europe à la fin de l'âge de la pierre*, Prague, 45–100.

GEORGIEV, G. I. and ANGELOV, N. 1957 Ausgrabungen des Siedlungshügels bei Russe in den Jahren 1950 und 1953, *Izvestiya* (Sofia) 21, 125–7.

GRBIĆ, M. 1929 *Pločnik*, Belgrade.

HILLEBRAND, J. 1931 A prehistória néhány segédtudományának jelentöségéröl, *Arch. Ért.* XLV, 248–51.

JOVANOVIĆ, B. 1971a *Metalurgija Eneolitskog Perioda Jugoslavije*, Belgrade.

1971b Early Copper Metallurgy of the Central Balkans, in *Actes du VIII*e *Congrès ISPP* 1, 131–8.

1972 Technologie minière de l'Enéolithique Ancien centrebalkanique, *Starinar* XXIII, 1–14.

KALICZ, N. 1969 Die kupferzeitliche Balaton-Gruppe im Komitat Veszprém, *Mitteilungen der Museen des Komitates Veszprém* 8, 83–90.

KINGERY, W. D. and FRIERMAN, J. D. 1974 The Firing Temperature of a Karanova Sherd and Inferences about South-East European Chalcolithic Refractory Technology, *Proc. Prehist. Soc.* XL 204–5.

KOHL, G. and QUITTA, H. 1966 Berlin Radiocarbon Measurements II, *Radiocarbon* 8, 27–45.

KOREK, J. and PATAY, P. 1956 The Settlement at Herpály-halom from the Late Neolithic and Copper Ages, *Folia Arch.* 8, 40–2.

MIRTCHEV, M. and ZLATARSKI, D. 1960 Le tell de Sava, *Izvestiya* (Varna) XI, 1–26.

NESTOR, I. 1955 Sur les débuts de la métallurgie du cuivre et du bronze en Roumanie, in *Nouvelles Études d'Histoire présentées au X*e *Congres des Sciences Historiques, Roma*, Bucharest, 47–63.

NOVOTNÁ, M. 1955 Kupfergeräte und das Problem der ältesten Kupfergewinnung in der Slowakei, *Slov. Arch.* 3, 96–8.

NOVOTNY, B. 1958 *Die Slowakei in der jungeren Steinzeit*, Bratislava.

PETRESCU-DÎMBOVIȚA, M. 1965 Evolution de la civilisation de Cucuteni à la lumière des nouvelles fouilles archéologiques de Cucuteni-Baiceni, *Rivista di Scienze Preistoriche* 20, 157–78.

PIGGOTT, S. 1965 *Ancient Europe from the beginnings of agriculture to classical antiquity*, Edinburgh.

POPOV, R. 1921 Materialy za issledovanija na praistoriata v Sofijskata kotlovina, *Materialy za istoriata na Sofia* 5.

PULSZKY, F. 1884 *Die Kupferzeit in Ungarn*, Budapest.

RENFREW, C. 1969 The Autonomy of the East European Copper Age, *Proc. Prehist. Soc.* XXXV, 12–39.

1973 Sitagroi and the independent invention of metallurgy in Europe, in *Actes du VIII*e *Congrès ISPP II*, 473–81.

ROSKA, M. 1942 *Thesaurus antiquitatum Transsilvanicarum* I, *Praehistorica*, Kolozsvár.

ROSETTI, D. 1934 Sapaturile dela Vidra, *Publicațiile Museului Minicipiului București* 1, 1–59.

SERGEEV, G. P. 1963 Rannetripolskij klad u s. Karbuna, *Sovetskaya Arkheologiya* 1, 131–51.

ŠIŠKA, S. 1964 Gräberfeld der Tiszapolgár-Kultur in Tibava, *Slov. Arch.* XII, 293–356.

SKORPIL, H. and SKORPIL, K. 1898 *Mogili. Pametnitsi iz Bulgarsko*, Plovdiv.

SLOBOZIANU, H. 1959 Considérations sur les établissements antiques situés autour des lacs de Tekirghiol et d'Agigea, *Materiale și Cerc. Arh.* V, 751–2.

STALIO, B. 1964 Dépot d'objets métalliques nouvellement mis au jour à Pločnik près de Prokuplje, *Recueil du Musée National* 4, 41.

SCHMIDT, H. 1924 *Vorgeschichte Europas*, Berlin-Leipzig.

1932 *Cucuteni in der Oberen Moldau*, Berlin.

SZEKELY, Z. 1962 Les sondages faits par la Musée Régional de Sf. Gheorghe, *Materiale și Cerc. Arh.* 8, 339–40.

1964 Découvertes néolithiques tardives dans l'établissement de Reci, *Studii și Cerc. Ist. Veche* 15, 121–6, 288.

SZTÁRAY, A. 1881 Lucskai lelet, *Arch. Ért.* 258–9.

TODOROVA-SIMEONOVA, H. 1971 Spätneolithisches Gräberfeld bei der Stadt Devnja, *Bulletin du Musée National à Varna* VII (XXII), 3–26.

TOMPA, F. 1929 *Die Bandkeramik in Ungarn*, Budapest.

1937 25 Jahre Urgeschichtsforschung in Ungarn 1912–1936, *Bericht der Röm.-Germ. Kommission* 24–5, 27–127.

VLASSA, N. 1967 Quelques problèmes du néolithique de Transylvanie, *Acta Musei Napocensis* IV, 423.

VULPE, A. 1964 Sur la chronologie des haches doubles en cuivre à tranchants opposés, *Studii și Cerc. Ist. Veche* 15, 457–66.

VULPE, R. 1957 *Izvoare*, Bucharest.

WERTIME, T. A. 1964 Man's first encounters with metallurgy, *Science* 146:3649, 1266.

1973 How metallurgy began, *Actes du VIII*e *Congrès ISPP II*, 181–92.

WILKE, G. 1923 *Kulturbeziehungen zwischen Indien, Orient und Europa*, Mannus Bibl. 10.

10

MARIJA GIMBUTAS

Ideograms and Symbolic Design on Ritual Objects of Old Europe (Neolithic and Chalcolithic South-east Europe)

THIS article will deal with the ideograms and symbolic designs incised or painted on ritual vases, sacrificial containers, seals, figurines, and other objects related to cult practices performed in domestic shrines or communal sanctuaries.

The purpose of this essay is to draw attention to the consistent use of ideograms and symbolic designs throughout the Neolithic (*c.* 7000–5300 BC) and Chalcolithic (*c.* 5300–3500 BC), and their influence on and relationship to the numerous linear signs widely used in Old Europe from the beginning of the Chalcolithic era. In the Central Balkans the proliferous use of linear signs starts *c.* 5400–5300 BC (true age)[1] with the beginnings of the Vinča civilization. In other parts of the Balkan peninsula and the Danube basin – in Greece (Dimini and later complexes), in the East Balkans (Karanovo-Gumelniţa complexes), in Moldavia (Cucuteni), Transylvania (Petreşti), Hungary (Tisza and Lengyel complexes) – signs of similar nature are likewise present during the Chalcolithic.

The dissertation of Milton M. Winn entitled 'The Signs of the Vinča Culture: an Internal Analysis; Their Role, Chronology and Independence from Mesopotamia' (UCLA 1973) has identified the Vinča sign corpus and thus prepared the ground for further evaluation and understanding of this extremely interesting phenomenon of European prehistory. It is of utmost significance that such a system is present in the Vinča culture (5500/5400–4000 BC), itself a culmination of a long development. The great lengths of the Neolithic and Chalcolithic periods are confirmed by stratigraphies and radiocarbon dates obtained in recent excavations in all parts of Old Europe and particularly in the Central Balkans at such sites as Anza, Divostin, Lepenski Vir and Obre in Yugoslavia (Gimbutas 1974a; 1974b; McPherron and Srejović 1975; Srejović 1972). The theoretical necessity of a foreign source in Mesopotamia is obviated, nor is it necessary to lower the chronology of the Vinča culture to assume contemporaneity with Troy I (Hood 1968).

I WHAT ARE IDEOGRAMS?

A small number of the signs are identified as ideograms – specific, permanent configurations with religious connotations. Fixed ideograms – as independent abstract signs, not pictographs – are as early as the beginning of pottery decoration in Europe, and some of them originate in the Upper Palaeolithic, while others begin in the Neolithic. Certain signs consistently recur in all parts of Old Europe in the course of three millennia, i.e. *c.* 6500–3500 BC, and persist in the Aegean area down to the Geometric period or even later. Ideograms appear in isolation, or are flanked by symbolic designs apparently intended to extend, intensify, or emphasize the inherent theme.

The analysis of Vinča signs led Dr Winn to the following conclusions:

1. Vinča signs do not reflect sentence writing. 2. They do not reflect the use of phonemes. 3. The system is not a pictographic writing. 4. Some signs possibly represent concepts as specific as words. 5. Many repetitions of the same sign have intentional significance, i.e. the meaning of a multiple form is distinct from that of a single form. 6. The signs are not pot marks. 7. The majority of signs fall into a graphic system representing concepts, wherein more than 200 signs are used; they occur within sign groups or as isolated signs; they are distinct from the decoration.

The use of a complicated system of concept writing must have had antecedents and appropriate conditions for the emergence of the script. Such conditions were present in the circumstances I have elsewhere designated as the *Civilization of Old Europe*, in recognition of the collective identity and achievement of the different cultural groups of Neolithic and Chalcolithic South-east Europe. The fifth and fourth millennia witnessed the blossoming of this earliest European civilization. In this region

[1] In dendro-chronologically calibrated radiocarbon dates.

the inhabitants developed a social organization more complex than that of their western and northern neighbours. The settlements, often amounting to small townships, involved craft specialization and the formation of religious and governmental institutions (Gimbutas 1974a). The presence of an elaborate religious ceremonialism is attested by remains of shrines and their models, by cult equipment, and by thousands of figurines, some of which seem to have been used in the re-enactment of rituals. Sophistication of cult equipment reached its climate at the beginning of the Chalcolithic, in the second half of the sixth millennium BC.

Ideograms and symbolic designs of seals, vases, sacrificial containers, ladles, and figurines occur for millennia before the concept writing of the Chalcolithic. In much the same way they continue into the Chalcolithic era as a parallel phenomenon to the linear signs. It is therefore important to distinguish the latter from the ideograms and symbolic designs, as well as to see how they were related.

Several distinct levels of ideas connected with different images of goddesses or gods, and the accompanying symbols, have been distinguished by this author in *Gods and Goddesses of Old Europe* (1974a). The first and the most abundant group are the symbols pertaining to goddesses connected with water, rain, nourishment and cosmogonical myths. The underlying idea seems to have been the concept of hydrogenesis: that the cosmos, indeed all life, comes from water. The goddesses are reified in the shape of a fish, a water-bird, or a water snake; they also appear as fish-woman, bird-woman, and snake-woman hybrids. The symbols that accompany such images either have bird, fish, or snake characteristics, or iconographically represent water or rain. The second level of symbols entails the idea of regeneration, birth and death. To this level belong the cyclical female nature deities and the male year-gods. The associated symbols are those of 'becoming': chrysalises, caterpillars, insects, the crescent moon and its visual counterpart in the horns of the bull, whirls and circles. The third level, as a natural response to an agrarian way of life, reflects concern for the insurance and recurrence of life. The deity of fecundity is a pregnant goddess. Her associated symbols represent the germination of the seed, the fertility of fields and animals: dots, lenses, vulvas, lozenges, plants and pigs.

Within the framework of this essay we cannot cover the totality of known symbolic designs and ideograms. We shall restrict the analysis and illustrations to the first group, i.e. to the symbolic designs

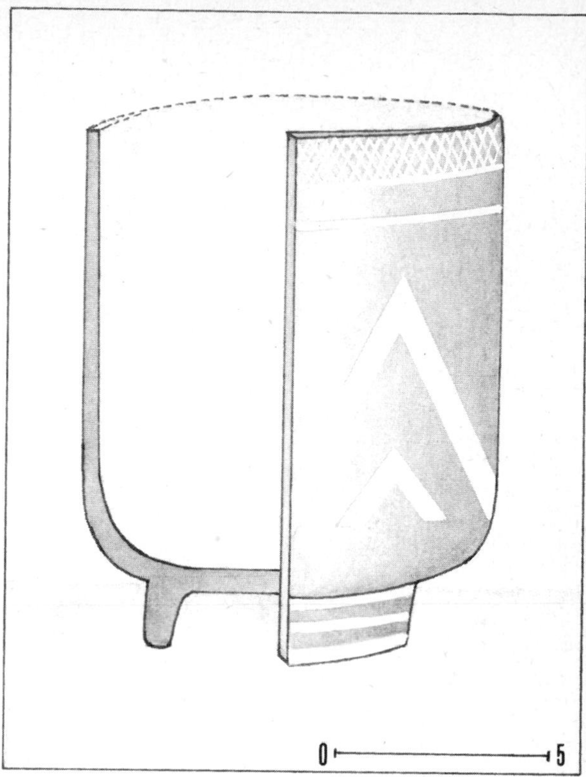

1 A Neolithic vase of the Karanovo I period, early sixth millennium BC, Muldava, central Bulgaria. An isolated double chevron is painted in white on a red background in the centre of the vase (after Detev, 1968).

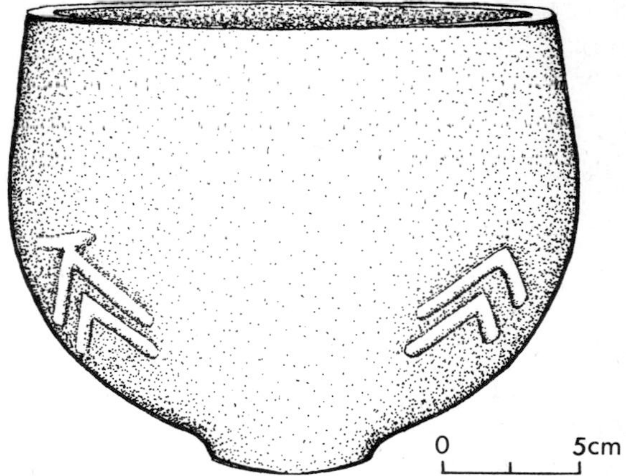

2 Isolated chevrons in relief on a vase from Obre I, Bosnia, Yugoslavia. Starčevo complex, first half of the sixth millennium BC. Radiocarbon dates for Obre IA: 6710 ± 60 (UCLA 1605 G) and 6795 ± 150 (Bln 636) BP. True age: 5780–5750 BC (after Benac, 1973).

3 Head of the Bird Goddess with excised chevrons above the beak. Kalojanovec site south-east of Stara Zagora in central Bulgaria. Karanovo IV period, approx. early part of the fifth millennium BC. The width of the head is 6 cm (published in Gimbutas, 1974a).

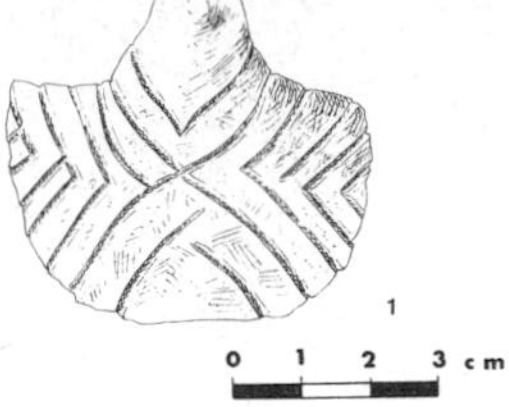

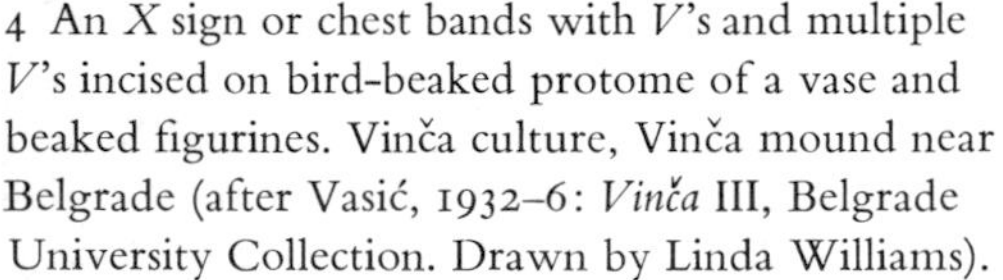

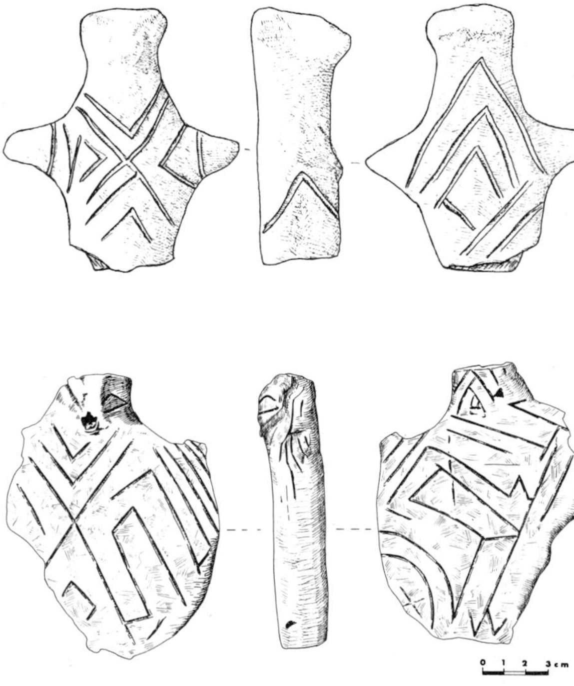

4 An *X* sign or chest bands with *V*'s and multiple *V*'s incised on bird-beaked protome of a vase and beaked figurines. Vinča culture, Vinča mound near Belgrade (after Vasić, 1932–6: *Vinča* III, Belgrade University Collection. Drawn by Linda Williams).

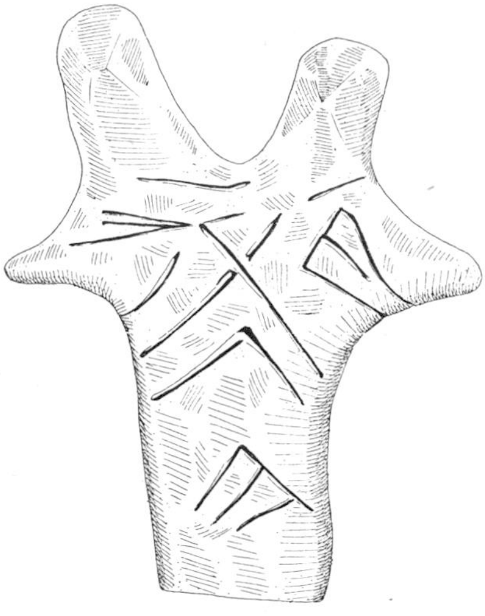

related to cosmic waters or to rain, rain clouds, and rain magic, and to the ideograms of divinities associated with nourishment by rain, water and milk. These divinities appear as water-bird, snake, fish, or hybrids such as the bird-woman, snake-woman, and fish-woman. The basic ideogram associated with this concept is the *V* sign as illustrated here by Neolithic vases of the Karanovo I (*Ill. 1*) and Starčevo (*Ill. 2*) complexes.

Chevrons on head, neck or body of beaked figurines (*Ill. 3*), or in association with the chest-band on the bird-masked figurines or bird protomes (*Ill. 4*), connect this ideogram with the Bird Goddess. *V*'s, chevrons, and *X* or ('chestband') designs combined with *V*'s are the most frequent emblems on seals (*Ill.* 5). The appearance of the same signs on seals emphasizes their function as ideograms; chevrons and *X*'s are not decoration. We may postulate that these signs are ideograms of the beaked Goddess expressing her immanence within, or identification with, the object.

Because of complementary distribution, repeated or grouped items are regarded as constituting an ideogram different from that of the motif as a single instance. Such an ideogram is the banded *V*'s. It most frequently occurs on handles of vases (*Ills.* 6, 7) or in an isolated column on the shoulder of

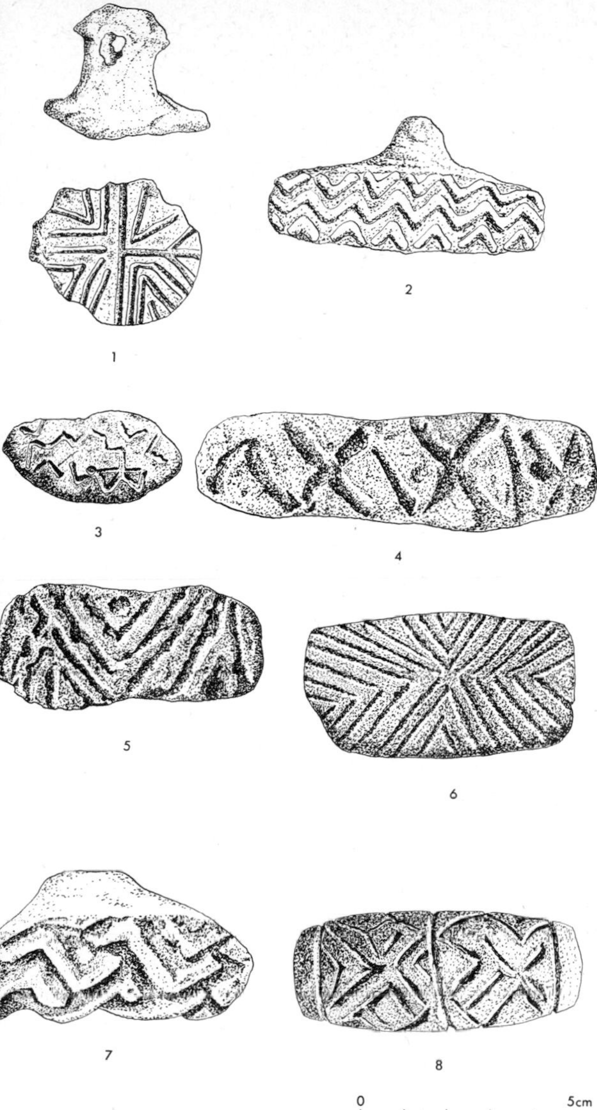

5 *V*'s and chest-band signs on seals. 1–7, handled type, Neolithic; 8, cylindrical, Chalcolithic. 1, Sesklo culture at Volos, Thessaly; 2, Nea Nikomedeia near Veroia, Macedonia; 3,6, Kotacpart-Vata-Tanya, south-eastern Hungary; 4,5, Kopancs-Zsoldos-Tanya, south-eastern Hungary; 7, Perieni, Moldavia, north-eastern Romania; 8, Sitagroi III, Drama Plain, north-eastern Greece (1, after Tsountas, 1908, 341; 2, after Rodden, 1965, 98; 3–6, after Bognár-Kutzián, 1944, Pl. XLVI; 7, after Petrescu-Dîmbovița, 1957, Fig. 715; 8, Philipi Museum, Greece. Excavation by Renfrew and Gimbutas 1968–69. Drawn by J. Oudshoorn).

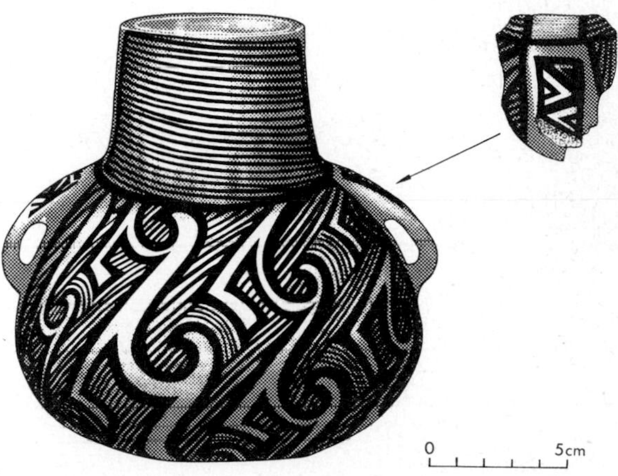

6 Ideogram of banded *V*'s on the handles of a spiral-decorated vase. Black paint on a red background. Rakhmani II, Thessaly. Dimini period, *c.* 5000 BC (after Wace and Thompson, 1912. Drawn by V. Anagnastopoulos).

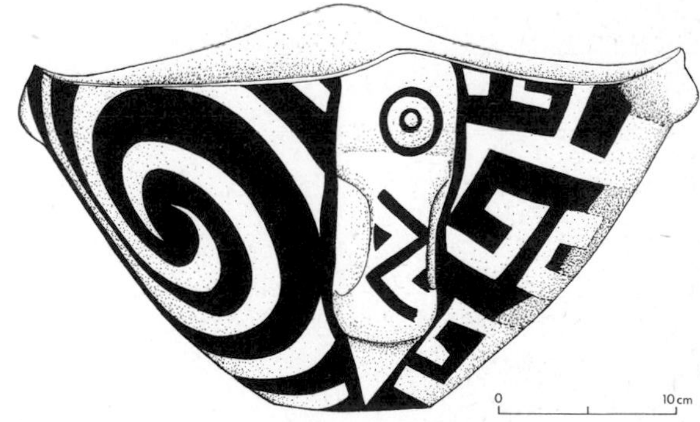

7 Vase from Dimini in Thessaly, painted dark brown on ochre-orange. Phase: Dimini IIIA. Note snake spiral in one section, meander design in another, and band of *V*'s on the handle (after Tsountas, 1908. Drawn by J. v.d. Marel).

8 Butmir vase with four columns of banded *V*'s on the shoulder. H. 23.5 cm. Nebo, Bosnia.

9 Beaked stand or lid bearing two columns of banded *V*'s and multiple *V*'s on the forehead above the beak. Vinča culture. Crnokalačka Bara near Ražanj, south of Niš, southern Yugoslavia.

a vase (*Ill. 8*), on lids (*Ill. 9*), on ladle handles and on figurines. Because it occupies a special and specific place on such articles and occurs on objects related to cult practices in all cultural groups of Old Europe, we assume that this sign is meaningful. The illustrations here are from the Dimini (*Ills. 6, 7*), Butmir (*Ill. 8*), and Vinča (*Ill. 9*) complexes. *Ill. 9* shows the relation of *V*'s to the chevron ideogram. *Ill. 8* shows the relation of the banded *V* column to the fish. On the Dimini vases (*Ills. 6, 7*) the banded *V*'s are accompanied by snakes and meanders. From these associations it can be postulated that the ideogram consisting of interconnected or banded *V*'s does not imply specifically the Bird Goddess, Snake Goddess, or Fish Goddess, but perhaps is a reference to an element common to them all, a reference to some cosmogonic idea. The interconnected *V*'s evoke such images as a winding snake, a bird in flight, or a fish. As an ideogram, it may be conceived to refer to them all as a mystic unity. During the Neolithic and the Bronze Age this sign is often painted or incised on figures of flying birds and of swimming fishes (*Ill. 10*). In the Aegean and the Mediterranean Bronze Age, and in the Geometric period, the actual effigy of a quite naturalistically portrayed snake, on handles or shoulders of vases (*Ill. 11*), is often substituted for the banded *V*'s.

Another example of such compounding is the ideogram consisting of a *V* connected to a meander, as can be seen on an Early Vinča vase (*Ill. 14*) and figurines (*Ill. 15*). This sign may be interpreted as an extension of the connotation of the chevron combined with the connotation of the meander, reflecting a particular affinity of attributes or identity, or perhaps indicating metaphorically the identity of air and water, or else the ambivalent ambiguity of a single divinity as both bird and snake.

2 EXPLODED IDEOGRAM AS SYMBOLIC DESIGN

Through duplication, inversion, and other permutations, the chevron constitutes the basic component of symbolic design on a certain class of ritual vases. Thus we find large pithoi and ornithomorphic vases where the centrally placed chevron is enhanced by the addition of an indefinite number of *V*'s to form a soaring chevron (*Ill. 16*). Bands of interconnected chevrons envelop bowls and dishes inside and out (*Ill. 17*). Multiple chevrons sometimes extend across the whole vase and constitute the sole ornament (*Ill. 18*). That such decoration of a pot seems strange and not particularly suitable points to usage primarily for a ritual purpose. The fact that the areas of the spreading chevron are

10 Wings and fishes marked with interconnected *V*'s. Painting on vases from Susa, Iran. 'Second style' of Susa (after Pottier, 1912).

11 Early Bronze Age vase from Thessaly with columns of winding snakes in relief on the shoulder (after Milojčić, 1949, Taf. 13. Drawn by Petra Rozendaal).

12 1, An ideogram – a rectangular snake meander – on a polychrome painted potsherd from Argive Heraeum, Peloponnese, Late Neolithic; 2, framed meandroid ideogram incised above the handle and flanked by snake coils. Early Vinča, end of sixth millennium BC. Predionica in Priština, southern Yugoslavia (1, after Blegen, *Prosymna*, 1937; 2, after Galović, 1959, Pl. 713).

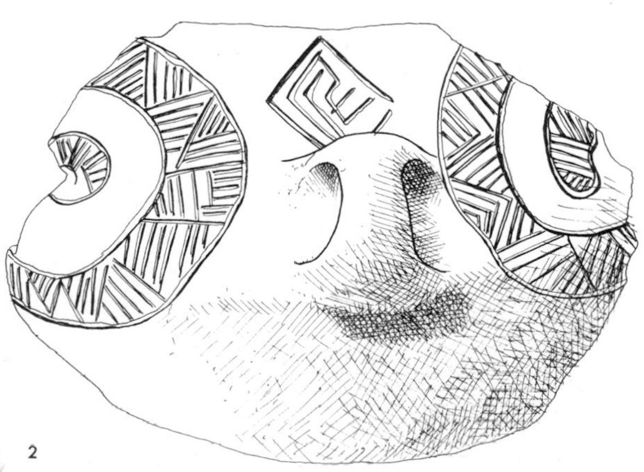

13 Terracotta stamp and cylinder seals bearing snake-coil ideograms: 1, Starčevo-Körös cultural complex. Kotacpart-Vata-Tanya site, south-eastern Hungary; 2, Chalcolithic Adriatic civilization. Malik IIA, Albania; 3–5, Cucuteni civilization. Chalcolithic. Frumușica near Peatra Neamț, Moldavia, north-eastern Romania (1, after Bognár-Kutzián, 1944, Pl. XLVI; 2, after Prendi, *Studia Albanica* I, Pl. X; 3–5, after Mataša, 1946).

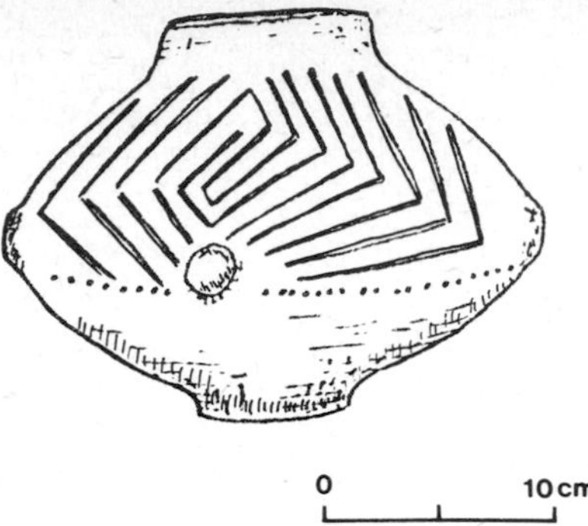

14 Vinča vase from Malča near Niš, southern Yugoslavia, decorated with an ideogrammatical design – a meander flanked with chevrons (after Winn, 1973. Courtesy Archaeological Museum, Niš).

often outlined or delimited links the decorative chevron with the isolated chevron as a concept.

Vases decorated with an infinite number of snake spirals on a striated background (*Ill. 6*) offers examples of the transformation of ideogram into decorative motif. In this case the snake ideogram or *S* sign has been repeated and transformed into a design of interconnected spirals.

A small snake coil, or an *S* sign, or an angular *S* (meander) independent of the decoration, are as frequently encountered as *V*'s. Very often isolated snake coils or meanders as ideograms are flanked by large snake coils (*Ill. 12*). The same signs appear on seals in all phases of the Neolithic and Chalcolithic (*Ill. 13*). Both the ideogram and the 'snake design' emerge not later than 6000 BC. The snake-inspired running spiral decorating the wares of Old Europe reached its climax in the Dimini, Vinča, Butmir, and Cucuteni civilizations.

3 DECORATIVE DESIGN AS AN ABSTRACTION OF NATURALISTIC SYMBOLS

The schematization or geometrization of the snake symbol is only one instance of this phenomenon. That of the *V* is another. It is our contention that the

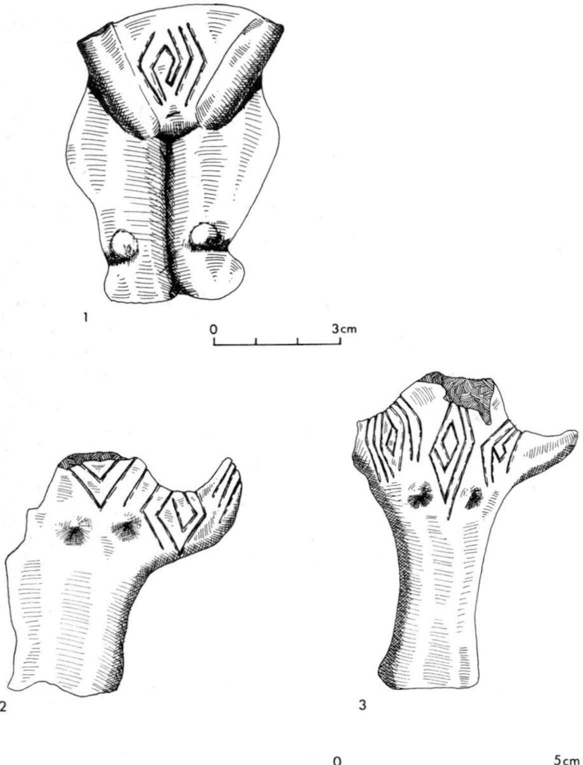

15 Ideogram of *V*'s connected with a meander, incised on Vinča figurines: 1, Fafos near Kosovska Mitrovica, southern Yugoslavia; 2, Jela near Šabac, northern Yugoslavia; 3, Gomolava near Sremska Mitrovica, northern Yugoslavia (after Winn, 1973. 1, Kosovska Mitrovica Archaeological Museum; 2, Šabac Museum; 3, Novi Sad, Vojvod Museum, Drawn by Linda Williams).

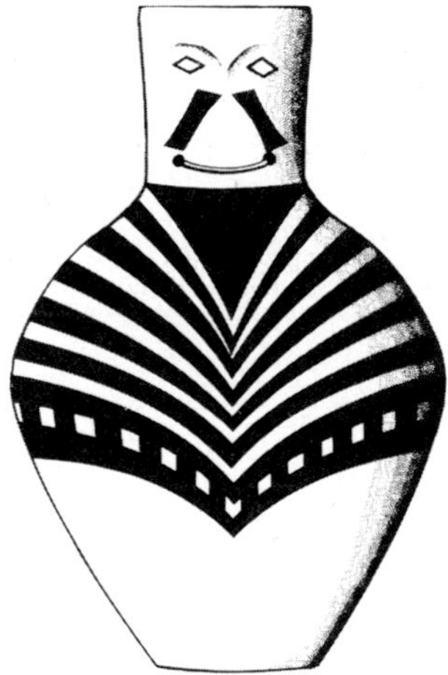

16 Bird Goddess as a pithos, painted with alternate cream and red bands forming a multiple *V* design in front. Eyes, beak and a necklace marked on the neck (necklace in relief). Red bands slant down the cheeks below the beak. H. 92 cm. Early Vinča settlement at Anza (Anza IV), between Titov Veles and Štip in eastern Macedonia, southern Yugoslavia. True age: 5300–5000 BC (after Gimbutas, 1972).

3

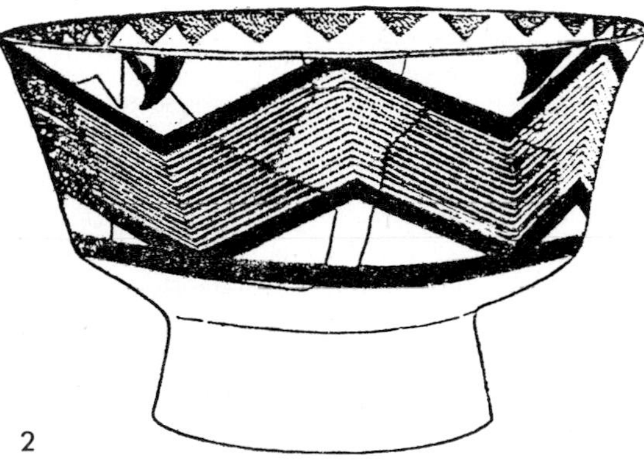

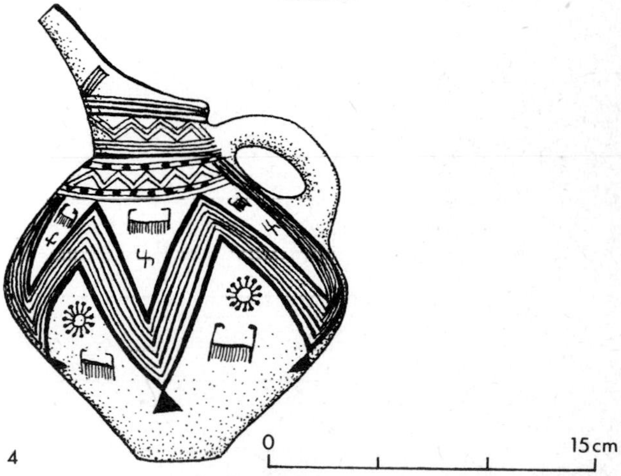

4

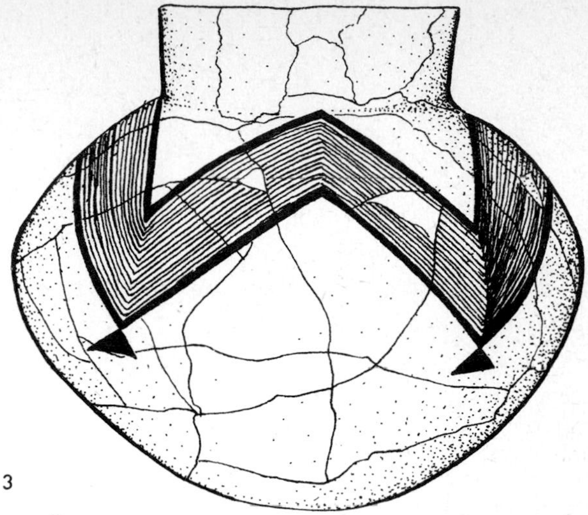

0 15 cm

17 Chevron and beak design on Neolithic and Bronze Age vases: 1, Starčevo vase from Žitkovac at Kosovska Mitrovica, southern Yugoslavia. Painted in dark brown: chevrons inside, interconnected diagonal lines on the outer surface. First half of the sixth millennium BC; 2, Asea, Argolid, Peloponnese. Painted in dark brown. Late Neolithic/ Chalcolithic; 3, Chaeroneia, central Greece. Middle Neolithic, Sesklo complex. Red-on-white painted; 4, pitcher from Kültepe, western Turkey. Early Bronze Age (1, after Galović, 1968, Taf. 15; 2, after Holmberg, *Asea, Götebergs Högskolas Årsskrift* XLV (1939); 3, after Wace and Thompson, 1912, Fig. 140; 4, after Matz, 1928, Abb. 113. Drawn by J. Oudshoorn).

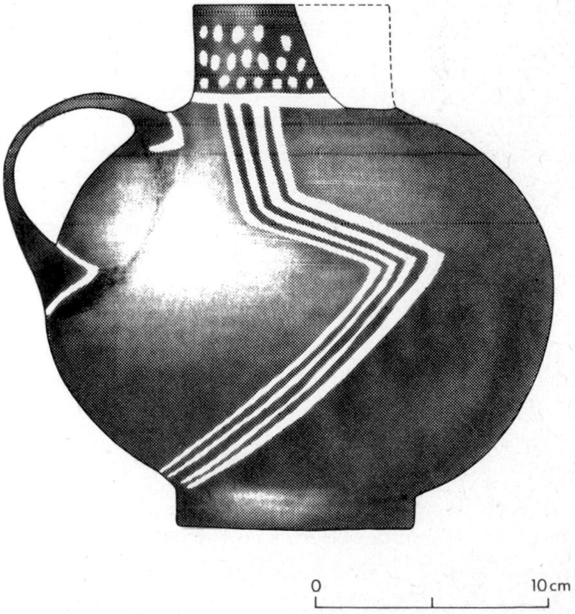

18 Exploded chevron on a Sesklo vase. Note *V*'s (beaks or wings) at base of handle. Tsangli near Farsala, Thessaly, northern Greece. White-on-red painted, *c.* 6000 BC (after Wace and Thompson, 1912. Drawn by V. Anagnastopoulos).

0 10 cm

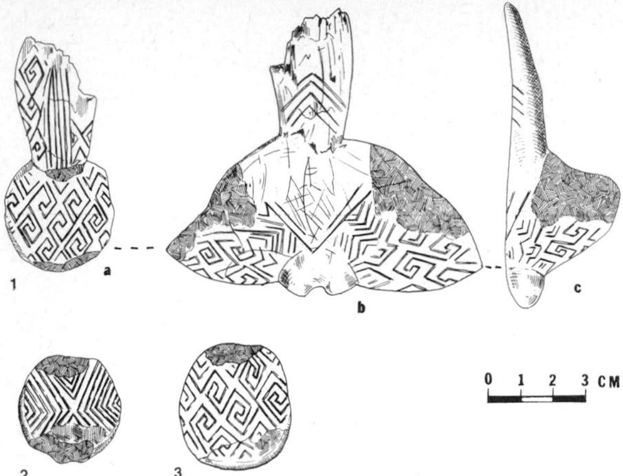

19 Chevron as an ideogram and decorative design in association with meanders and parallel lines on Upper Palaeolithic ivory figurines portraying water bird-women hybrids. Mezin, western Ukraine, *c.* 14000 BC (after Salmony, 1949, 107. Reproduced from Gimbutas, 1974a).

20 Sesklo vases decorated with 'stair' design (abstract ram-horn motif) associated with 'beak' design on the neck and an isolated chevron below the handle. Tsani Magula, Karditsa Plain, Thessaly (after Theocharis, 1973).

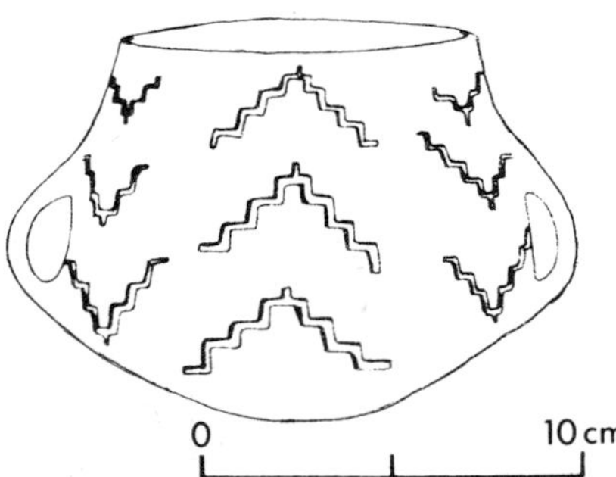

21 Vase decorated with geometricized horn motif. Dimini near Volos, Thessaly, *c.* 5000 BC (after Theocharis, 1973).

V represents an abstract or 'shorthand' rendering of the beak of a bird, and by extension, a bird in general; this symbolization is a very early one. *V*'s appear on Upper Palaeolithic ivory sculptures representing bird-woman hybrids, known from the site of Mezin located on the Desna in the western Ukraine. On these figurines (*Ill. 19*) chevrons also appear in association with meanders. Another example, having no antecedents in the Palaeolithic, is the ram, a domesticated animal. The naturalistically portrayed ram hardly appears. Its symbolic reference is the head, or the horns alone. Further abstracted it appears on the exquisite Sesklo vases of Thessaly, painted in red on a white-slipped background, as a 'stair' design (*Ill. 20*). Variants of this motif continue into the Late Neolithic (*Ill. 21*). At first glance this design seems to be purely geometric decoration, but observation of many instances shows its relationship to the ram horn. This is most evident where horns are used not in a continuous pattern, but in isolation (*Ill. 21*). A vase from Chaeroneia, a Middle Neolithic site of central Greece (*Ill. 22*), shows the motif completely geometricized. It is important also to observe that the stair design quite regularly appears in association with the *V*, the interconnected *V*, and the beak design (*Ills. 20, 22*). Analogous schematization of the ram horn can be seen on the Hacılar pottery of central Anatolia. Some of the designs can easily be recognized as ram horns but others are totally abstracted (*Ill. 24*).

The use of ram horns as an ideogram can be traced back to the Early Neolithic. At Nea Nikomedeia, an Early Neolithic settlement in Greek Macedonia, for example, it appears on a number of seals. In geometric form, the motif of inverted and opposed horns is frequent (*Ill. 23*) as in the decoration of pottery. Seals with the ram horn ideogram must have had a functional significance similar to those bearing chevrons, *X*'s, and snake coils.

4 ACCUMULATION OF SYMBOLS AND VARIATIONS OF A THEME

Certain patterns often occur in combination. Thus we find consistent association of the snake, bird, and ram (*V* sign, beak, or chevron) with the net, checkerboard, bands of parallel lines, and striated area patterns. The Dimini style vase from Sesklo (*Ill. 25*) presents a classic example of an accumulation of symbols on a single object: inside the dish two isolated snake coils are on a background of bands of parallel lines alternating with stair design. Outside the surface is separated into sections of meander, checkerboard, and parallel lines. Such orchestration

22 Sesklo vase decorated with continuous *V*'s and abstract ram-horn motif. Chaeroneia, central Greece, *c.* 6000 BC (after Theocharis, 1973).

24 Ram horns on Hacılar V-II vases, central Anatolia (after Mellaart, 1970).

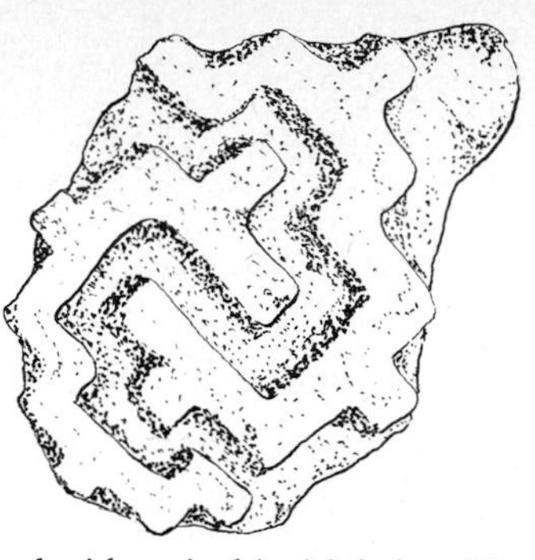

23 Clay seal with excised 'stair' design. Nea Nikomedeia near Veroia, Macedonia, *c.* end of the seventh millennium BC (after Rodden, 1965, 98).

25 Dish of classical Dimini style: a, interior decorated with two snake coils, band of parallel lines and 'stair' design; b, exterior decorated in sections of meander, checkerboard and parallel lines. *c.* 5000 BC (reproduced from Theocharis, 1973, 288 and Pl. IX. Originally published by Tsountas, 1908).

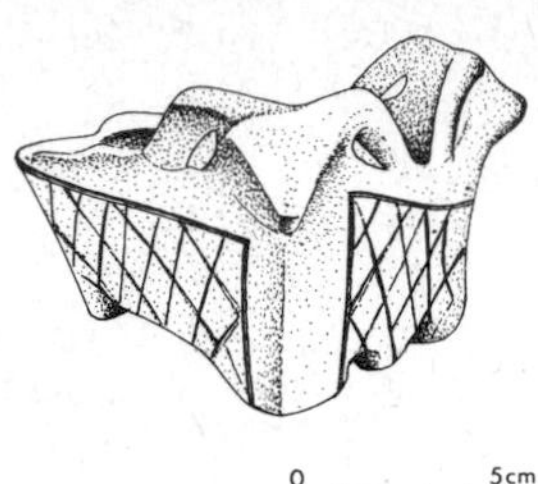

26 Triangular container with ram-head protomes, decorated with framed net-patterns. Fafos I, Early Vinča site at Kosovska Mitrovica. The net decoration was originally encrusted with white paste (courtesy Archaeological Museum, Plovdiv. Drawn by J. v.d. Marel).

27 Ram-headed three-legged vessel from Jasatepe in Plovdiv, central Bulgaria. The sides are decorated with snake coil, parallel lines and semi-circles. Three horizontal lines cross the nose of the animal. The excised decoration is encrusted with white paste (courtesy Archaeological Museum, Plovdiv. Excavation by P. Detev. Drawn by J. v.d. Marel).

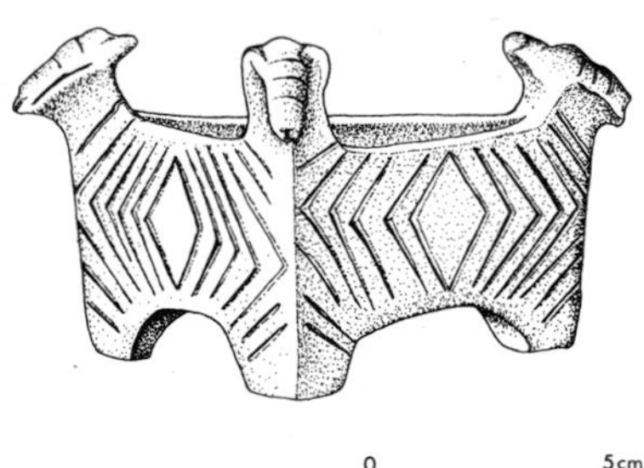

28 Triangular container with ram-head protomes. Sides bear multiple opposing chevrons. Three horizontal lines cross the heads of the animals. Vinča near Belgrade. Early Vinča period, end of the sixth millennium BC (after Dimitrijevič, 1969. Drawn by J. v.d. Marel).

of the symbolic motifs resembles a treatment of musical themes, with some motifs dominant, and others in the background serving as accompaniment. On this vase the snake coils are clearly dominant; the bands of parallel lines are subordinate, and the stair design is of still less importance; the meander, checkerboard, and parallel line patterns support the background theme.

During the Chalcolithic, stylized ram heads which adorn triangular or rectangular sacrificial containers are consistently combined with an incised design on the sides of either a net and checkerboard pattern (*Ill. 26*), bands of parallel lines, a snake coil, or coils (*Ill. 27*), or, more frequently, with *V*'s, simple chevrons, or duplicated, inverted, and opposing chevrons (*Ills. 28, 29*). Three incised or painted lines on the nose (*Ills. 27, 28*), groups of three parallel lines painted over the horns and nose, and sometimes three horns instead of two indicate some connection of the ram with the sacred number three. Stylized horned heads of rams in groups of three serve as handles for lids (*Ill. 30*). The sides of this elegant 'three ram head' container are encrusted with net and checkerboard design. The lids of sophisticated Gumelniţa vases are furnished with stylized ram handles in which a *V* motif predominates in the design of the painted surface (*Ill. 31*).

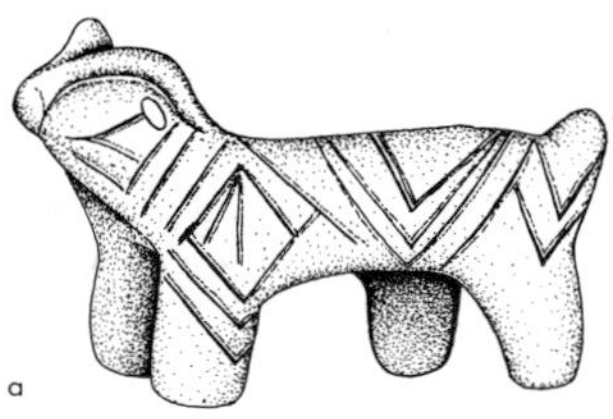

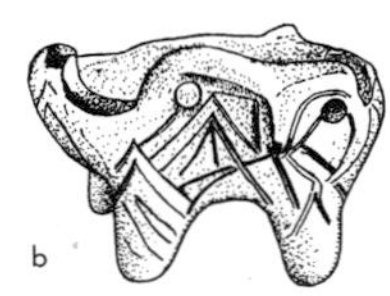

29 Ram-headed vessel incised with *V*'s and chevrons: a, profile; b, front. Vinča near Belgrade. Early Vinča period (after Vasić, *Vinča* II, Pl. LXXVIII, Fig. 335).

In rare cases, ram-head protomes have fortunately been discovered in association with other ceremonial equipment such as vases, ladles, plaques, and other objects. On these the painted designs are similar to those of the ram-headed containers. At the site of Ghîrbom near Alba Iulia in Transylvania which forms a part of the Petreşti cultural complex, large pedestalled vases, a spouted pot, a lid with a small handle, and a round disc inscribed on both sides were found together with a ram head, originally part or protome of a vase (*Ill. 32*). Presumably these objects were kept as a group on a table, perhaps for use in sacrificial ceremonies. The head of the ram has painted groups of parallel lines and incised *V*'s and simple lines on the neck. The clay disc is randomly incised with groups of parallel lines and *V*'s. The units of parallel lines and *V*'s on the disc, on the ram head, and on the vases strongly suggest a related conceptual intent. Other frequently used motifs are snake spirals in bands of parallel lines, multiple *V*'s, checkerboard, and the net or ladder. The constant application of this characteristic group of designs to vessels for ritual use emphasizes their referential character as symbols.

Symbolic design in combination with ideograms can ideally be studied on Vinča lids, illustrated below. The covered vases with richly decorated lids (*Ill. 33*) rank, by virtue of their temporal and spatial distribution in the Vinča culture, as one of the most characteristic creations of the ceramic art of this civilization. They have been found in almost all systematically explored Vinča settlements. The aggregate of symbols used in the decoration of the lids – the meander, bands of parallel lines, meandering dotted snakes, single and multiple *V*'s, rows of striated triangles, diagonal lines in groups of two or three, and framed columns of banded *V*'s – is a familiar one, and apparently constitutes a system of related attributes of a certain divinity. Their ramified associations offer some insight into the function of the vessels, as dedicated for specific use, in a certain sort of rite.

The catalogue of motifs occurring on lids is tabulated in *Ill. 34*. The semicircles or triangles indicated by two, three or multiple parallel lines are anthropomorphic eyes. Their exaggerated size is clearly intended to imply the supernatural (*Ills. 34–40*). This implication is further stressed in the area below the plastically rendered pupils by the symbolic diagonal bands of parallel lines (*Ill. 39*), groups of three diagonal lines connected at the top by four lines running in the opposite direction (*Ills. 36, 40*), vertical columns of horizontal striations

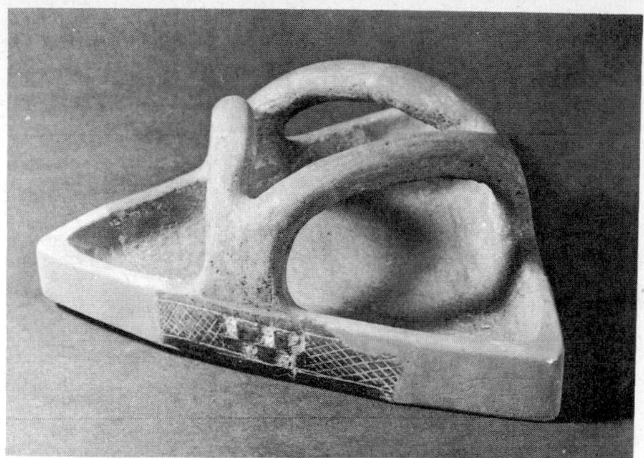

30 Triangular black-polished container with three stylized ram-horn handles. Alternating checkerboard and net designs around the exterior are white-encrusted. Baniata at Plovdiv, central Bulgaria. Karanovo III, East Balkan civilization. End of the sixth millennium BC (excavation by P. Detev, 1947–8).

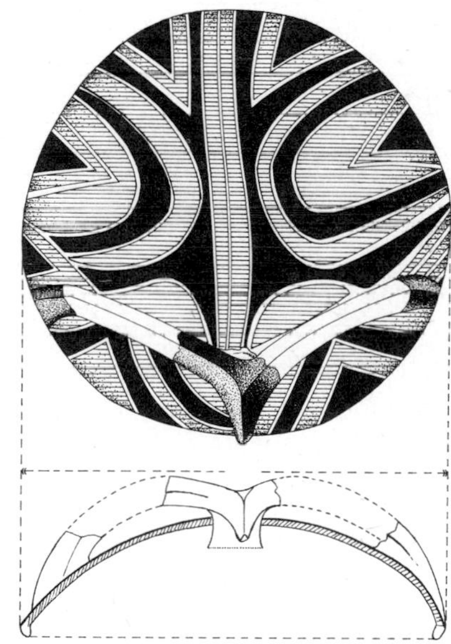

31 Lid with ram-head handle from Gumelniţa, southern Romania. East Balkan civilization. Polychrome painted designs include chevrons, semicircles and a central dividing panel. Colours: white-bordered purplish-red stripes on a brown ground. Diameter 25.5 cm (after Dumitrescu, 1966. Drawn by J. v.d. Marel).

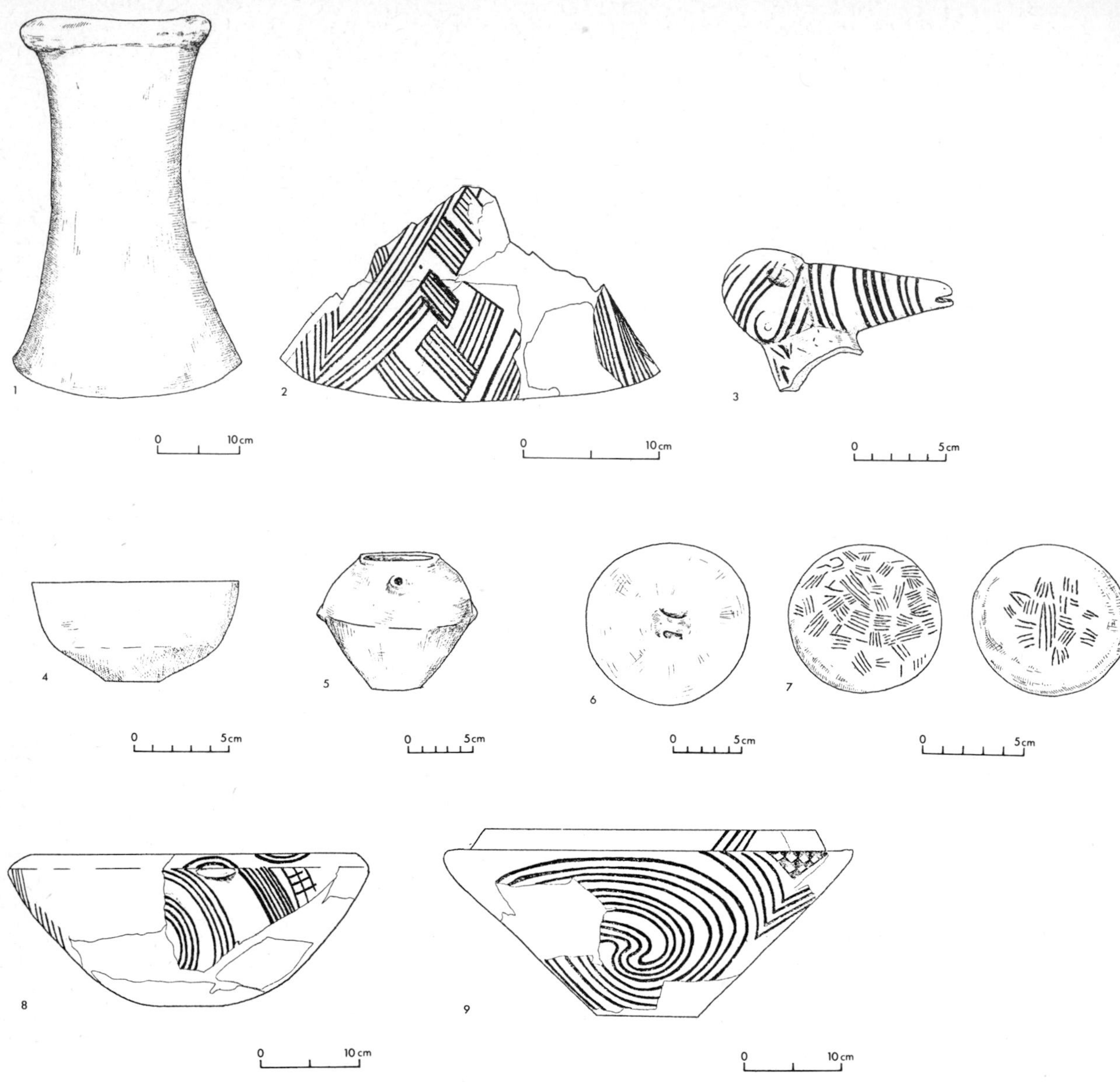

32 Assemblage of ritual objects: 1,2, pedestalled vases; 3, ram head (probably a protome of a large vase); 4, dish; 5, spouted vase; 6, small lid; 7, plaque with incised signs found in a house at the site of Ghîrbom near Berghiu, district of Alba in Transylvania. Petreşti complex, *c.* 4500 BC (courtesy I.A. Aldea, Muzeul Regional, Alba Iulia. Drawn by Linda Williams).

(*Ill. 42*), or meandering bands. On many lids this area is framed (*Ill. 40*). Between the eyes the prognathic protrusion is obviously not a nose, but the beak of a bird (*Ills. 37–39*). Above the beak and eyes, the upper part of the lid is filled with striations (*Ill. 40*), bands of parallel lines (*Ill. 42*), dotted bands (*Ill. 36*), striated triangles, or a large dotted meander (*Ill. 38*). Immediately above the beak is a multiple *V* (chevron), an ideogram of the Bird Goddess (*Ills. 35, 39*). Further identification is furnished by a framed column of banded *V*'s incised above the beak, another ideogram discussed above (*Ill. 36*).

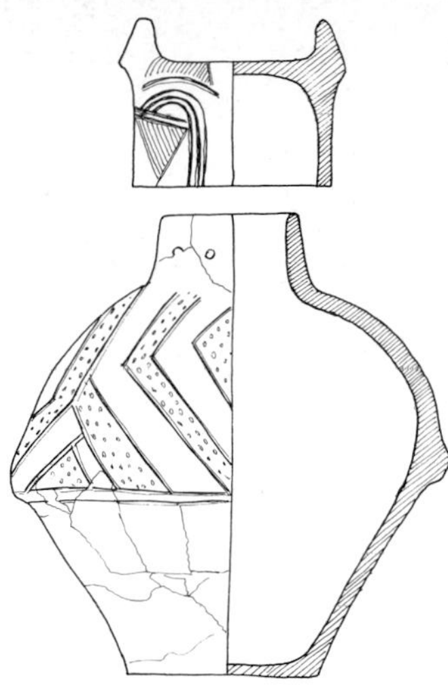

33 Classical Vinča vase with lid. Decoration by incision and encrustation of white paste. Brown fabric. Over the body are dotted meandering bands; on the lid are parallel lines around eyes, striated triangles below eyes, striated areas above eyes. Early Vinča, end of the sixth millennium BC or beginning of the fifth millennium. Found 7–6.6 m deep at Vinča (after Vasić, *Vinča* II. Belgrade University Collection. Drawn by J. v.d. Marel).

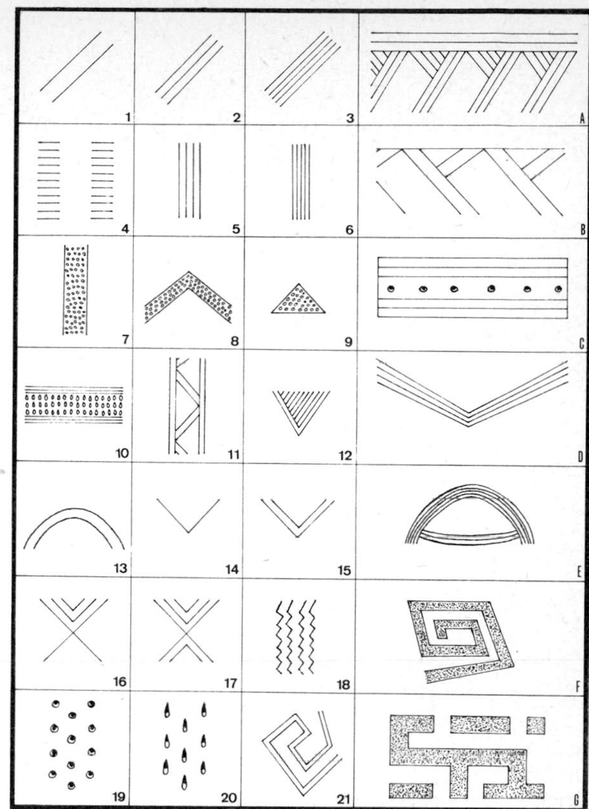

34 Motif catalogue of Vinča lids (after Vasić, *Vinča* II).

35 Early Vinča lid with double chevron above the beak. Enormous triangles emphasize the supernatural character of the eyes of the Goddess. Four dotted 'rain bands' above the eyes. Vinča site (after Vasić, *Vinča* II. Belgrade University Collection. Drawn by J. v.d. Marel).

The ears represent an animal of mythic significance, perhaps an owl.

Analysis of the decorated lids shows that the sign content, as well as the associations between the sign groups, is consistent. The following ideograms can be recognized: a chevron (or multiple *V*'s), a chevron combined with an *X* sign, a column of banded *V*'s, an isolated meander, a framed meander, and framed bands of interconnected groups of diagonal lines (see catalogue of motifs in *Ill. 34: 11, 14–17, D, F, 21, A, B*). Each of the motifs expresses a concept, either as a fixed ideogram or as amplifications of ideograms by symbolic design. Their repetitious association with parallel lines, dotted or striated bands and triangles emphasizes the intimate relationship with rain and streams. The framed area of interconnected diagonal lines might very well be an ideogram of rain. Quite probably then, the peculiar lidded vases served in the cult of the Bird Goddess, perhaps in a rain (or nourishment) invocation rite. The same set of ideograms appears on the Bird Goddess' masks (*Ill. 41*).

36, 37 Two early Vinča lids. Random striations over eyes. Framed areas of diagonal parallel lines, probably an ideogram connected with rain, over the lower part. Banded *V*'s, chevrons, dotted bands and parallel lines (after Vasić, *Vinča* II. Belgrade University Collection. Drawn by J. v.d. Marel).

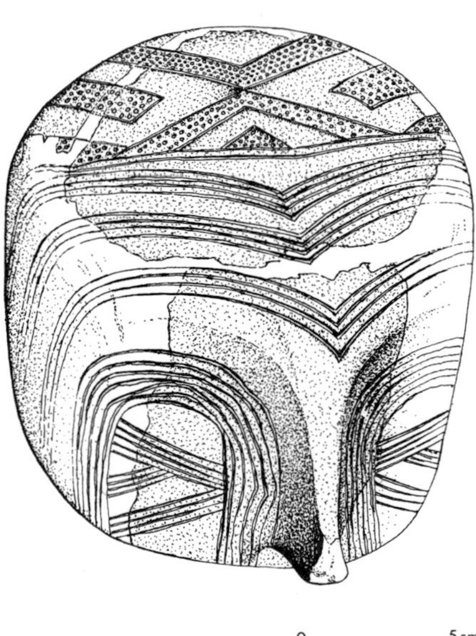

39 Lid of the mid-Vinča period from the site of Potporanj at Vršac, eastern Yugoslavia. Multiple chevrons above the beak, 'streams' around the eyes and bands of dotted meanders in the back (courtesy Vršac Museum. Drawn by J. v.d. Marel).

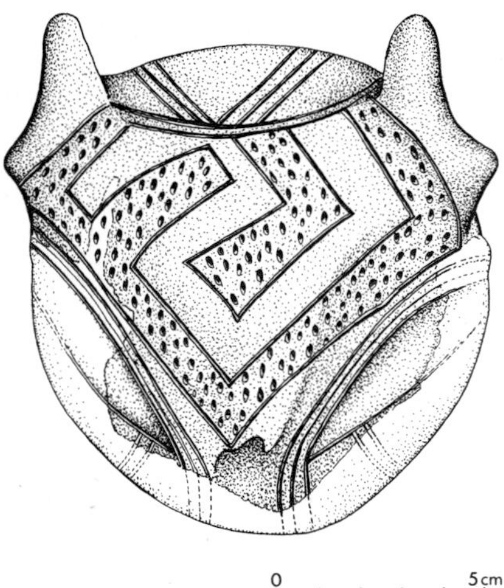

38 Punctuated snake meander above the beak, chevron on the back of the head. 'Streams' around the eyes. Lid of the Vinča IIB phase, found at a depth of 7.2 m at Vinča (after Vasić, *Vinča* II. Belgrade University Collection. Drawn by J. v.d. Marel).

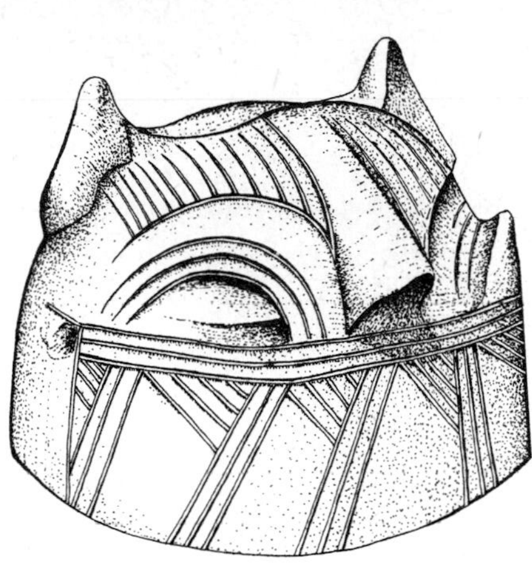

40 Lid from the site of Vinča, found at a depth of 6.6 m. The framed area of interconnected diagonal lines covers the whole lower part of the lid. Striations above the eyes (after Vasić, *Vinča* II. Belgrade University Collection. Drawn by J. v.d. Marel).

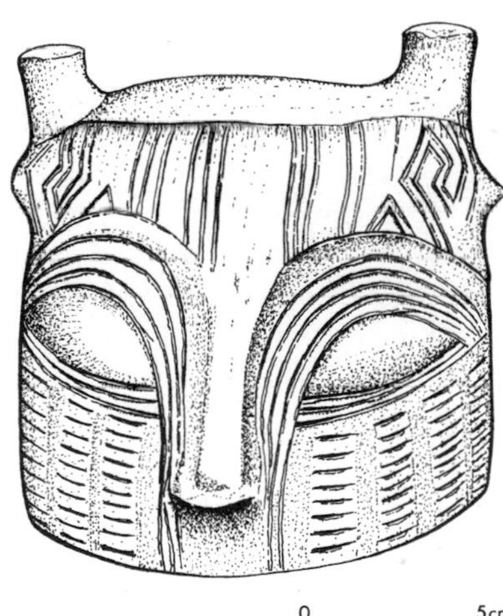

42 Lid of mid-Vinča period decorated with vertical bands of horizontal striations below the eyes and bands of parallel vertical lines above. Fafos II near Kosovska Mitrovica, southern Yugoslavia (courtesy Kosovska Mitrovica Museum. Drawn by J. v.d. Marel from the author's photograph).

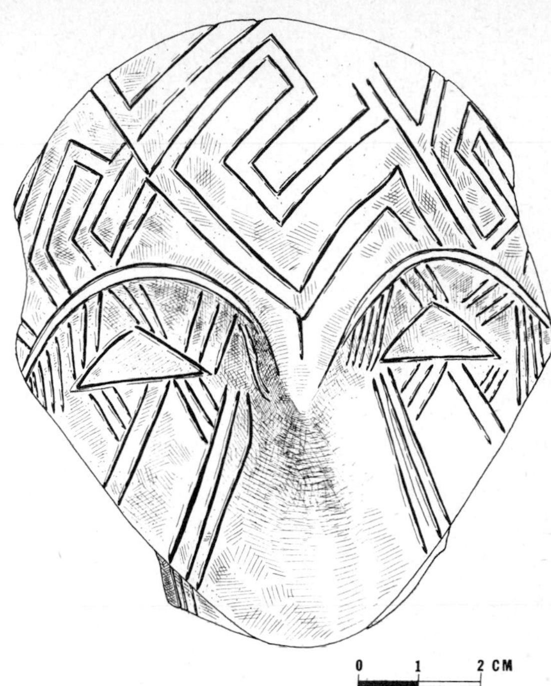

41 Bird Goddess' mask decorated with meanders over the top and groups of parallel lines (rain ideograms?) round the eyes. Vinča site at Potporanj, eastern Yugoslavia, *c.* early fifth millennium BC (courtesy National Museum, Belgrade. Originally published by M. Grabić, 1929).

5 DELINEATED AREAS OF SYMBOLIC DESIGN AND FRAMED IDEOGRAMS

On pottery, framed areas defined by vertical and horizontal lines, in which duplicated or enlarged ideograms are placed, appear at the threshold of the Chalcolithic period in the Early Vinča, Butmir, Tisza, Early Lengyel, Proto-Cucuteni, Karanovo III, and Dimini complexes. This interesting development can be interpreted as an effort to emphasize certain concepts and to separate one concept from the next. Objects with such delineated areas of design, randomly chosen from different cultural groups, illustrate the practice of 'concept painting' in all parts of Old Europe. The examples are from the Dimini (*Ill. 43*), Cucuteni (*Ill. 44*), Vinča (*Ill. 45, 46*), and Butmir (*Ill. 47*) cultures.

The appearance of the device of framing concepts is synchronous with the beginning of the use of

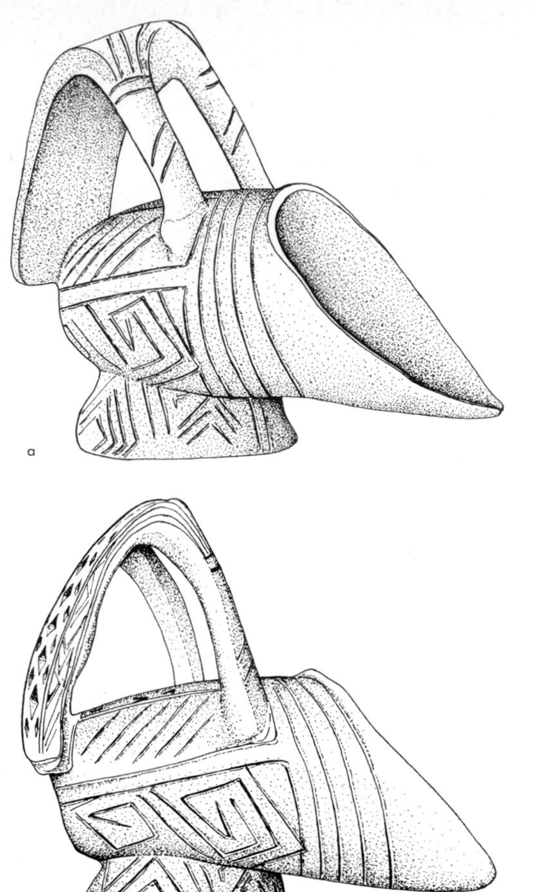

43 Bird-beaked 'scoop' (libation vase?) with handle merging bird's wings and tail. Three views. The ideograms – chevrons, striations and meanders – and a line of signs (c) are framed. Sesklo, Thessaly. Dimini period (after Tsountas, 1908. Drawn by J. v.d. Marel).

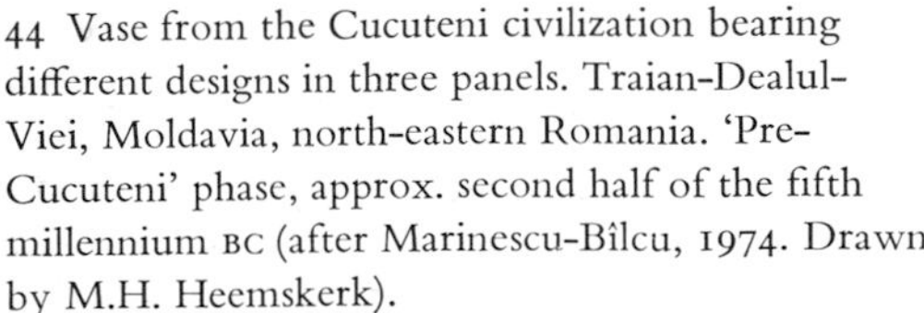

44 Vase from the Cucuteni civilization bearing different designs in three panels. Traian-Dealul-Viei, Moldavia, north-eastern Romania. 'Pre-Cucuteni' phase, approx. second half of the fifth millennium BC (after Marinescu-Bîlcu, 1974. Drawn by M.H. Heemskerk).

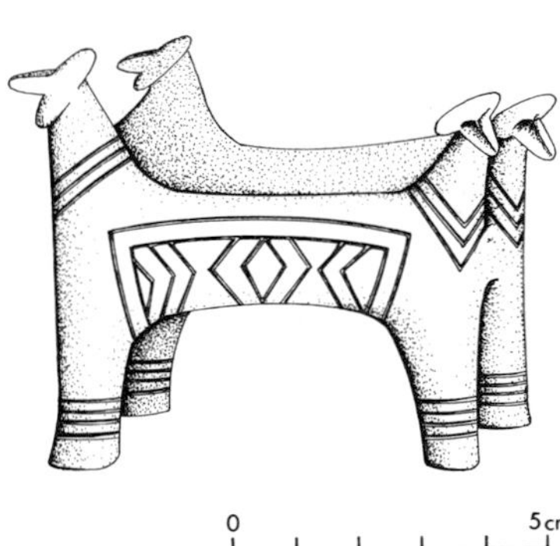

45 Four-legged vessel with an animal head (stylized ram?) at each corner. An ideogram of opposing chevrons is incised on the long sides; triple chevrons adorn the neck of the animals. Early Vinča. Priština, southern Yugoslavia (courtesy of Priština Regional Museum. Drawn by J. v.d. Marel).

many linear signs. Some vases and figurines exhibit both framed symbolic designs and completely abstract linear signs (*Ill. 43*). Others show intensification of a theme by duplication, inversion, or enlargement of a sign. This device is illustrated by a Vinča figurine from Gomolava (*Ill. 46*), decorated by inscribed panels separated by straight lines. The arrangement and size of *V*'s is different in each compartment. The impression is that each of the delineated areas implies a slightly different concept, or stresses a variation of the same concept.

6 IDEOGRAMS WITH ADDITIONS OF LINES

To express a more complicated concept, or another aspect of a particular concept, an extra sign was added to an ideogram. These additional signs usually appear as simple lines or longer dashes. Such compounds are in evidence in the Neolithic period on cult vessels, seals, and spindle whorls of the Starčevo (Criș) and Sesklo cultural groups (see *Ill. 5:3* and *Ill. 48*). The consistent use of additional lines, and their combinations into characteristic groups, eventually crystallized the entire corpus of signs visible at the beginning of the Vinča culture.

The ideograms of the Neolithic period constituted the basis of the sign system. Through the addition of a line at the side, above, or across, there are more than thirty signs derived from the *V* or chevron alone (*Ill. 49*). Such amplified signs are found in columns and lines, around circular objects, on miniature vessels, on figurines, spindle whorls, sacrificial containers and on anthropomorphic

46 Schematic figurine from the Vinča settlement of Gomolava near Sremska Mitrovica, northern Yugoslavia. The entire body is incised with multiple *V*'s and chevrons in panels (after *Rad Vojvod. Muzeja*, Novi Sad 14 (1965), 166 and Tab. XIII. Drawn by Linda Williams).

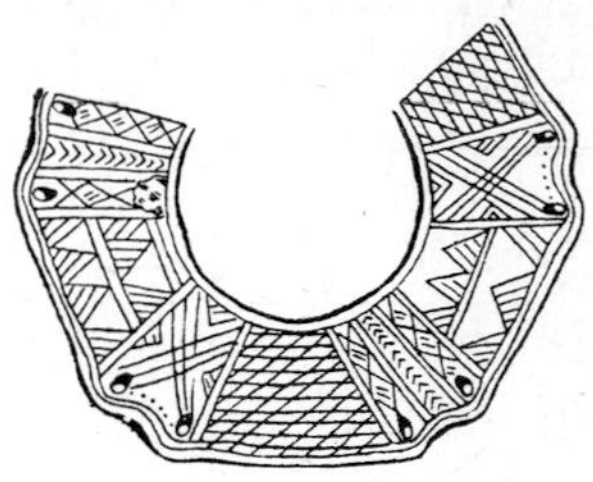

47 Panel or register decoration of multiple *V*'s, striated triangles, chest-band design with *V*'s, net-pattern and interconnected lozenges with striations inside a Butmir vase from Jablanica, Bosnia, Yugoslavia (after Matz, 1928, 226 and Abb. 97).

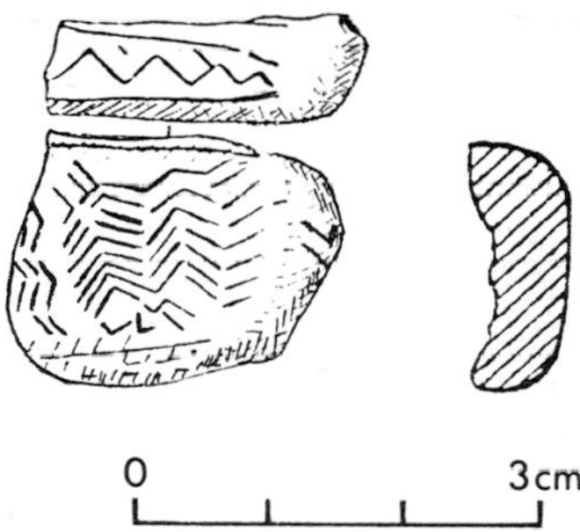

48 Fragment of a clay vessel incised with lines of interconnected *V*'s to which isolated *V*'s and simple lines are added. Starčevo (Criș) site of Perieni, Moldavia, north-eastern Romania. First half of the sixth millennium BC (after Petrescu-Dîmbovița).

49 *V*'s and *X*'s with additional lines, duplications and invertions: Vinča signs as they appear incised in isolation or groups (from the corpus of Vinča signs by Winn, 1973).

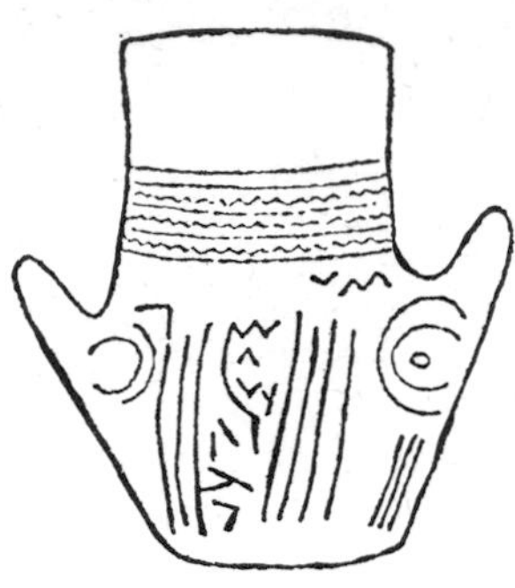

50 Vase with anthropomorphic features (breasts and handles as upraised arms) bearing a column of signs consisting of *V*'s and *V*'s with additional lines flanked with parallel lines. At the lower right side – three lines, an isolated ideogram. Szegvár-Tüzköves near Szentes, Hungary (Tisza group) (after Csalog, 1959, 23:2).

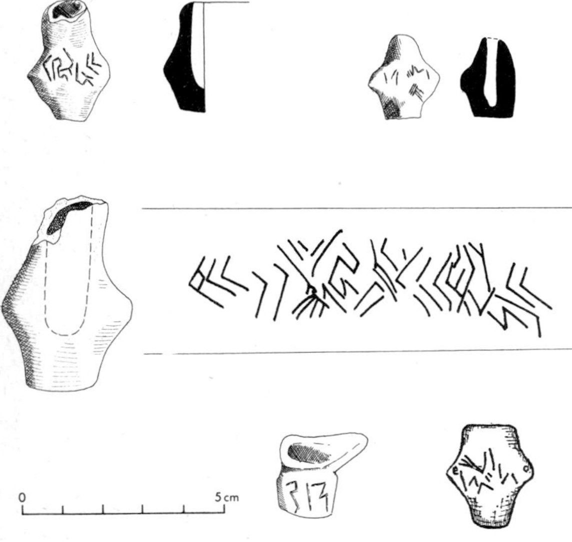

51 A miniature vessel from the Early Vinča period with circular band of inscribed signs: multiple *V*'s, *V*'s with addition of extra lines, and meanders (after Letica, 1967).

vases (*Ills. 50, 51*). Preconditioned by a long use of ideograms and symbolic design, and by a similar process of development, the limited number of basic ideograms developed during the course of the sixth millennium BC into the sign writing of Old Europe.

CONCLUSIONS

1. Ideograms in use during the Neolithic and Chalcolithic derive from symbols of mythical figures and ideas. Through duplication, inversion, amplification, and the device of framing, their number and meaning steadily expanded.
2. Ornamental design on vases, sacrificial containers, ladles, and other cult objects was based on stylization and abstraction of concrete symbols, and on the multiplication or 'explosion' of ideograms related to specific divinities for whose cult they were produced.
3. Characters of the script of Old Europe such as are known from the Vinča corpus, dated to the period 5300–4000 BC, are intimately related to ideograms. In fact, many signs are derived from ideograms through the addition of lines or dashes, by duplications or inversions, and by their combination into groups.

Bibliography

BANNER, J. 1959 Anthropomorphe Gefässe der Theisskultur von der Siedlung Kökénydomb bei Hódmezövásárhely (Ungarn), *Germania* XXXVII, 14–35.

BENAC, A. 1952 *Prehistorijsko Naselje Nebo I problem butmirske kulture* (French résumé 151–64), Sarajevo.

1971 Obre II. Neolitsko naselje Butmirske grupe na Gornjem polju, *Glasnik Zemaljskog Muzeja* XXVI. In English translation: Obre II, A Neolithic settlement of the Butmir group at Gornje polje, *Wissenschaftliche Mitteilungen des Bosnisch-Herzegowinischen Landesmuseums* III, A (1973).

1973 Obre I Neolitsko naselje starčevačko – impresso i kakanjske kulture na Raskršću, *Glasnik Zemalijskog Muzeja*.

BIBIKOV, S. N. 1958 *Poselenie Luka-Vrublevetskaja = Materialy i Issledovanija po Arkheologii SSSR*, 38, Moscow and Leningrad.

BOGNÁR-KUTZIÁN, I. 1944–47 *The Körös Culture* 2 vols, Budapest.

BREGANT, T. 1968 *Ornamentika na neolitski keramiki v Jugoslaviji*, Ljubljana.

CSALOG, J. 1959 Die anthropomorphen Gefässe und Idolplastiken von Szegvár–Tüzköves, *Acta Archaeo. Hung.* XI, 7–38.

DETEV, P. 1965 Modèles de decoration de l'énéolithique, *Archaeologija* (Sofia) VII: 4, 65–73.

1968 Praistoricheskoto selishche pri selo Muldava, *Godishnik* (Arch. Mus. Plovdiv) VI, 9–48.

DIMITRIJEVIĆ, S. 1969 *Starčevačka kultura u Slavonsko – srijemskom prostoru i problem prijelaza ranog u srednji neolit u srpskom i hrvatskom podunavlju*, Gradski Muzej, Vukovar.

DOMBAY, J. 1960 *Die Siedlung und das Gräberfeld in Zengövárkony* = *Archaeol. Hung.* 37.

DUMITRESCU, V. 1945 La station préhistorique de Traian; fouilles de 1936, 1938 et 1940, *Dacia* IX–X, (1941–44).

1954 *Habaşeşti*, Bucharest.

1959 La civilisation de Cucuteni, *Berichten van de rijksdienst voor het oudheidkundig bodemonderzoek* 9, 7–48.

1966 New discoveries at Gumelniţa, *Archaeology* 19, 162–72.

GALOVIĆ, R. 1959 *Predionica: Neolitsko naselje kod Prištine* (*Predionica: Äneolithische Ansiedlung bei Priština*), Priština.

1968 Die Starčevo Kultur in Jugoslawien, in *Die Anfänge des Neolithikum vom Orient bis Nordeuropa* II, ed. H. Schwabedissen, 1–22, Fundamenta A: 3.

GEORGIEV, G. I. 1961 Kulturgruppen der Jungstein- und Kupferzeit in der Ebene von Thrazien (Südbulgarien), in *L'Europe à la fin de l'âge de la pierre*, ed. J. Böhm and S. J. De Laet, 45–100.

GEORGIEV, V. I. 1970 *Pismenostta v'rkhu glinenata pločka ot Gradešnica.* (Résumé in French: L'écriture sur la plaque en argile du village Gradešnica). In a joint article with Bogdan Nikolov, Débuts d'écriture du chalcolithique dans les terres bulgares, *Archeologija* (Sofia) XII: 3, 7–9.

GIMBUTAS, M. 1972a Excavation at Anza, Macedonia, *Archaeology* 25, 112–23.

1974a. *The Gods and Goddesses of Old Europe 7000–3500 BC. Myths, Legends and Cult Images*, London.

1974b Anza, ca. 6500–5000 B.C. a cultural yardstick for the study of Neolithic Southeast Europe, *Journal of Field Archaeology* I: 1, 22–26.

1974c Achilleion: A neolithic mound in Thessaly; Preliminary report on 1973 and 1974 excavations, *Journal of Field Archaeology* I, 277–302.

GRBIĆ, M. 1929 *Pločnik. Äneolithische Ansiedlung*, Belgrade.

HOOD, M. S. F. 1968 The Tartaria tablets, *Scientific American* 215: 1, 30–7.

KALICZ, N. 1970 *Dieux d'Argile. L'âge de pierre et de cuivre en Hongrie*, Budapest.

KANDYBA, O. 1937 *Schipenitz. Kunst und Geräte eines neolithischen Dorfes* = *Bücher zur Ur- und Frühgeschichte* V, Berlin.

KARMANSKI, S. 1968 *Žrtvenici, statuete i amuleti sa lokaliteta Donja Branjevina kod Deronja*, Odžaci.

LETICA, Z. 1967 Minijature sudovi iz Vinča, *Zbornik* of the National Museum in Belgrade, V, 77–126.

MAKKAY, J. 1968 The Tartaria Tablets, *Orientalia* 37, 272–89.

1971 A Chalcolithic stamp seal from Karanovo, Bulgaria. *Kadmos* X, 1–9.

MARINESCU-BÎLCU, S. 1974 *Cultura Precucuteni peteritoriul României*, Bucharest.

MARSHAK, A. 1972 *The roots of civilization. The cognitive beginnings of Man's first art, symbol and notation*, New York.

MAŢASĂ, C. 1946 Frumuşica. *Village préhistorique à céramique peinte dans la Moldavie du Nord*, Bucharest.

1964 Asezarea eneolitica Cucuteni B de la Tîrgu Ocna-Podei (raionul Tîrgu Ocna, reg. Bacău), *Arheologia Moldovei* II–III, 11–66.

MATZ, F. 1928 *Die frühkretischen Siegel: Eine Untersuchung über das Werden des minoischen Stiles*, Berlin and Leipzig.

MCPHERRON, A. and SREJOVIĆ, D. 1975 *Divostin*, Belgrade.

MELLAART, J. 1970 *Excavations at Hacılar* I–II, Edinburgh.

MIKOV, V. 1959 The prehistoric mound of Karanovo, *Archaeology* 12, 88–97.

MÜLLER-KARPE, H. 1968 *Jungsteinzeit* = *Handbuch der Vorgeschichte* II, Munich.

NIKOLOV, B. 1970 Glinena pločka s pismeni znaci ot s. Gradešnica, Vračanski okryg. (Résumé in French: Plaque en argile avec des signes d'écriture du village Gradešnica, dép. de Vraca) *Archeologija* (Sofia) XII: 3, 1–9.

PASSEK, T. S. 1949 *Periodizatsija tripol'skikh poselenii* = *Materialy Issledovanija po Arkheologii SSSR* 10, Moscow and Leningrad.

PAUL, I. 1965a Ein Kulttisch aus der jungsteinzeitlichen Siedlung von Deutschpien (Pianul de Jos), *Forschungen zur Volks- und Landeskunde* (Bucharest) 8: 1, 69–76.

1965b Un complex de cult descoperit in asezarea neolitica de la Pianul de Jos (Ein in der neolithischen Niederlassung von Pianul de Jos entdeckter Kultkomplex), *Studii şi Comunicari/Sibiu/*, 5–20.

PETRESCU-DÎMBOVIŢA, M. 1957 Sondajul stratigrafic de la Perieni, *Materiale şi Cercetări Arheologice* III, 65–82.

1963 Die wichtigsten Ergebnisse der archäologischen

Ausgrabungen in der neolithischen Siedlung von Truşeşti (Moldau), *Prähistorische Zeitschrift* XLI, 172–86.

1966 *Cucuteni. Monumentale Patrie Noastre*, Bucharest.

PEZARD, M. and POTTIER, E. 1913 *Les antiquités de la Susiane: Catalogue, Musée du Louvre*, Paris.

POTTIER, E. 1913 *Étude historique et chronologique sur les vases peints de l'acropole de Suse = J. de Morgan 1912 Delegation en Perse, Memoires* XIII, Paris.

RODDEN, R. J. 1965 An Early Neolithic Village in Greece, *Scientific American*, 212:4, 82–93.

SALMONY, A. 1949 Some Palaeolithic ivory carvings, *Artibus Asiae* 12, 107–12.

SCHMIDT, H. 1903 Tordos, *Zeitschrift für Ethnologie* 35, 438–69.

1932 *Cucuteni*, Berlin.

SCHWEITZER, B. 1969 *Die geometrische Kunst Griechenlands. Frühe Formenwelt im Zeitalter Homers*, Cologne.

SREJOVIĆ, D. 1972 *Europe's first monumental sculpture: New discoveries at Lepenski Vir*, London.

THEOCHARIS, D. 1967 *The prehistory of Thessaly*, Volos.

1973 *Neolithic Greece*, Athens: National Bank of Greece.

TICHÝ, R. 1972 K otázce pisma v mladši dobe kamenne (zur Frage der Schrift in der jüngeren Steinzeit), *Vlastivedny vestnik moravsky* XXIV:1, 7–11.

TITOV, V. S. 1969 *Neolit Gretsii*, Moscow.

TODOROVIĆ, J. and CERMANOVIĆ, A. 1961 *Banjica, naselje vinčanske kulture. (Banjica, Siedlung der Vinča-Gruppe)*, Belgrade.

TSOUNTAS, Ch. 1908 *Ai proistorikai akropoleis Diminiou kai Sesklou*, Athens.

VASIĆ, M. M. 1932–36 *Preistoriska Vinča* 4 vols, Belgrade.

VASILJEVIĆ, M. 1963 Neolitsko naselje Jela u Šapcu, *Ustvari* (Šabac) 26, 120–38.

VLASSA, N. 1963 Chronology of the Neolithic in Transylvania, in the light of the Tărtăria's Settlement's Stratigraphy, *Dacia* VII, 485–94.

1970 Kulturelle Beziehungen des Neolithikums Siebenbürgens zum vorderen Orient. *Acta Musei Napocensis* VII, 3–39.

VULPE, R. 1957 *Izvoare: Săpăturile din 1936–1948*, (*Izvoare: Les Fouilles de 1936–1948*), Bucharest.

WACE, A. J. B. and THOMPSON, M. S. 1912 *Prehistoric Thessaly*, Cambridge.

WINN, M. MC. 1973 *The signs of the Vinča Culture: an internal analysis; their Role, Chronology and Independence from Mesopotamia* University of California, Los Angeles, Ph. D. History, archaeology, Ann Arbor.

ZERVOS, C. 1962 *Naissance de la civilisation en Grèce*, Paris.

11

P. J. R. MODDERMAN

The Aveburys and their Continental Counterparts

1 Stuart Piggott lecturing at Avebury, 14 August 1949.
Left to right: M. Ørsnes-Christensen, Denmark; Major R.C. Allan, British Council; P.J.R. Modderman, Netherlands; R.J.C. Atkinson; Stuart Piggott; Sir Mortimer Wheeler; Thabit Hassan Thabit, Sudan; F.S. Nelson, Netherlands; M.E. Mariën, Belgium.

AVEBURY, a hot summer afternoon in August 1949. In the shadow of the trees, east of the southern entrance, a small group of archaeologists is spread out against the rampart facing the re-erected stone circles. Stuart Piggott is explaining what is known about this extraordinary monument to the members of a course organized by the British Council. They come from Belgium, Denmark, the Netherlands, Italy, and the Sudan (*Ill. 1*). Most of them are young; the only clear exception seems to be Professor A. E. van Giffen.

Piggott naturally knew what he was talking about, particularly since he had been involved in the original excavations at Avebury, but he also knew how to communicate his story to the audience. I think that all who had the privilege to listen to Stuart Piggott's lectures have the same memory of him. As an acknowledgment for all that I have received from Stuart Piggott, I should like to contribute to this Festschrift a continental counterpart to Avebury.

The sobriquet 'The Averburys' is given by me to that diversified group of monuments which are individually known as causewayed camps and henge monuments. Avebury itself is in my opinion the most impressive of all of them; therefore I choose its name to cover the associated earthworks for which a non-military purpose is generally accepted. They have in common the formation of an enclosure. The easiest to recognize are those consisting of ditches and banks or settings of standing stones. However, it is apparent that geology and land use have strongly influenced the present situation of these monuments. We realize that the English Downs until the middle of the twentieth century have preserved all types of earthworks very favourably because the latter have been left virtually untouched after going out of use. Modern research has made it clear that the Averburys are not restricted to chalk, but may be found wherever ancient man had the impetus to construct them. The problem is that under many soil conditions the ditches are totally silted up and the banks are eroded by natural agencies. Man himself may have been the final levelling factor in cases where the site of the monument now lies on arable land. It is my impression that this is the main reason why the continental counterparts of the British Avebury's are still rare. Aerial photography may reveal more of them, but I am sure this is not the only way to trace them. Extensive excavations of settlement sites are another way to find them, as is shown by the example of Hienheim, which will be described in more detail below.

As a continental archaeologist I feel myself excused from attempting a summary of the genealogical register of the Averburys in Great Britain and Ireland. The recent reviews by Isobel Smith (1971) and G. J. Wainwright (1969) are in every respect sufficient for the purpose of this contribution. From these studies we learn that the enclosures were created over a long period of time, the first quarter of the third millennium BC being the oldest period according to the radiocarbon dates for the causewayed camps (Smith 1971, 90). The henge monuments have produced dates between 2500 and 1500 bc; later dates are unknown. The need to build them might have declined, or the structures may have been so temporary that they are beyond the powers of the archaeologist to trace them, or the purpose for which enclosures were made may have at least partly been absorbed by some of the barrows. The idea of separating a certain space for religious and/or social purposes is so human that it might appear at every time in any place. Quite rightly several authors have pointed to the Iron Age *Viereckschanze* as late prehistoric examples.

To produce a classification of the Aveburys seems to me unnecessary, not only since others with detailed knowledge have already done it, but also since in my opinion it would obscure the general idea behind these enclosures, which is perhaps best defined as socio-religious and certainly not military. To prove this purpose is decisive.

THE CHAMER ENCLOSURE AT HIENHEIM, LDKR. KELHEIM, BAVARIA

The Institute of Prehistory of Leiden University is currently carrying out excavations at Hienheim on the Danube (Modderman 1966; 1971). The point where the Roman *limes* meets the river is visible from the site. The main object of this research, which started in 1965, is a *Linearbandkeramik* and Stroked (or better stiched!) Ware settlement. The habitation was apparently continued, as clear traces of Rössen occupation, some pits with Altheim ware and quite an extensive quantity of Chamer material were found. To make the story complete a late Corded Beaker grave, an Early Bronze Age pit dwelling, Ha B pottery, and some forty remarkable rectangular pits in which burned stones have been found, must be mentioned. For our present purposes only the traces left by man in the Chamer period will be of interest.

For Hienheim two radiocarbon dates are available: one from a pit with Chamer pottery, 2270±55 bc (GrN 5732), and another from the inner ditch of the enclosure to be discussed, 2390±55bc (GrN 6425). These results seem to be in general agreement with the short chronology proposed on typological grounds by R. A. Maier (1964).

A plan (*Ill. 2*) shows the area excavated up to and including 1974; this area covers some 1.25 hectares with the Chamer pits and a double ditch having causeways which certainly can be reckoned to date to the Chamer period. There are some house plans which are considered to belong to the same period.

Another important feature clear from the plan is the site's location in the landscape (*Ill. 2*). The settlement originally lay on a terrace of the Danube

2 Plan of the excavation at Hienheim, Ldkr. Kelheim, Bavaria.

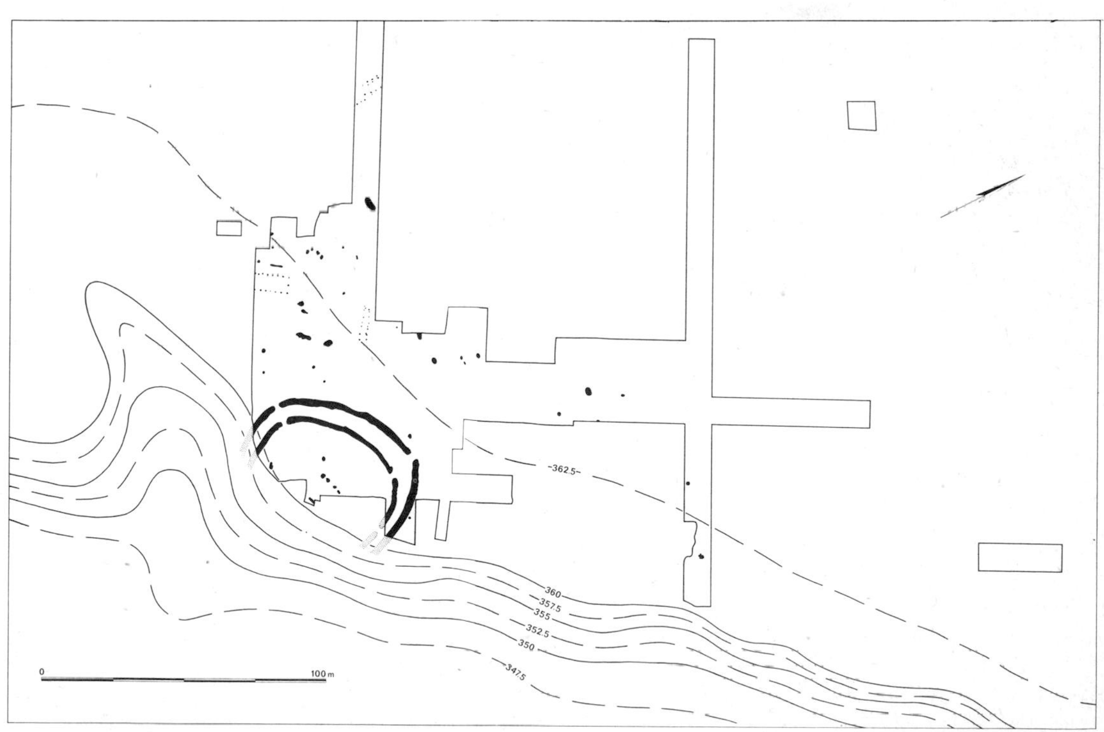

3 The 1967 excavations at Hienheim, looking southward; the Danube is visible at the top.

which flows some 500 m east of the site in a south-north direction. There is a difference of 10–12 m in height between the lower terrace, which is still flooded occasionally, and the upper terrace surface. The steep slope between both terraces is a very striking feature of the landscape, and the settlement site has a natural boundary in this escarpment. To the south there is a small valley, which has silted up considerably since the medieval occupation of Hienheim started in about AD 1000. In the Chamer period the valley will have served as another natural boundary. Although to the north and west there are no obstructions for the occupation, as the plan shows, we are fairly sure that the extension to the north is well established.

The double ditch system has been almost totally excavated and its continuation up to the steep slope examined by borings. The ditches are dated by sherds of Chamer ware, some of which were lying on the bottom of the filling, and by the radiocarbon date already mentioned of 2390 ± 55 bc.

The enclosure within the inner ditch measures 48 × 37 m while the dimensions are 58 × 44 m for the outer ditch. Although there is no doubt that both ditches were made with the same intention, there are some indications that one was dug in succession to the other after a lapse of many years. At the outset one may point to the fact that the inner ditch incorporates three causeways whereas the outer one has only two. The north-eastern interruption is not repeated, which can be explained by the proposition that there was no more need for it when the outer ditch was constructed. Secondly the ditches do not run parallel; the shortest distance between them is about 3 m but over 6 m near the the northern entrance. Thirdly, the width of the inner ditch is considerably smaller (1.05–1.65 m) than that of the outer ditch (1.80–2.35 m). Finally the cross-sections through the ditches show clear differences (*Ill. 4*). The inner ditch tends to be nearly perpendicular on both sides and the end. This can be observed in three cross-sections and in two of the ends. For the outer ditch four cross-sections and three of the ends are at our disposal. They show steep slopes on the inside of the ditch but they are never vertical, while the outer slope is even less steep and more rounded. To complete the description, mention must be made of the depth of the ditch, which in principle is the same for both. Known measurements for the inner ditch vary between 0.80 m and 1.40 m, and for the outer ditch are between 1 m and 1.30 m, all measurements being taken from the present land surface.

The ditches were dug through a layer of loess and into the river gravel. Part of the gravel was washed from the throw-out back into the filling of the ditches. The inner ditch north of the western entrance shows clearly that this gravel came from the outside, an indication that there was originally an external bank. This observation leads to the conclusion that the enclosure had no military purpose. Probably the outer ditch also had an external bank because the filling up of the ditch occurred most rapidly on that side.

We have no idea at all what happened inside the enclosure. A row of four pits containing amongst other objects Chamer ware, arrowheads and a stone axe was discovered in 1974, but we are in the dark as to the purpose of the pits as well as that of three small pits nearby. There are a number of post-holes near the centre forming part of some wooden structure, but as the only dating for them is post-*Linearbandkeramik* they are not included on the plan (*Ill. 2*).

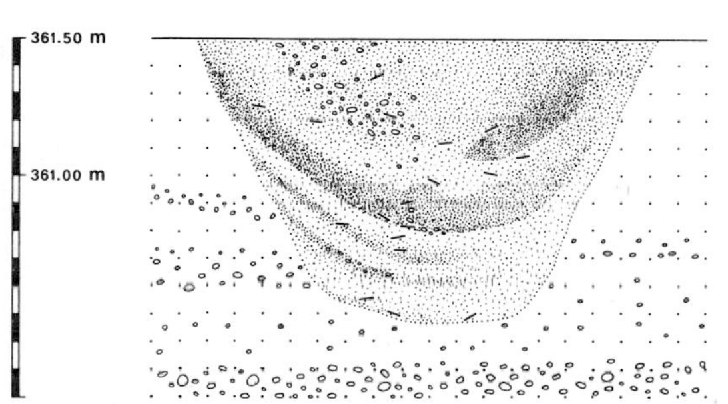

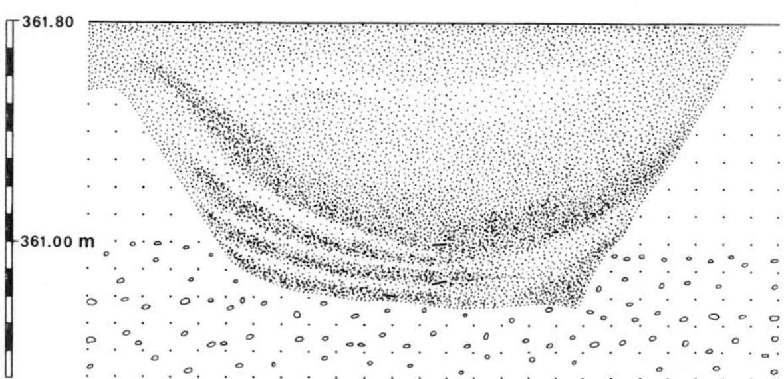

4 Sections through the inner and outer ditch of the Chamer enclosure at Hienheim. The outside of the ditch is on the left.

The investigations at Hienheim have shown that during the Chamer period a relatively small part of the settlement was enclosed by a system of ditches with first three and then two causeways. There are indications that the banks lay outside these ditches and that the whole structure was renovated and enlarged after some time. I have no real doubt that the Hienheim enclosure is in some way related to Avebury.

OTHER CONTINENTAL COUNTERPARTS

Some 74 km east-south-east of Hienheim is situated the well-known ditch system of Kothingeichendorf. According to R. A. Maier (1962) there is only sufficient certainty about the northern circular ditches; the southern one (Wagner 1928) is omitted by Maier. A recent study of the original documents in the Aussenstelle Landshut der Abteilung für Vor- und Frühgeschichte vom Bayerischen Landesamt für Denkmalpflege and in the Prähistorische Staatssammlung at Munich (for which I want to thank Dr R. Christlein, Dr R. A. Maier and Dr H. P. Uenze), has convinced me of the correctness of Wagner's plan. There is no reason why we should doubt what Reinecke (1923) writes about Kothingeichendorf. The northern of the two ring-ditches is greatly filled with material dated by *Spiralkeramik* whereas the upper part contained Rössen pottery. The southern and more oval-shaped ditch-system is dated by Münchshöfen ware and is documented by photographs. There is indeed no certainty about the dating of the ditches *between* the enclosures, but they are in all probability contemporaneous with the southern system. The inner diameter of the northern circular ditch measures *c.* 50 m, which is of the same scale as Hienheim. The southern one measures some 100 × 150 m.

The circular enclosures of Bochum (Günther 1973) and Langweiler (Ihmig *et al.* 1971; Kuper 1972) are better dated and do not differ much in age. Bochum is dated to early Rössen, whereas Langweiler is slightly earlier in Grossgartach. Bochum has a circular ditch (diam. 46 m) with between nine and eleven causeways. Langweiler is much larger (diam. *c.* 80 m) and apparently oval in form; only half of the latter could be excavated. Nothing can be said about the relation between bank and ditch. There are hardly any occupation traces inside the ditches. Altogether the possibility that the enclosures of Bochum and Langweiler had some non-military purpose can surely not be excluded and it may be pointed out that, from the Aldenhovener Platte, earthworks with deep and sharp V-shaped ditches are known. Those which must be considered as defence works are of very late *Linearbandkeramik* date (Ihmig 1971). In contrast the ditches of Bochum and Langweiler are flat-bottomed and their depth is not much over one metre.

Preliminary notes were published on a rectangular ditch system at Bochum-Laer which measures some 40 × 60 m (Wilhelmi 1969–70; Finke 1971). It is dated by Rössen pottery but further comment must await more detailed publication.

There is strong evidence that the earliest examples of man's intentions to enclose a field by a ditch without fortificatory needs were accomplished in Western Europe between about 4200 and 3600 bc in uncalibrated radiocarbon dates. This is considerably older than the causewayed camps of the Windmill Hill Culture.

Several years ago Stuart Piggott mentioned (1954, 31) the resemblance of the causewayed camps in Great Britain to similar structures on the continent of Michelsberg date. In the meantime a number of radiocarbon dates for both cultures have become available. They show that the Michelsberg and Windmill Hill Cultures are contemporaneous. On the other hand the similarity between the causewayed enclosures in Britain and the Michelsberg earthworks is open to considerable doubt. Smith (1971) does not even hint at the possibility that causewayed camps might have had a 'military' purpose, whereas Lüning (1967, 113) concludes on good grounds that the defensive value of the Michelsberg ditch and wall systems must have been paramount. Recent research in Belgium near Spiennes (Hubert 1971a) and at Boitsfort (Hubert 1971b) are in agreement with German experience. Although the outward resemblance between the earthworks on the continent and in Great Britain is striking, the motives for their construction must have been different.

The conclusion we just arrived at seems to have one interesting exception: the well-known earthwork of Altheim in the valley of the River Isar near Landshut. Maier's (1962) suggestion, that the site was used for cult and served special rites, is imposing. Human sacrifices seem to be connected with the practices because of the disjointed skeletal remains in the filling of the ditches. This peculiarity is the main reason for comparison with the causewayed enclosures of the Windmill Hill Culture. The supposition that the three-fold ditch system at Altheim was meant as a fortification is, however, not very convincing. The situation in the landscape is not in agreement with what one would expect (see Maier 1962, Beilage 1). The size of the Altheim enclosure is on the scale of those from Bochum, Langweiler, Kothingeichendorf and Hienheim. The interior surface measures some 40 × 60 m, whereas the entire monument is 88 m in width and 120 m in length. It is interesting to note that the inner ditches of the Windmill Hill enclosures give for Windmill Hill 80 × 62 m, for Whitehawk Camp 100 × 70 m, Combe Hill 105 × 90 m and for Robin Hood's Bay 118 × 90 m, all measurements being internal and exclusive of the ditches. There are of course many examples of wider enclosures, certainly when one regards the outer rings (Smith 1971, 94).

When using the diameters of the enclosures as an indication of the character of these monuments, I want to make it clear that these are included in the discussion solely because of lack of other arguments. The only trend which may be derived from the diameters is that the smaller the enclosure, the more probable it is that it did not contain a complete settlement, which means in turn an increasing possibility of the use of such sites as socio-religious centres.

Looking for continental Aveburys one is naturally curious as to how the situation was in France. Apparently ditch digging was not an uncommon feature of man in the French Middle Neolithic period (Bailloud and Mieg de Boofzheim 1955). The most general form is that of the *éperon barrée*, which strikes us as an incontestable example of a fortification.[1] Air photography has been a great help in the search for other types of ditch systems. However, both the well-known double-ditched enclosures of les Matignons (Burnez and Case 1966) are apparently not the type of enclosure we are after. The dimensions are those of a settlement. The older ditch system surrounded one in fact, but the authors claim that the second system embraced only part of the habitation. During the last few years two examples of causewayed ditches have been observed on air photographs. Agache (1971) announces the first one found in the Somme district with seven or eight causeways; it encloses an area of 270 × 200 m. A second example which has a striking resemblance to that of Urmitz (except for its size: 260 × 150 m)

---

1 Some more recently published examples are Chariez (Thévenin 1958), Roquefort (Sireix and Roussot-Larroque 1968), Lavans-les-Dole (Petrequin 1970) and le Camp de Myard (Nicolardot 1973).

was published by the brothers Mordant (1972). They tend to compare the enclosure of Noyen-sur-Seine with the Windmill Hill causewayed camps, which assumes a non-military purpose. It is very hard to decide upon this question as long as no attempt has been made to collect further information of such a site by extensive excavations. In sum it can be said that in France traces of Aveburys are so far doubtful, but all possibilities of finding one or more splendid examples are by no means exhausted.

CONCLUSION

The Aveburys are a group of prehistoric monuments for which it is often difficult to tell whether their makers had a socio-religious enclosure in mind instead of fortification. The bank outside the ditch is generally accepted as decisive. So are the rapid silting of the ditches and a relatively high amount of human bones. Hardly considered till now is the relation of the enclosure to habitation traces of the same period both inside and outside the earthworks. Was the enclosure a solitary monument or was it part of a settlement?

The impetus to enclose a certain terrain is only too human, but the way to fulfill that wish differs greatly. In this respect it is worth mentioning the Danish 'Stonehenge' near Kalundborg (Ramskou 1970). Three stone circles with a largest diameter of 320 m were discovered around a small barrow with a stone cist. Repeatedly authors have recalled the fact that the Iron Age knew its *Viereckschanze* no less than the Goloring itself (Röder 1948), showing that the tradition is indeed a long-lasting one.

Bibliography

AGACHE, R. 1971 Camp néolithique à accès multiples découvert à l'Etoile (Somme), *Bull. Soc. préh. franç.* 68, 195–6.

BAILLOUD, G. and MIEG DE BOOFZHEIM, P. 1955 *Les civilisations néolithiques de la France dans leur contexte européen*, Paris.

BURNEZ, C. and CASE, H. 1966 Les camps néolithiques des Matignons à Juillac-le-Coq, *Gallia préhistoire* 9, 131–245.

FINKE, W. 1971 Notiz über Bochum-Laer, *Westfälische Forschungen* 23, 173.

GÜNTHER, K. 1973 Die Abschlussuntersuchung am neolithischen Grabenring von Bochum Harpen, *Archäol. Korrespondenzblatt* 3, 181–6.

HUBERT, F. 1971a Fosses néolithiques à Spiennes, *Archaeologica Belgica* 136.

1971b Neue Ausgrabungen im Michelsberger Erdwerk in Boitsfort (Belgien), *Germania* XLIX, 214–18.

IHMIG, M. 1971 Ein bandkeramischer Graben mit Einbau bei Langweiler, Kr. Jülich, und die zeitliche Stellung bandkeramischer Gräben im westlichen Verbreitungsgebiet, *Archäol. Korrespondenzblatt* 1, 23–30.

IHMIG, M., KUPER, R. and SCHRÖTER, I. 1971 Ein Grossgartacher Erdwerk in Langweiler, Kr. Jülich, *Germania* XLIX, 193–6.

KUPER, R. 1972 Langweiler 12, *Bonner Jahrb.* 172, 380–6.

LÜNING, J. 1967 Die Michelsberger Kultur. Ihre Funde in zeitlicher und räumlicher Gliederung, 48 *Bericht Röm.-German. Kommission*, 1–350.

MAIER, R. A. 1962 Fragen zu neolithischen Erdwerken Südbayerns, *Jahresber. der Bayerischen Bodendenkmalpflege* 3, 5–21.

1964 Die jüngere Steinzeit in Bayern, *Jahresber. der Bayerischen Bodendenkmalpflege* 5, 9–197.

MODDERMAN, P. J. R. 1966 Linienbandkeramische Bauten aus Hienheim, Ldkr. Kelheim, *Anal. Praehist. Leidensia* II, 1–5.

1971 Neolithische und frühbronzezeitliche Siedlungsspuren aus Hienheim, Ldkr. Kelheim, *Anal. Praehist. Leidensia* IV, 1–25.

MORDANT, C. and D. 1972 Das neolithische Erdwerk in Noyen-sur-Seine (Dép. Seine-et-Marne), *Archäol. Korrespondenzblatt* 2, 253–9.

NICOLARDOT, J.-P. 1973 Structures et datations par mesure du radiocarbone, du rempart et de l'habitât néolithique du Camp de Myard, commune de Vitteaux (Côte d'Or), *Bull. Soc. préh. franç.* 70, 70.

PETREQUIN, P. 1970 Le camp néolithique de Moulinrouge à Lavans-les-Dole, *Revue arch. de l'Est* 21, 99–120.

PIGGOTT, S. 1954 *Neolithic cultures of the British Isles*, Cambridge.

RAMSKOU, T. 1970 Et dansk Stonehenge? *Nationalmuseets Arbejdsmark*, 59–66.

REINECKE, P. 1923 Ergebnisse der Vorgeschichtsforschung in Bayern aus den letzten Jahren, *Der bayerische Vorgeschichtsfreund* 3, 38–42.

RÖDER, J. 1948 Der Goloring. Ein eisenzeitliches Heiligtum vom Henge-Charakter im Koberner Wald (Landkreis Koblenz), *Bonner Jahrb.* 148, 81–132.

SIREIX, M. and ROUSSET-LARROQUE, J. 1968 Le camp de Roquefort à Lugasson (Gironde), *Bull. Soc. préh. franç.* 65, 524–44.

SMITH, I. F. 1971 Causewayed enclosures, *Economy and Settlement in Neolithic and Early Bronze Age Britain and Europe*, ed. D. D. A. Simpson, Leicester, 89–112.

THEVENIN, A. 1958 Brève étude sur le camp préhistorique de Chariez (Haute-Saône), *Revue arch. de l'Est* 9, 97–112.

WAGNER, F. 1928 Prehistoric Fortifications in in Bavaria, *Antiquity* II, 43–55.

WAINWRIGHT, G. J. 1969 A Review of Henge Monuments in the Light of Recent Research, *Proc. Prehist. Soc.* XXXV, 112–33.

WILHELMI, K. 1969/70 Notiz über Bochum-Laer, *Westfälische Forschungen* 22, 99.

12

PIERRE-ROLAND GIOT

Cross-cousinly Relations: a Breton Viewpoint

TWENTY years ago I published a short paper on prehistoric relations between Brittany and Britain (Giot 1954). Since the Second World War, I had been struck by the flocks of strange archaeologists coming over to Brittany and fishing everywhere, poking around in search of origins and prototypes or at the very least looking for parallels. They used to be persuaded that exactly what they were seeking certainly existed, but that it must be hidden in some storeroom or just awaiting publication. I used to reply to these visitors: 'Were the prehistoric inhabitants of Britain incapable of making inventions of their own?' In my paper I began calling this psychological tendency or disease 'the insularity complex'. I had, myself, been on a long search the same year around south-west Britain looking at anything that might have been of interest in the way of connections, and my conclusion was that there were many more local particularisms of innovations than there were effects of diffusions. Apparently twenty years ago I may well have been in advance of my time: in recent years I seem to have heard or read more variations on this theme, composed sometimes in a most extravagent style.

Of course we still have the pleasure of plenty of visitors, following the tracks of prominent forerunners with Stuart Piggott amongst the most welcome (Crawford 1913; Piggott 1937; 1938; 1953; Daniel 1939; Wheeler 1939; Forde 1927; 1930; 1932; Case 1969; and many others). Many have learnt to take a look at Normandy or more northern France at the same time. But Brittany has always been a special focus of interest. It may be an unconscious effect of the historical and ethnic relations between the British and early Breton populations in the Dark Ages; the similitude of the name of the countries reflects this down to the present day in spite of so many divergences since those far-off times. Of course for Cornwall and the Cornish this is only natural (Doble 1924). But when we deal with prehistory or protohistory, things are somewhat different, and it is only with the passing of time that we can observe relations between the two areas becoming closer or more frequent, as the following brief notes attempt to demonstrate.

Before the Bronze Age, visitors must indeed have come seldom. From the point of view of the western end of the Channel, after the marine transgression and formation of the Dover Straits during Mesolithic times, and thus after the last possibilities for pedestrians to get over, the archaeological resemblances of the Neolithic cultures can only be substantiated from a very general point of view. There is of course on both sides of the Channel the general idea of megaliths, the general idea of passage graves, the general form of pottery such as that exemplified by the style of Hembury ware, at least. But if one goes into further detail, one does not find the same megalithic tombs on each side of the Channel, nor the same art, nor the same flint artifacts, and frequently not the same pottery at all. It is as difficult a topic to develop as it is a negative one: Cornwall and Devon, for instance, are so near to northern Brittany, and yet there are many things one does not find there, and why? Why, in spite of such similar topography and geology, are there in Cornwall no huge cairns such as Carn or Barnenez? and in a later period, no gallery graves of the style so common from Armorica to the Paris Basin and on to Normandy?

One cannot, of course, pretend that there were no relations at all between the Neolithic populations on both sides of the Western Channel. Since vague or even detailed similarities in style are always a disputable argument – as much so as the problem of the 'megalithic yard' – let us take hold of the only material evidence of such contacts. This is confined to half a dozen stone axes of which the source material must have come from Brittany. Even here, one must always be suspicious of objects from museums and private collections. For example, there is a stone axe of porcellanite marked as coming from 'Northern Ireland, 1872' amongst the collection assembled in the last century by Monseigneur David, Bishop of Saint-Brieuc; had the label been lost, there might well have been a problem....

The extensive petrological work on stone axes from Brittany and the neighbouring regions has in fact shown no single case of an import from the British Isles. But four axes of the Breton Group A

1 Group 'A' axe from Gommené (Côtes-du-Nord). Length 16.7 cm.

(British Group X), coming from the extensive Neolithic dolerite quarries and factories at Plussulien (Le Roux 1971), are known from Somerset, Worcestershire, and Hampshire (two examples) (Evens, Smith, and Wallis 1972, nos. 319, 333, 536 and 1071). Two axes of fibrolite (sillimanite) are known in Cornwall (*loc. cit.* nos. 170 and 1305), though this might be considered a less specific proof, as some fibrolite is known from Scotland, in spite of its frequent use as a material for stone axes in Brittany (about 20 per cent of the total). Of course dolerite Group A axes (*Ill. 1*) constitute about 40 per cent of the stone axes of Brittany, and a large proportion of the stone axes are of crystalline rocks from the provinces adjoining Brittany (from 15 to 30 per cent according to Le Roux' recent investigations) with plenty of examples farther beyond. And what are four axes of Group A in south-west Britain, compared to the hundreds, if not thousands, exported to Normandy, Maine, Anjou, Vendée, Touraine and adjacent districts?

Surely, if connections were close in Middle and Late Neolithic times between Brittany and south-west England, we should expect to find in the latter region some hundreds of Breton axes, as many as in Normandy or in Touraine, for instance. To go on with some negative enumerations, one should remember that in Britain up to now one has recognized no Grand Pressigny flint, no variscite (so-called 'callais') beads, and no Breton battle-axes. And once more one could prolong the list.

In Neolithic times, the Channel was still a very formidable barrier. There is little point in wondering whether the few stone axes that got over were the result of 'commercial' or ceremonial exchanges, or spoils from plunder, or simply things brought over occasionally by boats lost in a storm. One way or another, there obviously were from time to time some contacts, but no massive exchanges of goods or of population. No Roscoff–Plymouth or Cherbourg–Southampton ferryboats, no return tickets then but, every once in a while, these rare or accidental contacts were enough to spread, as necessary, new technical or ideological ideas.

The very early radiocarbon dates obtained for some of the Breton megalithic tombs has often been stressed (Giot 1971), nearly a score of such dates now being available. Often these dates have been utilized without realizing that most of them were provided by the charcoal from my own excavations or those of my fellow-workers (and not from the excavations of Professor Colin Renfrew, as I was more than once puzzled to learn from my reading of *Paris-Match*; Farkas 1974). But in fact not only is thermoluminescence dating of pottery vindicating the order of magnitude of tree-ring recalibration of radiocarbon dates; it is equalizing the dates of the megalithic tombs from most parts of Western Europe – Professor Renfrew (1973) has heard of some of these although seemingly not those from Portugal.

Before 2000 bc the Channel was perhaps no more a semi-permeable barrier than the Bay of Biscay.

From the Bronze Age onwards, perhaps already from the time of the earlier Bell-Beakers, great progress in boat-construction and in navigation must have been made in Western Europe, progress which resulted in quite frequent inter-relations and exchanges. To make lists and to sort out once more parallels from the Wessex and Armorican barrow-cultures onwards – a task pioneered nearly 40 years ago by Stuart Piggott – would be a classic exercise and would need a whole Festschrift. In some cases, criticism, caution and restraint might be necessary, in others more imagination than was once considered to be advisable.

Again, the problem of migrations of populations over the Western Channel at different times during the Iron Age is quite open. But do such culture changes really need this type of explanation?

Bibliography

CASE, H. J. 1969 Neolithic explanations, *Antiquity* XLIII, 176–86.

CRAWFORD, O. G. S. 1913 Prehistoric Trade between England and France, *L'Anthropologie* XXIV, 641–9.

DANIEL, G. E. 1939 The Transepted Gallery Graves of Western France, *Proc. Prehist. Soc.* V, 143–65.

DOBLE, G.-H. 1924 Les relations durant les âges entre la Bretagne et le Cornwall, *Bulletin diocésain d'Histoire et d'Archéologie* (Quimper) 23, 203–11, 279–95.

EVANS, E. D., SMITH, I. F. and WALLIS, F. S. 1972 The petrological identification of stone implements from South-West England, *Proc. Prehist. Soc.* XXXVIII, 235–75.

FARKAS, J.-P. 1974 Désolé, mais la civilisation vient du froid, *Paris-Match* no. 1288, 66–9.

FORDE, C. D. 1927. The megalithic monuments of Southern Finistère, *Antiq. Journ.* VII, 6–37.

1930 On the use of greenstones in the megalithic culture of Brittany, *Journ. Roy. Anthrop. Inst.* XL, 211–34.

1932 The typology of the Breton megalithic tombs, *Proc. First Intern. Congr. of Prehist. Protohist. Sciences* London, 114–17.

GIOT, P.-R. 1954 Quelques mots sur les relations préhistoriques entre Bretagne et Grande-Bretagne, *Annales de Bretagne* LXI, 252–7.

1971 The Impact of Radiocarbon Dating on the Establishment of the Prehistoric Chronology of Brittany, *Proc. Prehist. Soc.*, XXXVII, 208–17.

LE ROUX, C.-T. 1971 A stone-axe factory in Brittany, *Antiquity* XLV, 283–8.

(In press) La fabrication des haches polies en Bretagne, bref état de la question, *98ème Congres des Sociétés Savantes 1974*.

(In press) L'industrie de la pierre polie dans la Bretagne néolithique, *Archéologia*.

PIGGOTT, S. 1937 The Long Barrow in Brittany, *Antiquity* XI, 441–55.

1938 The Early Bronze Age in Wessex, *Proc. Prehist. Soc.* IV, 52–106.

1953 Les Relations entre l'ouest de la France et les Iles Britanniques dans la Préhistoire, *Annales du Midi* LXV, 5–20.

RENFREW, A. C. 1973 *Before Civilization: the radiocarbon revolution and prehistoric Europe*, London.

WHEELER, R. E. M. 1939 Les camps de l'Age du Fer dans le Nord-Ouest de la France et le Sud-Ouest de la Grande-Bretagne, *Revue Archéologique* 6ème série, XIII, 103–24.

13

R. J. C. ATKINSON

Lukis, Dryden and the Carnac Megaliths

As his friends know, and as his writings amply testify, Stuart Piggott's many interests include both megalithic monuments and the history of archaeological thought and practice. It is as a small contribution to both these fields that I offer him, with affectionate regard, this sketch of two British archaeologists of the nineteenth century, the Reverend W. C. Lukis and Sir Henry Dryden. Neither has so far received the notice he deserves; and their work together in 'illustrating the monuments' of the Carnac region of south Brittany a century ago has recently acquired a new significance.

William Collings Lukis was born in Guernsey in 1817, the third son of F. C. Lukis, the founder of archaeological studies in the Channel Islands and a noted amateur of natural history (Kendrick 1928, 99–101). He went to school both in Guernsey and in France, and there acquired a fluency in French which doubtless served him well in his later work at Carnac. He graduated from Trinity College, Cambridge, in 1840, and was ordained the following year at Salisbury. Thereafter he held a curacy at Bradford-on-Avon (where he wrote a monograph on church plate), and subsequently the livings successively of three Wiltshire parishes, East Grafton, Great Bedwyn and Collingbourne Ducis. From 1861 until his death in 1892 he was Rector of Wath in the North Riding of Yorkshire. He was evidently an enterprising and conscientious pastor, and in each of his parishes he oversaw either the restoration of the church or the rebuilding of the village school, or both. In view of his long summer absences in pursuit of megaliths at home and abroad (and sometimes in the spring or autumn as well) one imagines, however, that his curates felt that they had earned their stipends.

Whilst at Great Bedwyn he helped to found the Wiltshire Archaeological Society in 1853, and was one of its joint General Secretaries for its first four years. His first paper in the Society's *Magazine* (Lukis 1854) was addressed to entomologists, and enjoined on them the need for the same systematic and accurate recording of data that was to be his precept and practice in the study of megaliths; but this seems to have been his only printed contribution to natural history. His other interests included church architecture, plate and bells, on the last of which he published a number of papers; but his ruling passion was for megalithic monuments, on which he was rightly regarded, both in Britain and abroad, as one of the leading authorities of his time.

The earliest of his plans of chambered tombs, one of the Le Couperon site in Jersey, is dated 1839, when he was still an undergraduate. From then on, for more than forty years, he conducted an astonishing series of surveys of megalithic tombs, circles and alignments in England, Scotland and Wales, in various parts of France, and especially in the Carnac area, and in the Netherlands and Algeria. The results of these he recorded in neat and workmanlike plans and elevations on cartridge paper to a uniform series of scales and conventions, stones in horizontal or vertical section being tinted pink, stones in elevation in grey, and fallen stones in buff. Most of this work was done during long summer holidays – far longer, indeed, than a parish priest could now afford in either time or money – and some of it with the help of grants made by the Society of Antiquaries, to which he made a series of reports (Lukis 1879–81a–c; 1881–83a,b; 1883–85; 1885b). On the occasion of the first of these he announced his intention of presenting all his plans to the Society's library, where most of them now are; but he retained some in his possession, notably two bound volumes entitled *Chambered Barrows*, which now form part of the Lukis collection in Guernsey. Some of the plans in the second volume, and a number of those in the Antiquaries' library, bear Dryden's name as well, but the draughtsmanship is clearly that of Lukis.

In 1880 the Society of Antiquaries tentatively adopted a proposal to publish all Lukis's plans of megaliths if sufficient support were forthcoming (Evans 1956, 337) and a brochure was circulated, inviting subscriptions. In the event, however, only the first section appeared, its publication having been delayed by a disastrous fire at the printers'

(Lukis 1885). There can be no doubt that had this project been completed it would have ranked as one of the major British archaeological publications of the nineteenth century, and would have earned for Lukis in the eyes of posterity a place no less honoured than those occupied, say, by Sir John Evans or General Pitt-Rivers. As it is, however, both he and his work have remained in a relative obscurity from which they deserve to be rescued.

His published work on megaliths, listed in the bibliography below, reflects a life-long insistence on the importance of accurate and systematic record as a basis for comparative studies, and is remarkably free from the tortuous complexities of typology which have subsequently for so long bedevilled megalithic research, and are only now being shown, through the application of radiocarbon dating, to be largely sterile. His writing contains, however, a few recurrent themes on which he was particularly insistent, and occasionally roundly outspoken, in opposition to the views of some of his contemporaries – especially, perhaps, James Fergusson, the author of *Rude Stone Monuments* (1872), whose ideas Lukis clearly regarded as not merely mistaken, but pernicious. He constantly reiterates his own belief that all dolmens (a term which he disliked) were originally 'tumular', even if in many cases little survived now of the mound or cairn; and he attacks vigorously the concept of the 'demi-dolmen' or 'earth-fast dolmen', a supposed type of chambered tomb in which one side of an inclined capstone rested on orthostats and the other on the ground. On both of these points he would have the support of most students of megaliths today, though it is interesting to note that neither concept had been wholly abandoned even sixty years after Lukis died (Raftery 1951, 116).

His own ideas about the classification of megalithic tombs were admirably simple (Lukis 1864a). Having distinguished first of all unchambered from chambered tumuli, he divided the second category into those with and without 'covered ways or passages', thus implicitly anticipating the adoption of the term 'passage-grave' for morphological description. His only attempt at any finer sub-division (Lukis 1868b) was based on the method of roofing the burial-chamber, where he cautiously regarded the use of capstones and of corbelling, respectively, as significant criteria and allowed in general the priority of the former. On this basis he constructed in outline a chronological sequence of types. 'But I do not assert', he says, 'that the position of each monument in the two series is strictly correct.' If this example of cautiousness had been more widely known and more closely followed, there might have been fewer false starts and dead ends in subsequent megalithic enquiries.

Two papers published in 1864 show that Lukis was then already familiar with at least some of the megaliths of the Carnac region, and in that year and in five others subsequently (1866–69 and 1872) he spent a great deal of time in recording them in detail. During parts of the last five of these seasons he joined forces with Sir Henry Dryden (*Ill. 1*).

Henry Edward Leigh Dryden (1818–99), fourth baronet of Canons Ashby in Northamptonshire, belonged to that class of energetic and enlightened *dilettanti* (in the original sense of that term) to which British archaeological and antiquarian studies owe so much. His interests were wide, and included church architecture and other ecclesiastical remains, and medieval armour and other artifacts, as well as megalithic monuments. Politically, as might be expected, he was a high Tory, and used to open his grounds to meetings of the Primrose League; but he was also a frequent and popular speaker on archaeological subjects at meetings of Radical societies. The collection of his drawings of French sites in the Ashmolean includes a number of large maps and plans of the Carnac region, boldly painted, with their corners perforated by many drawing-pins, which were evidently used to illustrate some of these talks. He also had a strong interest in church music, and trained three local choirs by the methods of Hullah, then in vogue; and to one of these, three miles from his home, he walked each week to supervise choir-practice in his capacity of Lay Rector. Despite his relative wealth and his position in the society of his day he was evidently an engagingly modest man. It is said that when he was poor as a young man, before he succeeded to the baronetcy and its estates in 1837, he had his clothes made by the village tailor, and that he never thereafter took his custom elsewhere.

During a long and active life as an archaeologist and antiquary he made a vast number of plans, drawings, squeezes and watercolours of architectural and archaeological monuments, of which he presented relevant collections to the Royal Irish Academy in Dublin, the Society of Antiquaries of Scotland in Edinburgh and, of Cotswold chambered tombs and barrows, to the public library at Gloucester. Despite these gifts, however, the remainder of his records, presented to the Northampton Central Library a year before his death, comprised the contents of no less than five hundred portfolios.

The catalogue of that collection (George 1912) records that after his death the French government tried unsuccessfully to buy his plans of sites in France, and that at their instigation they were acquired by the Ashmolean Museum at Oxford.

Dryden was renowned amongst his contemporaries as a skilled surveyor, with an almost obsessive regard for accuracy, and a story was told of him, doubtless with a mixture of admiration and wry amusement, that having on one occasion found a discrepancy of half an inch in his measurements of an architectural monument in France he made a journey of 200 miles for the sole purpose of rectifying the error. This is probably not apocryphal, because his field-notes preserved at Oxford show that the framework of some of his surveys of French chambered tombs was measured to the nearest millimetre, a standard of accuracy which even today would seldom be adopted, in such a case, by an archaeological field-worker.

It was probably from Dryden that Lukis acquired his own competence as a single-handed surveyor. Their collaboration began soon after they both came down from Cambridge, with the survey and excavation of three sites in the Cotswolds (Crawford 1925, 159–61, 165–8), and it continued at intervals up to at least 1878, when they spent the summer together planning the *hunebedden* of Drenthe in the Netherlands.

Dryden's printed contribution to the literature of the Carnac megaliths seems to be confined to two short papers (Dryden 1870; 1876). In the second of these he says that he had spent five summers in France, 'assisting Mr W. C. Lukis to make plans of these remains, and the literary part of the matter was left to Mr Lukis'. Some of his assistance took the form of making watercolour sketches of the tombs and alignments (*Ills. 2, 3*), in colours rather more brilliant than those of nature, and often with the aid of a *camera lucida*, an instrument now superseded by the photographic camera, though it still has a useful part to play in archaeological draughtsmanship for those who, like myself, need all the help they can get. I suspect, however, that Dryden's use of it was merely another expression of his passion for accuracy.

The dates on the drawings catalogued below

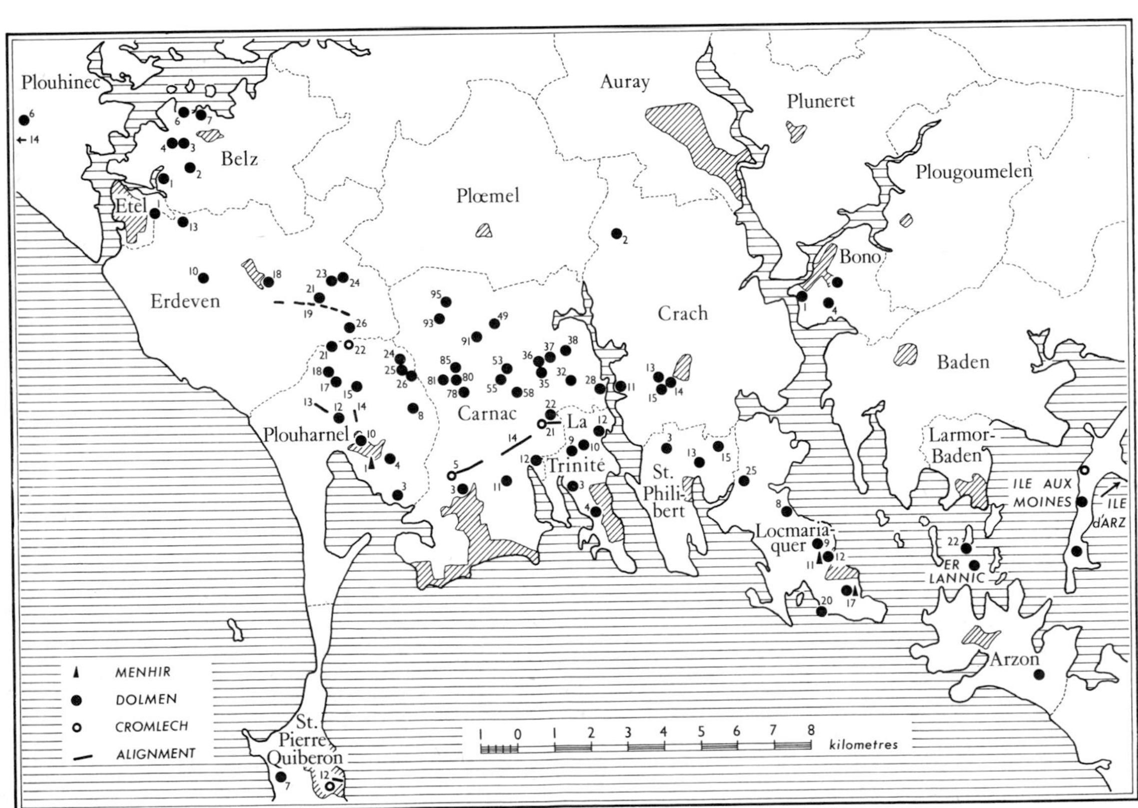

1 Map of the Carnac area, showing the sites surveyed by Lukis and Dryden.

show a number of gaps and these, I suspect, were given over to the planning of churches and other architectural monuments, where the roles of surveyor and assistant were reversed, with Lukis holding the end of the tape and sometimes, perhaps, exercising a little Christian forbearance. Clearly his own tastes and those of Dryden did not always coincide, for the latter's drawings at Northampton include a detailed architectural survey of the little Flamboyant chapel of Nôtre Dame des Fleurs at Plouharnel (the next village west of Carnac, where Lukis habitually stayed at the Hotel du Commerce), of which Lukis himself said (1875, 122) that it 'scarcely invites attention'. He was a freemason, and therefore hardly a high churchman, and he may have found the Flamboyant style a little too florid for his middle-of-the-road Anglican sensibilities.

Between them, separately and together, Lukis and Dryden planned all the major megalithic monuments of the Carnac area, and excavated a number of them as well. Most of these excavations must have been confined to the sieving of the residual of burial chambers already despoiled by others, or even, as Lukis disapprovingly records, to searching the dumps left by previous explorers, which often yielded a surprising harvest of disregarded or unnoticed finds to augment his private collection, now in the British Museum.

The immediate product of these surveys was a guide-book written by Lukis for the tourist with an interest in megaliths, many of whom he had encountered in the course of his work in the Morbihan (Lukis 1875). In the preface, referring to his seven summers spent in the area, he says: 'As I was not pressed for time, and had no occupation to hinder a daily ramble over the country, which I accomplished chiefly on foot, I became familiar with most parts of it.' His daily ramble, as the dates on his plans reveal, commonly included the planning of three or four chambered tombs and the sifting of the contents of at least one of them; and on one memorable day, 27 October 1866, he appears to have planned no less than eight separate sites on a walk of at least fifteen kilometres, or nine miles.

He evidently expected no less of the readers of his *Guide*, for whom he set out seven well-planned but strenuous daily itineraries, with useful details about transport and hotels. For one of these, the traveller is recommended to stay the previous night at Lukis's own habitual headquarters at Plouharnel. 'Supposing, then, the latter course to be adopted, the tourist, who is an early riser, may visit several

2 Watercolour by Sir Henry Dryden of the Dolmen de Crucuno, Plouharnel (no. 21), Morbihan.

3 Watercolour by Sir Henry Dryden of stones at the head of the Ste-Barbe alignment, Plouharnel (no. 13), Morbihan.

dolmens before breakfast.' This confident assertion is not quite as daunting as it sounds, because breakfast here means a meal which today would be called 'brunch'; but perhaps just as well, because the itinerary suggested involves a walk of ten kilometres, or six miles, to visit six chambered tombs and a prehistoric potters' site on the shore. After breakfast our tourist, having engaged the services of an intelligent lad from the village as his guide, proceeds to inspect another ten chambered tombs, three alignments, a rectangular 'cromlech' and a long barrow, and returns to Plouharnel in time for a much-needed dinner, having covered a further fifteen kilometres, or nine miles. Even the most vigorous and dedicated of today's professional field-workers would hardly regard such a day's programme with anything but misgiving, let alone an amateur on holiday.

Very few of the long list of surveys catalogued below have been published. Reduced versions of eight of them were used to illustrate the reports of the Brittany meeting of the Cambrian Archaeological Association in 1889 (Anon. 1890); and among the Dryden papers in the Ashmolean there are proofs and finished versions of a large lithographed plan of the Kerlescant 'cromlech' and adjacent long barrow, with another of the same size and style of the great *allée couverte* at Essé (Ile et Vilaine), the Roche aux Fées. I have not so far been able to discover, however, if these were ever published, or were merely the beginning of a larger project later abandoned.

Apart from their value as documents in the history of British field archaeology, there are two other reasons why these Carnac surveys deserve to be better known. The first is that they were made before the extensive restorations, both of alignments and 'cromlechs' and of chambered tombs, which have since been carried out and not always, it is clear, with sufficient regard for ascertaining and preserving the original form of the monument. They thus have a special significance in the light of the recent and current researches in the Carnac area of Professor Alexander Thom and his collaborators (Thom 1971–74; Atkinson, 1975).

Amongst the chambered tombs the effects of restoration can be illustrated by two plans (*Ill. 4*) of Clud-er-Yer (Carnac 85), the first made by Lukis and Dryden in July, 1867 and the second by the writer and his wife in April, 1974. Some of the differences in detail result from the different levels at which the plans were; but even when allowance is made for this, a number of marked changes are evident. Moreover an even earlier but more schematic plan, made by Lukis' elder brother Frederick in 1854, shows in the south-east side-chamber now missing, an upright of the back wall and a capstone; and in the terminal chamber a pair of transverse jambs forming the entrance from the passage. Only one of these survived in 1867, and today both have been rearranged. Comparison may usefully be made also with the plan made by Le Rouzic at the time of his restoration of the site in 1921 (reproduced in Daniel 1939, Fig. 5, A).

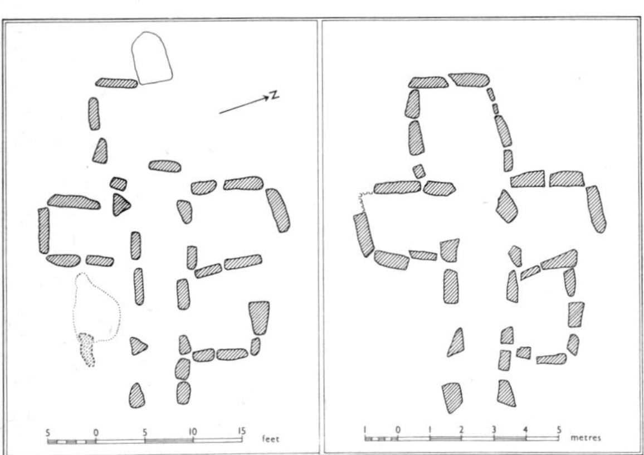

4 The chambered tomb of Clud-er-Yer (Carnac 85). Left, as planned by Lukis and Dryden in 1867, with additional features noted by F.D. Lukis in 1854; right, as planned in 1974.

It is in the cromlechs and alignments, however, that the most extensive restoration has been undertaken. By way of example, the plan of the west end of the Kermario alignment (Carnac 14), made by Dryden and Captain S. P. Oliver in June, 1870, shows that little more than one third of the stones were then standing (*Ill. 5*). A recent survey (Thom 1974, Fig. 2) makes it clear that almost all the fallen stones have since been re-erected.

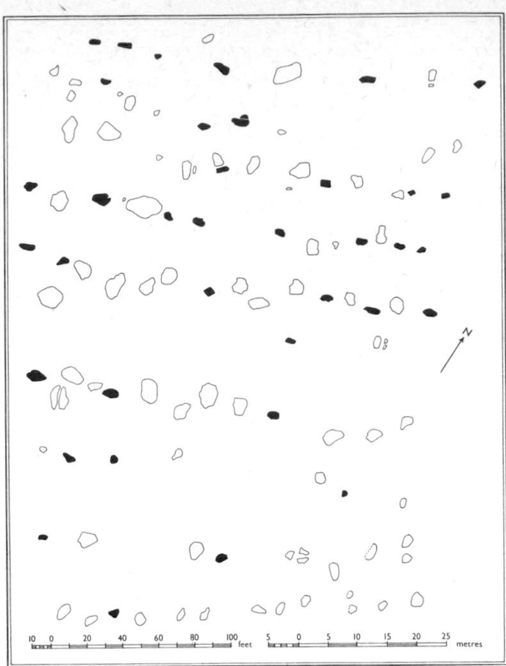

5 The west end of the Kermario alignment (Carnac 14), as planned by Dryden and Oliver in 1870.

The value of the Lukis and Dryden plans is also enhanced by the changes which have taken place in land use in the region. A century ago almost all the chambered tombs were in or on the boundaries of cultivated ground, and were thus clearly visible and easily accessible. Since 1945, however, all but the most fertile land has gone out of cultivation, and either has been planted with pines or has reverted to scrub, mainly gorse, which is no longer regularly cut, and often not cut at all, as it was formerly. The result is that many of the minor or more ruined tombs, including some protected by legislation, are now lost in impenetrable thickets of gorse, bramble and broom standing up to three or four metres high. This affords, of course, some protection against vandalism, though not against the slower destruction wrought by the roots and stems of trees and bushes. Already the location, and sometimes even the existence, of a monument appears to be known only to the oldest inhabitants of the neighbouring hamlet, so that it is increasingly at risk of inadvertent destruction during the occasional clearances, with bulldozers, of patches of woodland and scrub. For both these reasons, therefore, all students of the Carnac megaliths, in which joyful company Stuart Piggott has been numbered for many years, have reason to be grateful to Lukis and Dryden that more than a century ago they chose with such systematic energy to illustrate these monuments.

Catalogue

The plans, elevations, sketches and watercolours of the Carnac megaliths made by Lukis and Dryden are contained in the following collections:

I *Lukis Collection, St Peter Port, Guernsey.* Formerly in the Lukis Museum, now closed, and presently stored in the offices of the Ancient Monuments Committee in Castle Cornet. The majority are in two bound volumes entitled *Chambered Barrows,* whose pages (435 × 280 mm) are numbered in pencil in the top right corner of right-hand pages only. Manuscript annotations on separate slips, made by Miss V. C. C. Collum in 1928, mainly identifying the sites by their modern names, are attached to a number of pages.

II *Society of Antiquaries of London.* Portfolio in bottom drawer of plan-chest A in Room 1, mezzanine floor of back staircase, which also contains the other plans of megaliths presented by Lukis. Most of the Carnac plans are on half-imperial cartridge paper (nominally 560 × 380 mm).

III *Department of Antiquities, Ashmolean Museum, Oxford.* Dryden's plans of French sites are contained in two rolls, and in six unnumbered portfolios, here arbitrarily identified for reference as follows:

a. Grey binder's cloth, foxed, 575 × 415 mm (rough plans only).
b. Brown moiré binder's cloth, quarter-bound red morocco, 355 × 240 mm.
c. Ditto, 405 × 300 mm.
d. Ditto, 405 × 300 mm.
e. Ditto, 575 × 410 mm, labelled '1st ½ imp.' inside front cover.
f. Ditto, 575 × 410 mm, labelled '2nd ½ imp.' inside front cover.

IV *Dryden Collection, Central Library, Northampton.* Twenty-seven watercolour or pen-and-wash sketches of sites, of which the published catalogue (George 1912, *s.v.* France, Morbihan) omits: Crucono quadrilateral, Vieux Moulin alignment and Rondossec, all in the Commune of Plouharnel; and Mané Kerioned, Carnac. One sheet of elevations of sculptured stones, Mein Drein, Locmariaquer. A catalogued drawing of the design on the underside of the capstone of the Table des Marchands, Locmariaquer is missing or misplaced.

For ease of reference by field-workers the sites are arranged below in alphabetical order in each commune, using their modern names. Former names used on the drawings are given in brackets if they differ significantly. The first column, headed 'Inventory', gives the number allotted to the site in the (non-alphabetical) list by communes prepared by Zacharie Le Rouzic and published (1965) by Monsieur Maurice Jacq of the Carnac Museum. Sites not otherwise identified as alignments, 'cromlechs', menhirs, etc., are chambered tombs. The term 'cromlech' is used in its Breton sense of a non-linear (and usually non-circular) setting of standing stones. The following abbreviations are used:

A Ashmolean Museum
CB Chambered Barrows
cl *camera lucida*
D Sir Henry Dryden
e elevation
f facing
FL F. du B. Lukis
G Guernsey, Lukis Colln.
L W. C. Lukis
N Northampton Central Library
O Captain S. P. Oliver
pf portfolio
pl plan
r roll
SA Society of Antiquaries of London
ss elevation of sculptured stones
w watercolour or wash sketch

Inventory	Site		Scale or size	Date	Name	Coll.	Remarks
BELZ							
3	Clermont Roh Clour, Kerlutu	pl	1:48	2.10.66	L	G	*CB* I, 62
1	Kerbrevost (Kerbrohost)	pl	1:48	2.10.66	L	G	*CB* I, 63
2	Kergallon	pl	1:48	10.11.66	L	G	*CB* I, 81
7	Kerhuen	pl	1:48	2.10.66	L	G	*CB* I, 64
4	Mané er Run, Kerlutu	pl	1:480, 1:48	2.10.66	L	G	*CB* I, 62
6	Moulin des Oies	pl	1:48	2.10.66	L	G	*CB* I, 5
	(La Petite Bossen)	pl	1:48	2.10.66	L	SA	
CARNAC							
35	Clos Pernel, Kerguarec	pl	1:48	27.10.66	L	G	*CB* I, 72
85	Clud er Yer	pl, e	1:64	67	DL	A	pf. d
		pl, e	1:48	7.67	DL	G	*CB* II, 1
		pl, e	1:48	7.67	DL	SA	
		ss	1:16	7.67	DL	SA	
3	Cruz Menquen (Crux Motten)	pl, e	1:48	5.9.66	L	G	*CB* I, 58
		pl, e	1:48	5.9.66	L	SA	
80	Keriaval	pl, e	1:48	8.7.67	DL	G	*CB* II, 3
		pl, e	1:48	8.7.68	DL	SA	? wrong date
		w	340 × 240	8.7.67	D	N	cl.
21	Kerlescant alignment	pl	1:240	67–69	DL	A	pf. e
		e	1:240	68–69	DL	A	pf. e
		e	1:64	68–69	DL	A	pf. e
		e	1:64	—	—	A	r (pencil)
		e	1:64	68–69	DL	SA	
		e	1:64	68–69	DL	SA	
		w	340 × 240	26.8.69	D	N	
		w	340 × 240	26.8.69	D	N	cl.
21	Kerlescant cromlech	pl	1:240	7.67 and 7.68	DL	A	pf. e
		e	1:64	68, 69	DL	A	pf. e
		pl, e	1:64	13.7.67	DL	SA	
		e	1:64	7.67 and 7.69	DL	SA	
21, 22	Kerlescant alignment,	pl	1:240	67–69	DL	A	pf. e
	cromlech and long borrow	pl	1:240	67–69	DL	SA	
24	Kerlescant North	pl, e	1:480, 1:48	27.10.66	L	G	*CB* I, 74 and f.
	Long Barrow	pl	1:480, 1:48	68	D	A	pf. d (copy)
		e	1:48	18.7.67	D	A	pf. d
12	Kercado	pl	1:480, 1:48	8.64	L	G	*CB* I, 49 and f.
14	Kermario alignment	pl	1:240	6.70	DO	A	pf. e
		e	1:64	6.70	DO	A	pf. 3
		pl	1:240	6.70	DO	SA	
		e	1:64	6.70	DO	SA	
		w	340 × 245	22.7.67	D	N	cl.
		w	340 × 240	22.7.67	D	N	cl.
32	Lannec er Roch, Kerlagat	pl	1:48	27.10.66	L	G	*CB* I, 73
		pl	1:48	67	L	G	*CB* II, 11
78	Lannec Rocolan, Noterio (Notriou)	pl	1:48	27.10.66	L	G	*CB* I, 70
37	La Madeleine	pl	1:48	27.10.66	L	G	*CB* I, 71
53	Mané Brisil, Le Moustoir	pl, e	1:48	3.7.67	DL	G	*CB* II, f.6

Inventory	*Site*	*Scale or size*		*Date*	*Name*	*Coll.*	*Remarks*
91	Mané Gardreine, Kergrim	pl	1:48	8.8.68	L	G	*CB* II, 23
55	Mané Graver (Lan er	pl, e	1:32	3–4.7.67	DL	A	pf. d
	Gravor)	pl, e	1:48	3.7.67	DL	G	*CB* II, 1
81	Mané Kerioned (Grionec or	pl, e	1:48	7.67	DL	A	pf. f
	Kerozille)	pl, e	1:48	7.67	DL	SA	
		ss	1:16	7.67	DL	SA	
		w	340 × 245	8.7.67	D	N	cl.
93	Mané Lavarec, Quelvezin	pl	1:48	6.11.66	L	G	*CB* I, 76
5	Le Menec alignment,	pl	1:240	67	DL	A	pf. e
	W. end	w	340 × 240	24.8.69	D	N	
	Le Menec alignment,	pl	1:240	1.8.69	DL	A	pf. e
	middle	pl	1:240	1.8.69	DLFL	SA	
	Le Menec alignment,	pl	1:240	67	DL	A	pf. e
	E. end	e	1:64	7.67, 8.68, 69	DL	A	pf. e
		e	1:64	7.67, 8.68	DL	SA	
		w	340 × 240	24.8.69	D	N	
5	Le Menec, W. cromlech	pl	1:240	67	DL	A	pf. e
		pl, e	1:64	67	DL	A	pf. e
58	Le Moustoir	pl	1:32	3.7.67	D	A	pf. d
95	Queric la Lande (Mané Bras)	pl	1:48	5–6.11.66	L	G	*CB* I, 75
36	Roch Feutet (Pierre Fendue)	pl	1:48	27.10.66	L	G	*CB* I, 71
11	Er Roch Vihan, Kerluir	pl	1:48	8.64	L	G	*CB* I, 32
38	Rogarte (Kerjarec)	pl	1:48	27.10.66	L	G	*CB* I, 72
49	Er Rohallec, Kergo	pl	1:48	66–67	L	G	*CB* II, 12
28 ii	Er Velannec, Kerlearec	pl, e	1:48	14.11.66	L	G	*CB* I, 82 and f.
CRACH							
13	Coët Kersu	pl	1:48	9.11.66	L	G	*CB* I, 76
11	Luffang (Lufant)	pl	1:48	9.11.66	L	G	*CB* I, 77 and f.
14	Er Mar (Roch de Parc-Lan)	pl	1:48	9.11.66	L	G	*CB* I, 5
2	Parc er Roh, Kervin Brigitte	pl	1:48	26.8.64	L	G	*CB* I, 25
15	Peudrec	pl	1:48	9.11.66	L	G	*CB* I, 78 and f.
ERDEVEN							
10	Kerangre	pl	1:48	10.11.66	L	G	*CB* I, 79
24	Keredo, Er Run	pl	1:48	17.10.66	L	G	*CB* I, 65 and f.
		pl	1:48	17.10.66	L	SA	
23	Keredo, Er Trion	pl	1:48	15.9.66	L	G	*CB* I, 64
13	Kerhuel (Kerivil)	pl	1:48	10.11.66	L	G	*CB* I, 80
19	Kerzerho alignment, W. end	pl	1:240	18.8.69 and 5.9.72	DL	A	pf. e
		pl	1:480	18.8.69	DL	A	pf. e
		e	1:64	8.69	DL	A	pf. e
		w	340 × 240	9.9.72	D	N	cl.
		pl	1:480	18.8.69	DL	SA	
		pl	1:240	18.8.69 and 5.9.72	DL	SA	
		e	1:64	8.69	—	SA	
	Kerzerho alignment,	pl	1:240	17.8.69	DL	A	pf. e
	E. end	pl	1:240	17.8.69	DL	SA	

Inventory	Site	Scale or size		Date	Name	Coll.	Remarks
19	Kerzerho North alignment	pl	1:240	30.6.70	DO	A	pf. e
		pl	1:480	18.8.69	DL	A	pf. e
		pl	1:240	30.6.70	DO	SA	
		w	340 × 240	9.9.72	D	N	
		w	340 × 240	6.70	D	N	from sketch by O.
21	Mané Bras	pl	1:480, 1:48	31.8.64	L	G	*CB* I, 8 and f.
		pl	1:48	8.66	L	G	*CB* I, 59 and f.
26	Mané Groh	pl	1:48	29.8.66	L	G	*CB* I, 57
		w	340 × 240	28.6.67	D	N	cl.
18	Ty er Mané	pl	1:48	11.10.66	L	G	*CB* I, 66
ETEL							
1	Roh er Argant	pl	?1:48	10.11.66	L	G	*CB* I, 80 Scale not given
LARMOR-BADEN							
22	Gav'r Inis	pl, e	1:240	29.7.68	DL	A	pf. f
		pl, e	1:48	1.8.68	DL	A	pf. f
		pl, e	1:240	29.7.68	DL	SA	
		pl, e	1:48	1.8.68	DL	SA	
		ss	1:8	1.8.68	D	A	pf. b
		ss	1:16	—	D, DL	SA	
		w	340 × 240	29.7.68	D	N	from Île Longue
LOCMARIAQUER							
11	Er Grah (The Great Menhir)	pl, e	1:64	29.7.68	DL	A	pf. e
		pl	1:480	29.8.64	L	G	*CB* I, 29 and f.
		pl	1:48	29.8.64	L	G	*CB* I, 29 and f.
		pl.	1:64	29.7.68	DL	SA	
		w	340 × 240	31.7.68	D	N	cl., from SW.
		w	340 × 240	31.7.68	D	N	cl., from SE.
25	Kercadoret	pl, e	1:48	—	L	G	*CB* II, 7
17	Mané er H'röek	pl, e	1:48	31.7.68	DL	A	pf. f
		pl, e	1:240	31.7.68	DL	A	pf. f
		pl, e	1:48	31.7.68	DL	SA	
		pl, e	1:240	31.7.68	DL	SA	
		ss	1:16	29.8.64	L	SA	
17	Mané er H'röek Menhirs	pl, e	1:48, 1:240	31.7.68	DL	A	pf. f
		pl	1:48	31.7.68	DL	SA	
9	Mané Lud	pl, e	1:48	24.7.67	DL	A	pf. d
		pl, e	1:48, 1:480	24.7.67	DL	SA	
		ss	1:16	24.7.67	DL	SA	
8	Mein Drein, Kerveresse	pl, e	1:48	26.8.67	L	G	*CB* II, 8
		pl, e	1:16, 1:48	26.8.67	L	SA	
		ss	1:8	69	D	N	'from W.C.L.'
16	Men er Mère	pl	1:64	68	L	A	pf. c
20	Les Pierres Plates	pl, e	1:48	24.7.67	DL	A	pf. f
		pl	1:48	24.7.67	DL	SA	
		ss	1:48	—	—	SA	
12	Table des Marchands (Dol ar Marchand)	pl, e	1:48	24.7.67	DL	G	*CB* II, 4
		pl, e	1:48	24.7.67	DL	SA	
		w	340 × 245	31.7.68	D	N	cl.

Inventory	*Site*	*Scale or size*		*Date*	*Name*	*Coll.*	*Remarks*
PLOUGOUMELEN (*now in Bono*)							
—	Le Bono (destroyed)	pl	1:48	25.8.64	L	G	*CB* I, 24
4	Mané Verh	pl	1:48	4.9.67	L	G	*CB* II, 10
1	Le Rocher (Kernoz)	pl, e	1:48	68	D	A	pf. f. (copy)
		pl	1:48	25.8.64 and 28.8.67	L	SA	
		pl, e	1:96	28.8.67 and 4.9.67	L	SA	
		ss	1:16	—	—	SA	
PLOUHARNEL							
21	Crucuno (Kerconno)	pl, e	1:48	64	L	A	pf. f
				67	DL		
		pl, e	1:48	5.7.67	DL	G	*CB* II, 2 and f.
		w	340 × 240	28.6.67	D	N	cl.
		w	150 × 90	5.7.67	D	N	
22	Crucuno quadrilateral cromlech	pl, e	1:240	7.67	DL	A	pf. c
		pl	1:240	7.67	D	G	pf. xxviii
		w	345 × 240	29.6.67	D	N	cl.
12	Kerberenne	pl	1:48	22.8.66	L	G	*CB* I, 58
3	Keroch	pl	1:48	21.9.66	L	G	*CB* I, 59
24	Er Mané, Cohquer (Cosquer)	pl, e	1:48	29.8.68	L	G	*CB* II, 25
		pl, e	1:48	29.8.68	L	SA	
25	Mané beg er Heur, Cohquer (Cosquer)	pl	1:48	25.9.66	L	G	*CB* I, 60 and f.
15	Mané Remor	pl, e	1:48	7.8.68	L	G	*CB* II, 23
26	Men er Roh, Cohquer (Mané er Huhr, Cosquer)	pl, e	1:48	29.8.68	L	G	*CB* II, 24
1	Menhir near chapel	e	1:8	6.70	D	A	pf. c
4	Er Roh, Kergavat	pl, e	1:48	54	FL	A	pf. d (copy)
		pl, e	1:48	1.9.64 and 8.68	L	G	*CB* I, 30 and f.
18	Roch er Vredir (Roch Verhdihr, Roch Breder)	pl, e	1:48	1.9.68	L	G	*CB* II, 24
17	Er Roheu, Kernehue (Roch du Chapelet)	pl	1:48	27.8.64	L	G	*CB* I, 28
10	Rondossec (Roch Guyon)	pl, e	1:48, 1:240	7.67	DL	A	pf. f
		pl, e	1:48	2.7.67	DL	SA	
		w	340 × 245	23.7.67	D	N	
8	Runesto	pl	1:64	15.7.67	DL	A	pf. d
		pl, e	1:48	15.7.67	DL	G	*CB* II, 5
13	Sainte Barbe alignment	pl, e	1:64	7.67	DL	A	pf. c
		pl	1:240	12.8.69	—	A	r.
		w	340 × 245	10.7.67	D	N	cl.
14	Vieux Moulin alignment	pl, e	1:64	7.67	DL	A	pf. c
		pl	1:64	10.9.72	DL	A	pf. c
		w	340 × 245	28.6.67 and 11.7.67	D	N	cl.

Inventory	Site		Scale or size	Date	Name	Coll.	Remarks
PLOUHINEC							
14	Gueldro (Kerzine)	pl	1:240	19.8.69	DL	SA	
		e	1:64	8.69	DL	SA	
6	Kervelhue	pl	1:240	19.8.69	DL	A	pf. c
		pl	1:64	19.8.69	DL	SA	
		w	340 × 240	69	D	N	
ST PHILIBERT							
13	Kermané (Porher)	pl, e	1:48	26.8.67	L	G	*CB* II, 9
3	Petit Kerambel (Roch Maneac, Kernehue)	pl, e	1:48	3.8.68	DL	A	pf. d
		pl, e	1:48	3.8.68	DL	G	*CB* II, 22
		w	160 × 95	3.8.68	D	N	
15	Roh Vras, Kerhan	w	340 × 240	3.8.68	D	N	cl.
ST PIERRE—QUIBERON							
7	Mané Beker Noz	pl	1:64	67	DL	A	pf. b
12	St Pierre alignment	pl	1:240	7.67 and 8.68	DL	A	pf. e
		e	1:64	67 and 68	DL	A	pf. e
		w	340 × 245	12.7.67	D	N	cl.
12	St Pierre cromlech	pl	1:240	12.7.67	DL	A	pf. e
		e	1:64	and 17.8.68			
LA TRINITÉ SUR MER							
9	Kermarker	pl	1:48	12.10.66	L	G	*CB* I, 68
10	Mané Bras, Kervilor	pl	1:48	12.10.66	L	G	*CB* I, 67
4	Men er Roch, Kerdro Vihan	pl, e	1:48	31.8.68	L	G	*CB* II, 25
3	Queric en Arvor	pl	1:48	12.10.66	L	G	*CB* I, 66
12	Er Rohec, Kervilor	pl	1:48	16.10.66	L	G	*CB* I, 69
ILE D'ARZ							
*	Pen Liousse (Maison des Poulpiquets)	pl	1:48	2.9.64	L	G	*CB* I, 21 and f.
ILE AUX MOINES							
*	Er Bouglio, Penhap	pl	1:48, 1:480	9.64	L	G	*CB* I, 14
		pl	1:48	2.8.69	DL	G	*CB* I, f. 14
		w	160 × 95	2.8.69	D	N	
*	Kergonan cromlech	pl, e	1:48, 1:240	2.8.69	DL	A	pf. e
		pl	1:240	—	—	SA	
		pl, e	1:48	2.8.69	DL	SA	
*	Roh Vraz, Kerno	pl	1:48	9.64	L	G	*CB* I, 32
ER LANNIC							
*	Er Lannic cromlech	pl	1:240	1.8.68	DL	A	pf. c
		e	1:64	1.8.66	DL	A	pf. c
SARZEAU (*now in Arzon*)							
*	Tumiac	pl	1:48, 14:80	—	—	G	*CB* I, 15

Note: sites marked * lie outside the area covered by Le Rouzic's *Inventory*

Bibliography

ANON. 1890 Report of the Brittany meeting, *Archaeologia Cambrensis* 5 ser. VII, 43–80, 161–76.

ATKINSON, R. J. C. 1975 Megalithic astronomy: a prehistorian's comments, *Journ. Hist. Astron.* VI, 42–52.

CRAWFORD, O. G. S. 1925 *The Long Barrows of the Cotswolds*, Gloucester.

DANIEL, G. E. 1939 The transepted gallery graves of western France, *Proc. Prehist. Soc.* V, 143–65.

DRYDEN, Sir H. 1870 Notes of three chambered tombs in the parish of Carnac, Brittany, *Proc. Soc. Ant. Scot.* VII, 394–5.

1876 On some megalithic remains in France, *Proc. Soc. Ant. Scot.* XI, 235–6.

EVANS, J. 1956 *A history of the Society of Antiquaries*, Oxford.

GEORGE, T. J. 1912 *Catalogue of the Dryden Collection*, Northampton.

KENDRICK, T. D. 1928 *The archaeology of the Channel Islands: I, the Bailiwick of Guernsey*, London.

LE ROUZIC, Z. 1965 *Inventaire des monuments megalithiques de la region de Carnac*, Vannes (reprinted from *Bull. Soc. Polymathique du Morbihan* July, 1965).

LUKIS, W. C. 1854 A few words to Wiltshire entomologists, *Wilts. Arch. Mag.* I, 95–6.

1864a On cromlechs, *Journ. Brit. Arch. Assoc.* XX, 228–37.

1864b Danish cromlechs and burial customs, compared with those of Brittany, the Channel Islands, and Great Britain, *Wilts. Arch. Mag.* VIII, 145–69.

1864–67 Chambered tombs in Wiltshire, *Proc. Soc. Ant. Lond.*, 2 ser. III, 213.

1866 On some peculiarities in the construction of chambered barrows, *Journ. Brit. Arch. Assoc.* XXII, 249–63.

1868a On a remarkable chambered barrow at Kerlescant, Carnac, Brittany, *Journ. Brit. Arch. Assoc.* XXIV, 40–4.

1868b On the various forms of monuments, commonly called dolmens, in Brittany, pointing out a progress in their architectural construction, with an attempt to reduce them to chronological order, *Trans. Internat. Congr. Prehist. Arch., third session*, Norwich, 218–23.

1870–73 On certain erroneous views respecting the construction of French chambered barrows (summary), *Proc. Soc. Ant. Lond.* 2 ser. V, 366.

1872 On the stone avenues of Carnac, *Wilts. Arch. Mag.* XIII, 78–91.

1875 *A Guide to the chambered barrows, etc. of South Brittany*, Ripon.

1876–78a The Devil's Arrows, Boroughbridge, Yorkshire, *Proc. Soc. Ant. Lond.* 2 ser. VII, 134–8.

1876–78b Stonehenge and the Avenue, *Proc. Soc. Ant. Lond.* 2 ser. VII, 268–71.

1877 On some megalithic remains in western Cornwall, *Journ. Brit. Arch. Assoc.* XXXIII, 291.

1879–81a Report on the *hunebedden* of Frenthe, *Proc. Soc. Ant. Lond.* 2 ser. VIII, 46–55.

1879–81b Report on the prehistoric monuments of Devon and Cornwall, *Proc. Soc. Ant. Lond.* 2 ser. VIII, 285–92.

1879–81c Report on the prehistoric monuments of Dartmoor, *Proc. Soc. Ant. Lond.* 2 ser. VIII, 471–81.

1881–83a Report on the prehistoric monuments of Avebury and Stonehenge, *Proc. Soc. Ant. Lond.* 2 ser. IX, 141–57.

1881–83b Prehistoric monuments of Wilts, Somerset and S. Wales, *Proc. Soc. Ant. Lond.* 2 ser. IX, 344–55 (with correlation in *op. cit.*, 2 ser. X, 148–9).

1883–85 Report of the survey of certain megalithic monuments in Scotland, Cumberland and Westmoreland, *Proc. Soc. Ant. Lond.* 2 ser. X, 302–20.

1885a Egyptian obelisks and European monoliths compared, *Archaeologia* XLVIII, 421–30.

1885b *Prehistoric Stone Monuments: Cornwall*, Society of Antiquaries of London.

RAFTERY, J. 1951 *Prehistoric Ireland*, London.

THOM, A. and THOM, A. S. 1971 The astronomical significance of the large Carnac menhirs, *Journ. Hist. Astron.* II, 147–60.

1972a The Carnac alignments, *Journ. Hist. Astron.* III, 11–26.

1972b The uses of the alignments at Le Menec Carnac, *Journ. Hist. Astron.* III, 151–64.

1973 The Kerlescan cromlechs, *Journ. Hist. Astron.* IV, 168–73.

1974 The Kermario alignments, *Journ. Hist. Astron.* V, 30–47.

Acknowledgments

This paper could not have been written without the help of my wife, both in compiling biographical information about Lukis and Dryden, in cataloguing the second volume of *Chambered Barrows* in Guernsey, and in checking many of the plans in the field in Brittany. For permission to study, catalogue and copy drawings I am indebted to the Ancient Monuments Committee of the States of Guernsey and to Mrs H. R. Cole, the curator of the Island Museum; to the Ashmolean Museum, Oxford and to Mr A. G. Sherratt, Assistant Keeper, Department of Antiquities; to the Northampton Central Library; and to the Society of Antiquaries of London and its Librarian, Mr J. H. Hopkins.

14

MICHAEL J. O'KELLY

Some Thoughts on the Megalithic Tombs of Ireland

Professor Piggott has contributed much to the study of the Neolithic in these islands as well as in Europe, and part of that valuable contribution has been his work on the megalithic tombs. I hope therefore that he will find the following thoughts on these structures of some interest.

The four-fold classification proposed by de Valera and Ó Nualláin (1961, xii-xiv), for the 1200 or so tombs which they have listed in their survey, has received fairly general acceptance. The tombs are classified into court cairns, portal dolmens, passage graves, and wedge-shaped gallery graves. There is of course a residue of sites which are unclassifiable for one reason or another. While the classification is intended as no more than a convenience to facilitate the study of such a large body of material, it seems to have created a notion in the minds of some that the different classes of tomb were being built in splendid isolation, and that there was little or no communication between the sects of this elaborate cult of the dead. But manifestly this cannot have been so; and if one lists the points of similarity in the various types of tomb instead of the differences, it becomes obvious that there was a good deal of dialogue indeed.

For instance, court cairn and portal dolmen builders were working very much in the same area, the northern third of Ireland, and were building their tombs contemporaneously, for the grave goods are largely the same in both classes of tomb. There are similarities of detail in the entrance structures and in orientation, while both tomb types have long mounds, though there is some evidence that early portal dolmens had small circular mounds which were later incorporated into long mounds as was clearly the case at Dyffryn Ardudwy in Wales (Powell 1963, 20). The subsidiary chambers added onto some existing court cairns can look like miniature dolmens, and so on.

A court cairn gallery which has transept cells can be said to have a cruciform plan like that of many passage graves, even if there are differences of detail; the sill slabs set across the passages of some passage graves, Dowth North, Mound of the Hostages, Carrowkeel, cairns G, H and K for instance, compare with the sill type of segmentation in some court cairns. The high western ends of some wedges which have marked porticos can be compared to the high frontal structures of certain portal dolmens. The flat or very slightly dished façades of some wedges are not unlike the very shallow façades of some court cairns. Some wedges have circular cairns with orthostatic kerbs just like those of the passage graves. Whether these comparable features are valid evidence of dialogue between the sects or of the influence of one group of builders on another is debatable; but since there is overlap of tomb types both in space and in time, communication amongst the people building them is certain to have taken place. Under those circumstances, interaction of tomb types could hardly have been avoided, especially as the basis of the effort for all the builders appears to have been the *provision of a house for the dead*.

But while there is distributional overlap of tomb types, there is also evidence of mutual exclusiveness, particularly amongst the court cairns and the wedges. The virtual confinement of the court cairns to the northern third of the country and the preponderance of wedge-galleries in the south must mean that areas of sect influence could be maintained over a period of time.

How is this tomb building activity to be related to what we already know of the Neolithic period in Ireland? It is now becoming clear that stock-raising had begun here before 3000 bc, and it is reasonable to think that food production would need to have been well established before a community could undertake the building of a very elaborate megalithic tomb, since this needed time and a group of men free from other chores to undertake the collection and transport of the stones to the selected site – and this was no easy matter if the land was as heavily forested as the palaeobotanists would have us believe. As we know, however, from the layers of turves incorporated into the Newgrange cairn, cereal agriculture had been introduced into that area before the tomb was built, that is before 2500 bc, and the surroundings were composed of woodland and open spaces at the time of building.

Perhaps this work could have been done at any time of the year except in spring and autumn when even small-scale farmers are likely to have been most busy. Once the tomb orthostats had been set up, everyone in the community including the older children could take part in the collection of stones, and in piling them against the outside of the structure to create the ramp on which the roof stones were moved up into place. When the roof was completed the stone-collecting and piling-up went on until the cairn was finished.

It must be realized, however, that as yet no tomb in Ireland has been dated to a time as early as the beginning of farming here and that, whenever megalithic tomb building began, present evidence suggests that the practice must be spread over a period of some centuries, so that some tombs may be centuries later in date than others even in the same class. The C14 dates for the tomb structure at Newgrange centre on 2500 bc, while the Mound of the Hostages passage grave at Tara has a C14 date of about 2000 bc (Watts 1960, 114–15, D.44).

But was this tomb-building a normal part of the Neolithic way of life from the beginning in Ireland, or was it a cult practice which found ready adherents when it was preached here? The cult is poorly represented at Lough Gur and not at all at Lyles Hill, two of the most prolific Irish settlements of the period. It would seem that megalithic tombs were not intended merely as repositories for the dead, but rather were built as *houses* in which the spirits of the dead would continue to live for a very long time, and so the most durable materials had to be used in order that the house should last forever. Hence the great stone slabs in contradistinction to the ephemeral materials, wood and thatch, used for the houses of the living.

This concept of a house for the dead has been supported in a remarkable way by the new discoveries at the Newgrange passage grave. Admittedly this is an extraordinary monument in any case, but the lessons learnt from it must surely be applicable to some extent, if not in detail, to tombs of the same and of the other classes. Newgrange was not a cenotaph; it was used as a tomb. Cremated and unburnt skeletal remains have been found inside it accompanied by some of the characteristic beads, pendants and 'marbles'.

Every precaution was taken by the builders to ensure that the inside should remain dry, as it does today, thousands of years after it was built. The corbel slabs of the roof of the chamber were laid with an outward fall, so as to run rain-water coming down through the cairn off to the outside of the tomb structure. Where the roof of the passage joins into that of the chamber, great care was taken to pack the interstices between the slabs with clean sea sand (brought from the shore 20 miles away) and burnt soil so that no water should run through to the inside. Farther out, where the corbelled inner portion of the passage roof comes down onto the outer part done in flat slabs, an elaborate system of channels was chiselled into the upper surfaces of the roof slabs so as to collect the percolating water and run it off to the sides. Where the water spilled down onto the corbel slabs below, these also were grooved so as to run it still farther out and dissipate it into the body of the cairn, thus preventing it from getting inside. Not only this: the interstices between all the slabs here too were packed – 'puttied up', one might say – with burnt soil. This seems to have come from turves which were cut for the purpose, stacked and burnt. The resulting grey soil was probably mixed with water before it was put into the joints. It is charcoal from this packing which has given two separate C14 dates: 2475 ± 45 bc (GrN-5462-C)[1] and 2465 ± 40 bc (GrN-5463). These figures are virtually the same and can be taken to indicate an uncorrected round figure date of 2500 bc. On present evidence, this is the earliest satisfactory date achieved for *any kind* of megalithic tomb in Ireland. There is no evidence that the court cairns are older or even as old. If the bones of the persons inside were mere bones, it should not have mattered whether they got wet or not and there should have been no need for such elaborate and troublesome precautions to keep them dry. Obviously, the matter was not as simple as this.

That it was not so simple is further shown at Newgrange by the provision of the 'roof box' (*Ill. 1*). This curious and so far unique feature consists of a box-like structure open at the front, and set up so as to form a roof over a deliberately contrived slit in the roof of the passage. The leading edge of the roof-lintel of the box is ornamented.

A curious fact is that on 21 December, the winter

---

[1] GrN-5462-C was originally published (M. J. O'Kelly 1969, 140; C. O'Kelly 1971, 96; Shee and O'Kelly 1971, 75) as 2550 ± 45 bc (GrN-5462). The corrected number and date has been supplied by Dr W. G. Mook of the Groningen Laboratory in a letter to me dated 9 February 1972.

1 Entrance and 'roof box' over it. Newgrange, Co. Meath.

solstice, at exactly 08:54 GMT, the top edge of the disc of the sun appears above the local horizon opposite the east edge of the roof-slit, and at 08:58 a direct ray passes through the slit and down the 20 m-long passage and, as a very thin pencil of light, strikes across the chamber floor to the front edge of the basin stone in the end chamber, dramatically and brightly illuminating the tomb. During the next six minutes, the ray widens to 17 cm and, at 09:04 having moved across the floor, begins to narrow again when it strikes the base of R21, the last orthostat at the inner end of the right-hand side of the passage. At 09:15 exactly, direct sunlight to the chamber is cut off. During the whole period of 17 minutes of illumination, the strength of the light in the chamber is such that the details of the structure are clearly visible right up to the capstone of the roof 6 m above the floor. The effect must have been even more dramatic when the tomb was first built, for an inward movement of some of the passage orthostats, principally L18 and L20, has reduced the width of the beam of light from an original 40 cm or so to the present maximum of 17 cm. A very careful and detailed survey, recently done (Patrick 1974), proves that the sun has shone through the passage to the chamber since the time of construction and is likely to continue to do so forever, regardless of changes in the obliquity of the ecliptic. John Patrick says 'it seems likely that its orientation is deliberate' (Patrick 1974, 519).

We know that the roof slit was lightly closed by placing two blocks of quartz against it, and that these were pulled out and pushed back a number of times – one block has survived and the movement has left scratch marks on the front lintel of the passage. Should one then imagine a mid-winter ceremony when, on the shortest day, people gathered before the entrance to the tomb to watch the quartz blocks being drawn back, in readiness for the admission of the sunlight into the house for the dead? And then what?

It may be that the 'roof-box' feature was used at times other than the winter solstice in some recurring ritual, perhaps on special or anniversary days. If this is so, it is obvious that those who were inside were not just dead people who were finished with when they were put in and had the door closed on them. Presumably too they were 'special' people, since it is only for such that one can envisage the building of a tomb as great as that of Newgrange. The amount of bone found inside was small and can only represent a few people, though we do not know how much of the original deposit may have been removed since the tomb was opened in AD 1699. Nor do we know whether any or all of those who worked at its building, or who contributed in some other way to the effort, had rights of burial in it or not.

When we look at other megalithic tombs, the same points seem to emerge – a great effort was made to build a tomb to house only a few bodies. Admittedly, the amount of excavation done is not only small but is also selective in all classes of tombs. Such as it is, however, the evidence suggests special people in all cases. Fourknocks and the Mound of the Hostages have so far contained the largest numbers of people – Fourknocks twenty-four and the Mound of the Hostages many more. Apart from them, the numbers of persons are small in each case; and in several of the court cairns, only a single youth was found in the tomb.

Megalithic tomb building seems therefore to have come in the Middle Neolithic period in Ireland, and to have been something that was done only for special people. The cult must have been practised over a long period of time, probably for 500 years or more. If one brings the number of tombs up from the surviving 1200 to about 1500 to allow for all those destroyed, and if these are spread over 500 years, this gives an *average* building rate of three per year. One may then see the tombs not as the result of large colonizing or invading forces, but rather as a cult practice implanted here and there by a small group led by an accomplished preacher, who addressed a mixed population of Larnians and those Neolithic folk who had already been in Ireland for a long time.

This interpretation can also explain the differences in tomb types not only in Ireland but outside it as well. Once the missionary implanted the idea of the building of a house for special dead people and had indicated the general form which, according to his sect, it should take, the details of construction were largely a matter for the builders. In this way local variations and exuberances easily came into being, and this must be why it is so difficult to find really close parallels for tombs as between one area or country and another. If this was happening, our neat evolutionary or devolutionary series of tomb types have little validity! Passage graves are known in Spain, Portugal, France, Britain, Ireland and Scandinavia; and while a basic thread of recurrent features connects them all, not many tombs in Ireland are exactly or even closely paralleled in one of the other areas – each tomb was an individual effort. Nevertheless, passage graves make the strongest claim to be regarded as the international tomb type (Fleming 1969, 248–9).

Court cairns as we know them in Ireland do not occur on the continent and, while they are similar to tombs in Scotland and on both sides of the Severn estuary, there are important differences of detail. When one compares small scale plans of Irish wedge-gallery tombs with small scale plans of the *allées couvertes* of Brittany, close similarities seem to exist; but seen in the field, the tombs do not appear to be at all so nearly related. Indeed one can see the wedge-gallery graves *evolving in Ireland* from the V-shaped or undifferentiated passage graves!

The strong coastal concentrations of court cairns have given rise to arguments as to whether the builders arrived in force on the east coast of Ireland and spread westward or vice versa. But are such arguments legitimate? If a group of tombs is on or near the coast, does this necessarily mean that they were built by people who had lately come in from the sea? Is it not possible that such concentrations merely mean that coastal land was more amenable to settlement because, let us say, forest growth had been inhibited by the salt-laden winds from the sea?

The Sligo passage graves have been said to be the degenerate offspring of tombs first built in Ireland by people who arrived by sea on the east coast and who gradually spread westward across Ireland. But surely this is a doubtful concept. There is nothing degenerate about the Carrowkeel tombs – indeed their builders showed great expertise and resource. The fact that they are *different* in some details from some of those on the east and that they have no art need not mean any more than that they were built by people who had a slightly different notion of how the house-for-the-dead idea should be carried into effect; and if the builders arrived by sea at all, they are as likely to have come in on the west as on the east, or indeed at several places at the same time!

One can now identify the remains of a single cruciform passage grave in the Carrowmore cemetery. Otherwise, the tombs of this group are somewhat different from the rest of the Irish passage graves, but this is not to say that they are degenerate or developed structures. Indeed the *simplest* of them bear some resemblances to the *simplest* passage graves of Scandinavia, particularly to those of Denmark, but the more complex Carrowmore tombs differ in many respects from Danish monuments that at first sight might appear comparable. The superficial similarities are probably due to the fact that split glacial boulders have been used at Carrowmore and in Denmark as building material. The Carrowmore tombs are likely to have been very early in the Irish passage grave series.

Because some passage graves occur in the Dublin-Wicklow mountains – a gold and copper bearing area – and because some wedge-gallery graves in the south-west are near the copper ore deposits, it has been argued that their builders were attracted to the particular areas by the presence of these minerals, but there is no evidence that this was so. No metal object of any kind has been found in a primary position in any Irish passage grave, and the same is true of the wedge-gallery tombs because all of the supposed metal associations with them can be questioned. It should be remembered that the county which has the greatest number of wedges, Clare (over 100 of the tombs), has no known copper deposits. And the occurrence of Beaker pottery in five wedge tombs is surely due to secondary intrusion into pre-existing structures, just as it is in Brittany and elsewhere.

Because the wedge-tombs are found on hill slopes of medium height above sea level up to levels above the present-day cultivation line, it has also been argued that their builders were herdsmen who occupied these levels because they provided sufficient grazing on which to winter their cattle (de Valera and Ó Nualláin 1961, 11, 112, 116). It is difficult to prove or disprove this, for the presence of the tombs in such areas does not necessarily mean that the people who built them lived or herded animals anywhere near them. Obviously, the several issues raised by these fascinating megalithic structures will not be answered until many more of them have been fully excavated. There has been too much *sampling* of sites. The chambers have been emptied, but the cairns and what lies below them have rarely been fully examined. Findings and interpretations have been conditioned by too many preconceived notions. There must be a more critical assessment of the evidence from every site and the older findings must be firmly re-interpreted in the light of the best recent work.

MEGALITHIC ART

Probably the best known feature of the Irish passage graves is the 'art' which is so well exemplified in the Boyne and Loughcrew cemeteries and at Fourknocks, all in Co. Meath. It does not occur at Carrowkeel or Carrowmore, the two Sligo cemeteries. One site, Cloverhill, in the Carrowmore area is often mentioned as an example of the art, but the structure is not a passage grave and the devices on its stones do not resemble anything in the repertoire of any passage-grave artist – they are of the early Iron Age or the early Christian period. Other examples of the art are found at Kings Mountain and Tara (Mound of the Hostages), Co. Meath; at Seefin, at Baltinglass and Tournant,[2] Co. Wicklow; at Sess Kilgreen and Knockmany, Co. Tyrone; at Carnanmore and Lyles Hill,[3] Co. Antrim; at Kiltierney, Co. Fermanagh; at Drumreagh, Co. Down and at Clear Island,[4] Co. Cork. Seen on a map, this distribution is markedly eastern and northern in extent if one regards the Kiltierney and Clear Island sites as outliers.

The devices on the stones are geometrical in concept and entirely non-representational and, while it is probable that they are symbolic, religious or magical in content, it is unlikely that we will ever discover what any of them meant since we cannot know the minds or the emotions of a people who did not know how to write and who are separated in time from us by more than four thousand years. Needless to say, speculations as to the meanings of various devices are many, but it must be remembered that the interpretations offered are not only purely personal, but also conditioned by the strength of the interpreter's imagination and by the climate of thought and psychology in which he has grown up.

At Newgrange the panel on orthostat 19, on the left side of the passage as one walks towards the chamber, is a case in point. At the top is a band of zigzags below which are two spirals set side by side. Below them is a lozenge, and below that a spiral. This is seen by some as the stylized representation of a face – the spirals being eyes and mouth, while the lozenge between is the nose and the zigzags are a head of wavy hair. Having found a face, the imagination then leaps on to identify it as that of the 'eye goddess' or 'earth mother' or 'goddess of fertility', a concept now largely discredited (Fleming 1969). Others see sex symbols and fertility cult indications in much of the work and, while such possibilities cannot be excluded, neither can they be substantiated. In her recent and very valuable discussion of the art of the Boyne passage graves, C. O'Kelly (1973) has demolished many misconceptions including the notion that there is an anthropomorphic element in it.

I have written the word 'art' in inverted commas since there is no means of knowing whether the carvings were meant to be art in our modern sense of the term, or even whether they were thought of as ornament or decoration. In some instances it is obvious that the carver was aware of the shape of the slab and that he laid out an overall pattern to fit the available space. The outstanding example of this is the entrance stone (K1) at Newgrange where an integrated pattern of lozenges, spirals and concentric arcs was exactly fitted not only into the outline of the stone but also to its surface curvature (*Ill. 2*). This carving is regarded as one of the great achievements of prehistoric art in Western Europe.

The kerb-stone no. 52, which is diametrically

[2] This stone is now in the National Museum of Ireland.

[3] The stone from this site is in the Ulster Museum, Belfast.

[4] This stone is in the Cork Public Museum, on loan from the Department of Archaeology, University College, Cork.

2 The entrance stone at Newgrange.

3 Kerb-stone no. 52 at Newgrange.

opposite the entrance stone, has much of the same quality and may well have been carved by the same master hand (*Ill. 3*). In this case, the artificer set out to bring into his overall pattern a series of cup marks which occurred entirely naturally on the slab. He improved the cups a little and framed some of them in cartouches, and thus provided some archaeologists with the basis for an urge to compare them with certain parts of the ornament on the orthostats of '. . . Les Pierres Plates, whose *shields* are found on Kerbstone K52 of Newgrange' (Herity 1974, 193)! Other examples at Newgrange which bear patterns designed to fit the respective stones are the relief saltire on the leading edge of the lintel of the roof box and the 'false relief' pattern of lozenges, triangles and zigzags on a corbel in the western cell of the tomb. The entrance stone of the western tomb at Knowth has an organized pattern of boxed rectangles fitted to the shape of the stone (Eogan 1967, Pl. XXXIX) and the Fourknocks stones lettered a, b, c, e and f are other good examples (Harnett 1957, 224–7).

For the rest, there are individual devices of high quality such as the S-spiral on kerb-stone 67 or the three-spiral design in the end-chamber at Newgrange (C. O'Kelly 1971, Pls. 7, 8b, 30), or the wheel-like motifs on a kerb-stone at Dowth, or the rosette-like devices on stone 8 in the chamber of cairn T at Loughcrew. But as well as these, there are many items which can only be looked upon as doodles or graffiti executed by prentice hands in moments of idleness, so carelessly are they done in comparison with the best formal work described above.

Excavation and survey both inside the Newgrange tomb and along the kerb at the periphery of the cairn have brought to light many new examples of carvings that are in positions in which they could not ordinarily have been seen once the construction of the tomb was complete. These are on the edges and backs of orthostats or on the parts of them embedded in the ground, or on the under or upper surfaces of corbel slabs, on the upper surfaces of the lintels of the passage roof and on the backs as well as the fronts of the newly exposed kerb-stones. Those on the backs of the kerb-stones and on the upper surfaces of the passage roof slabs were very effectively covered up by the completed cairn.

These 'hidden' decorations, being protected from the weather and all other destructive forces, are so completely fresh that each chisel mark is as clearly visible now as the day it was made. In some cases also, extremely finely scratched graffiti are perfectly preserved. It seems unlikely therefore, that slabs such as these have come from pre-existing monuments dismantled to provide building material for a new tomb as has sometimes been suggested. Indeed it is more likely that the carving was done on the stones while they were lying about the site. If the important thing was the act of carving a device, it would not matter whether it was visible or not when the slab was built into place in the tomb structure. At Newgrange the builders seem to have been more concerned to utilize the slabs to the best structural advantage, rather than to place them where their areas of ornament could be seen. There is no doubt, however, that some of the carvings were done after the slabs had been set into their permanent positions in the structure. A notable example of this is the Newgrange entrance stone. Here the decoration stops along the bottom of the face at a line which corresponds exactly with the level at which the ground surface stood in front of the finished tomb. Another marked instance is K52 at Newgrange, while a number of stones at Loughcrew and at Knockmany also show the feature.

The actual carving was done by picking and the implements used were most probably flint points and a wooden mallet. A study of the individual pick marks shows that at least three grades of point were used – broad, medium and fine, and in some instances broad and fine points were used to give texture to a pattern. A good example of this is orthostat no. 8 on the right of the Newgrange passage as you enter. Here a panel of horizontally divided lozenges is picked with a fine point in the upper half of each lozenge and a broad point in the lower. Researchers have made several experiments with such flint points and it has thus been proved that they are quite adequate for the purpose. There is no evidence from any Irish passage grave that metal tools were known to or used by the builders, nor is there any evidence that paint was used, either alone or as an infilling in the carved patterns. Some incised work is also known where the point or the cutting edge of a flint blade was used to cut the lines of the pattern into the surface of the stone.

A feature of the Boyne cemetery tombs is the all-over pick dressing of the surfaces of some of the kerb-stones, of most of the orthostats and of some of the corbels of the roof. This treatment is especially noticeable at Newgrange where in several instances it has almost obliterated motifs previously carved on the surfaces. Good examples are K2 and K97, the kerb-stones on each side of the entrance stone. The pick dressing of K2 has almost removed a long double zigzag and a spiral on the bevelled top of the slab and a single zigzag lower down on the face. On K97 ghost-like traces of three pre-existing spirals are visible in certain lights behind the all-over pick dressing.

It is strange that none of the other Irish types of megalithic tomb have any comparable art work. One court cairn at Malinmore, Co. Donegal has some picked designs on two structural stones but, like those on the Clover Hill structure at Carrowmore, Co. Sligo, these appear to be of the Iron Age or early Christian period. A number of the wedge-shaped gallery graves have artificial cup-marks on some of their capstones, but there are no picked devices which would compare with those of the passage graves. In two instances, Baurnadomeeny, Co. Tipperary, and Scrahanard, Co. Cork, there are crudely incised criss-cross patterns on structural stones (O'Kelly 1960, 91). The Baurnadomeeny example is certainly ancient but there is some doubt about the other.

Claire O'Kelly (1973, 380) finished her study of the Boyne Valley art with a quote from Professor T. G. E. Powell, a life-long friend of Stuart Piggott, and it will not be amiss if I repeat it here. Powell says (1966, 114), 'As the evidence stands, there are two great provinces of megalithic stone-cut art: Brittany and Ireland, and although both share with the Peninsula a basic symbolism, both display such emphatic and large scale divergent achievements that they cannot have relied solely on that one southern source'.

Bibliography

EOGAN, G. 1967–68 Excavations at Knowth, Co. Meath, 1962–1965, *Proc. Roy. Irish Acad.* LXVI, C, 299–400.

FLEMING, A. 1969 The myth of the mother-goddess, *World Archaeology* 1, 247–81.

HARTNETT, P. J. 1957 Excavation of a Passage Grave at Fourknocks, Co. Meath, *Proc. Roy. Irish Acad.* LVIII, C, 197–277.

O'KELLY, C. 1971 *Illustrated Guide to Newgrange*, 2nd edn, Wexford.

1973 Passage-grave art in the Boyne Valley, Ireland, *Proc. Prehist. Soc.* XXXIX, 354–82.

O'KELLY, M. J. 1960 A Wedge-shaped Gallery Grave at Baurnadomeeney, Co. Tipperary, *JCHAS* LXV, 85–115.

PATRICK, J. 1974 Midwinter sunrise at Newgrange, *Nature* 249, 517–19.

POWELL, T. G. E. 1963 The Chambered Cairn at Dyffryn Ardudwy, *Antiquity* XXXVII, 19–24.

1966 *Prehistoric Art*, London.

DE VALERA, R. and Ó NUALLÁIN, S. 1961 *Survey of the Megalithic Tombs of Ireland* I: *Co. Clare*, Dublin.

WATTS, W. A. 1960 C14 Dating and the Neolithic in Ireland, *Antiquity* XXXIV, 111–16.

15

TREVOR WATKINS

Wessex without Cyprus: 'Cypriot Daggers' in Europe

THE finds of 'Cypriot daggers' in Europe seem to date from the last quarter of the nineteenth century. Reinecke (1933), in response to an article by Davies (1930), showed that the reports of these daggers were not reliable; many were not 'Cypriot daggers' at all, and none of those that were could be shown to have an authenticated provenance in Europe. Nevertheless, many scholars have preferred to take the position that 'an occasional wandering of these hook-tang daggers to Europe remains a possibility' (Hawkes 1938, 158, n. 2), or a more actively contrary position like that of Branigan (1970) to whose hypothesis the authenticity of these daggers and their contexts is fundamental. Various scholars believe in this dagger or that, and the effect has been cumulative as the beliefs become collected until authors like Branigan and Gerloff (1975) accept every dagger for which a claim to be Cypriot in origin and found in Europe has been advanced.

This essay is concerned only to restate the known facts about 'Cypriot daggers' in Europe, adding information not available to Reinecke. The standpoint of the author is that of someone acquainted to some extent with the products of the metal industry of Cyprus and the Levant in the Early and Middle Bronze Ages. The type in question is a blade, long and pointed, with a midrib or medial thickening extending into a long, thin tang, which is bent at the extremity into a hook or loop used as a means of fixing the tang in the haft. Since the type was not Cypriot in origin, the label 'Cypriot' seems inappropriate, and even the word 'dagger' would rankle in some quarters. Schaeffer (1936, 42–5) firmly believes them to be spearheads, which some indubitably were, while Catling (1964, 56) speaks of swords, dirks, daggers and spearheads. A neutral, general title is required; we may call them *hook-tang weapons*, and leave aside for the present purpose both Catling's verminous dirks with their 'rat-tailed tangs', and all concern for their precise use. The various forms are discussed by Maxwell-Hyslop (1946, 29ff.), Stronach (1957, 104ff.), Åström (1957, 136–8), Stewart (1962, 242–4), Catling (1964, 56ff., 117ff.) and Renfrew (1967, 10 and Pl. 7; 1972, 322–3).

One most important observation to emerge from a consideration of all the hook-tang weapons in Europe (the two Aegean Early Bronze Age examples apart) is that they are all Cypriot in origin. But a second observation is that not all the objects called 'Cypriot daggers' are Cypriot hook-tang weapons. Particularly unfortunate in this respect is the Winterbourne Basset Down dagger (Goddard 1912, 100, and Fig. 3 on Pl. IV; Annable and Simpson, 1964, No. 352), which is certainly a dagger, very probably Cypriot, but not, *pace* Branigan (1970, 93), a 'Cypriot dagger', in that it is not a hook-tang weapon. In other cases there has been either simple error or complete lack of documentation as with the 'Cypriot daggers' said by Ohnefalsch-Richter (1899, 320) to have been found in Albania and south Italy. Reinecke (1933, 256) dismissed the dagger from Stillfried-am-der-March in eastern Austria, pointing out that on the one hand its tang was flat and spatulate and not rod-like and hooked, and on the other hand that its original publisher (Menghin 1916, 20) made no claim that it was anything more than 'dem kyprischen Typus auffallend nähere'. However one now views that opinion, it was Davies (1930, 76) who misconstrued the object as a 'Cypriot dagger'. Reinecke similarly discarded the Aranyos dagger from Hungary (Reinecke 1933, 257; Hampel 1896, 74–5), and he has also shown that another Hungarian piece described by Davies (1930, 76) as from Arad is a confusion for one of the four weapons from Csorvás. The one quoted by Gordon Childe (1929, 218) as from Ó Szöny is the piece illustrated by Pulszky (1884, 414 and 416, no. 4), who said it was 'supposedly' from Uj-Szöny, but had reached the museum through the hands of a dealer in antiquities named Kraus, whom we shall meet again. Besides its doubtful origins, it is not a hook-tang weapon, nor is it recognizably Cypriot for that matter. It was Reinecke (1933, 257–8) who pointed out also that, of the two so-called 'Cypriot daggers' from Switzerland, the one which was found near the site of the pile-dwelling at Lüscherz (Gross 1883, Taf. 10, Nr. 26) is not a Cypriot hook-tang weapon.

With all Reinecke's dismissals I fully agree, having

consulted the literature and considered available illustrations. And to that list should now be added four more pieces. Of the group of weapons from the south of France only one is a Cypriot hook-tang weapon. That reportedly found at Tour de Trinitaire, Marseille, is not only not a Cypriot hook-tang weapon, but was apparently 'frauduleusement introduit dans ce gisement' (Benoît 1965, 64, no. 108; Jacobsthal and Neuffer 1933, 37; also Bossert 1954, 33: '*keine* cyprische Lanzenspitze', having seen it in Marseille). The dagger from the rock-cut tomb of Bounias at Fontvieille, near Arles (Bouches-du-Rhône) is patently not a hook-tang weapon and has no Cypriot affinities of any kind (Arnal and Latour 1953, 44 and Fig. 9:11; Bill 1973, 18 and Taf. 14, 22). The little knife from Abri 2, Romanin, near St-Rémy, is similarly perfectly at home in its bell-beaker context and innocent of all Cypriot claim (Bill 1973, 18 and Taf. 6, 2). The fourth addition to the list of errors is the weapon reported (at second hand) to have been found in an *allée couverte* at Tertre de l'Église en Plévenon, Côtes-du-Nord (Douillet 1874, 100). It survives only as a 'dessin médiocre' reproduced by Briard (1965, 62 and Fig. 15B). From the poor illustration and the precise description it is clear that it is not a Cypriot hook-tang weapon (Giot 1955, 523 agrees); it has no hook at the end of the tang, which is square in section and pointed, and its faceted blade is unparalleled among all the blades from Cyprus.

Having dismissed those objects wrongly attributed to the class we are still left with a number of genuine hook-tang weapons from various countries, in particular the Plouguerneau and Taillebourg hoards and a number of other single finds from other parts of France, a single weapon from Switzerland, the Csorvás quartet from Hungary, and the Egton Moor weapon from Yorkshire, England. The circumstances of these finds, their contexts and associations, we should now review.

In France the Plouguerneau hoard from Brittany is the most important single 'find' (*Ill. 1*). Besides the seven Cypriot hook-tang weapons there were two flat axes and two 'flesh-hooks', all four of which could well also be Cypriot, and certainly none of the group can be thought to be native to Brittany. The hoard was bought around 1900 by a collector, P. du Chatellier, and is now in the Musée des Antiquités Nationales, St Germain-en-Laye, to whom I am indebted for the drawings from which my illustration is reproduced. Du Chatellier himself, we are told (Déchelette 1910, 195), held doubts about their discovery in an otherwise unrecorded

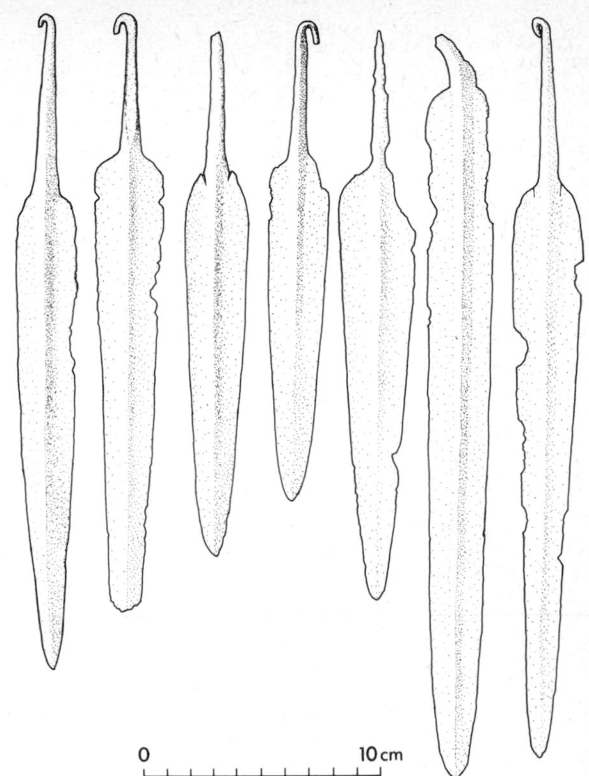

1 Cypriot hook-tang weapons of the 'Plouguerneau hoard'.

tomb; he scarcely mentioned the weapons or their alleged find-spot in an article to which they would have been of fundamental importance if he had believed in them (Chatellier 1903, 172). Déchelette added cryptically but with a certain air of authority (1910, 195): 'nous avons nous-mêmes des raisons de croire que ces objets ont été apportés de la région de Chypre, par quelque matelot breton, à une date récente'. Briard (1965, 62) and, following him, Branigan (1970, 100) argue for the authenticity of the Plouguerneau hoard on two grounds. On the one hand the comparatively more secure provenance of the Plévenon dagger is supposed to compensate for the poor provenance of the Plouguerneau hoard (but we have seen that the Plévenon dagger has little in common typologically with the unprovenanced Cypriot hook-tang weapons); and on the other hand the second argument says that the carvings on the uprights of two Breton *allées couvertes*, at Prajou-Menhir, Trébeurden (Côtes-du-Nord), and Mougau-Bihan, Commana (Finistère) (Giot 1955; L'Helgouach 1957), represent hook-tang weapons

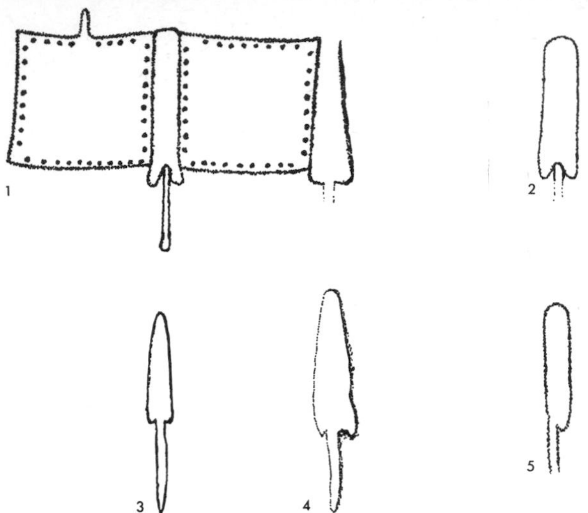

2 Breton rock-carvings alleged to be of Cypriot hook-tang weapons: 1, 2, from Prajou-Menhir; 3–5, from Mougau-Bihan (after L'Helgouach).

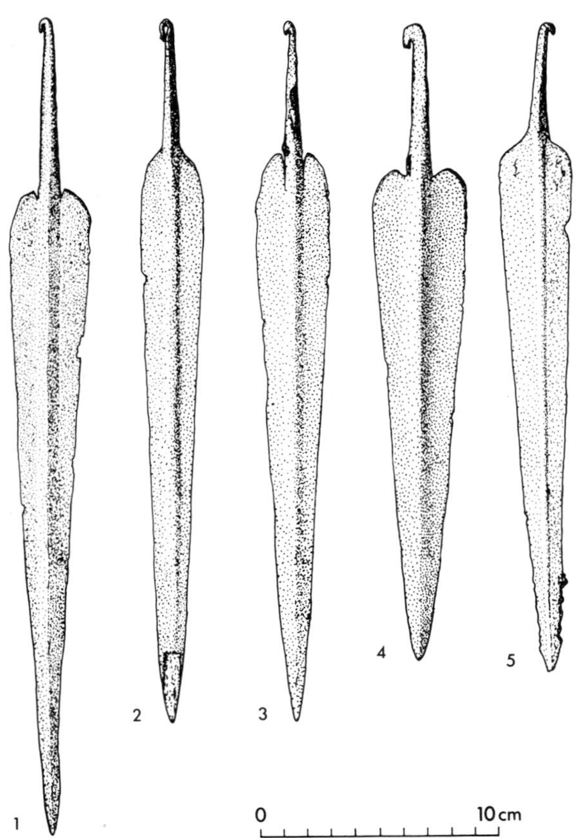

3 1–4, weapons from 'Taillebourg'; 5 from Saintes.

of Cypriot type, thereby demonstrating that the type was known (and therefore had been imported) in ancient times in Brittany (*Ill. 2*).

The difficulty here is in accepting that Cypriot hook-tang weapons are in fact depicted. L'Helgouach argues (1965, 278) that these carvings are of Cypriot hook-tang weapons on three grounds: he says that they look like Cypriot hook-tang weapons, as long as one grants artistic licence to the Prajou-Menhir sculptor; that they are depicted accurately in scale (when in fact they are more than twice life size); and that they compare well in typological detail. It seems to me that juxtaposition of carvings and hook-tang weapons will show clearly enough that there is rather little correspondence of typological detail; most important of all, if we are to believe that the carvings represent hook-tang weapons, where are the hooks on the tangs? And no one has attempted to explain the rectangular objects between the 'daggers'. An argument could more easily be made out that the Prajou-Menhir carvings represent sacred mushrooms. The carvings at Mougau-Bihan (L'Helgouach 1965, 278) may well be daggers or lance-heads, but there is no reason whatsoever to prefer a Cypriot prototype, for they exhibit no Cypriot traits, and no hooked tangs in particular. And so, without the security that might have been afforded by the carvings, and deprived of the association of the Plévenon dagger, whose comparatively more respectable provenance would have been a most useful support, the Plouguerneau hoard itself must once more be consigned to archaeological limbo, recent Cypriot exports not ancient Breton imports.

A second group of Cypriot hook-tang weapons for which a French provenance has been claimed is that said to be from Taillebourg (Gomez and Bourhis 1974 for fuller discussion of the doubts and details, and now Gomez 1974). The group consists of four weapons which are now in the municipal museum at Angoulême, whither they came with the collection of a Dr Lhomme (*Ill. 3:1–4*). The catalogue of Dr Lhomme's collection was missing when the collection was transferred to the museum, and the provenance 'Taillebourg' was attributed on the basis that the objects were wrapped in a piece of paper labelled thus. Later, the catalogue was rediscovered, in which the weapons are shown as having no known provenance. The collection, however, includes a number of pieces of medieval armour from Taillebourg. Incidentally, in the same museum and deriving from the same private collection are two flat axes of unknown provenance, which seem likely to be of Cypriot or Levantine origin, thus increasing the resemblance of this group to the Plouguerneau 'hoard'. Gachina (1972) notes the presence in the region of three further Cypriot hook-tang weapons, but that in the Musée Mestreau at Saintes (Charente-Maritime (*Ill. 3:5*) has lain there a long time and has no known provenance, while a second, in the Collection Lugol at Mansle (Coffyn, Gomez and Bastien 1973), is ascribed to the excavations at Bois-du-Roc, Vilhonneur (Charente) because the object bears that superscription. Gomez (personal communication) has the gravest doubts of this supposed origin, since the records of the excavation, published and unpublished, contain no mention of it.

The fine Early or early Middle Cypriot weapon in the Musée Borély, Marseille, said to have come from Mont Bassan, Auriol (*Ill. 4*), in fact has a very dubious background, and reached the museum from a private collection formed long ago by the brothers Bosq, who bought as well as excavated to augment their collections. I am indebted to M. Jean Courtin for his opinion that 'cet objet ne vient pas d'Auriol. Je pense qu'il s'agit d'une supercherie'. Another Cypriot hook-tang weapon for which a French provenance has been claimed is that from Dricourt, Lorraine, now in the municipal museum at Charleville (Fromols 1938, 161–2; Hawkes 1937, 158). Fromols reported that the weapon was supposed to have been found in 1877, but he was doubtful as to the real existence of the site and its excavation. Once again no record of any such excavation or site survives, and the association claimed for the Cypriot weapon, which would date somewhere between 1650 and 1400 BC, is ludicrous – an Italian fibula which cannot be dated earlier than the middle of the eighth century BC. Finally, a weapon reputed to have been found at Clermont-Ferrand (Puy-de-Dôme), and now in the Musée des Beaux-Arts, Lyon, has recently been drawn into the list of ancient Cypriot imports (Briard 1965, 62). Millotte (1963, 94), however, saw the weapon, and illustrates it simply for the record, remarking nothing beyond its existence in the museum.

Doubtless there are more Cypriot hook-tang weapons scattered through French collections, but to date none has been shown to have an authentic French provenance. Once more we meet the plea 'une telle concentration (in the Charente basin) . . . plaide en faveur d'une provenance française pour une certaine nombre de pieces' (Coffyn, Gomez and Bastien 1973, 138); but surely this is no more than a hope, and one might better argue that when so many objects share a dubious, or even fraudulent, ancestry the only safe conclusion is that one can rely on none of them.

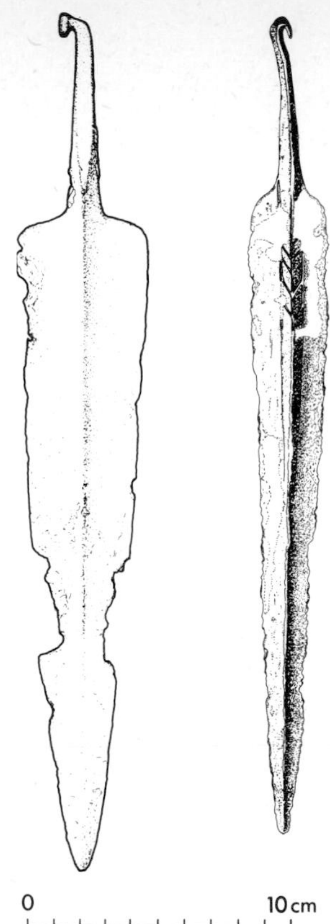

4 Weapon from Mont Bassan, Auriol.
5 Weapon from Egton Moor, Yorkshire.

Among the many Cypriot hook-tang weapons in British museums, that from Egton Moor in Yorkshire (Elgee 1936) is the only one for which the claim of a British find-spot has been advanced (*Ill. 5*). The weapon is in Whitby Museum, and from the museum records and Elgee's note in the local newspaper it can be traced tenuously back through three or four pairs of hands to a date somewhere between 1875 and 1885, when it was supposed to have been found on the moor by a 'lad' herding sheep. Whatever the truth of the origin of the Egton Moor dagger it can hardly be treated other than with some suspicion, noting how well it conforms to the general pattern of mysterious appearances in the late nineteenth century.

The Swiss hook-tang weapon in Bern Museum is a clear Cypriot import (*Ill. 5:5*). It was reported by

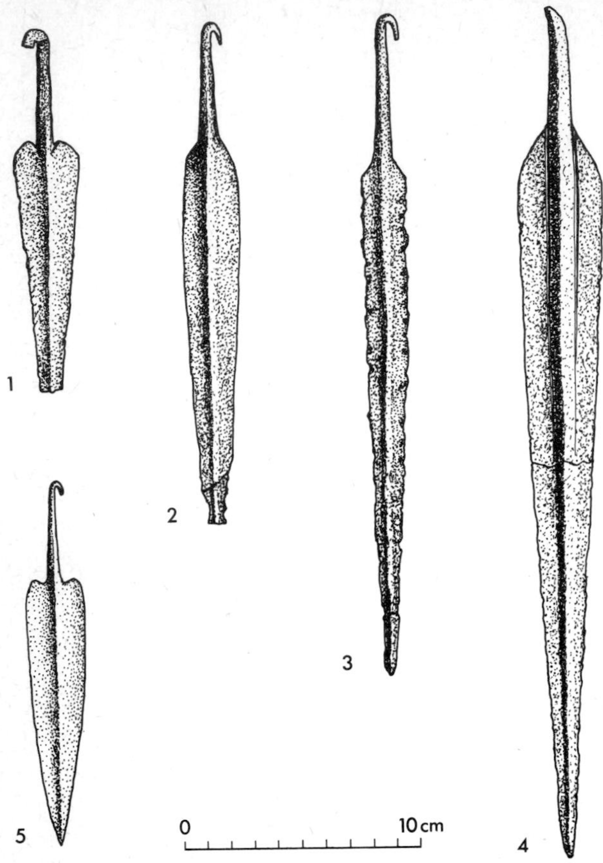

6 1–4, weapons from Csorvás, Hungary; 5, from the River Zihl, Switzerland (1–4, after Pulszky; 5, after Montelius).

Forrer in *Antiqua* for 1885 as having come to Bern among a variety of objects of different materials and dates dredged from the River Zihl. Reinecke (1933, 259) acutely noted that the weapon has the characteristic patina exhibited by many of the bronzes from Cypriot rock-cut tombs. The implication is clear that the weapon lay in a Cypriot tomb for some long time before it reached Bern; whether it came from the River Zihl is of little consequence, for even if it did it is scarcely a context of great usefulness in any argument concerning trade, culture contact or chronology.

The Csorvás weapons (Pulszky 1884, 414 and 416, nos. 3, 5–7; Montelius 1900, 100) were mistakenly counted as three by Davies (1930, 76), who thought the fourth came from Arad. Childe twice spoke of two weapons from Csorvás (Childe 1927, 89; 1929, 218), while Déchelette (1910, 195) equally inexplicably counted five. The primary source is Pulszky, who writes of and illustrates four weapons, all of them undoubtedly Cypriot in origin (*Ill. 6: 1–4*). They were sold to Budapest Museum by the antiquities dealer Kraus, whose name we have already met. According to the information supplied by Kraus they had been found at an un-named and otherwise unknown site near Csorvás. There is no reason to doubt the dealer's word, but the context is in any case not a good one, and again there is nothing known to be associated with them. Like the Plouguerneau hoard, these weapons are supposed to represent a hoard in Europe composed entirely of Cypriot goods with not even a scrap of local pottery or metal-work in association.

And now we may pause to review the evidence so far, before passing on to three general considerations. There are two classes of 'Cypriot dagger' in Europe, a first group of mistaken identities, those that are not Cypriot hook-tang weapons, and a second group which are Cypriot hook-tang weapons, but which have no associations and no secure or satisfactory provenance. Thus in some respects the 'Cypriot daggers' are similar to the Aegean double axes in Britain, recently re-examined by Briggs (1973). The three general considerations concern the lack of context or associations, the supposed typological and chronological homogeneity of the group, and their distribution as viewed from their source, Cyprus.

Concerning the lack of associations of the Cypriot hook-tang weapons little can be said except to remark that even where as many as eleven Cypriot objects apparently occur together in Europe, as at Plouguerneau, they occur without association, an altogether remarkable coincidence. The single exception is the weapon from Dricourt, 'associated' with an Iron Age Italian fibula. On the other hand if one were to suppose that the Cypriot hook-tang weapons were introduced into Europe about the time they appear in the literature (i.e. the late nineteenth century) the lack of associations and reliable provenances would fall into place; and in this context one may note the involvement of a Budapest antiquities dealer, Déchelette's suspicions concerning the Breton sailor, and Hawkes' general musing on the same profession (1974, 210). At the same time we may note how all the weapons have appeared within a certain time range, just the time that Cyprus came under British control, and just the time when wholesale looting, excavation, trading and collecting reached an early peak. In

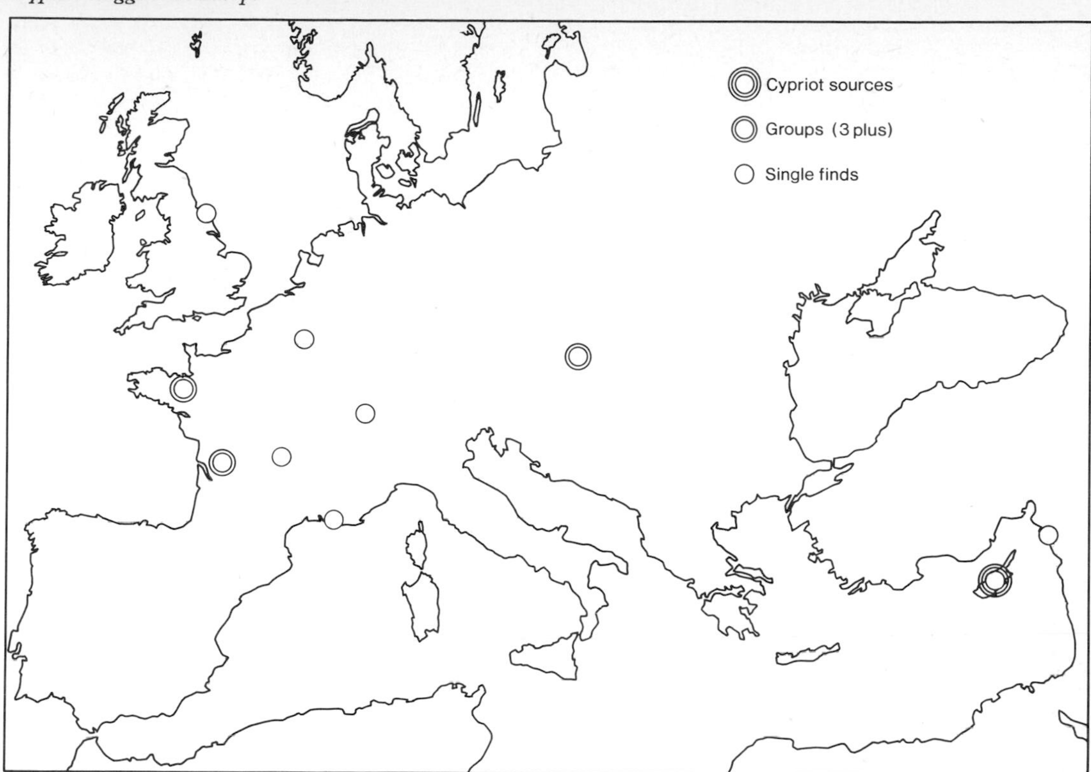

7 Distribution of Cypriot hook-tang weapons claimed as ancient imports.

spite of the ever-growing interest in European prehistory and the ever-increasing number of excavations in most countries of Europe, no Cypriot hook-tang weapon has come to light in an excavated context in this century.

Again, if one started from the idea that these Cypriot hook-tang weapons were modern imports into Europe, one would expect a more or less random selection of types rather than only Late Cypriot I weapons to be represented (cf. Branigan 1970, 105). As it happens the great majority of cemeteries looted and excavated (and at the end of the nineteenth century there was no great distinction in technique) belonged to the later parts of the Bronze Age; Early Bronze Age tombs were excavated in any number only between the two World Wars. Therefore it is no surprise to find that the weapons encountered in European museums and collections come predominantly from the Middle and Late Bronze Ages. There is not space here to enter into detail, but it is not difficult to see that there is a range of typological variation, particularly around the shoulders and root of the tang, among the hook-tang weapons found in Europe. For the sake of brevity let it serve to refer readers to Catling's account of Late Cypriot hook-tang weapons as distinct from those of the earlier phases of the Bronze Age (Catling 1964, cf. Figs. 1 and 2, 12 and 13). As Catling and others have shown there are typological variations of detail, and there are also tendencies for the general proportions of the weapons to change through time: both typologically and proportionally the European hook-tang weapons cover at least the half millennium from 1900 (or even earlier) to 1400 BC. *Contra* Branigan, who would like to see a *floruit* of Cypriot exports into Europe as close as possible to 1400 BC, it may be noted that Catling can only find a handful of hook-tang weapons for the Late Cypriot I period (approximately 1600–1400 BC), for these are the last examples of a long-lived type. Thus, while LC I weapons are found in European collections, Middle Cypriot Bronze Age types are also represented, and we are asked to believe in a trade in Cypriot hook-táng weapons, flat axes and meat-hooks that persisted for at least five hundred years. Moreover, a group like that supposedly from Csorvás contains not only weapons of LC I date, but others which can only be Middle Cypriot; if one accepts the hoard as genuine then one is driven to conclude that traders were handling very assorted goods, some of distinct antiquity it would appear. And at the same time one may wonder what was the demand for obsolete Cypriot flat axes in Europe.

When one considers the distribution map of Cypriot hook-tang weapons of the Bronze Age as a whole (*Ill. 7*), the pattern is indeed a strange one; large numbers of them are known to have been found in tombs in Cyprus, but only one weapon from the whole of the rest of the East Mediterranean can be identified as a Cypriot export, and that from Ras Shamra, ancient Ugarit, on the Syrian coast immediately opposite Cyprus (Schaeffer 1938, 219, Figs. 18 and 23A, Pl. XXII:1). Looking westwards, one finds no Cypriot hook-tang weapon in the Aegean area at any period. There is indeed little reason to expect to find many in the Mycenaean world, for serious Mycenaean contact with Cyprus in general post-dates the end of the hook-tang weapon's history, and in any distribution of these weapons through Europe the Mycenaeans would have had little part to play. In short, the erratic distribution in Europe conforms with no imaginable pattern of ancient exchange; it is, however, consistent with the pattern one might expect to be produced by the activities of modern dealers, collectors, merchants, sailors and travellers at the end of the last century.

There is only a negative and repetitive conclusion to this essay: scholars have already dismissed the Cypriot hook-tang weapons in Europe, and this is but a fuller dismissal. Such a class of objects is of no usefulness in chronological or cultural considerations. It cannot help us to date any phase or horizon in European prehistory, and it cannot be used to tie the ultimate knot in a line of argument that binds Wessex and Mycenae across Europe. Wessex with or without Mycenae is another matter entirely, and perhaps harder to resolve for want of evidence, but a Wessex (and a Europe) without Cyprus is clear and certain.

Bibliography

ÅSTRÖM, P. 1957 *The Middle Cypriot Bronze Age*, Lund.

ANNABLE, F. K. and SIMPSON, D. D. A. 1964 *Guide Catalogue of the Neolithic and Bronze Age Collections in Devizes Museum*, Devizes.

ARNAL, J. and LATOUR, J. 1953 Les monuments et stations néolithiques de la région d'Arles-en-Provence, *Etudes Roussillonaises* III, 27–61.

BENOIT, F. 1965 Recherches sur l'hellenisation du Midi de la Gaule, *Annales de la Faculté des Lettres, Aix-en-Provence* XLIII.

BILL, J. 1973 *Die Glockenbecherkultur und die frühe Bronzezeit im französischen Rhonebecken und ihre Beziehungen zur Südwest-Schweiz*, Basel.

BOSSERT, E.-M. 1954 Zur Datierung der Gräber von Arkesine auf Amorgos, *Festschrift für P. Goessler*, ed. W. Kimmig, Stuttgart, 23–34.

BRANIGAN, K. 1970 Wessex and Mycenae: Some Evidence Reviewed, *Wilts. Arch. Mag.* 65, 89–107.

BRIARD, J. 1965 *Les depôts bretons et l'âge du bronze atlantiques = Travaux du Laboratoire d'Anthrop. Préhist. de la Faculté des Sci.*, Rennes.

BRIGGS, C. S. 1973 Double Axe Doubts, *Antiquity* XLVII, 318–20.

CATLING, H. W. 1964 *Cypriot Bronzework in the Mycenean World*, Oxford.

CHATELLIER, P. DU 1903 Un Âge du Cuivre ayant precédé l'Âge du Bronze a-t-il existé en Armorique? *Revue de l'École d'Anthropologie*, 169–72.

CHILDE, V. G. 1927 The Danube thoroughfare and the beginnings of civilization in Europe, *Antiquity* I, 79–91.

1929 *The Danube in Prehistory*, Oxford.

COFFYN, A., GOMEZ, J. and BASTIEN, J.-M. 1973 L'Âge du Bronze dans la collection Lugol à Mansle (Charente), *Bull. Soc. préh. franç.* LXX, 138–44.

DAVIES, O. 1930 The Copper Mines of Cyprus, *Ann. Brit. School at Athens* 30, 74–85.

DÉCHELETTE, J. 1910 *Manuel d'archéologie préhistorique celtique et gallo-romaine* I:1, 2nd edn, Paris.

DOUILLET, C. 1874 Tumulus du Tertre de l'Église de Plévenon, *Bull. Soc. Arch. Hist. Côtes-du-Nord* VI, 93–103.

ELGEE, F. 1936 A Unique Bronze Dagger, *Whitby Gazette* 27 November 1936.

FROMOLS, J. 1938 Découvertes et communications régionales, *Bull. Soc. Arch. Champenoise* XXXII, 161–2.

GACHINA, J. 1972 Poignard à soie de type 'chypriote' et hallebarde du Musée Mestreau à Saintes (Charente-Maritime), *Bull. Soc. preh. franç.* (*Comptes rendu, séries mensuelle*) LXIX, 283–5.

GERLOFF, S. 1975 *The Early Bronze Age Daggers in Great Britain = Prähist. Bronzefunde* VI:2, Munich.

GIOT, P.-R. 1955 Présence de gravures sur les supports de l'allée couverte de Prajou-Menhir en Trébeurden, Côtes-du-Nord, *Bull. Soc. préh. franç.* LII, 522–3.

GODDARD, E. H. 1912 Notes on Implements of the Bronze Age found in Wiltshire, *Wilts. Arch. Mag.* XXXVII, 92–116.

GOMEZ, J. 1974 La question des poignards chypriotes, dits de Taillebourg, du Musée municipal d'Angoulême. Une affaire classée, *Bull. Soc. préh. franç.* LXXI, 229–30.

GOMEZ, J. and BOURHIS, J. 1974 Les poignards chypriotes, dits de Taillebourg du Musée Municipal d'Angoulême, *Bull. Soc. préh. franç.* LXXI, 49–51.

HAMPEL, J. 1896 Neuere Studien über die Kupferzeit, *Zeitschrift für Ethnologie* XXVIII, 57–91.

HAWKES, C. F. C. 1937 The Double-Axe in Prehistoric Europe, *Ann. Brit. School at Athens* 37, 141–59.

1974 Double Axe Testimonies, *Antiquity* XLVIII, 206–12.

JACOBSTHAL, P. and NEUFFER, E. 1933 *Gallia Graeca: recherches sur l'hellénisation de la Provence = Préhistoire* 2, fasc. 1.

L'HELGOUACH, J. 1957 L'allée-couverte de Prajou-Menhir en Trébeurden, Côtes-du-Nord, *Annales de Bretagne, Notices d'Archéologie Armoricaine* LXIV, 1–8.

1965 *Les sépultures megalithiques en Armorique = Travaux du Laboratoire d'Anthrop. préhist. de la Faculté des Sci.*, Rennes.

MAXWELL-HYSLOP, K. R. 1946 Daggers and Swords in Western Asia, *Iraq* VIII, 1–65.

MENGHIN, O. 1916 Vorgeschichtliche Sammlungen in Niederösterreich, II, *Weiner Prähistorische Zeitschrift* III, 15–23.

MILLOTTE, J.-P. 1963 Matériaux pour servir à l'étude des époques protohistoriques en France centrale. II. Quelques objets inédits de L'Age du Bronze et leur signification, *Revue Archéologique du Centre* II, 91–9.

MONTELIUS, O. 1900 *Die Chronologie der ältesten Bronzezeit in Nord-Deutschland und Skandinavien = Archiv für Anthropologie, Ethnologie und Urgeschichte* = appendix *Zeitschrift für Ethnologie*, Berlin.

PULSZKY, F. 1884 *Die Kupferzeit in Ungarn*, Budapest.

REINECKE, P. 1933 Kyprische Dolche aus Mitteleuropa?, *Germania* XVII, 256–9.

RENFREW, A. C. 1967 Cycladic Metallurgy and the Aegean Early Bronze Age, *American Journal of Archaeology*, LXXI, 1–20.

1972 *The Emergence of Civilization*, London.

SCHAEFFER, C. F. A. 1936 *Missions en Chypre 1932–1935*, Paris.

1938 Les fouilles de Ras Shamra–Ugarit; neuvième campagne (Printemps 1937), rapport sommaire, *Syria* XIX, 193–255.

STEWART, J. R. B. 1962 *The Early Cypriot Bronze Age = Swedish Cyprus Expedition* IV:1A, Lund.

STRONACH, D. 1957 The Development and Diffusion of Metal Types in Early Bronze Age Anatolia, *Anatolian Studies* VII, 89–126.

Acknowledgments

Without the advice and help of many people this essay could not have been written. On the other hand it was written by one hand and I bear responsibility for any views expressed or errors incorporated. I most gratefully acknowledge the help of M. Jean Courtin, Dr Claudine Dauphin, M. José Gomez, Dr Sabine Gerloff, Dr Anthony Harding, Gordon Thomas, and many museum curators, all of whom sought and provided information willingly, and not forgetting Stuart Piggott, who contributed willingly but unwittingly.

16

DAVID AND FRANCESCA R. RIDGWAY

From Ischia to Scotland: Better Configurations in Old World Protohistory

For nearly thirty years, by his example in the field and his teaching in the Edinburgh Department, the illustrious recipient of these pages has been both a source of illumination and a reflector of European light in Scotland. Recently, the authors of the present essay were pleased to receive the following intimation, penned in an unmistakably fair hand:

In ancient Pithekoussai
They frequently invoked the Mousai –
And like me, got friskier and friskier
On the excellent wine of Ischia.

Clearly, ancient Europe was never the same again after the foundation of the first Greek colony in the West: we attempt below to illustrate this momentous episode in terms of certain new (and better) configurations that are currently emerging in European protohistory as a whole. In doing so, we are mindful of Stuart Piggott's own thoughtful summary of the events that came to a head in Italy in the eighth century BC: 'it is not my lack of courage that persuades me to take a position of compromise, and see a complex mixture of indigenous, central and eastern European and oriental elements in the Etruscan people, accumulating over some centuries of trade and other contacts and culminating in a strongly orientalising phase; archaeologically it looks probable and fits more of the evidence than the extreme views' (Piggott 1965, 193). It seems to us that this passage underlines the necessity for a working relationship between exponents of different disciplines: south of the Alps, the protohistorian must explain his paraphernalia of Villanovan tomb-groups, typology and association tables to the ancient historian in terms that the latter is likely to understand, and vice versa. Ideally, the conversation should also include an art historian and a comparative philologist, for in this period even single items can provide grist for more than one mill. The Shipwreck Krater from Pithekoussai, for example, may (or may not) be a valid piece of evidence for one of the possible themes of Attic heroic poetry and its diffusion in the mid-eighth century BC (Webster 1958, 176): it is also a reflection of the hazards of contemporary commercial life encountered by Euboean merchants in the far West ('there *are* sharks in the Mediterranean': Boardman 1973, 166).

The Euboean diaspora to the East (Al Mina at the mouth of the Orontes: *c.* 825 BC) and to the West (Pithekoussai in the Bay of Naples: *c.* 770 BC) is now a fact of life (recent summary with bibliography, not repeated here: Ridgway 1973). The chronological difference (see chart: *Ill. 1*) between the two ends of the network may well turn out to be more apparent than real: Euboeo-Cycladic Middle Geometric pottery, earlier than any so far known from Pithekoussai, is well represented in mainland Campania and southern Etruria; at Veii, it includes two examples of a type that has much in common with the earliest Greek pottery at Al Mina (Ridgway and Dickinson 1973 with Fabbricotti and Healey 1972, 246, Fig. 36: grave AAβγ, 1).

The earliest Euboeans so far found at Pithekoussai arrived with a formidable and fully formed combination of taste, technology and oriental connections. Since 1965, the impressive evidence from their cemetery has been complemented by the excavation of a no less remarkable 'Metalworking Quarter' in the suburban Mazzola district of Lacco Ameno, in use from the mid-eighth to the beginning of the seventh century BC (Buchner 1971; Klein 1972); bronze-working as well as iron-working was involved. There is good reason to suppose that precious metals, too, were weighed out there on the Euboean standard: an appropriate weight has been found, and thus 'jewellery' or 'goldsmiths' workshops' (Strabo *Geography* V, C247 = V. 4. 9) are as archaeologically possible as they are (now) philologically respectable (Mureddu 1972). In addition, the same site has revealed the previously unsuspected existence of a locally produced variety of Euboean Late Geometric figured pottery – of which the Cesnola Krater, recently and independently transferred from Naxos to Euboea (Coldstream 1971), acts as a useful illustrated dictionary of motifs.

The western Euboeans maintained their connections both with the Near East and with the Italian mainland. The 'Lyre-Player Group' seals from north Syria or Cilicia, abundant at Pithekoussai in the third quarter of the eighth century BC, are well known; and so is the Villanovan spiral amphora associated in an LG II tomb with the Early Protocorinthian pottery illustrated most recently by Snodgrass (1971, 93, Fig. 50). But perhaps the best illustration of Pithekoussai as a clearing house for foreign influences, and well before the LG II = Early Protocorinthian period at that, is a recently excavated LG I tomb (provisional no. 944) which contains *inter alia*: (a) a locally made oinochoe; (b) an imported skyphos of the Thapsos class, with panel; (c) a spiral amphora, imported from mainland Italy; (d) an imported aryballos with conspicuous Levantine affinities – and silver fibulas (not yet restored). Taken with the considerable body of supporting evidence, this association underlines the status of the Bay of Naples as the Euboean 'missing link' on the route from the Near East to Etruria; and it shows, too, that the route was in use by the third quarter of the eighth century BC.

Two attempts have been made to evaluate the impact of the commercial and industrial activities at Pithekoussai on the formative stage of the western Euboeans' neighbours in Etruria (Ridgway 1972; Buchner 1973). There can no longer be any doubt that the metal resources of Etruria constituted one of the prime attractions for the first western Greeks. An opponent of this model has asked 'What primary products were the Greeks offering the Etruscans?' (Graham 1971, 45). Interestingly enough, precisely the same question – 'What had Greece to offer in return?' – has also been asked at the other end of the Mediterranean, in a stimulating paper on Cypro-Aegean exchanges in the ninth and eighth centuries BC (Coldstream 1972). Unlike Graham, Coldstream answers his question: 'Greece's greatest contribution to Cyprus during the Geometric period is not at all materialistic. . . . The greatest gift to Cyprus from the Aegean . . . was the diffusion of the Homeric poems in the late eighth century, which inspired the people of Salamis and Paphos to honour their rulers with a manner of burial which recalled in detail the funeral rites already immortalized in the Homeric poems.'

Could not something similar have happened in the West? After all, the 'Nestor Cup' itself (in an LG II tomb at Pithekoussai) and the unstratified 'Ajax and Achilles' seal impression have implications for the circulation of the Homeric poems; so does the fact that early pyres at Pithekoussai were quenched (like Patroclus': *Iliad* XXIII, 255f.) with

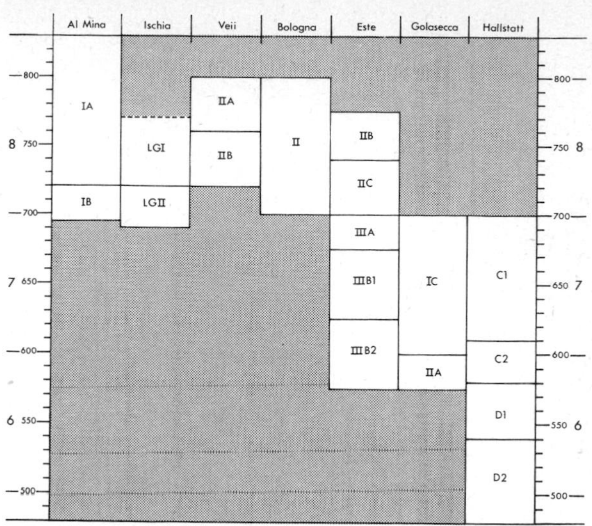

1 Table of chronological periods relevant to the text. (Al Mina: Ridgway 1973, 10; Ischia: LG I covers the earliest material found so far, LG II = Early Protocorinthian (*c*. 720–690, following Coldstream 1968, 327); Veii: Close-Brooks 1967a, 329; Bologna: Müller-Karpe 1959, Fig. 64; Este, Golasecca and Hallstatt: *Studi sulla cronologia*. . ., forthcoming, and Peroni 1973, Fig. 20.)

the contents of local LG I oinochoai, found unbroken and unburnt in many cremation graves. And on the mainland, orientalising chariot burials are currently being excavated at Castel di Decima (inland between Rome and Lavinium), associated in one case with a pair of Thapsos cups, a spiral amphora and an Early Protocorinthian aryballos (Zevi and Bedini 1973). The Pithekoussai-like aspects of this late eighth-century combination in *Latium vetus* are not in fact as surprising as they may have appeared: sherds from Pithekoussan LG I vases have just been recognized among the heterogeneous material yielded by the soundings carried out some years ago in the sacred area of Sant'Omobono in Rome itself. These sherds are not the only wares exported to the mainland from Ischia: the newly discovered Pithekoussan Late Geometric style provides many parallels for 'Cycladic' (Blakeway 1935) decorative ideas in Etruria.

Apart from actual Pithekoussan products, however, it is also instructive to examine the distribution of other people's goods, present *en masse* at Pithekoussai and sporadically in Etruria. The 'Lyre-Player Group' seals are a case in point; another good

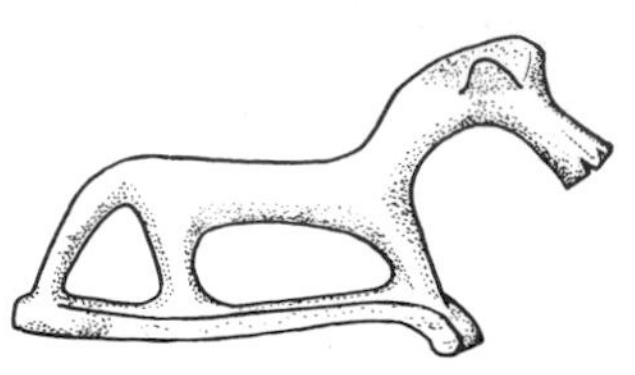

2 1, Bronze horse figurine found near Birkwood, Lesmahagow, Lanarkshire; 2, terracotta mules and cart from Pithekoussai (Ischia), *c.* 635–620 BC.

example is that of the 'Rhodian' – or Near Eastern, or Phoenician? – 'Kreis- und Wellenbandstil' globular aryballoi, collected most recently by Cristofani Martelli (1973, (II) IID, Pl. 33: nos. 1–4). There are about a hundred of them in LG II tombs at Pithekoussai, which must be the source of the four known to us in Etruria. Of these, three – surely too many for a coincidence? – are in highly suggestive contexts:

a. Casaletti di Ceri, tomb 2 (near Cerveteri: Colonna 1968): associated with one of the very earliest Etruscan inscriptions;
b. Tarquinia, Poggio Gallinaro, tomb 8 (Hencken 1968, 346, Fig. 344b): this tomb-group has closer links with Pithekoussai than any other known to us in Etruria;
c. Vulci, Tomba del Carro di Bronzo (Necropoli dell'Osteria, 1965 excavations: Scichilone 1967, 43, no. 56): associated with an exceptionally fine range of local orientalising metalwork.

In the circumstances, there is no need to stress unduly the non-materialistic effects of the earliest Greek presence in the West – tempting though it is to speculate on the probable fate of a Greek bard or schoolmaster who offered an unsolicited recitation at, say, Veii in Villanovan times. The reality is likely to have been comparatively down to earth. The metallurgical purpose in the link between southern Etruria and the earliest and most northerly Greek colony in the West has been expounded elsewhere: it is now time to say that the 'primary product' – Graham's phrase – brought by the first western Greeks to the Iron Age Etruscans was the foundation of the Etruscan orientalising style, fashion, period or phenomenon and all that that implies in terms of exotica, craftsmen and raw materials (including precious metals). Could not, in fact, Etruscan orientalising be to some extent the outward and visible (commercial and *artigianale*) sign of the consolidation in the West of the Homeric/heroic idea, on the model postulated so convincingly for Cyprus by Coldstream? Could not the 'Lyre-Player Group' seals and 'Kreis- und Wellenbandstil' aryballoi be not so much the seeds as the trace-elements of this process? Could not Pithekoussan jewellery or goldsmiths' workshops in Strabo have something to do with the trinkets at Cumae and Veii 'hawked to the natives by Euboean or Cycladic merchants . . . traders with Levantine contacts' (Coldstream 1968, 355), active in Etruria and mainland Campania from the time of the 'pre-colonial' Euboeo-Cycladic Middle Geometric pottery there? The subsequent (if it really was!) foundation of the colony at Pithekoussai would have strengthened the 'Levantine contacts' with Etruria, and could have meant that some of the earlier trinkets were made at Pithekoussai (see much further, Buchner 1973).

In short, the story of the eighth century BC on the Tyrrhenian side of Italy emerges as no less complex than that of Iris Origo's *Merchant of Prato* and his fourteenth-century AD contemporaries: there is no need to look farther afield for ethnographic parallels. Shedding our white coats, we have wallowed in the difference between history and prehistory as defined by a not entirely apocryphal First Year student at Edinburgh: 'in history, people don't have to stay at home and invent everything independently'. Can the result be of any use to the specialist, domiciled in Scotland, whose studies lie in barbarian Europe? One small example must suffice.

A sporadic bronze horse figurine from Birkwood in Lanarkshire (*Ill. 2:1*) has close affinities with those on five of the *Zierbeile* (ceremonial axes) in the Hallstatt cemetery (Scott and Powell 1969). On the most recent analysis of the Hallstatt material, this type (Peroni 1973, 31, Fig. 2:3) is one of a number that make their first appearance in Ha C1 and continue into Ha C2. Of the Hallstatt graves with *Zierbeile* surmounted by horse figurines, in fact, 507 (Kromer 1959, Pl. 99: 2) is Ha C1 while 697 (Kromer 1959, Pl. 127: 4; Scott and Powell 1969, 119, Fig. 1c) and 504 (Kromer 1959, Pl. 94: 2) are Ha C2. The examples from graves 329 (Kromer 1959, Pl. 55: 15) and 734 (Kromer 1959, Pl. 147: 15a-b; Scott and Powell 1969, 119, Fig. 1b) do not have enough associations to win a place on Peroni's invaluable *Tabella delle associazioni*: such associated pieces as they have, however, do not suggest any significant divergence.

Not the least important feature of Peroni's stimulating contribution to Hallstatt chronology is the fact that it appears in the wake of excellent work carried out under his supervision in the circum-Adriatic area (Lo Schiavo 1970), in the north Tyrol (Fugazzola 1971) and – particularly relevant for our present purposes – in the area covered by a major collective volume of *Studi sulla cronologia delle civiltà di Este e Golasecca* (in press). We are therefore treated to authoritative typological correlations between Ha C1 and Este III A, III B1, the early part of III B2 and most of Golasecca I C; Ha C2 is synchronized with the greater part of Este III B2, the rest of Golasecca I C and most of Golasecca II A (Peroni 1973, 55, Fig. 14 and 57, Fig. 15 for the fifty-two relevant Este and Golasecca types; 67, Fig. 20 for comparative chronological table; text, 52–8). The associations of the finest and most informative of the Hallstatt *Zierbeile*, namely that from grave 697 – an 'elegant production portraying a distinctive breed of small horse' (Scott and Powell 1969, 120) – are a case in point; they include examples of:

(a) the Ha C2 *Mehrkopfnadel mit Faltenwehr* (Kromer 1959, Pl. 127: 1, 2): cf. the Este III B2 *spillone con capocchia a globetti e costolature tipo Benvenuti* (Peroni 1973, Fig. 14: 12);

(b) the Ha C2 *profilierte Spitzenschutz* of one of the above (Kromer 1959, Pl. 127: 1): cf. the Este III B2 *puntale di spillone tipo Rebato* (Peroni 1973, Fig. 14: 14);

(c) the Ha C2 – D2 *Deckel mit eingenietetem, profiliertem Knauf* (Kromer 1959, Pl. 128: 1): cf. the Este III B2 and Golasecca II A *coperchio di situla con presa a corolla* (Peroni 1973, Figs. 14: 16 and 15: 14);

(d) the Ha C2 – D2 *Situla* (*'an doppelten Attaschen sind 2 gewundene Tragreifen angebracht . . .'*: Kromer 1959, Pl. 128: 7): cf. the Este III B2 and Golasecca II B *situla con doppia ansa mobile ed attacchi ad anello* (Peroni 1973, Figs. 14: 15 and 15: 20);

(e) the Ha C1 – D2 *Situla aus mehreren Teilen zusammengenietet* (Kromer 1959, Pl. 128: 5, 6): cf. the Este III B2 – III C *grande situla a collo distinto tipo Franchini* (Peroni 1973, Fig. 14: 20).

The Este and Golasecca sequences (full particulars in *Studi, cit.*) have been defined and dated in their turn by comparison with the material from the Bologna cemeteries and the peninsula. The synchronisms between the Bologna sequence and those in southern Etruria are well attested from Müller-Karpe's (1959) Bologna I onwards; for Veii, Dr Close-Brooks (1967a, 327) has noted the presence of two Bologna II fibulas – of a type that is also characteristic of Este II B – in grave AA 12A of the Quattro Fontanili cemetery (Cavallotti Batchvarova 1965, 72, Fig. 13n). This Veii grave is assigned by Dr Close-Brooks to the initial stages of her local period II A (*c.* 800–760 BC) – precisely the period which sees the arrival at Veii of the 'pre-colonial' Euboeo-Cycladic Middle Geometric pottery referred to at the beginning of this paper, and the associated sudden awareness there of metallurgy. In addition to the Bolognese fibulas, in fact, Quattro Fontanili AA 12A also yielded a Villanovan bronze belt (Cavallotti Batchvarova 1965, 70, Fig. 11) of a type that apparently reached Euboea (Close-Brooks 1967b).

All of which provides yet another illustration of a golden rule: 'All the accepted system of dates, Greek and Italian, historical and archaeological, is interdependent . . .' (Dunbabin and Hawkes 1949, 142). Since this has brought us to Veii, let us examine the context there of the small horse-tripod (Hencken 1957, Pl. 3, Fig. 10; Scott and Powell 1969, 119, Fig. 1d, see our *Ill. 3: 1*) mentioned by Professor Powell in connection with the Birkwood horse.

The piece was found, securely associated, in Grotta Gramiccia grave 785 – one of 1200 graves excavated at Veii between 1913 and 1916 and still unpublished. As it happens, chronologically valuable data about some of the associated pieces in this particular tomb have long been available. They combine to show that the date – 'reasonably consistent with the first half of the seventh century' – proposed by Hencken and accepted by Powell is much too low. The pieces in question are two painted skyphoi (Blakeway 1935, 196, note 1; Müller-Karpe 1962, 29; Gjerstad 1966, 326, note 2; Ridgway 1967, 313) and a painted plate (Blakeway *loc. cit.*; Hencken 1957, Pl. 3, Fig. 11). These three pieces suggest

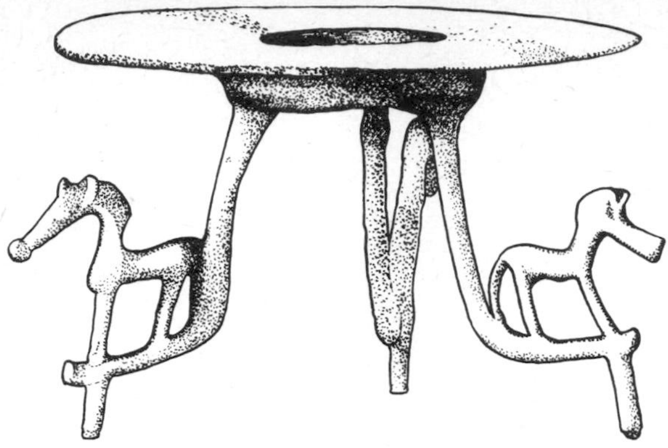

3 1, Bronze horse tripod from Veii (Period IIB), Grotta Gramiccia tomb 785; 2, Pithekoussan LG I horse panel: restored (after Klein).

very strongly that Grotta Gramiccia 785 falls into Dr Close-Brooks' Veii II B (*c.* 760–720 BC) – a date that also fits the only other published items from the grave: variants of von Hase's 'Veji-typus' of horse-bit (von Hase 1969, Pls. 16: 182–3 and 17: 184). In other words, the horse-tripod cited by Powell (mainly as an indication of the kind of mounting the Birkwood horse might originally have had) is now found to be a product of the metallurgical boom initiated in Etruria in the first half of the eighth century BC by the first western Greeks. LG I at Pithekoussai – we have seen that a major source of its distinctive new figured style is the 'Metalworking Quarter' there – has roughly the same chronological range as Veii II B: and the contact between the two areas at this time is symbolized by the contents of Pithekoussai tomb 944.

One of the more frequent and characteristic motifs of the Pithekoussan LG I style is a virtually heraldic representation of a horse (*Ill. 3: 2*). Clearly, it would be rash to jump to any hasty conclusion based on stylistic resemblances – length of muzzle, stiffness of mane, type of tail – between two contemporary renderings in different media. The really important fact is that the Pithekoussai LG I and the Veii II B horses demonstrate knowledge of the sprightly Greek horse – 'probably with Levantine blood' (Scott and Powell 1969, 122): cross-breeding at Al Mina? – and western capacity to produce it in bronze by the middle of the eighth century BC.

However, a more closely contemporary parallel for the horses on the Hallstatt *Zierbeile* and for their Scottish cousin may be cited, also from Pithekoussai. The rescue excavation of a votive deposit there, dated *c.* 635–620 BC by its Transitional and Early Corinthian pottery, has produced a number of locally made terracotta mules and carts (*Ill. 2: 2*). Stylistically, and in spite of the difference in medium, these surely do have much in common with the Transalpine examples: the heads are large in proportion to the body; the necks and the tails are long; the manes are stiff; the ears are pointed; the muzzles are expanded; the mouths are indicated by transverse slits; a position of stubborn arrest is indicated by the forwards-sloping forelegs.

The latter feature in particular may, of course, be no more than an expression of independently acquired perversity common to the small steppeland horse and to the south Italian *ciuccio*. If, however, this *sconclusionato discorso* has a conclusion, it is this: the fact that late seventh-century representations of ill nature in small equids on both sides of the Alps have anything in common at all is a result of contacts made not only 'in the night-clubs of Sparta' (Scott and Powell 1969, 124) but also – and nearly a century and a half earlier – in those of Ischia.

Bibliography

BLAKEWAY, A. 1935 Prolegomena to the study of Greek commerce with Italy, Sicily and France in the eighth and seventh centuries BC, *Ann. Brit. School at Athens* 33, 1932–3 (1935), 170–208.

BOARDMAN, J. 1973 *The Greeks Overseas* (2nd edn), Harmondsworth.

BUCHNER, G. 1971 Recent work at Pithekoussai (Ischia), 1965–71, *Archaeological Reports for 1970–71*, 63–7.

1973 Nuovi aspetti e problemi posti dagli scavi di Pithecusa con particolari considerazioni sulle oreficerie di stile orientalizzante antico. Paper read at the Centre Jean Bérard, Naples, in Autumn 1973; forthcoming in *Contribution à l'étude de la societé et de la colonisation eubéene.*

CAVALLOTTI BATCHVAROVA, A. 1965 Veio-Quattro Fontanili: quarta campagna di scavo, *Notizie degli Scavi*[8] 19, 65–155.

CLOSE-BROOKS, J. 1967a Considerazioni sulla cronologia delle facies arcaiche dell'Etruria, *Studi Etruschi* 35, 323–9.

1967b A Villanovan belt from Euboea, *Bulletin of the Institute of Classical Studies* 14, 22–4.

COLDSTREAM, J. N. 1968 *Greek Geometric Pottery*, London.

1971 The Cesnola Painter: a change of address, *Bulletin of the Institute of Classical Studies* 18, 1–15.

1972 Cypro-Aegean exchanges in the ninth and eighth centuries BC, *Praktika tou protou Diethnou Kyprologikou Synedriou* A[1] (Nicosia), 15–22.

COLONNA, G. 1968 *s.v.* 'Caere', *Rivista di Epigrafia Etrusca = Studi Etruschi* 36, 265–71.

CRISTOFANI MARTELLI, M. 1973 *Corpus Vasorum Antiquorum – Gela: Museo Nazionale.*

DUNBABIN, T. J. and HAWKES, C. F. C. 1949 Review-discussion of *Der Geometrische Stil in Italien* (Å. Åkerström: Lund-Leipzig, 1943), *J. of Roman Stud.* 39, 137–42.

FUGAZZOLA, M. A. 1971 Contributo allo studio del 'gruppo di Melaun-Fritzens', *Annali dell'Università di Ferrara* (sez. XV) 2, 1–141.

GJERSTAD, E. 1966 *Early Rome IV: Synthesis of archaeological evidence*, Lund.

GRAHAM, A. J. 1971 Patterns in early Greek colonisation, *J. of Hellenic Stud.* 91, 35–47.

HENCKEN, H. 1957 Horse tripods of Etruria, *American Journal of Archaeology* 61, 1–4.

1968 *Tarquinia, Villanovans and Early Etruscans*, Cambridge, Mass.

KLEIN, J. 1972 A Greek metalworking quarter: eighth century excavations on Ischia, *Expedition* 14:2 (Winter), 34–9.

KROMER, K. 1959 *Das Gräberfeld von Hallstatt*, Florence.

LO SCHIAVO, F. 1970 Il gruppo liburnico-japodico: per una definizione nell'ambito della protostoria balcanica, *Memorie della Accademia Nazionale dei Lincei*[8] 14, 363–523.

MÜLLER-KARPE, H. 1959 *Beiträge zur Chronologie der Urnenfelderzeit nördlich und südlich der Alpen*, Berlin.

1962 *Zur Stadtwerdung Roms*, Heidelberg.

MUREDDU, P. 1972 χρυσεῖα a Pithecussai, *Parola del Passato* 27, 407–9.

PERONI, R. 1973 *Studi di cronologia hallstattiana*, Rome.

PIGGOTT, S. 1965 *Ancient Europe from the beginnings of agriculture to classical antiquity*, Edinburgh.

RIDGWAY, D. 1967 'Coppe cicladiche' da Veio, *Studi Etruschi* 35, 311–21.

1972 Rapporti dell'Etruria meridionale con la Campania: prolegomena pithecusana, in *Aspetti e problemi dell'Etruria interna* (= *Atti dell'VIII Convegno Nazionale di Studi Etruschi ed Italici, 1972*, Florence (1974), 281–92).

1973 The first Western Greeks: Campanian coasts and southern Etruria, in (eds.) C. and S. Hawkes, *Greeks, Celts and Romans*, London, 5–38.

RIDGWAY, D. and DICKINSON, O. T. P. K. 1973 Pendent semicircles at Veii: a glimpse, *Ann. Brit. School at Athens* 68, 191–2.

SCICHILONE, G. 1967 La tomba del carro di bronzo di Vulci, in *Arte e Civiltà degli Etruschi* (exhibition catalogue: Turin), 25–44 (cat. nos. 24–56).

SCOTT, J. G. and POWELL, T. G. E. 1969 A bronze horse figurine found near Birkwood, Lesmahagow, Lanarkshire, *Antiq. Journ.* XLIX, 118–26.

SNODGRASS, A. M. 1971 *The Dark Age of Greece*, Edinburgh.

VON HASE, F.-W. 1969 *Die Trensen der Früheisenzeit in Italien* (= *Prähistorische Bronzefunde* 16:1), Munich.

WEBSTER, T. B. L. 1958 *From Mycenae to Homer*, London.

ZEVI, F. and BEDINI, A. 1973 La necropoli arcaica di Castel di Decima, *Studi Etruschi* 41, 27–44.

Acknowledgments

We are grateful to Giorgio Buchner (Ischia) for much discussion of the Pithekoussan end of this story, and for supplying *Ill. 2:2* and the original (Klein 1972, 38, Fig. 4) of *Ill. 3:2*; to Eugenio La Rocca (Rome) for permission to refer to the unpublished Pithekoussan material from Sant'Omobono; to T. G. E. Powell (Liverpool) and J. G. Scott (Glasgow) for their courtesy in supplying Margaret Scott's original drawings of the horse from Birkwood (*Ill. 2:1*) and of the horse-tripod from Veii (*Ill. 3:1*: after Hencken 1957, Pl. 3, Fig. 10). As stated in the text, *Studi sulla cronologia delle civiltà di Este e Golasecca* is in the press: the authors are R. Peroni, G. L. Carancini, P. Coretti Irdi, L. Ponzi Bonomi, A. Rallo, P. Saronio Masolo and F. R. Serra Ridgway.

17

ANTONIO ARRIBAS

A New Basis for the Study of the Eneolithic and Bronze Age in South-east Spain[1]

[1] I am indebted to my friend Derek Simpson of the University of Leicester for inviting me to England in March 1975, an occasion which provided the impetus for this paper. My original Spanish and subsequent English texts were kindly read by Jon C. van Leuven and Derek Simpson respectively.

The starting point for the study of the Bronze Age in south-east Spain goes back to the second half of the nineteenth century when Louis and Henri Siret began excavations in the north of the province of Almería; from Almizaraque and Herrerías they extended their investigations throughout the province of Almería, reaching the River Andarax where Louis Siret excavated the famous settlement of Los Millares. In the north he went as far as the region of Mazarrón-Lorca in the province of Murcia. In the west he explored the region of Guadix-Fonelas-Baza in the province of Granada, but not in the plain (*Vega*) of Granada, nor to the south-west; the area of Jaen remained practically unexplored.

Louis Siret published several works (1890; 1893; 1907), but much unpublished material was incorporated by G. and V. Leisner (1943) in a corpus of megalithic chamber tombs entitled *Die Megalithgräber der Iberischen Halbinsel.* This study deals, however, with only part of the problem of the Eneolithic-Bronze Age in south-east Spain, taking account of only one aspect of the cultural complex – the tombs themselves and their funerary ritual. In this period there was hardly any other published evidence of the prehistory of the area, apart from isolated studies by individual archaeologists with no economic backing and lacking real teamwork. These efforts, however, give us some idea of the occupation of this area at the time of the first metallurgists.

In the First National Congress of Archaeology, held at Almería in 1949, the necessity was expressed for wider investigation using modern methods of archaeological excavation. As a result excavations were begun in the Eneolithic settlement of Tabernas (Almería), under the direction of Professor Julio Martínez Santaolalla, but unfortunately the site has not been published. Investigations in the Bronze Age settlement of La Bastida de Totana (prov. Murcia) followed; without a good stratigraphy, it was impossible to establish a cultural and chronological sequence. After this excavation Professor Santaolalla turned to the Eneolithic settlement of El Campico de Lebor (Totana, prov. Murcia) (Santaolalla 1947). Since 1953, Professor Almagro and the author have re-excavated the necropolis of Los Millares (Santa Fé, Almería) as well as its contiguous settlement (Almagro and Arribas, 1963).

The settlement at Los Millares revealed much information, including the now well-known fortification wall with bastions and round houses in the interior. After these discoveries, knowledge of peninsular Eneolithic-Bronze Age settlements was expanded with work by Sangmeister and Schubart at Vilanova de São Pedro and Zambujal in Portugal and at Lébous in France.

In the 1950s in Granada, a group formed around the Provincial Archaeological Museum by the Swiss J. Christian Spahni, the archaeologist M. Pellicer and the anthropologist M. García Sánchez, decided to re-excavate the megalithic chamber tombs of the region of Gor-Gorafe (García Sánchez and Spahni 1959; García Sánchez 1963; cf. G. and V. Leisner 1943). M. Pellicer presented his stratigraphic sequence from the Neolithic to the Bronze Age based on his excavations at Cueva de la Carigüela (Piñar, Granada) (Pellicer 1964) and later at Cueva de Nerja (Málaga) (Pellicer 1963). To this may be added the work of Professor Mergelina in Montefrío in the 1930s and of Professor M. Tarradell in the 1940s in Montefrío itself and in Monachil, which is referred to below. In 1965 Beatrice Blance produced the first ordered and scholarly study of all this material for her doctoral thesis on the beginning of metallurgy in the Iberian Peninsula, published in 1971.

Other archaeologists have been working in the same area. M. Almagro and Manuel Pellicer have re-excavated at Almizaraque (Almería). Maria Josefa Almagro has published her excavations at the necropolis of El Barranquete (Almería), which has tholoi very similar to those of Los Millares (M. J. Almagro 1974). F. Gusi has opened several trenches in the settlement of Tabernas (Almería).[2] Ana

[2] Two C14 dates shed some light on the unpublished recent excavations by F. Gusi. A date of 3420 bc suggests a very early Eneolithic occupation. A date of 2080 bc may belong to the upper levels of the Beaker horizon.

Maria Vicent and Ana Maria Muñoz have published the results of their excavations in the stratified cave of Los Murciélagos de Zuheros (Córdoba), which have given a satisfactory number of C14 dates for the so-called 'Cave Culture' (Vicent and Muñoz 1973; Hopf and Muñoz 1974, 9–27).[3] The most interesting work, however, has been the excavation by Professor Wilhelm Schüle in two settlements in the north of the province of Granada: Cerro de la Virgen (Orce) (Schüle 1967a, b; 1969b; Schüle and Pellicer 1966; Kalb 1969) and Cerro del Real (Galera) (Schüle 1968; 1969a, b; Schüle and Pellicer 1964; Pellicer and Schüle 1966; von den Driesch 1972, 8–12).

In *Cerro de la Virgen* (*Orce*) three main phases have been identified, beginning with the Eneolithic and ending in the Early Bronze Argaric period. *Period I* is represented by a settlement with large round huts of mud brick, covered with a dome like a tholos. The huts follow the tradition of the simple huts of the lower layers, normally constructed of posts and wattle and occasionally oval in plan. The settlement had a fortified wall, as at Los Millares; a special feature is an artificial irrigation system (the first identified in Spain). This first period may be compared with Los Millares I, Vilanova I and Zambujal I.

Period II represents a cultural decay with the appearance of the Beaker Culture. Houses are circular in plan and built in mud brick; they are smaller and of cruder construction than those of the previous period. In this period the fortification wall collapsed. Pottery follows the previous tradition but with this Beaker phase wrist guards (*Armschutzplatten*) and V-perforated buttons of ivory begin to appear.

In *Period III* beakers disappear but wrist guards and V-perforated buttons are predominant. Burials are now below the floors of the settlement. In sub-phase IIIA the burials are all in pits but in IIIB they are in both pits and pithoi. In IIIB the classic Argaric cup appears, together with objects of silver (gold is very rare) which are known from IB onward. The plans of huts in this phase are difficult to ascertain, being built of organic material with mud but without posts. They were, however, probably round or oval.[4] Just as with the architectural traditions, it is interesting to see how the ceramic tradition continues throughout the life of the settlement, evolving in a slow and gradual way. It is certain that some types of the lower levels disappear, especially those of better quality, and that the beakers appear and disappear in the same manner as with the typical cups.

Cerro del Real (Galera, prov. Granada) provides a cultural and chronological sequence following on from that of Cerro de la Virgen (Orce). The lower Late Bronze Age levels (Real I) belong to a post-Argar phase, hitherto almost unknown, and continue the ceramic and architectural traditions of Cerro de la Virgen. The settlement of Real I is relatively large (500 × 200 m); the huts are of mud-brick construction, circular or oval in plan with an average diameter of 12 m. They do not appear to have been domed, but have vertical walls, being roofed with esparto grass laid on wooden rafters. The mud-brick walls are plastered, and in some cases have a low internal bench running all round. The many thin layers of plaster on the walls and floors indicate prolonged occupation. They are very different to the rectangular and juxtaposed houses of the Argar period in Almería. The material shows some continuity with the Eneolithic and Argar levels of Cerro de la Virgen. It is evident that there are gradual changes and some earlier forms disappear – for example, hemispherical cups and carinated vessels with high neck. Carinated bowls and burnished dishes with everted rim are abundant and of good quality, unknown since the Beaker phase at Cerro de la Virgen. Two intrusive and exotic sherds of dark pottery, painted in red and yellow, are best paralleled at Monachil. Schüle thinks they are 'indigenous imitations' of the eastern pottery of El Carambolo (Lower Guadalquivir). There is a sherd of Cannelee pottery typical of the urnfields of Catalonia and southern France at the beginning of

[3] Several C14 dates between 3980 bc and 4345 bc belong to layers IV and V, related to the 'Cave Culture'. Agriculture is attested by the presence of *Triticum diccoccum* (Emmer), *Triticum aestivum* and *Hordeum vulg.*; domestication by *Bos*, *Ovis* and goat, and to a lesser extent, pig (Hopf and Muñoz 1974).

[4] There are five C14 dates for the Beaker levels between 3920 BP and 3800 BP. The date (GRN-5594) for Argar A is 3735 ± 55 BP which is archaeologically acceptable, unlike the single date for Argar B (GRN-5595): 3865 ± 50 BP. The date for Argar B in Cerro de la Virgen is calculated by Schüle as *c.* 1500 bc (Vogel and Waterbolk 1972).

the first millennium BC. Among coarse wares, the number with flat bases increases and large vessels with protuberances are typical. At the end of this phase there are some sherds of stroked pottery, also indicating contact with the area of the Lower Guadalquivir.

Unfortunately the location of the cemetery belonging to this phase is unknown. The conservatism of these settlements is reflected in pottery and architecture, although metal tools and weapons show a certain degree of technological development. Schüle believes that in these settlements one must take into account not only the Eneolithic tradition but also other roots from the Eastern and Central Mediterranean and from Atlantic Europe. Although these phases of the post-Argar Bronze Age are in some ways archaic, on the other hand they reflect contact with, and influence from, other metallurgical centres. This phase (5/6 m deep) had a long and slow development; but at the end it shows a sharp change.

The new phase (Real II), or 'Proto-Iberian', was a short one (judging by its total stratification of less than half a metre); in it appears a quite different pottery form, a wheel-turned, well-fired burnished ware painted with red lines. The origin of these new wares lies in the Phoenician colonies on the coast of Málaga and Granada.

Phase III corresponds to the typical Iberian Age, shown by the classic Iberian pottery painted with horizontal lines thinner than before, semicircles, wavy lines and so on, so well known in the south of Spain.

Since 1966, when the Department of Prehistory at the University of Granada was founded under the author's direction, the principal aim has been to create a team of archaeologists to embark on a systematic study of the period from the Eneolithic to the Late Bronze Age in the area of eastern Andalusia. The prime research tasks were:

1) to select the potentially most rewarding settlements,
2) to excavate them carefully and scientifically.

As a centre for this programme Granada had several points in its favour:

1) the proximity to the settlements,
2) the possibility of establishing a regional stratigraphic sequence for the sites,
3) the launching of a long-term programme unhindered by the need to produce spectacular results.

The following is a résumé of the work carried out by the Department since 1968 in the three main settlements that have been chosen for the purpose of providing the basis of a synthesis of the region from the Eneolithic to the Bronze Age. The settlements are: Cerro de la Encina at Monachil, Los Castillejos at Montefrío and Cuesta del Negro at Purullena, whose stratigraphy covers the period from the Neolithic of the 'Cave Culture' to the Late Bronze Age.

Cerro de la Encina is a hill situated near the River Monachil, about 3 km from Monachil village at an altitude of 870 m, and about 7 km from the town of Granada. Life in the river valley shares the characteristics of the Granada depression and the Penibetic, the valley extending along the slopes of the Sierra Nevada. The shape of the upper terrace of Cerro de la Encina is that of a plateau (*meseta*) with a sharp drop on the south facing the river. In the east the slope is more gentle. In the north-west the plateau faces a deep gorge produced by the erosional effect of the River Monachil. The top of the upper terrace dominates the view of the outflow of the river into the plain (*vega*) of Granada, providing a route to the west between two hills which form the end of the series of mountains bordering the plain.

The name of Monachil appeared in archaeological literature as early as 1921 when D. Juan Cabré opened two tombs excavated below the calcareous and conglomerate rock on the slope of the Cerro (Cabré 1922). In one of the tombs there were remains of four skeletons while in the smaller of them were the remains of two skeletons. Cabré drew the pots and other objects found in them and showed them to be of Argaric type.

In 1946 Tarradell decided to restudy the settlement with the object of examining the settlement un-noticed in the earlier work. In the small trenches he dug, bed rock was reached at 40/50 m, but only sherds of pottery were found without association structures. Discouraged, he thought that erosion and cultivation had completely destroyed the settlement (Tarradell 1947–48).

Since 1968 the Department of Prehistory of Granada, under the direction of the author, has been carrying out excavations almost every year until 1973, with, in some years, two or three campaigns in spring and autumn. Trenches excavated from 1968 until 1973 in Cerro de la Encina at Monachil (prov. Granada) have provided a broad picture of this settlement, and established a stratigraphical sequence. The elaboration of this stratified sequence will, it is hoped, provide the basis for the interpretation of future excavations in other settlements in south-east Spain.

Study of the structures and parallels for the

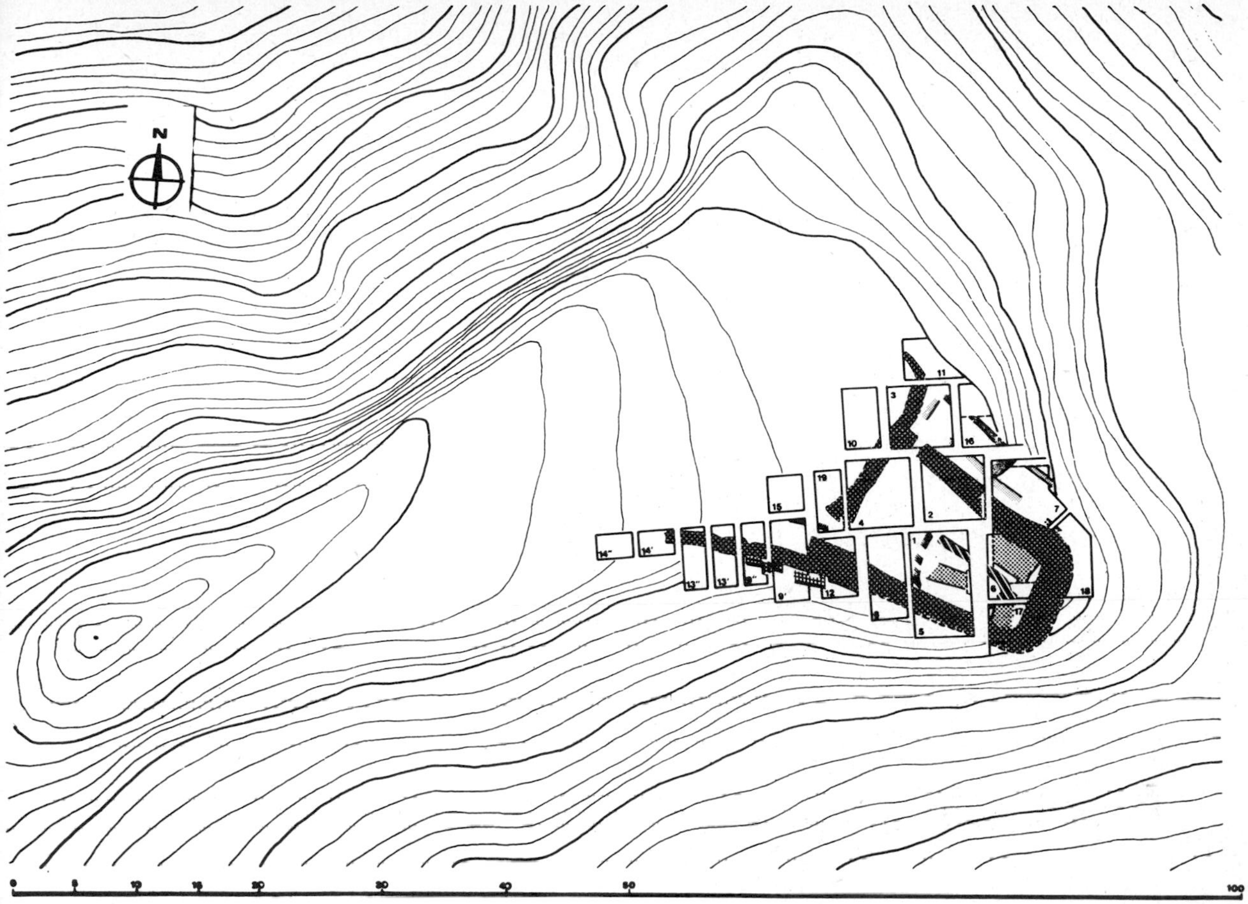

material have established three phases of the settlement. Phase I, barely represented in some of the trenches, belongs to an early stage of Argar B. The structures belonging to this phase are built directly on virgin soil, although in other areas of the settlement traces of even earlier structures have been found. The walls of the settlement are wide, built with stones bonded with grey clay; a special feature consists of post-holes on both sides of the wall and strengthened with stones.

Phase II, dated between 1200 and 1000 bc, belongs to the climax of Argar B. Structures include a broad rectangular building with an apsidal end which is termed the 'bastion'; it has two post-holes. The walls are very thick, with stones bonded with light brown clay and plastered with red clay, and in some cases they had to be reinforced with short parallel walls in the areas of greatest destruction. The tradition of the post-holes at both sides of the walls continues. After a fire, the structures of phase IIa collapsed; the ruins were razed

1 Plan of trenches opened at Cerro de la Encina, Monachil (prov. Granada). Total length of scale 100 m.

2 View of the excavations at Cerro de la Encina, looking north-west.

and the floors levelled at a higher position than before. An external area served partly as a refuse dump. New interior walls show that occupation continued during phase IIb, until the final abandonment and gradual collapse of the stone walls. It is difficult to say how much time lapsed between the abandonment and the re-occupation during Phase III.

Phase III shows a radical change in the system of building, pottery and in the economy of the settlement. The earlier inhabitants based their economy mainly on horse, and to a lesser extent on sheep, goat cattle and pig. Now sheep and goat are more numerous, with smaller quantities of cattle and pig; the horse is virtually absent.

Above the ruins of the Argaric 'bastion' were built huts of mud brick or wattle and daub; the insides of the wall were covered with yellow-white stucco, decorated with grooves forming geometric patterns; the rooves were thatched. The few small finds typical of the central Meseta (pottery decorated with stab and drag, excisions, incisions and pointillé), of the Ebro valley (specific forms of loom-weights, and the use of stucco) and lower Andalusia (pottery with geometric burnished patterns) suggest changing patterns of trade rather than population movement. This last phase must be dated between 1000 for its beginning and 700 bc for its end when there appeared wheel-turned Phoenician pottery from workshops on the Mediterranean coast.[5] These wares are found in the surface layers of the settlement and provide a chronological horizon.

The settlement of *Las Peñas de los Gitanos* is situated 7 km from the village of Montefrío (prov. Granada). The 'Peñas', extending about 2 km in an east-west direction, are formed by a series of gorges, terraces and canyons, contrasting with the rounded hills in the valley. The prehistoric settlement is situated on the upper terrace (100 × 20 m) at an altitude of 1000 m, with steep cliffs on three sides. The easiest approach is from the west.

In the 1930s excavations were conducted by Professor Mergelina who was able to locate traces of an Iberio-Roman settlement, but he did not excavate beneath this period (Mergelina 1942; 1946). He excavated the megalithic necropolis in the area, however, and from the metal tools was able to demonstrate that the tombs continued in use until the Argaric period.

In 1946–47 Tarradell opened a long trench along the major axis of the terrace and exposed the stratigraphy to bed rock. He also excavated in several caves in the area but was unable, in the short time available, to locate any structures other than a short line of stones which could belong to the Bronze Age (Tarradell 1952).

With the aim of finding the types of structures of Eneolithic and Bronze Age date we began to open several trenches in the spring of 1971; these were continued in the summer of 1974. Trench 1 was finished in 1974 and has so far provided the most comprehensive stratigraphical sequence:

I) The basal levels (VI, Vc) can be related to the 'Cave Culture'; the most characteristic vases are hemispherical bowls and *ollas* (spherical bowls) with narrow mouths. Decoration includes incisions (long, short, radiated, crossed lines, parallel lines, and so on). Characteristic are two large spoons, one with a massive handle, the other with a vertical handle like that of a tea cup. There are also sherds of almagra painted pottery; one fragment has a dark painted angular band on a light ground. The flint assemblage has a high percentage of nuclei and some trapezes, giving the impression that this is a local industry.

II) A transitional phase to the Eneolithic is represented by levels Va and Vb. Along with the usual hemispherical bowls and the *ollas*, the characteristic shape of this phase is a large flat dish. Decoration follows the earlier tradition. There are also clay horns, polished stone axes and adzes, and large, coarsely flaked flint knives. Several vases can be related to the Almerian Culture (conical and carinated globular forms). In 1974 several fragments of maritime Beakers were found.

III) An Eneolithic phase is represented by levels IVb and IVa. Typical pottery forms are part- and hemispherical bowls, associated with dishes with broad rims and some carinated forms. All were undecorated with the exception of a single sherd of painted 'almagra' ware. There were large numbers of clay horns, bone awls (*punzones*) and concave-based flint arrowheads, while in 1974 Beaker sherds were found associated with bone conical buttons and also fine clay horns, but thinner than normal and burnished.

IV) A transitional phase is represented by level III; the typical flat dishes have disappeared and large storage jars characteristic of levels II and IA make their first appearance. Some Beaker sherds were also found in this level in 1974.

V) Levels II and I both produced part- and hemi-

[5] A C14 date for phase IIa of 3625 + 40 BP (GRN-6634) appears to be too high in my opinion.

spherical bowls, carinated vases and *ollas* with undulating rim and large storage jars, both carinated and smooth profiled. Flint sickle blades are common. A small knife of copper also comes from this level.

It appears that this phase shows an evolution from the lower levels into a new stage which, although not containing typical Argaric material, is, as in the case of Cerro de la Virgen, contemporary with it.

The conclusions and interpretations based on this excavation of this settlement may be summarized as follows:

1) The original settlement appears to have been a rock shelter (100 m long and 20 m wide), protected on the north by an enormous rock wall and on the south by a steep cliff facing the valley.

2) The archaeological deposits are up to 4 m deep with few stone structures (except in the Ibero-Roman levels), this earth deposit resulting from the decay of huts constructed of clay and organic material, although a number of Eneolithic huts do have stone foundations.

3) The population of Las Peñas de los Gitanos was very conservative, judging by the thick transitional levels Va and Vb, (from the Cave Culture to the Eneolithic) and level III (from the Eneolithic to the Early Bronze Age). This conservatism is also seen in the long retention of certain pottery forms and their decoration (as in the so-called 'almagra' ware). This conservatism must relate to the site's marginal position in relation to the cultural foci of Almería (Los Millares, El Argar).

4) Some pottery forms and metal artifacts certainly reflect contact with these centres. Thus in levels

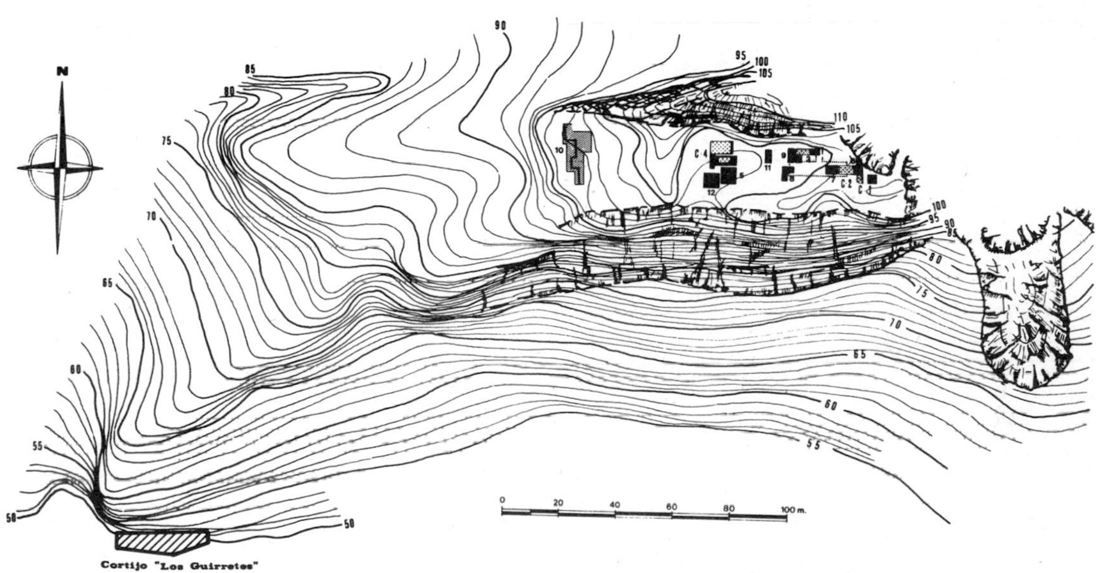

3 Plan of Las Peñas de los Gitanos, Montefrío (prov. Granada).

4 Trenches 4, 5 and 12 at Las Peñas de los Gitanos.

Va and Vb pots are found typical of the Neolithic Almerian complex, here in the context of the Cave Culture. The presence of Beakers in levels IVA, IVB and III also demonstrates contact with other cultural regions.

5) The most insular phase appears to be that of levels II and I. There is no real Argaric pottery to show influences from outside the region. Rather it is characterized by the presence of large storage jars (as in Cerro de la Virgen, Orce).

6) The same conservatism is apparent in the tombs. The only known tombs were those of the megalithic necropolis containing 'Argaric' material. At the end of the 1974 season we were able to locate shaft graves in the levels belonging to the Cave Culture and those of the transition to the Eneolithic. Future excavation of this area is planned. It is possible that the megalithic chamber tombs were built during the Neolithic-Eneolithic and continued in use until Early Bronze 'Argaric' times.

7) Detailed ecological information must await the reports of Peter Uerpmann on the animal bones and of Dr Maria Hopf on the cereals.

8) The C14 samples have been sent to the laboratory of Gronigen.

The settlement of *Cuesta del Negro* is situated near the village of Purullena, about 50 km north-east of Granada.[6] It is located in the south-west of the region of Hoya de Guadix, one of the most characteristic areas of all east Andalusia. It consists of a high plateau with an altitude of 1000 m, partly eroded by the rivers along it and bordered by a great belt of mountains (Sierra Nevada, Baza, El Mencal and Harana). In some places the mountains are cut by deep canyons which provide access to Almería and the Upper Guadalquivir.

The landscape is one of the most spectacular in all of Spain; the network of rivers rising in the Sierra Nevada have eroded the Quaternary deposits to produce the landscape of 'badlands' characteristic of this zone. In the centre of the depression are a series of deep and elongated gulleys (*hoyas*). One of these gulleys is that formed by the River Fardes; Cuesta del Negro is situated in one of these canyons which opens to the plain of that river. The climate is clearly continental (long, cold winters and short, hot summers) due to the altitude and the belts of mountains which inhibit maritime influence. Purullena has no more than 300 cubic mm of rain annually, very irregularly distributed. As a result the typical vegetation is scrub, composed of thyme, rosemary and esparto.

The settlement is situated in the border between the depression of the River Fardes and the high plateaux formed by an elongated band 300 m wide, part of a landscape of badlands extending for several kilometres on a natural route from the River Fardes to the uplands. The settlement is strategically placed both from the point of view of suitable arable land and of pasture for stockraising, with several springs in close proximity. It extends 500 m from east to west, and 130 m from north to south. The bed rock is formed by a mixture of alternating levels of conglomerates and sands of Quaternary age.

The settlement of Cuesta del Negro has two clearly defined cultural phases.

I) The lower levels correspond to Argar B and can be dated from their archaeological content between 1400/1300–1000 BC. In the 3–4 m depth of these levels there are several superpositions of huts cut in the virgin soil. They are more or less circular in plan with diameters of 3–4 m. These rock-cut huts must have had timber walls, as is suggested by the numerous thin organic layers. The floors of the Argaric levels have a marked slope. Graves were found beneath the hut floors in the form of an excavated pit with a chamber at a lower level. Sometimes the pit (*pozo*) is wide and the chamber small; or the reverse may be the case. The contracted burials lay on a bed of esparto grass and have various orientations. There are cases of double burials of a man and woman and one example of a jar burial, the body being that of a child less than one year old. Ritual activities are represented by the lighting of fires in the burial chamber, and the covering of the bones with red ochre.

The local evolution of pottery forms is apparent from a study of the contents of successive levels. In the lower levels vases and bowls with high carinations appear. These carinated vases represent at least 20 per cent of the pottery; there are a very few cups typical of Argar. The upper levels show a different development: the carination of vases and bowls is set low on the body, lenticular bowls appear and the number of pedestal cups increases. Grave goods normally consist of carinated pots, bowls and pedestal cups, copper bracelets and earrings and some beads of stone and shell. There is a small tronco-conical piece of gold.

[6] Excavations at this site by the Department of Prehistory at Granada in 1971–73 were directed by Fernando Molina and Enrique Pareja.

II) The upper levels belong to the Late Bronze Age. A tentative date for them would be 1000–700 BC. The settlement of this period covers an area roughly 200 × 100 sq. m. There are at least four superpositions of houses with different orientations. The houses are rectangular in plan and their average size is 7 × 4/5 m. The stone foundations are preserved to a height of 0.50–1 m; these cut Argaric levels and are sometimes sunk into the virgin soil in order to level the floors. Occasionally they are rock cut. The stone walls are bonded with clay, without any revetment. Slight post-holes occasionally occur in the interior. The roofs were of flat wattle-and-daub construction, in some cases with wooden rafters. Little is known of the internal fittings, but one house had a small semi-circular enclosure of clay, set close to the wall, within which were found large storage jars (one containing wheat) and flat querns.

Half the pottery is coarse but the remainder is very carefully made. The most common shapes are large flat dishes, tronco-conical and carinated, and small flat-bottomed carinated vases, also with high carination. About 5 per cent of the pottery is decorated with excision (*Kerbschnitt*), 'stab and drag', furrows arranged in pendant semi-circles combined with 'barbed wire' lines, and triangles and bands filled with pointillé. This pottery is very similar to that from the settlements of the central Meseta (El Berrueco, for example).

Unfortunately it has not been possible to locate the cemetery (as in Monachil, Purullena, Cerro del Real) belonging to this phase of the Late Bronze Age, which would help considerably in determining the physical nature of these new settlers.

A special feature of this settlement is the presence of a bastion and a fort, probably defensive in function.

The bastion is located in the central part of the terrace, dominating the area. It is built of stone (in a similar way to the 'bastion' of Monachil) and mud brick. Its plan is apsidal and in the 30–40 cm deep stratigraphy it was possible to identify several occupation layers, including a level with burning and the subsequent collapse of the stones of the fortification. From the material found it appears that the fort was built in the Argaric period and that its destruction took place at the end of this period.

The fort about 500 m away, has the highest strategical position, dominating the surrounding area and providing a defence against possible attack from the uplands. It was built during the Argaric period in the same technique as the bastion, and has post-holes inside the wall. It was rebuilt during the Late Bronze Age, re-using some features and adding others, thus modifying the earlier plan slightly.

The study of the animal bones has been undertaken by Dr Hans Peter Uerpmann (Institute of Archaeology, Tübingen) and the human bones by the Laboratory of Physical Anthropology, Granada. Samples of organic material for C14 dating have been sent to the Laboratory at Groningen. A programme of dating of the three settlements by means of thermoluminescence is being carried out by the Research Laboratory for the History of Art and Archaeology at Oxford.

Addendum

Results of C14 tests on several samples from Montefrío and Purullena were received in the summer of 1975 from the Laboratory of Groningen. This preliminary note gives a date of *c.* 1865 bc for Montefrío level II, corresponding to the Early Bronze Age. For Purullena a date of 1645 bc has been obtained from one of the graves of early Argar B (phase I) which agrees with the date given for early Argar B at Monachil (1635 bc). Two dates (1120 and 1185 bc) from the last period of a Late Bronze Age house at the same settlement are too high if we tentatively place the beginning of the Late Bronze Age in Almería *c.* 1000 bc (Sangmeister 1967). The five C14 dates now available for the three settlements agree fairly well in themselves but not, however, with results from previous archaeological studies throughout south-east Spain. This is a problem requiring future discussion.

Bibliography

ALMAGRO, G. M. J. 1974 El poblado y la necrópolis de El Barranquete (Almería), *Acta Arq. Hisp.* 6.

ALMAGRO, G. M. 1974 Cincuenta nuevas fechas para la prehistoria y la arqueologia peninsular, *Trabajos de Prehist.* 31.

ALMAGRO, M. and ARRIBAS, A. 1963 El poblado y la necrópolis megalíticos de Los Millares, *Bibl. Praehist. Hisp.* III.

BLANCE, B. 1971 Die Anfänge der Metallurgie auf der Iberischen Halbinsel, *SAM* 4.

CABRÉ, J. 1922 Una necrópolis de la Primera Edad de los metales en Monachil, Granada, *Mem. Soc. Esp. Antrop. Etnogr. y Preh.* I.

DRIESCH, A. VON DEN 1972 Ostarchäologische Untersuchungen auf der Iberischen Halbinsel, in Studien über frühe Tierknochenfunde von der Iberischen Halbinsel, 3, *Deutsches Arch. Inst. Abteilung Madrid*, Munich, 8–12.

GARCIA SÁNCHEZ, M. 1963 El poblado argárico del Culantrillo, en Gorafe (Granada). *Arch. Preh. Levantina* X, 69–96.

GARCIA SÁNCHEZ, M. and SPHANI, C. 1959 Sepulcros megalitícos de la región de Gorafe (Granada), *Arch. Preh. Levantina* VIII, 43–114.

HOPF, M. and MUÑOZ, A. M. 1974 Neolitische Pflanzenreste aus der Höhle Los Murciélagos bei Zuheros (prov. Córdoba), *Madr. Mitt.* 15, 9–27.

KALB, F. 1969 El poblado del Cerro de la Virgen de Orce (Granada), *X Congr. Arq. Nac., Mahón*, Zaragoza.

LEISNER, G. and V. 1943 *Die Megalithgräber der Iberischen Halbinsel*, Berlin.

MARTINEZ SANTAOLALLA, J. *et al.* 1947 Excavaciones en la ciudad del Bronce Mediterraneo II de la Bastida de Totana (Murcia), *Informes y Memorias de la Comisaria Gral. de Exc. Arq.* 16.

MERGELINA, D. DE 1942 La estación arqueológica de Montefrío (Granada), 1°: Los dólmenes, *Bol. Sem. Arte y Arq. Univ. Valladolid.*

1946 La estación arqueológica de Montefrío (Granada), 2°: La acropoli de Guirrete (Los Castillejos), *Bol. Sem. Arte y Arq. Univ. Valladolid.*

PELLCER, M. 1963 Estratigrafia prehistórica de la Cueva de Nerja, *Exc. Arq. en España* 16.

1964 El Neolitico y el Bronce de la Cueva de la Carigüela de Piñar, *Trabajos de Preh. del Sem. Hist. Prim. del Hombre* 15.

PELLICER, M. and SCHÜLE, W. 1962 El Cerro del Real, Galera (Granada), *Exc. Arq. en España* 12.

1966 El Cerro del Real, Galera (Granada), *Exc. Arq. en España* 52.

SANGMEISTER, E. 1967 Die Datierung des Rückstroms der Glockenbecher und ihre Auswirkung auf die Chronologie der Kupferzeit in Portugal, *Palaeohistoria* XII, 395–407.

SCHÜLE, W. 1967 El poblado del Bronce Antiguo en el Cerro de la Virgen de Orce (Granada) y su acequia de regadio, *IX Congr. Arq. Nac. Valladolid*, Zaragoza, 113–121.

1967 Feldbewässerung in Alt-Europa, *Madr. Mitt.* 8, 79–99.

1968 Fauna del Bronce y Hierro en Orce y Galera (Granada), *Papeles del Lab. de Arq. de Valencia* 5, 5–7.

1969a Die prähistorische Siedlung auf dem Cerro del Real, in Studien über der frühe Tierknochenfunde von der Iberischen Halbinsel, I, *Deutsches Arch. Inst. Abteilung Madrid*, Munich.

1969b Tartessos y el hinterland, in *V Sympos. Internac. de Preh. Penins. Jerez de la Frontera, 1968*, Barcelona, 15–32.

SCHÜLE, W. and PELLICER, M. 1964 Excavaciones en la zona de Galera (Granada), *VIII Congr. Arq. Nac. Sevilla-Málaga 1963*, Zaragoza, 387–392.

1966 El Cerro de la Virgen, *Exc. Arq. en España* 46.

SIRET, L. 1893 L'Espagne préhistorique, *Rev. des Questions Scientifiques*, October.

1906 Orientaux et Occidentaux en Espagne aux temps préhistoriques, *Rev. des Questions Scientifiques*, October.

1907 Orientaux et Occidentaux en Espagne aux temps préhistoriques, *Rev. des Questions Scientifiques*, January.

SIRET, L. and E. 1890 *Las primeras edades del metal en el Sudeste de España*, Barcelona.

TARRADELL, M. 1947–48 Investigaciones arqueológicas en la provincia de Granada, *Ampurias* 9–10, 223–36.

1952 La Edad del Bronce en Montefrío (Granada). Resultados de la excavaciones en yacimientos de las Peñas de los Gitanos, *Ampurias* 14, 49–80.

VICENT, A. M. and MUÑOZ, A. M. 1973 La Cueva de los Murciélagos, Zuheros (Córdoba), 1969, *Exc. Arq. en España* 77.

18

T. G. E. POWELL†

South-western Peninsular Chariot Stelae

† Terence Powell died on 8 July 1975 after a brief illness. The text remains as originally submitted and has been seen through the press by the Editor.

THOSE singular monuments of Peninsular prehistory, the decorated slabs of the south-west, have claimed wide interest since their first recognition at the end of the nineteenth century. Not only are the *estelas decorades* informative about a phase of Peninsular prehistory in its own right, but they also convey inferences, perhaps direct lessons, for larger European issues. Attention has more especially been focussed on the dead warrior's equipment: the outlined sword and shield, sometimes but not invariably of Carp's-Tongue and V-notch types, the spear, helmet, and other rather less determinate objects. The whole material has been splendidly brought together by Almagro (1966), and the present lines are deeply indebted to his foundations for the following up of certain problems that may contribute to that fuller appreciation for which he has laboured. In seeking to honour Stuart Piggott, who has so illuminated the path of exploration in European prehistory, the wheeled vehicles depicted on some of these stones are paraded with an invitation to consider more closely what was intended in the ancient wheelwright's shop, and the funerary tradition that prompted their inclusion among the adjuncts of the dead warrior.

Of the forty-one stones classified by Almagro as *estelas decoradas*, it is necessary to exclude sixteen high-relief carvings of his *tipo alentejano*, and of the remaining twenty-four stones, all *de tipo general*, only six display vehicles. A carved stone from Substantion, Montpellier, in the south of France, is listed by Almagro, and is certainly related, but while showing a V-notch shield, spear, and a row of three disconnected wheels, it does not contribute directly to the present enquiry. A discovery of major significance was, however, made in 1968 at Ategua, 20 km south of Córdoba, and this brings the present total of vehicle carvings in the Peninsular south-west to seven. An important paper on the Tartessian panorama in eastern Andalucía by Blanco Freijeiro, Luzón Nogué, and Ruiz Mata (1969), gives a first account of work in progress at the 'oppidum' of Ategua, and the discovery of the decorated stone at the exterior foot of a substantial stone wall which surrounds a settlement with houses of rectangular plan. The pottery of this settlement includes hand-built incised ware, and fragments of Phoenician amphorae. It is believed that this defended settlement was the work of an intrusive element in the population of Andalucía who were active in the exploitation of metal, and maintained long-distance relations with Phoenician, and possibly other, colonies on the south coast. It would appear that the decorated stone should be accepted as a funerary memorial to one of the chieftains who had ruled within the wall probably about the turn of the eighth and seventh centuries BC.

Not only is this stone the first of the decorated stelae to have been found in such an archaeological context, but the quality and precision of work in presenting the whole funerary scene is far in advance of the designs revealed on previously discovered stones. The stele from Ategua goes far to elucidate the question as to what type of vehicle was really intended on the other stones, quite apart from opening new issues about the origin of the iconography as a whole. The Ategua stele has also been published by J. Bernier (1969) whose line-drawing clarifies the composition (*Ill. 1*).

The stele from Ategua is complete. It measures 1.60 × 0.80 × 0.30 m, and appears to have stood upright with a pointed butt in the ground. The broad face of the stone shows, on the upper part, a schematized human figure with circular shield lying to left, and short sword, spear, probable belt-clasp, and unidentified circular object ('roundel') all lying to right. Below the warrior's side-turned feet is a small, apparently prone, figure laid crosswise, and below this figure is a small rectangle filled with obliquely drawn lines. To the left of the rectangle is a headless four-legged animal with tail executed in single line, and to the right is a small human figure, standing or lying horizontally, below which is another schematic animal. The lower face of the stone is occupied by a two-wheeled vehicle with attendant figures. The plan of the vehicle is carefully outlined, and consists of a rectangular floor with semi-circular front. The axle-beam is marked, and the two wheels each have four spokes. The pole runs through as a single line from the rear edge of the floor to the yoke which is represented as a line joining a pair of headless animals providing traction. Beyond the curved front of the vehicle, the pole is flanked by a pair of lines that spring from the double edge outline of the body or 'basket'. At the rear corners, the body is provided with a pair of loops that can easily be understood as hand-holds or guards widely portrayed on chariots of varying date around the Eastern Mediterranean. It remains to note the large presiding functionary standing behind the vehicle, and with arm outstretched to it, and the two groups of hand-holding participants standing below.

That this vehicle is a version of the *biga*, as understood in Greek contexts, is the opinion of Blanco Freijeiro and his co-authors (1969, 161), and it would be difficult to press any other interpretation. This is an important point as it goes far to

1 Stele from Ategua, Córdoba. Ht. 1.60 m. (after Bernier).

2 Comparative table of warrior's adjuncts carved on south-western Peninsular stelae with chariots.

	Ategua (Córdoba)	Torrejon del Rubio I (Caceres)	Fuente de Cantos (Badajoz)	Solana de Cabañas (Caceres)	Cabeza de Buey (Badajoz)	Cortijo de Cuatro Casas Carmona (Sevilla)	Valencia de Alcantara II (Caceres)
Vehicle	×	×	×	×	×	×	×
Sword	×	×	×	×	×	×	×
Shield	×	×	×	×	×	×	×
Spear	×	×	×	×	×	—	—
Helmet	—	—	×	—	?	—	—
Bow and arrow	—	×	—	—	—	×	—
Fibula	—	×	—	×	×	—	—
Belt-clasp?	×	—	×	—	—	—	—
'Roundel'	×	×	×	×	×	—	—
Additional human(s)	×	—	—	—	—	—	—
Additional animals	×	—	—	—	—	—	—
Total	8	7	7	6	6	5	3
Catalogue and map nos. (Almagro, 1966)	—	xxiv (30)	xli (20)	i (29)	xix (22)—	xxxii (1)	xxxvi (35)

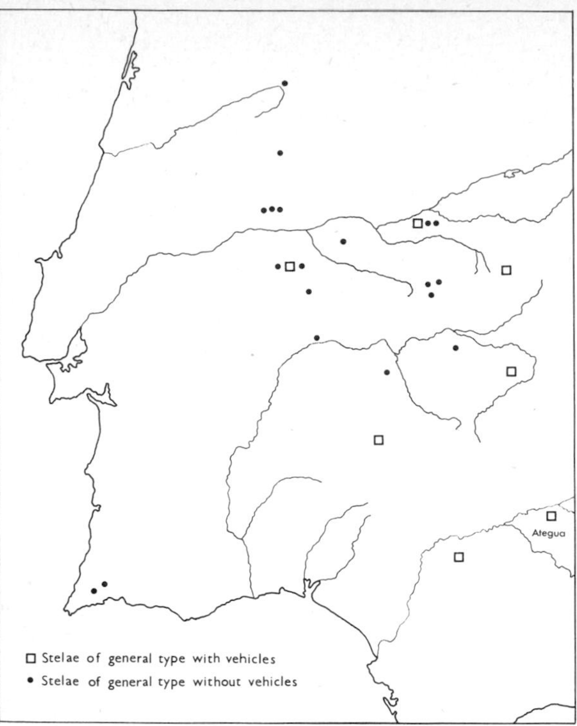

3 Map of stelae of Almagro's general type.

resolving the question as to whether any of the vehicles within the group of *estelas decoradas* were intended to possess more than two wheels. Some misunderstanding on this point has occurred in the past, and has perhaps led to cultural inferences of too definite a kind. The stele at Ategua is the most easterly as yet discovered, so that it was thought worthwhile to consider first those geographically nearest to it, to see if there was any line of stylistic deterioration from nearest to farthest among those stelae showing vehicles. This does not emerge, but it can be said that the six stelae published by Almagro hang together in their infantile drawing more than do any of them with the Ategua stele. A simple analysis of the representation of adjuncts shows that Ategua scores 8 points, followed by two with 7, two with 6, and two with 5 and 3 respectively (*Ill. 2*). Some stones are more damaged than others, and have almost certainly lost various carved items, but it can be seen that the inventory of equipment is very consistent for vehicles, sword, shield, and spear, throughout the whole territory involved. This territory is somewhat smaller than that of all stelae of Almagro's general type, and lies south of the Tagus, and east of the Portuguese frontier within the provinces of Córdoba, Sevilla, Badajoz, and Carceres (*Ill. 3*). The position of the vehicle in relation to that of the warrior on the face of the stone is not more formalized than that of other adjuncts, but at least two lie up and down the stone, to one side of the warrior, while the rest lie across the foot as in the case of Ategua. The absence of a warrior on two of the stones leaves any decision to rest on factors of shape and space available, just as shape and space determine that other stelae were never intended to display a vehicle, or a warrior, but only a selection of weapons.

The question of wheels may now be confronted (*Ill. 4*). In all cases a pair lie on either side of the approximate mid-point of the vehicle, and in four cases the axle-beam is drawn in a correct relative position, but in only two examples is it extended to the centre of the wheel. Only two cases show spoked wheels, the rest being open circles, in one instance with a dot at centre. The stone from Solana de Cabañas shows an additional pair of wheels springing from the pole well in front of the body of the vehicle and touching the draught animals' rumps. These wheels are closer together than the other pair, and must surely be regarded as an initial error in execution of the design. They could not easily be erased, and have thus become the principal witness in arguments for a four-wheeled vehicle or waggon. The rear loops on this vehicle are over-large and stick out like ears, but although such loops on other vehicles have been accepted as wheels no one has pressed a case for a six-wheeled vehicle at Solana de Cabañas. In the light of the evidence furnished by this stele, backed by that of Ategua, it is suggested that the interpretation of the remaining vehicles as possessing only one pair of wheels need not be laboured. In English terminology these all can be accepted as 'chariots': light two-wheeled vehicles normally drawn by a pair of matched horses, in other words *bigae* as already suggested by the excavators of Ategua for their own. Not much can be said about the drawing of the horses if such they were intended to be. Heads are hardly attempted, and are generally absent. Yoke traction was certainly intended. The drawing of the animals as if lying flat, like the wheels, is generally accepted as a primitive convention widespread in the Old World, yet in late European prehistory it mingles with a style of drawing that is clearly intended to convey a side view of horses under yoke, and probably in motion. Of this latter style of portrayal may first be instanced the incised chariot frieze on a pottery vessel from a cremation burial of an early phase of

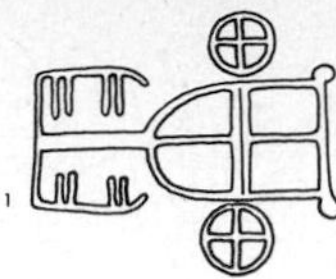

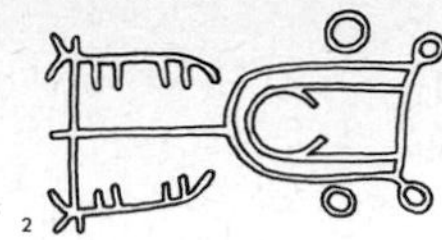

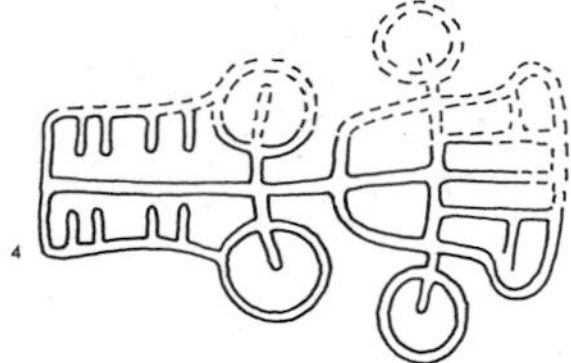

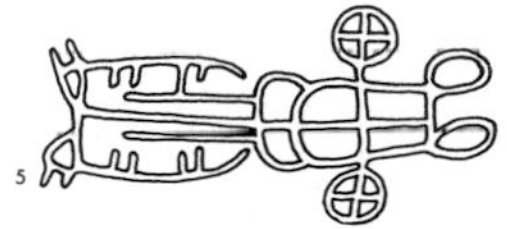

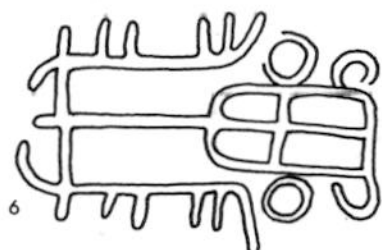

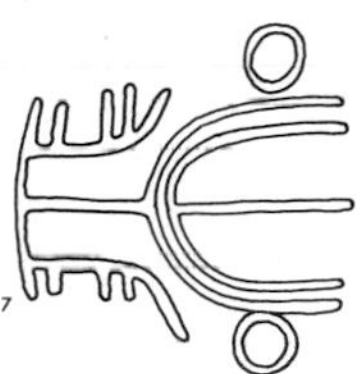

4 Comparative outlines of chariots (not to scale): 1, Ategua; 2, Torrejón del Rubio; 3, Fuente de Cantos; 4, Solana de Cabañas; 5, Cabeza de Buey; 6, 'Cuatro Casas' Carmona; 7, Valencia de Alcántara II (1, after Bernier; 2–7, after Almagro).

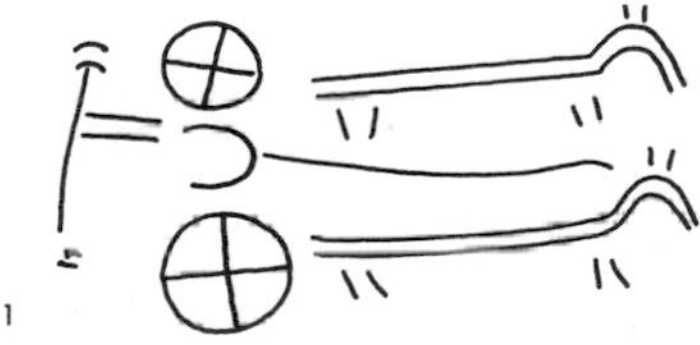

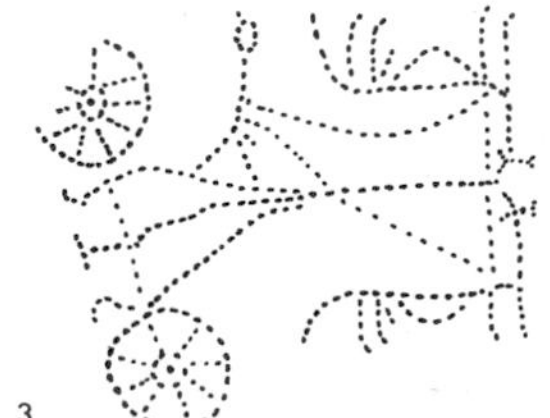

5 Men and horses in relation to vehicles on some funerary urns: 1, Vel'ke Raškovce, Slovakia; 2, Sopron-Burgstall, north-western Hungary; 3, Rabensburg, Lower Austria; 4, Darslub, Pomerania.

the Piliny Culture at Vel'ke Raškovce in Slovakia (Vizdal 1972), and the famous chariot slab from Kivik, Skåne (Powell 1966, Ill. 157; Sandars 1968, Pl. 188). These are both likely to date some five centuries earlier than the Peninsular stelae, but much closer in time must be the side-view funeral processions on two of the urns from Sopron-Burgstall (Gallus 1934, Pls. II:4 and VI:1). Side-view depictions of horses drawing four-wheeled vehicles are known from a number of Face Urns of the East Pomeranian group of the Lusatian Culture (La Baume 1928; 1950), Almagro (1966, Fig. 78c) has illustrated an example from Elsenau, and another from Darslub emphasizes a wider position in funerary vehicle iconography (*Ill. 5:4*). A seeming instance of compromise is given by the dot-incised chariot and pair on the shoulder of an urn, of Bernhardsthal type, from Rabensburg, Lower Austria (Felgenhauer 1962, Fig. 1) where a man standing in the chariot holds reins for a pair of horses with feet lying outwards on either side (*Ill. 5:3*). This certainly looks like a lack of co-ordination of techniques in design. One may then go back to Scandinavian rock-carvings, again of relatively early date, to observe yoked pairs of draught animals with feet lying outwards or in-wards. Good examples of both, attached to chariots, occur on the same rock surface at Frännarp (Piggott 1965, Fig. 77). Within the Hallstatt Iron Age world again, a waggon with a pair of horses with outward-lying feet is shown in the carving on a bone handle, of Platěnice context, from Dobřcice, Moravia (Forman and Poulík 1956, Pl. 116, for good photo; Neustupný 1961, Ill. 60). It does not appear that the type of vehicle, waggon or chariot, is of import-ance in relation to the way in which the animals are drawn, although of course the late Middle Bronze Age vehicles are all two-wheeled. The Rabensburg chariot is, for the moment, exceptional in the Hall-statt world if it is accepted as representing a funerary car, and not perhaps a vehicle performing an acces-sory rôle in funeral games or procession.

Blanco Freijeiro and his co-authors (1969, 160–1) have written of 'El expresivo lenguaje geométrico de la estela de Ategua', so it is permissible to take note here of the model funerary car from Vari, Attica, with its four wheels (Demargne 1964, Ill. 491; Kurtz and Boardman 1971, Pl. 16), and move thence to the superb compositions of funeral scenes on Geometric marker vases from the Dipylon cemetery at Athens (Hampe 1952; Kurtz and Boardman 1971, for cult; Snodgrass 1971, Pl. 138, for cortège; Ahlberg 1971, for detailed study). Here again paired horses pull four-wheeled hearses. The geometric idiom touching Andalucía need not, however, be directly Greek, and is more likely to have stemmed from Cyprus and Asia Minor (Al-magro 1966 for V-notch shield, fibulae, etc.). Almagro had also foreseen the possibility that the wheeled vehicles on the stelae might have been introduced by seaways from the other end of the Mediterranean. It is therefore appropriate on all counts to turn to the elaborate burial tradition manifest in the necropolis at Salamis in Cyprus, where the two-wheeled chariot, having presumably carried the corpses to the tomb, was buried in the *dromos* with its slain horses still beneath the yoke (Karageorghis 1967). Although there is no evidence to warrant affirmation, it may be suggested as a possibility for the Peninsular stelae that the drawing of the chariot horses was intentional to show that they lay dead, felled in their place before completion of the ceremony. If this interpretation should prove tenable it would at least establish the likelihood that the Peninsular stelae were intended to show not such funerary episodes as *prothesis* or *ekphora*, but rather a final act of arraying the corpse with all its attributes of rank and valour. The Salamis necropolis provides a generally approximate chronological backcloth. Unfortunately there is as yet no equivalent testimony from Asia Minor so far as funerary vehicles are concerned, except for sculpture of the late sixth and early fifth centuries BC from such sites in Phrygia as Aksakal-Daskyleion, where it can be seen how a two-wheeled vehicle can convey a prone body under a pall with all proper dignity (Borchhardt 1968).

An explanation of the general funerary tradition exemplified at Salamis as a development of Phrygian practice leads to consideration of the background for the great tumuli at Gordion with their splendidly constructed timber-built graves. The associated ritual may well have owed much to earlier Hittite observances, but more barbaric Pontic traditions, with or without horse burials, are likely to have been involved. Especially is this so in the device of sinking a pit in which to place the timber chamber, and the heaping up of a substantial tumulus over all. It is in this same direction that one must look for the promptings that led to the construction of pit-sunk timber chamber graves under tumuli, princip-ally in Bohemia and Bavaria, often with small waggons or representative parts, and all integral to the early iron-using phase of Hallstatt culture (Hallstatt C) (Kossack 1970, 139–48). It is thus permissible to compare such few indications as survive of funerary ritual in the Peninsular south-west and the north Alpine region without straining for any direct connections, but only to recognize a shared inspiration, and that, most probably, emanating from Asia Minor.

The hand-holding participants seen on the Ategua stele promise much for future comparative studies, but the tall personage standing behind the chariot cannot be altogether ignored here. He recalls the tall schematic figure that stands, or walks, behind each of the four chariots in the frieze on the vessel from Vel'ke Raškovce, but perhaps more cogently he should be compared with the individuals behind the waggons on two of the Sopron urns (*Ill. 5:2*). Nor in this connection can the tall figure standing behind the bier on the model hearse from Vari be forgotten; but perhaps even more relevant for Ategua, as showing a continuance of this posture in Asia Minor, is the man walking behind, and touching with outstretched arm, a bier mounted on a two-wheeled vehicle, carved on one of the stelae from Aksakal-Daskyleion (Borchhardt 1968, Pl. 49).

Finally, a cautionary note must be sounded on the rôle of chariots, as differentiated from utilitarian two-wheeled carts and four-wheeled waggons, in the overall material equipment of the 'Tartessian' chieftains of the Peninsular south-west. It cannot be assumed, on the evidence of memorial stelae alone, that in or about the eighth and seventh centuries BC chariots were integral to native culture or functional for other than funerary and ceremonial purposes. A dimension is added to the impact on Iberian life, brought about by oriental trader-colonists, that reached beyond immediate skills and crafts to awareness of how great occasions were conducted among admired but far distant peoples.

Bibliography

AHLBERG, G. 1971 *Prothesis and Ekphora in Greek Geometric Art*, Göteborg.

ALMAGRO, M. 1966 *Las estelas decoradas del sudoeste peninsular* (Biblioteca praehistorica hispana VIII), Madrid.

BERNIER, J. 1969 Una nueva estela grabada junto a las murallos ibericos de Ategua en la provincia de Córdoba, *Zephyrus* XIX-XX, 181–4.

BLANCO FREIJEIRO, A., LUZÓN NOGUÉ, J. M., RUIZ MATA, D. 1969 Panorama tartésico en Andalucía oriental, in *Taressos y sus problemas*, ed. J. M. Maluquer de Motes, 119–62.

BORCHHARDT, J. 1968 Epichorische, gräko-persisch beeinflusste Reliefs in Kilikien, *Istanbuler Mitt.* 18, 161–211.

DEMARGNE, P. 1964 *Aegean Art*, London.

FELGENHAUER, F. 1962 Eine hallstattliche Wagendarstellung aus Rabensburg, N.Ö., *M.A.G.W.* XCII (Festschrift Hans Hančar), 93–111.

FORMAN, W. and B., POULÍK, J. 1956 *Prehistoric Art*, Prague and London.

GALLUS, S. 1934 Die figuralverzierten Urnen vom Soproner Burgstall, *Arch. Hungr.* XIII.

HAMPE, R. 1952 *Die Gleichnisse Homers und die Bildkunst seiner Zeit*, Tübingen.

KARAGEORGHIS, V. 1967 *Excavations in the necropolis of Salamis, I* (*Salamis* III), Nicosia.

KURTZ, D. C., and BOARDMAN, J. 1971 *Greek Burial Customs*, London.

LA BAUME, W. Bildliche Darstellungen auf Östgermanischen Tongefässen der fruhen Eisenzeit, *I.P.E.K.*, 25–56.

1950 Zur Bedeutung der bildlichen Darstellungen auf Gesichtsurnen der frühen Eisenheit, *Prähistoriche Zeitschrift* 34/35, 158–78.

MALUQUER DE MOTES, J. M. (ed.) 1969 *Tartessos y sus problemas*, Barcelona.

NEUSTUPNÝ, J. and E. 1961 *Czechoslavakia before the Slavs*, London.

PIGGOTT, S. 1965 *Ancient Europe from the beginnings of agriculture to classical antiquity*, Edinburgh.

POWELL, T. G. E. 1966 *Prehistoric Art*, London.

SANDARS, N. K. 1968 *Prehistoric Art in Europe*, Harmondsworth.

SNODGRASS, A. 1971 *The Dark Age of Greece*, Edinburgh.

VIZDAL, J. 1972 Erste bildliche Darstellung eines zweirädiges Wagens vom Ende der mittleren Bronzezeit in der Slovakei, *Slovenská Archeológica* 22, 223–31.

19

OTTO-HERMAN FREY

The Chariot Tomb from Adria: Some Notes on Celtic Horsemanship and Chariotry[1]

[1] Translated by Peter Golden and J. V. S. Megaw

GAULISH chariotry is, as we all know, a subject of great interest to Stuart Piggott. It has led him for instance to make a full-scale reconstruction of a war-chariot and to try to discover how horses harnessed to the yoke were managed. In an earlier note I put forward, among other things, views concerning the side screens of such chariots, which conflicted with the Edinburgh reconstruction (Frey 1968). I was thereby perhaps guilty of delaying study of the subject, and want to offer by way of compensation this small paper, which takes up and expands some ideas about the use of the chariot which were first propounded by Stuart Piggott.

Several years ago Piggott cited examples of Roman coins which unequivocally depicted Gallic chariots (Piggott 1952; see also Harbison 1969, 47ff.). Of these coins, one group had been minted at the end of the second century BC, the other in the middle of the first century BC. The written record, however, does not entirely agree with this testimony. It is true that King Bituitus of the Arverni, when he supported the Allobroges in their struggle against Rome in the year 121 BC, had fought from a chariot decorated with silver.[2] One can therefore draw on Florus' account as an explanation for the portrayal of chariots on the older coins; but this does not follow for the more recent group. As Piggott observes in his article:

> By 58 BC the total absence of any reference to chariot warfare by Caesar, and his surprised recognition of its survival in Britain a few years later, shows that by that date it had been dropped from tactical use by the Gauls.

It thus seems unlikely that these coins can be regarded as representations of contemporary Gallic chariotry.[3] Piggott thinks that they are either an anachronism or depict contemporary British vehicles encountered by Caesar in his campaigns of 55 and 54 BC.

When this observation was made, archaeological evidence for corresponding Late La Tène chariots from the continent was almost totally absent. The only well-known exceptions were the tombs from Hoppstädten which had produced such vehicles (Dehn 1938; see now Haffner 1969). But other discoveries had in fact been made, and recently the material has increased markedly, so that today one can say with certainty that in the first century BC a light two-wheeled chariot was common over much of the Celtic world. Hence the appearance of a typical Celtic *essedum* on coins of the first century BC should no longer be in question. The inclusion of such a chariot in a grave must indeed have been a general custom for the upper stratum of Celtic society (Joachim 1969, n. 2, 5; 1973, n. 1; 1974, n. 11), for example in the territory of the Treveri. Schindler, who has recently discussed such burials, is inclined to think that these chariots were no longer used in war (Schindler 1971, 65). They were merely a status symbol for a warrior of the nobility who himself had ridden into battle. Schindler is led to this interpretation by several points, for instance the extremely long swords known from such tombs. These swords are usable only as cavalry weapons. Spurs in the graves (Joachim 1973, 40) are of a type which show the dead to have been not a charioteer but a mounted warrior. With this in mind, is it not possible to suppose that the *esseda* represented on the coins were not actual war chariots, but nothing more than traditional symbols of rank? The chariot of King Bituitus with its precious silver decoration may have been also primarily a badge denoting his social status.[4]

[2] Florus (I.37.5) reports that the king was brought to Rome to take part in the triumph 'discoloribus in armis argenteoque carpento quali pugnaverat'. A collection of the references to the Celtic chariot in Classical literature is given by D'Arbois de Jubainville (1888).

[3] The arguments seem convincing, but there must have been a strong tradition concerning the use of war-chariots, since Strabo (IV.5.2) writes of chariots as though they still existed. For Diodorus (V.29.1) see Tierney 1960, 250.

1 Adria: chariot burial.

There are numerous parallels from the Mediterranean world for the symbolic use of the chariot. We may recall the triumphal chariot of the Roman emperors (Wiesner 1944, 67ff.) and the richly decorated vehicles from central Italian tombs of the sixth century BC; here one need only mention the famous example from Monteleone (Richter 1915, 17ff., no. 40). These chariots can only be interpreted as ceremonial vehicles, as at the time the phalanx proved to be the favoured form of battle-order in Etruria (Snodgrass 1965, 116ff.), and it is unthinkable that the chariot still had any rôle to play in warfare.

In the Celtic world the custom of a mounted warrior being buried with a chariot as a symbol of rank appears not to have been confined to the Late La Tène phase. Perhaps the Early La Tène chieftain-grave from Kärlich can be interpreted in this manner, since besides a chariot and other grave-goods a small mounting was found depicting a rider (Driehaus 1965; Joachim 1970; Osterhaus 1966, 169; Megaw 1970, no. 33). A similar rite can be found in the chariot-burial from Adria and, as an example from the regions north of the Alps, in a burial from Léry (Eure).

2 Adria: chariot burial. Surviving fragments of the curb-bit of the charger.

The tomb at Adria was excavated in 1938 in a cemetery beside the Bianco Canal (Fogolari and Scarfì 1970, 73f., nos. 44–5). In the grave itself were discovered the remains of a two-wheeled vehicle with iron tyres and with linch pins and nave hoops of bronze and iron (*Ill. 1*). Also found in good condition were the skeletons of two horses that had been harnessed to the chariot. In their mouths were simple iron ring bits; nearby lay four iron rein-rings. A third horse skeleton behind the chariot was provided with harness typical for a charger, as is shown by the presence of a curb-bit. The mouthpiece itself was made of iron, the omega-shaped cheek-pieces being of bronze as were the rein-hooks and the rods which had been provided with three holes

[4] The reports of war between Bituitus and the Romans are not precise enough to give a clear idea about the method of fighting used by the Allobroges, the Arverni, or the Sallyes who started the struggle (Jullian 1909, 3ff.). Only in the case of the Sallyes is a cavalry force mentioned by Strabo (IV.6.3). It remains an open question whether there was still a great number of charioteers or not.

for attachment to the curb. Unfortunately the curb was not recovered, even though the horse skeletons and underlying earth matrix were brought intact to the Adria museum for conservation (*Ill. 2*).

No human remains were found in the grave, but there may have been a burial in the area immediately behind the chariot and the horses, where there were definite signs of disturbance suggesting to the excavators that a grave had been tampered with at some time in antiquity. The Bianco Canal cemetery contains, besides Roman cremations, 'Celtic' inhumations of the third and second centuries BC. Apart from a Roman burial, three inhumation graves of the third century BC lay in the vicinity of the chariot tomb; however, this can only be regarded as weak support for dating the chariot to the third century BC. Each of two other graves from the same cemetery also contained a skeleton of a war-horse. In both cases there can be no doubt of a pre-Roman date, even though detailed investigation of the associated grave-goods is not yet complete.[5]

The pre-Roman cemetery of Adria is normally considered to be 'Celtic'. But this is hardly precise since Adria in the fifth and fourth centuries BC was inhabited by Greeks, Etruscans and Veneti, as is attested by graffiti on contemporary pottery (Fogolari and Scarfì 1970, 27ff.). Whether, perhaps in the fourth century BC, a real Celtic invasion did or did not take place must remain uncertain. The only definite indication is the Celtic influence shown in the grave-goods. This strong cultural impact is seen not only at Adria but also in the whole Angulus Venetorum, which was never invaded by the Gauls. This is proved too by Polybius (II.17.5) who, writing in the second century BC, states that the Veneti, apart from their language, differed only slightly from the Gauls in both customs and costume. Thus, at least in this respect, one may claim that the chariot-burial from Adria was indeed Celtic. The tomb from Léry reveals that, nearly contemporary with the Adria cemetery, similar rites concerned with equipment for the after-life are also found north of the Alps (Coutil 1901, 128f. and Pl. 2, 13–15; Jacobi 1974, 184, no. 798). Léry represents the burial of a warrior with his sword and spear. Other grave-goods include two iron ring-bits, obviously for a team of horses, and third bit, once more a curb-bit, such as could only have been used for a charger. So here again is evidence for a warrior who was at once a charioteer and a horseman.

These grave finds, on the one hand, pose the question of the development and function of the Celtic horseman, and on the other hand they beg the purpose of the associated chariots which, as already observed to have been no longer employed in the field during the Late La Tène phase, had instead at that time a symbolic rôle. It remains to pursue these problems in greater depth, setting our discussion in a wider time perspective.

To assess the function of the horseman in battle, we must first try to consider horse harnesses in detail. The omega-shaped cheek-pieces from Adria, combined with the curb-bit, were originally examined by Werner Krämer (1964) and more recently discussed by Jacobi (1974, 182ff.). While in Central Europe a few examples have come to light, a whole series has been found in north and central Italy. Similarly these cheek-pieces can be seen on a group of Apulian vases and in other representations of the fourth century BC. Although earlier evidence for these bits is unknown, derivations of the form survived into the first century AD.[6]

It is interesting to note that in Italy omega-shaped cheek-pieces are also associated in several other finds with curb-bits. But this combination with the typical harness of a charger does not seem to be obligatory, because on representations of chariots the horses are shown with such cheek-pieces too.[7] Curb-bits of different forms are ubiquitous in Italy from the second half of the fourth century BC onward.[8] Of this type of bit, several examples have also been found in the southern Balkans, although from Central Europe there have been hitherto only very few finds. But since a clear relationship in customs of horse-rearing is demonstrated by the distribution of these cheek-pieces, it may be suggested that the

[5] Dr B. M. Scarfì, Milan, is preparing a complete publication of the cemetery, and I am most grateful for her advice. Professor G. dei Fogolari, Padua, very kindly provided the illustrations for *Ills. 1,2*.

[6] Jacobi 1974, 187, n.803. The small omega-shaped cheek-pieces listed by Jacobi are well known from Dacian findings; see for example the catalogue *The Illyrians and Dacians* (Belgrade 1971), D 148.

[7] Besides Apulian vases see for instance a stele from Padua: Prosdocimi 1963–64; Frey 1968; Megaw 1970, no. 102.

[8] For references see Jacobi 1974, 184ff. A well-dated example is known from a tomb of Canosa, Apulia: Jacobsthal 1944, 146ff., Pl. 258d:4, 4a; Oliver 1968, 13f., text Fig. 2:4, 4a.

curb-bit, so important for fighting on horseback, was also more widespread in the Celtic world than might at first sight be concluded from the present evidence.

Recently the actual function of the curb-bit has been the subject of a survey by Nylén (1972–73; see also Anderson 1961). Because a horse when confronted with an obstacle tends to shy to one side, it must be controlled through some special device, since otherwise it can play no effective role in close fighting. This essential task of controlling the horse is best fulfilled by the curb-bit, whose discovery thus constitutes a critical advance in the deployment of cavalry in warfare. Of course the curb-bit, though the most effective, is not the only device to allow mastery of a spirited war-horse. Typical in the East Mediterranean and the southern Balkans are bits with spiked mouthpieces, a powerful restraint indeed (Anderson 1961). In the present stage of research it is difficult to tell when these rough bits were introduced. As a first step, one could consider the application of a muzzle strap whereby, in addition to harnessing of the horse's mouth, pressure would have been exerted on the sensitive bridge of the muzzle. Nylén for instance (following Cowen 1967, 416ff.; see also Piggott 1965, 177ff.; Powell 1971) believes that, in Central Europe, relatively effective horse-fighting had existed since the beginning of the Hallstatt period. But these conclusions are largely hypothetical and, despite considerable work on the subject, progress has been slow in answering precisely the outstanding questions about horse-harness and cavalry technique in the area north of the Alps as well as around the Mediterranean. In view of the many unsolved problems, we must rely on evidence from outside the Celtic domain in order to clarify the function of mounted warriors at this period.

Turning to Greece, it is for example interesting to note that, in the seventh and sixth centuries BC, the descendants of Homer's chariot-using heroes are not in fact described as heavily armed cavaliers fighting directly from horseback, even though riding was known from Mycenaean times onward (Wiesner 1968; contrast Greenhalgh 1973). Instead of cavalry it is the foot-soldiers of the closely formed phalanx who play the vital rôle.[9] The chief reason for this was undoubtedly the new social system evolved by the Greek city-states. Also of interest is that the art of horse-fighting does not seem to play an important part at all in the seventh and early sixth centuries BC. In the earliest representations of military scenes on vases, apart from hoplites, fighting on foot and using the horse only as a means of transport to the battlefield, one finds only lightly armed cavalry. Only from the late sixth century onward does one find illustrations of riders richly equipped with body-armour but without shield, who may have been relatively effective in close combat. In contrast to other peoples it was certainly the foot-soldier, and not the knight fighting from horseback, who held the key position in early Greek warfare.

The development just described also had an influence on wealthy barbarians in the Balkans and Italy. In the Balkans where we have considerable evidence for riding amongst the upper classes, there are some archaeological finds which show that it was nonetheless the equipment of the Greek foot-soldier, and not that of the true cavalryman, which became the model for the outfit of an effective warrior.[10] For instance, in the graves of the famous cemetery of Trebenište near Lake Ohrid the dead were buried with a thrusting-spear, sword, helmet, and the heavy hoplite shield[11] developed for fighting in

[9] See already Helbig 1902. His views have been modified for instance by Alföldi 1967, who shows that an aristocratic cavalry existed also in early Greece since Aristotle referred to it in his *Politics* 4.12 (1297b). But it quickly became ineffectual when the hoplite phalanx was evolved. Of the ample bibliography on this topic I cite here only a few other recent articles: Snodgrass 1965; Anderson 1965; Wiesner 1968; Greenhalgh 1973.

[10] Of all the Greek weapons in the Balkans only the so-called 'Illyrian helmets' have been collected systematically (Lahtov 1965a). The oldest finds date back to the late seventh century BC (Ha C2) (Vejvoda and Mirnik 1971). Of course these open-faced helmets could have been good protection for cavalry no less than the Boeotian helmets (Snodgrass 1967, 94). The preference for the former type of helmet in the Balkans may be explained by strong connections with Macedonia where it is well attested (Snodgrass 1967, 114ff.). But it is impossible to interpret the outfit of the wealthy dead of Trebenište otherwise than as a hoplite outfit; see below.

[11] Filow 1927; Popović 1956; Lahtov 1965b. The similarity of the finds with the Greek hoplite outfit is so striking that Filow thought of 'vornehme griechische Söldner' (Filow 1927, 107f.).

close formation – in other words the complete equipment of the Greek hoplite. But according to Thucydides (IV.126) the Illyrians were almost totally ignorant of Greek discipline and tactics in warfare. Therefore the Trebenište chieftains' expensive Greek weapons must be considered as purely symbols of rank.

A different situation is to be observed in the reception accorded to the hoplite outfit in Italy where, as in the Balkans and from the seventh century BC on, noble Etruscans for example were buried with Greek helmets, greaves or other weapons (Snodgrass 1965, 116ff.). Here the influence of the Greek city-states was so strong that as time went by, first in the Etruscan cities and later also in Rome, the battle-order of the phalanx was adopted, even though in Rome the *equites* may have played a more significant rôle – as is suggested by their status in society – than their counterparts elsewhere (Alföldi 1967). Heavily armed soldiers carrying the characteristic hoplite shield appear even on north Italian metalwork (Lucke and Frey 1962; Taf. 26, 64–65; Frey 1969, Taf. 50, 58, 66, 69, 78; Frey 1975). It is thus possible that some of the central Italian development in warfare filtered into this area. But how far these changes affected military tactics north of the Alps remains uncertain.

In fact we know very little about Hallstatt warfare in Central Europe (Kossack 1959, 93ff.; 1972, 93f.) Certainly there are some representations, for instance of armed horsemen, in the East Hallstatt region from the seventh century BC on.[12] By contrast, in the West Hallstatt area such portrayals are completely absent, and the evolution of arms and armour can only be deduced from grave-goods. It is of course possible that the long Hallstatt cutting-sword, the typical weapon for a single combatant, was used mainly from horseback.[13] And one can well imagine that the increase of weapon-graves with probable thrusting-spears in the later Hallstatt phase is an indication of relatively well-regimented units of foot-soldiers. But all these interpretations are rather weak, and a reconstruction of war-practice seems difficult. For in contrast to the south-east Alpine area, where the dead was buried with his complete armour (Gabrovec 1966), in the West Hallstatt area he was generally provided only with a single weapon.

For instance, in the central grave VI of the great Hohmichele barrow near the Heuneburg, the buried chieftain was provided only with a long bow and a quiver full of arrows (Riek and Hundt 1962, 156ff.), which can hardly have constituted a nobleman's total armoury. Should we regard this bow with arrows as serving only the purpose of equipment for hunting in the afterlife? Or are we dealing here with a weapon comparable to Odysseus' highly prized bow (Homer, *Od.* 21.11ff.)? In other Late Hallstatt graves, one commonly finds either spears or daggers; and again one thinks of Homer's descriptions where, for example, Menelaus rises from his bed to greet Telemachus and puts on a sword to show his lofty status (*Od.* 4.308). Similarly Athena enters Odysseus' house with a spear in her hand when appearing as Mentes, chief of the Taphians (*Od.* 1.104, 121, 127), and Telemachus goes to the assembly armed with his sword and spear (*Od.* 2.1ff.; 17.62; 20.125ff, 145). Here then are instances of the wearing of certain weapons in the daily life of leaders as proof of their social position (cf. Helbig 1909, 49); and the same may have been done in the Hallstatt area, as a result of which there are only single weapons in the Celtic tombs rather than complete warrior outfits. Naturally, from this evidence one cannot be certain whether these people fought as riders or as foot-soldiers, or indeed as charioteers.

From the beginning of the Early La Tène period, however, the problem becomes less intractable, as the tombs are now far more richly furnished with weapons (Osterhaus 1966). But the clearest testimony comes from the scene depicted on the sword scabbard from grave 994 of the Hallstatt cemetery (Kromer 1959, 182f., Taf. 201–2; Megaw 1970, no. 30; Dehn 1970, Taf. 78–81). This shows a frieze of foot-soldiers and riders, the former lacking armour and provided only with shield and spear, being clearly inferior to the mounted warriors who – besides a long spear and in one case a sword as well – are given both helmets and body armour (*Ill. 3*). It is certain that these riders did not use the horse merely for transport to the battlefield, following

[12] See for instance the figures on the famous cult waggon from Strettweg (Schmid 1934; Pittioni 1954, 620f., Abb. 439; Modrijan 1962, 18ff.; Megaw 1970, no. 38). Other examples of mounted warriors with helmets are seen on the bronze vessels from Klein-Klein (Schmid 1933, Abb. 10a, Taf. 1a, c).

[13] Cowen 1967, 416ff. A different evolution of the sword is assumed by Schauer 1971, 213ff., who also thinks that the long sword types served as cavalry weapons.

3 Hallstatt, grave 994. Details of incised sword-scabbard showing Celtic cavalry (courtesy R-G. Z. M.).

the Greek fashion, but must have actually fought from horseback.[14] This is revealed not only by the fallen enemy against whom one rider is directing his spear, but also by the lack of shields, since shields are preferable for horse-fighting but not for combat on foot. This Central European find, in contrast to the Mediterranean evidence, displays an effective cavalry force with an obviously high degree of control over its horses. One may trace a direct line from the riders on the Hallstatt scabbard to the noble Celtic knights of the Late La Tène phase, who have such a significant part in Caesar's *De Bello Gallico*.

Together with the Celtic mounted warrior who features so prominently at the beginning of the La Tène period, one must also consider the rôle of the charioteer. In the battles of Sentinum in 295 BC and Telamon in 225 BC, the presence of chariots is still attested although it seems, according to the accounts of Livy (X.28–30) and Polybius (II.28–9), that chariotry amongst the Celts was by then already obsolescent (Anderson 1965, 350) and that the cavalry were paramount in battle. But when one finds chariots in the Early La Tène chieftain graves of Central Europe (Harbison 1969) it is likely that, along with the war-horse, they still had the function of an actual item of military equipment, though probably reserved by tradition for those of high rank and thus preferred as grave-goods for warriors.[15] At the same time, the chariot may have had a supplementary use in carrying the body to the cemetery and symbolically onward to the afterlife. The chariot-tomb from Adria must also be seen in terms of this tradition, while it is not impossible that the chariot had partly lost a military function by then. For otherwise how could one interpret the representation on a gravestone from Padua, of about the same period, showing a typical Celtic *essedum* taking a woman on the journey to the next world (Frey 1968, 317)?[16]

The origin of the Celtic chariot is, of course, a much-discussed topic (e.g. Osterhaus 1966). But whether this problem can be solved on the basis of evidence from graves is debatable in the light of what has just been said. It is possible that, in the West Hallstatt culture, the chariot was already used even though it was not buried with the dead, and although only in the East Hallstatt region do we have clear evidence for chariots (Felgenhauer 1962). Instead of chariots, the dead were placed on a four-wheeled waggon together with only a few characteristic weapons which had been carried in everyday life as signs of their owner's rank. In contrast, the chieftains of the Early La Tène period, for instance in the Marne region, were buried with a complete collection of weapons for both defence and

14 Polybius (III.115.1–3) tells how, at the battle of Cannae, the Celtic and Iberian cavalry leapt down to fight on foot (see Anderson 1965, 350). But this may have been a special situation and not typical of Celtic war practice in general.

15 Only in the Early La Tène tomb of Moscano di Fabriano is the dead clearly equipped as a rider (now in Ancona; Frey 1971, 174). For references to other possible horseman-graves see Joffroy and Bretz-Mahler 1959, 32. For the whole question see also Joachim 1974, 163.

16 In one of the Late La Tène chariot-tombs from Hoppstädten a woman was buried (Haffner 1969, 110; see also Schindler 1971, 65). The absence of weapons in the English cart-burials suggests that there also two-wheeled vehicles were not necessarily war-chariots (Stead 1965, 5).

attack; one may cite the well-known chariot-graves of Somme-Bionne and Gorge Meillet (Morel 1898; Fourdrignier 1878; see also Joffroy and Bretz-Mahler 1959). Here the dead are represented as warriors who naturally pass into the afterlife with the same chariots they had used in battle.

This is not the place to study in detail the cultural change which occurred with regard to burial practices and their origin. But I hope that these brief comments may help towards a more thorough examination of the function of the Celtic chariot from the beginning of the La Tène period on.

Bibliography

ALFÖLDI, A. 1967 Die Herrschaft der Reiterei in Griechenland und Rom nach dem Sturz der Könige. Gestalt und Geschichte (Festschrift K. Schefold), *Antike Kunst* 4, 13–47.

ANDERSON, J. K. 1961 *Ancient Greek Horsemanship*, Berkeley and Los Angeles.

1965 Homeric, British and Cyrenaic Chariots, *American Journal of Archaeology* 69, 349–52.

COUTIL, L. 1901 L'époque gauloise dans le sud-ouest de la Belgique et le nord-ouest de la Celtique, *Bull. Soc. Normande d'études préhist.* 9, 48–138.

COWEN, J. D. 1967 The Hallstatt Sword of bronze on the Continent and in Britain, *Proc. Prehist. Soc.* XXXIII, 377–454.

D'ARBOIS DE JUBAINVILLE, H. 1888 Le char de guerre des Celtes dans quelques textes historiques, *Revue Celtique* 9, 387–93.

DEHN, W. 1938 Ein Trevererfriedhof bei Hoppstädten an der Nahe, *Rheinische Vorzeit in Wort und Bild* 1, 109–13.

1970 Ein keltisches Häuptlingsgrab aus Hallstatt, *Krieger und Salzherren = Röm.-Germ. Zentralmuseum Mainz, Ausstellungskataloge* 4, 72–81.

DRIEHAUS, J. 1965 Eine frühlatènezeitliche Reiterdarstellung aus Kärlich, *Bonner Jahrb.* 165, 57–71.

FELGENHAUER, F. 1962 Eine hallstättische Wagendarstellung aus Rabensburg, N.-Ö. *Mitt. der Anthrop. Gesell. in Wien* 92, 93–111.

FILOW, B. D. 1927 *Die archaische Nekropole von Trebenischte am Ochrida-See*, Berlin and Leipzig.

FOGOLARI, G. and SCARFÌ, B. M. 1970 *Adria antica*, Venice.

FOURDRIGNIER, E. 1878 *Double sépulture gauloise à char de la Gorge Meillet*, Paris and Chalons-sur-Marne.

FREY, O.-H. 1968 Eine neue Grabstele aus Padua, *Germania* XLVI, 317–20.

1969 *Die Entstehung der Situlenkunst, Röm.-Germ. Forschungen* 31, Berlin.

1971 Das keltische Schwert von Moscano di Fabriano, *Hamburger Beiträge zur Archäologie* I, 173–7.

1975 Bemerkungen zur hallstättischen Bewaffnung im Südostalpenraum, *Arheološki Vestnik* 24 (forthcoming).

GABROVEC, S. 1966 Zur Hallstattzeit in Slowenien, *Germania* XLIV, 1–48.

GREENHALGH, P. A. L. 1973 *Early Greek Warfare: Horsemen and Chariots in the Homeric and Archaic Ages*, Cambridge.

HAFFNER, A. 1969 Das Treverer-Gräberfeld mit Wagenbestattungen von Hoppstädten-Weinsbach, Kreis Birkenfeld, *Trierer Zeitschrift* 32, 71–128.

HARBISON, P. 1969 The Chariot of Celtic Funerary Tradition, *Marburger Beiträge zur Archäologie der Kelten: (Festschrift W. Dehn) = Fundberichte aus Hessen* 7, Beih. I, 34–58.

HELBIG, W. 1902 Les ἱππεῖς athéniens, *Mém. de l'Académie des Inscriptions et Belles-lettres* 37, 157–264.

1909 Ein homerischer Rundschild mit einem Bügel, *Jahreshefte des Österreichischen Arch. Inst. in Wien* 12, 1–70.

ILLIRI ŞI DACI 1972 *Muzeul Naţional Beograd-Muzeul de Istorie al Transilvaniei Cluj*, Cluj and Bucharest.

JACOBI, G. 1974 *Werkzeug und Gerät aus dem Oppidum von Manching = Die Ausgrabungen in Manching* 5, Wiesbaden.

JACOBSTHAL, P. 1944 *Early Celtic Art*, Oxford (reprinted with corrections 1969).

JOACHIM, H.-E. 1969 Unbekannte Wagengräber der Mittel- bis Spätlatènezeit aus dem Rheinland, *Marburger Beiträge zur Archäologie der Kelten: (Festschrift W. Dehn) = Fundberichte aus Hessen* Beih. I, 84–111.

1970 Zur frühlatènezeitlichen Reiterfigur von Kärlich, Ldkr. Koblenz, *Jahrbuch d. Röm.-Germ. Zentralmuseums Mainz* 17, 94–103.

1973 Ein reich ausgestattetes Wagengrab der Spätlatènezeit aus Neuwied, Stadtteil Heimbach-Weis, *Bonner Jahrb.* 173, 1–44.

1974 Ein spätlatènezeitliches Reitergrab aus Kollig, Kreis Mayen-Koblenz, *Hamburger Beiträge zur Archäologie* IV, 159–70.

JOFFROY, R. and BRETZ-MAHLER, D. 1959 Les

tombes à char dans l'est de la France, *Gallia* 17, 5–36.

JULLIAN, C. 1909 *Histoire de la Gaule* III, Paris.

KOSSACK, G. 1959 *Südbayern während der Hallstattzeit = Röm.-Germ. Forschungen* 24, Berlin.

1972 Hallstattzeit. In *Vor- und frühgeschichtliche Archäologie in Bayern*, ed. O. Kunkel, Munich, 85–100.

KRÄMER, W. 1964 Latènezeitliche Trensenanhänger in Omegaform, *Germania* XLII, 250–7.

KROMER, K. 1959 *Das Gräberfeld von Hallstatt*, Florence.

LAHTOV, V. 1965a La tombe du guerrier illyrien découverte dans le village Rečica près d'Ohrid et le problème de casque gréco-illyrien, *Situla* 8, 47–78.

1965b *Problem Trebeniške Kulture*, Ohrid.

LUCKE, W. and FREY, O.-H. 1962 *Die Situla in Providence (Rhode Island) = Röm.-Germ. Forschungen* 26, Berlin.

MEGAW, J. V. S. 1970 *Art of the European Iron Age*, Bath.

MODRIJAN, W. 1962 *Das Aichfeld = Judenburger Museumsschriften* 3.

MOREL, L. 1898 *La Champagne souterraine*, Reims.

NYLÉN, E. 1972–73 The warriors horse and the curb-rein-bit, *Tor* 15, 68–83.

OLIVER, JR., A. 1968 *The Reconstruction of two Apulian Tomb Groups = Antike Kunst*, 5.

OSTERHAUS, U. 1966 *Die Bewaffnung der Kelten zur Frühlatènezeit in der Zone nördlich der Alpen*, Unpublished Dissertation, Philipps Universität Marburg/Lahn.

PIGGOTT, S. 1952 Celtic Chariots on Roman Coins, *Antiquity* XXVI, 87–8.

1965 *Ancient Europe from the beginnings of agriculture to classical antiquity*, Edinburgh.

PITTIONI, R. 1954 *Urgeschichte des österreichischen Raumes*, Vienna.

POPOVIĆ, L. 1956 *Katalog nalaza iz necropole kod Trebeništa*, Belgrade.

POWELL, T. G. E. 1971 The Introduction of horse-riding to Temperate Europe: A contributory note, *Proc. Prehist. Soc.* XXXVII:2, 1–14.

PROSDOCIMI, A. 1963–64 Un'altra stele paleoveneta patavina, *Memorie della accademia patavina di SS. LL.AA. = Classe di Scienze Morali, Lettere ed Arti* 76, 1–15.

RICHTER, G. 1915 *Greek, Etruscan and Roman Bronzes*, The Metropolitan Museum of Art, New York.

RIEK, G. and HUNDT, H.-J. 1962 *Der Hohmichele. Röm.-Germ. Forschungen* 25, Berlin.

SCHAUER, P. 1971 *Die Schwerter in Süddeutschland, Österreich und der Schweiz I: Griffplatten-, Griffangel- und Griffzungenschwerter = Prähistorische Bronzefunde* IV, 2, Munich.

SCHINDLER, R. 1971 Ein Kriegergrab mit Bronzehelm der Spätlatènezeit aus Trier-Olewig. Zum Problem des vorrömischen Trier, *Trierer Zeitschrift* 34, 43–82.

SCHMID, W. 1933 Die Fürstengräber von Klein Glein in Steiermark, *Prähistorische Zeitschrift* XXIV, 219–82.

1934 *Der Kultwagen von Strettweg = Führer zur Urgeschichte* 12, Leipzig.

SNODGRASS, A. M. 1965 The Hoplite reform and history, *J. of Hellenic Stud.* 85, 110–22.

1967 *Arms and Armour of the Greeks*, London.

STEAD, I. M. 1965 *The La Tène Cultures of Eastern Yorkshire*, York.

TIERNEY, J. J. 1960 The Celtic Ethnography of Posidonius, *Proc. Roy. Irish Acad.* 60, C, 5.

VEJVODA, V. and MIRNIK, I. 1971 Excavations of Prehistorian Barrows at Kaptol, *Vjesnik Arheološkog Muzeja u Zagrebu* 3, Ser. 5, 183–210.

WIESNER, J. 1944 Reiter und Ritter im ältesten Rom, *Klio* 36, 45–100.

1968 *Fahren und Reiten = Archaeologia Homerica* I F, Göttingen.

20

TADEUSZ SULIMIRSKI

The Celts in Eastern Europe

MUCH has been written on the Celts in Western and Central Europe, but very little is known of Celtic participation in the cultural development of Eastern Europe. In this contribution to the sixty-fifth birthday of my friend Stuart Piggott, I propose to give a brief review of some questions relating to the presence of Celts in the countries north-east of the Carpathians.

Archaeological evidence suggests that early in the third century BC, some Celtic tribes had reached the north-eastern corner of the Great Hungarian Plain, northern Transylvania and the Carpathian Ukraine (Krushelnitskaya 1965, 119–22; Bidzila 1964, 92–143; Woźniak 1974). Soon afterward, however, some of them moved across the mountains and imposed themselves there as rulers over the native population of Thracian stock. Consequent on this action was the formation of the Lipica Culture (*Ill. 1*), a culture basically of a mixed Geto-Romanian and Celtic character (Smiszko 1932; 1934; 1935, 155–64; 1936, 125–39; 1948, 98–127; Kozłowski 1939, 82, 90ff.; Krushelnitskaya 1965; Berciu 1966, 75–93; Woźniak 1970, 76ff.; Sulimirski 1974, 89ff.). Its territory extended north of the East Carpathians, approximately east of the River San to about the pre-War south-eastern frontier of Poland. Its northern border ran in an arc, with its top somewhere north of Lwów.

Remains of the culture (some thirty sites) consist of settlements and cemeteries, mostly with inurned cremations; inhumations were an exception (Sveshnikov 1957, 73–74). Of importance are two richly furnished princely inhumation burials (Smiszko 1935, 155; 1957, 238–43), one at Kołokolin in the vicinity of the type-site of Lipica, the other at Chizhikov near Lwow, both secondary burials in Neolithic barrow graves situated outside the cemeteries of the later culture. Both had been disturbed, but their burial ritual and the surviving portion of their contents imply that both graves belonged to the Lipica Culture. Some articles bear a definite La Tène Celtic character (*Ill. 2*), and imported Roman pottery and other items put the date of the graves in the first half of the first century AD.

Several settlements of the Lipica Culture have been investigated (Smiszko 1934; Sulimirski 1934, 33–43). In a hut of the settlement at Nowosiółka Kostiukowa near Zaleszczyki, a genuine Celtic socketed iron axe was found and, outside the huts, sherds of the typical Celtic painted ware; the finds imply that the settlement was inhabited in the first century BC. More important, however, was the discovery of a Celtic settlement at Bovshiv (Krushelnytska 1964, 130–8; 1965), some 10 km north-west of Halicz, in which hand-made and wheel-turned ware was discovered characteristic of the La Tène period of the first century BC. In the settlement at Horosheva, situated in a meander of the Dniester *c.* 12 km south of Ivanie Puste (Pachkova 1972, 320), remains of two pit-dwellings were uncovered. Besides pottery similar to the wheel-turned ware characteristic of the Geto-Dacian settlements in Romania, many sherds were also found there of hand-made vessels modelled on Celtic prototypes, and sherds of a grooved vase of a type known from Celtic settlements of the second century in Bohemia. In a few other sites single La Tène brooches or bronze bracelets were found. Mention may be made of two hoards of gold and silver coins, a Celtic one from Sokal, and imitations of Macedonian *tetradrachmae* from Skomorochy; single coins, similar imitations, have been found at Trembowla, Łuck-Lutsk and Lipovets (Kukharenko 1959a, 31–51; Sulimirski 1936, 40, Fig. 5; Ambroz 1966, 12, 14, 19).

The height of the Lipica Culture was in the first century AD. The first century BC was its formative period, although the beginning of this process may have started in the second century BC, soon after the arrival of the Celts in the region. The culture was in existence up to the late second or the third century AD, when most of its territory was seized by other cultures. Kozłowski (1939, 91; Sulimirski 1974, 98, 104ff.) points out that the material culture of the modern Ukrainian population of the ancient Lipica territory, and of the mountains south of it, exhibits many features characteristic of the ancient local Thracian culture. This, in turn, suggests

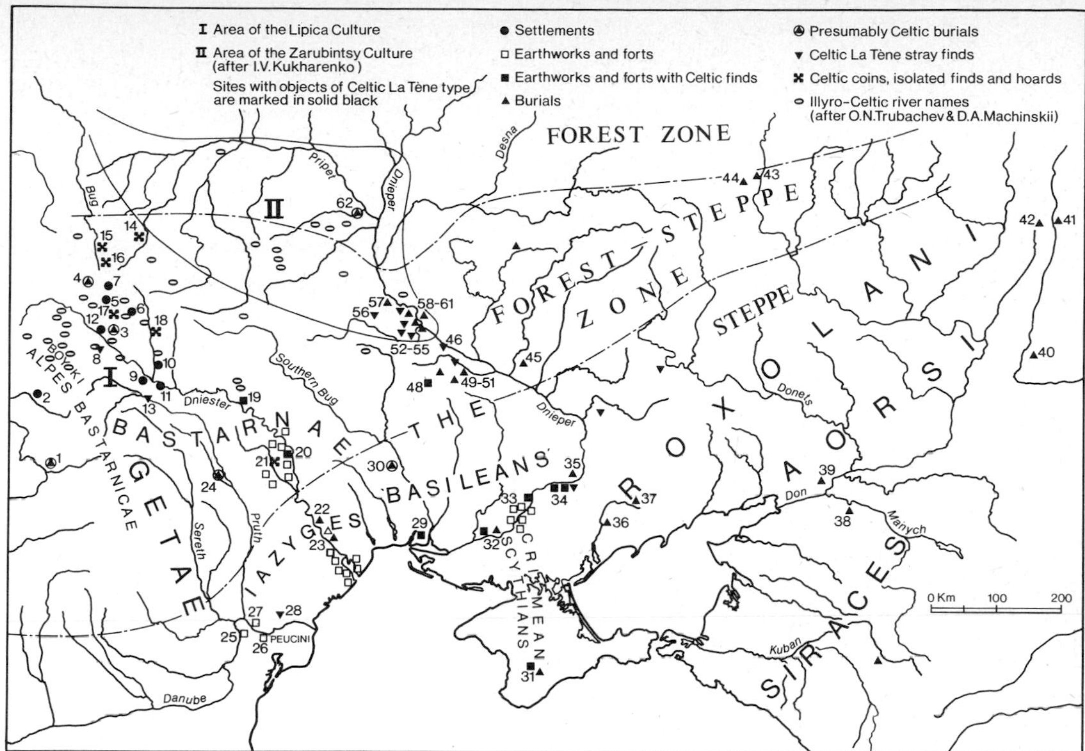

Fig. 1 Map of the North Pontic area in the late third to mid-first centuries BC.

1 Ciumeşti
2 Halish-Lovachka
3 Kołokolin
4 Chizhikov
5 Zvenigorod
6 Lipica
7 Niesluchov
8 Komarów
9 Horodnica
10 Nowosiółka Kostiukowa
11 Horosheva
12 Bovshiv
13 Stefanówka-Stefanivka
14 Łuck-Lutsk
15 Sokal
16 Skomorochy
17 Lipovets
18 Trembowla
19 Grigorovka
20 Sakharna
21 Bucheny
22 Parkany
23 Glinnoe
24 Glavaneşti Vechi
25 Arbium-Măchin
26 Noviodunum-Isacea
27 Aliobrix-Orlovka
28 Izmail
29 Olbia
30 Marievka (Bougakom)
31 Scythian Neapolis and Tavel-Krasnolesie
32 Nikolaevka-Kozatskoe
33 Zolota Balka
34 Znamenka and Kamenka earthworks and Vodianoe
35 Verkhna Tarasovka
36 Novo-Filipovka
37 Mogila-Tokmak
38 Veselii
39 Sadovy
40 Kalinovka
41 Tonkoshurovka (Marienthal)
42 Bolshaya Dimitrievka
43 Chastie Kurgany at Voronezh
44 Antipovka
45 Verkhnaya Manuilovka
46 Cherkassy
47 Lubentsy
48 Pasterskoe
49–51 Yablonovka, Mikhailovka-Prusy, Medvedovka
52–55 Grishchintsy, Kurilovka, Trostianets, Pishchalniki
56 Olshanitsa
57 Stretovka
58–61 Kanev, Pekary, Liplava, Bukrin
62 Zalesie

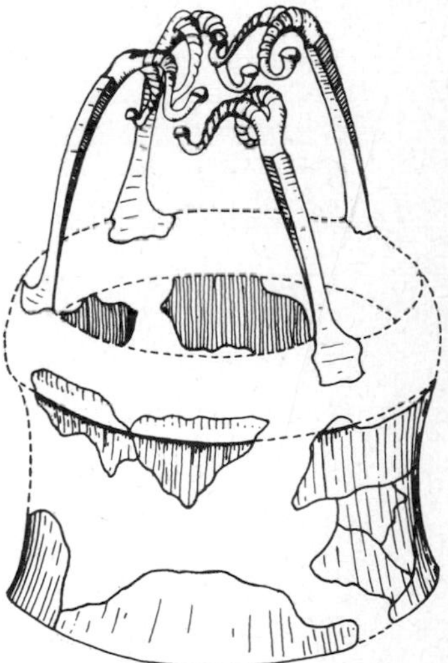

2 A Celtic ritual vessel from the princely barrow grave of the Lipica Culture at Kołokolin near Halicz, Galicia (after Smiszko).

the survival up to the present day of the ancient hybrid Geto-Thracian-Celtic population of the Lipica Culture slavicized in the course of time.

Tribal names of the Celts responsible for the formation of the Lipica Culture are still a matter for dispute. Perhaps among the makers of the Lipica Culture were some splinter groups of the Boii who, after being crushed by the Getae, may have crossed the Carpathians. Some Ukrainian scholars (Skoryk 1931, 6–23, 172f.) connect with the Boii the name 'Boyki', given to a large section of Ukrainian highlanders in the Eastern Carpathians. Ptolemy (III.5.7) places the Bastarnae in that part of the Carpathians, where also the name 'Alpes Bastarnicae' figures on the Tabula Peutingeriana. This implies that the region must have been inhabited by, and possibly in possession of, the Bastarnae. But the question then arises, who in fact were the Bastarnae? Were they a Celtic or a Germanic (Teutonic) people? This dilemma has been widely discussed in archaeological literature and, it seems, opinions of the scholars concerned reflect mainly their own preconceived convictions as to the Celtic or Germanic origin of the people.

That the Bastarnae were a Celtic people is indicated by several circumstances. The name 'Alpes Bastarnicae', just mentioned, speaks decidedly in favour of their Celtic origin. Moreover, the names of their chiefs, or princes, which have come down to us are all exclusively Celtic; Celtic also is the name of their hero, Teutagonus. Some ancient authors simply state that they were a Celtic people; for example Livy (XL.57–8; XLIV.26–7) calls Clondicus, their chief, in one place 'Regulus Gallorum', and in another passage 'Dux Bastarnorum'. But most important is the opinion of Polybius, who was a high-ranking officer of the Roman army and a diplomat as well as one of the most reliable ancient historians. Polybius considered the Bastarnae as a Celtic people: he says that they do not differ from the Celtic Scordisci either in their language or in their customs.[1] Pompeius Trogus was of the same opinion; the Celts who arrived in about 240–230 BC in the Danubian delta were called by him the Bastarnae, and their invasion 'Basternici motus' (*Prolog*. XXVIII). Some other ancient authors call them the 'Galatians',[2] a designation which went out of use as soon as their tribal names became widely known and the names 'Bastarnae' or 'Peucini' came into common use. The presence of the Celts in the Danubian delta is confirmed by Celtic names of a few strongholds, at present earthworks, at the western limit of the delta,[3] Noviodunum (modern Isaccea) and Arrubium (modern Macin); Aliobrix (Orlovka) also bears a Celtic name: it lay on the northern bank of the Danube in Bessarabia (*Ill. 1*). According to Much (1890, 75–80) the latter name means 'the castle in a foreign country'. Farther east, still on the northern bank of the Danube, lies the town of Izmail, where a Middle La Tène Celtic brooch has been found.

The Bastarnae were divided into several tribes, but only three are known by name. Two of these, the Atmoni and Sidoni, have been located by some authors somewhere in the north-east Carpathians, while those on the Danubian island of Peuce, mentioned above, were called the Peucini.

Many scholars believe in the Germanic or Teutonic origin of the Bastarnae. Their views are based chiefly on works by ancient historians who, like Tacitus, although hesitantly, classify the Bastarnae as Germans. Professor Radu Vulpe was the first to attribute to them the Poienești-Lukashevka group of Bessarabia and Moldavia (Vulpe 1955; Zaharia *et al.* 1970, 54ff., 640f., Machinskii 1966, 82–96; Fedorov 1957, 51–62; 1960, 8–56). This group contains material similar to that of the Przeworsk Culture of Poland, and is even closer to the Jastorf Culture in north Germany. A few cremation cemeteries and a number of settlements have been attributed to the Poienești-Lukashevka Culture. They extend over a strip of land from about the middle Dniester, across the middle of Bessarabia to Iași, and then along the central part of Moldavia nearly to the junction of the River Birlat with the Sereth.

The erroneous assumption underlying this theory of the relationship of the Bastarnae and the Poienesti-Lukashevka group has already been exposed in the literature (Gajewski 1959, 286–92; Nosek 1946, 46ff., 142). The most important refutation of its credibility is the gap between the time of the recorded arrival of the Bastarnae in the North Pontic

1 Quoted after Nosek (1946, 48f.) who cites the relevant passage of Polybius (*Livius* XL.57): 'facile Bastarnis iter daturos: nec enim aut lingua aut moribus obhorrere'.

2 Powell (1958, 21) points out that the name 'Galatae' was widely used by Gréek writers as an equivalent for Keltoi-Celtae.

3 *Tabula Imperii Romani*, L 35 Bucharest. Bucharest 1969, 22, 24, 53, 78. The entry on 'Arubium' mentions the 'ruins of a Celtic citadel'.

area, who reached the Danubian delta in 240–230 BC, and the date of the earliest remains of Poienești-Lukashevka type, placed at the very end of the second or rather in the first century BC. No traces of this culture have been found in the region of the Danubian delta, the area where the presence of the Bastarnae has been well attested by ancient records. Remains of Poienești-Lukashevka type are concentrated mostly along the central part of Moldavia, in the regions which have not been connected with Bastarnian settlement as recorded by the ancients.

The Bastarnae were a hybrid race. Strabo (VII.3.2) says that their tribes are mingled with the Geto-Thracians, and also with the Celtic tribes, the Boii, Scordisci and the Teurisci. Plutarch (Much 1890, 76) considers them as a kind of warrior-caste or nobility, whose necessities of life were provided by their bondsmen. They seem to have been a troop of well-armed, experienced and tough warriors who imposed themselves on the indigenous Dacian population; but in mingling with the natives, they were gradually absorbed by them, although probably remaining the ruling class. They must have been in close contact with the surviving groups of the Scythians, with the smaller intrusive Germanic tribes, and with the Sarmatian Iazyges, with whom they freely intermarried (Tacitus, *Germania* XLVI).

Since their arrival in the region of the Danubian delta, the activities of the Celtic Bastarnae were frequently recorded by ancient writers; this was due mainly to the proximity of Greek coastal cities, and subsequently of the Roman frontier. This territory is, however, beyond the scope of our present study.

The position was different farther north, where in the North Pontic area the Bastarnae were barred from direct contact with the Greek cities by peoples living in the intermediary zone. The only recorded activity of the Bastarnae in that area was the destructive raid (in which they appear under the name of the Galati) undertaken jointly with the Scires around 190 BC, a raid which reached the estuary of the Southern Bug and threatened Olbia. Archaeological investigations in the neighbourhood of Olbia and along the sea coast up to the lower Dniester have revealed the extent of the destruction of rural settlements in that area at the beginning of the second century BC (Synytsyn 1959, 32; Viazmitina 1962, 5f.). This destruction most probably occurred during the raid of *c.* 190 BC and suggests the route it must have taken.

A glimpse of the situation in the North Pontic area in the second and first centuries BC is given by Strabo (VII.3.17) who says that between the Danube and the Dnieper extended, first, the 'Desert of the Getae' (the Bessarabian steppe), then the country of the Tyregetae on the estuary of the Dniester; next was the country of the Sarmatian Iazyges and that of the 'Basileans' ('the Royals'), probably descendants of the Royal Scythians; and then that of the 'Urgi' whose name is usually regarded as a corruption of Herodotus' 'Georgi'. Further, Strabo says '. . . and in the interior dwell, first the Bastarnae, whose country borders on that of the Tyregetae and Germans . . .'. We may assume accordingly that the country of the Bastarnae lay within the forest-steppe zone and extended from the Pruth north of Iași north-eastwards over the area of the middle Dniester into southern Podolia, where the Bastarnae bordered on the Iazyges 'with whom they freely intermarried'.

In the absence of written records, we have to examine both the archaeological evidence for Celtic activities in the North Pontic area, and the impact of Celtic culture on that of the native population of the region. Thus four sites on the middle Dniester, quoted by Ptolemy (III.5.15), Carrodunum, Eractum, Maeotonium and Vibrantavarium, all Celtic names, attest to Celtic presence in the country mentioned above as the land of the Bastarnae. The actual position of these sites has not been established, but they should be identified with some of the earthworks on the middle Dniester, supposedly built by the Getae in the fourth or third century BC (Meliukova 1958, 96ff., Fig. 30:22; Kukharenko 1959a, 45; Ambroz 1966, 12, 19; Fedorov 1960). In one of these, the earthwork at Grigorovka near Mogilev Podolskii, two bronze brooches of respectively Early and Middle La Tène type found together with a ribbed bronze bracelet, are probably attributable to the Celts. La Tène objects were also found in the earthworks of Sakharna and Bucheny near Rezina farther down the river.

Brooches of so-called 'Middle La Tène form' were also found in two 'Scythian' barrow graves in the steppe on the lower Dniester in the region of Tiraspol (Meliukova 1962, 152ff.; Kukharenko 1959a, 45; Ambroz 1966, 14, 21). The burials were in fact Iazygian, as indicated by the date of the brooches, late second to early first century BC, the time at which, according to Strabo, the Iazyges lived in the area.

The diffusion of Celtic La Tène objects in the North Pontic countries east of the Lipica territory is very uneven, and their distribution is different in the three areas distinguishable there (Kukharenko

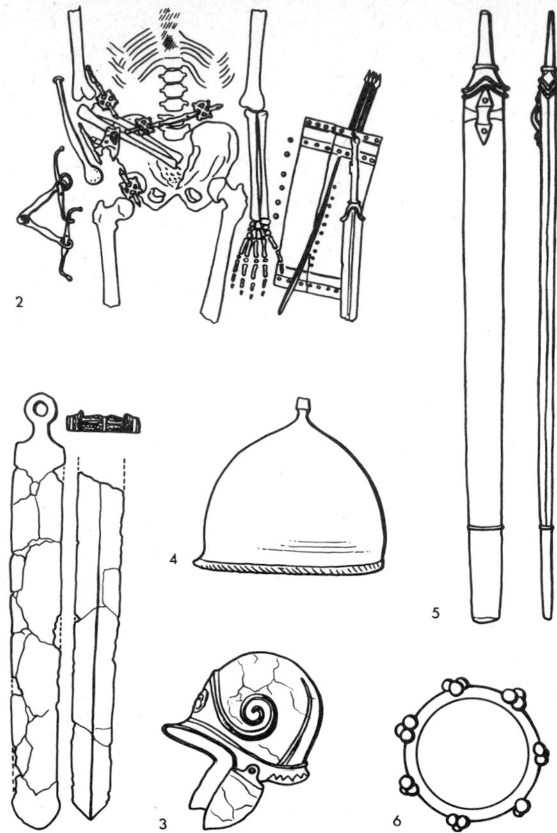

3 Celtic weapons found in Eastern Europe: 1–3, from a princely burial in the mausoleum at Scythian Neapolis in the Crimea; 4, bronze La Tène helmet from Mogila-Tokmak near Melitopol; 5, Middle La Tène sword from a grave at Verkhna Tarasovka near Nikopol; 6, bronze ring of the fourth to third century BC from a grave at Prusy near Smiela (after Pogrebova).

1959a; Woźniak 1974, 139ff.). The first of these areas is the steppe in the south of the country; the second extends over the forest-steppe zone in the middle, and the third one embraces the southern part of the deciduous forest zone up to about the Pripet marshes in the north.

First, to deal with the steppe zone in the south. Brooches of Middle and Late La Tène type have been found scattered over the area, either as isolated finds or in Late Scythian barrow graves on the lower Dnieper, the Molochna and the Donets south of Kharkov (Kukharenko 1959a).[4] Some thirty Middle and Late La Tène brooches have been found in the ruins of ancient Olbia while a few come from 'Scythian' barrow graves at Ostrovka (formerly Marizin) nearby.

A number of Celtic weapons have been discovered in this area also (Bodianskii 1962, 272ff.; Viazmitina 1962, 120f., Fig. 61, 230; 1969, 69ff., 74). From a Late Scythian burial at Verkhna Tarasovka on the lower Dnieper near Nikopol comes an iron sword of the second century BC (*Ill. 3: 5*); and two iron swords were excavated in the Late Scythian earthwork of Zolota Balka in the same region farther down the river. The impact of Celtic culture is also noticeable in the archaeological material from other Late Scythian earthworks on the lower Dnieper. The Crimea was also affected; in the earliest, second century BC, royal burial in the mausoleum at Scythian Neapolis (Pogrebova 1961, 103–213, Fig. 4:2; Sulimirski 1970, 128ff., Fig. 46:c), Celtic swords, a bronze helmet and some other items formed part of the grave-goods (*Ill. 3: 1–3*).

The most important find from the region is however the burial at Marievka (formerly Bugovskii near Romanova Balka;[5] *Ills. 4, 5*). The site lay at a distance of about 5 km west of the Southern Bug and some 40 km north-west of Voznesensk, near the border of the steppe and forest-steppe zones. This was an inhumation barrow grave of the first century BC, opened by local peasants.[6] Items saved from the grave-goods consist of a bronze helmet, bronze situla, two bronze and three iron cheek-pieces, a pair of iron bits, two iron spearheads, and a few other items. The imported helmet and some smaller items of the equipment suggest that a Celtic prince may have been buried there. The horse-gear is Scythian or Sarmatian: cheek-pieces of the same type have been found in the Sarmatian princely burial at Antipovka near Voronezh (Gushchina 1961, 241–7), but also in the remains of the Celtic settlement at Halish-Lovachka near Mukachevo, Carpathian Ukraine (Bidzila 1964, 122, Pl. VI:7–10); the second bit (*Ill. 4:6*) has its counterpart in the hoard from Bravicheni in Bessarabia (Fedorov 1960, 9, Fig. 1:16).

The helmet from Marievka (*Ill. 4:8*) represents an

[4] Stray: Lepinskaya, Vodianoe; Scythian burials: Kamenka, Znamenka, Nikolaevka-Kozatskoe; Sarmatian burials: Novo-Filipovka, Petrovskoe.

[5] Iakounina-Ivanova (1927, 100–8), erroneously published the find as from 'Bougakom near Romanko-Balkovo'.

[6] A. M. Tallgren in a note at the end of the article by Iakounina-Ivanova (1927).

Italo-Celtic or Graeco-Italic type.[7] Four specimens of this type were found in four Sarmatian princely graves farther east, sites about 400 to 600 km distant from each other.[8] The easternmost of these lies near Saratov on the lower Volga, the northernmost at Antipovka, mentioned above. All helmets are to be dated in the first century BC. That from Marievka seems to have been brought overland from Central Europe. It cannot be ascertained, however, whether the other specimens which reached sites on the Molochna (Mogila Tokmak, *Ill. 3:4*), the lower and upper Don and on the lower Volga were brought overland through Celtic commercial channels, or by sea and imported by merchants from the Bosporus. None the less, a few Celtic-type bracelets and Middle La Tène brooches found in Sarmatian barrow graves in the Volga steppe, and a Celtic bronze cauldron from the Sarmatian burial at Sadovy near Novocherkassk (Kaposhina 1969, 76–9, Fig. 22), imply that the influence of Celtic culture had spread as far as the Volga.

Different was the diffusion of 'Celtic' objects, mainly brooches and bracelets, in the Ukrainian forest-steppe zone (Kukharenko 1959a, 48f.). East of the Dnieper they have been found in only a few scattered sites. The bulk of finds come from the country west of the river, where they appear mainly in two concentrations situated quite close to each other, a smaller concentration on the River Tiasmin south of Cherkassy, and a larger one in the region of Kanev. Outside these two areas only a few isolated finds have been recorded. Mainly Middle but also some Late La Tène brooches have been found, sometimes several examples at one site. In the Tiasmin group some brooches occur in Late Scythian burials, while within the territory of the Zarubintsy Culture, (Kukharenko 1964, 30ff., 48ff.; Tretiakov 1966, 200–20), which also embraces the area of the Kanev group (*Ill. 1*), La Tène fibulae are often found in burials sometimes together with specimens of the local 'Zarubintsy type', a variant of the classic Celtic brooches (Kukharenko 1961; Ambroz 1969, 184–90).

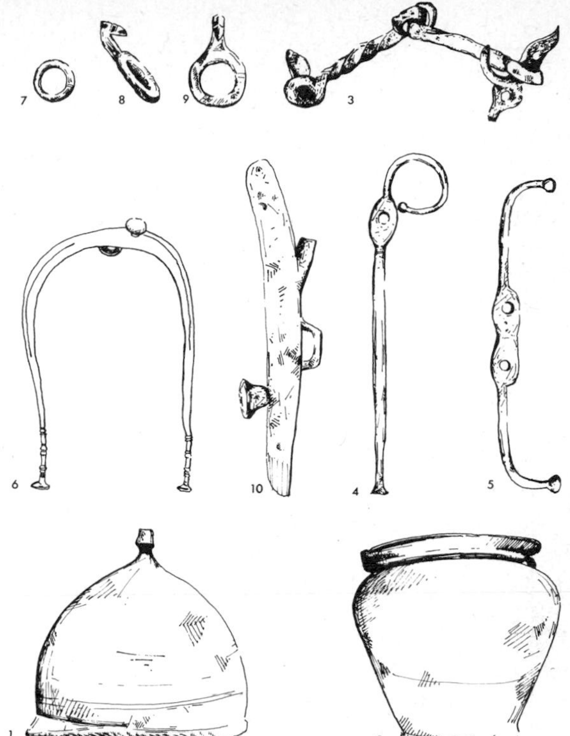

4 1, Bronze helmet; 2, situla; 3, bridle-bit; 4–6, cheek-pieces; 7–9, parts of horse harness from the burial at Marievka (Bougakom) (after Iakounina-Ivanova).

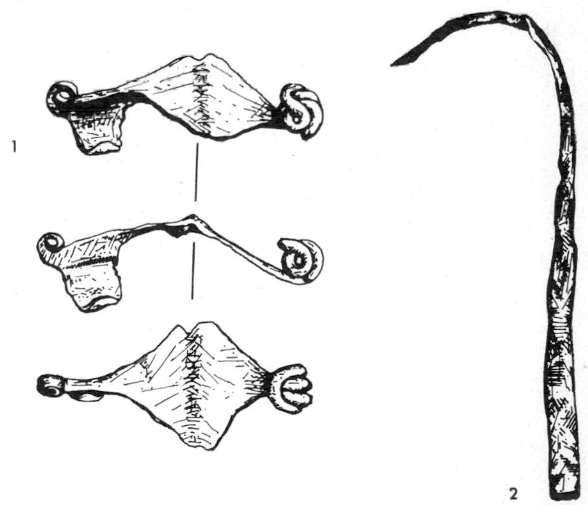

5 1, Bronze brooch with incised tremolo ornament (inset); 2, iron spearhead from the burial at Marievka (after Iakounina-Ivanova).

[7] A. Mahr, quoted by A. M. Tallgren at the end of the article by Iakounina-Ivanova (1927).

[8] a) Mogila-Tokmak, 60 km north-east of Melitopol (*Ill. 3:4*); Reinecke (1948, 90–6); b) Veselii on the Manych; Artamonov (1935, 208; c) Tonkoshurovka (formerly Marienthal), *c.* 50 km north-east of Saratov; Kukharenko (1959, 50); d) Antipovka, 40 km west of Voronezh; Gushchina (1961), from a princely grave.

Bracelets of La Tène type were not common, but of interest are ring-pendants with small decorative birds or bear figurines as found at Pasterskoe, Kanev and Pekary; at Pekary iron Celtic spurs and a small bronze pendant of Celtic character were found (*Ill. 6:4*), the latter in the shape of a human face or mask (Machinskii 1973, 3–9, Fig. 1–6).

The sole find in the northern area attributable to the Celts is the cremation burial in a grey wheel-turned urn found at Zalesie near the junction of the Pripet with the Dnieper (*Ill. 6:1,2*); the burial included an Early La Tène type brooch (Machinskii 1973, Fig. 1:1,2; Kukharenko 1959a, 48; 1959b, 27ff.). This isolated grave, probably of the second century BC, lay in the centre of the original territory of the Zarubintsy Culture, which developed there in turn out of the local substratum of the Milograd Culture; the southern division of the latter culture, south of the Pripet, was strongly affected by the Scythian Culture. The formative agent in the Zarubintsy Culture seems to have been the Pomeranian Culture influence which infiltrated there from the west, as postulated by some Soviet scholars (Nikitina 1964, 43–7; 1965, 194–204; Kukharenko 1957, 91–3; 1960, 289–300). Celtic elements seem to have also been active in the process of the final development of the culture either directly, or possibly by the intermediary of the Pomeranian Culture, which was already affected by Celtic influence (Woźniak 1970, 176ff.; 1971, 504–19; Shchukin 1973, 17–23). The brooches of the Zarubintsy type, a development of Celtic La Tène fibulae forms, support this assumption.

Of particular interest is the diffusion (according to Trubachev)[9] of Illyro-Celtic, or perhaps rather Thraco-Celtic, toponyms in the country south of the River Pripet, within the original area of the Zarubintsy Culture, and in a still larger number in the territory of the Lipica Culture (*Ill. 1*). The Celts seem to have been responsible for this phenomenon, the Illyrian and Thracian elements having been absorbed by them during their period of settlement in the Alpine region and Bohemia, and subsequently in the Carpathians.

The character of Celtic La Tène finds in Eastern Europe and other phenomena briefly reviewed here seem clearly to attest the presence of the Celts in the western part of the North Pontic area from the late third to the first century BC. Their presence in the region of Olbia has been recorded by ancient writers. To deny this factor, as well as their sojourn in the region of the upper Tisza and the territory of the Lipica Culture,[10] is contrary to the incontestable facts. The Celts, that is the Bastarnae, were not the sole inhabitants of any one area of the regions described here; they lived amongst the indigenous

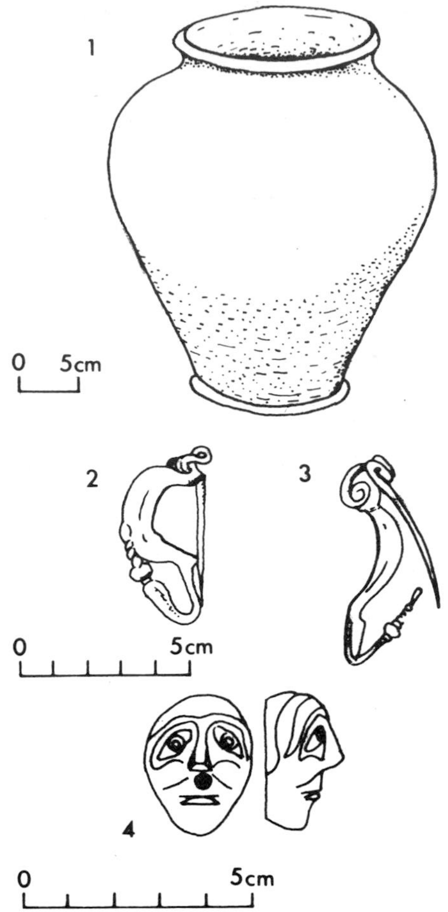

6 1,2, La Tène urn and bronze brooch from Zalesie; 3, bronze brooch from Liniaevo; 4, bronze 'mask' from Pekary, probably representing a Celtic goddess (after Machinskii).

[9] Quoted by Machinskii (1973, 9; Fig. 2). It may be mentioned in this context that the topographical names in Germany and Poland which used to be regarded as 'Illyrian', have lately been considered mostly 'Venetic'.

[10] E.g. Braichevskii and Bidzila (1966, 57–64, 267f.). Woźniak (1966, 65–82, 265f.) demonstrates the baselessness of such a theory.

population, forming its leading or upper class, exercising a considerable and lasting influence on the culture of the peoples of a large part of Eastern Europe (Kukharenko 1959a, 41–3).

In discussing the presence of the Celts in Eastern Europe the gradual transformation of the culture of migrating tribes from still farther east should always be taken into account. As shown by Abramova (1961, 108ff.), as time elapsed since leaving their country of origin, during their westward advance the Sarmatians progressively lost several features characteristic of their culture proportionately to the distance which actually separated them from their former homeland. A good example of this process can be seen in the considerable difference between the culture of the Iazyges on the Hungarian Plain, and their culture at the time when they still lived on the North Pontic steppe (Sulimirski 1970, 133f., 171ff.; Párducz 1941; 1944; 1950; Harmatta 1950). The same undoubtedly applies to the Celtic tribes, who not only had gradually lost some features characteristic of their original culture, but had also progressively adopted elements of the cultures of those natives among whom they temporarily settled during their drive eastwards. The final result of this development was the loss of their identity.

Bibliography

AAC	Acta Archaeologica Carpathica
AO	Arkheologicheskie Otkrytiya
KSIAM	Kratkie Soobshcheniya Instituta Arkheologiyi AN SSSR
KSIIMK	Kratkie Soobschcheniya Instituta Istorii Materialnoy Kultury
MIA	Materialy i Issledovaniya po Arkheologii SSSR
SA	Sovetskaya Arkheologiya
SVOD	Svod Arkheologicheskikh Istochnikov, Arkheologiya SSSR

ABRAMOVA, M. P. 1961 Sarmatskie pogrebeniya Dona i Ukrainy – II v. do n.e. – I v.n.e., *SA* (1), 91–110.

AMBROZ, A. K. 1959 Fibuly Zarubinetskoy kultury, *MIA* 70, 184–90.

1966 Fibuly Iuga Evropeyskoy Chasti SSR, *SVOD* D-1-30, Moscow.

ARTAMONOV, M. I. 1935 Raboty na stroitelstve Manychskogo kanala, *Izvestiya Gosudarstvennoy Akademii Istorii Materialnoy Kultury* 109, 208.

BERCIU, D. 1966 Les Celtes et la Civilisation de La Tène chez les Géto-Daces, *Bulletin of Institute of Archaeology* No. 6, 75–93.

1967 *Romania before Burebista*, London.

BIDZILA, V. I. 1964 Poselennya Halish-Lovachka, *Arkheologiya* XVII, 92–143.

BODIANSKII, A. V. 1962 Skifskoe pogrebenie s latenskim mechom v Srednem Podneprovie, *SA* (1), 272–6.

BRAICHEVSKII, M. and BIDZILA, V. 1966 Problema Keltov v Severo-Vostochnom Prikarpati, *AAC* VIII, 57–64, 267–8. In Russian; Polish summary.

FEDOROV, G. B. 1957 Lukashevskii mogilnik, *KSIIMK* 68, 51–62.

1960 Naselenie prutsko-dnestrovskogo mezhdurechya v I tysyacheletii n. e, *MIA* 89, 8–56.

FILIP, J. 1956 *Keltové ve střední Evropě*, Prague.

GAJEWSKI, L. 1959 Review in Polish of Vulpe (1955), with French résumé, *AAC* I/2, 286–92.

GUSHCHINA, I. I. 1961 Sluchaynaya nakhodka v Voronezhskoy oblasti, *SA* (2), 241–7.

HARMATTA, J. 1950 *Studies in the History of the Sarmatians*, Budapest.

IAKOUNINA-IVANOVA, L. 1927 Une trouvaille de l'âge de La Tène dans la Russie méridionale, *Eurasia Septentrionalis Antiqua* I, Helsinki, 100–8.

KAPOSHINA, S. I. 1969 Keltskii kotel iz Sadovogo kurgana u Novocherkasska, *KSIAM* 116, 76–9.

KOZŁOWSKI, L. 1939 *Zarys pradziejów Polski południowo-wschodniej*, Lwów.

KRUSHELNYTSKA, L. I. 1964 Doslidzhennya verkhnikh shariv poselennya bilya s. Bovshiv, Ivano-Frankivskoy oblasti, u 1961 r. *Materialy i Doslidzhennya z Arkheologii Prykarpattya i Volyni* V, 130–8, Kiev.

1965 Keltskii pamyatnik v Verkhnem Podnestrovie, *KSIAM* 105, 119–22.

KUKHARENKO, I. V. 1957 Nekotorye itogi izucheniya Pripyatskogo Polesya, *Kratkie Soobshcheniya Instituta Arkheologii* 7, 91–3, Kiev.

1959a Rasprostanenie latenskikh veshey na territorii Vostochnoy Evropy, *SA* (1), 31–51.

1959b Pamytniki Zarubinetskoy kultury v oblasti Verkhnego Podneprovya, *MIA* 70, 22–31.

1960 K voprosu o proiskhozhdenii Zarubinetskoy kultury, *SA*, 289–300, map on 288.

1961 Pamiatniki zheleznogo veka na territorii Polesia, *SVOD* D-1-29, Moscow.

1964 Zarubinetskaya kultura, *SVOD* D-1-19, Moscow.

MACHINSKII, D. A. 1966 K voprosu o datirovke, proiskhozhdenii i etnicheskoy prinadlezhnosti pamyatnikov tipa Poianeshti-Lukashevka, *Arkheologiya starogo i novogo sveta*, 82–96, Moscow.

1973 O kulture Srednego Podneprovya na rubezhe Skifskogo i Sarmatskogo periodov, *KSIAM* 133, 3–9.

MELIUKOVA, A. L. 1958 Pamyatniki skifskogo vremeni lesostepnogo Srednogo Podnestrovya, *MIA* 64, 5–102.

1962 Skifskie kurgany Tiraspolshchiny, *MIA* 115, 114–66.

MELNIKOVSKAYA, O. N. 1967 *Plemena Iuzhnoy Belorussii v Rannem Zheleznom veke*, Moscow.

MUCH, R. 1890 Die Bastarnen, *Mitt. d. Anthrop. Ges.* XX, 75–80.

NIKITINA, V. B. 1964 Vnov otkrytie pamyatniki Pomorskoy kultury, *KSIAM* 102, 43–7.

1965 Pamyatniki Pomorskoy kultury v Belorussii i na Ukraine, *SA* (1), 194–204.

NOSEK, S. 1946 *Kultura grobów skrzynkowych i podkloszowych w Polsce południowo-zachodniej*, Kraków.

PACHKOVA, S. P. 1972 Raskopki na srednem Dnestre, *AO*, 320.

PÁRDUCZ, M. 1941 Denkmäler der Sarmatenzeit Ungarns, *Arch. Hungr.* XXV.

1944 Denkmäler der Sarmatenzeit Ungarns, *Arch. Hungr.* XXVIII.

1950 Denkmäler der Sarmatenzeit Ungarns, *Arch. Hungr.* XXX.

POGREBOVA, N. N. 1961 Pogrebeniya v mavzolee Neapola Skifskogo, *MIA* 96, 103–213.

POWELL, T. G. E. 1958 *The Celts*, London.

REINECKE, P. 1948 Ein neuer Bronzehelm italischer Form, *Festschrift für O. Tschumi*, 90–6, Frauenfeld.

RUSSU, I. I. et al. 1969 *Tabula Imperii Romani. Romula-Durostorum-Tomis*, Bucharest.

RUSU, M. and BANDULA, O. 1970 *Mormintul unei Căpeteni Celtice de la Ciumeşti*, Baia Mare.

SHCHUKIN, M. B. 1973 Chernyakhovskaya kultura i yavlenie keltskogo renessansa, *KSIAM* 133, 17–23.

SKORYK, M. 1931 Pro nazvu 'Boyky', *Litopys Boykivshchyny* I, 6–23, 172–3, Sambor.

SMISZKO, M. 1932 *Kultury wczesnego okresu epoki cesarstwa rzymskiego w Małopolsce Wschodniej*, Lwów.

1934 Osady kultury lipickiej, *Prace Lwowskiego Tow. Prehistorycznego* Nr. 1, Lwów.

1935 Znalezisko wczesnorzymskie z Kołokolina, pow. rohatyński, *Wiadomości Archeologiczne* XIII, 155–64.

1936 Stan i potrzeby badań nad okresem Cesarstwa rzymskiego w południowo-wschodniej Polsce, *Wiadomości Archeologiczne* XIV, 125–39.

1948 Doba poliv pokhovan v zakhidnikh oblastyakh URSR, *Arkheologiya* II, 98–127.

1957 Bogatoe pogrebenie nachala nashey ery vo Lvovskoy oblasti, *SA* (1), 238–43.

SPROCKHOFF, E. 1925 *Reallexikon d. Vorgeschichte* V, ed. M. Ebert, 294–7, Pl. 90a.

SULIMIRSKI, T. 1934 Trzy chaty przedhistoryczne, *Prace Lwowskiego Tow. Prehistorycznego* Nr. 1, 33–43, Lwów.

1936 *Scytowie na Zachodniem Podolu*, Lwów.

1970 *The Sarmatians*, London.

1974 Trakowie w północnych Karpatach i problem pochodzenia Wołochów, *AAC* XIV, 89–105.

SVESHNIKOV, I. K. 1957 Mogilniki lipitskoy kultury v Lvovskoy oblasti, *KSIAM* 68, 63–74

SYNYTSYN, M. S. 1959 Naselennya Dnistro-Buzkoho Prychornomorya Skifsko-Sarmataskoho chasu, *Materialy z Arkheologii Pivnichnoho Prichornomorya* II, 13–35, Odessa.

TRETIAKOV, P. N. 1966 *Finno-Ugry, Balty i Slaviane na Dnepre i Volge*, Moscow-Leningrad.

VIAZMITINA, M. I. 1962 *Zolota Balka*, Kiev.

1969 Kultura naseleniya Nizhnego Dnepra posle raspada edinoy Skifii, *SA* (4), 62–77.

VULPE, R. 1955 *Le probléme des Bastarnes à la lumière des découvertes archéologiques en Moldavie*, Bucharest.

WOŹNIAK, Z. 1970 *Osadnictwo celtyckie w Polsce*. Wrocław-Warsaw-Cracow.

1971 Die jüngste Phase der keltischen Kultur in Polen, *Archeologické Rozhledy* XXIII, 504–19.

1974 *Wschodnie pogranicze kultury lateńskiej*, Wrocław-Warsaw-Cracow.

ZAHARIA, N., PETRESCU-DÎMBOVIŢA, M. and ZAHARIA, E. 1970 *Ascezări din Moldova*, Bucharest.

ZIRRA, V. 1967 *Un cimitr Celtic în Nord-Vestul României*, Baia Mare.

21

SIGFRIED J. DE LAET

Native and Celt in the Iron Age of the Low Countries

IT is always tempting to try and combine archaeological sources with the earliest written documents available for a particular area. This exercise has often been attempted for northern Gaul in the period of the Roman conquest of the middle of the first century BC. The two main problems which have most frequently been discussed are firstly the ethnic affinities of the inhabitants of northern Gaul, and secondly the attribution of the archaeological remains to the different tribes mentioned by Caesar as living in this region.

There is no need to consider extensively here the first of these problems, which originates in the apparently contradictory statements of Caesar's *De Bello Gallico.* This author stresses that the River Rhine was the frontier between *Galli* and *Germani*, and he includes northern Gaul – the territory of the *Belgae* – within the Celtic area; on the other hand he designates several Belgic tribes – namely the *Eburones, Condrusi, Caeroesi, Paemani* and *Segni* – as *Germani cisrhenani*; he adds that most of the *Belgae* were descendants of *Germani* who earlier crossed the Rhine to settle in northern Gaul. A partial solution of this problem is to be found in recent studies by C. F. C. Hawkes (1965) and Rolf Hachmann (1971; see also Hachmann, Kossack, and Kuhn 1962; De Laet 1974, 519ff.). Both authors have drawn attention to the fact that the first mention of *Germani* is to be found in Posidonius, who uses the name to indicate a group of Celtic tribes living initially on the right bank of the Rhine to the north of the Helvetii. For political reasons it would seem that Caesar wanted to distinguish clearly these Celtic-speaking *Germani* from the other Celtic tribes because, among other reasons, he wished to give the impression in Rome that he had conquered the entire Celtic area (*Gallia omnis*), despite his failure to subdue the Celtic territory east of the Rhine. Afterwards, the Romans transferred the name of these Celtic-speaking *Germani* to the Germanic-speaking peoples, who never actually called themselves *Germani*, and who subsequently, in the time of the civil wars and the reign of Augustus, gradually occupied the territory of the real *Germani* (Schönberger 1952; Hachmann and Kossack in Hachmann, Kossack, and Kuhn 1962). For the present argument it is important to point out that archaeological sources, as well as numismatics, the history of religion and linguistic studies, all indicate that Celts were living in northern Gaul at the time of the Roman conquest, which indeed supports the evidence of the earliest written sources (De Laet 1974, *loc. cit.*).[1]

I do not think, however, that the tribes living in this area formed a homogeneous Celtic unity, and I am of the opinion that only the upper classes – kings, aristocracy, priests, and warriors – must undoubtedly be regarded as Celts, but that the lower classes had a different ethnic origin and were not yet completely celticized in Caesar's time. This brings us to the second problem, which was for the first time seriously discussed in Mariën's *Oud België* published in 1952. In 1958, I also tried to group the archaeological finds from the La Tène III period and to ascribe each of these several groups to one particular tribe. It becomes clear that the solutions proposed originally by Mariën and by the present writer are unsatisfactory, in view of the continual need to revise our groupings and their tribal interpretations in the light of new discoveries (Mariën 1952; 1961a; 1961b; 1970; 1971; De Laet 1958; De Laet and Glasbergen 1959; De Laet and Van Doorselaer 1973). Amongst the main difficulties encountered in studying this problem is the fact that it is almost impossible to give a precise date to the majority of La Tène sites in northern Gaul, and that most of these sites show a number of separate and individual characteristics; this means that it is seldom possible to group the sites in geographical

[1] According to Kuhn (in Hachmann, Kossack, and Kuhn 1962) and to Gysseling (1960; 1962a; 1962b), place-name studies indicate traces of an Indo-European language which is neither Celtic nor Germanic. These indications, however, cannot be dated with any degree of precision, and could even go back as far as the Early Bronze Age (De Laet 1974, 523–4).

and archaeological units (De Laet and Van Doorselaer 1973). The main cause of this failure, however, probably lies in the mistaken premiss that in Caesar's time a tribe formed not only a political unit but also a homogeneous cultural entity. It is the last notion that we shall discuss in this paper.

The starting-point of my hypothesis is the existence in the Celtic world of a strongly differentiated social structure, which is already mentioned by the earliest authors. The contrast is especially clear between the upper classes, the aristocracy (kings, nobles, druids) and its client-warriors on the one hand, and on the other hand the lower classes (craftsmen, peasants, fishermen and so on). In our opinion it is possible to show, through a close examination of the ethnogenesis of the Celtic tribes in the south of the Low Countries, that at least in this area these different social classes had distinct ethnic origins. If this is indeed the case, then it must also be possible to show that the contemporary archaeological material is not the reflection of the different tribes, as had previously been accepted, but displays the different social classes within these tribes (De Laet 1974, Ch. 11). We must therefore first of all consider briefly the ethnogenesis of the tribes concerned.

During the Late Bronze Age, between the north and south of the Low Countries, a clear cultural frontier came into existence, following the Lower Rhine from its delta to its confluence with the River Lippe and farther east along this same river. The frontier survived during the entire Iron Age, with the south forming part of the Hallstatt and La Tène cultural provinces, while the area to the north of the Great Rivers continued essentially to maintain Late Bronze Age traditions and exhibits completely different characteristics. This cultural frontier has its origin in the immigration, into the region between the Lower Rhine and the North Sea, of new populations belonging to the Urnfield Culture. Their arrival here can be dated to Ha A2 and Ha B, or relatively late in the evolution of this culture (Desittere 1968; De Laet 1974, Ch. 9). Many authors in the past have discussed the question of whether the Urnfield people were already Celts, that is, Celtic-speaking. In my opinion this problem is insoluble, since one cannot really ascertain whether certain populations were indeed speaking Celtic as early as the eleventh to ninth centuries BC. Yet it is certain that the Urnfield people played an important part in the genesis of the Iron Age Celts, since they formed the main ethnic component in those regions – Switzerland, southern Germany, eastern France – which were the cradle of the Celts; this does not exclude the possibility that other elements may also have played a rôle in the same process of cultural growth. As far as can be determined archaeologically, the arrival of Urnfield groups in the south of the Low Countries seems to have been a peaceful immigration rather than a violent invasion, since almost immediately after their arrival they apparently became intermingled with the indigenous population. This is shown by the pottery, burial rite, and grave structures (De Laet 1963; Desittere 1968). As a result of this peaceful and rapid integration of these immigrants into the native communities, a number of local cultural groups came into being in the south of the Low Countries. It is not relevant to enter here into the basically unimportant controversy about the names to be given to these groups: do they still belong to the Urnfield Culture, or must the continuity of the native elements be emphasized (cf. Desittere 1974)? Actually there is general agreement that both Urnfield elements and indigenous survivals are present, and it seems gratuitous to try and find out which elements were quantitatively the more important. It is more useful for our analysis to note the existence in this area, at the transition from the Bronze Age to the Iron Age, of several cultural groups showing a number of common traits as well as obvious differences. Notwithstanding the prominence of Urnfield elements in these groups, it is difficult to call them Celtic or proto-Celtic. During the whole of the Iron Age the lower classes must have been composed of descendants of these native groups.

During the seventh century BC, the make-up of the population in our area was greatly modified by the invasion of several groups of Hallstatt warriors, who subdued the native population and settled there as a ruling class (Mariën 1958). Traces of these conquerors have been found in several regions, in the valleys of the Rivers Dyle and Haine, in the south of the province of Namur, and in the South Flemish hills, the Campine, and Dutch Limburg. This distribution does not rule out the possibility of more settlements in other areas where they have not yet been found. The intruders came from the south, some of them perhaps from Bourgogne or France-Comté; but the best-known group, that which settled in the Dyle Valley, more than probably had its origin in Bavaria, as is evident from the very characteristic grave-goods such as horse-trappings, chariot-fittings, and weapons (Mariën 1958; Kossack 1953; 1959). The cemetery of La

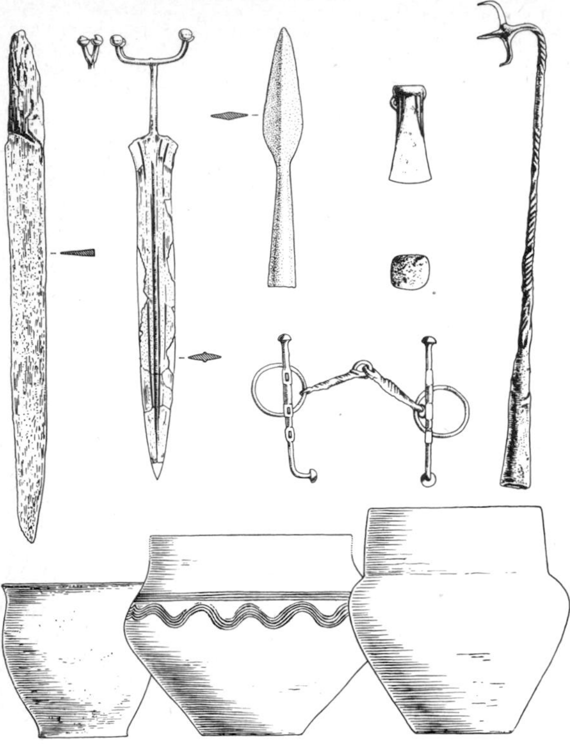

1 Court-Saint-Etienne, La Quenique, grave-goods from Tomb 3. Scale c. 1:8.

Quenique at Court-Saint-Etienne (*Ill. 1*) provides vital information about the relations in this Dyle group between the Hallstatt overlords and the native population: the indigenous urnfield, with its poor flat graves, already in use before the arrival of the Bavarian Hallstatt warriors, shows a strong contrast with the rich barrows of the latter. It is obvious that that natives had become no more than a subservient lower class. But already traces of the first stages of acculturation are to be seen: the pottery found in the barrows of the rulers is identical in shape and manufacture to that of the natives; it is equally far from impossible that the cremation rite as used by the warrior class was borrowed from the natives, since the Hallstatt people in eastern France used only the inhumation rite, while in Bavaria most of the graves were inhumations and cremation was rare.

The arrival of these Hallstatt warriors in the south of the Low Countries had two main consequences: the development of communities with clear social stratification dominated by a Celtic-speaking aristocracy, and the emergence of political structures which were new to this area – namely tribes. As regards the Celtic character of the aristocracy, I am personally convinced that the Celtic ruling classes which, as already noted, we find in the south of the Low Countries in Caesar's time were for the greater part descendants of the Hallstatt warriors who arrived here during the seventh century BC. The Hallstatt Culture which they introduced here at that time had a normal development, and the transition from the Hallstatt to the La Tène Culture took place almost everywhere with no interruption in the occupation (De Laet 1974, Ch. 10–11).[2] The Hallstatt warriors of the seventh century are in our opinion the very first elements in the prehistoric population of the Low Countries which may be surmised with a certain degree of probability to have been Celtic-speaking.

We have just mentioned that the arrival of these conquerors resulted in the introduction of new social and political structures. As far as can be deduced from the archaeological material, no political organization larger than the village existed in the south of the Low Countries during the Neolithic and the Bronze Age. It is true that different settlements of the same culture shared common traditions in many fields such as technology, houses, burial rites, religion and art; but there is no indication whatsoever that a larger political unit bound together these different villages. Within the villages themselves social differences undoubtedly existed, but they must have been relatively unimportant. This lack of an overall political structure, and the small distinctions between the social classes, might explain why during the Late Bronze Age the immigrant Urnfield groups were so easily and quickly integrated into the indigenous population. In the focal areas of the Hallstatt Culture, however, a further stage in social and political development had been reached already at the beginning of the Iron Age: tribes arose, that is, political units each with their own relatively large territory including several villages and settlements, each with a central authority exercised by a tribal chieftain assisted by a high social class whose surviving material wealth contrasts sharply with the miserable archaeological remains of the lower classes. It is, of course, possible that within one and the same tribe

[2] The problem of the transition from the Hallstatt to the La Tène period in Belgium is to be treated more extensively by the present writer and A. Van Doorselaer at the IXth International Congress of Prehistoric and Protohistoric Sciences to be held at Nice in 1976.

a cultural dichotomy existed: on the one hand an aristocracy with its own culture, religion and language, and on the other hand the lower classes – descended from the vanquished native population – with perhaps other traditions and customs and even a different language.

This seems precisely to have been the case in the south of the Low Countries. It is probable that, after having subjugated the native Late Bronze Age population, the various groups of Hallstatt warriors each settled in a particular area. These conquerors, travelling on horseback and coming from considerable distances away, may have not been accompanied by their wives but married local women, such as the daughters of village headmen; this could have favoured some acculturation and promoted better relations between the conquerors and at least part of the native populace. But most of the latter from then on formed a proletariat of craftsmen and peasants. When the tribal territories were defined, the conquerors did not take into account the different native groupings, thereby making it possible that one of these groups could thenceforth be spread over two or three tribes, or alternatively that one new tribe could include two or three of the earlier groups. Within the tribes, not only might a cultural opposition between upper and lower classes have existed, but also a cultural heterogeneity within the lower classes themselves.

During the six centuries separating the arrival of the Hallstatt warriors from the coming of Caesar, many political events transpired: here as in other parts of the Celtic world, the Iron Age was a period of unrest. We know little of what took place then, but doubtless further raids of Celtic warriors must have occurred, and a number of tribes or segments of them left the Low Countries to participate in the great Celtic expansion of the fifth and fourth centuries. Inter-tribal wars were common, and tribes were often divided internally by political struggles and *coups*. All this resulted in continuously changing boundaries between the different tribes. The principal actors in these events were the aristocracy and its warrior-clients, but the natives must have felt the consequences of the changes. Sedentary farmers tried obstinately to retain their ancestral fields, but in many cases war surely drove them away. A typical example of this is provided by the excavations in the Trou de l'Ambre at Eprave, where during the Late La Tène period a group of fugitives found a temporary refuge only to be exterminated soon afterwards (*Ill. 2*) (Mariën 1970). What emerges more often, however, is the fact that the

2 Trou de l'Ambre, Eprave. Late La Tène material.

3 Altrier, Luxembourg. Italic *stamnos*, sword, fibula and torque from chieftain's grave.

lower classes acquired new masters during such continual changes in tribal territory, and that villages closely related in culture came to form parts of different tribes. This fluid political situation certainly constituted a formidable obstacle to the progress of acculturation already mentioned. In addition, it seems that these political changes may have emphasized the established social oppositions.

In the present writer's opinion it is just this social contrast which we find reflected in the archaeological material. At present we cannot of course study the evidence in detail, but a few typical instances may illustrate the point (cf. De Laet 1974, Ch. 10 and 11). What is immediately apparent, when considering

4 The Kemmelberg. General view.

the material remains of the aristocracy and the warrior class, is that although on the one hand they bear an unmistakable pan-Celtic character, and their closest parallels are found in other parts of the Celtic world, on the other hand the influence of the native population is detectable in a number of features. One notes this dual character *inter alia* in a series of chieftain's burials, both from the Late Hallstatt period (Wijchen, Oss, Overasselt, Baarlo) and from the Early La Tène period (Eigenbilzen, and the recently excavated Altrier barrow: *Ill. 3*; cf. Thill 1972). Because of their typically Celtic grave-goods and Mediterranean luxury imports, they fit perfectly into the 'classic' Hallstatt and La Tène cultures, although certain elements in grave-structure and burial rite may indicate native influence: for example the circular ditch around the Oss barrow, and the fact that in all these chieftain's graves cremation was practised in contrast to the inhumation of such graves in other Celtic areas. The fortified princely dwellings, of which the best known are the Aleburg at Befort and the Kemmelberg (*Ill. 4*) in Western Flanders, can easily be compared to the *Fürstensitze* farther south. Despite the severe bombing of the site during the First World War, the Kemmelberg has yielded unmistakeable proof of the wealth of the chieftains who lived there in the Late Hallstatt and Early La Tène periods. It is for example the most north-westerly site where Attic pottery has been found. While the finer ware which was probably made locally shows typical Celtic characteristics, native survivals are visible in the coarse pottery (Van Doorselaer 1971; Van Doorselaer, De Meulemeester, and Putman 1974). We must leave aside other evidence of this leading Celtic aristocracy, such as the cemetery of La Courte at Leval-Tragegnies excavated poorly almost three-quarters of a century ago (Mariën 1961b). It would also exceed the limits of this paper to discuss a number of hoards, for instance that from Frasnes-lez-Buissenal, and surface finds which illustrate the wealth of the ruling class. But it is useful to mention here, because of their unusual nature, the Early La Tène barrows of the Crête Ardennaise groups (*Ill. 5*). They are the only Iron Age inhumation graves in the south of the Low countries. Although some of them are chariot-burials, the grave-goods are not rich enough to belong to the nobility; perhaps they are to be ascribed to a group of mercenaries in the pay of a local princeling.

The remains of the lower classes clearly differ from all this. A common characteristic is firstly their great poverty: luxury goods are lacking in both graves and settlements, and even modest ornaments and metal objects such as fibulae are exceptional. A second trait is the heterogeneity of the sites: rarely is it possible to group several sites into one unit. Thirdly we find both a remarkable number of survivals which go back to the Urnfield period, and also clear Celtic influences. Ancestral customs are evident in burial ritual and grave-structure, showing only a slow and relatively unimportant evolution since the arrival of the Urnfield people. Peasant conservatism is obvious in domestic pottery with its antiquated ornamentation, such as the coarsening of the surface and the finger-impressions on the rim, which continues throughout the Iron Age, and in which typical Urnfield shapes are still present in La Tène times. But it is also in pottery that the influences of the upper classes are visible: the so-called 'Marnian' pottery with its carinated profile, which one finds in Early La Tène cemeteries and settlements, is in the present writer's opinion a copy of the finer luxury pottery as it is known for instance from the Kemmelberg. Political instability must have been the reason why farmers sometimes fortified their villages (such as the Kesselberg) or erected hill-refuges which were used only in times of danger (such as Hastedon at Saint-Servais, *Ill. 6*, and Montauban at Buzenol). The method of construction of these fortifications differs from site to site, but here also the native traditions continue: elsewhere I have attempted to demonstrate that the wall at Hastedon is more closely related to some fortifications of the Urnfield period than to the Celtic *murus gallicus* (De Laet 1971).

To summarize, we think that the archaeological material from the Iron Age in the south of the Low Countries reflects not the political division of the population into tribes, but instead the social structure of a community in which two components are

5 Ste-Marie-Chevigny, Crête Ardennaise group. Pot (Tomb III), iron spearhead (Tomb V), bronze torques (Tomb III), and bronze bracelets (Tomb IV).

6 Saint-Servais, Hastedon. General view.

clearly to be seen: a ruling class of nobles and warriors who were doubtless Celts, and a lower class composed essentially of descendants of the earlier indigenous population which was vanquished by the Hallstatt warriors from the seventh century BC on. During the following six centuries a certain cultural rapprochement and a mutual influencing of both elements occurred, but social rivalries and unstable political circumstances made a complete integration impossible.

One is all too conscious of the fact that only new excavations can show the value of this new approach to archaeological material. Yet I trust that it will meet with Stuart Piggott's approval as an approach which might perhaps be usefully employed in other regions conquered by the Celts.

Bibliography

De Laet, S. J. 1958 *The Low Countries*, London.

1963 Eléments autochtones dans la civilisation des Champs d'Urnes en Belgique et aux Pays-Bas, in *A Pedro Bosch-Gimpera en el septuagésimo aniversario de su nacimiento*, Mexico, 119–27.

1971 Fortifications de l'époque de La Tène en Belgique, *Archeologické Rozhledy* 23, 432–50.

1974 *Prehistorische kulturen in het Zuiden der Lage Landen*, Wetteren.

De Laet, S. J. and Glasbergen, W. 1959 *De voorgeschiedenis der Lage Landen*, Groningen.

De Laet, S. J. and Van Doorselaer, A. 1973 Groupes culturels et chronologie de l'époque de La Tène en Belgique, in *Études Celtiques* XIII = *Actes du 4e Congrès international d'Études Celtiques*, 571–82.

Desittere, M. 1968 *De Urnenveldenkultuur in het gebied tussen Midden-Rijn en Noordzee* = *Dissertationes Archaeologicae Gandenses* XI, Bruges.

1974 Quelques considérations sur l'âge du bronze final et le premier âge du fer en Belgique et dans le sud des Pays-Bas, *Helinium* XIV, 105–34.

Gysseling, M. 1960 *Toponymisch woordenboek van België, Nederland, Luxemburg, Noord-Frankrijk en West-Duitsland (voor 1226)*, 2 vols, Tongeren.

1962a La genèse de la frontière linguistique dans le nord de la Gaule, *Revue du Nord* 44, 5–37.

1962b De Germaanse kolonisatie in Noord-Gallië volgens de teksten, *Handelingen van de koninklijke Commissie voor Toponymie en Dialectologie* 36, 39–48.

Hachmann, R. 1971 *The ancient civilization of the Germanic Peoples*, London.

Hachmann, R., Kossack, G. and Kuhn, H. 1962 *Völker zwischen Germanen und Kelten*, Neumünster.

Hawkes, C. F. C. 1965 Celtes, Gaulois, Germains, Belges, *Celticum* 12, 1–7 = *Suppl. à Ogam-Tradition Celtique* 98.

Kossack, G. 1953 Pferdegeschirr aus Gräbern der älteren Hallstattzeit Bayerns, *Jahrbuch d. Röm.-Germ. Zentralmuseums Mainz*, 111–78.

1959 Südbayern während der Hallstattzeit, *Röm. Germ. Forschungen* 24, Berlin.

Mariën, M. E. 1952 *Oud-België: van de eerste landbouwers tot de komst van Caeser*, Antwerp.

1958 Trouvailles du Champ d'Urnes et des tombelles hallstattiennes de Court-Saint-Etienne, *Monographies d'archéologie nationale* 1, Brussels.

1961a *La céramique en Belgique, de la préhistoire au Moyen Age*, Brussels.

1961b La période de La Tène en Belgique. Le groupe de la Haine, *Monographies d'archéologie nationale* 2, Brussels.

1970 Le Trou de l'Ambre au bois de Wérimont, Eprave, *Monographies d'archéologie nationale* 4, Brussels.

1971 Tribes and archaeological groupings of the La Tène period in Belgium. Some observations, in *The European Community in Later Prehistory. Studies in honour of C. F. C. Hawkes*, ed. J. Boardman, M. A. Brown and T. G. E. Powell, London, 211–41.

Schönberger, H. 1952 Die Spätlatènezeit in der Wetterau, *Saalburg Jahrbuch* XI, 21–130.

Thill, G. 1972 Frühlatènezeitlicher Fürstengrabhügel bei Altrier, *Hémecht* 24, 487–98.

Van Doorselaer, A. 1971 Inleidende beschouwingen over de Kemmelberg na drie opgravingscampagnes, *Archaeologia Belgica* 131.

Van Doorselaer, A., De Meulemeester, J., Putnam, R. and J.-L. 1974 Resultaten van zes opgravingscampagnes op de Kemmelberg, *Archaeologia Belgica* 161.

22

D. F. ALLEN†

Wealth, Money and Coinage in a Celtic Society

† Derek Allen died suddenly at his home on 14 June 1975. The text has been seen through the press by Dr John Kent, Deputy Keeper of Coins and Medals at the British Museum.

THE first cognoscenti of Celtic coins, not least William Stukeley, for whose divagations Stuart Piggott has so amiable an affection, were much preoccupied with the purposes for which Celtic coins were made; amongst the favoured choices were druidical offerings and prizes at the secular games. Later writers, preoccupied with legends, such as TASCIO, which they found hard to account for, turned to more prosaic explanations, such as the payment of taxes or the demands of commerce. Sir John Evans in England and Adrien Blanchet in France put the study on a less speculative basis, and writers have since been more concerned with dates, distributions and attributions than with less tangible interpretations. Nevertheless those early questions remain unanswered and, in an age when we are all too familiar with the jargon of social, economic and monetary theory, it is time to look at them again.

Current literature on Celtic coins leaves no doubt of the universal assumption that they existed to serve the interests of Celtic trade. However perverse the comment may seem, this is a highly questionable proposition. An imitative coinage – and all Celtic coinage from the Balkans to Gaul was essentially imitative – will never have been more sophisticated than the coinage which it imitated. It is becoming ever more widely recognized that the underlying purpose of the silver and gold coinage of the Greeks was to enable the issuers to buy services or supplies or otherwise to meet inescapable obligations (Kraay 1964, esp. 88f.). Its purpose was not to facilitate trade. No doubt, once made, it could be and was used as and when required in the course of trade, but this was a secondary and incidental by-product of its essential purpose. The coinage of Rome, likewise, represents the conversion into a buying and paying medium of the colossal amounts of booty and tribute resulting from her recurrent military successes (Crawford 1970; Cook 1958). Its issue was directly connected with payments to Roman soldiers and auxiliaries and the purchase of their equipment and supplies. There is evidence for the presence of Roman merchants in different parts of Europe long before we find there traces of their money.

Ancient trade, on any scale exceeding that of the local market place, was conducted by barter. If proof of this were needed, it is that the greatest trading nation of the ancient world, the Carthaginians, had no use for money until a relatively late date, and only after they had gathered colonial responsibilities and military ambitions. There is no trail of coined money in the wake of Carthaginian trade. In so far as precious (or other) metals changed hands in the course of that trade, as they certainly did, their status was that of a commodity like any other; disfigurement into the form of barbarian coinage would have in no way enhanced their trading value.

The purpose of coining money in Celtic Europe was no different in kind from the purpose on the Mediterranean coast. Until a late date, when there are other explanations, Celtic coins are scarcely found outside the area in which they originated. These narrow distributions indicate plainly enough that the coins were made for use within groups of communities, not for a wider circulation. It is, indeed, not until the whole pattern of these communities was in course of revolution as a consequence of Roman influence or intervention that we start to find on any scale coins of one territory displaced to another. The vast majority of these displaced pieces are of small denomination, found isolated and not in hoards. The primary function of Celtic coinage in precious metals must be sought within the communities to which they were confined.

Ancient writers give us few clues, and these are not always revealing. Thus it is told of Luernius, father of the Arvernian Bituitus, who lived in the mid-second century BC, that he scattered gold and silver amongst a crowd of followers at a potlach, much as coronation medals were, until the eighteenth century, thrown to the spectators in Westminster Abbey (Athenaeus IV. 37; cf. Strabo IV. II. 3). Here money is being used, not for a commercial purpose, but as a royal prerogative; the tradition of rewarding court poets with gifts survived into medieval Ireland (Williams 1971, 105, 107). There are other reasons for believing that the main purpose underlying the coining of money was to facilitate compliance with the requirements of the complicated social structure of Celtic life.

We find some evidence for this in the surviving Irish laws, which refer to a state of affairs many centuries earlier than when they were written down. There was no publicly enforced criminal law, only personal rights dependent on social status. To these were given relative conventional values, expressed in Ireland first in slave girls and later in cattle of recognized qualities. Even in Ireland, where the use of coined money did not penetrate until many centuries later, these were in due course converted into currency terms, namely Roman scruples of silver (Hennessy *et al.* VI, 645, V, sub. *scrépall.*) There can be little doubt that, in those parts of the Celtic world where money was in use, this conversion took place very much earlier, even though we lack positive proof. The legal and social conventions which called for compensation for injury also laid down, for instance, the amounts of dowries and ransoms, which were more easily paid, even within the community, in money than in kind.

The importance of the dowry in Celtic society is well established (Caesar *De Bello Gallico* VI. 19; Holmes 1911, 510–11). We may legitimately compare the practice in Massalia, so closely linked with southern Gaul, whereby dowries were limited by law to 100 pieces of gold, plus five for a dress and five for golden ornaments (Strabo IV. 1. 5). Such indications as we have from the Irish tales are that, on the contrary, it was a minimum dowry which convention there demanded. The wife's *pecunia* could be measured in cattle and land rights, but also in precious metal (Kinsella 1970, 52–3).

For ransoms we have the story of how, when a Gaulish chieftain's severed head was carried off as a trophy by his enemies, his own family offered to buy it back for its weight in gold, an offer which, incidentally, was refused (Strabo IV. 4. 5; Diodorus V. 29. 4). Of course, we are not told whether the gold was paid in coin, torques or ingots, but there is other evidence of head-ransom amongst the Celtic peoples.

When we hear, as we so often do, of Gauls who were rich, their wealth will generally have been demonstrated by the possession of cattle, land and slaves, rather than by the accumulation of money. But we hear almost as often of Gauls who have fallen into debt. The cause of these debts is not stated, but, in a primitive community, their origin is often to be sought, then as now, in an inability without a loan to comply with some conventional requirements of society, such as an elaborate funeral. In such matters the Celts had a reputation for unbridled ostentation. One may recall the rich Ariamnes, who offered a year's free feasting to his brother Celts and engaged a smith a full year in advance to construct a large enough cauldron (Athenaeus IV. 34). Such action might have led a lesser man into debt, for which in the Celtic world there existed a form of slavery (Caesar I. 4; VI. 13; Holmes 1911, 514–17). Then there is the extraordinary custom whereby at a feast, in return for gold, silver, amber, or jars of wine promised to his family, a man would lie down on his shield and offer himself for slaughter (Athenaeus IV. 195; cf. IV. 110). Was this a method of escape from the burden of debt and risk of slavery?

We hear not infrequently of bribery. This can be conducted in other ways, but the only simple and inconspicuous means of bribery is by the transfer of money. When Convictolitavis, the Aeduan, was bribed to support the cause of Vercingetorix, we are told that he was *sollicitatus pecunia* (Caesar VII. 37). One may guess that this was with coins in Vercingetorix' own name.

We can obtain some information about the uses of money from the circumstances in which Celtic coins are found, although too often the details are not adequately recorded. By and large hoards of Celtic coins are features of the countryside; they are not found in the urban centres. In Britain it is noticeable that even the isolated gold coins tend to come from sites not otherwise recorded in Celtic occupation. One hoard from Podmokly, Bohemia, is notable because it apparently represents the savings of a family, rather than of an individual, over half a century or more, a coin at a time (Fiala 1902; Castelin 1964, 63). But this is exceptional; the majority of hoards are sufficiently consistent in their contents to indicate that they have been brought together over a relatively short period. A special type of deposit is the offering of coinage at a sacred site; one example is the series of gold coins found at the site of La Tène (Allen 1973); another is the first stratum of coinage at the Romano-British temple at Harlow (Allen 1964; 1967; 1968). However, the vast treasure of gold and silver found by the Romans in the sacred lake at Tolosa in 106 BC was composed, not as might have been expected of the local *monnaies-à-la-croix*, but of ingots (Strabo IV. 1. 3).

One must not expect the story to be clear-cut nor the evidence decisive, but the picture which emerges is of a situation in which the primary demand for money was to play a part in the internal life of the narrow communities into which the Celtic world was divided. This proposition need not conflict with secondary uses of coinage, nor with the evolution of new uses over time. There are, in particular, two classes of coinage for which a different explanation is required.

In the early first century BC there grew up in Gaul an enormous coinage based in character, weight and standard on the Roman quinarius (Colbert de Beaulieu 1965; 1966; 1973, 217ff.). It had its origin in the tribe of the Allobroges, within the frontiers of the Roman Provincia, and was quickly followed by a comparable coinage amongst the pro-Roman Aedui, which circulated equally in the territories of the Sequani and the Lingones. It is to this coinage that Cicero must refer when he speaks of Roman merchants in the Provincia and the employment there of Roman money (Cicero *Pro Fonteio*, 1, 2f., esp. 5, 11).

Coinages on this scale were clearly not made solely for internal use within the community. It seems certain that the primary purpose was the payment of troops, a secondary one perhaps the payment of tribute. The quinarius coinage continued throughout the Gallic War (and even after), a phase during which actual Roman coinage is demonstrably absent from Gaul (Rolland 1953–4). Even if the earlier coinage of the Aedui played its part in the obscure transactions between the Aedui, the Sequani and Ariovistus, the bulk of the coinage was struck for the pay of the Roman troops in Gaul. A Roman legionary earned 120 denarii a year, from which the cost of his food and clothing was deducted, a figure increased by Caesar to 225 (Brunt 1971, 14). The use of the quinarii by Roman soldiers and auxiliaries meant that the distribution of the coinage was no longer confined to the area in which it was made; the quinarii are, in fact, the first Gaulish coinage to have a distribution in bulk far wider than the tribal areas of origin. The largest hoard of all, and one of the earliest, that from Robache, St Dié, consisted of at least 15,000 pieces, and was found in the territory of the Lingones; it must have been a tribal treasure chest, to be compared with the Whaddon Chase hoard in Britain, which was hidden to avoid capture by an enemy and never recovered (Blanchet 1905, 603, tr. 269).

In parallel with the growth of the quinarius coinage, there is found in Gaul a bronze and 'potin' coinage, part struck, part cast. Its origin lies in the bronze coins of Massalia, but it always had a local and independent character. It is to be distinguished in principle from the precious metal coinages, since from the start it must have been a fiduciary issue, even if some gold and silver coinages eventually became so debased as to be almost indistinguishable from it. The essence of these bronze and cast potin coinages is that the vast majority are found in known settlements and oppida, not in hoards but as isolated finds. It is plain that, unlike the coins in precious metals, one is here dealing with a market currency, coins made for use in small-scale local transactions or at travelling fairs. They are, when and where found, an indication of a change in social life and economic practice, the movement away from rural life to the quasi-urban existence which we eventually associate with the Roman empire. Some types, particularly those of potin circulated over wide regions, are scarcely ever identifiable with a particular tribe; the struck bronze coins tend, in contrast, to be extremely local, many types hardly being known outside a single settlement or town.

On a much less advanced scale the same phenomenon is seen amongst the Danubian Celts. Local bronze coinages are frequent at such sites as Szalacska, Regöly and Dunaszekscő (Sey 1972), and at the same date as those of Gaul (Pink 1939, Abb. 491–8, cf. 202–3). For small change other eastern Celts preferred silver minims, as at Stradonice (Píč 1903; Déchelette 1901, Pl. II) and Magdalensberg (Bannert and Piccottini 1972). Even in Gaul the silver minim played a much larger rôle than the number now in collections suggest. These minute coins, the reflection in Celtic Gaul of the obol of Massalia and its hinterland, were scarcely hoarded, and owing to their size are frequently missed by excavators. It is of some interest that in Britain the only areas where bronze coins are lacking are those in which we find silver minims. The rôle in society of the bronze coin and the minute silver minim was the same.

It is far from obvious by what means the Celtic peoples acquired the precious metals from which their coinage was made and how, once made, it was put into circulation. Precious metals were mined in the countries from which coins come, but the amounts were limited and the location of the mines, so far as we know them, bears little relationship to the scale of the coinage. Thus we learn that the Tarbelli in Aquitaine (Strabo IV. 2. 1) had gold mines; if they had any coinage at all, it was confined to formless blobs of silver. Similarly the gold mines of the Tolosates (Strabo IV. 2. 13) lay in an area of extensive silver coinage, the metal for which came from the territory of the Ruteni (Strabo IV. 12. 13). The Helvetii had a reputation for their gold production, no doubt panned from the Rhine and the Rhône, and this can be related to the moderate output of gold coins from Switzerland (Strabo IV. 3. 3; VII. 2. 2; Athenaeus VI. 233). But there are, so far as we know, no convenient gold mines to account for the vastly greater gold output of the Armorican and Belgic tribes. Panned gold from the Beroun no doubt accounts for the Bohemian gold coinage, but again the quantity is moderate (Castelin 1964, 96–7). There was a famous gold mine in Noricum, but effectively no gold coins (Polybius XXXIV. 10. 10; Strabo IV. 6. 12). One must envisage the silver mines, first exploited by the Macedonian kings, as providing the bulk of the silver for the extensive Danubian coinage, and the hideous but good standard tetradrachms imitating those of Thasos are clearly the conversion into a currency medium of the product of the Thracian silver mines.

There is no need to underestimate the extent to which the coinage of Gaul represents the proceeds of rapine. Raids such as those on Rome and Delphi are only the most famous episodes of a continuing story. When the Gauls were at the gates of Rome in 390 BC, there was not enough gold in the city to buy them off, less than 1000 pounds (Livy V. 48–9; Justin 42; Pliny *De rerum natura* 33. 5). This implies that the Gauls were no strangers to being bought off with precious metal. In the case of the Scordisci in Hungary we are specifically told that they did not import gold into their country, but were willing to pillage silver; the coins from this area are, in fact, exclusively of silver (Athenaeus VI. 234).

In this context, too, we should not overlook the contribution made by the remittances, if one may use the term, of Gaulish mercenaries; they were scattered far and wide in the Mediterranean and, by definition, earned good money and the bonus of occasional booty.

At the same time it is probable that the Celts enjoyed what we would now call a favourable balance of trade, though no more than a modest one. Like most ancient societies, the Celts in the main sought self-sufficiency in agricultural produce. No Celtic land ever became a granary of Greece or Rome. We often hear of the dense population of Celtic lands; we also hear of frequent movements in search of new agricultural land (Jullien 1907–30, II, 333). Despite the popularity in Rome of Gaulish hams and geese, there is no reason to think that there were any large agricultural surpluses from which money was earned. In iron, but not in other metals, the European Celts were broadly self-sufficient. The exports from which they could earn were largely ores, hides, and pre-eminently slaves. But there is every reason to think that the proceeds of this traffic were spent up to the hilt on the sought-for imports from the Mediterranean world. These included luxury goods, traces of which occur on so many Celtic sites, but more especially a commodity which had passed almost out of the luxury category into that of necessity, namely wine. It was no coincidence that the value of a slave and of an amphora of wine were equal (Diodorus V. 26. 3). The Roman trader in Gaul was often a speculator in land, rather than in commodities, and any ultimate balances accumulated in Gaul were eventually paid back with interest to Rome in the form of booty and tribute.

One particular service which Gaul could provide was in the provision of transport facilities across its territory, especially for the passage of ores from Spain and Britain, but for other traffic too. The river fleets on the Rhône, Seine, Loire and Rhine will have earned profits, much of which is likely to have been settled in money payments. In addition we have explicit evidence for river dues on the Rhône and Seine, the collection of which was disputed between riparian tribes (Aedui and Sequani) (Strabo IV. 3. 2). As regards Britain, it was commented with interest that Britain was accepting imports from Gallia Celtica on which they were ready to pay duty (Strabo IV. 5. 2). The payment of duty in kind on goods in transit tends to defeat the purpose of the transport and will generally have been settled in money. It is the trader who, in the first instance, pays the duty on such goods. All the evidence is that the initiative came from the Roman side and it will, therefore, in all probability have been the Romans who provided this finance.

It is not to be expected that the supply of precious metal for coinage represented a consistent flow; on the contrary, there is reason to think that the production of coinage was intermittent and episodic, depending on the supply of metal available to the issuer and the circumstances for which it was required. One can gain some indication of this from the study of coin dies, which show the coinage in disconnected blocks. Old dies, rusty or disfigured, could be brought out for re-use when something happened which demanded a sudden production of coinage (Allen 1972, 131–2, nos. 7–26), or in other cases what look like emergency dies were hastily made for a purely temporary purpose as for example the coins of SEQVANOIOTVOS (Blanchet 1905, 402, fig. 419). Any attempt to read a complete history of any people into the surviving relics of its

1 The Moneyers of Nancy, a Gallo-Roman sculpture, Espérandieu VI (1915) 56, no. 4606; limestone, 0.34 × 0.26 × 0.26 m. Presumably found at Charpeigne, Meurthe-et-Moselle, and now in the Musée de Lorraine, Nancy. The scene must be intended as a version of the *Dieu au Maillet*, but in fact it is a crude but dramatic representation of the normal scene in a forge or mint – the smith with hammer, one assistant holding the object to be hammered, and another working the furnace behind. The process will scarcely have changed from the period of independence.

coinage is bound to mislead; in all probability the coinage tends to reflect only the moments of prosperity and disaster.

It is clear, in both the east and the west, that the supply and quality of gold available was richer at the earlier stages of the coinage, beginning in the third century BC, than towards the end. This is not solely the consequence of Gresham's law, bad money driving out good, but a reflection of the fact that, with growth in the use of and demand for money, the metal supply gradually became attenuated. Even in Rome the supply of metal for coinage went through phases of plenty and dearth; while in Rome consistent standards could be maintained, the consequence of dearth in less organized lands was debasement. Nevertheless, the extent to which the process of debasement was parallel between one place and another is notable (Castelin 1964, 120–1). In Britain, for instance, it is difficult not to believe that in the long gap between Caesar and Claudius there was a monetary convention between the tribes, whereby consistent weights, qualities and denominations were maintained. The gold stater represented by weight exactly two thirds of the Roman aureus, though in poorer metal, the silver coin one third of a denarius. Conditions in Britain were exceptional; apart from a tentative trace in late Belgic Gaul, it is the only Celtic land where a consistent policy of trimetallic coinage was maintained.

It has been much debated over the years who actually issued Celtic coins, and the question still remains open (Colbert de Beaulieu 1973, 169–70, n. 212). A distinction must be drawn between making and issuing. There is no reasonable doubt that the coins were made by the smiths who played such a prominent rôle in Celtic life. The skill of coin making lies in the manufacture of the dies; thereafter the actual process of striking the coins out of metal of chosen standard was relatively simple. An ancient mint also was easily mobile. Security apart, one does not have to envisage any elaborate structure; a mint need not differ in scale or kind from any smithy or forge (*Ill. 1*). The making of dies, however, was a rare skill, which must in the first place have been learned from Mediterranean craftsmen (*Ill. 2*, and note 1, p. 205). Most of the early copies are remarkably close to the originals, and the techniques, apart from cast potin coins, never varied far from those employed in the mints of Greece and Rome. But the ability to make new dies was, like the supply of metal, intermittent. In Bohemia, for instance, after interesting beginnings, the art of die engraving was virtually lost, and individual dies went on in use long after the types had been beaten to destruction and then marginally rendered serviceable again (Paulsen 1933, esp. Pls. 3–29). Even in Noricum, where for a short time in the middle of the first century BC there was an active production of partly Romanized dies, there is an instance of one obverse die being employed by no less than four different issuers, named singly on the reverse (Göbl 1973, 23). In much of the quinarius coinage more than one obverse die was engraved onto a single block, so that an individual coin may show parts of more than one obverse die. This economy device is known in the Hellenistic world, but it is rare and scattered. Its wide adoption in Gaul shows that the

2 Dies for Celtic coins: 1–3, bronze; 4, iron; 5, bronze set in iron. 1, from Corent; 2, from Bar-sur-Aube; 3, from Moirans; 4, from Cerikovo, Bulgaria; 5, from Avenches, Switzerland.

Notes on dies for Celtic coins shown in Ill.2.

The dies here illustrated are all mentioned in Vermeule (1954). With the exception of no. 4, they are also mentioned in Blanchet (1905). Although they have all been illustrated in different places, they have not been brought together before, as here.

1 Musée des Antiquités Nationales, St-Germain-en-Laye, no. 12273 (Vermeule 1954, n. 11; Blanchet 1905, 52, n. 2). Found at Corent, Les Martres-de-Veyre, Puy-de-Dôme, 1845. Bronze head, originally set in iron shaft. Die for the reverse of a silver coin attributable to the Bituriges Cubi, horse with sword above. a, Side view of die; b, bottom view of die.

2 Bibliothèque Nationale, Paris. (Vermeule 1954, 15, n. 9; Blanchet 1905, 32 n. 4; see also Babelon 1901, I, 907–8, fig. 26). Found at camp of Sainte-Germaine, Bar-sur-Aube, Aube. Bronze head, originally set in iron shaft. Die for reverse of silver coin of Aedui or Lingones with legend TOGIRI over horse. a, Angular view of die; b, cast of die face; c, cast of resulting coin.

3 Bibliothèque Municipale, Grenoble. (Vermeule 1954, 16, n. 12; Blanchet 1905, 52, n. 5; see also Babelon 1901, I, 908). Found probably at Moirans, Isère. Bronze head, originally set in iron shaft. Die for reverse of a silver coin of the Allobroges with legend VOL below horse. a, Cast of die face, from cast in Musée des Antiquités Nationales, St-Germain-en-Laye, no. 25836; b, cast of resulting coin.

4 National Museum of Archaeology, Sofia. (Vermeule 1954, 12, n. 6; see also Babelon 1901, I, 905, fig. 24; Kubitschek 1925, 133–5, pl. 13, fig. 1). Found at Cerikovo, Lukovit, Plevna, Bulgaria, in 1897. Iron shaft. Die for reverse of early imitation to tetradrachm of Philip II from the mint of Amphipolis. a, Die from side; b, cast of die face; c, cast of resulting coin.

5 Musée d'Avenches, Vaud. (Vermeule 1954, 15, n. 8; Blanchet 1905, 51, n. 3; see also Meyer 1863, iv; Forrer 1908, 31; von Kaenel 1972, 60–61, pl.11:17). Found in or near the theatre, Avenches, in 1859. Bronze head set in iron base. Obverse die for stater of type attributable to the Sequani. Die from above.

These are, I believe, the only dies for Celtic coins of which photographs are obtainable. The other dies from France mentioned by Vermeule and Blanchet are lost, and those found at Szalacska, Somogy, Hungary, (Gohl 1907, 170–83; Forrer, (ed.) Castelin 1969, II, pl. 20), were destroyed during the Second World War. The dies for imitations of Roman Republican denarii from Tilişca, Sibiu, Romania, (Lupu 1964, 5–31; Forrer 1908, pl. 19) are in another category.

Celtic smiths kept contacts outside their own narrow world.[1] One may recall that it was Elico, an Helvetian smith resident in Rome, who summoned Brennus and his raiders to destroy the city (Pliny 12. 5).

It could be that the earliest Celtic coinage was an independent enterprise of the smiths; the name EIQVITIVICO, found on an early imitation of a Philippic stater, may well be that of a smith (Blanchet 1905, 219, Fig. 59). But it is the nature of coinage that it should soon receive the stamp of authority, warranting its weight and content. This is a natural function of government and, moreover, both the profits and the relatively subservient position of the smiths in Celtic society will have ensured the involvement of the chieftains or kings. All indications are that, prior to the introduction of the quinarius coinage, minting in precious metals was conducted on a tribal basis, and that individual types can properly be linked with the names of particular tribes. In Gaul and in Britain, where we have some knowledge of the tribal structure in the twilight before the Roman conquest, it is not too difficult in most cases to assign coinage to a known tribe; in the east this remains much more hazardous.

It is therefore disappointing that, of the very large number of personal names surviving on later Celtic coins, so very few can be connected with the names known from history. Of more than a hundred chieftains in Gaul mentioned by Caesar we have coins of no more than a dozen, if that (Colbert de Beaulieu 1962; Blanchet 1905, 287, Fig. 160). Amongst them we have only one instance of a ruler who calls himself *rex*, Adietuanus; he is barely Celtic, since his tribe, the Sotiates, lay in Gallia Aquitania. The list includes some that Caesar calls kings, such as Tasgetius (Strabo VII. 3. 11; VII. 5. 2),[2] but for the most part the names are those of leading citizens, whose right to issue coins in their own name would in most countries not be self-apparent. Perhaps conditions during Caesar's war were exceptional; we have, for instance, the coins, including the siege money, of Vercingetorix himself. Nevertheless, there are too many instances where a ruler's name is known to history, yet coins which are apparently contemporary do not bear his name. Thus, amongst the Boii we have no less than sixteen names on coins issued during the mid-first century BC, which do not include that of Kritasiros (the only coin purporting to bear this name being a modern forgery) (Göbl 1973, 77–9). There are scarcely fewer names on related Norican silver coins, which equally appear to have been in issue through the ascendancy of Voccio (Alföldi 1974, 42; Göbl 1973, 71–6).[3] It has long been a puzzle that the name of Galba[4] has not been found on coins of the Suessiones, who undoubtedly were coining extensively at the relevant time. Similarly, the absence of coins with the name Indutiomarus amongst the Treviri has prompted the attribution to him of the only coins in a generally epigraphic range which happen to be uninscribed; all the other names are otherwise unknown (Scheers 1972). The implication is that the principal rulers in Gaul were not in general the moneyers whose names the coins bear. The function or privilege of issuing coins fell to those who did not exercise the chief authority.

There are cases amongst the bronze coins of post-conquest date where we have titles on the coins indicating issue by an *arcantodan* or in one instance a *vergobret* (Blanchet 1905, 85). These titles may well be more widely applicable, especially in those cases where there are two names on the coins, implying a shared magistracy, comparable with the triumviri monetales of Rome or the duumviri of many Spanish coinages. The AR monogram on the number of Norican coins may well mean *arcantodan* (Göbl 1973, 30; cf. Blanchet 1905, 100–1). Very few coins bear inscriptions which imply the issue by a tribe as such and only one of the letters EX S C, giving it an official municipal character (Blanchet 1905, 86 and 126).

The main constituents of the quinarius coinage present a problem on their own. Coins with the names Caletedu, Q. Doci Sam F., Togirix and Q. Iulius Togirix, to name only the chief constituents, were produced on so vast a scale that it is surprising we know nothing of the issuers from any other sources. Some of the coins may merely reproduce an 'immobilized' name on a familiar coin type, but

[1] For Greek analogies see Hill (1922, 37–8 and Pl. I: 1823 – coins from Segesta, Lycia, Alzia, Velia and Phlius); a good example in the British Museum showing parts of these obverse dies is a bronze coin of Demetrius I of Antioch (162–150 BC).

[2] The 'kings' mentioned by Caesar are listed in Holmes (1911, 504); of the eleven named, coins are known of four.

[3] A few coins are known which read VOKK in an Etruscan script (Göbl 1973, 86).

[4] Galba is unmentioned for example by Colbert de Beaulieu (1964) and Scheers (1970); but see Caesar II. 4. 13, and Blanchet 1905, 84.

this does not eliminate the problem. The likelihood is that we are here dealing with appointed procurators or officials, charged with the duty of producing a coinage required for special purposes. Much the same applies to the later bronze coinage with the name Germanus Indutilli L, focused on the Treviri and found over most of northern Gaul and Germany; it looks as if we have here an otherwise unrecorded freedman acting as an imperial commissioner to make the small money required on the *limes* and in its hinterland (Todd 1965, 3–7).

In Britain we have a later phase and a different situation: a higher proportion of the names found on the coins can with certainty, or at least plausibility, be identified with characters known to history, some six of whom call themselves *rex* or a Celtic equivalent. But even here, it is less than happy that we should not have the name Prasutagus on the coins of the Iceni, but be required to identify his coins amongst the issues bearing the anonymous tribal name *Ecen* (Allen 1970, 16–17). It may well be that even in Britain responsibility for the coinage, other than in the principal kingdoms of the centre and south, resided with magistrates. We can read too much into names for which there is no direct historical explanation (Scheers 1972).

This paper has ranged cursorily over a very wide field, one that deserves more attention than has recently been fashionable. In the absence of more cut-and-dried evidence than exists, any views expressed run the risk of being thought speculative. But I hope that, in the context of this tribute to an archaeologist who has never feared to look beneath the surface, my suggestions will not be considered out of place.

Bibliography

Alföldi, G. 1974 *Noricum*, London.

Allen, D. F. 1964 Celtic coins from the Romano-British temple at Harlow, Essex, *Brit. Numis. J.* XXXIII, 1–6.

1967 Celtic coins from the Romano-British temple at Harlow, Essex, *Brit. Numis. J.* XXXVI, 1–7.

1968 Celtic coins from the Romano-British temple at Harlow, Essex, *Brit. Numis. J.* XXXVII, 1–6.

1970 The coins of the Iceni, *Britannia* I, 1–33.

1972 The fibula of CRICIRV, *Germania* L, 122–32.

1973 The coins found at La Tène, *Études Celtiques* XIII:2, 477–521.

Babelon, E. 1901 *Traité des monnaies grecques et romaines* I: *Introduction*, Paris.

Bannert, H. and Piccottini, G. 1972 *Die Fundmünzen vom Magdalensburg*, Klagenfurt.

Blanchet, A. 1905 *Traité des monnaies gauloises*, Paris.

Brunt, P. A. 1971 *Social conflicts in the Roman Republic*, London.

Castelin, K. 1964 *Die Goldprägung der Kelten in den Böhmischen Ländern*, Graz.

(ed.) 1968–69 Forrer, R. *Keltische Numismatik der Rhein- und Donaulande* enlarged and rev. edn, 2 vols, Graz.

Colbert de Beaulieu, J.-B. 1962 Les monnaies gauloises au nom des chefs mentionnés dans les Commentaires de César, *Coll. Latomus* LVIII = *Hommages à A. Grenier*, 419–46.

1964 'Criciru' et 'Roveca', les Belges sur la Marne, *Rev. Belge de Numis.* CX, 69–112.

1965 Les monnaies de Caletedu et le système du denier en Gaule, *Cahiers numismatiques* VI, 163–80 = *Bull. de la Soc. d'Études numis. et archéol.*

1966 La monnaies de Caletedu et les zones du statère et du denier en Gaule, *Rev. arch. du Centre* XVIII, 101–29.

1973 *Traité de monnaies Celtiques* I: *Méthodologie des Ensembles*, Paris.

Cook, R. M. 1958 Speculations on the origins of coinage, *Historia* VII, 257–62.

Crawford, M. H. 1970 Money and exchange in the Roman world, *J. Roman Stud.* LX, 40–8.

Déchelette, J. 1901 *Le Hradischt de Stradonitz en Bohème et les fouilles de Bibracte*, Paris.

Fiala, E. 1902 Der Podmokler Goldfund, *Numis. Zeitschr.* XXXIV, 149–56.

Forrer, R. 1908 *Keltische Numismatik der Rhein- und Donaulande*, Strasbourg. See also Castelin, K. (ed.).

Göbl, R. 1973 *Typologie und Chronologie der Keltischen Münzprägung im Noricum*, Vienna.

Gohl, O. 1907 Usine monétaire et fosderie celtique à Szalacska-Hongrie, *Rev. Numis.* 170–83.

Hennessy, W. M. et. al. (eds.) 1856–1901. *Ancient laws of Ireland*, Dublin.

Hill, G. F. 1922 Ancient methods of coining, *Numis. Chronicle* 5 ser. II, 1–43.

Holmes, T. Rice 1911 *Caesar's conquest of Gaul*, Oxford.

Jullien, C. 1907–30 *Histoire de la Gaule*, Paris.

Kaenel, H. M. von. 1972 Die Fundmünzen aus Avenches, *Schweiz. Num. Rundschau* 51, 60–1.

Kinsella, T. (trans.) 1970 *The Táin*, Oxford.

Kraay, C. 1964 Hoards, small change and the origin

of coinage, *J. Hellenic Stud.* LXXIV, 76–91.

KUBITSCHEK, W. 1925 Münzstempel des Nationalmuseum in Sofia, *Numis. Zeitschr.* 58, 133–5.

LUPU, N. 1964 Die Münze in der dakischen Burg von Tilişca, *Forsch. zur Volks- und Landeskunde* VII, 5–31.

MEYER, H. 1863 Beschreibung der in der Schweiz aufgefunden Gallischen Münzen = *Mitt. der antiquarischen Ges. in Zürich* XV: 1.

PAULSEN, R. 1933 *Die Münzprägung der Boier*, Vienna.

PÍČ, J. L. 1903 *Hradiště u Stradonic: Starožitnosti Země České* II:2, Prague.

PINK, K. 1939 *Die Münzprägung der Ostkelten und Ihrer Nachbarn*, Budapest.

ROLLAND, H. 1953–4 Monnaies de la République romaine trouvées en Gaule, *Actes du XXVIIe et XXVIIIe Congrès: Fédération hist. du Languedoc mediterranéen et du Roussillon*, 1–19.

SCHEERS, S. 1970 L'histoire monétaire des *Suessiones* avant l'arrivée de Caesar, *Anc. Society* I, 135–61.

1972 Coinage and currency of the Belgic tribes during the Gallic War, *Brit. Numis. J.* XLI, 1–6.

SEY, K. B. 1972 The question of the chronology of the Transdanubian Celtic Bronze coins, *Acta Archaeol. Hung.* XXIV, 359–63.

TODD, M. 1965 GERMANVS INDVTILLI L, Remi ou Treveri, *Schweiz. Münzblätter* 15, 3–7.

VERMEULE, C. C. 1954 *Ancient dies and coining methods*, New York.

WILLIAMS, J. E. C. 1971 The court poet in medieval Ireland, *Proc. Brit. Acad.* LVII, 85–135.

23

KONRAD JAŻDŻEWSKI

The 'Princes' Graves' and Associated Industrial Settlement of the Second and Third Centuries AD at Przywóz, Central Poland[1]

[1] Translated by Maria Abramowiczowa

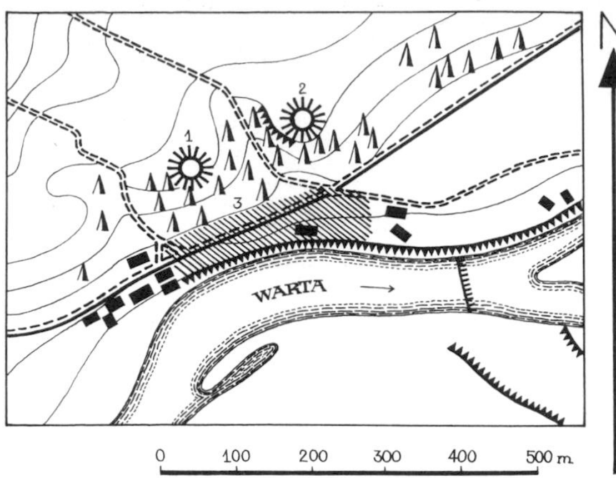

1 Plan of Site 1, Barrows 1 and 2, and settlement 1a of the second-third centuries AD, Przywóz, Wieluń district, Sieradz province.

1 Barrow 1
2 Barrow 2
3 Settlement = 1a

WITH this modest contribution I wish to join the group of colleagues gathered together on the present occasion to honour Stuart Piggott for all that he has done for the development of European archaeology. I am very happy indeed that I am able to express not only my admiration for Piggott and his great achievements, but also my gratitude for the inspiration I have derived from his works, marked as they are by an enviable breadth of approach and scope.

Some 400 km north of the ancient Roman frontier towns and the *castra* of the legions which stretched along the Danube in the northern margin of Pannonia, there existed in the second and third centuries AD a small settlement and two associated barrows, situated on the Upper Warta (a tributary of the Odra) in the area of the so-called *barbaricum* (*Ill. 1*). The presence of these features was revealed only by archaeological investigations conducted there in 1964–74. This paper does not pretend to give a comprehensive account of the excavations; its purpose is to draw attention to this interesting habitation and sepulchral complex discovered in an area which so far has been little noted for finds of this kind. Later in the paper it will be demonstrated that the connections between this now forgotten part of the region and the Roman Empire were once active and important. For this reason I hope that the results of the excavations at Przywóz may be of interest to archaeologists not only in Poland but also abroad.

The investigations were pursued in the village of Przywóz, which lies on the border of two historical provinces of Poland, Great Poland and Silesia. The village is situated in the southern part of central Poland, in Wieluń district, Sieradz province, on the left bank of the River Warta. The soil here is poor and sandy; outcrops of Jurassic limestone occasionally appear. The only commodity valued in the Roman period and later until the late Middle Ages was iron ore which, in the form of flat ferruginous concretions, occurred in a wide area just under the surface and was exploited for several centuries.

The excavations at Przywóz were conducted on behalf of the Archaeological and Ethnographical Museum in Łódź under the direction of the present writer, aided by the Museum Conservator, Stanisław Madajski. Other members of the excavation team included Irena Jadczyk, Tadeusz Makiewicz, Małgorzata Kowalczyk, Eleonora Kaszewska, Jiro Hasegawa.[2]

The results of the excavations can be summarized as follows. Where the edge of the high terrace of the *pradolina* of the Warta rises some 16 m above the river, at a distance of 140 and 170 m north of its left bank, the presence of two barrows has been recorded. These lie some 165 m apart, divided by a gully cutting into the edge of this terrace, and have been designated as Site 1. Beneath, on the lower river terrace which rises some 2–5m above the water horizon, remains of a settlement site contemporaneous with the two barrows, have come to light in the area between the river bank and the foot of the upper terrace. The settlement, which stretched for 250 m along the river and was some 50 m wide, is marked as Site 1a in *Ill. 1*.

Of the two barrows, the western one (no. 1) has been much better preserved than its eastern

[2] The original drawings for this paper were made by the following: Alicja Bobowska (*Figs. 1, 2, 4–12, 14–59*); Krystyna Trzebiatowska (*Figs. 3, 13, 62*); and Agineszka Kuśnierzowa (*Figs. 60, 61*).

neighbour (*Ill. 3*). At present it is 4 m high, although its original height was probably about 5 m, and it measured 24 m in diameter. The outer layer of the mound is of marl, brought from a distance of several hundred metres probably because of its considerable compactness, which contrasts markedly with the sandy gravel subsoil and the immediate surroundings. Beneath this capping was the central part, which consisted of a cairn of large and small field stones, about 6.5 m across and some 1.7 m high. The cairn was built over the cremation layer which in turn overlay ancient humus and the primary sterile layer. The cremation layer marks the remains of the funeral pyre on which the dead was cremated. It was slightly irregular in outline and occupied a smaller area than the mound, and consisted of burnt soil, numerous pieces of charcoal, ashes, lumps of burnt daub, and small artifacts either broken or charred or molten in the funerary fire. In the centre of the mound under the cairn was the pit of the main grave, measuring 75 cm across and 1.15 m deep (*Ill. 2*). It contained an urn represented by a black shining hollow-pedestalled vase with four lugs, ornamented with meander pattern and a zone of triangles (*Ill. 4*). In addition to charred human bones, there were a few lumps of molten bronze and some *terra sigillata* potsherds. The cremation layer around the urn contained more cremated human bones scattered at random, sherds of another ornamented hollow-pedestalled vessel of clay (*Ill. 5*), sherds probably of a *terra nigra* and a broken *terra sigillata* vessel with moulded decoration of grape-vine and grapes (*Ill. 6a–d*), a brooch with a wide strap bow and three ridges (on the head, in the middle of the bow and at the foot) inlaid with silver gilt plates with decoration imitating interlacing (Almgren type V:96) (*Ill. 7*), 50 g of gold in the form of several hundred tiny globules and grains from a molten ornament (*Ill. 8*), five identical bronze strap-ends once probably fixed to a broad belt (*Ill. 9a–e, f*), remains of a wooden casket with bronze mounts, the central one ring-like and surrounded by four trefoil-shaped fittings (*Ill. 10a–b*), and lumps of molten glass.

Under the cremation layer, or beyond its extent under the marl of the mound, was the primary humus in the form of a grey-brown layer marking the former surface of the field. After removal of the humus, traces of plough-marks made by an ard before the building of the barrow were noticed on the pale sand of the old land surface. The plough-marks were light-grey strips 10 cm wide, cutting only 2 to 3 cm into the ground. They stretched in

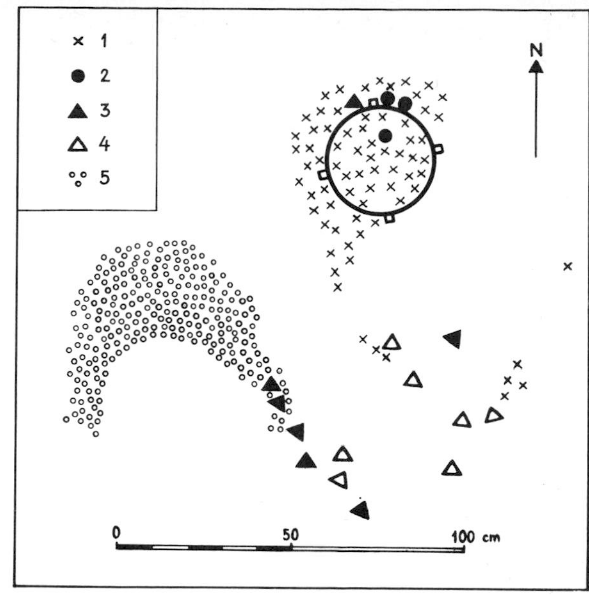

2 Przywóz, Site 1. Ground plan of the central grave in Barrow 1.
1 Cremated bones
2 Pieces of molten bronze
3 Terra sigillata
4 Other pottery
5 Grains of molten gold

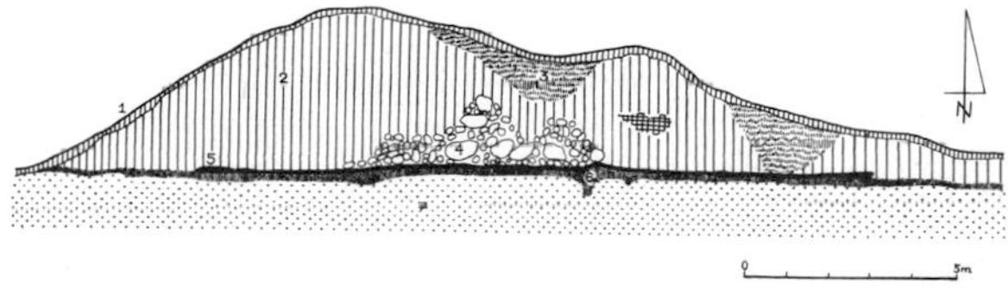

3 Section through Barrow 1, Przywóz, Site 1.
1 Present-day humus
2 Mound of marl
3 Modern disturbances
4 Stone core
5 Cremation layer
6 Original turf line
7 Old land surface

4 Przywóz, Site 1. Urn from the central grave in Barrow 1.

5 Przywóz, Site 1. Vessel reconstructed from sherds scattered around the urn in the central grave in Barrow 1.

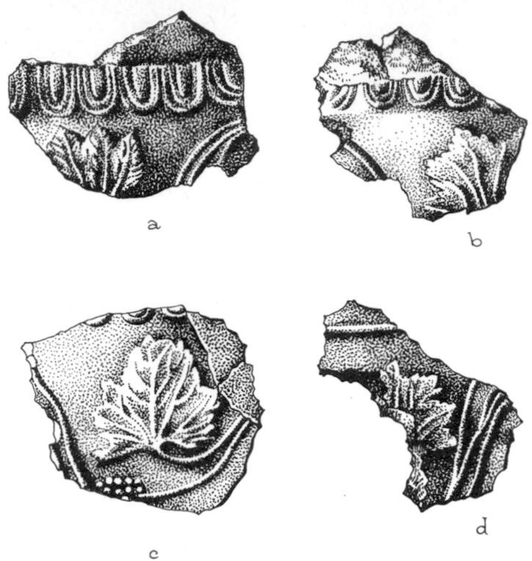

6 Przywóz, Site 1. Sherds of a terra sigillata vessel from the central grave in Barrow 1.

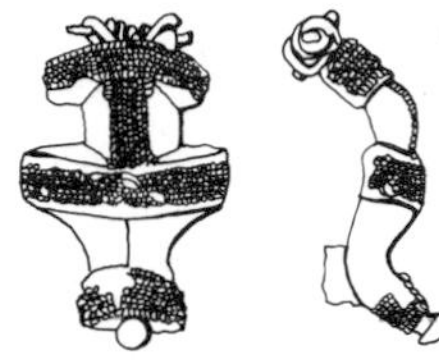

7 Przywóz, Site 1. Bronze brooch with bow and crest inlaid with silver plaques with embossed ornament from the central grave in Barrow 1.

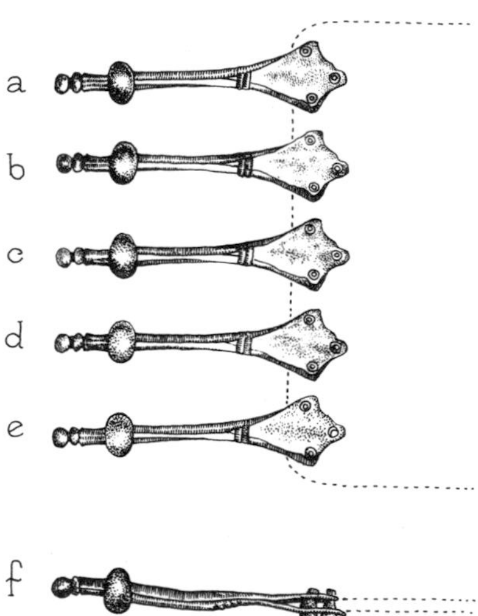

9 Przywóz, Site 1. Bronze strap-ends of a broad belt from the cremation layer near the central grave in Barrow 1: a–e, view from above; f, profile.

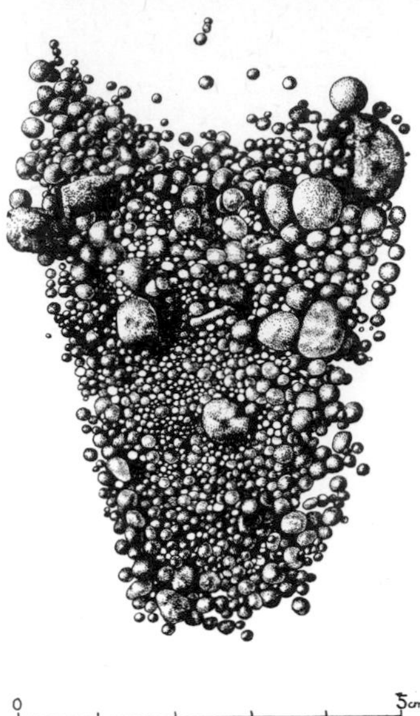

8 Przywóz, Site 1. Globules of gold ornament melted in the cremation fire from the central grave in Barrow 1.

parallel rows averaging 12 cm apart, forming a criss-cross pattern over an area slightly smaller than the primary extent of the mound (*Ills. 11, 12*).

Under the mound, at a distance of some 2.5 m from the central grave described above, a pit 1.75 m in diameter and about 30 cm deep was uncovered. It contained a skeleton of a dog with a skull about 20 cm long, and a fragment of iron slag. Perhaps the idea behind this burial was that the dog should continue to protect its master in the other world (*Ill. 13*). Another pit under the same mound yielded a number of loom-weights shaped as truncated cones, which had been parts of a vertical loom (*Ill. 14*).

Barrow 2 had a mound also of marl which was levelled by farming activities, and its central core of field stones had been almost completely dismantled in the last century. The barrow was once surrounded by a ditch about 1 m wide and some 50 cm deep, with an inner diameter of 22 m (*Ill. 15*). Among the stones of the core were numerous lumps of iron slag, derived from broken furnaces where iron ore was smelted, and there were also lumps of unworked ore. Potsherds of the Roman period lay scattered at random in the make-up of the mound. But the grave was not found, probably because it had been destroyed before systematic excavations were undertaken. On the other hand, an unusual

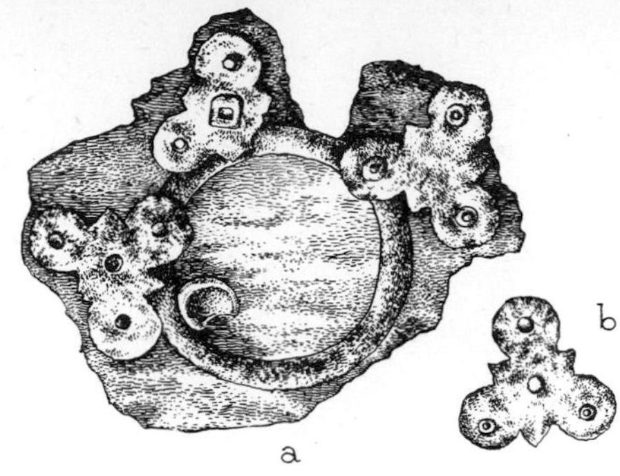

10 Przywóz, Site 1. Remains of a wooden casket with bronze mounts from the cremation layer around the central grave in Barrow 1: a, fragments of the casket with the mounts as found; b, the mounts.

11 Przywóz, Site 1. General ground plan of plough-marks beneath the cremation layer and of the central grave in Barrow 1.

1 Central grave with urn and stones from the cairn over the grave pit
2 Criss-cross furrows

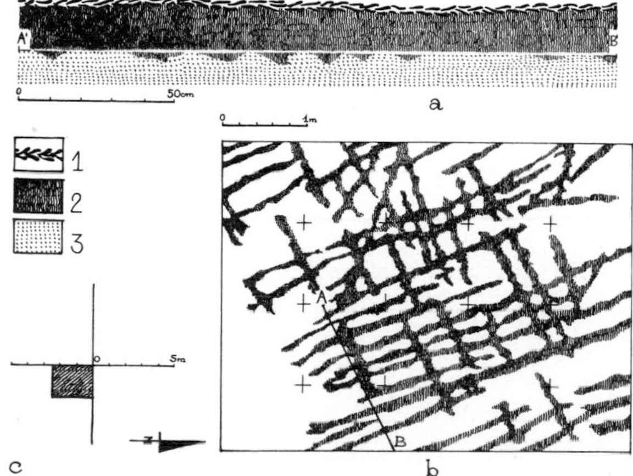

12 Przywóz, Site 1. Section of the ground plan (at right-angles to the plan in *Ill. 11*) of the plough-marks beneath the cremation layer in Barrow 1.

a Section along A-B
b Part of the ground plan in the south-east sector of the Barrow
c Section of the ground plan
1 Cremation layer
2 Original turf line and cross-sections through the plough-marks visible beneath it
3 Old land surface

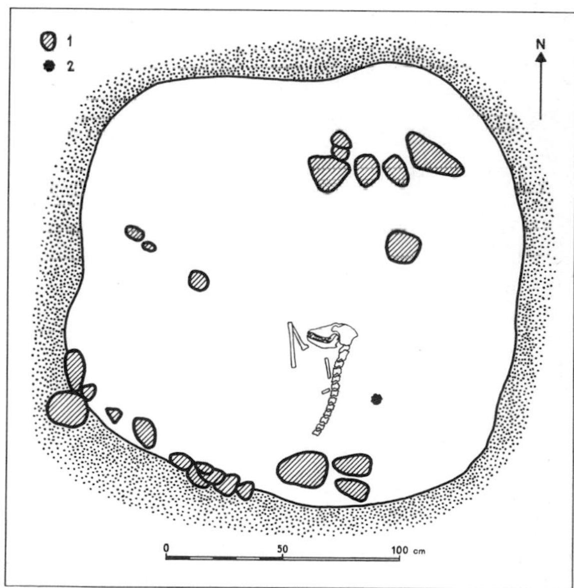

13 Przywóz, Site 1. Ground plan of the dog burial near the central grave in Barrow 1.

1 Stones
2 Slag from the iron-ore smelting

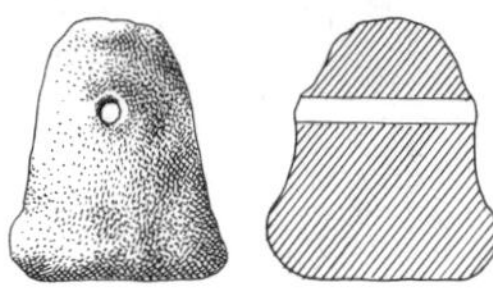

14 Pryzwóz, Site 1. Clay loom-weight from the pit under the mound of Barrow 1.

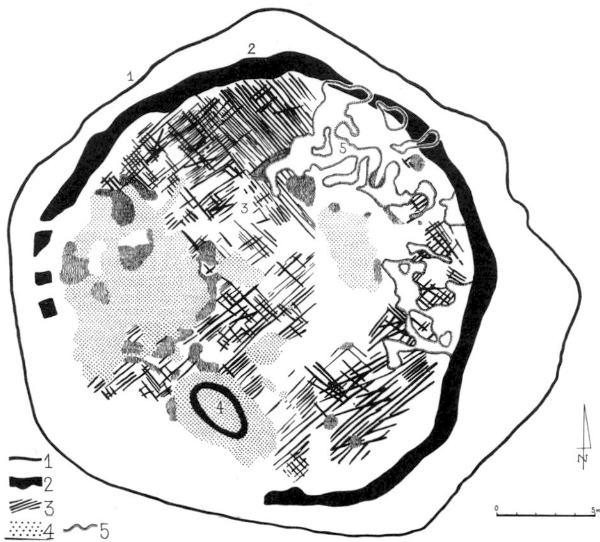

15 Przywóz, Site 1. Ground plan of Barrow 2 after the removal of the mound and stone core.

1 Edge of the mound
2 Surrounding ditch
3 Marks of criss-cross cultivation
4 Position of the well-like pit with cylindrical vessel (cf. *Ill. 16*)

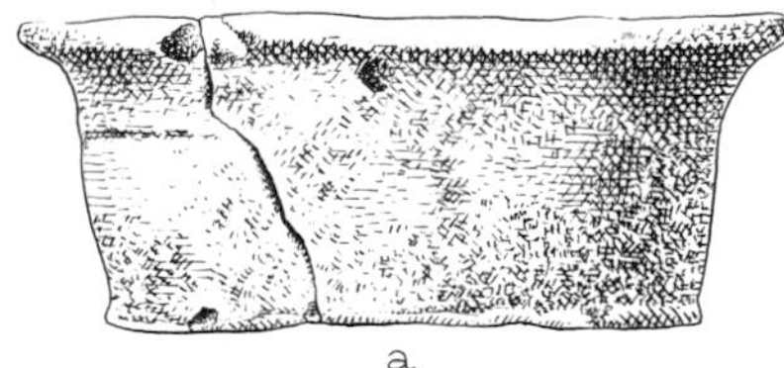

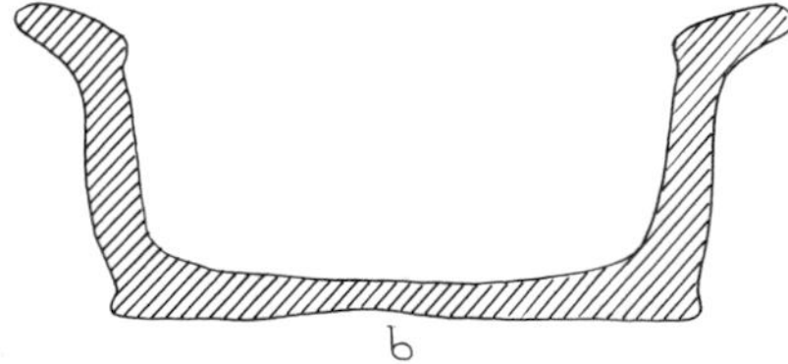

16 Przywóz, Site 1. Wheel-made vessel from the bottom of the deep well-like pit under Barrow 2.

small squat vessel was discovered at the bottom of a deep well-like pit 2 m in diameter and reaching to a depth of 5 m, situated under the mound near the edge of the barrow. This bowl-like vessel was conical in shape, wheel-made and well fired, with a markedly everted rim and a slightly rusticated dull surface, and was yellowish in colour (*Ill. 16*). It was found broken and blackened by soot, and is certainly of alien and probably provincial Roman origin, Pannonia being a possible source of manufacture. Also under this barrow, plough-marks have come to light. They appeared as criss-cross furrows, 10 to 15 cm wide and 10 to 20 cm apart. It is noteworthy that the deep well-like pit mentioned above has produced a big lump of iron slag from a smelting furnace. This find is yet another proof of the interrelations between the barrows and the settlement (Kowalczyk 1968).

The settlement itself, located at the foot of the barrows, occupied nearly the whole width of the lower terrace, reaching as far as the river. The dependence of the settlement on the river is also shown by the position of the houses, whose long axes usually ran parallel to the course of the Warta. Almost the entire area of the settlement has been explored. Its small peripheral zone probably still lies buried under the woods bordering the area on the west and north. More than half a hectare has been examined. About one third of the settlement either was unsuitable for habitation because of the erosive activity of water – which after heavy rainfall flowed down the fairly steep bank into the river – or has been washed away in ancient or modern times, or has been destroyed recently by digging for gravel (*Ill. 17*).

The settlement was presumably unfortified since no traces of a surrounding rampart, moat, or palisade have been found on its outskirts. Two roads seem to have intersected at the site: one running along the river in the middle of the lower terrace, and the other meeting it at a right-angle and leading from the plateau behind the edge of the upper terrace, through the gully separating the two barrows. The excavations have revealed a large number of various features, including the remains of twenty-one houses probably built in several rows parallel to the road by the river, dozens of rubbish pits, hundreds of post-holes, a dozen or so hearths, a number of smelting furnaces some of which were fairly well preserved and a few others much ruined, extended dumps of slag lying in channels grooved by seasonal streams, and occasional single large storage jars (Kaszewska, Makiewicz 1969; Jadczyk 1971).

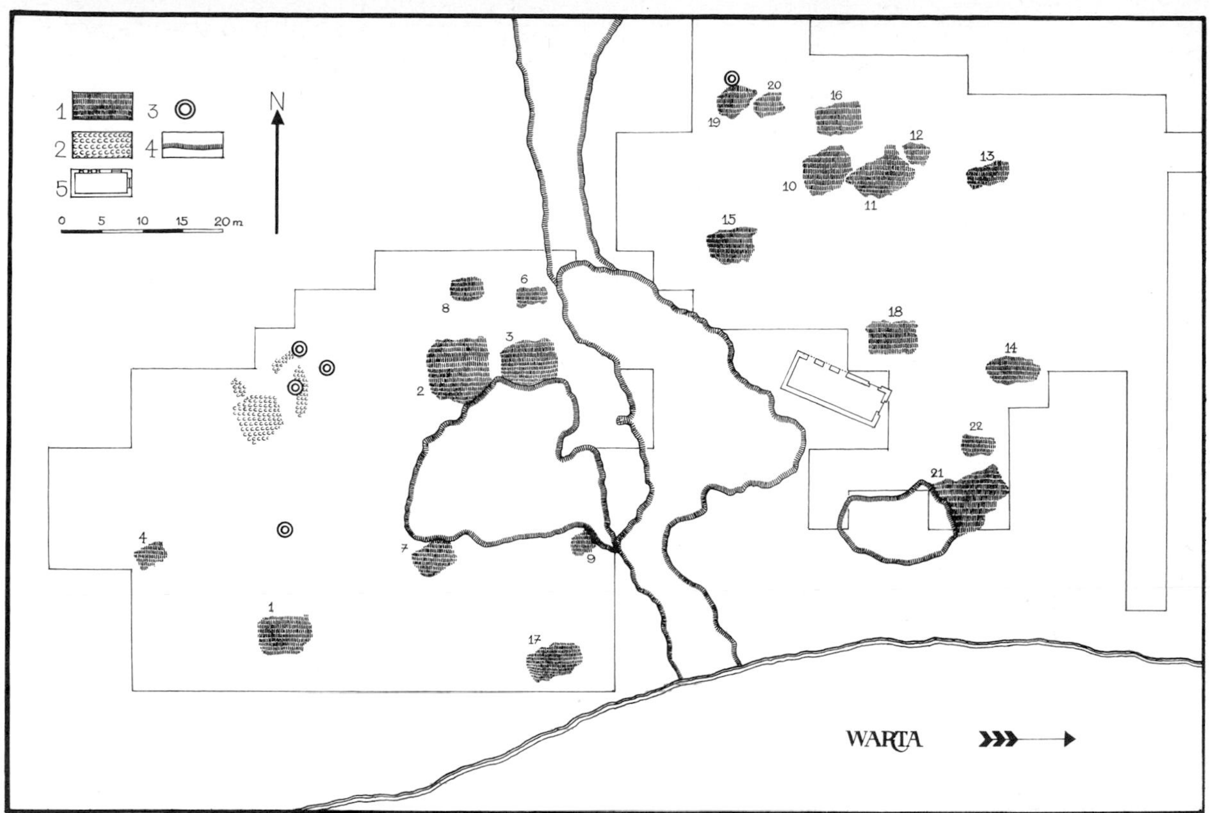

17 Przywóz, Site 1. Plan of the settlement at the foot of Barrows 1 and 2.

1 Semi-subterranean houses
2 Larger concentration of iron slag from iron-smelting
3 Smelting furnaces
4 Limits of the area destroyed in modern times
5 Modern house

The dwellings are represented by pits approaching a squat rectangle in ground-plan. They are the remains of shallow or deep semi-subterranean huts of small or medium size. The presence of over-ground post houses cannot be entirely excluded, as is suggested by numerous post-holes uncovered there. Unfortunately the post-holes form such a chaotic maze that no logical pattern can be detected. Overground block houses might also have existed, but have not survived due to the absence of foundations and the poor conserving properties of the subsoil. In view of this, our conclusions as to the extent, size and layout of the settlement are necessarily based on the semi-subterranean houses only. If we assume that at least one third of the settlement has been destroyed by various factors, there is reason to maintain that it had consisted of at least thirty houses during the hundred or hundred and fifty years of its existence. As shown by observations made on well-dated multi-layer early medieval settlements such as Gdańsk, Opole and Novgorod Velikiy, a timber house did not last much longer than twenty-five years. Consequently, some five to eight houses might have existed here at any one time.

These semi-subterranean houses were usually sunk into the soil to a depth of 60 to 120 cm, and occasionally only 15 to 60 cm. Their horizontal measurements varied between 7.5 by 7 m, giving 52.5 sq. m (*Ill. 18*), and 3.6 by 2.4 m giving 8.6 sq. m. The average dwelling space was between 20 and 30 sq. m. The foundation levels of the houses were flat and there were probably neither timber nor clay floors. Some houses had walls built of short timber planks with ends tenoned into the slots of vertical timber posts which were sunk into the sandy subsoil. The others were built of long horizontal beams in 'block house' style. The walls were plastered as is shown by the surviving lumps of

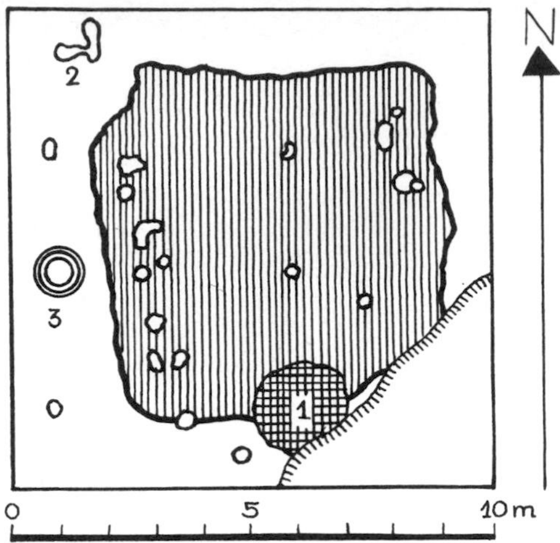

18 Przywóz, Site 1a. Ground plan of House 2.
1 Hearth
2 Post-holes
3 Wheel-made storage jar (cf. *Ill. 19*)

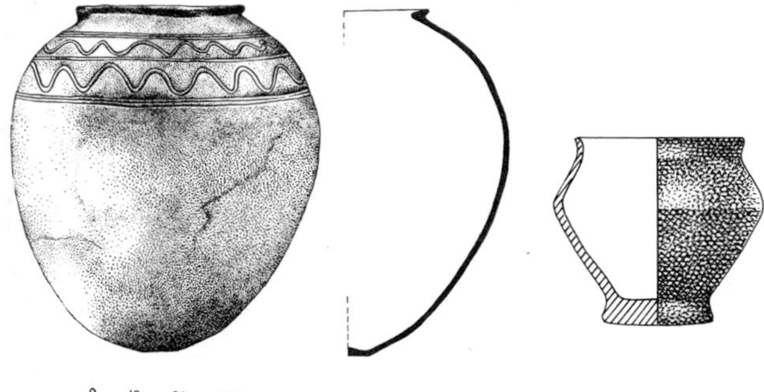

19 Przywóz, Site 1a. Large wheel-made storage jar buried up to its mouth near the wall of House 2.
20 Przywóz, Site 1a. Clay hand-made pot from House 10.

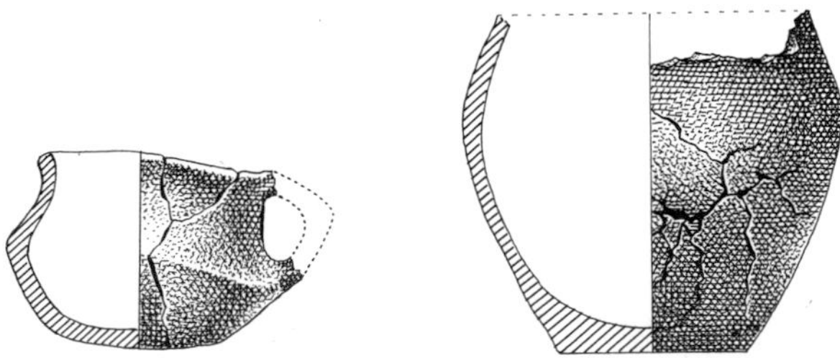

21 Przywóz, Site 1a. Hand-made mug from House 3.
22 Przywóz, Site 1a. Hand-made egg-shaped pot from the occupation layer in square CXL.

daub with impressions of beams. There are also indications that the roofs were supported by longer or shorter uprights with their upper parts forked. The hearths were usually open, built of small stones and clay. They were situated near the walls or sometimes partly beyond the extent of the dwelling pit in a sort of roofed porch. The houses seem to consist of only one room (Jadczykowa 1973, 6).

The cultural layer, both inside and outside the houses, has yielded a vast quantity of artifacts, among which the pottery – mostly fragmentarily preserved – predominates. An exceptional find is a large ornamented and wheel-turned storage jar (*Ill. 19*) found outside the wall of one of the largest houses. The bulk of pottery from Przywóz, which on a rough estimate consisted of some 1000 to 1500 vessels, was however made by hand. The prevailing forms are coarse medium-sized vessels, either undecorated or with only scanty ornament, with rusticated or partly smoothed surface, and mostly yellow or grey-brown in colour. This is the common kitchen ware, samples of which are shown in *Ills. 20–22*. The second group includes thin-walled pottery, mostly with a black and burnished surface, more varied in shape, often on high or low hollow pedestal feet, and frequently ornamented. The more attractive though seldom-used motifs include meanders composed of engraved lines or dots (*Ill. 23a–b*), or zones formed of alternating groups of diagonal lines. A few unusual forms also occurred, for example a fragmentary vessel on a high hollow and openwork pedestal (*Ill. 24*), or another vessel on which a country-woman of some seventeen centuries ago made fanciful lines of the kind we make today when trying out a new pen (*Ill. 25*). Some of the ornaments, such as vertical ribs pressed from the inside (*Ill. 26*) or circular hollows pressed from the outer surface on the bases of bowls or walls of small pots, distinctly point to imported provincial Roman glass ware as the source of inspiration. The pottery includes forms with large decorative handles (*Ill. 27a–d*), deep cups and pots (*Ills. 28, 29*) and vessels which performed some specific domestic functions such as a clay strainer (*Ill. 30*) or a thick-walled pot with a large hole inside which was probably used in tar-making (*Ill. 31*). The favourite motifs used to decorate the body of the vessels include extensive trellis patterns, perpendicular lines (*Ill. 29*), a maze of strokes running in all directions, zones of combing scattered at random, and simple fingernail impressions (*Ill. 28*) or rows of pinchings (*Ill. 32*). The third category of pottery, accounting for only

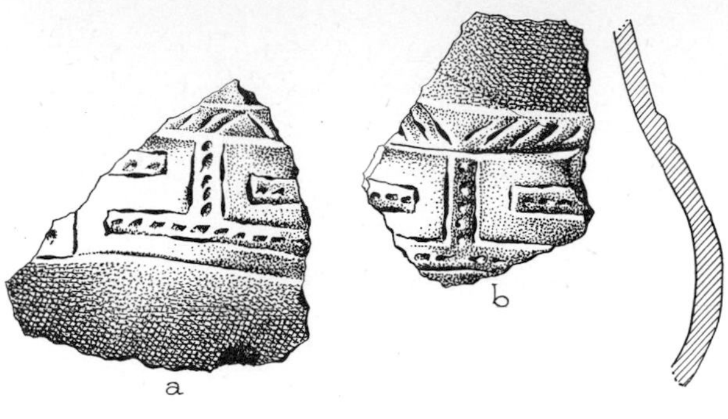

23 Przywóz, Site 1a. Sherds of a hand-made black-burnished pot with meander ornament (the background and the ornament are reversed) from the occupation layer in square XIX.

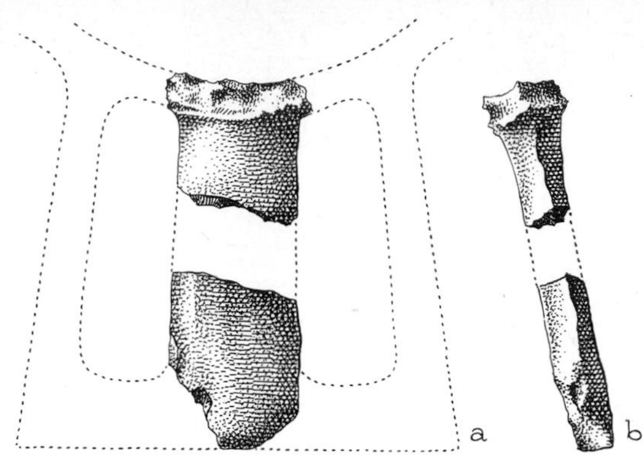

24 Przywóz, Site 1a. Sherds of a hand-made vessel with a high open-work pedestal, from House 15: a, front view; b, side view.

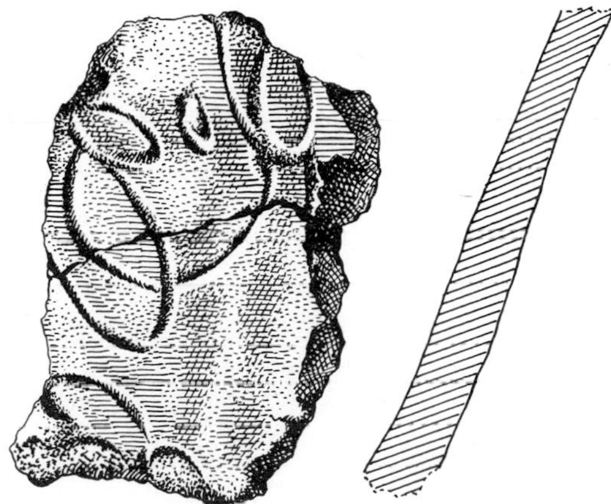

25 Przywóz, Site 1a. Sherd of a large, hand-made, thick-walled vessel, ornamented on its lower body with abstract designs, from House 16.

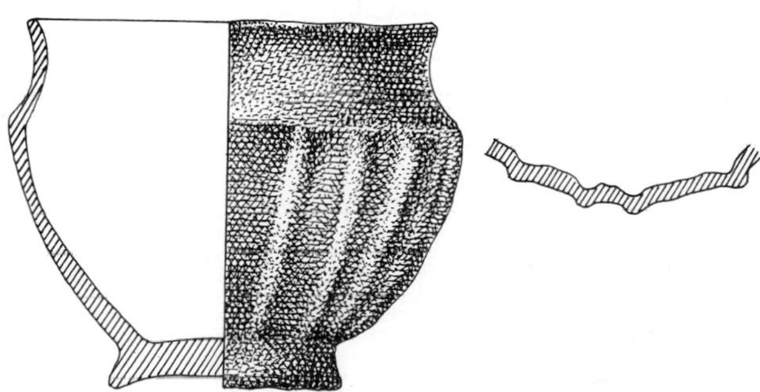

26 Przywóz, Sire 1a. Hand-made vessel with vertical ribs pressed from inside, imitating imported glass vessels, from House 3.

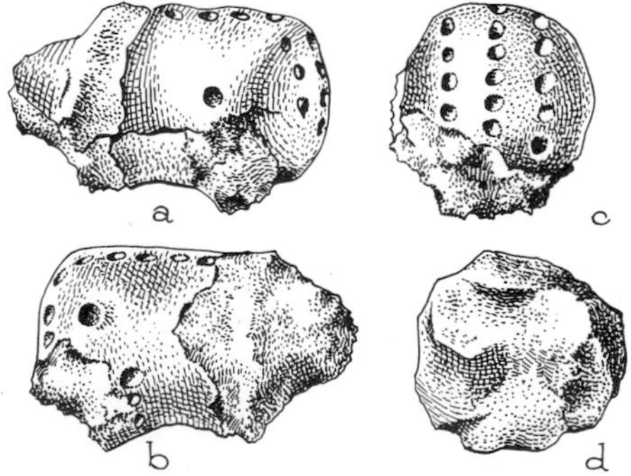

27 Przywóz, Site 1a. Fragment of a decorated handle of a big hand-made vessel from the occupation layer in square XIII.

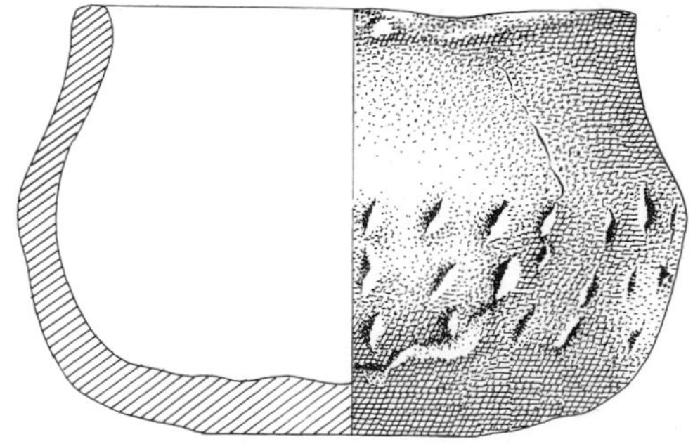

28 Przywóz, Site 1a. Thick-walled, hand-made cup of clay with finger-nail impressions, from rubbish pit no. 107.

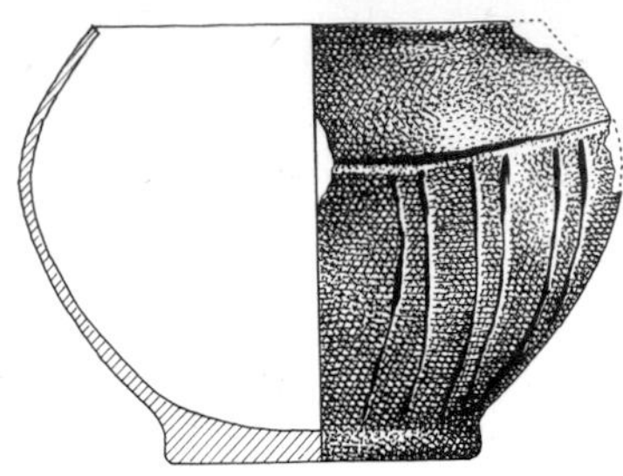

29 Przywóz, Site 1a. Hand-made clay vessel decorated with a horizontal line and vertical grooves, from House 16.

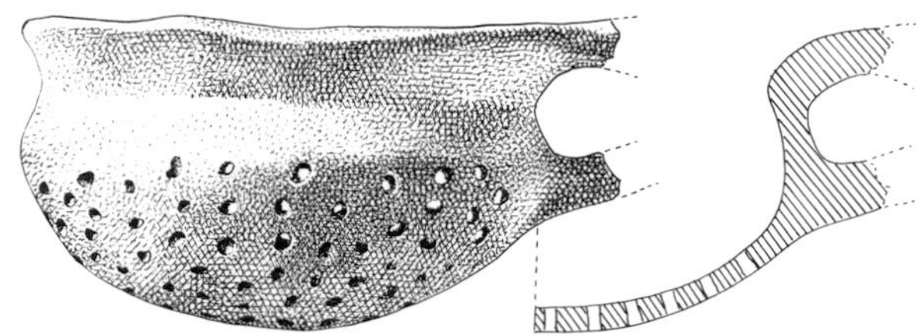

30 Przywóz, Site 1a. Hand-made clay strainer from rubbish pit no. 172.

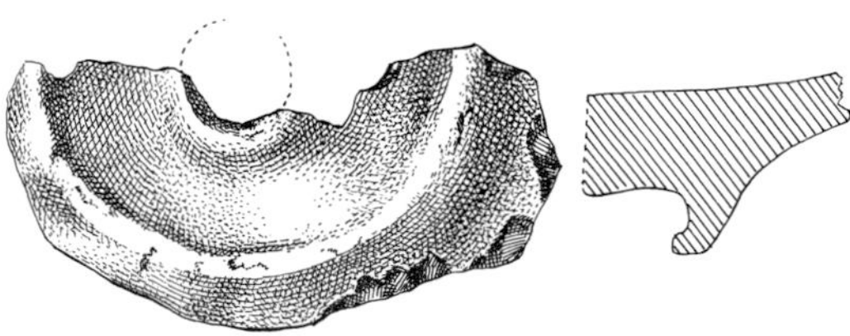

31 Przywóz, Site 1a. Fragmentary base of a hand-made clay pot with a ring-like foot and a big hole in the centre, perhaps used in tar-making, from House 12.

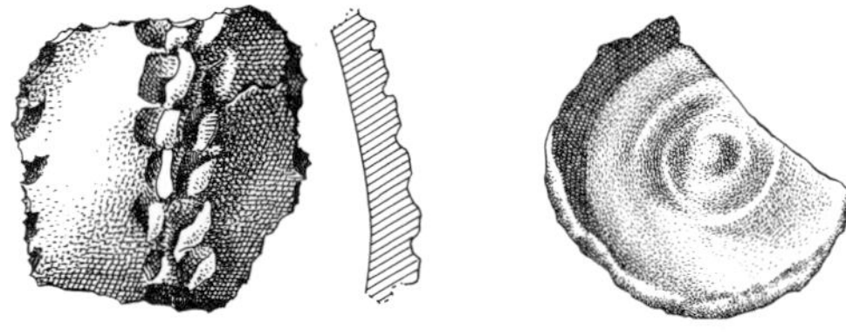

32 Przywóz, Site 1a. Fragment of a hand-made pot ornamented with vertical rows of 'pinchings', from House 2.

a small percentage of the whole, includes wheel-made vessels or vessels shaped by hand and finished on the wheel. One sub-group of this class, preserved in small fragments, consists of thin-walled vessels made of fine clay grey in colour (the so-called 'grey ware'), ornamented with dense diagonal lines (*Ills. 33, 34*), plastic circular ribs, or horizontal straight and wavy lines. This group can be designated as table-ware. The other part includes the already mentioned big storage jars with capacity up to 100 litres, of which as many as three have been discovered in House 2 or near it (*Ills. 18, 19*). They have an egg-shaped body, a thick wide everted and inturned rim (*Krausengefässe*), and are decorated with zones of horizontal or wavy lines (*Ill. 35*). The storage jars were made of clay with added sand and are dark-grey and reddish in colour. The clay artifacts, found in quantity at Przywóz, include spindle-whorls, which are usually biconical and sometimes bear varied ornaments (*Ill. 36*), and loom-weights shaped as truncated cones. The latter belonged to vertical looms and were occasionally found in groups of more than ten (*Ill. 14*). To sum up, the pottery of Przywóz is typical of the Przeworsk group of the Venedian culture, dated to the second half of the second and to the third centuries AD.

In comparison with other typical settlement sites of this period in Poland, Przywóz has produced an exceptionally large number of metal objects, some quite unique in this area. These include firstly a pair of iron compasses, doubtless of provincial Roman origin (*Ill. 37*), an iron trident or leisterprong which could have been used in fishing no less than fighting (*Ill. 38*), an iron balance scale also imported from the Roman provinces (*Ill. 39*), and a large cylindrical padlock of iron and bronze which served to fasten a casket (*Ill. 40*) and was also an import. Other metal objects included iron and bronze brooches (*Ills. 41–45*) similar to Almgren types II:43, IV:75, 79, 80, 92, VI:159, and VII:195 (Almgren 1923), and a number of bronze pins (possibly hair-pins) (*Ills. 46, 47*). An iron plough-share (*Ill. 48*), some iron coulters (*Ill. 49*), an iron sickle (*Ill. 50*), and parts of rotary querns indicate agricultural activities, whereas an iron fish-hook (*Ill. 51*) and the above-mentioned trident show that the inhabitants of the river settlement were engaged in fishing as well. Attention should also be called to a bronze strap-end of the same type as that found in Barrow 1 (*Ill. 52*), an ornamented bronze mount (possibly part of a belt or casket) (*Ill. 53*), an iron spur (*Ill. 54*), an iron spear- or arrowhead (*Ill. 55*), an unidentified iron object which may be a damaged key (*Ill. 56*),

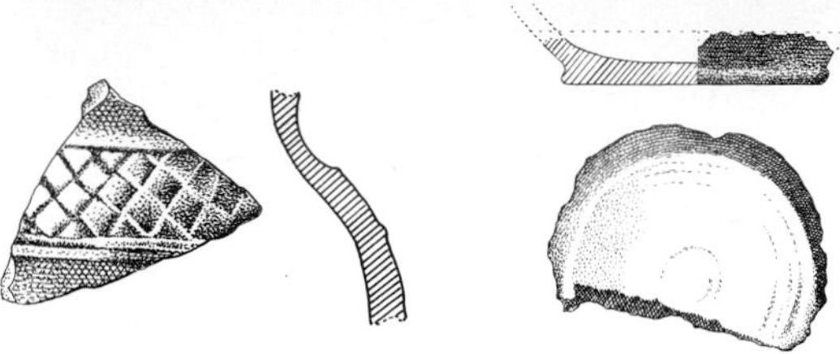

33 Przywóz, Site 1a. Fragment of a small wheel-made vessel of 'grey' clay, ornamented on the upper part of the body with trellis pattern, from the occupation layer in square XXII.

34 Przywóz, Site 1a. Bottom part of a wheel-made vessel of 'grey' clay, from the occupation layer in square XXII.

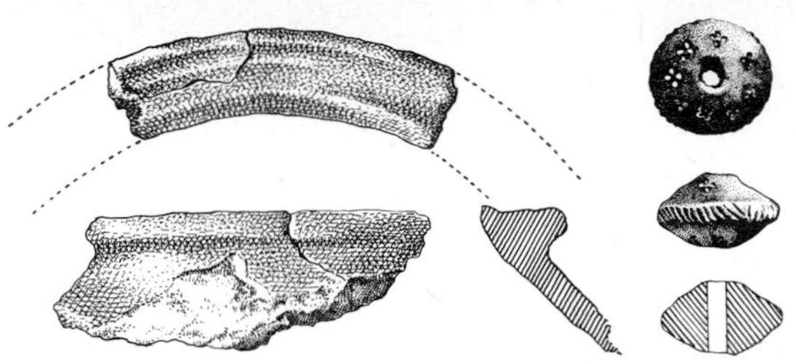

35 Przywóz, Site 1a. Fragment of the rim of the large storage jar, shaped by hand and finished on the wheel, made of clay with an admixture of sand, from the occupation layer in square XXII.

36 Przywóz, Site 1a. Ornamented clay spindle-whorl from the occupation layer in square LIII.

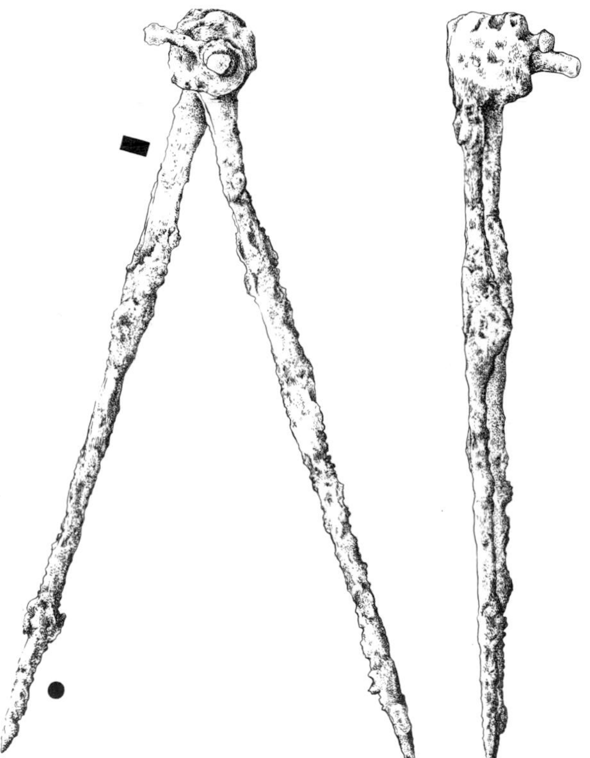

37 Przywóz, Site 1a. A pair of large iron compasses with a clamp-wedge, from House 10.

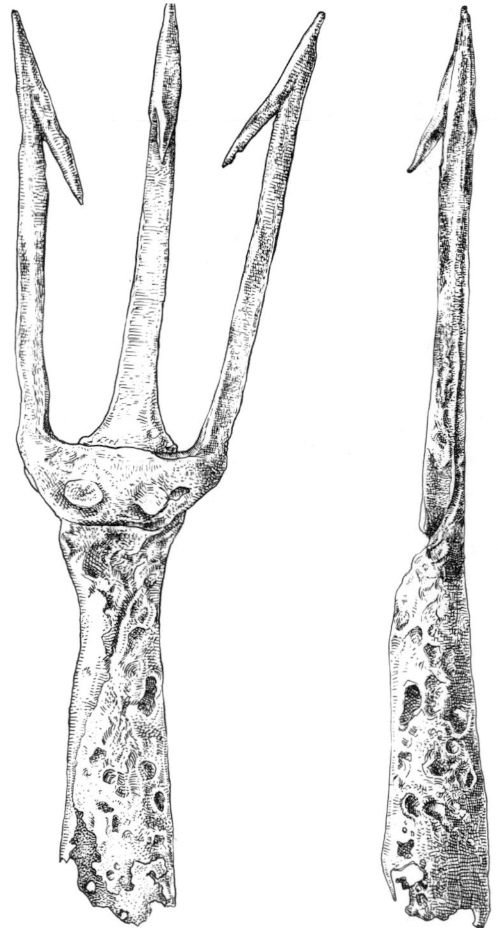

38 Przywóz, Site 1a. Socketed iron trident or leister, scorched in the fire, with a rivetted bow with two flanking barbs and one barb on the middle prong, from section LXXXIV.

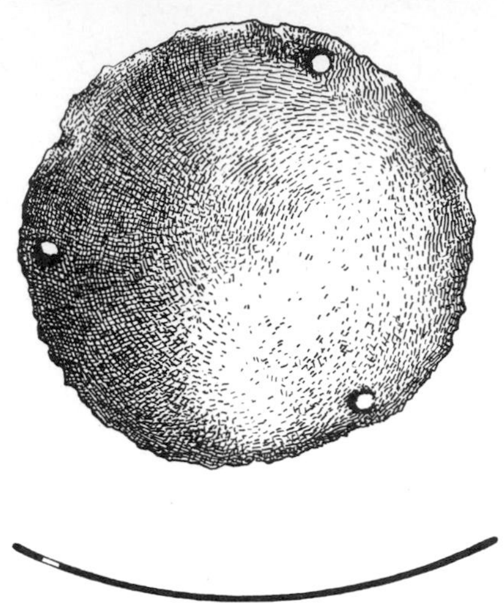

39 Przywóz, Site 1a. Iron scale pan from a balance from the hearth in House 2.

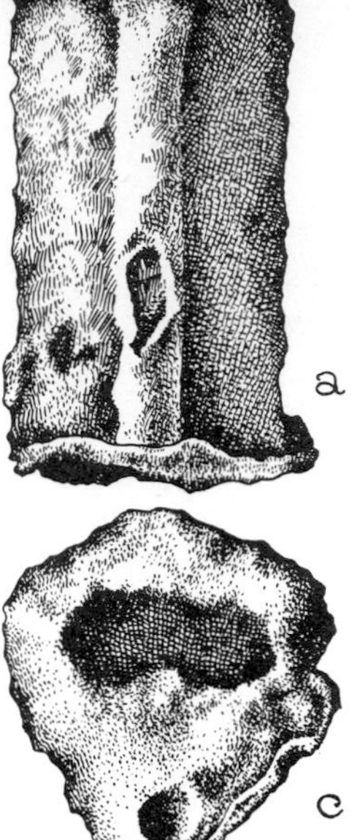

40 Przywóz, Site 1a. Padlock, probably of a casket, with the cylinder of iron sheet, and the top, bottom and side tubes of bronze: a, front view; b, side view; c, top view. From the occupation layer in square XXII.

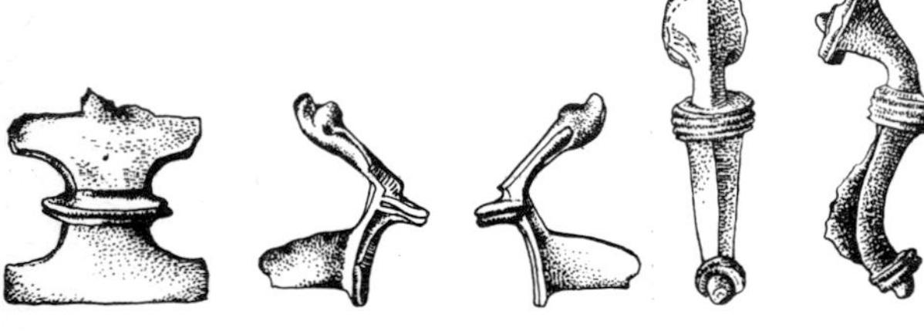

41 Przywóz, Site 1a. Iron brooch found above House 2.
42 Przywóz, Site 1a. Bronze brooch from House 14.

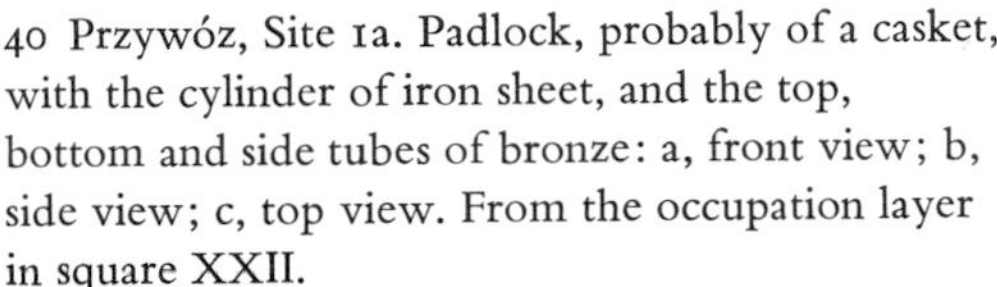

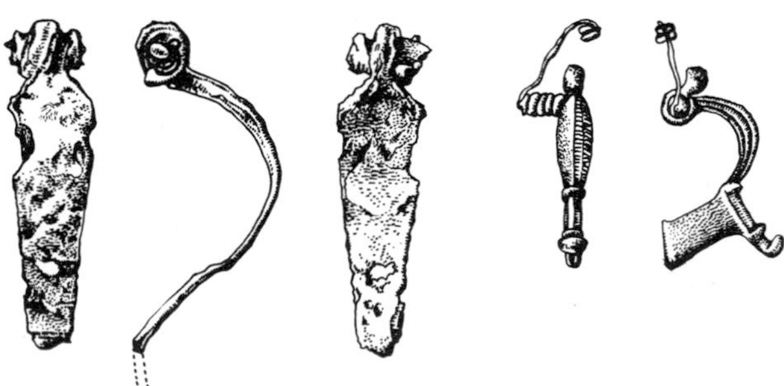

44 Przywóz, Site 1a. Iron brooch from the occupation layer in square LII.
45 Przywóz, Site 1a. Bronze brooch from House 1.

46 Przywóz, Site 1a. Bronze pin with a moulded head from the occupation layer in square LXIII.
47 Przywóz, Site 1a. Bronze pin with a hammer-like head from the occupation layer in square LXXXIV.

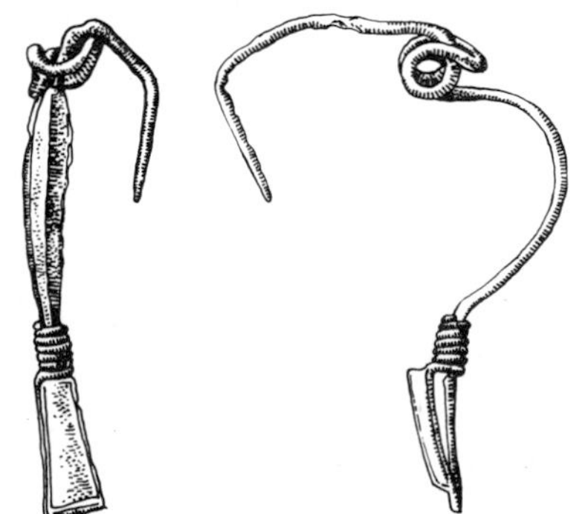

43 Przywóz, Site 1a. Bronze brooch from House 10.

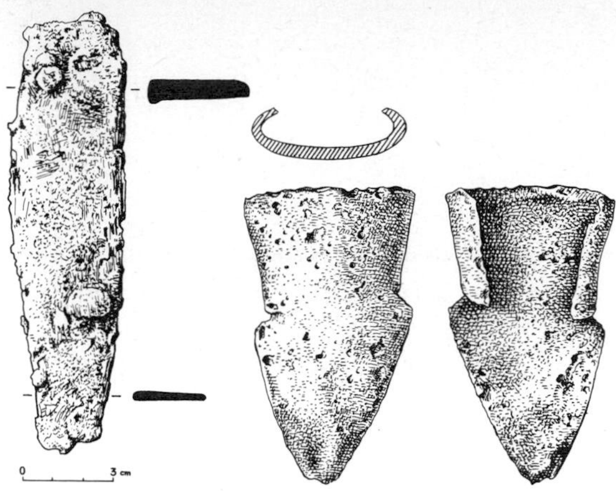

48 Przywóz, Site 1a. Asymmetric plough-share of iron from the occupation layer in square LX.
49 Przywóz, Site 1a. Iron ard-coulter from the occupation layer in square XV.

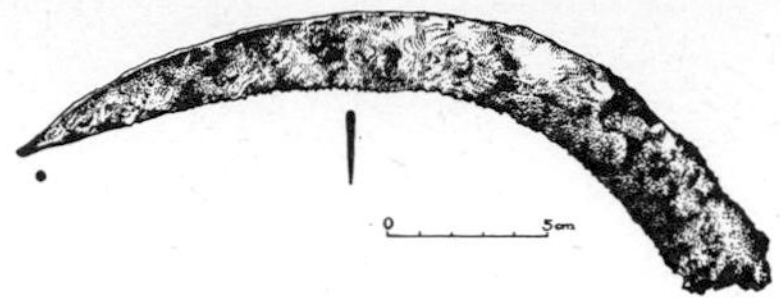

50 Przywóz. Site 1a. Iron sickle with indented blade from pit 16.

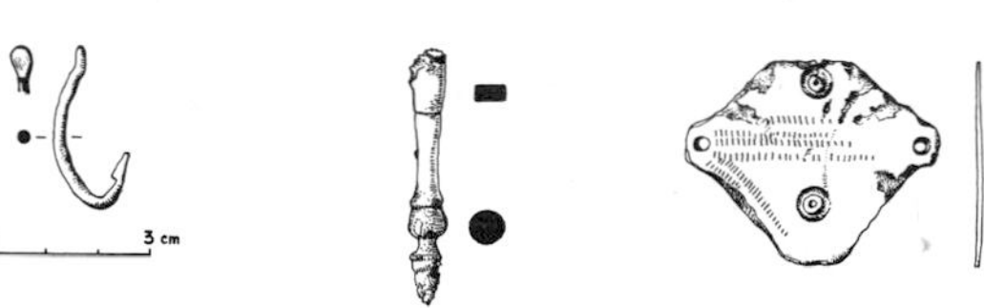

51 Przywóz, Site 1a. Iron fish-hook from pit 18.
52 Przywóz, Site 1a. Bronze strap-end from House 11.
53 Przywóz, Site 1a. Bronze ornamented strap-end or casket mount from the occupation layer in square XXXVIII.

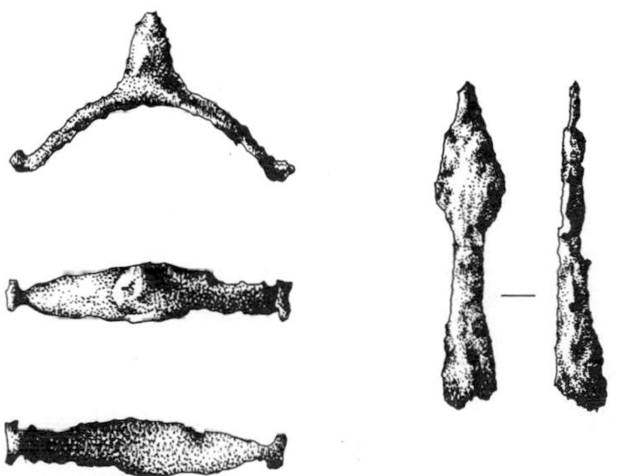

54 Przywóz, Site 1a. Iron spur from the occupation layer in square XIX.
55 Przywóz, Site 1a. Iron arrow- or spearhead from the occupation layer in square XXII.

simple iron knives (*Ills. 57, 58*), as well as fragmentary axes and numerous small fragments of other damaged metal objects.

The find which assists most to establish the absolute date of the settlement is a silver *denarius* of Faustina Maior (Mater) (AD 104–141), the wife of Antoninus Pius (AD 138–161). This coin is considerably worn by long use and weighs 1.86 g (*Ill. 59*); its obverse bears the head of the empress with a diadem and the inscription DIVA FAUSTINA, and the reverse, inscribed AETERNITAS, shows the symbolic representation of Aeternitas with a globe in hand.

56 Przywóz, Site 1a. An iron key(?) with the lower end broken off, from House 9.
57 Przywóz, Site 1a. Iron knife from the occupation layer in square CCXXVII.
58 Przywóz, Site 1a. Iron knife from the occupation layer in square LXXVII.

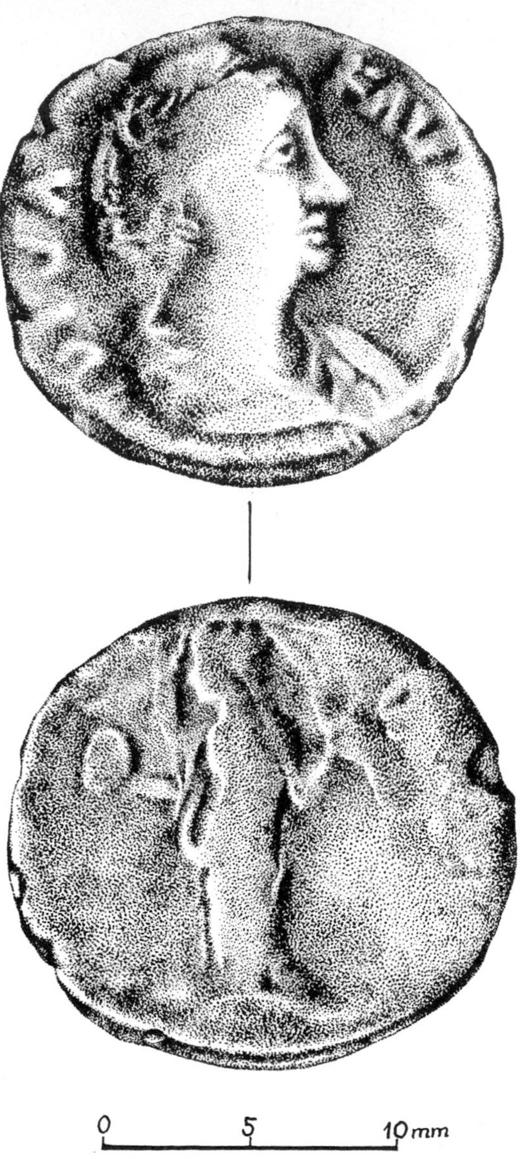

59 Przywóz, Site 1a. Silver *denarius* of Faustina Mater (AD 101–141), wife of Antoninus Pius (AD 138–161), found in post-hole no. 19.

The *denarius*, discovered in a post-hole, probably found its way there in the third quarter of the second century AD at the earliest.

A separate chapter in the history of the Przywóz settlement is the iron-working pursued by its inhabitants. This activity is attested by several small smelting furnaces where the local iron ore was smelted. These were mostly concentrated in the west part of the site, though single furnaces occur in the northern part as well (cf. *Ill. 17*). Other finds in this group include big lumps of slag mostly discovered in beds of seasonal streams, and many single lumps of slag of various sizes scattered all over the settlement in the cultural layer, houses and refuse pits, and in the make-up of the two barrows as well. The furnaces were sunk into the ground, one of the better preserved being of cylindrical shape with an internal diameter of 80 cm and external diameter of 128–135 cm and surviving height of 90 cm. Its clay walls were between 20 and 30 cm thick, the fill consisting of some 100 kg of slag with a layer of charcoal at the bottom. Traces of a channel filled with grey earth were visible partly to one side and partly under the clay walls of the furnace. This seems to be an air channel through which, during the smelting process, air was introduced into the furnace by means of bellows (*Ill. 60*) (Makiewicz 1960). Large hearths represented by vast stone pavements covered by a layer of charcoal and ash may also have been associated with iron smelting. They were found in the neighbourhood of smelting furnaces and may have served for working iron bloom.

Due to the non-farming activities of its inhabitants, the settlement had an industrial character. It is possible that these very activities contributed most to the wealth of the Przywóz population, notably of the members of the local tribal aristocracy. This wealth is reflected in a larger number of various metal objects than is usually encountered in settlements of this period and culture group, and in the presence of rather unusual imports from the Roman provinces. The pair of compasses, for instance (*Ill. 37*), the only object of this kind to be found in Poland during the period (Jadczyk 1973a), has counterparts from Heilbronn-Böckingen, in the region of the Lower Neckar, Baden-Württemberg, in a nearly identical carpenter's pair of compasses which was part of a smith's hoard deposited in the first half of the third century AD in an abandoned Roman *castellum* (Schönberger 1967, 142, Fig. 10:16). A similar specimen has been found at ancient Lauriacum near Linz on the Danube (Groller 1925, col. 125, Fig. 3), whereas less close parallels occur in Dacia Apulensis, at Sarmizegetusa (*Ulpia Traiana*), the ancient capital from the period of the war between the Dacian king Decebalus and Trajan (AD 101–107), and in Illyricum dating to the first or second centuries AD. Another import from the Roman provinces is the balance, whose introduction to Polish territory is documented by the iron scale (*Ill. 39*). Also of provincial Roman origin are other objects found at Przywóz yet rarely

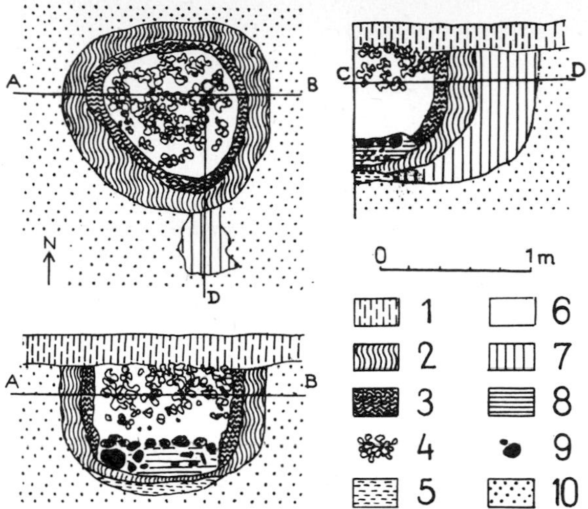

60 Przywóz, Site 1a. Ground plan and sections along A-B and C-D of a smelting furnace between squares XXVIII and XXVI.

1 Present-day arable layer
2 Clay
3 Heavily burnt clay
4 Slag
5 Burnt sand
6 Fill of the furnace
7 Dark grey soil
8 Soil with a large amount of charcoal
9 Larger pieces of charcoal
10 Sand

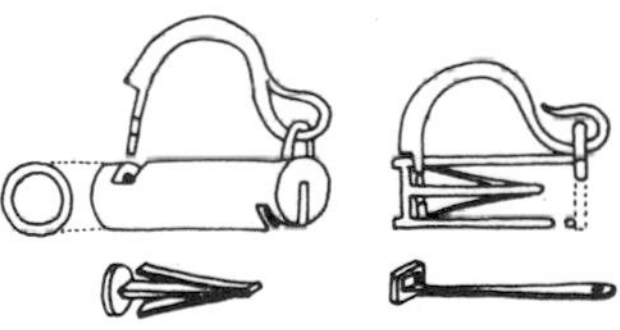

61 Echzell, Kr. Büdingen near Frankfurt-am-Main, West Germany. Roman *castellum* from the end of the first and beginning of the second century AD. Left, outer view of a Roman cylindrical padlock with a bow and a spring inset; right, section through the padlock shut after the insertion of the spring inset; below, the key which served for clamping the spring leaves of the inset and thus for opening the padlock by drawing out the inset (after Gaheis).

encountered in other parts of Poland at that time. Examples in this category are the bronze-iron cylinder padlock (*Ill. 40*), to which analogies occur for instance at the Roman *castellum* of Echzell, Kr. Büdingen near Frankfurt-am-Main, dating from the first half of the second century AD (*Ill. 61*) (Gaheis 1930, col. 257, Fig. 122a), and the trident (*Ill. 38*), so common in the Greco-Roman world as for instance the well-known symbol of Neptune. Contacts with the Roman provinces are also clearly shown by the finds from the two barrows. Thus the *terra sigillata* vessel ornamented with grape-vine motifs, found in fragments in Barrow 1 (*Ill. 6a–d*) and dating from the last quarter of the second century, probably originated in the East Gaulish workshop of Comitialis I (it bears the stamp SECUNDINUS-AVITUS) at Rheinzabern, the Roman Tabernae or Tabernis, on the left bank of the Upper Rhine (Rutkowski 1960; Majewski 1949; 1960). By way of Raetia, Noricum and Pannonia, the vessel must have reached Carnuntum on the Danube, whence along the River Morava, via the Moravian Gates and along the Upper Odra, it finally arrived on the Upper Warta (Eggers 1951, 68, map D). A similar journey was probably made by other objects found in this barrow, such as the molten glass from the funerary pyre which originally constituted vessels or beads, sherds of presumed *terra nigra*, and possibly the gold object represented by tiny globules (*Ill. 8*) and the casket with the unusual bronze mount (*Ill. 10a–b*). The unique wheel-made cylindrical vessel, well-fired and with a coarse and yellow surface, discovered at the bottom of the deep well-like pit in Barrow 2 (*Ill. 16*), is also obviously of alien and perhaps Pannonian origin, since the nearest analogy is provided by a vessel of similar shape found in Gorsium (present-day Tác in western Hungary) in Pannonia Inferior, a settlement lying between Lake Balaton (ancient Lacus Pelso) and the auxiliary *castrum* (Castrum Stativum) of Intercisa on the Danube south of Budapest.[3]

The objects which reached Przywóz by way of trading exchanges of more limited range comprise a few wheel-made pots, representing the 'grey ware' which lasted in Poland for some three centuries from its original appearance in the mid-third century AD. It was most popular in southern Poland at the end of the third and during the fourth century, became less frequent in the northern parts of Poland, and decreased in the course of time. This grey ware

[3] Information from Dr Jenő Fitz, Director, István Király Múzeum Székesfehérvár, Hungary.

was mainly produced in Little Poland and Silesia, but it is impossible to identify the workshop which created the 'grey' bowls and jugs whose fragments have been found at Przywóz. The most likely guess is Upper Silesia, and the same applies to the large storage jars (Godłowski 1960; 1969).

We lack conclusive evidence for regarding the six complete brooches and the few undiagnostic fragments discovered at Przywóz as local products. No two specimens are of the same form and, as mentioned above, similar examples were assigned by Almgren to various types. The earliest forms date from the second half of the second century AD, possibly from its last quarter, and the latest survived into the second half of the third century. Generally speaking, a considerable part of the extent of their distribution corresponds with the basins of the Odra and Vistula, an area dominated by the Venedian culture with its larger southern Przeworsk group and its smaller northern Oksywie group, and also by the West Baltian or Old Prussian culture in the north-eastern part of Poland. In the basin of the Elbe and east of the Bug, these brooch types are seldom if ever encountered. Nor have any close analogies been found in the south and southwest, though that area certainly inspired their emergence. They are in fact most frequent in the northern, western and central parts of Poland (Almgren 1923). It may therefore be assumed that at Przywóz the demand for brooches was met by products made within the broad culture area to which the inhabitants of Przywóz themselves belonged. Since the group clearly possessed sources of raw material, they probably produced by themselves at least some of the less complicated iron objects.

A number of diagnostic artifacts consistently date the Przywóz settlement to the close of Eggers' phase B2, the transitional phase B2/C1, the whole of phase C1, and to the beginning of phase C2. In terms of absolute chronology, the settlement dates from about AD 150 to about AD 260/270 (Eggers 1951; Godłowski 1970). The contemporaneity of the barrows and the settlement is established by a number of objects, such as the brooch of Almgren type V:94–97 (*Ill. 7*), the strap-ends (*Ills. 9; 52*), and the hand-made pottery (e.g. *Ills. 4; 23a–b*) many examples of which, similar in form and decoration, were found both in the barrows and in the settlement. The interrelation between the settlement and the two barrows is also manifested by iron slag and by sherds of common hand-made pottery belonging to the same cultural group and the same period. Barrow 1 can be assigned to the last quarter of the second century. As regards Barrow 2, which unfortunately did not yield diagnostic finds, it can be generally assigned to the third century (AD 260/270) on the grounds of the cylindrical vessel, to which a close analogy, as already mentioned, has been discovered at Gorsium. It would thus appear that Barrow 1 was built a few decades after the emergence of the settlement, and that Barrow 2 was constructed several decades later, just before the settlement was abandoned.

The barrows at Przywóz doubtless marked the last resting places of persons of high rank and wealth. At that time, the common grave type in the Venedian culture and in its regional groups was the flat grave (Kostrzewski, Chmielewski, and Jażdżewski 1965). Several graves in the basins of the Odra and Vistula, though distinguished by rich furniture, were unmarked by mounds of either earth or stone. But at Przywóz the two dead were honoured by large mounds approaching 1000 cubic metres in volume. The building of these mounds involved great effort since the marl used had to be brought from a considerable distance. The transport of several cubic metres of stone also must have demanded a large labour force. It would seem that the task of constructing the mounds must have far exceeded the capabilities of the community that lived at the foot of the barrows, whose population in one generation (i.e. 25 years) has been estimated at about 40 persons of all age-groups. It thus appears that, apart from the local people, the population of neighbouring settlements must have also participated in this task.

The two barrows were situated symmetrically on either side of a gully, along which a road ran to the settlement and the ford. This road was on the same edge of the river terrace, at the same altitude above water-level, and commanded the same extensive view over the settlement, the river and the region beyond. The connections between the barrows and the settlement are obvious. The barrows are isolated: despite a thorough search, no cemetery where the bulk of the Przywóz population might have been buried has come to light. Barrow 1, which was better preserved, unmistakably demonstrates an intention to distinguish the dead not only by the great collective effort involved in raising the mound but also by the specific burial rite. The body, as has been shown, was cremated on the spot, on a particularly large pyre, whose remains together with the grave-goods, partly deformed in the fire, were scattered over the whole area subsequently covered by the mound. He was buried with his dog, and moreover was furnished with especially valuable goods such as the gold ornament, *terra sigillata, terra nigra*, bronze and glass objects. Moreover it is possible that, prior to raising the mound, ritual ploughing was performed – although of course the plough-marks may be the remains of simple cultivation. The same applies to Barrow 2 in a lesser degree, though differences have been noted, namely the presence of the surrounding ditch, a smaller mound, and the absence of evidence for cremation which suggests inhumation burial.

In Poland as in other areas such as north-east Bohemia, south-west and northern parts of the German Democratic Republic, the region of the Lower Elbe in West Germany, Denmark and southern Norway, the Roman period is marked by the appearance of a special group of unusually rich graves, which are conventionally termed 'princes' graves'. There is no doubt that increasing social differentiation led in the first century AD to the emergence of a tribal aristocracy whose distinctiveness was reflected in its burial rite. These graves can be divided into several categories. One of the earliest categories, which coincides with Eggers' phases B1 and B2, and is marked by the dominance of inhumation, has been studied in detail by Eggers who labelled it the 'Lubieszewo – or Lübsow – group' after Lubieszewo in the district of Gryfice, Szczecin province, some 40 km east of the mouth of the Odra (Eggers 1953). The other categories, usually of later date, have not yet been attributed to definite groups. In any case they lasted in Poland throughout the whole Roman period, and occasionally survived until the Migration period (*Ill. 62*). Naturally, not every barrow or every richly furnished grave must *ipso facto* be a 'prince's grave'. At Siedlemin, in the Jarocin district of Great Poland, there is a cemetery dating from the end of the third and the early fourth centuries. It consists of nine barrows each of which, under a stone cairn, sometimes also covered by an earthen mound, contained a cremation layer with fairly rich grave-goods, including provincial Roman imports such as molten bronze and glass vessels (Karpińska 1926). Similar barrows with a cremation layer occur in other places in Greater Poland, Pomerania and central Poland (Godłowski 1968; 1969). The assemblage of features characteristic of these barrows seems to indicate that the personages buried there were members of a tribal aristocracy, perhaps tribal chieftains, but it is rather doubtful that they were in fact 'princes'. In any case it is by no means easy to determine the

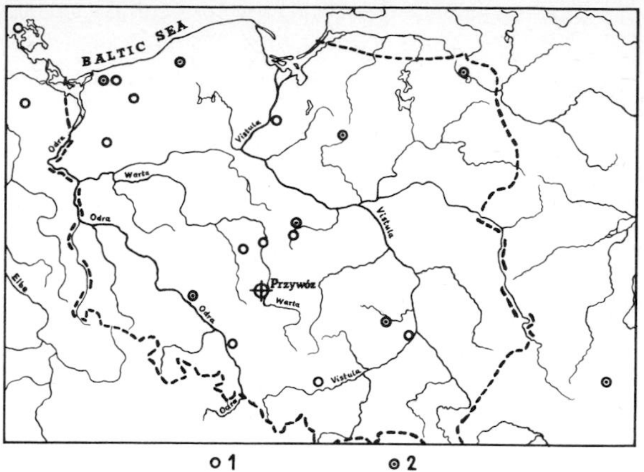

62 Map showing the position of the site at Przywóz against the background of other sites with more certain evidence for 'princes' graves' of the Roman period in Poland and in neighbouring regions (after Łowmiański and Humnicki).

1 'Princes' graves' of the Early Roman period
2 'Princes' graves' of the Late Roman period

exact position occupied by the foremost representatives of this aristocracy in the social hierarchy during this transitional period, marked as it was by the emergence of relatively short-lived social units and centres of the earliest territorial communities. As is known, the demarcation line between the military chieftains who wielded limited power during particular campaigns, the tribal chieftains and the princes who succeeded in ruling over a definite territory for a longer or shorter period, is extremely vague.

The political and military activity of such *duces, reguli* or *reges* as, for instance, Arminius among the Cherusci, Maroboduus or Tudrus or Vannius among the Marcomanni and the Quadi, is recorded by Roman writers of the first to third centuries AD as having taken place in the neighbourhood of the Roman Empire along its frontiers on the Danube and the Rhine. As regards the territories far removed from these frontiers, the main sources of information are archaeological rather than written, since the latter are much too scanty. In any case, when in any one region or in its immediate vicinity there occur graves which are distinguished by their structure or furniture, and which represent a characteristic time-sequence for example with intervals of 25 to 30 years, it seems feasible to assume the existence of a dynasty of princes who succeeded in ruling over an area for several generations. As far as the Celtic culture area is concerned, an area where more advanced social and political forms had crystallized much earlier than in Poland, there occur 'dynastic' princes' graves of this kind, which show a significant time-sequence occasionally lasting for several centuries. One of the best examples is in the neighbourhood of the well-known Heuneburg near Sigmaringen, in Baden-Württemberg, dating from Ha D1-D2 and LT A, with the nearby and impressive barrow of Hochmichele in the neighbourhood of Heiligkreuztal, Kr. Saulgau. Not far away at Asperg, Kr. Ludwigsburg, is a Late Hallstatt barrow, the 'Grafenbühl', with an early La Tène barrow of the same name at Klein Aspergle, both being near the contemporary princely residence of the Hohenasperg (Jażdżewski 1968, 86–91). The existence of a dynasty of princes in Poland may be testified by the concentration of princes' graves of the Lubieszewo type at Łęg Piekarski, near Turek in Konin province, which lies on the Middle Warta 85 km north of Przywóz (Leciejewicz 1960; Kietlińska 1961). A similar situation has been recorded at Lubieszewo itself, east of the mouth of the Odra, where a dynasty of princes seems to have ruled for a considerable period in the first and second centuries AD; at Rządz near Grudziądz on the Lower Vistula, in the first half of the first century AD (Eggers 1953); perhaps also at Zakrzów near Wrocław on the Middle Odra in the second half of the third century AD, and at Szwajcaria, in the Suwałki province, from the second half of the third to the second half of the fourth century AD – a site which is in the territory of the West Balts or Galindai-Sudovians (Okulicz 1973). In the last three places cited, the dynasties seem to have ruled for comparatively brief periods.

The question now arises in this context of how to interpret the barrows at Przywóz. Compared with both the Lubieszewo and the Siedlemin types their position is somewhat different, and chronologically they fall between the two types. Barrow 1 with its cremation layer is similar to the Siedlemin type, and Barrow 2 on account of its assumed inhumation rite, although somewhat later in date, is closer to the earlier mounds of the Lubieszewo type. However, the princes' graves of the Lubieszewo type differ distinctly in grave-goods from the barrows at Przywóz. The absence of various bronze vessels, and silver and glass cups, so characteristic of the Lubieszewo graves, is compensated at Przywóz by the *terra sigillata* and perhaps the *terra nigra* vessels, by the imported cylindrical vessel of provincial Roman and perhaps Pannonian origin, by the massive gold ornament, not to mention the large mounds built with great expenditure of time and labour. In status, the two last-mentioned categories of barrows seem equal. Barrow 2 seems to be later than Barrow 1 by several decades, perhaps by a quarter of a century. Unfortunately we do not know if anyone was actually buried in Barrow 2, though in the light of the analogies cited this seems highly probable. It is therefore possible – while by no means certain – that the barrows at Przywóz were the burial places of two male representatives of the tribal aristocracy who died within the space of one generation. If this surmise is true, we would be dealing here too with a short-lived dynasty of princes. The economic basis for its formation and brief existence of at most a century was provided by fairly advanced agriculture employing an animal-drawn ard with an iron share and iron coulter, by the exploitation of the large local deposits of iron ore, and by iron smelting carried out on a rather large scale at several points of the ore-bearing area, which stretched for over 100 km from Wieluń to Częstochowa and beyond. An analogy for this socio-economic model is provided by the situation which seems to have occurred some centuries earlier in the area between the Rhine, the Mosel and the Saar. In this area the concentration of Celtic princes' graves of the La Tène period corresponds to the area of rich deposits of haematite, siderite and spherosiderite. In the same region, at the well-known sites of Schwarzenbach, Waldalgesheim and Weisskirchen, occur funerary monuments which can be interpreted with a fair amount of certainty as the last remains of the dynasties of princes who once ruled over the area (Driehaus 1965, esp. 32ff.).

A centre of power, albeit a short-lived one, must be associated with a finite territory. In our case, we can only guess that the area concerned was rather small, mostly limited to the northern part of the ore-bearing zone, to the region on the Upper Warta, of a size which may be equated with one or two modern districts, covering approximately 2000 to 2500 sq. km. Territorial communities of this kind, grouped round a centre of power, however temporary, can be regarded as an intermediate stage between two distinctive political structures. First are the earlier tribal organizations of a kind which, for many centuries, down to at least the beginning of our own era, were the only form of political structure known to the communities living in the basins of the Odra and Vistula. Subsequently we have the states proper, the nuclei of which did not appear until the ninth century AD (Łowmiański 1963, I, 348–414). These short-lived proto-states of the Germanic Marcomanni and Quadi, who lived north of the Danube, were sometimes defined by the Romans with the term *regnum*. It is true that these later organizations were much larger and more advanced, partly due to the heritage of the Celts with their semi-civilization, who had inhabited Bohemia, Moravia and Slovakia, and partly due to the direct and strong influence of the Roman Empire itself. But the presence of the 'princes' graves' suggests that in the northern part of the barbarian world, in the sphere of influence exerted by the small monarchic client states in the Roman frontier area, there existed medium-sized and quite small ephemeral proto-state organizations. Great and sudden changes in ethnic and social relations, caused by the coming of the Huns and the migrations of peoples, were responsible for the disappearance of these organizations. It was not until much later that these proto-states began to re-emerge, in a different form and under different circumstances (Jażdżewski 1968, 86–91).

In conclusion, I would like to deal briefly with two miscellaneous details concerning the settlement and barrows at Przywóz. So far no separate seat of these putative princes has been discovered. It is possible that they lived in the settlement on the river, perhaps in one of the largest houses, such as House 2 or 3. In this period, the differences in mode of living between the tribal aristocracy and the rest of the free population were not as marked as in later centuries. Servants, members of the war-band, and artisans could all have lived in smaller houses in the neighbourhood.

We do not know why the settlement was abandoned in the second half of the third century AD. A sudden disaster seems implausible since – apart from a few houses destroyed by fire, a common fate for structures of this type and not necessarily the result of warlike activities – there are no indications that the whole settlement was destroyed. It is possible that the population moved some two kilometres down the river to another place in the neighbourhood, namely to the settlement at Toporów, in the district of Wieluń, since the beginning of this site coincides with the decline of Przywóz.[4]

63 Obelisk with granite slab containing information, seen against the background of the reconstructed 'Princes' grave' no. 1 at Przywóz.

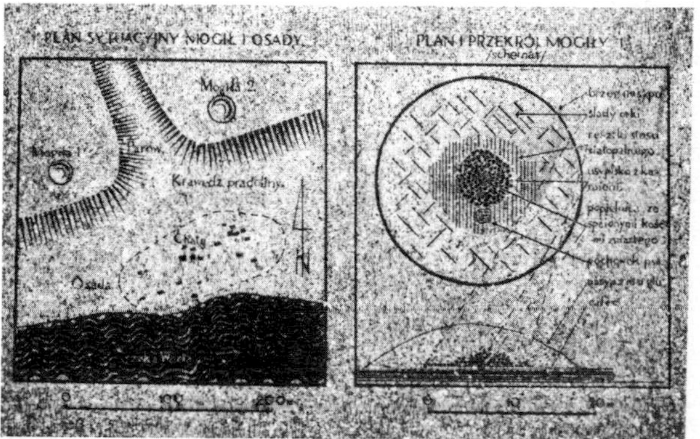

64 Granite slab measuring 70 × 100 cm, from the obelisk shown in *Ill. 63*.

[4] It should be added that in the final stage of the excavation at Przywóz in 1974, a large obelisk was set up near Barrow 1, incorporating a granite slab which presents basic information about the barrows and the settlement with schematic plans and sections (*Ills. 63, 64*).

Bibliography

Polish titles are given also in translation

ALMGREN, O. 1923 *Studien über nordeuropäische Fibelformen*, 2nd edn, Leipzig.

DRIEHAUS, J. 1965 Fürstengräber und Eisenerze zwischen Mittelrhein und der Saar, *Germania* XLIII, 1, 32–49.

EGGERS, H. J. 1951 *Der römische Import im freien Germánien* = *Atlas der Urgeschichte* I, 1–2, Hamburg.

1953 Lübsow – ein germanischer Fürstensitz der älteren Kaiserzeit, *Prähistorische Zeitschrift* XXXIV/V, 1949/50, 58–111.

1955 Zur absoluten Chronologie der römischen Kaiserzeit im Freien Germanien, *Jahrbuch d. Röm.-Germ. Zentralmuseums Mainz* 2, 166–244, = *Sprockhoff-Festschrift* 1.

GAHEIS, A. 1930 Das römische Tür- und Kastenschloss, *Österreichische Jahreshefte* 26; Beiblatt, columns 231–62.

GODŁOWSKI, K. 1960 *Studia nad stosunkami społecznymi w okresach późnolateńskim i rzymskim w dorzeczu Odry i Wisły. Próba interpretacji cmentarzysk* (English summary – A Study of Social Conditions in the Late La Tène and Early Roman Period in the Odra and Wisła Basin. An Attempt to Interprete Cemeteries) = *Biblioteka Archeologiczna* 13, Warsaw–Wrocław.

1969 *Kultura przeworska na Górnym Śląsku* (English summary – The Przeworsk Culture in Upper Silesia), Katowice–Cracow.

1970 *The Chronology of the Late Roman and Early Migration Periods in Central Europe* = *Prace Archeologiczne* 11, Cracow.

VON GROLLER, M. 1925 Die Grabungen im Lager Lauriacum im Jahre 1918, *Der römische Limes in Österreich* XV, ch. II, col. 99.

JADCZYK, I. 1971 Wyniki badań wykopaliskowych prowadzonych w Przywozie, pow. Wieluń, na stanowisku 1 i 1a z okresu wpływów rzymskich (Results of Excavations carried out at Przywóz, district of Wieluń, on sites 1 and 1a from the Roman Period), *Sprawozdania Archeologiczne* XXIII, 169–80.

1973 Bogactwo cyrklem mierzone (Wealth measured with a pair of compasses), *Z otchłani wieków*, XXXIX 3, 171–3.

JADCZYKOWA, I. 1973 Budynki mieszkalne osady produkcyjnej w Przywozie, pow. Wieluń, I (English summary – Houses of the Industrial Settlement at Przywóz, district of Wieluń, part I), *Prace i Materiały Muzeum Archeologicznego i Etnograficznego w Łodzi, Seria archeologiczna* 20, 129–52 (part II in press).

JAŻDŻEWSKI, K. 1968 *Z problematyki początków Słowiańszczyzny i Polski* (The Problem of the Origin of the Slavs and of Poland) = *Acta Archaeologica Lodziensia* 16, Łódź.

KARPIŃSKA, A. 1926 *Kurhany z okresu rzymskiego w Polsce ze szczególnym uwzględnieniem typu siedlemińskiego* (French summary – Les tumulus de la période romaine en Pologne et plus particulièrement ceux du type de Siedlemin), Poznań.

KASZEWSKA, E. 1969 Sprawozdanie z badań w Przywozie, pow. Wieluń w 1966 roku (English summary – Report on the Excavation at Przywóz, Wieluń, in 1966), *Sprawozdania Archeologiczne* XX, 147–51.

KIETLIŃSKA, A. 1961 Tombe 'princière' à inhumation No. 1–No. 2 – Łęg Piekarski, distr. de Turek, dep. de Poznań, Pologne, *Inventaria Archaeologica – Pologne* fasc. V, Pl. 32: 1–3; Pl. 33: 1–4, Łódź.

KOSTRZEWSKI, J., CHMIELEWSKI, W. and JAŻDŻEWSKI, K. 1965 *Pradzieje Polski*. (French summary – Préhistoire de la Pologne), 2nd ed., Wrocław–Warsaw–Cracow.

KOWALCZYK, M. 1968 Sprawozdanie z prac wykopaliskowych prowadzonych na cmentarzysku kurhanowym z wczesnego okresu rzymskiego w Przywozie, pow. Wieluń (Report on the Excavations of a Cemetery of Burial Mounds of the Early Roman Period at Przywóz, distr. of Wieluń), *Sprawozdania Archeologiczne* XIX, 113–22.

LECIEJEWICZ, L. 1960 Tombe 'princière' à inhumation No. 3 – Łęg Piekarski, distr. de Turek, dep. de Poznań, Pologne, *Inventaria Archaeologica – Pologne*, fasc. IV, Pl. 26: 1, 2, Łódź.

ŁOWMIAŃSKI, H. 1963, 1967, 1970, 1973 *Początki Polski* I–V (The Beginnings of Poland), Warsaw.

MAJEWSKI, K. 1949 *Importy rzymskie na ziemiach słowiańskich* (Roman Imports in Slavonic Lands), Wrocław.

1960 *Importy rzymskie w Polsce. Wybór źródeł archeologicznych do dziejów kontaktów ludności ziem Polski z Imperium Rzymskim*. (French summary – Importations romaines en Pologne. Choix de sources archéologiques pour l'histoire des contacts entre la population du territoire de la Pologne et l'empire romain), Wrocław.

MAKIEWICZ, T. 1969 Dalsze badania w Przywozie (Further Excavations at Przywóz, district of Wieluń), *Sprawozdania Archaeologiczne* XXI, 103–7.

OKULICZ, J. 1973 *Pradzieje ziem pruskich od późnego paleolitu do VII w.n.e.* (English summary – A History of the Ancient Prussian Territory from the Palaeolithic to the 7th Century AD), Wrocław–Warsaw–Cracow–Gdańsk.

RUTKOWSKI, B. 1960 *Terra sigillata znalezione w Polsce* (English summary – Terra Sigillata Pottery found in Poland) = *Bibliotheca Antiqua* 2, Wrocław.

SCHÖNBERGER, H. 1967 Ein Eisendepot, römische Flossfesseln und andere Funde im Bereich des Kastells Heilbronn – Böckingen, *Fundberichte aus Schwaben* 18:I, 131–51.

24

ANNE ROSS AND RICHARD FEACHEM

Ritual Rubbish? The Newstead Pits

ANY consideration of Stuart Piggott's formidable bibliography immediately reveals that from the period of his earliest publications he has had a deep understanding of the importance of the nature and organization of religion in the ancient European world. He has also long appreciated the value of the cautious use of contemporary custom and belief as an aid to understanding this complex and elusive subject. It is, therefore, particularly apposite that we have in Scotland one of the most fascinating presumptively votive sites in the British Isles. The interest is heightened in that this was brought to light in and around a Roman fort, at Newstead, in the Ettrick and Lauderdale District of the Borders Region. The deposits discovered here by James Curle (1911) early in this century are suggestive of the pan-Celtic custom, attested by the archaeological, literary and folklore records, of making votive offerings into holes in the ground – shafts, pits, wells – or simply on the surface of a sacred spot (Ross 1968).

Our knowledge of this extensive complex of deposits depends upon James Curle's remarkably conscientious analysis of what one feels might, if not so meticulously recorded, have been dismissed as mere rubbish pits, and accorded no further attention. Before proceeding to the evidence recorded by Curle at Newstead it will be instructive to refer to another Roman fort, at Maryport, in the Allerdale District of Cumbria. Here too is a large group of 'pits', situated in a restricted area about 300 m east of the fort. When excavated in 1870 and again in 1880 some of the pits were found to contain, amongst other items, Roman altars – in one case three in one pit (Birley 1961, 220); others included pieces of inscribed stone among their contents. Some forty pits contained nothing but what was described as rubbish, but no details of this, or of the number or the distribution of the pits, were recorded. A study of the occurrence of these altars in pits, recorded by Birley (1961, 222), concluded that their presence was a result of the Roman army's regular renewal of vows for the emperor's health and safety on his birthday and on 3 January, when new altars were set up 'and those that stood by the side of the parade-ground for the previous twelve months were accorded honourable burial'. The fact that in one particular year the emperor seemingly had three birthdays does not appear to have affected the argument. In fact, a few examples of altars being found in pits have been recorded here and there, but there is no body of evidence such as would support any general practice of annual disposal of altars at Roman forts in this manner, which leaves the postulated situation at Maryport in an isolation uncharacteristic of the general atmosphere of conformity evinced by the Roman army. Apparently all the altars at Maryport are assignable to the second century AD, and the pits in which they were found were in the area where the third-century civilian settlement seems to have expanded along the roads leading from the fort to the north and north-east. There was no opportunity to search for further pits before that part of the site was built over in 1922. Such a threat does not, as far as is known, apply at Newstead. The land around the fort has not been disturbed other than by cultivation, and it remains one of the most potentially rewarding and informative archaeological sites in Scotland.

As noted by Ross (1968), the distribution of most of the single or grouped ritual shafts and wells is within that part of Britain over which the Belgic influence spread to greater or lesser extent, though of course this was only one particular manifestation in the British Isles of the pan-Celtic custom of making offerings into the ground. There are, for example, no ritual shafts in Ireland although the literature provides evidence which has not yet been confirmed archaeologically. At the same time it has long been recognized that a Belgic element is discernible in southern Scotland independent of that which ultimately arrived there with the Roman army.

Let us now consider the nature of the contents of the Newstead pits in the light of the illustrations (*Ills. 2–11*) which provide us, for the first time, with a visual picture based on James Curle's admirable excavation reports. The amount of information here made available to the reader is so generous that to ask for more might seem presumptuous. But the fact remains that, as a result of the existence of gaps in the evidence, pursuit of any particular theme or line of study within the mass of the work may not inevitably lead to a completely clearly demonstrated conclusion. Such gaps would not necessarily interfere with a broad interpretation of the work, but the study of the various holes in the ground recorded by Curle and which, at the start, we can term pits, is a case in point. The information upon which this study must be based includes the number and distribution of the pits, their shape and identity, and the date and nature of their fillings. Careful scanning of the text reveals plenty of information on all these points, but it is not quite as comprehensive as might have been hoped for. Nevertheless it is perfectly possible, by systematic marshalling of facts and eradicating inconsistencies, to present the vital information in a form from which further discussion about their significance and purpose can proceed. References in brackets are to pages in Curle, 1911.

I THE NUMBER AND DISTRIBUTION OF THE PITS

The absence of a detailed plan of the excavations presents a challenge at the start. At various places in the narrative we learn that a considerable but unspecified area was excavated by means of parallel trenches a few feet apart (18); that various stretches of ditches were dug out and others left (18, 19); that while the *principia* was entirely excavated, other buildings were 'outlined' by following the walls and digging diagonal trenches across any 'chambers' which were discovered (42). Particular note is made of the fact that ground in the north-west corner of the fort was carefully trenched down to the subsoil with the discovery only of an oven (71). It is recorded (86) that at the west annexe 'a considerable portion of the ditches was cleared out'; that 'no part of the ditch' of the south annexe was cleared out (87); that 'no buildings', but plenty of pits, were found in the south annexe (88); and so on. Thus, although it is possible to produce a plan of the distribution of most if not all of the pits recorded (*Ill. 1*), it is not possible to tell how many more there might have been in the area covered by the existing distribution. This applies both to certain areas bounded by defences and to an area outside and north of the fort where the ground begins to fall towards the right bank of the river Tweed.

With these limitations in mind, then, we can

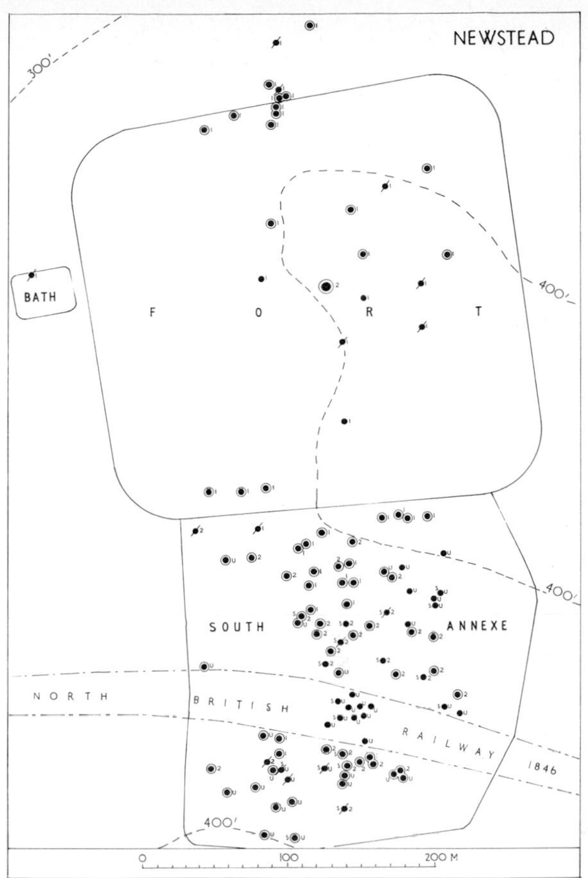

1 The pits at Newstead.

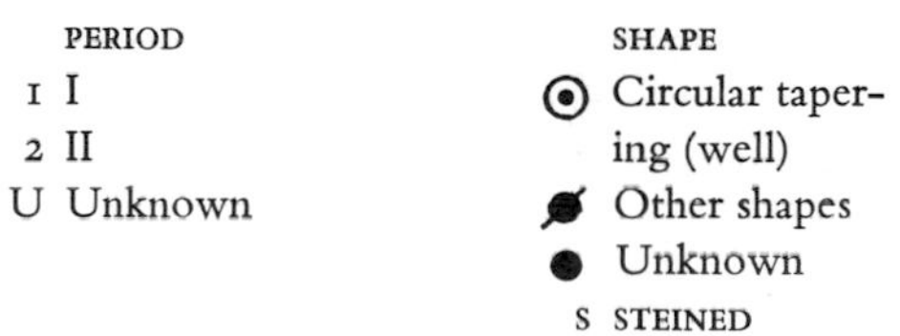

proceed to consider the 107 pits recorded, and those discovered in 1846 when the North British railway cutting was made across the south annexe. Curle, restating an earlier report on the 'railway pits', says (5) that a space of some 30 ft square in the cutting gave about 10 pits measuring from 10–20 ft in depth and 2–5 ft in diameter – measurements which, as appears below, are perfectly credible in the context – and in addition some 16 other pits about 3 ft deep and 3 ft in diameter, plastered over sides and bottoms with a lining of whitish clay five to six inches thick. Interesting though these little pits are, they seem to have no parallels in the

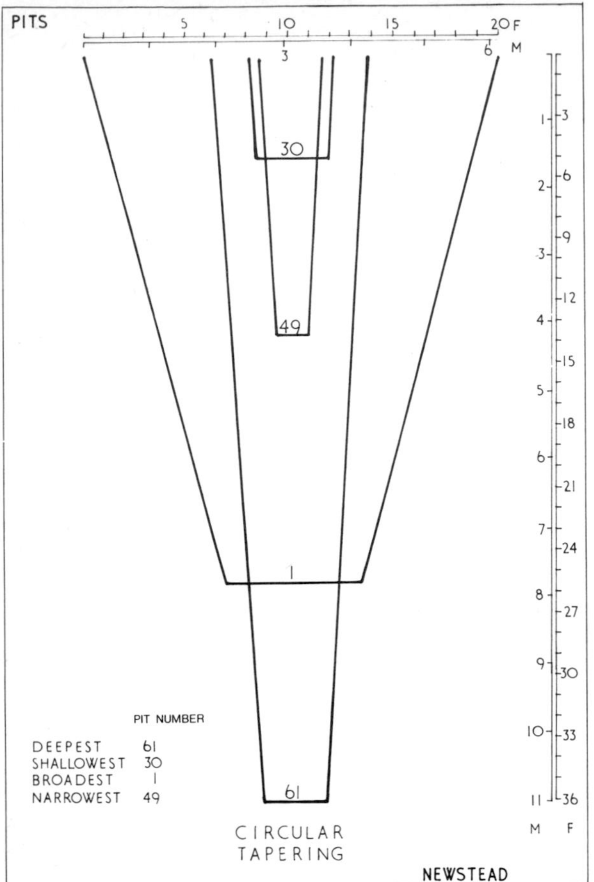

2 Pits of circular tapering shape.

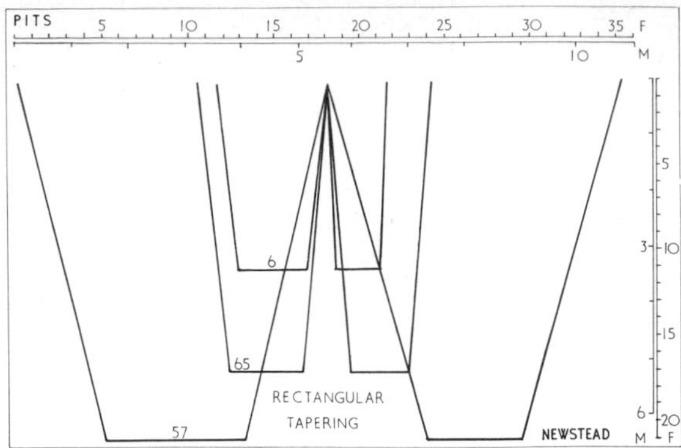

3 Pits of rectangular tapering shape.

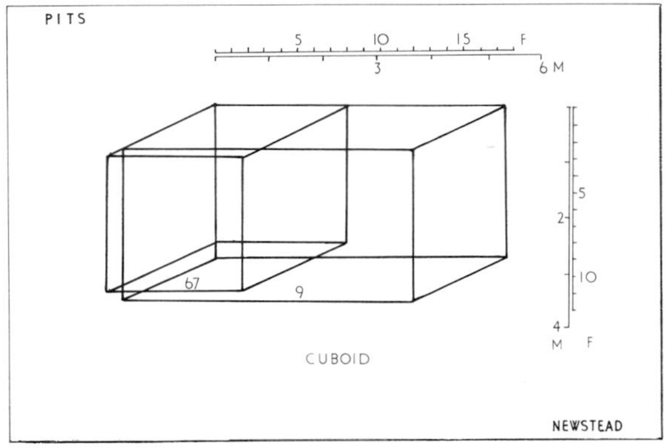

4 Pits of cuboid shape.

main narrative and no affiliation with the pits which form the subject of the present study, so no further reference will be made to them here. We have, then, a total of 117 pits – 10 from the railway cutting of which only a little information is known, and 107 from Curle's list.

2 THE SHAPE AND IDENTITY OF THE PITS

The pits thus distributed and counted can now be described according to their various shapes, and their identities determined. Curle does not include in his descriptions of every example he records all the measurements that are necessary to enable a complete and perfectly reliable, comprehensive picture to be reconstructed; but enough information is available to provide a useful and reasonably reliable sketch of the characteristics of the majority. This shows that there are seven shapes of pit, one of which – the circular tapering shape – is by far the most widely represented (*Ill. 2*); the extremes of measurement recorded among the 76 pits of this shape are indicated by outlines of the deepest, shallowest, broadest and narrowest examples.

A circular tapering pit such as number 1 (*Ill. 6*), supposed to have originated when the *principia* of the first Antonine fort was built (47–9, 116–17), is of such proportions that neither 'pit' nor 'well' can properly describe it. 'Water hole' bears too feral an implication; 'cistern', although not without an irrelevant connotation today, is probably the word most suited to such a shape. Cistern, too, is indubitably the word for the three rectangular tapering pits (*Ill. 3*) which include the huge example at the bath house – pit 57 (*Ill. 9*). The two cuboid pits, 9 and 67 (*Ill. 4*) can also be called cisterns. These two are the only examples of this shape that can be recognized among Curle's descriptions; but at Bar Hill, on the Antonine Wall, seven out of nine pits were cuboid, the other two circular tapering.

All the other circular tapering pits at Newstead, however, are of proportions which invite description as wells – numbers 49 and 61 in *Ill. 2*, for example. The same word suits the simple cylindrical class of which four are recognizable in Curle's descriptions, the oval tapering class, the circular churns and the biconic (all in *Ill. 5*).

By simplifying descriptions to cisterns and wells, then, of the 117 pits recorded by Curle we have 10 of unknown shape in the railway cutting (all of which were nevertheless probably wells), 15 others of which Curle's descriptions are insufficient to allow certain identification, and 92 which can be recognized as cisterns or wells. This is 78.6 per cent of the total or, with the 10 railway pits, 87 per cent. As in every kind of typological classification there are certain examples which are not as amenable as the majority – number 30 in *Ill. 2*, for example, a stocky member of the circular tapering class which might be described either as a cistern or as a well. But without any doubt the majority of the Newstead pits were wells, some of them steined (S in *Ill. 1*), the minority cisterns.

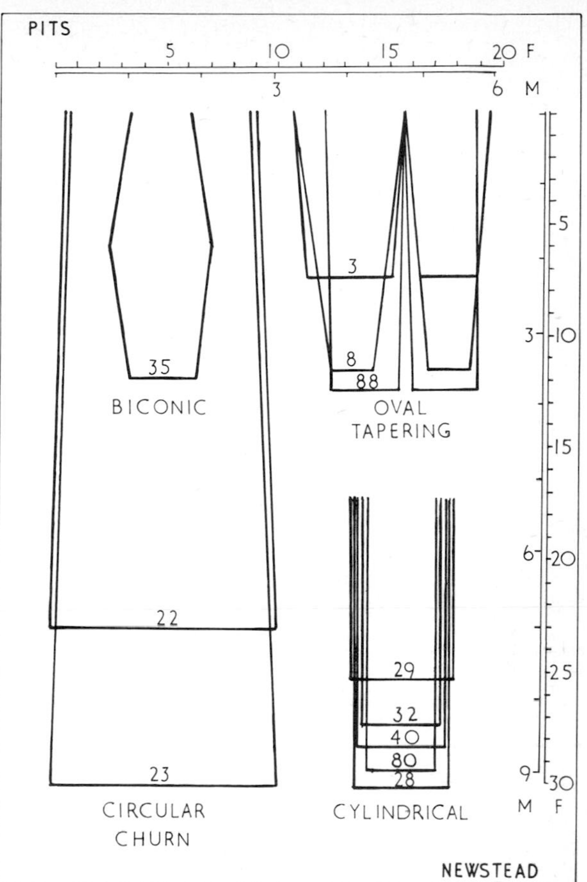

5 Pits of other shapes.

3 THE DATING AND NATURE OF THE FILLINGS OF THE PITS

The process of dating the fillings of the cisterns and wells suffers, more than does the determination of their number, distribution or shape, from a degree of deficiency in Curle's descriptions. It is clear that the fillings of some pits are described with minute thoroughness, that accounts of others are more generalized, that those of others again include only items regarded as being of particular interest, and that those of yet others are perfunctory to the point of being virtually useless. The same lack of consistency applies to what is handed on about the relationship between certain pits and certain structural features. Nevertheless, a useful body of conclusions may still be assembled, big enough to form a significant sample for purposes of discussion.

The recorded position of a pit *vis-à-vis* a dated structure often provides evidence at least of a date at which the pit contained filling, though not necessarily just exactly when the filling was done. The well number 2 (*Ill. 7*), for example (65, 117), was sealed by the foundations of one of the *contubernia* of the northernmost barrack block of the early Antonine fort; and there are several examples of such juxtapositions of filled cisterns or wells and the foundations of buildings. Those which, like number 2, were sealed by the construction of the early Antonine fort may be referred to as belonging to Period I; insofar as they contain Roman material they are unlikely to pre-date the arrival of Romans at the site, and so were probably filled between the end of the first-century occupation of the site and the construction of the early Antonine fort. Other cisterns or wells containing only first-century objects but not physically related to second-century buildings can also be included in Period I. The questions arise, when were the cisterns or wells dug, and were they filled by the Romans departing at the end of the first century, by Britons at or after this departure, or by the next Romans arriving to build the first Antonine fort?

The comings and goings of Roman forces in North Britain during the second century provide problems of dating so complex, and in many cases so scantily revealed, that no scholar has yet emerged triumphant from wrestling with them. We can, though, at least seek agreement for the supposition that there was a gap in the Roman military occupation of the Newstead site between about AD 100 and the construction of the early Antonine fort; and that in this gap certain cisterns and wells were filled, and some of the latter possibly dug. There eventually came a time, or times, when others were filled – now without any first-century material but including a variety of second-century material. The precise dating or datings of this second series of fillings need not be determined for the present purpose; all that must be established is that a good many of Curle's accounts of these fillings allow these to be recorded as belonging to Period II – that is, after the temporary and the final withdrawings of the Roman garrison from the site. Here, however, the choice of who did the fillings is reduced to two – was it the Romans at the moment of their departure, which presupposes that the pits were there to be filled – or was it the Britons, at or after departures?

Thus we have fillings of Period I, fillings of Period II, and of course a number which cannot be assigned to either period – whether because no datable material was present or because the record is deficient. Within the rather broad limits laid down by the nature of Curle's accounts of the fillings, there would appear to be 45 assignable to Period I, 33 to Period II, and 39 unassignable, including the 10 railway pits. That is to say, 78 of the 117 recorded pits – 66.6 per cent – are assignable; of these, 58 per cent are assignable to Period I and 42 per cent to Period II.

Before discussing the nature and significance of the fillings of selected examples at Newstead and elsewhere, reference must be made to the existence of another kind of deep hole, the shaft, which without any doubt was made and used solely for ritual purposes. This is now so well known a subject that it suffices here simply to refer to the examples in continental Europe and in Britain summed up by Ross (1968). The situation can be seen thus:

i) shafts or pits were on occasion designed and used only for ritual purposes, and filled ritually;
ii) cisterns or wells originally made for the storage or supply of water were on occasion ultimately used and filled ritually;
iii) cisterns and wells were on occasion filled
a) naturally and slowly, as a result of the dwelling places they served having been abandoned;
b) when the water had become impure or had dried up, to remove the hazard they then represented; and, allegedly,
c) on abandonment by Roman forces, to get rid of material which might be of use to an enemy; and
d) on the return of Roman forces to a site previously abandoned by them, to clear up before reconstruction.

The spread of the cisterns and wells at Newstead does include, as has been noted above, a few north of the fort in an area not known to have been included within any defensive system (cf. Maryport). This is of course no ground upon which to suppose that these outliers pre-date the Roman occupation of the area; for not every part of every *vicus* was necessarily within an earthwork enclosure, nor has every such enclosure necessarily been located yet at Newstead. While cuboid cisterns are certainly of Roman origin, as many examples elsewhere attest, the great number of wells recorded at Newstead is itself remarkable, and must give rise to consideration of whether any of them existed before the Romans came to the site – either as wells or as ritual shafts, at a British settlement or *locus* (? Segloes). Vital evidence for or against this possibility is missing in that no excavations took place outside the fort or annexes (except the small area to the north), and we do not know, but may certainly expect, that in fact significantly more wells or shafts remain to be found in the immediate vicinity. The potentially relevant oval earthwork on Red Rig has not been investigated. So, failing any proof that wells or shafts existed here before the Romans arrived, but bearing the possibility very much in mind, can we detect in the fillings any examples which can be identified as ritual, done in the absence of Romans, as in (i) or (ii) above, rather than as being due to any of the circumstances mentioned in (iii)? And if so, are we to suppose that a proportion of the wells were dug between the Roman occupations purely for the purpose of ritual?

'Railway pit' 10 (*Ill. 7*) (5, 6)
Period unknown; about 11 ft deep, about 3 ft 6 in in diameter; contained the skeleton of a man 'erect or nearly so'.

Pit 1 (*Ill. 6*) (47–9, 116–17)
Period I; circular tapering; diameters mouth 20 ft, bottom 6 ft 6 in; depth 25 ft 6 in.
In the courtyard of the *principia* of the first Antonine fort; probably lined with red sandstone blocks; over 40 cartloads were removed which, placed on the ground, measured 41 sq. yds.
Apparently this cistern was constructed as part of the first Antonine fort but was not in use with the

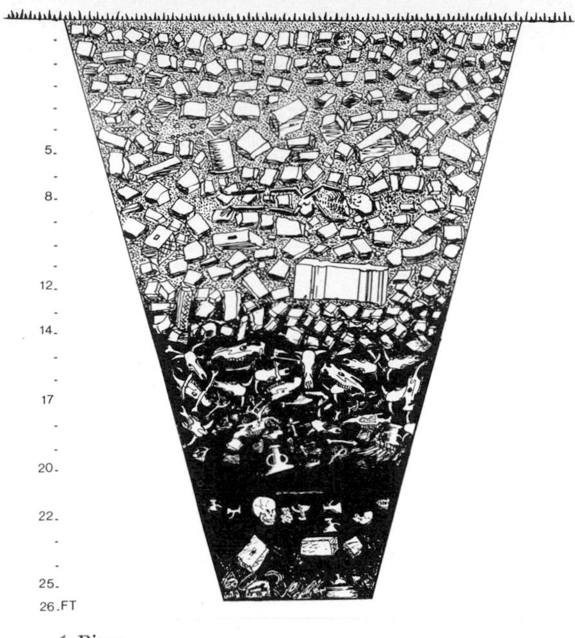

6 Pit 1.

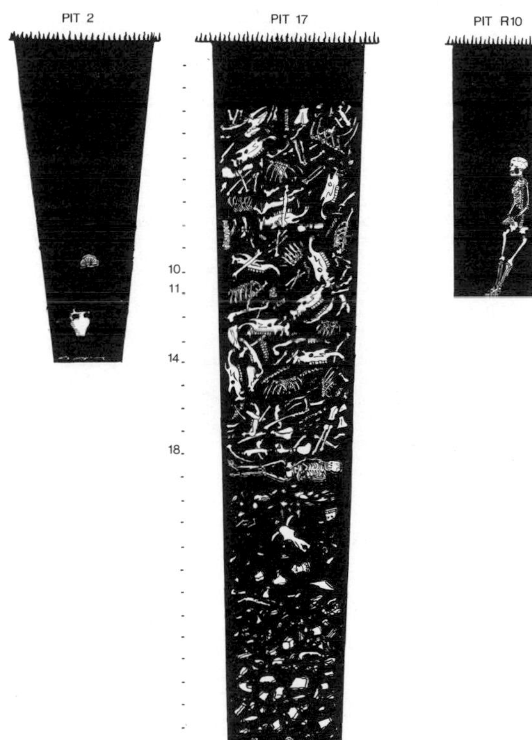

7 Pits 2 and 17, and 'railway pit' 10.

second Antonine fort. The filling included, right at the bottom, an upper quern stone, iron knife with bone handle, another iron knife, linch pin, iron bar, sickle, iron and brass armour, staves and bottom of oak bucket, rim of large bucket, two stones with boars incised on them, five iron arrowheads, chain armour, shield boss and brass fragments, brass coin of Titus or Vespasian (first century), iron hold-fast, wall plaster, necks and sides of several amphorae, many nails. From a depth of 20 ft down and reaching to this bottom layer were an iron bar, a human skull and part of another, the necks of five amphorae, brass armour scales, the bottom of a second-century Samian cup. From the depth of 14 ft to 20 ft were 'frequent' ox skulls, horse skulls, deer horns, shoe-soles and leather scraps, some stone mouldings, amphorae sherds, undecorated Samian, and a deer-horn pick. At about 12 ft down was an altar to Jupiter with, immediately beneath it, a first brass of Hadrian. A few feet above this was a male skeleton placed horizontally, along with a bronze penannular brooch, four glass beads with gold foil, and two pieces of what had been a bronze brooch. The cistern was filled from about the 20-ft level upwards with the red sandstone blocks already mentioned – the altar, skeleton etc. were among these as, higher up, were a bronze chain of 12 links, a length of twisted silver wire, part of a penannular brooch and two bronze rings. Very near the top was a fragment of an inscribed tablet (Curle, Pl. XVIII: 4).

Pit 2 (*Ill. 7*) (65, 117)
Period I; circular tapering; diameters mouth 6 ft, bottom 2 ft 10 in; depth 14 ft.
Sealed by walls of two *contubernia* of the northernmost barrack block of the early Antonine fort.
At the bottom was a mass of corroded iron and bronze with part of a wooden shaft or handle adhering, and fragments of burnt bone. Two feet from the bottom was a perfect bronze oinochoe (Pl. LV). A little above this was part of a lava quern. Then, right at the top, was a bronze buckle (Pl. LXXVI: 1).

Pit 17 (*Ill. 7*) (120)
Period I; circular tapering; diameters mouth, 6 ft 6 in, bottom 4 ft 10 in; depth 31 ft 9 in.
In the south annexe.
Sealed with thick clay below which was a very dark coloured deposit. A little below the top was a sherd of Castor ware; then the bones of nine horses. At 18 ft 9 in, the skeleton of a woman, horizontal (thought by Curle to be a dwarf but now shown to

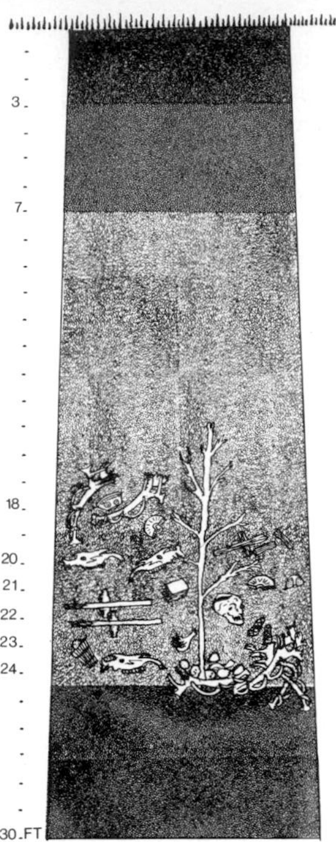

8 Pit 23.

be a woman). Immediately below the skeleton, the skull of a dog, the skull of an ox, oyster shells, mussel shells and, continuing downwards, leather including discs, fragments of Samian (including some illustrated on 111, 1.); bricks, tiles, large iron hammer (Pl. LVII: 6), small saw, deerhorn handle (Pl. LXVIII: 6), iron stylus, iron finger ring, more oysters, mussels and many hazel nuts.

Pit 23 (*Ill. 8*) (122, 220, 292)
Period II; circular churn; diameters mouth 8 ft, bottom 10 ft; depth 30 ft.
In the south annexe.
At the bottom yellow sludge, probably washed down when the well was open. At 6 ft from the bottom a birch branch 9 ft high standing up. Just below this a 'number' of red-deer antlers, five dog skulls, a horse skull and a bucket (Pl. LXIX: 4). Then, at a somewhat higher level, beside the lower part of the branch, a piece of elk antler and a pair of shoe-soles. A little higher, a human skull with a cut in the crown and two complete wheels with hubs (Pl. LXIX: 2). Above these, two horse skulls, parts of two querns, a brick, oak scantling. Higher still, part of another quern and a piece of Samian which, if it is Antonine as stated, dates the filling. Near the top of the branch, a pair of red-deer antlers. Above this up to 7 ft from the top was a fill of bluish-grey matter containing wood and moss; above this a layer of yellow clay and, to cap all, two or three feet of soil. Somewhere in this well were an iron axe (Pl. XLI: 1) and pieces of cloth and rope.

Pit 57 (*Ill. 9*) (128)
Period I; rectangular tapering; sides at mouth 17 ft, 18 ft; sides at bottom, 5 ft 6 in, 8 ft; depth 21 ft.
'Beneath the foundations of the wall of the baths.' Close to the bottom at 20 ft, a bronze ewer (Pl. LVI); just above this two bronze pots (Pl. LIII: 3, 5); then a gap. At 16 ft to 15 ft a bronze mask helmet (Pl. XXX), iron lamp (Pl. LXXIX: 6), a sword (Pl. XXXIX: 11), a hub ring. Above this an iron strigil (Pl. LXVI: 22), a sword bent double (Pl. XXXIV: 13), a small sword (Pl. XXXIV: 10), part of the blade and tang of another sword, a hippo-sandal, five iron hub rings, a die (Pl. XCIII: 3). At 13 ft the stamped bottom of a Dragendorf 18 vessel, piece of charred oak beam, bronze pot (Pl. LIII: 1), bronze tankard handle (Pl. LIV: 7). At 12 ft a rim of a Dragendorf 37 vessel and a human skull. At 8 ft hypocaust pillar bricks and wall bricks. In washing out the silt, the pieces of a coarse earthen-ware bowl were found; animal bones were scarce. At the top a clay sealing.

Pit 95 (*Ill. 10*) (138)
Period II; circular tapering; diameters mouth 9 ft, bottom 4 ft; depth 17 ft.

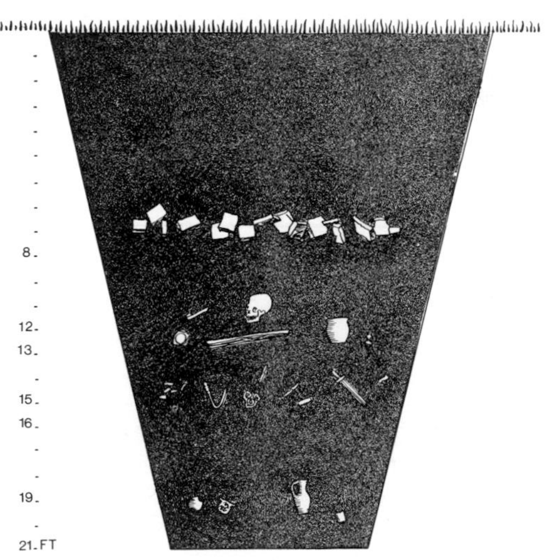

9 Pit 57.

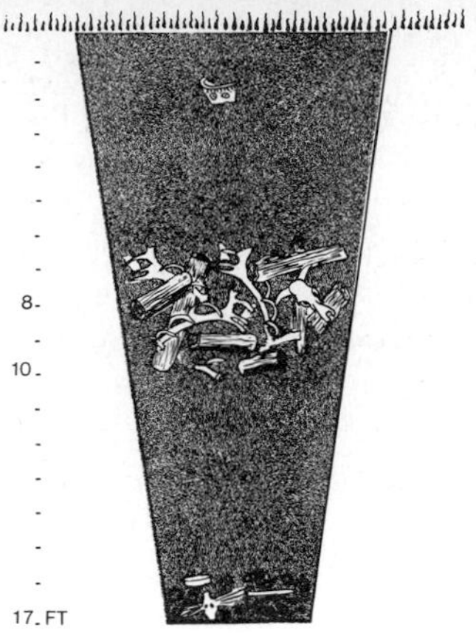

10 Pit 95.

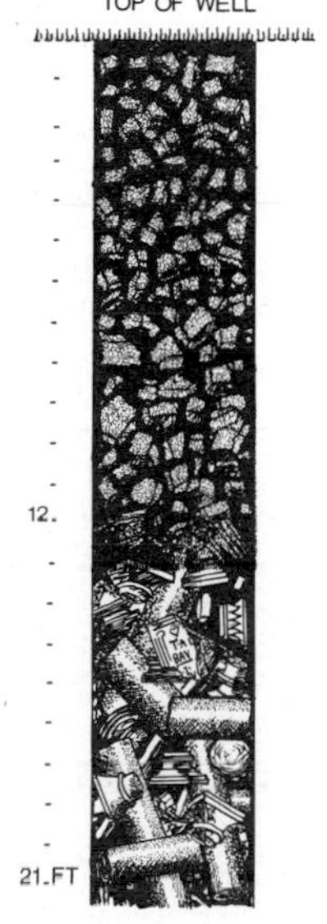

11 Well, Bar Hill.

In the south annexe.
At the bottom a hub with parts of spokes still in it; four hanging ornaments of brass with an iron ring, one small brass tongue on a brass ring, a brass disc – all harness fittings. Two iron buckles, a key, a mounting of hammered iron, a ? lynch pin, a Dragendorf 33 cup with stamp, small cup type 17 (Pl. XL), sherds of a bowl type 41 (Pl. XLVIII), sherds of types 48, 49. Two pots type 47 (Pl. XLVIII); a 1st brass of Trajan. From 8 ft to 10 ft down, logs of wood, skull of *bos longifrons*, several antlers of red deer, one probably a pick. In 'upper levels' a sherd of Dragendorf 37.

Well at Bar Hill fort, Cumbernauld District, Strathclyde Region (*Ill. 11*) (MacDonald 1906; Feachem 1969).
Second century; cylindrical; diameter 4 ft; depth 43 ft.
In *praetorium*.
At about 38 ft, above a layer of mud and shingle, a large amphora, broken, with a bag of tools and other iron objects. At 33 ft an inscribed altar, a red-deer horn, a coin, bits of squared oak and the frame and pulley wheel of the original well gear, pieces of iron. Between 12 ft and 33 ft building stones, bases, capitals and round columns, fragments of an inscribed tablet, pieces of oak. Above 12 ft building stone. With some difficulty all the filling was brought out of the well 'which had plainly been filled up of set purpose'. Details of pottery, stonework, wood, leather, iron, bronze, lead and horns, bones and skulls comprising the filling appear in MacDonald 1906, 535–6.

These descriptions of a selection of the fillings of the Newstead 'pits' and the well at Bar Hill argue strongly in favour of their being ritual rather than casual in nature. At Newstead, then, we have a complex of which there may still remain an extensive area as yet undisturbed, where modern techniques of excavation could still be applied. While not necessarily unique in Britain, the Newstead complex could well prove to be one of the most important ritual sites in Europe. In view of Stuart Piggott's deep interest in this sphere of European archaeology, there could be no more fitting tribute to his scholarship than further investigations here.

Bibliography

BIRLEY, E. B. 1961 *Researches on Hadrian's Wall*, Kendal.

CURLE, J. 1911 *A Roman Frontier Post and its People*, Glasgow.

FEACHEM, R. W. 1969 *Medionemeton*, on the *limes* of Antoninus Pius, Scotland, *Collection Latomus*, 103, 210–16.

MACDONALD, G. 1906 The Roman Forts of the Bar Hill, Dunbartonshire, *Proc. Soc. Ant. Scot.* XL, 403–546.

ROSS, A. 1968 Shafts, Pits, Wells – ? Sanctuaries of the Belgic Britons, in *Studies in Ancient Europe*, ed. J. M. Coles and D. D. A. Simpson, Leicester, 255–85.

25

C. E. STEVENS

The Sacred Wood

HAVING never published a word on prehistory, I can only give the praise of an admiring amateur to Stuart Piggott's great presentations of the prehistoric scene. But there is another aspect of his genius which delights both amateur and professional. It is his love for what is curious and strange; he is not the biographer of William Stukeley for nothing. He has taken time off to find Red Indians on a tomb in an Oxfordshire church, and Winston Churchill at an assembly of crack-pot 'Druids'. I shall try to please him by examining the curiosity of a Sacred Wood in central Devon, though I doubt whether a prehistorian – or anyone else – can make much of it. A novelist, perhaps.

Among names in the Ravenna Cosmography there appears, evidently west of Exeter, a place written as *Nemetotatio* (or *Nemetotacio*, the difference being immaterial for a medieval scribe); it is punctuated as a single word in our three manuscripts (Richmond and Crawford 1949, 17, 42; Pinder and Parthey 1860, 424, 7). The *-tatio* termination seems impossible to parallel, so that Richmond and Crawford emended it to (*s*)*tatio*. On Gallic analogies, this should mean a customs house on a frontier (Grenier 1925, 656),[1] and there is another *statio* somewhere in these parts (*Statio Deventia Steno* according to the punctuation of the manuscripts: Richmond and Crawford 1949, 17, 31; Pinder and Parthey 1860, 15–16); but it can also denote something like a local police station (Hirschfeld 1891; 1913).[2] If we were certain of the emendation, and certain too that *Nemeto* was *statio*, we could have scope for ingenuity. I shall try a guess, making clear that this is all it can be.

It is quite different with *Nemeto*. There is a Gallic word *Nemeton* which means a sacred place and should be cognate with Latin *nemus*, a grove. A Gallic inscription in Greek characters from Vaison states that Segomaros made a *nemeton*; the context seems to be religious (Dottin 1918, no. 7, 149–50). The Council of the Galatians, says Strabo (XII.5.1), met at 'what is called Drunemeton', and our own *Vernemetum* (Willoughby on the Fosse Way) has a variety of the intensive prefix (Rivet 1970, 49, 80). Both should mean a 'very sacred grove' and, if a temple was built there, a 'great temple' – which is how Venantius in the sixth century translated what he called a Gallic word (*Carmina* I.9–10: 'nomine Vernemetis voluit vocitare vetustas/quod quasi fanum ingens Gallica lingus refert'). In Ireland, according to W. J. Watson (*History of the Celtic Place-names of Scotland*, 1926,) the word *nemed*, occasionally found in a pagan context, is, in Irish literature, 'not uncommon in the sense of holy place, sanctuary, church.' The equivalent *nyfet* means shrine in Welsh, and we have the Cornish parish name of Lanivet. We can presume that an open area (in Latin a *lucus*[3]) in a forest was a *nemeton* and that any building placed there, whether Romano-Celtic temple or Christian church, was a *nemeton* too.

But the forest itself could be a *nemeton*. A Breton Cartulary of 1031 speaks of the 'Wood (*silva*) which is called *Nemet*' (*Cartulaire de Quimperlé* quoted by Holder 1922, 712); and the forest of the Ardennes has its *dea Arduinna*.[4] One can guess that

[1] Richmond and Crawford 1949, 42, suggest a mining office (with parallels). This will hardly do for a *Nemeto Statio*: there are no mines in the district.

[2] But if we do take the word *Statio* out of *Nemetotatio*, it might go with the next name in the list of the Cosmography, Tamaris (so, in their commentary, Richmond and Crawford 1949, 14).

[3] We may notice a dedication in 'Lucubus' (Groves) from Nîmes: *ILS* 4768.

[4] *ILS* 4663, 4697. Holder 1922, 712, believed that, on a dedication 'Silvano deo et Montibus Numidis' (erected by quarry-masters in the Pyrenees), 'Numidis' was a cutter's error for 'Nimidis' ('Sacred Mountains'). This is very attractive (what are Numidian Mountains doing in the Pyrenees?), though I wonder whether the shift from 'nemet' to 'nimid' can be so early.

the forest of Rouvray, near Rouen, was a *nemeton* of this type: within it are no less than ten Romano-Celtic temples, each presumably a *nemeton* itself (see map in Grenier 1934, 768).

It looks as though there was such a forest *nemeton* in central Devon. Thirteen Domesday Book manors exist there called Nimet, Nimetone and Limet, the last clearly one of the usual Domesday Book mis-spellings. The skill of two West Country clergymen, O. J. Reichel and T. W. Whale, has tracked them down (Reichel 1897; Whale 1903). Eight are still recognizable in modern villages and farms containing Nympton, Nymet and Nymph. The five now bearing different names are all close by. And there are a Nymet and two Nymphs outside, though not far from, the area of these manors.

Ekwall (1928, 304–5)[5] noticed that these Nimet names were all near the rivers Mole and Yeo, which can be shown to have borne in early times variations of this Nimet name; and Finberg has shown that the Troney, just south of the manorial group, should be a third (Finberg 1953, commenting on Napier and Stevenson 1895, No. 1).[6] The farm of Nymetwood is close to its bank. Ekwall should thus be right in implying that these manorial names are relatively late and that the English, settling this area from the seventh century onward (Hoskins 1954, 41–5), had only the river-names to inspire their 'Nimet' nomenclature.

But this does not at all imply that the notion of a 'Sacred Wood' is misconceived. 'Nimet' or anything resembling it has, as a river-name, no certain parallel outside our three.[7] Nor should it have. A sacred river should be called *Deva* (Ekwall 1928, 6, 117–18); it should not, as such, be called by the name for a Sacred Grove or a Sacred Wood. These rivers should thus have received their names because they flowed through a 'Sacred Wood'. It follows that the rivers and the manorial names, covering a rectangle of some ten miles by three, may only be giving us a sample area of a 'Sacred Wood' that may have been much larger.[8]

Plotted on the geological map (Geological Sheets 309 and 324; cf. Edmonds, McKeown, and Williams 1969, 34–42), these names are all on or very close to the Carboniferous Culm Measures of central Devon, with a total area of more than 1200 square miles; and to quote Lady Fox (1973, 19), 'they break down into a stiff yellow clay, water-logged in winter, hard-baked in summer, and supporting a dense mixed oak-wood with a heavy undergrowth unfit for early settlement.' In fact, a little to the east of our names, we find the villages of Cruwys Morchard and Morchard Bishop, which are shown by old forms to correspond with Welsh 'Mawr Coed', the 'Great Wood'.[9] The higher ground of the Culm Measures (the 'Welcombe Formation' of Edmonds, McKeown, and Williams 1969, 42), however, around the contour of 700 feet, and poorly drained rough pasture for the most part today, was utilizable for settlement in the more favourable conditions of the Bronze Age. Thus there is a group of Round Barrows, four miles east of a manorial name, in the parish of East Worlington; and Round Barrows with three Standing Stones near one of them are in the parish of Witheridge to the east. But from the Iron Age until the coming of the English, the 'Great Wood', the *Nemeton*, was very sparsely if at all populated.

In summing up, we should be able to say with reasonable certainty that there was a 'Sacred Wood' in central Devon which we can locate in the southern

5 The Editors of *PND*, 348, favour the explanation of Napier and Stevenson 1895, 58, that *Nymet* was originally the name of a forest, and I am following them. Ekwall regards the Mole as a back-formation from North and South Molton, and notices that Yeo, a frequent river-name in Devon, is a dialectal form of Anglo-Saxon *ea*, river. There may be, as he says, 'nothing remarkable in the fact that two streams not far apart have the same name.' But three is, for me, another matter.

6 Troney as a river-name is actually a back-formation according to *PND* 15, 104.

7 Ekwall 1928, 304–5, and *PND* 348, produce *Nymet* names elsewhere, and I am not convinced that their example from Baltonsborough, Somerset, is a stream name. Why the parish should have a 'Sacred Wood' is not my concern.

8 Back-formations and Anglo-Saxon river-names seem uncommon in the area of the Culm Measures (*PND* 1–19). It is possible, therefore, that our *nemeton* did not have a larger extent than the catchment area of these three *Nymed* streams, themselves, as I am arguing, back-formations. But I would not build much on this.

9 *PND* 380, 408. Domesday Book forms are Morcet, Mochet, Morceth, Morcets. To doubt 'if the same word can be referred to in the two names' is to forget the geology.

stretches of the Taw (itself a Celtic river-name: Ekwall 1928, 304–5) and its neighbourhood. But it might have been much larger: as large, at a maximum possibility, as the 1200 square miles of the Culm Measures. It was called by the Iron Age natives a *nemeton*; and the Ravenna Cosmography produces, in its manuscript tradition, a name *Nemetotatio* which ought to have been derived from a Roman road-book.[10] Yet we do not know its exact form, and we can only locate it somewhere west of Exeter. Thus we are entitled to speak of a 'Sacred Wood'. But we cannot say why it was 'Sacred' at a time when there were apparently very few people in it to conduct sacred rites, and we cannot say what the rites were. We do not know, and it is very unlikely that we ever shall.

Still, remembering how Stuart Piggott has revealed the fancies of William Stukeley and the crack-pot Druidism that he inspired, I bid him follow my fancies into the 'Sacred Wood' on the edge of which I live. There are things curious, things strange about it (*Ill. 1*).

The Romans seem to have been interested in it with the *Nemeto-* site that should have been on a Roman road. There is such a road running west from Exeter, at least as far as North Tawton parish inside the southern boundary of Nimet names; and somewhere near Crediton it threw off a branch to the north-west, passing through the Nimet area to an unknown destination in the Culm Measures (Margary 1973, 120–1, 123). Air photography has shown what looks like a fort and its annexe in North Tawton parish, which is likely to be in the *nemeton* area; and there may well be another astride the road six miles east of it in Colebrooke parish, very close to the *Nymed* stream which is now the Troney.[11] No field archaeologist has, as yet, followed the lonely road to the north-west in search of forts.

Roman roads with the possibility of more forts than one in a virtually uninhabited area – here are things strange and curious. One might think of police control over desperate men 'out in the maquis', if one had any notion where they came from to take to it.[12]

Has this area really nothing 'Sacred' to show but its Celtic appellative of a 'Sacred Wood'? We have, it seems, to look backwards in time to the Round Barrows of the Bronze Age on the high hills and the Standing Stones which might be the remains of a Stone Circle on Witheridge Moor. And this is not all. In East Worlington parish, a mile or so from the Round Barrows and on ground considerably lower, between the Barrows and the Little Dart river, there is a solitary Standing Stone, called the granite 'Long Stone', which must, like the Witheridge Stones, have been carried at least a dozen miles from Dartmoor. It must already have stood alone in the time of German de la Stane in the fourteenth century (*PND* 402). But perhaps it was not always alone. For the land of Wilson farm runs close up to it, and the Place-Name Editors think that Wilson may be the 'Weofod Stan' (Altar Stone) from which they derive 'Weveston', a medieval manor connected with Worlington (*PND* 401–2). What the English settlers saw as an 'Altar Stone' should be not the upright 'Long Stone' but a large stone lying flat. Yet if it was close to the 'Long Stone', one might think of another Stone Circle, already in ruins when the settlers arrived, perhaps deliberately ruined (as Stonehenge was seemingly ruined: Atkinson 1956, 77, 92) by Roman orders. Here, indeed, are the fancies which I have promised Stuart Piggott. But I will seriously suggest that, if we are looking for traces of ancient religion in our *Nemeton*, this is the place to find it. Moreover there is an old report of Roman coins in one of the East Worlington barrows (Lysons 1822, cccviii), almost the only record of Roman coins from the Culm Measures. I noticed many years ago the appearance of Roman pottery at henge sites (including Stonehenge) with reference to the Roman henge-like 'rotunda' at Frilford

[10] As Richmond and Crawford 1949, 2–5, have demonstrated. On their doctrine, there should be more roads beyond Exeter than we know, and it might be worth checking by field-work what Bennet, Bishop of Cloyne (Lysons 1822, cccxv), had 'little hesitation in supposing' to be a Roman road running north and south across Witheridge parish.

[11] The line of the Exeter-North Tawton road in Colebrooke parish was given to Margary by the late M. Lambert. I can add that road metalling is visible in the east bank of the Troney. There is a suspicious-looking square field (O.S. 6″ SX 79NE) astride the line to the west of the Troney, which is perfectly placed for a Roman fort. I have walked it in vain for pottery but am hoping for an air-photograph and a trial excavation.

[12] *Aulularia* (a parody of Plautus from the Later Empire) has an amusing picture of the 'maquis' in Gaul (Peiper, 16, ll. 22–6). I fear that there is no English translation.

(Berks.) and I suggested a religious continuity (Stevens 1940).

The youthful Stuart Piggott took my ideas further and uttered the dangerous word Druids as transmitters of such continuity (Piggott 1941). Though he has consigned these wild oats to the furnace, they are regarded as good grain by Professor Hawkes (1970, 13–14). Perhaps my old friend, as he follows me into the 'Sacred Wood', will accept the continuity – without the Druids. I will ask him to wonder whether the Roman authorities anticipated St Samson at some place in the *pagus Tricurius*, the modern Hundred of Trigg in Cornwall. The Saint, as Piggott reminded his readers, showed, in a practical manner, his disapproval of men whom he found making 'Bacchic revels' at a Standing Stone (Fawtier 1912, 143).

But Roman authorities might have been tolerant, as was their usual policy in religious matters.[13] If this were so, we might find a parallel in their treatment of unromanized natives to the north of Hadrian's Wall, as Richmond (1940, 97) worked it out. They were allowed recognized meeting-places (*loca*), and one of them, the *locus Maponi* (Richmond and Crawford 1949, 15, 19, 39; Pinder and Parthey 1860, 436, 17–20), takes its name from a local deity, being thus both an administrative and a religious centre. Moreover it would appear that its sanctity was displayed by a Standing Stone, or possibly a Stone Circle.[14] We might therefore think of the East Worlington/Witheridge complex as the equivalent, more or less, of a *locus* in the north. If the authorities were not tolerant (and even if they were), a *Nemeto Statio* (if there was a place so named) could be regarded (wherever, in relation to the 'Sacred Wood', it actually was) as a centre for public control of activities inside it. These are speculations, more appropriate, it may be, for a novelist than a scholar, but I can plead that it is the imaginative genius of Stuart Piggott that inspires them. Speculations, however, they must remain

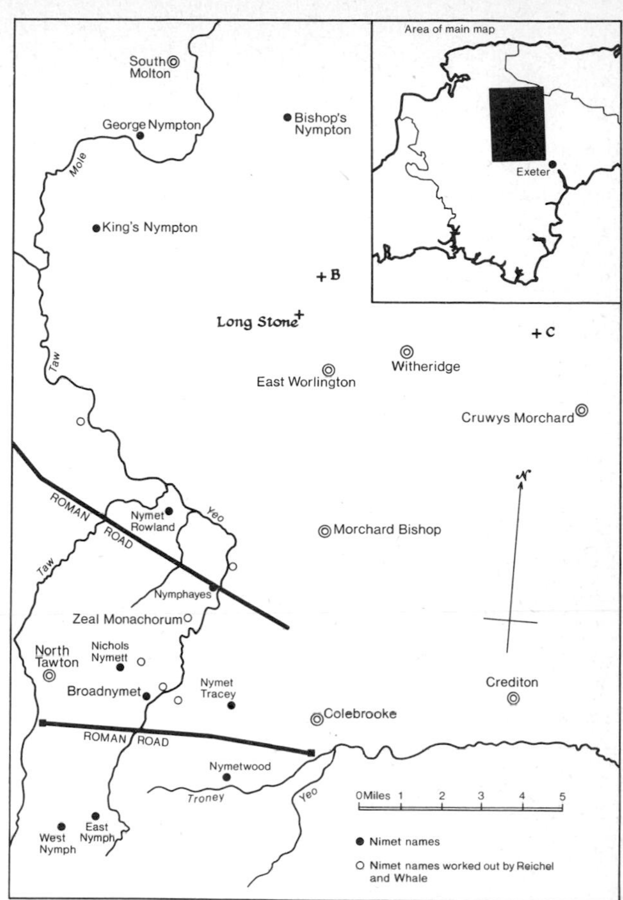

1 'The Sacred Wood.' B Barrow C Stone circle ■ Roman fort (?)

until our knowledge of *Dumnonii* to the west of Exeter during the Roman period is much enlarged.[15] But the 'Sacred Wood' should be a fact.

I have a tail-piece for Piggott from a hundred years ago. In the parish of Nymet Rowland there lived a family called Cheriton on a largish farm that was their freehold. They went down-hill and became objects of local horror. Their house was a

[13] The magnificent language of Gibbon (ed. Bury 1909, 31) is worth repeating. 'The various modes of worship which prevailed in the Roman world were all considered by the people as equally true; by the philosophers as equally false; and by the magistrate as equally useful.' The exceptions are the Christians – and the Druids.

[14] Radford (1954) argues that Richmond had picked the wrong Stone Monument for the *locus Maponi*. But this does not affect his conclusions.

[15] Devon, west of Exeter, and Cornwall are, for the student of Roman administrative practice, a curious region. It was inhabited mostly by unromanized natives and yet, after the early stages of the occupation, it seems to have been very short of, even perhaps totally lacking in, military garrisons. I am hoping for a paper on this 'frontier zone', which seems to have no parallel elsewhere, at a future 'Congress of Roman Frontier Studies' – when it can be written.

roofless ruin, and twelve or more of them slept in a pit the size of a waggon. Their 'dreadful superstitions' attracted the notice of a journalist who wrote them up for the *Daily Telegraph*. He pointed out that, had they been living in Patagonia, they would have received the attentions of missionaries. A writer on a local paper told how a man from the group who takes, without marriage, a woman for his mate, agrees with her to 'defy decency and goodness in any shape for the remainder of their lives.' Their language was disgusting and obscene, their clothes rags when they wore any. They were known far and wide as the 'North Devon Savages'.[16] Did their ancestors enjoy the freedom of the *Nemeton*? Were they perpetuating such 'dreadful superstitions' as St Samson observed in the Hundred of Trigg? I am afraid that we must refuse a connection between the men, whoever they were, in the *Nemeton* and the short-lived existence of the 'Savages'. Only a novelist could bridge the gap between them. Yet Stuart Piggott is the man to understand the novelist who bridges the gap.

Bibliography

ATKINSON, R. J. C. 1956 *Stonehenge*, London.

BARING-GOULD, REV. S. 1898 *An Old English Home*, London.

DOTTIN, G. 1918 *La Langue gauloise*, Paris.

EDMONDS, E. A., MCKEOWN, M. G. and WILLIAMS, M. 1969 *British Regional Geology, South-west England*, 3rd edn, London.

EKWALL, E. 1928 *English River-Names*, Oxford.

FAWTIER, R. 1912 *Vie de St. Samson, Bibliothèque de l'École des Hautes Études* CXCVIII.

FINBERG, H. P. R. 1953 *Early Charters of Devon and Cornwall*, Leicester.

FOX, Aileen, 1973 *South-West England*, 2nd edn, Newton Abbot.

GIBBON, E. 1909 *Decline and Fall of the Roman Empire* I, ed. J. B. Bury, London.

[16] The 'Savages', who lived not in an empty valley (like the Doones) but within a mile of a railway station, have not been well reported from a sociological point of view. The *Daily Telegraph* article is in the issue of 23 October 1871. The fullest account is that of 'Tickler' (1871, 128–38). There is a short mention of them in Baring-Gould (1898, 10–18). The Exeter City Library has a file on the 'Savages' which I have inspected by the kindness of Mr G. J. Paley.

GRENIER, A. 1934 *Manuel d'Archéologie gallo-romaine*, Paris.

HAWKES, C. F. C. 1970 in Wallace-Hadrill, J. M. and McManners, John, *France, Government and Society*, 2nd edn, London.

HIRSCHFELD, O. 1891 *Die Sicherheitspolizei im römischen Kaiserreich, Sitzungsberichte der Berliner Akademie* 859–67 (= *Kleine Schriften* 1913, 591–600, Berlin).

HOLDER, A. 1922 *Alt-Celtischer Sprachschatz* II, Leipzig.

HOSKINS, W. G. 1954 *Devon*, London.

ILS = Dessau, H. 1906 *Inscriptiones Latinae Selectae* II, Pt. 1, Berlin.

LYSONS, REV. D., and S. 1822 *Magna Britannia* VII *Devonshire*, London.

MARGARY, I. D. 1973 *Roman Roads in Britain*, 3rd edn, London.

NAPIER, A. S. and STEVENSON, W. H. 1895 *The Crawford Collection of Early Charters and Documents*, Oxford.

PEIPER, R. (ed.) 1885 *Aulularia*, Leipzig.

PIGGOTT, S. 1941 The Sources of Geoffrey of Monmouth II. The Stonehenge Story, *Antiquity* XV, 305–19.

PINDER, M. and PARTHEY, G. 1860 *Ravennatis Anonymi Cosmographia*, Berlin.

PND = Gover, J. M. B., Mawer, A. and Stenton, F. M. 1931–2 The Place-Names of Devon, *English Place-Name Society* VIII and IX, Cambridge.

RADFORD, C. A. R. 1954 'Locus Maponi', *Dumfriesshire and Galloway Transactions*, 3rd series, XXXI, 35–8.

REICHEL, REV. O. J. 1897 The Hundred of North Tawton, *Trans. Devon Assoc.* XXIX, 245–74.

RICHMOND, I. A. 1940 The Romans in Redesdale, in *History of Northumberland* XV, Newcastle-upon-Tyne.

RICHMOND, I. A. and CRAWFORD, O. G. S. 1949 The British Section of the Ravenna Cosmography, *Archaeologia* XCIII, 1–50.

RIVET, A. L. F. 1970 The British Section of the Antonine Itinerary, *Britannia* I, 34–82.

STEVENS, C. E. 1940 The Frilford Site, A Postscript, *Oxoniensia* V, 166–7.

'TICKLER' (Tozer, Elias) 1871 *Devonshire Sketches*, 2nd edn, (Newspaper Articles reprinted), Exeter.

VENANTIUS FORTUNATUS 1883–85 *Monumenta Germaniae Historica, Auctores Anticuissimi* IX, ed. B. Krusch, Berlin.

WHALE, REV. T. W. 1903 Analysis of the Exeter Domesday in Hundreds, *Trans. Devon Assoc.* XXXV, 679–83.

26

ROBERT B. K. STEVENSON

The Earlier Metalwork of Pictland

WHEN in 1320 the nobles wrote a letter to the Pope from Arbroath in the name of the Scottish nation, and boasted of its history regardless that among them Norman, Norse and English names together outnumbered Gaelic, the most factual part of the historical introduction included the phrase *expulsis Britonibus et Pictis omnino deletis*. In the mythology of their cultural amalgam the Britons had been rolled back, but the Picts, with an echo of Rome versus Carthage, had been blotted out. If not then, at any rate in the later Middle Ages and on into the last century, the sculptured monuments of the Picts were liable to be attributed to the Danes; and the stresses of national mythologies continue to influence the study of both Dark Age and current problems. A valuable function of archaeology as represented by the second Abercromby professor is to try to track the elements in the amalgam of any particular culture, and to distinguish mythologies from models.

The amount of metalwork from Pictish times and territories is almost unbelievably small and it has been little studied (Henderson 1967). The corresponding amount for the Gaelic-speaking Scots during their supremacy, say 850–1100, is much less, apart possibly from hand-bells, some of which should be Pictish (Anderson 1881). The discovery, however, of 28 silver objects at St Ninian's Ise in Shetland, and their recent exemplary publication (Wilson 1973), encourages the hope that excavations on sites in richer mainland areas will yet change the picture radically. For these few objects have led to the firm identification of a type of brooch as characteristically Pictish, and have more than doubled the amount of information about metalwork used in Pictland in the eighth century at the height of its power and at the early stages of its finest sculptured monuments; but the areas of origin of all but the brooches remain unproven. At the risk of circular argument Pictland, for this survey, is indicated by Pictish sculpture at its greatest extent: everywhere on the east of modern Scotland north of the Forth and on the west the Outer Isles and Skye, but not Mull – Argyll, and northern Ireland being the country of the Scots.

Though sculpture is distinctive in the different kingdoms of the period, despite its amalgamating the same traditions of what we may for convenience call Celtic, Mediterranean and Germanic art, the mobility of metalwork as well as of metalworkers produced at least the appearance of greater homogeneity and broader divisions. This was so both before and after the revolution in the decoration of Celtic brooches introduced about AD 700 by the Hunterston or Tara type and its cast counterparts, and more or less contemporary changes in other objects (Henry 1965, I, 96–7; Stevenson 1975). Paradoxically even those with finest gold filigree, such as the Hunterston brooch designed (?) by an Anglo-Saxon goldsmith, were probably fostered by the renewed dominance in the Anglo-Saxon kingdoms of 'chip-carved' gilt bronze or silver over goldwork (Wilson 1960).

Less is known of Pictish history before 700 though, following the Anglo-Saxons' conquest of the Britons in south-east Scotland before the mid-seventh century, there had been a period when they controlled at least some of Pictland; and the archaeological chronology is vaguer still. When the name 'Picts' was first used by Latin writers about AD 300, it seems to have referred to the peoples on the mainland north of the Forth previously called Caledonians. Persistence into the ninth century among them of a non-Indo-European language alongside 'Gallo-Brittonic' has been stressed by K. H. Jackson, but perhaps too much (Jackson 1955; Nicolaisen 1972). Certainly the arrival of Celtic speakers at the end of the Bronze Age, then conceived as in the first century BC (Piggott 1955, 64), must now be pushed back 500 years because of typological studies and C14 dates, and one may more readily think that the Beaker people, arriving by about 2000 BC, were already in some sense Celtic. Yet some lasting difference in the area we are calling Pictland is indicated by distributions peculiar to it. For example Gordon Childe once dated the carved stone balls (later recognized as pre-1500 BC) to correspond to the eighth-ninth century AD symbol sculpture; both distributions resemble that of the early first millennium AD stone cup-lamps, except that it extends round the Clyde estuary (Stevenson 1966, 37 and Fig. 7; Steer 1958, Fig. 7). However, for several centuries there is no metalwork of much consequence attributable to those parts after the mainly second-century AD heavy ornamental bronzes, including armlets (Simpson 1968), ascribed to the Caledonians (Stevenson 1966b, Fig. 5). It is as if Severus' punitive campaigns around 210 had put an end to an aristocratic society's patronage of artistic craftsmen, perhaps altering the balance of elements within the population. Southwards to Hadrian's Wall, later ambitious work is not known either. What there is, mostly small brooches and pins, is similar in both areas and indeed spreads to other parts of the British Isles at the close of the Roman empire and afterward.

The pins draw on the two traditions that continue to be basic to cultural development far into the post-Roman centuries, the pre-Roman Iron Age tradition and the Roman or Romano-British. This continuity makes dating objects often extremely difficult, for they can easily be much later than they seem at first sight – the opposite to Charles Thomas' attempt to push back the late-Pictish symbols towards a local early animal art of a kind for which evidence is hard to find (Thomas 1963).[1] In her full reappraisal of pins and brooches Elizabeth Fowler showed how there grew, probably from straight disc-head pins first seen at a Roman fort in south-east Scotland, a native type with a very stylized animal head, snout downwards (Fowler 1964). By the late third and fourth century this is widespread from Gloucestershire and Ireland to Pictish Morayshire, but mainly between Forth and Tyne. Brooches with similar hoop-swallowing heads grew a little later from small Romano-British clenched-end penannulars, and by the fifth century have rather slight corrugated or plain hoops up to 9 cm in diameter. They are well represented at and around Traprain Law just south of the Forth, are widely distributed in England and Wales, reach Orkney, Shetland and the Hebrides, and Ireland but apparently not initially. These Type E or zoomorphic pins and Type E and F brooches were probably widely made as well as used, but may have begun in southern Scotland and probably represent the only animal-art style there then; Mrs Fowler has convincingly suggested that the heads derive from the Caledonian snake-armlets.

More fully in the Roman tradition are the pins, of bone as well as bronze, derived from the Roman ball-headed pin (Stevenson 1956a). Perhaps by the fifth century in southern England they developed 'hips', a swelling which may be marked or replaced by a band of ornament. They are frequent from northern Scotland and known in Ireland. A disc-head edged and belted with ladder-pattern, from Pictish Orkney, is linked by the polygonal faceting of its point to a nail-head pin from the seventh-eighth-century Buston crannog in British Ayrshire, and to the well-known eighth-century Witham pins from eastern England which have highly decorated disc-heads.

Another even longer tradition was that of the pin with a ring head. This functional feature, doubtless to hold a string that could be looped round the point, ensured its continuity from the earliest Iron Age on into Viking times. The type with a plain projecting head is very widespread in Scotland but rare elsewhere, and from it there developed in the fourth century a number of variants (Fowler 1964). The new ring head is formed wholly or partly of large or small beads, or corrugations. Most varieties are best represented from Scotland. Clay moulds come from Orkney and Caithness, and several from Traprain. Ten pins from Covesea cave in Pictish Morayshire comprise three kinds including the 'ibexhead', and a silver specimen. One of these kinds made at Traprain, which has three to five beads above and a plain surface below, leads to the important type resembling a row of fingers with a semi-circular palm and therefore called a hand-pin (Henderson 1967, Pl. 16). The 'proto-hand-pins' include one from the Outer Hebrides. A variant from Hadrian's Wall and probably a couple of Irish silver examples had enamelled spiral decoration on the flat surface.

It was in Ireland, as far as the evidence goes, that from the fifth century onwards the heads of hand-pins and the terminals of the zoomorphic brooches were progressively enlarged and elaborated to catch the eye. Presumably some smaller and less ambitious pins and brooches should be contemporary with the others; examples of degeneration series should be looked for, and indeed are probably the most numerous. The brooches have been well illustrated

[1] The decorated cup from West Lothian is untypical in its kind of stone, square handle and *drilled* perforation, but except for its animal does resemble a Faroese lamp which is *modern* (*Proc. Soc. Ant. Scot.* I, 1851–54, 117). Similarly the carved symbols in his comparison to a Caledonian terret, are almost certainly modern.

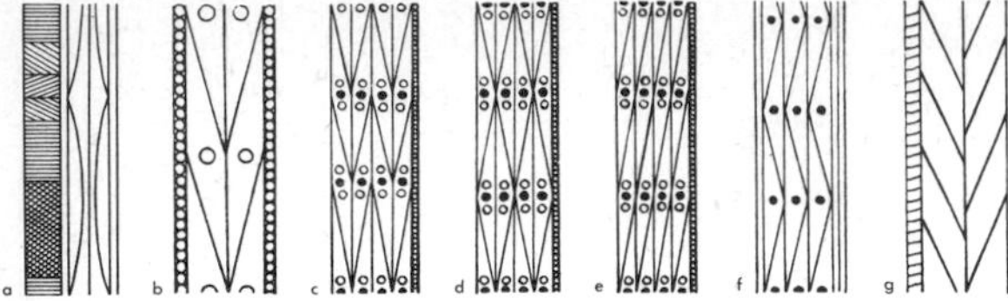

1 Diagrams of patterns: a, Sutton Hoo large hanging-bowl, escutcheon frame; b-f, Norries' Law silver: b,g, edge of hand-pins, c-f, knife-handle (?) fragments (courtesy National Museum of Antiquities of Scotland).

(Kilbride-Jones 1937) but there are hardly any satisfactory dating points. It evidently took, however, two centuries to reach the imposing brooch from Ballinderry, Co. Meath, for Françoise Henry has pointed out that details of its finely corrugated hoop, and the millefiori decoration on the terminals, are matched on the applied escutcheons of the great bronze hanging-bowl from Sutton Hoo (Henry 1965, I, Pl. 24–5; Bruce-Mitford 1972, Pl. A). A date around AD 600 may be suggested for the bowl, which was not new when buried about 630, and the comparison with the undoubtedly Irish brooch makes Irish workmanship most probable.

We may also compare for technique and general style, and so perhaps broadly for date, the Sutton Hoo bowl's champlevé hair-line spirals and birds' heads with the ornament on fully developed silver hand-pins, of which the finest comes from Gaulcross in Morayshire, *Ill. 1a* (Stevenson, 1966a). Its 'dodo-heads', and the comma ends of the better known pins from Norries' Law in Fife, are closer in detail to the best of the Irish 'latchets' (Henry 1965, I, Pl. 13). The production of their spirals is illuminated by a finely incised lead disc from Orkney, for as pointed out by Norman Robertson it is a negative (Curle 1976). Three methods have been proposed for such Dark Age work: cutting back the metal surface of a cast or hammered blank (likely only for soft metal), or impressing a fully-tooled lead or other pattern into a clay mould made in two pieces to allow its removal, and keyed for reunion, or by *cire perdue* using a wax pattern that was left to be lost in baking the mould, which did not need to be two-piece. Decorated keyed moulds are known in Britain and Scandinavia, but apparently not unkeyed moulds (Stevenson 1975), so that the only evidence for lost-wax casting is the unevenness of some plain surfaces (Henry 1965, I, 94). A metal positive could not have been cast directly from the lead negative or from an impression of it, but a beeswax pattern formed on it could have been re-used by a canny Pict from a keyed mould – a *cire* technique but not *perdue*.

One Norries' Law pin has two features that point to further connections. First, like some others, it has little punched circles on its back in threes and in lines, and forming pseudo-beaded-filigree collars at the base of the 'fingers'. Many Irish brooches have circles used in these ways, occasionally beside 'dodo-heads' and small curvilinear triangles with central dots (Kilbride-Jones 1937a, Fig. 10). Secondly the diverging parallelograms on the edge of the pin-head, *Ill. 1b*, are an example of a system of decorative parallelograms and triangles enhanced by punched circles and dots. This is known only on other pieces from Norries' Law, *Ill. 1c-f*, tentatively identified as from knife-handles, but might be an elaboration of the elongated curvilinear pattern on the outside of the central hatched frame of Sutton Hoo's large hanging-bowl already mentioned, *Ill. 2a*. The second Norries' Law pin, *Ill. 1g*, is inferior, indeed a later copy of the first (Stevenson 1966a).

There are widely differing views on the dates of the hand-pins of which there are widespread later varieties, and for the concealment of the Norries' Law hoard a sixth-century date has been strongly argued (Thomas 1963, 42–5; Fowler 1964, 128–9). But if the Gaulcross and Norries' Law pins follow the Sutton Hoo bowl they can be early, and the imitation late in the seventh-century, giving a time-span for hand-pins like that of zoomorphic brooches. This fits the view that Pictish symbols start late, at least in the form in which we have them: to put it in a nutshell, 'primitive' symbols are degenerate, while the best at the beginning include the dog-like heads on two plaques from Norries' Law and the imaginary beast on sculptured monuments whose ear is elongated to a lappet, both typologically related to the Lindisfarne Gospels and later than the Book of Durrow; the scrolls at the joints of the Pictish animals are a mannerism constantly used in many other ways in the manuscripts, but isolated in Pictish art; the animal art in Pictland is derived about AD 700 from the symbols of the Evangelists in the manuscripts, and not earlier or the other way round (Stevenson 1972, 67–70).

The Norries' Law hoard still awaits even an inventory of the 750 g of it discovered after an estimated nearly 12.5 kg was melted down in 1819. Part of a fourth-century inscribed spoon is a Roman survivor (Stevenson 1956b), and so perhaps are a spiral finger ring with very worn bands of beading,

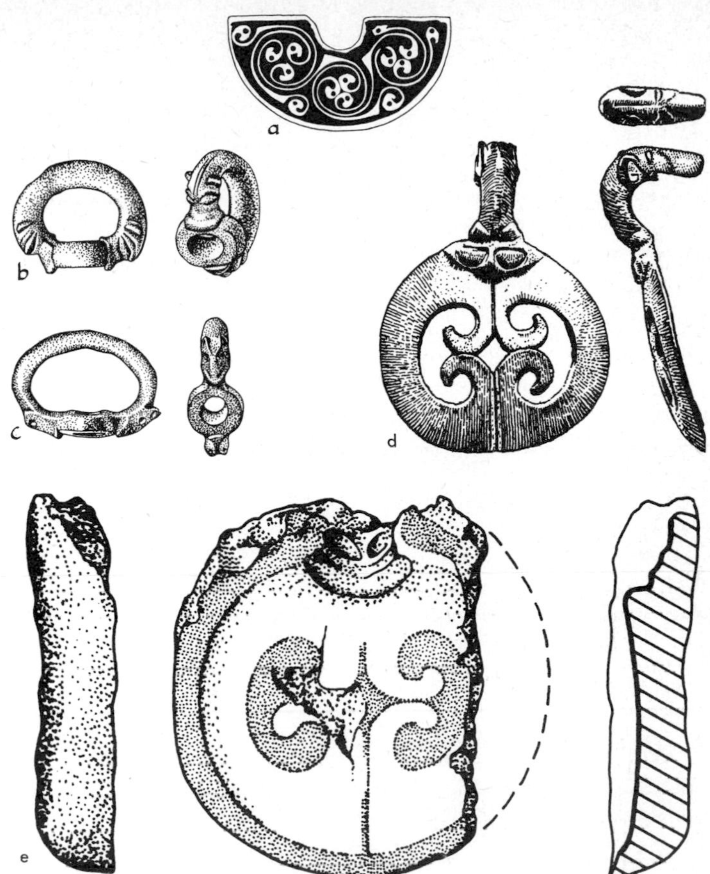

2 a, Gaulcross hand-pin detail, silver and champlevé red enamel; b,c, bronze swivel-rings from A'Chrois, Tiree and Vallay, North Uist; d, bronze hanging bowl escutcheon, Castle Tioram, Moidart; e, clay mould for a hanging-bowl escutcheon, Craig Phadrig, Inverness (courtesy National Museum of Antiquities of Scotland).

and part of another. The pieces of supposed Roman dish 40 cm in diameter are, however, too thin, and seem to have been all flat except for the surround of large *oblong* bosses. Marks show that two 4.5-cm discs have been rivetted on to it, though they do not survive. No less perplexing are three large spiral bosses with a sharp inner ridge and thin trumpet-ended stalks. They are cast hollow in a thick sheet from which a fourth has probably been cut away. Close parallels are on large Irish bronze disc-basins generally dated to about the second century AD (Piggott and Daniel 1951, Pl. 48), but also at the ends of interlocking peltas on the unique 'equal-armed' silver brooch, again Irish, dated, following Åberg, to the seventh century (Henry 1965, I, Pl. 10).

A similar fat scroll with sharp ridge is among the small designs embossed upon fragments of gold-covered copper sheet in seventh-century *Spangenhelm* style found in south-west Scotland (de Paor 1963, Fig. 1, 3). Though imported from abroad, to judge by the arcading, palmettes, classical drapery and figures, and geometric borders, besides lengths of vine-scroll, their technique may have been adopted in Scotland. For quite possibly a crescent in metal, cut through a stamped overall pattern of interlocking peltas, originated the design suggested on typological grounds as the prototype of those common Pictish symbols, the decorated crescents. The inner curls of truncated peltas are otherwise inexplicably left in their right places in the design on a stone in Sutherland (Stevenson 1955, Fig. 15; Henderson 1967, Fig. 18a). An actual cut-out metal crescent about 11 cm across, recorded from near Dundee, had a diaper of coffering, and so perhaps of the ninth century, and in relief the dog's-head and 'spectacles with floreated Z-rod' symbols found incuse on the Norries' Law plaques.

These, nearly identical, are perhaps the freshest objects in the hoard (Henderson 1967, Pl. 18). Pointed drop-shaped ovals 9 cm long and probably cast, their polished surface has contrasted with the bold symbols, originally red-enamelled. Despite a turban-shaped boss at the top there is no sign of fastening on the back, but only one has an engraved margin, so they may be unfinished. The spectacles' discs contain triple spirals in the hand-pin and hanging-bowl tradition. The symbol also occurs in the same form on one of the heavy silver chains, made up of paired rings flattened on their inner faces, which are peculiar to Scotland (Henderson 1967, Pl. 18; Stevenson 1956b). No chain is complete but five have a broad ring, like a modern napkin ring but penannular, which must have slipped over the single unflattened ring at the other end to form a 'choker' necklace. The lengths of most are similar, upwards of 45 cm, but the diameters of the links vary from 2.4 to 4.8 cm, and consequently the weights from 687 to 2877 g, in nine surviving examples. They are probably all Pictish though most have been found south of the Forth, because sunk symbols decorate each end of the 'napkin ring' in two instances, one from each area. In any case two things are clear from them, that silver was relatively common then (perhaps derived from hoards like the 24 kg of loot we have, buried at Traprain soon after AD 400), and that there was a fashion for plain or only slightly decorated surfaces. A differently made, and lighter, silver chain comes from the Gaulcross find, and so does a broad plain spiral bracelet. Parts of bracelets from Norries' Law may have been similar but for thickened disc ends.

Two large and heavy silver brooches from Norries' Law are also plain. It is unconvincing to interpret them as necklets just because the pins are missing and the hoops ornamentally twisted (Wilson 1973), for the one complete inner diameter is only 11.7 cm and the gap between the triangular terminals would nip a normal neck. Hammer marks on the back may indicate lack of finish; a coil of silver ribbon 92 cm long, and the bosses mentioned as perhaps being cut out, again suggest a silversmith's hoard. But there are comparable bronze brooches in Ireland up to 11 cm across, which are plain except for zoomorphic vestiges, and a smaller example from Mull. Of three silver brooches 6.5 to 8.0 cm across from Tummel Bridge in the central Highlands, two are slightly decorated: one with a double line of incised dots near the edge of the large terminals, rather like one from Lagore in Ireland (Fowler 1964, Fig. 5:2), the other with dots on the flat pin's widened centre and ridging on the head. The pin-shape is probably ancestral to that of eighth-century Pictish lobed brooches. Mrs Fowler, who suggests that the simplicity of her class H precludes typological analysis, inclines to a fifth- or even fourth-century date. But after the 'baroque' Ballinderry brooch a revulsion towards simplicity would be natural, and could accommodate in Ireland simultaneously brooches with curved designs including peltas (Kilbride-Jones 1937a, 12–14) and the large plain terminals, which in Pictland particularly perhaps, lost the zoomorph.

The strongest argument for an early date has been the sub-Roman character of the quite plain 4-pelta openwork escutcheon on the hanging-bowl found with the Tummel Bridge brooches (Henry 1936, Pl. 23; Kilbride-Jones 1937b, Fig. 2) to which Mrs Fowler, summing up other writers, has given an early fifth-century date (Fowler 1968, 299). The rim-sections have provided a supporting typology: the weak T-shape of the first openwork bowls is strengthened – flat folded-over rims and marked neck and shoulders go with elaborate patterns. However, regression in places cannot be ruled out. Another bowl, with a 2-pelta openwork escutcheon, comes from Castle Tioram (Kilbride-Jones 1937) on the west coast north of Mull, *Ill. 2d* after cleaning. A related clay escutcheon-mould, *Ill. 2e*, was excavated at Craig Phadrig near Inverness in association with 'E ware' (Small 1972), giving the first good evidence for a place of manufacture, but comparable escutcheons come from Wiltshire (4-peltas differently arranged) and Leicestershire (2-peltas). Others from Co. Londonderry, Cambridgeshire and Warwickshire (all 2-peltas), are decorated and enamelled, and have been dated to the seventh century (Haseloff 1959). They share with the plain ones details unlikely to have been kept by copyists at a different time, such as the central diamond and the vertical line through it. None have dot-and-circle or other immediately post-Roman patterns in characteristic form (Hawkes 1962). Little attention has been paid to the muzzle-shaped attachment at the base of the hook and the lentoid bosses higher up, which are normal on these openwork escutcheons. They may be compared to the animal heads of a swivel-ring from Tiree in the Hebrides, *Ill. 2b*. (A contrasting kind of head on a swivel-ring from North Uist is also shown.) Castle Tioram seems to have both eyes and ears. The large Sutton Hoo bowl too has eyes, and a muzzle comparable to the Ballinderry brooch; and this feature is also present in some form (becoming fan-shaped) on plain trefoil-shaped escutcheons from Leicestershire, on one that is heater-shaped with fine spirals, 'Faversham 3' from Kent, on another decorated one from Kent that is itself pelta-shaped, and on others quite degenerate. A further Sutton Hoo feature is a double-line round the edge of the suspension ring; Castle Tioram has comparable ladder-pattern (also found on the Sutton Hoo bowl's fish), and the Wiltshire 4-pelta bowl's rings are grooved.

It may from these comparisons be suggested that most of the bowls belong to the seventh century. Moreover one of the smaller Sutton Hoo bowls has a cruciform pattern of eight alternating fine-line peltas, the sort of design from which openwork ones might have grown, developing simultaneously with other styles such as the Durrowesque. Though like the earlier ornaments they were all probably made as well as used in various parts of the British Isles (the lead disc from Orkney is Durrowesque), the plain style may have had a regional, perhaps Pictish, emphasis in the later part of the century. Encouragement of originality, of which we have throughout seen signs on a small scale, really started to bear fruit in the seventh century, and it must have been a plain brooch that somewhere provided the *tabula rasa* which allowed the artist designing the Hunterston brooch's prototype such a free hand for his originality early in the eighth century.

Bibliography

ANDERSON, J. 1881 *Scotland in Early Christian Times* I, Edinburgh.

BRUCE-MITFORD, R. L. S. 1972 *The Sutton Hoo Ship Burial*, 2nd edn, British Museum, London.

COLES, J. M. and SIMPSON, D. D. A. (eds.) 1968 *Studies in Ancient Europe*, Edinburgh.

CURLE, C. L. 1976 Note in *Proc. Soc. Ant. Scot.* (forthcoming).

DE PAOR, L. 1963 Some vine scrolls and other patterns in embossed metal from Dumfriesshire, *Proc. Soc. Ant. Scot.* XCIV 1960–61, 184–95.

FOWLER, E. 1964 Celtic metalwork of the 5th and 6th centuries AD, *Archaeol. J.* CXX 1963, 98–160.

1968 Hanging bowls, in Coles and Simpson (1968), 287–310.

HASELOFF, G. 1959 Fragments of a hanging bowl from Bekesbourne, Kent and some ornamental problems, *Medieval Archaeol.* II 1958, 72–103.

HAWKES, S. and DUNNING, G. C. 1962 Soldiers and Settlers in Britain, 4th to 5th century, *Medieval Archaeol.* V 1961, 1–70.

HENDERSON, I. 1967 *The Picts*, London.

HENRY, F. 1936 Hanging bowls, *J. Roy. Soc. Ant. Ireland* LXVI, 209–46.

1965 *Irish Art of the Early Christian Period*, London.

JACKSON, K. H. 1955 The Pictish language, in Wainwright (1955), 129–66.

KILBRIDE-JONES, H. E. 1937a The evolution of penannular brooches with zoomorphic terminals in Great Britain and Ireland, *Proc. Roy. Irish Acad.* XLIII 1935–37, 379–455.

1937b A bronze hanging-bowl from Castle Tioram and a suggested absolute chronology for British hanging-bowls, *Proc. Soc. Ant. Scot.* LXXI 1936–37, 206–47.

NICOLAISEN, W. F. H. 1972 P-Celtic place-names in Scotland, *Studia Celtica.* 7, 1–11.

PIGGOTT, S. 1955 The archaeological background, in Wainwright (1955), 54–65.

PIGGOTT, S. and DANIEL, G. E. 1951 *A Picture Book of Ancient British Art*, Cambridge.

SIMPSON, M. 1968 Massive armlets in the North British Iron Age, in Coles and Simpson (1968), 233–54.

SMALL, A. *et al.* 1972 *Craig Phadrig*, University of Dundee, Dept. of Geography, Occasional Papers No. 1.

STEER, K. A. 1958 An early iron age homestead at West Plean, Stirlingshire, *Proc. Soc. Ant. Scot.* LXXXIX 1955–56, 227–51.

STEVENSON, R. B. K. 1955 Pictish Art, in Wainwright (1955), 97–128.

1956a Pins and the chronology of brochs, *Proc. Prehist. Soc.* XXI 1955, 282–94.

1956b Pictish chain, Roman silver, *Proc. Soc. Ant. Scot.* LXXXVIII 1954–56 (sic) 228–9.

1966a The Gaulcross hoard of Pictish silver, *Proc. Soc. Ant. Scot.* XCVII 1963–64, 206–9.

1966b Metalwork and some other objects, in *The Iron Age in Northern Britain*, ed. A. L. F. Rivet, 17–44.

1972 Sculpture in Scotland in the 6th-9th centuries AD, in *Kolloquium über spätantike und frühmittelalterliche Skulptur, Heidelberg 1970*, Mainz, 65–74.

1975 The Hunterston brooch and its significance, *Medieval Archaeol.* XVIII 1974, 16–42.

THOMAS, A. C. 1963 Animal art in the Scottish Iron Age, *Archaeol. J.* CXVIII 1961, 14–64.

WAINWRIGHT, F. T. (ed.) 1955 *The Problem of the Picts*, Edinburgh etc.

WILSON, D. M. 1960 *The Anglo-Saxons*, London.

1973 The treasure, in *St. Ninian's Isle and its Treasure*, Aberdeen University Studies, 152, ed. A. Small, 44–148.

27

V. M. MASSON

The Art of Altin-depe: the Artistic Traditions of the Urbanized Cultures between Sumer and India[1]

[1] Translated by Carol Vesecky and Tadeusz Sulimirski

IN 1944, Stuart Piggott visited the region of Quetta in northern Baluchistan and, after collecting a sufficiently representative collection of decorated pottery, distinguished a special complex which he conventionally named the 'Quetta Culture' (Piggott 1947). The correctness of discerning this group of early agricultural tribes was then fully confirmed by broader investigations conducted in the region by Fairservis (1956). At the same time Piggott, relying on the limited materials at his disposal, had already correctly apprehended the relationship between the Quetta complex and the materials of south Turkmenistan which were known at that time from the much restricted excavations of R. Pampelli (Piggott 1947; 1950). These observations were fully confirmed during continued work in Baluchistan as well as in Turkmenia (Masson 1964). As new data indicate, these connections lead us to the sources of such important phenomena as the formation of an urbanized culture in the region around the Iranian plateau (Lamberg-Karlovsky and Tosi 1973).

New archaeological discoveries clearly attest that, in the third and the beginning of the second millennium BC, a huge area between Mesopotamia and India was occupied not simply by settlements of agriculturists and cattle-herders, but by communities in which the process of formation of an urbanized culture of the ancient Eastern character proceeded intensively (Masson 1970). At present there are four chief sites whose material can be used in connection with the study of this problem: Mundigak in Afghanistan, Altin-depe in south Turkmenia, Shahr-i-Sokhta in Seistan and, to some degree, Tepe-Yahya in Kerman.

Characteristic manifestations of cultural complexes of this type include the emergence of large populated centres, intensive development of handicrafts, wide dissemination of seals, and the emergence of monumental architecture. Thus the area of Shahr-i-Sokhta at the time of its greatest flowering comprised 75 hectares, Namazga-depe in south Turkmenia 70, and Altin-depe 46. In comparison with these enormous centres, the size of Mundigak is much less significant. The mighty industrial centres of these settlements are most imposing. In Altin-depe, the artisan quarter with its numerous pottery kilns occupies an area of approximately two hectares (Masson 1972), and not far from Shahr-i-Sokhta there was even discovered a specialized settlement of artisan potters in which approximately fifty kilns were accounted for (Lamberg-Karlovsky and Tosi 1973). Data are available for the presence at Shahr-i-Sokhta of a specialized industry for the treatment of lapis lazuli (Tosi and Piperno 1973), and in Tepe-Yahya for the production of steatite vessels, which were in great demand in Mesopotamia, Baluchistan, and in adjacent areas (Lamberg-Karlovsky 1970).

True, an accurate chronology for this broad epoch has still not been fully worked out. The Namazga IV complex in south Turkmenistan, in which the initial stages of urbanization occurred, is dated approximately in the middle of the third millennium BC, followed in 2100–1850 BC by the early Namazga V complex. Lamberg-Karlovsky, who is trying to construct a long consecutive chronology of the Tepe-Yahya complexes, places Level IVC with its proto-Elamite tablets in the second half of the fourth millennium BC, thus proclaiming Tepe-Yahya to be presumably one of the most ancient cities in the world (Lamberg-Karlovsky 1971; 1972). Without going into the details of a careful analysis, it might be mentioned that a short chronology, which does not include subdivisions of the Yahya IV complex beyond the limits of the third millennium BC, seems more realistic to us. In particular, the study of the proto-Elamite tablets from Tepe-Yahya has shown that they belong to a later period than analogous tablets from Susa, which definitely eliminates their being dated to the fourth millennium BC (Vayman 1972). The possibility must not be excluded that in Tepe-Yahya we have a sort of far outpost of the Elamite civilization or even a trading station of the Elamites similar to that existing in Sialk IV (Childe 1956).

Be that as it may, there can be no question of the high level of cultural development represented by all the sites just mentioned. And what is more, at least some of them had a common initial cultural stratum characteristic of that particular ceramic tradition in which relations with south Turkmenistan on the one hand, and with the Quetta complexes in northern Baluchistan on the other, have been noted. This view has subsequently been developed by Tosi and his colleagues, who have discovered a quite specific pottery tradition in the lowest layers at Shahr-i-Sokhta, in which approximately 40 per cent of the decorated vessels have fairly precise counterparts in Geoksiur type pottery of south Turkmenistan (Lamberg-Karlovsky and Tosi 1973; Biscione 1973). This fairly characteristic style of geometric painting is well represented in Quetta, and its influence can also be traced in Mundigak III. Taking this into account, the Shahr-i-Sokhta I complex in particular appears to have been the cultural substratum for Seistan on which its further development was based. A study of layers with pottery of the Geoksiur period in Altin-depe has shown that they extend over at least half of the entire area of the settlement, and that this ceramic style formed the basis of the further evolution of the painted pottery of Altin-depe (Masson 1972). All these circumstances attest to the major role played by this Geoksiur substratum in the formation of the early urban civilizations in the area between Mesopotamia and India, especially in its eastern section, within which Tosi and Lamberg-Karlovsky have noted the existence of a special cultural area extending between Altin-depe and Shahr-i-Sokhta; this area they have named the 'South Turkmenistanian' (Lamberg-Karlovsky and Tosi 1973).

It seems that interesting evidence for explaining this problem might be obtained by the study of the art of these urbanized cultures. We shall attempt here to consider briefly the example of Altin-depe. We encounter there at least two artistic traditions, one of which goes back to local sources in the culture of early agricultural communities, while the other indicates definite influences from the direction of highly developed civilizations, predominantly from Mesopotamia. These artistic traditions are in varying degree revealed by several groups of artistic objects discovered at Altin-depe. The character of these groups is itself diagnostic. Thus the painted pottery, the characteristic mass product of the applied art of the early period, completely disappeared under conditions caused by the spread of the standardized production of artisan potters. The traditions of ornamentalism can be traced back through other forms of objects, in particular, through small pottery boxes. On the other hand, the wide diffusion of

1 Altin-depe. Small terracotta box.

female terracotta statuettes seems to continue the ancient tradition, although their style underwent considerable changes. Finally, such articles as the numerous seals, examples of sculpture, and monumental architecture are new phenomena, already connected with a society living in qualitatively different conditions.

Let us consider in detail the individual groups of objects. Small terracotta boxes (*Ill. 1*), which may possibly have been used as some kind of censer, are widespread in the upper layers of Altin-depe, their sides being decorated by carved ornaments with the separate elements painted red or black. The sides of these boxes are essentially square or rectangular with panels filled by geometric ornamentation based on motifs of crosses and semi-crosses. The decoration of the panels goes directly back to the painted pottery in the Geoksiur style. The shapes of multi-arm crosses, which emerge only at the time of late Geoksiur (Sarianidi 1965) and are widespread in the Altin-depe pottery of the Namazga IV period, already point to the refined nature of this traditional motif. The continuation of small ornamental boxes in the Namazga V period, when painting of pottery completely ceased, is interesting. Thus the rhythmic geometric ornamentation of these objects bears direct witness to the survival in south Turkmenia, into the epoch of urbanized culture, of the applied art traditions of the early agricultural communities.

Small pottery boxes with ornamented sides are also known from other areas of the region under consideration, in Shahr-i-Sokhta (Tosi 1969, Fig. 125) and in Mundigak (Casal 1961, II, Fig. 130); yet there they are decorated not by carving but by

2 Altin-depe. Seals made of silver, bronze, stone, and ceramics.

3 Altin-depe. Silver seal in the form of a fantastic animal.

painting which, incidentally, is traced back to the same Geoksiur traditions. Ornamentation in relief providing the play of light and shadow, and imparting to these articles a refined ornate look, was a specific feature of the South Turkmenistanian material.

We see the same ornamental traditions, possibly strengthened by the magic symbols of the separate elements, in the form of seals, the widespread products of Altin-depe (*Ill. 2*). The seals, which on the reverse generally had a small loop-shaped handle, were most frequently made in high relief of bronze and silver, which provided a good impression on malleable material. This type of seal, which Piggott at one time called 'partitioned' (Piggott 1950, 220), represents a characteristic feature of the area under consideration, one that differed from the cylinders of both Mesopotamia and Elam as well as from the square seals of Harappa. Among the relevant Altin-depe objects two different groups can be distinguished: the zoomorphic and geometric seals. Among the latter we encounter seals oval or square in shape, and those in the form of a pyramid with either one or two connected. However, the most common and important type is represented by cross-shaped seals which in the great majority of cases reproduce the shape of a multi-arm cross, like the ornament on the small terracotta boxes already described. The inner area of the seals is covered by pyramids or cogged lines, an ornament that can also be traced back to the geometric style of the local painted pottery of the Namazga IV period. It is interesting to note that the same style has been followed in the stone and clay seals, in which figures have been executed by boring a number of connected holes to form the unbroken line of the figure. Seals produced by this technique are diffused within the boundaries of the same cultural area as the partitioned seals and are well represented both at Shahr-i-Sokhta (Tosi 1969, Fig. 275) and at Mundigak (Casal 1961, II, Pl. XLV:11).

More rarely encountered are the zoomorphic seals, usually reproducing hoofed animals, mostly goats, as well as birds with wings outspread, and feline beasts of prey. All these subjects have direct counterparts in the pottery painting of the early agricultural communities of south Turkmenistan, where again the goat was the most popular theme (Masson 1970). Stylistic changes are expressed in a certain shortening of the animals' bodies, which is due to the utilitarian desire of obtaining an impression of the same length and breadth. The filling of the animals' bodies with a variety of lines and

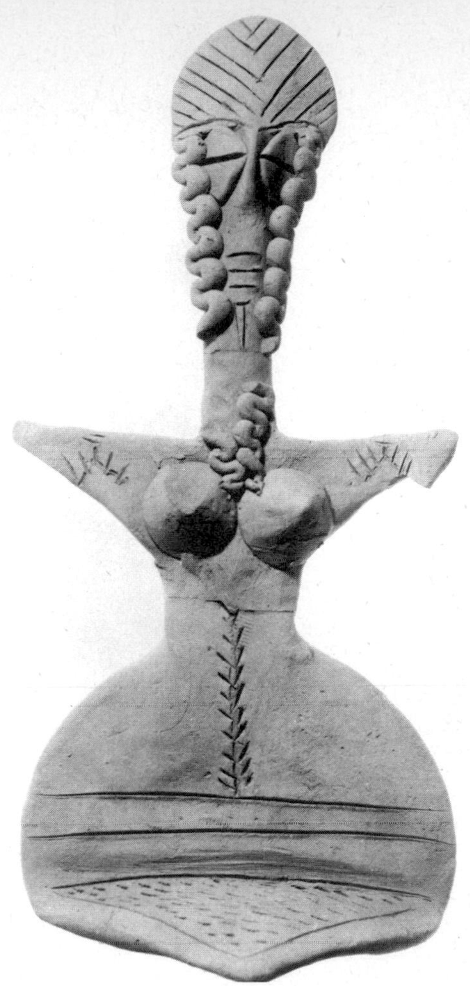

4 Altin-depe. Female terracotta statuette.
5 Altin-depe. Female terracotta statuette.

figures includes the seals of this group in that of the unified style of detailed ornamentation which is characteristic of partitioned seals as a whole.

Of special interest is a silver seal depicting a fantastic three-headed beast (*Ill. 3*), executed with outstanding artistic skill. Complementary fine engraving vividly exhibits the image of an animal with the body of a rapacious feline, one head of a bird of prey – probably an eagle – and two others closely suggesting the heads of reptiles. We have here undoubtedly an outstanding product of the toreutics of Altin-depe, with no direct parallels so far identified. As is known, the iconography of early Mesopotamia offers no three-headed motifs, and possibly in this instance the form of the three-headed beast comes from Indian contacts (Marshall 1931, III, Pl. CXII: 382). It is also known that in Mesopotamia, in a number of cases, monsters are simply a graphic combination of a god and his animalistic emblems (Deshayes 1969, 257). In Altin-depe such a combination was based on animalistic elements alone, two of which – the feline beast of prey and the eagle – are fairly well represented in the repertory of the painted pottery of the early agriculturists (Masson 1964, 156). In south Turkmenia the motif of reptiles was not quite so popular, although it appears on the painted vessels of the Namazga III period and on the grey pottery of Namazga IV.

In turning to the seals of Shahr-i-Sokhta, where their impressions on lumps of clay apparently covering the necks of vessels are especially numerous, we see their definite stylistic proximity, although Altin has the accentuated adherence to the cross-shaped seal motif. This similarity also relates to the zoomorphic seals, especially as regards the practice of filling the shortened trunks with ornaments (Tosi 1969, Figs. 288–9). At the same time images of birds and feline beasts of prey have not yet been encountered at Shahr-i-Sokhta, although impressions of seals have been found in the form of fish and

6 Altin-depe. 'The chieftain's house.'

7 Altin-depe. Religious complex. General view.

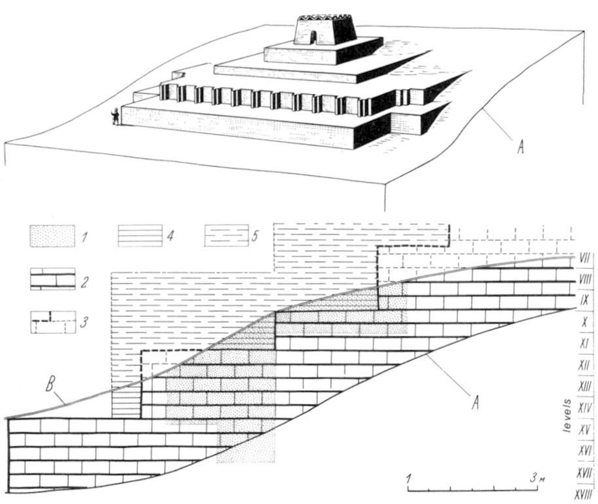

8 Altin-depe. Religious complex. Tower-shaped structure of the first period. Cross-section and reconstruction.

1 Excavated portion
2 Brick masonry of the first period
3 Reconstructed masonry of the first period
4 Brick masonry of the second period
5 Reconstructed masonry of the second period

even with the image of the head of a bearded man (Tosi 1969, Figs. 290–2).

A particularly abundant group of finds at Altin-depe is formed by terracotta female figurines (*Ills.* 4, 5), which literally represent the bulk of this widespread art. The style of these terracottas is restrained and accomplished. In a somewhat conventional, flat manner, they depict tall women with thin waists and broad hips, encircled by several rows of belts. Similar belts, consisting of many beads, were discovered in female burials at Altin-depe. The lower part of the figures, being inclined slightly forward, indicates a connection with a local tradition characteristic of the Neolithic when sitting women were predominantly depicted (Masson and Sarianidi 1973, 12–18). Individual details of the terracottas of this new style, fixed in the Namazga V period, find fairly firm parallels in Mesopotamian coroplastics: large, applied eyes, multistrand necklaces round the neck, belts on the hips and a triangle in the lower portion of the belly, covered with fine oblique incisions (Masson and Sarianidi 1973, 51–2). It is clear that the craftsmen, keeping to local traditions of the seated female statuette – all figurines from Mesopotamia are standing – applied here a number of graphic methods of Mesopotamian plastic art. But on the whole, the terracottas of Altin-depe are quite unique. Within the framework of the flat style possibly determined by the new ideological requirements of the epoch of urbanization, the masters of Altin-depe skilfully solved the task of creating a simple silhouette which is sufficiently elegant and refined. Determinative in the silhouette are the broad hips, spread arms, and head positioned on a slender neck or with a high headdress, which lighten this somewhat thick-set composition. Significant is the contrast between the flat torso, nearly devoid of detail, and the excessive detail of the upper part of the figurine with its multi-string necklace, the curling plaits, and occasionally the extremely complex headdress. It is as though this antithesis must lead the observer to the huge applied eyes, which concentrate all one's attention. In Sumer the eyes, as well as the ears, were considered organs of wisdom. As some investigators have suggested, the excessively magnified eyes of many Mesopotamian statuettes not only symbolized divine wisdom, but also, according to the laws of magic, gave divine wisdom to the representation itself (Afanas'eva and D'yakonov 1961, 14–15). Although the South Turkmenistanian terracottas possess definite parallels, for example in those of Shahr-i-Sokhta (Tosi 1969, Fig. 160), their style and wide diffusion remain specific features of the south Turkmenistan area.

Among the innovations characteristic of the culture of Altin-depe was the significant progress observed in the sphere of architecture. Utilitarian construction, expressed both in the small size of buildings and in the spontaneous irregularity of the settlement plans, was characteristic of the early agricultural communities of south Turkmenistan. In the period under consideration a tendency towards monumentality and a strict, almost geometric, regularity of plan has already been noted. As a striking example of the latter we might take the chieftain's house whose obviously restrained plan noticeably contrasts with the layout of the common quarters of Altin-depe (*Ill. 6*) (Masson 1969).

Of special significance is the large religious complex of Altin-depe (*Ill. 7*) which existed throughout three periods of construction and underwent substantial changes. At the first level of construction it consisted of three parts: the burial complex where, along with rich funeral gifts, apparently members of the priestly community were entombed (Masson 1974); commercial houses and buildings with adjacent three-room dwelling houses square in plan; and a tower-shaped structure on the outer edge of the complex (*Ill. 8*). The tower-shaped structure had four stepped platforms and its length along the lower step was 21 m. In its exterior aspect it strikingly imitated the ziggurats of Sumer, but unlike these the actual building formed only three-quarters of the total structure since it grew, as it were, out of the mound formed by the deposits of the Namazga IV period.

In the second period (*Ill. 9*) the tower was increased in length and height, and inside it the walled-in remains of an earlier structure have been found. By now the tower-shaped structure had attained the height of 26 m on the side of the façade. A complex of rooms was built onto the south of the tower and its foundation, a 3 m-high platform, was decorated with three step-like pilasters. Essential rebuilding also took place behind this frontal façade. The burial complex and the commercial buildings were filled in with quarry stone, while a square four-roomed house, resembling the chieftain's house in its clear layout, was erected on the foundation thus formed. The third period is marked by a definite decadence and many repair works.

The architecture of this religious centre of Altin-depe reveals definite ties with the architecture of Sumer. First of all this refers to the very method

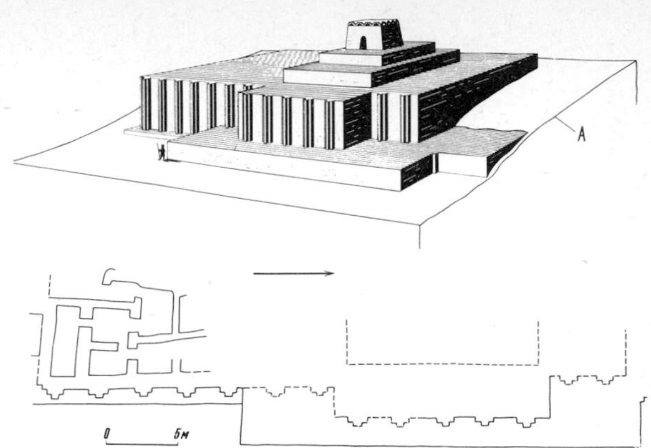

9 Altin-depe. Religious complex in the second period. Plan and reconstruction of the façade.

of building walls with rhythmically distributed buttresses. The step-like buttresses appear in southern Mesopotamia in the last third of the fourth millennium BC and were widely represented in the architecture of the third millennium BC, including the façade of the famous Ur Ziggurat (Woolley 1939, Pls. 68–72). The idea of the tower-shaped structure itself should be counted among the Mesopotamian influences, and in south Turkestan led to the rise of a particular type of vertical architecture. It should be noted that the early ziggurats of Mesopotamia were normally rectangular and not square in their layout. However, as distinct from Sumer, the tower-shaped structure of Altin-depe was oriented to the cardinal points not by its corners, but by its sides. A difference also exists in the form of the exterior, the frontal face of which proves to be substantially regular and monumental.

This combination of a spectacular façade and a unique type of elemental layout is also characteristic of the so-called Mundigak palace, which likewise belongs to the relics of monumental architecture (Casal 1961, I, 49–55). Furthermore, irregularity in layout is noted by Tosi in the case of monumental structures of Shahr-i-Sokhta (Lamberg-Karlovsky and Tosi 1973, 28).

Researchers unanimously conclude that the ziggurats discovered in the majority of the large centres of Mesopotamia were typically local structures which, outside Mesopotamia, were represented only in Elam (Deshayes 1969, 283–9). Moreover, a study of the cultures of the huge area east of Mesopotamia, which underwent a process of intensive urbanization, indicates that this spectacular architectural structure – the specific symbol of a city, performing moreover the function of an ideological and religious centre – was also adopted far beyond the border of the territory in which its origin has been traced. Alongside Altin-depe, we should turn our attention to the ruins of the settlement of Edit-Shahr in southern Baluchistan, where Fairservis noted the remains of a massive, mighty structure and treated it as a building of the ziggurat type (Fairservis 1967, 17; 1971, 195–6). Unfortunately, no excavations of this interesting site have yet been undertaken.

Finally, the last group of objects which we would like to discuss comprises small-scale sculpture. The golden heads of a bull (*Ill. 10*) and a wolf (*Ill. 11*) have been discovered in the above-mentioned burial complex of Altin-depe. The bull's head has inserted horns and ears, the horns being made of silver wire wrapped in gold foil. There are insets of turquoise on the forehead and the eyes. The somewhat conventional and stylized head of the bull from Altin-depe, like the terracottas of south Turkmenistan, reveals two connections. On the one hand, the schematic treatment of the animal's muzzle, looking almost like a pig's snout, is clearly reminiscent of the figurine of a bull made of marble-like limestone found in the Namazga III layer at Kara-depe (Masson 1960, Fig. 24). On the other hand, the treatment of the ears, the superciliary arch, and the manner of encrusted inlays on the forehead and eyes, manifestly leads us to the world of Sumerian toreutics, starting with the famous bull's heads on the resonators of harps from the royal graves of Ur (Woolley 1934, Pls. 107, 111, 115–17). Although combining the features of Mesopotamian tradition with local stylistic adaptations, the head of the Altin bull is closest to the head of a bull from a Bahrein temple, which also comes from beyond the confines of the Sumerian homeland (During-Caspers 1971).

10 Altin-depe. Religious complex. 'Tomb of priests.' Golden head of a bull.

11 Altin-depe. Religious complex. 'Tomb of priests.' Golden head of a wolf.

The new finds have substantially increased the number of objects of small-scale sculpture discovered in the area east of Mesopotamia. Thus, a bronze figurine of a woman carrying on her head a vessel supported by one hand was found in Shahr-i-Sokhta (Tosi 1971, Fig. 11). Tosi has already noted that parallels to this object occur in the culture of early dynastic Sumer. It seems possible that the closest analogies are the well-known anthropomorphic statuettes with vessels on their heads, which appear in both the early layers and the complexes of the period of the third dynasty of Ur (Parrot 1960, Fig. 292; Contenau 1931, 757, 788–9). The Mesopotamian figurines are close to the Shahr-i-Sokhta example not only in style but also in their size.

The Fullol treasure of gold and silver vessels discovered in northern Afghanistan is of even greater interest (Dupree *et al.* 1971; Tosi and Wardak 1972). While it contains objects from various periods, supporting the idea that this was some sort of temple treasure, the time of its deposition barely goes back beyond the second millennium BC, just the period at which the earliest relics of urban culture emerge there, closely resembling in their general appearance the relics of south Turkmenistan (Kruglikova and Sarianidi 1971). Among the objects in the treasure we see, on the one hand, obvious Mesopotamian imports, or their close imitations, represented by vessels covered with depictions of bulls. On the other hand, there are vessels ornamented in the tradition of Geoksiur style already mentioned, and closely corresponding with the remains in south Turkmenistan of the early Namazga III complex (Masson 1960, Table VIII, 3; XXX, 10). The possibility cannot be ruled out that these ancient ornamental traditions, applied to small-scale sculpture and to the above-cited small terracotta boxes, survived until the Bronze Age.

We may thus conclude that the formation of the art of Bronze Age Altin-depe was, in the first place, based on local traditions among which an especially outstanding rôle was played by the decorative elements whose roots go back to the painted pottery of the Geoksiur style. At the same time this society, which proceeded to witness urbanization developed within its own environment and on a local basis, had availed itself of the achievements of the highly evolved centres of Mesopotamia, the relations with which it is hardly possible to doubt although they may have been of a manifold nature. These same two aspects of Altin-depe can be noted in other ancient sites, at Shahr-i-Sokhta and Mundigak. A detailed study of the mutual relations of such cultural complexes, above all characterized by a very similar level of socio-economic development, ought to be the theme of future and more comprehensive investigations.

Bibliography

A. REFERENCES IN RUSSIAN

AFANAS'EVA, V. K. and D'YAKONOV, I. M. 1961 *Ob osnovnykh etapakh razvitiya izobrazitel'nogo iskusstva drevnego Shumera* (The fundamental stages of the development of representational art in ancient Sumer) = *Trudy Gosudarstvennogo Ermitazha* V, 5–23.

KRUGLIKOVA, I. T. and SARIANIDI, V. I. 1971 Ancient Bactria in the light of archaeological discoveries, *Sovetskaya Arkheologiya* 4, 154–77.

MASSON, V. M. 1960 *Kara-depe u artyka* (Kara-depe near the Artyk), = *Trudy YuTAKE* (Works of the South Turkmenistanian Complex Archaeological Expedition) X, Ashkhabad.

1964 *Srednyaya Aziya i Drevniy Vostok* (Central Asia and the Ancient East), Moscow-Leningrad.

1970a *Zona rannegorodskikh tsivilizatsiy mezhdu Shumerom i Indiey* (The zone of early urban civilizations between Sumer and India) = Abstracts of reports for a session devoted to the results of field investigations of 1969, Moscow.

1970b *Raskopki na Altyn-depe v 1969 g.* (Excavations in Altin-depe in 1969), Ashkhabad.

1970c K semantike znakov sobstvennosti epokhi bronzy, *Sibir' i ee sosedi v drevnosti* (The semantics of property symbols during the Bronze Age, in *Western Siberia and its neighbours in antiquity*), Novosibirsk.

1971 Excavations of a Bronze Age burial complex in Altin-depe, *Sovetskaya Arkheologiya* 4, 3–22.

1972 Shestoy sezon rabot na Altyn-depe (The sixth season of operations in Altin-depe). *Uspekhi sredneaziatskoy arkheologii* 1, 49–51.

MASSON, V. M. and SARIANIDI, V. I. 1973 *Sredneaziatskaya terrakota epokhi bronzy* (Central Asian terracottas of the Bronze Age), Moscow.

SARIANIDI, V. I. 1965 *Pamyatniki pozdnego eneolita Yugo-vostochnoy Turkmenii* (Antiquities of the late Chalcolithic of south-east Turkmenia), Moscow.

TOSI, M. 1971 Seistan in the Bronze Age, *Sovetskaya Arkheologiya* 3, 15–30.

VAYMAN, A. A. 1972 The links between the proto-Elamite and the proto-Sumerian written languages, *Vestnik drevney istorii* 3, 124–33.

B. REFERENCES IN OTHER EUROPEAN LANGUAGES

BISCIONE, R. 1973 Dynamics of an Early South Asian Urbanization: the First Period of Shahr-i Sokhta and its Connections with Southern Turkmenia, in *South Asian Archaeology*, ed. N. Hammond, London, 105–18.

CASAL, J. M. 1961 *Fouilles de Mundigak* I-II = *MDAFA* XVII, Paris.

CHILDE, V. G. 1956 *New Light on the Most Ancient East*, London.

CONTENAU, G. 1931 *Manuel d'Archéologie Orientale* II, Paris.

DESHAYES, J. 1969 *Les Civilisations de l'Orient Ancient*, Paris.

DUPREE, L., GOUIN, Ph. and OMER, N. 1971 The Khosh-Tepe Hoard from North Afghanistan, *Archaeology* 24, 28–34.

DURING-CASPERS, E. C. L. 1971 The Bull's Head from Barbar Temple, *East and West* 21: 3–4, 217–23.

FAIRSERVIS, W. A. 1956 *Excavations in the Quetta Valley*, New York.

1967 The Origin, Character and Decline of an Early Civilization, *Am. Mus. Novitates* 2302, 1–48.

1971 *The Roots of Ancient India*, New York.

LAMBERG-KARLOVSKY, C. C. 1970 *Excavations at Tepe Yahya, Iran, 1967–1969*, Cambridge, Mass.

1971 An Early City in Iran, *Scientific American* 224: 6, 102–11.

1972 Tepe Yahya 1971. Mesopotamia and the Indo-Iranian borderlands, *Iran* X, 89–100.

LAMBERG-KARLOVSKY, C. C. and TOSI, M. 1973 Shahr-i Sokhta and Tepe Yahya: Tracks on the Earliest History of the Iranian Plateau, *East and West* 23: 1–2, 21–57.

LENZEIN, H. 1941 *Die Entwicklung der Zikurrat von ihren Anfängen bis zur Zeit der III Dynastie von Ur*, Leipzig.

MASSON, V. M. 1972 Prehistoric Settlement Patterns in Soviet Central Asia, in *Man, Settlement and Urbanism*, ed. P. J. Ucko, R. Tringham and G. W. Dimbleby, London.

MARSHALL, J. 1931 *Mohenjo-daro and the Indus Civilization*, 3 vols, London.

PARROT, A. 1960 *Sumer*, London.

PIGGOTT, S. 1947 A New Prehistoric Ceramic from Baluchistan, *Ancient India* 3, 131–42.

1950 *Ancient India*, Harmondsworth.

SARIANIDI, V. I. 1971 The lapis lazuli route in the Ancient East, *Archaeology* 24, 12–15.

TOSI, M. 1969 Second campaign at Shahr-i Sokhta, *East and West* 19: 3–4, 283–7.

TOSI, M. and PIPERNO, M. 1973 Lithic Technology behind the Ancient Lapis Lazuli Trade, *Expedition* 16: 1, 15–23.

TOSI, M. and WARDAK, R. 1972 The Fullol or Khosh-Tepe Hoard: a new find from Bronze Age Afghanistan, *East and West* 22: 1–2, 9–17.

WOOLLEY, L. 1934 The Royal Cemetery, *Ur Excavations*, II, London-Philadelphia.

1939 The Ziggurat and its Surroundings. *Ur Excavations*, V, Oxford.

28

K. R. MAXWELL-HYSLOP

The Assyrian 'Tree of Life': a Western Branch?

THE origin of the ideas symbolized by the Assyrian sacred tree, as portrayed in its most elaborate form on the Neo-Assyrian reliefs of the ninth to seventh centuries BC, can be traced back to Sumerian religious belief in the third millennium BC and has been discussed by Gadd (1948), Widengren (1951), Van Dijk (1966), Hatto (1970), and Genge (1971). In this brief survey we shall attempt to follow the influences of this concept in early Christian iconography with reference to distinctive representations extant in the Near East, the Latin West, Egypt and North Africa, the Byzantine Empire and Armenia.

The subject has been chosen because its extent is comparable with the wide interests of Stuart Piggott, both geographically and chronologically; in the archaeological field his concern is world-wide and not confined to artifacts; ideas, documentary evidence, mythology or religious belief are all studied with the exactitude of scholarship which has characterized his work on prehistoric Europe and which remains a model for younger students. Meanwhile, the author hopes this *ballon d'essai*, written from an oriental viewpoint, may perhaps be a stimulus towards future investigation by those qualified to write on the many varying aspects of Christian iconography.

The Assyrian version of the Mesopotamian 'Tree of Life' is well known from reliefs and cylinder seals where the king, followed by a human or eagle-headed winged figure, is shown in front of a stylized tree engaged in a ritual, whose purpose was to endow the king with the magical powers of life and strength associated with the tree and thus to identify him with the source of these powers: the tree itself (Gadd 1948).

While the relationship between the distinctively Assyrian version of the sacred tree and Mitannian examples known from Syrian cylinder seals cannot be discussed here, we may note an infinite variety of types on cylinder seals, reliefs and wall paintings dating from the Middle Assyrian period to the end of the seventh century BC. This variety is aptly illustrated by a comparison of the trees on the frescoes from the palace of Tukulti-Ninurta I (1244–1200 BC) (*Ill. 1*) with a ninth-century seal of Mushezib-Ninurta showing the tree growing in a jar and two figures, followed by a pair of eagle-headed genii engaged in a ritual scene (*Ill. 2:1*). Middle Assyrian trees on cylinder seals are usually less stylized; the palm tree can be recognized as a date-palm, and the animals prance or browse in naturalistic vegetation (*Ill. 2:2; 3:1*). In the thirteenth century BC, the eagle-headed figure grasps the tree with one hand and puts his foot on the lower branches (*Ill. 3:2*). Again, in the ninth century BC, the king accompanied by human or eagle-headed genii performs the sacred tree ritual (*Ill. 4*). Winged gods, vulture- or eagle-headed genii are shown kneeling or standing at each side of the tree (*Ill. 5:1, 2*). While unfortunately we have no text actually describing the ritual, the discovery of new fragments of the Etana legend with mention of the *ṣarbatu* tree growing in the shadow of the shrine of the god Adad with nesting serpent (Kinnier Wilson 1969) provides new evidence for the ultimately Mesopotamian origin of some of the details of the Garden of Eden story in Genesis.

The Mesopotamian conception of the close association (or identification) of the king with the

1 Wall paintings from the palace of Tukulti-Ninurta I (1244–1208 BC). Ht. *c.* 55 cm (after Frankfort 1954, Pl. 74B).

2 1, Impression of a seal of Mushezib-Ninurta (*c.* 850 BC). From Tell Arban, north Syria. Ht. 4.9 cm. British Museum no. 89135; 2, Middle Assyrian seal impression. Late fourteenth-thirteenth centuries BC. Rampant bulls, eagle/vultures and a three-branched tree. Behind each bull is a sacred tree. Ht. 3.4 cm. British Museum no. 129547.

3 1, Middle Assyrian seal impression. Seal of Ashur-Rimani. Stag in front of a tree. Thirteenth century BC. Ht. 2.8 cm. Bibliothèque Nationale, Paris, no. 307; 2, Middle Assyrian seal impression. Winged eagle-headed genius picking a branch of the sacred tree. Thirteenth century BC. Ht. 3.8 cm. Pierpont Morgan Library, New York.

4 King Ashurnaṣirpal II (883–859 BC) with winged figures performing rites before the sacred tree. Alabaster relief from the North-west Palace at Nimrud. Ht. 1.78 m. British Museum no. 124531.

5 Impression of a cylinder seal. Neo-Assyrian period. Winged helmeted genii with cone and bucket watering the sacred tree. *c.* Eighth century BC. Ht. 1.8 cm. Musée du Louvre no. AO 22344.

6 Winged figures kneeling in front of the sacred tree. From the North-west Palace of Ashurnasirpal II at Nimrud. Ht. 1.18 m. British Museum no. 124580.

Tree or Plant of Life has been studied by Widengren in detail (1951) and he has followed the literary allusions to this concept from Sumerian and Babylonian sources to Israelitic-Jewish texts. Here it suffices to recall Daniel's identification of Nebuchadnezzar (or Nabonidus)[1] with the cosmic tree which symbolizes his rule over the earth, and also Ezekiel's allegorical description of the tree, the cedar of Lebanon whose 'top pierces the clouds . . .' whose 'boughs stretched wide . . . roots went deep into plentiful waters' and which was the 'envy of every tree in Eden, in the garden of God' (Ezekiel 31:1–9). If Babylonian ideas could have been picked up by Jewish writers as late as Hellenistic times, which may well be the case for the book of Daniel, one would expect to find examples of the artistic expression of these ideas. But how far can the Old Testament form a link between Mesopotamian and early Christian iconography?

The earliest representations of Old Testament scenes occur at Dura-Europos in the third century AD, where the painters of the Jewish synagogue included among the frescoes the vision of Ezekiel and a full-face figure of Abraham (Gough 1973, 29, Pls. 22, 23). As Michael Gough has pointed out, 'Considering that the Jews of Dura departed so far from the letter and spirit of the Second Commendment, it is hardly surprising that their Christian neighbours went farther, and the paintings in their baptistery were of scenes emphasizing the link between the prophecies of the Old Testament and their fulfilment in the New.' At Dura we can find a painting of Adam and Eve and the Tree of Knowledge, and a remarkably similar style for the same scene is used in the Catacomb of Januarius at Naples (*A.C.W.*, Pl. 99) dating from the third century AD.

In following the development of the northern Mesopotamian concept of the Tree of Life as portrayed on Mitannian and Middle Assyrian cylinder seals, it is important to remember that it was probably in the tenth century BC, a peculiarly barren period in Assyrian artistic history, that the author of Genesis 2:9 described the Garden of Eden where Yahweh 'caused to spring up from the soil every kind of tree, enticing to look at and good to eat, with the tree of life and the tree of the knowledge of good and evil in the middle of the garden.' Tradition differs as to the botanical species of the tree in the Israelitic Paradise. While the Assyrian cultic tree was basically a date-palm (Rabbinical sources suggest the olive, date or even a fig tree), the use of the vine in Christian iconography occurs as early as the mid-third century AD and, along with the acanthus, is discussed below.[2] In the Book of the Bee (Budge, ed. 1886) the tree of good and evil is stated to be a fig-tree, and the rod of Moses in this account is regarded as identical to the branch cut off the tree by Adam when he left Paradise. Space forbids discussion of the elaboration of this legend and the superb frescoes of Piero della Francesca at Arezzo;[3] here we will confine our remarks to representations of the Tree of Life in early Christian iconography. Can one differentiate between the use of a tree in Christian decoration when the motif has no apparent symbolic meaning, and its use to denote the ancient oriental concept of the tree watered by the Water of Life, a symbol of both god and king?

For a representation of the Tree of Life as opposed to the Tree of Knowledge, we can find in Egypt a fresco in the cupola of a burial chapel at El Baghawat west of Thebes (*A.C.W.*, Pl. 345; fifth century AD), which shows Daniel and Habakkuk with the *ankh* in his right hand standing by a tree which is nibbled by an animal. While the *ankh* symbol suggests that the artist was depicting the Tree of Life, on the same fresco both the trees of the Garden of Eden are shown, with Adam and Eve and the serpent. One may suspect that the tree grasped by Adam on the 'Carrand' diptych (*c.* AD 380–400) (*A.C.W.*,

[1] See David N. Freedman, The Prayer of Nabonidus, *Bulletin of the American Schools of Oriental Research* 145, 1957, 31 for the substitution of Nebuchadnezzar for Nabonidus by the Palestinian author of Daniel *c.* 165 BC.

[2] Robert Murray's *Symbols of Earth and Kingdom: A Study in Early Syriac Tradition*, Cambridge 1975, appeared after this article had gone to press. This invaluable work, where the rich literary imagery of the Early Syriac fathers is discussed in detail, will be an essential adjunct to the study of iconographical problems. For the symbolism of the Tree of Life and the use of the vine and olive themes in the fourth-century AD writings of Aprahat and Ephrem, see especially the sections 'Christ the Grape and the Tree of Life' (113–30), and 'Christ crucified as the Tree of Life, source of the sacraments' (320–4).

[3] Piero's interpretation seems to have been based on the fourth- and fifth-century versions of Athanasius of Alexandria, the Gospel of Nicodemus and Iacopo da Varazze's *Golden Legend* (1255–1266).

Pl. 196a) with the recently created birds and animals browsing in the branches is again intended to portray the Tree of Life.

An important mosaic which dates from the time of Constantine, in the church at Parenzo (Parentium in Istria, now Poreç in Yugoslavia), was discovered beneath the floor of the present sixth-century basilica. Here we have one of the earliest representations of the source of life (a vine) growing out of a large vase, presumably full of water (*A.C.W.*, Pl. 141), a popular motif which can be found again in the sixth century when a comparable version, with superimposed peacock occurs on the floor mosaic at Classis near Ravenna (*Ill. 7: 1*). A stone balustrade slab, again at Ravenna in S. Appollinare Nuovo (*A.C.W.*, Pl. 262), shows, in place of the peacock, the Cross, placed directly above the vase

7 1, The 'source of life'. Vine tendrils springing from a vase with a peacock perching on the rim. Floor mosaic from Classis, south of Ravenna. Sixth century AD. Accademia delle Belle Arti, Ravenna (after *A.C.W.*, Pl. 263); 2, the 'water of life'. Two deer drinking from an amphora, cf. Psalm 42,1. Floor mosaic from the bapistery of Salona, Dalmatia. Fifth century AD (after *A.C.W.*, Pl. 395).

8 Ivory throne of Bishop Maximianus of Ravenna, *c.* AD 546.

as though it is actually growing out of the vine, and the Cross is flanked by two peacocks to symbolize immortality. The sixth-century sarcophagus of Archbishop Theodore is again decorated with a pair of peacocks and two vines flanking the Chi-Rho monogram (Beckworth 1970, Pl. 101). Another splendid example of this 'source of life motif' from S. Appollinare Nuovo at Ravenna is the relief, on a chancel slab dating from the mid-sixth century, of vine tendrils growing from a vessel below the monogram of Christ and the peacock of immortality (*ibid.*, Pl. 99).

A more elaborate version of the same theme is repeated in ivory on the cathedra of Bishop Maxmianus of Ravenna (AD 546) (*Ill. 8*) where not only does a luxuriant vine grow from the vase, but the composition is elaborated by the

9 The 'water of life'. Two deer browsing by five streams of water in an acanthus scroll. Mosaic from a lunette in the mausoleum of Galla Placidia, Ravenna. *c.* AD 425/426 (after *A.C.W.*, Pl. 394).

addition of birds and two splendid lions at each side of the vessel with their front paws on the acanthus base. Animals, including monkeys, hide in the vine leaves; sheep, ducks, partridges and wild goats nibble the fruit while the opposing peacocks are placed above the heads of the Apostles.

Variations on the theme of the Tree of Life, with motifs obviously taken from Psalm 42 ('As the hart longs for flowing streams so longs my heart for thee O God . . .'), occur frequently in baptistery mosaics. At Salona in Dalmatia, the central vase is flanked by two deer who drink from its waters and there is no growing tree; small trees are shown in the field each side of the vase; the emphasis here is on the water (*Ill. 7: 2*), while on the mosaic forming the lunette on the Mausoleum of Galla Placidia at Ravenna the deer are browsing among the vine and acanthus leaves and the vase is replaced by five streams of water surrounded by flowers (*Ill. 9*).

The Tree of Life of Genesis 2:9, in contrast to the tree of good and evil, was also portrayed growing on a hill watered by streams, illustrating the concept of the tree in Paradise first expressed in literary form in Revelation 2:7 and 22:2: 'Those who prove victorious I will feed from the Tree of Life set in God's paradise' and 'on either side of the river were the trees of life'. Again Venantius Fortunatus, Bishop of Poitiers, in two of his magnificent hymns, identifies the tree with the Cross so that 'those return to life who fled the light of day . . .' and 'Thou shinest planted firm, hard by the running streams and spreadest forth thy leaves decked out with budding blooms and in thy branches hangs the same Vine, whence flows abundance of sweet wine – red with the red of blood.' The Bishop was writing in the sixth century AD, perhaps developing

10 1, The Cross as the Tree of Life. The Cross springs from an acanthus. Twelfth century AD, reproducing earlier motifs. The crucified figure and the two flanking figures were probably added in the thirteenth century AD. Below the acanthus (not shown) are four streams and a pair of drinking deer. Apse mosaic from the upper Church of San Clemente, Rome (after *A.C.W.*, Pl. 474).

10 2, Stylized tree flanked by two crosses. Early tenth century AD. Monastery of Deir es-Suranyi, Egypt (after Talbot Rice).

the old idea of the Christian cosmic tree expressed earlier by Bishop Hippolytus of Rome in an Easter sermon delivered in the third century AD.[4] An apse mosaic from the upper church of San Clemente, Rome, dating from the eleventh century but reproducing earlier motifs from the lower church, shows the development of the idea of the identification of the Cross with the Tree of Life (*Ill. 10: 1*). Here the Cross is planted in a large flowering acanthus whose tendrils form spiral patterns covering the background, while a pair of harts (not shown in *Ill. 10: 1*; see Decker 1958, Pl. 112) are drinking from four streams which water the roots of the tree. Birds perch in the foliage and doves decorate the shaft and arms of the Cross; the figure of Christ and the two flanking figures were later added in the thirteenth century. An earlier version of the acanthus with tendrils forming spiral patterns can be seen on the magnificent mosaics of the Baptistery of the Orthodox at Ravenna (Gough 1973, Pl. 82). Here the base of the plants which surround the medallions is undoubtedly that of an acanthus, but the spirals have more in common with vines than acanthus plants. In the stucco reliefs above with windows, the vine is depicted with realistic leaves and bunches of grapes springing from a pair of jars and deer browsing within the scroll, while on another relief the Cross rises from a stylized acanthus whose spiral tendrils again resemble vines. The plants on the centre dome mosaic (Gough 1973, Pl. 81), which reach the heads of the series of Apostles, bearing martyrs' crowns, to the edge of the circular scene of baptism, can perhaps more readily be described as trees. Michael Gough regards them as 'spikes of acanthus foliage' which are 'purely ornament with no likeness to real vegetation' but in Theodoric's Arian Baptistery the stylization has simplified the tree into a single trunk bearing little or no relation to a living plant (*A.C.W.*, Pl. 412).

While the acanthus combined with animals can be found on fifth-century mosaics at Mopsuestia, Cilicia (Gough 1973, Pls. 62, 66), the branches and vine tendrils, also combined with animals, occur at many sites, notably Dağ Pazari in Isauria; the Basilica of Justinian at Sabratha is also notable in this connection for the magnificent floor design of a huge acanthus plant, from which spring vine tendrils forming oval patterns down the length of the mosaic and clearly supporting vine leaves and bunches of grapes (*A.C.W.*, Pls. 360, 361).

After the period of the Iconoclast emperors ending with the accession of Michael III in AD 843, examples of the Tree of Life can again be found. We know from the accounts of early travellers that in the hall of the great palace at Constantinople there was 'an astonishing golden throne which could be raised into the air, and there was a golden tree beside it, with birds on it which twittered, and in front of it guardian lions that roared. It was made for the emperor Theophilus (AD 829–842) and was the wonder of all that saw it' (Talbot Rice 1962, 148f.). This, like so much of Byzantine art from the city itself, was destroyed. But with the Eastern inspiration of the designs of many of the rich textiles clearly evident, and the Sassanian influence also discernible in both jewellery and metalwork, it would be surprising if the concept of the Tree of Life with its long oriental history was not represented. The importance of Mesopotamia and Syria for the transmission of new ideas and Eastern motifs after the Islamic conquest cannot be overstressed. This has been discussed in detail by David Talbot Rice and we can still find, between the ninth and twelfth centuries, examples of the Tree of Life either as an essential part of the portrayal of the Fall or as the tree of Paradise or closely integrated with the symbol of the Cross.[5] Moreover, in Egypt after the Moslem conquests in the seventh century, the close connections between Coptic and Byzantine craftsmen resulted in a large production of ivories and wood carvings, while decorative work in wood and stucco was used for both Islamic and Christian buildings. Stucco in high relief was used for the wall decoration of the tenth-century monastery of Deir es-Suryani in the Wâdi 'n-Natrûn (*Ill. 10: 2*) and here a stylized tree, a mixture of acanthus, palm and vine, is clearly portrayed between two Crosses, while stylized acanthus foliage is lavishly used round the arches and in the borders of the wall decoration.

Reliquaries also provided an opportunity for the use of the Tree of Life motif, often as a 'leaved Cross'. A gold reliquary described by David Talbot Rice (1959, 318) as 'probably the most important and complete example of the Byzantine jeweller's

[4] P. Nautin, *Une homelie inspirée du traité sur la Pâque d'Hippolyte*, Paris 1950.

[5] Two earrings in the Archaeological Museum, Istanbul, are an apt illustration of the tree-Cross association, as one shows an oriental tree between two birds while on the other a Cross is flanked by the birds (Talbot Rice 1959, Pl.65).

11 Reliquary for the True Cross. Outer container of gold. *c.* AD 960. Limburg on the Lahn. Ht. 48 cm.

art' is closely dated by the inscription to between AD 945 and 963 (*Ill. 11*). The inscription states that the emperors Constantine and Romanos were responsible for its manufacture and, as we know that Constantine VII Porphyrogenitus (AD 913–959) was a practising goldsmith as well as a keen patron of the arts, it is possible that he worked on the frame of the relic himself. The Cross stands on a small stepped base but directly on the stalk of two large acanthus leaves which reach upwards to the cross-shafts. Other examples in silver gilt such as one of the twelfth century (Talbot Rice 1959, Pl. 166; a leaved Cross) and the Cross of Justin II (AD 565–578) (*ibid.*, Pl. 71) echo the close connection between Cross and tree aptly expressed by the Bishop of Poitiers in the sixth century AD. The sixth-century enamel Cross (*ibid.*, Pl. 70) traditionally presented to St Radegonde by Justin II is in the Convent of St Radegonde at Poitiers, and here the Cross is flanked by two stylized acanthus plants worked in different coloured enamels. In ivory, the Tree of Life in Paradise is portrayed on one of the finest Byzantine examples, the Harbaville triptych (*Ill. 12*). Here, on the back of the central panel, the Cross is shown in the Garden of Paradise with rosettes at the centre of the Cross and at the ends of each arm, and it is set among flowers, bushes and animals which are finely executed with a wealth of naturalistic detail. The Cross is flanked by two pointed trees entwined by vine scrolls and birds shown pecking at the bunches of grapes. The letters signifying 'Jesus Christ conquers' reinforce the theme of the Cross, the Tree of Life and Paradise.

The importance of the leaved Cross has been admirably demonstrated by David Talbot Rice with the history of the motif traced through examples dating from the sixth to the eleventh century AD. The development is traced from the naturalistic

12 The Cross in the Garden of Paradise. Reverse of the central panel of the Harbaville triptych. Ivory. Tenth century AD. Ht. 24.2 cm.

form, treated in a classical manner where the Cross is placed above the acanthus, to the more severely stylized representations where the plant has almost become a pattern and is more closely related to Eastern prototypes (Talbot Rice 1950). The stucco eighth-century panel from Ctesiphon (*Ill. 13:3*) is a clear example of the Eastern tree, and an early Christian Cross from Hira near Babylon (*Ill. 13:4*) dating from the eighth century shows the close relationship between the two motifs. Later examples from Greece (*Ill. 13:1, 2*) show an even closer connection between Cross and tree, whose roots form part of the base of the Cross; and for a clearer example of the Tree of Life identified with the Cross it is instructive to remember the unpublished relief at the monastery of Mar Behnam near Nimrud, where the figure of Christ is shown on a Cross which is a clearly stylized oriental sacred tree. Moreover, the Armenian version of the leaved Cross is closely related to the Mesopotamian, and this is well illustrated by a comparison between the leaved Cross carved in wood from Taqrit, Iraq (*Ill. 13:5*) and the *katchkars* mentioned below. A fragment of a stone lintel from the cemetery of Upper Artashet near Dvin (Soviet Armenia) is dated to the sixth-seventh century AD, and here the Cross is simply the upper part of a tree whose stylized leaves turn upwards and meet the arms of the Cross, while the lower roots turn into vine leaves with enormous bunches of grapes which are being picked by two figures (*Ill. 14:1*).

This type of Cross is well known in Armenia, where the *katchkars* (cross-stones) dating from the ninth century onwards portray fantastic Crosses

14 1, Fragment of a stone lintel with a cross framed by leaves and a vintage scene. Sixth-seventh centuries AD. Cemetery of Upper Artashet near Dvin, Soviet Armenia; 2, figure beside a pomegranate tree. Part of a sculptural scene with king and vine scroll. AD 915–921. The East façade of the Church of the Holy Cross, Aght'amar, Turkey (1,2, after Nersessian, Pls. 29, 34).

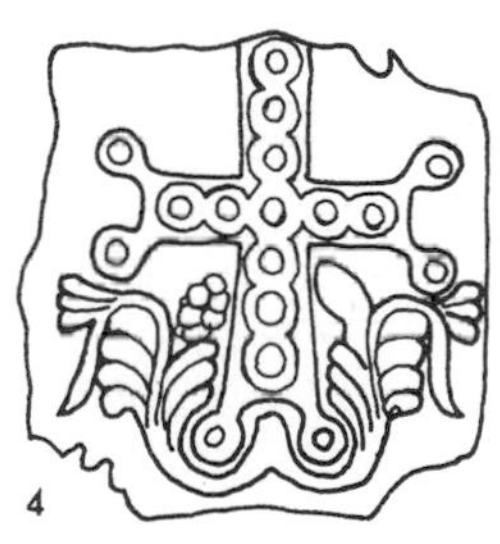

13 1, Leaved cross slab. Tenth or eleventh century AD. Byzantine Museum, Athens 2, leaved cross slab. Daphni, Greece. *c.* AD 1100; 3, stucco panel with tree and birds. Ctesiphon. Sixth century BC; 4, leaved cross on stucco plaque. Hira, Iraq. Eighth century AD; 5, leaved cross on carved woodwork. Taqrit, Iraq. Eleventh century AD (1–5, after Talbot Rice 1963, Figs. 4, 5, 10, 9, Pl. 3).

15 *Khatchkar* (cross slab). *c.* Thirteenth century AD. Geghard near Yerevan, Soviet Armenia.

springing from a naturalistic base of roots and foliage (*Ill. 15*). At Aghtamar, however, in addition to examples of leaved Crosses, the sculptures on the façade of the tenth-century church of the Holy Cross include a Tree of Life (recognizable as a pomegranate) with the animals and attendant (*Ill. 14: 2*) in a purely oriental style which, with the seated figure of the king feasting among the vine scroll, suggests Sassanian rather than Christian inspiration. In the margins of the Armenian manuscripts, while the acanthus is usually stylized and purely decorative, examples can be found where the connection with the Cross survives; the stylized acanthus ends in a Cross on the title page of St Mark's Gospel illustrated in 1262 at Hromlka (Nersessian 1969, Pl. 64), and on the title page of another St Mark's Gospel (*Ill. 16: 1*). For a more naturalistic style we must turn to the highly original Cilician school of illuminators, and to the end of the letters of Eusebius to Carpianius (Nersessian 1969, Pl. 63). Four trees, with birds and flowers growing from the roots, decorate the borders of the page with no

16 1, Acanthus and cross. Illumination from the margin of the first page of the Gospel of Saint Mark. Chester Beatty collection; 2, Christ with Adam and the tree. Part of a mosaic Creation scene. Twelfth century AD. Palatine chapel, Palermo (1, after Lang, Pl. 88; 2, after Talbot Rice 1963, Fig. 150).

17 The Nativity. Mosaic panel in the narthex of the Church of St Saviour in Chora (Kariye Cami), Istanbul. AD 1300–1320.

apparent symbolic significance; and similar plant or tree forms can be found as decoration of many of the canon tablets of Armenian manuscripts, or in the work of Toros Roslin in the thirteenth century. The use of the tree in Annunciation, Nativity and Life of the Virgin scenes, however, both by Roslin and in several of the superb mosaics in the Kariye Cami in Istanbul (*Ill. 17*) and again in a miniature mosaic now in Florence, perhaps echoes the idea of the tree cut down and felled by Ezekiel's 'foreigners, most barbarous of all nations' which has now begun to grow again. From the decapitated trunk a small shoot is carefully delineated, which could signify the Incarnation.[6] Alternatively it might be interpreted as the Tree of Life cut down by Adam's sin in the Garden of Eden, or as a reference to Isaiah 11:1, 'A shoot springs from the stock of Jesse' (Lang 1970, Pl. 85; Talbot Rice 1959, Pls. XXVII, XXXVI, XXXIX; Underwood 1967, 83f., Pls. 99, 100, 102).

The importance of Cilicia, especially in the post-Crusader period, for the transmission of oriental motifs such as the Tree of Life to the West cannot be treated here in a superficial survey. But we can note the fantastic half-human half-animal or bird figures combined with floral motifs of a Cilician gospel of the thirteenth century (Nersessian 1969, Pl. 65) as one of the many possible links with southern Italy and the visual imagery of Abbot Joachim of Fiore (*c.* AD 1135–1202) whose *Figurae* have been the subject of extensive and scholarly study by Marjorie Reeves and Beatrice Hirsch-Reich. Of the five motifs used by Joachim in his complicated system of figures which express his vision of the past and the future, the tree is a dominating image. Dr Reeves has stressed the fact that 'Joachim never attempted a direct representation of the Tree of Life or of the Tree of the Cross',

[6] See Murray (1975, 101f.) for Ephrem's hymns *On the Crucifixion* and *On the Nativity*, '. . . the vine of Egypt, which cut off the sweet stems of the house of Abraham. . . . One tiny shoot sprouted from it and see! it has overshadowed the world with its clusters' and 'The vinedressers came and rendered praise to the shoot that sprang out of the root and stock of Jesse.'

and yet the 'luxuriant and strange flowering of some of Joachim's trees' certainly recalls the vision of the 'trees of life, which bear twelve crops of fruit in a year, one in each month, and the leaves of which are the cure for the pagans' (Revelation 22:2; Reeves 1972, 29). It is impossible here to give even a cursory summary of the ideas behind the *Figurae* of Joachim, and one can only refer to Dr Reeves' magisterial treatment of the subject. While 'the idea of a tree first appears in Joachim's writings as a symbol of continuing human history whose branches must rise and spread throughout all centuries' (Reeves 1972, 30), his Trinitarian view of history required three different trees. There is evidence that Joachim's three interlinked circles can be traced to the influence of Petrus Alphonsi, a Spanish Jewish scientist and converted Christian. But can we find evidence of an oriental source for the form of the trees used in the *Figurae*? Here space forbids more than a hint of such a possibility. Joachim lived in a well-wooded part of Calabria (the Sila district) where magnificent trees were a common part of his environment; yet the trees drawn as the Tree of two Advents and the Tree of the Spiritus Sanctus are fantastic growths, with long straight trunks having sinewy branches of vine leaves or straight branches of stylized acanthus. The trees with side shoots are a mixture of pomegranate, vine and acanthus. The earlier and later Tables of Concords, however, suggest that the artist may well have been familiar with Armenian manuscript decoration; the acanthus decoration and the branches or roots at the base of these two figures are comparable with Armenian work, while the tree with the devil's head (Reeves 1972, Pl. 35) can be compared with the Cilician gospel mentioned above.

Joachim's treatment of the eagle, another leading motif, must also be noted. While the source is Biblical, based on Isaiah 40:31, Ezekiel 1:10 and Revelation 4:7, the bird as portrayed with its multitudinous captions, complicated number symbolism and unequal shaped wings recalls the eagles of Byzantine silks, such as the Chasuble of St Albuin at Bressanone or the Shroud of St Germain l'Auxerrois (Talbot Rice 1959, Pls. XII, 132). But it is the tree eagle figures from the *Liber Figurarum* which represents a tree with the eagle head forming the root and, when reversed, an eagle with the branches of the tree forming the eagle's wings which have been described by Dr Reeves as 'the most curious and magnificent of the whole Liber' (1970, 160). The visual imagery expressed by these superb figures, which can best be seen in the Oxford manuscripts in Bodley, was again based on Ezekiel; but one wonders whether, for Joachim, the close association between the Tree of Life and the eagle, which had existed for centuries before Christ in Mesopotamia and Syria, may have exercised a remote influence on the ideas behind the artistic expression of his complicated and involved system of thought. In Assyria, eagle- or vulture-headed figures were well known for their apotropaic character as guardians of the sacred Tree of Life, protecting the king, and on Phoenician and north Syrian type ivories from Nimrud the close connection between the eagle-headed figure and the tree is apparent in many examples (cf. also Mallowan 1966, II, Pl. 324, copper plaque representing sacred tree, jar with lustral water, antithetical winged griffins). The Etana legend concerning the *ṣarbatu* tree, the eagle, and the use of the plant to assist in the birth of Etana's son, the eagle, who soars up to heaven with Etana on his back, is again relevant here. Joachim of Fiore, when trying to understand the meaning of his vision, considered that divine truth had taken wings as an eagle and flown away above him. Later, he himself mounts the eagle and is carried aloft on the wings of the bird: the *intellegentia contemplativa* who has clarified the vision.

Here we can only suggest that we have a field which any orientalist interested, as was Frankfort, in the transmission of oriental influences (in the fields of both art and thought) to the West cannot afford to neglect. Many years ago Frankfort stressed the importance of silks and Sassanian textiles in the transmission of artistic motifs, and much can now be added to his survey at the end of *Mesopotamian Cylinder Seals* (1939, 316) where he wrote that 'from the ninth century onwards both Byzantium and the West began to receive an increasing number of a group of Oriental productions which were the true descendants of ancient Mesopotamian art.' In 1962 H. W. Saggs briefly referred to this subject (1962, 497f.) and today the extent of the influence of the Mesopotamian concept of the Tree of Life, transmitted via the Old and the New Testaments, the Apocrypha and early representations of the tree and Cross, needs reassessment and much further study. Visigothic Spain, English manuscripts

[7] Roger Cook's *The Tree of Life* (London 1974) was published after this article was completed. In his wide-ranging survey see especially Figs. 77–85 for illustrations from the *Legendary History of the Cross*, 1483 (ed. John Ashton, London 1937).

and Romanesque sculptural art are only some of the fields we might add to this brief survey, which could well end with the tympanum at Kilpeck, Herefordshire or the font at Hook Norton, Oxfordshire.[7]

Space will allow only two final instances where the identification of the king with the tree itself has been translated into a Christian framework. First, the curious nave mosaic of the Palatine chapel, Palermo (*Ill. 16:2*) where the tree is flanked by Adam and Christ, instead of Eve whose birth is shown in another part of the mosaic. Second, the illuminated manuscript of La Somme le Roy, attributed to the Parisian miniaturist Honoré and dated to *c.* AD 1290 (Millar 1953, Pl. IV). The text gives the instructions for the illuminator of the picture of the garden of virtues, and informs us that the centre tree signifies Christ under which grow the seven trees of virtues of which the book speaks. The seven foundations of the garden are the seven gifts of the Holy Spirit which water the garden. The seven maidens who draw from the seven fountains are the seven petitions of the gifts of the Holy Spirit. And for a final example of the distance in both space and time over which the idea travelled, with a magnificent transformation, it remains to quote Pope Alexander IV (1261–1264) who spoke of the University of Paris as the 'Tree of Life in Paradise, the Lamp of the House of God, a well of wisdom overflowing souls that thirsted after righteousness. . . .' (Creighton 1904, 108).

Bibliography

A.C.W. = Van der Meer, F., Mohrmann, C. 1958 *Atlas of the Early Christian World*, ed. M. Hedlund and H. H. Rowley, London.

Beckwith, J. 1970 *Early Christian and Byzantine Art*, London.

Budge, E. A. W. 1886 *The Book of the Bee*, Oxford.

Cook, R. 1974 *The Tree of Life*, London.

Creighton, M. (ed.) 1904 *History of the Papacy*, London.

Decker, H. 1958 *Romanesque Art in Italy*, London.

Frankfort, H. 1954 *The Art and Architecture of the Ancient Orient*, London.

1939 *Mesopotamian Cylinder Seals*, London.

Gadd, C. J. 1948 *Ideas of Divine Rule in the Ancient East* (Schweich Lectures of the British Academy), London.

Genge, H. 1971 Zum Lebensbaum in der Keilschriftkulturen, *Acta Orientalia Arch. Hung.* XXXIII, 321–4.

Gough, M. 1973 *Origins of Early Christian Art*, London.

Hatto, A. T. 1970 *Shamanism and Epic Poetry in Northern Asia*, London.

Kinnier Wilson, J. V. 1969 Some contributions to the Legend of Etana, *Iraq* XXXI, 8–17.

Lang, D. M. 1970 *Armenia, cradle of Civilisation*, London.

Mallowan, M. E. L. 1966 *The Nimrud Ivories*, 2 vols, London.

Millar, E. G. 1953 *An Illuminated manuscript of La Somme le Roy attributed to the Parisian miniaturist Honoré*, (Roxburghe Club) Oxford.

Murray, Robert 1975 *Symbols of Earth and Kingdom: A Study in Early Syriac Tradition*, Cambridge.

Nersessian, S. Der 1964 *Aght'amar. Church of the Holy Cross*, Cambridge, Mass.

1969 *The Armenians*, London.

Reeves, M. and Hirsch-Reich, B. 1970 *The Figurae of Joachim of Fiore*, Oxford.

Saggs, H. W. 1962 *The Greatness that was Babylon*, London.

Strommenger, E. 1964 *The Art of Mesopotamia*, London.

Talbot Rice, D. 1950 The Leaved Cross, *Byzantinoslavica* XI, 70ff.

1959 *Art of Byzantium*, London.

1962 *The Byzantines*, London.

1963 *Art of the Byzantine era*, London.

Underwood, P. A. 1967 *The Kariye Djami*, London.

Van Dijk, J. 1966 Les contacts ethniques dans la Mésopotamie et les syncrétismes de la religion sumérienne. In *Syncrétism*, ed. S. S. Hartman, Stockholm.

Widengren, G. 1951 *The King and the Tree of Life in Ancient Near Eastern Religion*, Uppsala.

Passages quoted from the Bible are from the *Jerusalem Bible*, London, 1966.

Acknowledgments

I would like to express my thanks to Mrs Jane Mackay who has drawn all the figures and to Miss N. K. Sandars, my husband and my father, Sir Charles Clay, for assistance on many points.

Addendum

I am grateful to Mr R. L. Van Nice for the following important note and drawings concerning Santa Sophia in Istanbul which was received during the publication of this article:

During the removal of eroded stucco left from the Fossati repairs of 1847 to '49, three crosses and the Tree of Life built into brickwork between the five windows of St. Sophia's apse were exposed for about two weeks and then again re-covered. The Tree (*Ill. 18*) stands between the last two windows at the north end of the curve of the drum of the aspe, brickwork in which is undoubtedly of the 6th century. The foliated cross (*Ill. 19*), located on the west face of the southeast pier at gallery level, is recorded in Salzenberg's transverse section, BL. IX of his *Altchristliche Baudenkmale von Constantinopel von V bis XII Jarhundert*, Folio Ed., Berlin, 1854. This was also painted over during the Fossati repair, and it remains obscured. . . . [One can note] that the upright stem of the cross is not vertical but inclines away from the nave at the same angle as the deformed face of the pier itself and that, therefore, the cross was *in situ* while deformation was underway.

These hitherto unsuspected details will be delineated in plates now being prepared for Volume II of our survey [R. L. Van Nice (ed.), *Santa Sophia in Istanbul: An Architectural Survey*, Dumbarton Oaks Center for Byzantine Studies, Washington (Vol. I, 1965)].

18 Tree of Life in brickwork of apse of Santa Sophia. Drawn by Diane Gurney after R. L. Van Nice.

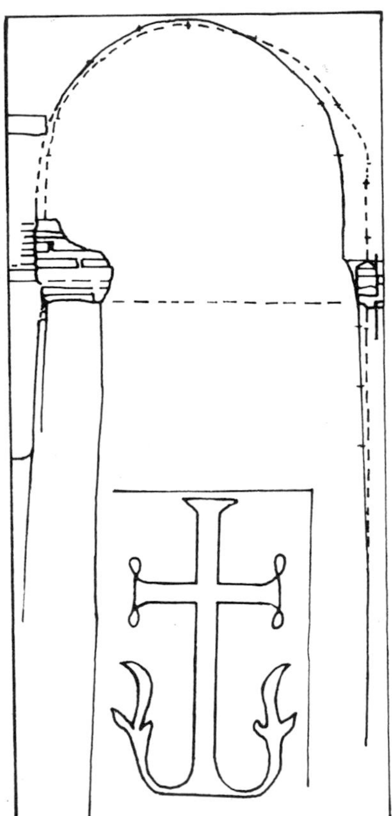

19 Foliated cross on inside of southeast pier of Santa Sophia. Drawn by Diane Gurney after R. L. Van Nice.

29

N. K. SANDARS

Are Myths Luggage?

A FEW years ago Stuart Piggott gave a wise and witty account of a subject too often overlaid with 'philosophy' and even fantasy, where a 'past-as-wished-for' eclipses the 'past-as-fact'. This subject, *The Druids*, is not alone in having suffered the conscious or unconscious manipulation that turns its materials into 'vehicles for the exemplification of a philosophical concept' (Piggott 1968, 14). The raw evidence of the documents is coloured, if not actually cooked, for ends abstract and aesthetic. Frazer was rightly rapped for finding dying gods under every bough, but the search for some 'universal of human nature' continues; preferring a system of symbols to the uncontrollable experience of life as it is lived by particular people (Levi-Strauss 1967, 25ff.). Applied to mythologies its justification is the 'internal relationship of reason' set over against external fact. Those who pursue mythologies pursue a chimaera; which being so, is it not folly in a prehistorian to venture onto such dubious ground?

The answer is that, as well as an anthropological and a sociological, there is an historical facet to mythologies which does indeed concern prehistorians. If 'themes of mythological thought' are really so alike, then either they owe the likeness to some 'universal of human nature', or to contact at an historical moment, and of an historically measurable kind. The question that I will put now (taking a specific example where likeness *has* been canvassed) is, *are* they after all so very alike? One kind of answer may be found in the unexciting particulars that, like the landscape in which a myth is set, are usually passed over as superficial and unimportant beside the universals of a theogony or a succession myth.

Comparisons between Greek and oriental myth and epic have been made ever since the cuneiform texts were first deciphered, and there seems to be, at the moment, something like unanimity in favour of a genetic connection between them. Since the oriental texts are earlier, *they* must be the source of whatever is not purely Greek in Greek mythology. There is *no* agreement, however, on the time, place or nature, of the connection. Professor Kirk is cautious, but he sees in Hesoid's story of Ouranos and Kronos a succession myth coming from early, pre-Hurrian, contacts between the Aegean and Anatolia, or (less plausibly) the Levant and the Aegean. Among oriental sources reflected in Greek mythology he includes the Babylonian Hymn, sometimes erroneously called a 'Creation Epic', the *Enuma Elish*, so named from the first line of its preamble, 'When on high the heavens . . .'. But the date of its composition (around 1100 BC according to Lambert) is incompatible with the early date at which he supposes the connection to have existed (Kirk 1970, 219–20; Lambert 1964, 3–13; but see now Kirk 1974, 259, 268).

Martin West in his commentary on the *Theogony* is also astray in dating *Enuma Elish* too early. According to West the Mycenaeans adopted the 'Succession Myth', which had come ultimately from Babylon, in either Anatolia or Syria or Cyprus, with Ras Shamra a likely point. He thinks that it is closer to Babylonian than to Hurrian writing and that it was handed down from the mid-second millennium BC. He concludes with a blunt and extreme statement, 'Greece is part of Asia, Greek literature is a Near Eastern literature' (West 1966, 31). Walcot, on the other hand, takes the ninth- or eighth-century BC for the crucial period, with a direct line of transmission from Mesopotamia to north Syria, and on to Euboea, with Al Mina 'the obvious place for the Greeks to have acquired knowledge of *Enuma Elish* or any other work of Babylonian literature' (Walcot 1966, 121). This sentence actually gives the game away, for whatever *Enuma Elish* is, it is not a work of literature, and to call it such is a misunderstanding of the known facts.

At first sight creation myths have a neat diagrammatic similarity – when X carried off Y, or A lay with B and begot C. These are interchangeable ciphers if X or A stands for heaven and Y or B for earth, and C their progeny. But my argument will be that, as well as embodying in these terms the major natural forces and solidities of the world, each of the great known cosmogonies presupposes a physical environment, a natural topography, peculiar to the earth as it was known by certain people at a certain time; and that these terms are *not* transferable. Similarities between Babylonian and other cosmogonies can be found by draining the names and actions of the gods of all proper meaning and treating them as a species of algebraic code. In this short article it will be impossible to display the arguments in any detail. My hope is simply that I may set off one or two warning signals.[1]

The names and characters of the Babylonian gods, as they appear in *Enuma Elish,* are a case in point. Even when we can analyze the parts of a name, like An as heaven and Ki as earth, to render *Anki* as cosmos, the modern word bears little relation to its meaning for an inhabitant of Babylon around the year one thousand BC. Akkadian Tiamat is a proper name for one of the primordial beings introduced in the beginning of *Enuma Elish* (Heidel 1951, 98; Speiser 1969, 60–72). Etymologically it is linked to Hebrew *tehom* 'the deep', which is not a proper name, but approximates rather to Akkadian *tamtu* meaning any large body of water.

The cosmogony is only a small portion of *Enuma Elish.* It is not even a true cosmogony because the material world of the Babylonians was eternal. It brings onto the scene the perpetual features of the physical world: swamp, reed-beds, the sea, the banks of silt and the empty skies, a vast theatre for wind, storm and hurricane; and the language of the Hymn reflects the nature of the beings it describes, watery, tempestuous inchoate. So Tiamat represents the sweet water under the earth. When she has been defeated by Marduk, the hero of the Hymn, and far-off mountains are piled on top of her, the rivers Tigris and Euphrates rise from her breasts. She is chaos and misrule, and she is also some sort of watery monster, part woman, part giant clam. The Babylonians found no difficulty in this multiple vision. Apsu, the other primordial being, the sweet waters of the abyss, Lahmu and Lahamu, Anshar and Kishar, the slow precipitation of silt and the low horizons of the swamp, and *Anu* the empty sky: the landscape materialized in these names is not simply a background for the wars and exploits of gods. It is itself those gods, and the names tell the story of the evolution from chaos to the contemporary and familiar earth. *Enuma Elish* is unthinkable away from the topography of the Persian Gulf and Lower Mesopotamia.

It is worth noticing, also, what is left out, for the things left out are precisely those that are put into Greek myths. Hesiod's *Theogony* begins on the top of a mountain. There is snow on the summits and springs of fresh water, oak tree and boulder. When Giants and Titans fight they throw stones at one another from the tops of mountains, but in *Enuma Elish* the only mountain is the one that Marduk piles onto Tiamat; and in the Mesopotamian marshland you must go a long way to find a sizeable stone. The gods there fight with winds, not rocks.[2]

There are many Mesopotamian cosmogonies, all different, and all evidently put together with some specific end in view: generally the glorification of an individual ruler, a city-state, or a technological discovery. The main business of *Enuma Elish* is the exaltation of Marduk and the glorification of his city Babylon. The council of gods, which in the Hymn proclaims the ordering of the universe and Marduk's supremacy, actually took place during the festival of the New Year at Babylon, when the statues of the gods were assembled from neighbouring cities, with the king of Babylon taking the place of Marduk. The festival included a recitation of the Hymn *Enuma Elish* by a priest standing in front of Marduk's statue. Both festival and recitation had the political purpose of securing right government. When Babylon was defeated and Marduk's statue removed by enemies there was no New Year Festival, no recitation, no fixing of destinies. Just as the cosmogony was peculiar to one landscape, the political theme belonged to Babylon alone (Falkenstein 1959, 147; Lambert 1964, 3).

It is difficult to see how this localized cult could have made sense to people living in an entirely different sort of society and natural environment; but this is what we are now asked to believe. We happen to possess an example of what occurred when *Enuma Elish was* taken outside Babylonia, and that no farther than to Babylon's northern neighbour Assyria, where many of the Babylonian gods were already known and worshipped. The Assyrian hero-god was not Marduk but Ashur, and we have the text of a programme of ceremonies performed in the Assyrian capital. In its course *Enuma Elish* was recited, but in very different circumstances to those at Babylon, for the purpose was the opposite one of discrediting Bel-Marduk, probably following the

[1] Some of the evidence was collected by the writer in a paper read to the Hibernian Hellenists at Ballymascanlon in 1973.

[2] Mountains play a greater part in Sumerian mythology but the view most generally held is that the Sumerians themselves were originally a mountain people.

conquest of Babylon by Sennacherib in 689 BC, when Marduk's statue was carried off captive and there was no festival in Babylon (von Soden 1955, 130–66). This travesty, a sort of popular pantomime in simple language, was misunderstood when it was first deciphered; it provides a caution against an optimistic resort to far-flung borrowings and 'influences', especially as the Greeks in the early first millennium (and for some time before) would have heard of the *Hymn*, if at all, through Assyria.

In Babylon itself *Enuma Elish* was still used during the Neo-Babylonian revival of the seventh century, and from there it did eventually reach the Greek world through historians like Berrosus and Phylo of Byblos; but these were learned men consciously collecting 'the wisdom of the ancients'.

Although Assyria blocked the way to the north and west in the ninth and eighth centuries BC, this had not been so in the second millennium when the Canaanite lands and the Phoenician coast lay open to Mesopotamian trade and diplomacy. Akkadian texts have been found at Ras Shamra and Tell el-Amarna, but the possession of a text does not mean that the contents were a part of the religious life and liturgy of the hosts, any more than did the antiquarian tablets in the library of Ashurbanipal at Nineveh. It *is* however necessary to take account of Canaanite and Phoenician writings alongside Greek myths; for Ras Shamra and Cyprus were accessible to Mycenaean Greeks, as well as to orientals.

Sea contacts are known through imported objects, some of which, including Kassite seals, reached mainland Greece. The Ugaritic archives give us a number of mythological writings whose style and tone is quite unlike that of Mesopotamia. The Sumerians and Egyptians had true cosmogonies; the Canaanites and Hittites did not, or none has survived. The Baal Epic is certainly not a creation myth. The gods contest for honours and power, but none really contests the authority of El who has the title 'Father of Mankind' and 'Creator of Created Things'; yet we have no text illustrating this rôle apart from the 'Birth of Dawn and Dusk'. El was not the father, or even grandfather, of Baal (Albright 1968, 104, 108; Gray 1965, 154 ff.; Driver 1956, 71–121). The principal theme of the epic, the introduction of a younger god into an established hierarchy, is too general and diffused to call for direct influences from elsewhere. Père de Vaux clarified the relationship of El and Baal in a careful argument that allows *some* assimilation of *some* aspects of Canaanite religion by a small people brought into sustained and sometimes violent contact with it (de Vaux 1969, 501). This sober assessment of the relationship between the beliefs of the early Israelites and their Syrian neighbours contrasts with more ambitious comparisons between Ugaritic and Greek myths. Only El, as the ideal of sovereignty, could be partially assimilated.

The tone of the Ugaritic writings is often sardonic; there are cutting speeches and harsh irony. When the young warrior goddess Anat comes storming over to El, threatening to make his grey hairs run with blood, El merely says 'I know thee daughter, that thou art gentle, there is no baseness in goddesses' (Driver 1956, 91). These poems from north Syria are set in a landscape that is closer to the landscape of Greek epic poetry than is that of Mesopotamia or of Anatolia. The Olympos of Ugaritic texts is Saphon, Mount Cassius, just visible from Ras Shamra. The seashore plays a part, and there are islands, on one of which lives the craftsman god; but there are also important differences. Gods and goddesses visit each other on donkey-back, the desert is always near, the sea is edged with dunes. In the 'Creation of Thunder and Lightning' the language is closer to that of the Psalms than to Greek poetry. It is possible to make the Ugaritic myths look more Greek by paring away, as irrelevant, all descriptive detail. Any people living in a mountainous coastal country and raising corn, may have gods of the sea, river gods and mountain gods, gods of storm and corn; and if these are interrelated, then parallel patterns are bound to appear. The presence of these parallels eases social contact between neighbouring peoples; they are not in themselves an argument for contact. When Hurrians came to Ras Shamra they had no difficulty in settling down among the local inhabitants, but they kept their own cult practices, only compiling some bilingual glossaries. Hurrian, Sumerian and Babylonian languages were all read at Ras Shamra, but no single Aegean text or name has yet been found, apart from a very little Cypro-Minoan.

The Hittites had a succession myth but it is not a true 'Creation'.[3] It was probably in the first place Hurrian and taken over, with so much else of Hurrian culture, by the Hittites. The sea plays a lesser part in the mythology of this inland people. There is nothing pastoral in the landscape. There

[3] The 'Song of Ullikummi', which is set in north Syria, contains a hint of some lost Creation in the passage beginning 'When they built heaven and earth upon me . . .' (Goetze 1969, 121–5).

are crags and stones; thunder roars; the most holy place, the sanctuary at Yazılıkaya, is a cleft rock where the carved gods stand or ride on mountain peaks. Boghazköy itself is a craggy hill strewn with rocks, quite unlike the tells of the Levant. The peculiar incident of the castrations of the Hurrian Anu and Greek Ouranos, and the subsequent births which, as is made clear in both Greek and Hurrian, are not the usual method of producing progeny, may owe something to each other (Gurney 1952, 190; Kirk 1970, 214; contrast, Walcot 1966, 3). 'The Song of Ullikummi', the diorite man, seems however to describe a local cataclysm, the appearance of an offshore volcanic island (of which the Aegean has not a few) and its extraordinary growth, like the Island of Surtsey that suddenly appeared off Iceland in 1963.

In Egypt, as in Mesopotamia, there were not one but many creation myths. The scenery of the Nile valley and the Nile inundation dominate them all, while the 'Memphite Theology of Ptah' is philosophical thought on a level very different from the myths we have been concerned with. Moreover an Egyptologist has pointed out the extremely limited nature of the interaction between lands as close as Syria-Palestine and Egypt (Kitchen 1969, 94). Even though deities and dedications from the one land appeared in the other, the impact on indigenous cult-practice and theology was minimal.

A creation myth is not the same as a succession myth, and it is cheating to wrench fragments out of other stories to make good the lack. It is also essential to bear in mind the difference between liturgical texts like *Enuma Elish*, and another sort of material which may once have been mythic, but which existed as 'tales of foreign wonders' that are heard and repeated for entertainment. They *can* be conveyed, and retold from chance and slight encounters, at ports and in foreign market-places. 'Wisdom Literature' may also be carried from place to place by itinerant wise men, or passed on by word of mouth between seekers and disciples. But all this is very different to Hesiod's noble structure, or the theogonic fragments scattered by Homer. These are not wonder tales like *Pandora* or *Sinbad the Sailor*. One people does not so lightly 'borrow' its liturgy, its creed, its justification for and picture of the physical world, and the springs of its political health, from another; nor, short of total conquest such as happened with the Aryan gods in India, can they be imposed. The Babylonian cosmogony cannot be thought of away from Mesopotamia and the Persian Gulf. This I believe is self-evident; but the same is true of Greek theogonies. The gods belong to the specific time, the landscape and the people among whom they grew; nor, with very rare exceptions, do they travel in anybody's portmanteau. Zeus and Enlil change places no more than Tigris and Scamander.

In summary my proposal is that the best method for estimating the independence or interdependence of specific myths is by staying nearest home: looking at what we know actually happened between neighbours. We do know something about the frequently bitter relations between Babylon and Assyria, between Israelites and Canaanites, between Egypt and Syria-Palestine; and in all these cases where some degree of documentation exists, the evidence is either for slight and superficial influences, or for rejection. Even where some of the names of the gods are the same, as between Hurrian-Hittite and Babylonian writings, or Israel and Ugarit, the characters and actions are quite different. This is hardly surprising, for between Mesopotamia and the Anatolian plateau lay Assyria, Mitanni and the peoples of north Syria. So before we drag Marduk over the mountains and the sea to the Aegean, we should take serious count of all the physical and political barriers as well as unknown factors such as: who were the gods of Mycenaean Miletus? of Troy and Tarsus? of Rhodes and Cyprus? We are in the dark except in the last case, where excavation has given some clues. Yet these are the places where either walls were raised over which the gods could not peep or, alternatively, Asiatic and Aegean mythologies rubbed shoulders.

My answer to Martin West's assertion is then an emphatic 'no'. Greek literature is *not* a Near Eastern literature, Greek cosmogonies are shaped by the islands, the capes and seas, the mountains and springs of the Greek peninsula and the Aegean coast. These are not decoration but lie at the heart of the poems, a firm anchor that prevents the myth being carried around like so much luggage.[4]

Bibliography

Albright, W. 1968 *Yahweh and the Gods of Canaan*, London.

Driver, G. R. 1956 *Canaanite Myths and Legends*, Edinburgh.

---

[4] I am grateful to Mrs K. R. Maxwell-Hyslop for reading this text and for suggesting improvements.

FALKENSTEIN, A. 1959 Akitu-Fest und Akitu-Festhaus, in *Festschrift Johannes Friedrich*, ed. R. von Rienle *et al.*, Heidelberg, 147–82.

GOETZE, A. 1969 Hittite Myths and Epics: The Song of Ullikummis, in *Ancient Near Eastern Texts Relating to the Old Testament*, ed. J. B. Pritchard, 3rd edn, Princeton, 121–5.

GRAY, J. 1965 *The Legacy of Canaan*, Leiden.

GURNEY, O. R. 1952 *The Hittites*, Harmondsworth.

HEIDEL, A. 1951 *The Babylonian Genesis*, 2nd edn, Chicago.

KIRK, G. S. 1970 *Myth, its meaning and functions in ancient and other cultures*, Cambridge.

1974 *The Nature of Greek Myths*, Harmondsworth.

KITCHEN, K. A. 1969 Interrelations of Egypt and Syria, in *La Siria nel Tardo Bronzo*, *Orientis Antiqui Collectio* IX, ed. M. Liverani, Rome, 77–95.

LAMBERT, W. G. 1964 The reign of Nebuchadnezzar I: a turning point in ancient Mesopotamian religion, in *The Seed of Wisdom, Essays in Honour of T. J. Meek*, ed. W. S. McCullough, Toronto, 3–13.

LEVI-STRAUSS, C. 1967 *The Scope of Anthropology*, London.

PIGGOTT, S. 1968 *The Druids*, London.

VON SODEN, W. 1955 Gibt es ein Zeugnis dafür, dass die Babylonier an die Wiederauferstehung Marduks geglaubt haben? *Zeitschrift für Assyriologie* 51, 130–66.

SPEISER, E. A. 1969 Akkadian Myths and Epics: The Creation Epic, in *Ancient Near Eastern Texts Relating to the Old Testament*, ed. J. B. Pritchard, 3rd edn, Princeton, 60–72.

DE VAUX, R. 1969 El et Baal, le Dieu des Pères et Yahweh, in C. F. A. Schaeffer, *Ugaritica* VI, Paris, 501–17.

WALCOT, P. 1966 *Hesiod and the Near East*, Cardiff.

WEST, M. L. 1966 *Hesiod Theogony*, Oxford.

30

JOSEPH NEEDHAM

Metals and Alchemists in Ancient China

It is a great pleasure to be allowed to contribute to this Festschrift for Stuart Piggott. Some thirty years ago I met him in India and the Middle East on one or another of my perpetual peregrinations to or from China; and since then I have followed his work with continuing admiration – most recently conferring on the ancient history of chariots, carts and waggons. My collaborators and I salute him with a *chhang shêng pu lao – ad multos annos*.

The piece here offered is an edited fragment from Volume V of *Science and Civilisation in China*, where anyone interested will find full references and documentation. To my collaborators, especially Dr Lu Gwei-Djen and Professor Ho Ping-Yü, I wish to acknowledge profound indebtedness; they have always been the *sine qua non* of Chinese history of science and technology.

The romanization system here adopted is that of Wade-Giles, with the substitution of an *h* for the aspirate apostrophe.

From early times it was possible for the Chinese alchemist to use certain ores, and to incorporate in his products certain metallic elements, which were not so readily available in other parts of the Old World. For a variety of different reasons, several of the more unusual or lesser known metals cannot be ruled out. We must reckon therefore with the possibility (or even probability) that some of the aurifictive or aurifactive alloys discovered by the proto-chemists of medieval China contained one or more of these, a circumstance which lends particular interest to the percentage table we shall discuss in what follows. About gold and silver themselves, copper and tin (constituents of age-old bronze), lead and iron in all its forms, nothing need here be said, because of their ubiquity common to all ancient civilizations, but zinc is another matter.

From a date most probably as early as the very beginnings of Chinese alchemy in the third (or even fourth) century BC, the discovery had been made that by adding zinc carbonate, calamine or smithsonite (*lu kan shih*[1])* to molten copper, a new yellow metal, capable of resembling gold very closely to the eye, could be produced. Brass, however, had also been known in Hellenistic and Roman, if not Greek, antiquity, and made in the same way, so there was nothing unique in the Chinese alchemist having zinc at his disposition – not, at least, until some time in the ninth century AD, when, long before competitors in any other culture, he succeeded in preparing systematically supplies of the isolated metal by a kind of distillation. Thenceforward the making of a great variety of brasses could be engaged in with much more precision.

The outstanding case of a metal which through many centuries the Chinese (in a sense) possessed while no one else did is nickel, and they were therefore far and away the earliest people to make cupro-nickel. Since we have been for years familiar with this as the 'silver' of our currency, one can see that there may have been something very real indeed about classical 'argentifaction' in China, and a new light is thrown upon My Lord of Verulam's remark about the Chinese being 'mad upon the making of silver'. China exported to the West ingots and objects made of 'paktong' (*pai thung*,[2] white copper, or better, white bronze) from the sixteenth century onwards, and this was nothing else but cupro-nickel. How far its making went back in that civilization need not detain us here; it is necessary only to add that nickel arsenide ore (the deceptively named kupfernickel, niccolite) simply took the place of calamine, and paktong was made instead of brass. Neither alloy was allowed to contain much tin, which is injurious to the properties of both. Metallic nickel, however, unlike zinc (which is to be our main concern in this essay), was never isolated in traditional China, but rather in Sweden in the eighteenth century. The related element cobalt is another metal which cannot be excluded from Chinese artificial alloys, especially after the beginning of the Ming, when indigenous supplies

* Notes appear on pp. 292–3.

of some cobalt ore were discovered and used for colouring the famous blue-and-white porcelain; but even before that time it had been imported from Persia (*Ills. 1–2*).

Some metals, of course, such as platinum, palladium, and probably cadmium, can be excluded from the medieval Chinese set of metals and minerals with a fair degree of certainty. But aluminium occupies a place by itself, and a somewhat controversial one, for during recent years it has been the centre of a kind of *cause célèbre*, by no means yet resolved. In 1956 a team of archaeologists from the Nanking Museum, headed by Lo Tsung-Chen (1957), excavated at I-hsing[3] in Chiang-su the tomb of a Chin dynasty worthy, Chou Chhu,[4] who died in AD 297. Some twenty metal belt-ornaments were found embedded in dust and dirt near the waist of the body, and many of the fragments of these were submitted to chemical analysis. Though some were mainly of silver and copper, others were almost wholly of aluminium, with up to 10 per cent of copper and 5 per cent of manganese. Since aluminium is a very difficult metal to smelt and was not isolated until after 1827, this discovery aroused intense interest in the realm of metallurgical-chemical history. The large-scale production of aluminium from bauxite by electrolysis was achieved only in 1889, so the discovery of an alloy dating from the third century AD yet having aluminium as its main constituent remains quite extraordinary. Further confirmatory analyses were presented by Yang Kên (1959), who reported a laboratory experiment in which charcoal was used as the reducing agent, aluminium oxide powder and finely comminuted copper as the materials, with borax as a flux; on heating, a small amount of a low aluminium-copper alloy was produced. No metallurgical chemist is prepared to believe, however, that an 85 per cent aluminium-copper alloy could ever be obtained by such methods, nor is there less scepticism about another proposed technique in which caustic alkali would release ionized metallic sodium or potassium to replace successive small quantities of aluminium which would then immediately dissolve in the molten copper. Yang Kên's communication gave rise to a considerable *retentissment* in Western technical journals, and chemists began to range themselves on opposite sides, in China as well as in Europe. While Chang Tzu-Kao (1964) accepted the findings whole-heartedly, they were strongly criticized by Shen Shih-Ying (1962), who himself, however, found high aluminium contents in some of the material, mixed with minor constituents

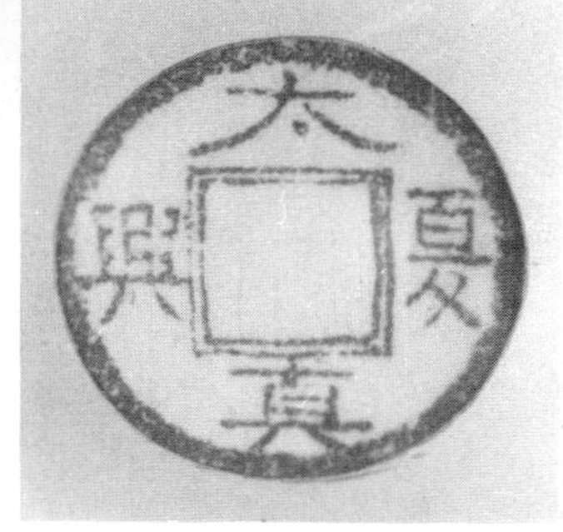

a

b

1 Cupro-nickel coins from medieval China: a, Ta-Hsia dynasty, Chen-Hsing r.p. (AD 419–425), a rubbing; b, Sui dynasty *wu chu* coin (AD 610), photo.

2 Cupro-nickel coins from Greek Bactria (*c.* 230–130 BC): a, Euthydemus II; b, Demetrius II; c, Pantaleon; d, Agathocles; e, Eucratides; f, Heliocles.

which would not be expected in modern aluminium produced by electrolysis – unless it had been re-melted in a not excessively clean workshop. What he threw doubt on was the exactness of the archaeological excavation, but this is just what is difficult to admit for those who are aware of the high scientific standards achieved in such work under the auspices of Academia Sinica during the past two or three decades. The dig was defended in a rejoinder by Lo Tsung-Chen (1963), but pending further developments some of the chemists are at loggerheads with the archaeologists on the matter.

For us the lesson seems to be that for the present it would be unwise to rule out the possibility that some medieval Chinese alchemical alloys may have contained aluminium. After all, the spagyrical metallurgists were constantly mixing metals and minerals and heating them together, while temperatures quite sufficient to melt cast-iron had been available since the late Warring States period. The question also remains to be answered whether these aluminium-copper alloys, if genuine, were obtained intentionally or by accident due to the use of particular ores. The argument that the secret, if such it was, could hardly have been altogether lost in later periods, is rather a weak one, for the Chinese alchemists were not inclined to be talkative about their special triumphs, and in the secretive period of medieval science, processes could only too easily be lost with their authors.

Now the most obvious way to imitate gold without using a lot of the precious metal was to dilute or 'debase' it with other metals, and this was always aided by the fact that gold keeps so much of its colour on dilution, though the tint changes very appreciably. Quite a variety of 'golden' tints can easily be produced. Lists of such appearances from ancient texts have been preserved from Babylonia and from Ancient Egypt. Debasement of one kind or another is of course the simple explanation of the *diplosis* so often referred to by the Alexandrian artisans and aurifactive philosophers. It must also be the meaning of the statement in the *Shen Nung Pên Tshao Ching*[5] that copper sulphate (*shih tan*[6]) can be used to 'prepare' gold and silver (*chhêng chin yin*[7]).

Table 1 contains mostly alloys that are still useful in the goldsmiths' trade today, but those which were made by the Hellenistic proto-chemists – and certainly by their colleagues in ancient China also – need not have been 'useful' in the modern commercial sense, where good malleability and ductility are required, as long as they looked attractive and were not too curiously enquired into by cupellation. Palladium and probably cadmium were no doubt impossible constituents for ancient and medieval workers at either end of the Old World, but aluminium is, as we have seen, just conceivable in China. Gold, silver and copper in many different proportions must have been the staple manufacture both in East and West, but it is clear from the texts that in the Hellenistic region, and doubtless in China also, other metals were frequently introduced, especially tin, lead, zinc, and arsenic. Sometimes these were all compacted first, as in the case of the whitish metal *claudianum*, so named from the emperor Claudius (AD 41–54) and consisting of a mixture of copper, tin, lead, zinc and arsenic, afterwards alloyed with small amounts of gold or silver. This was essentially a gold-containing brass, not unlike the Talmi or Abyssinian gold of more recent times, though also possessing a little lead and arsenic; the last would have increased the hardness and brittleness though perhaps this effect was cancelled out by the lead. The only other noteworthy compositions in Table 1 are the Japanese alloys. The discovery here was that very small amounts of gold in an alloy give it the property of accepting certain remarkable colours when 'bronzed' in a dip, and it seems most probable that this kind of thing was first done in China, though, as so often, brought to perfection in Japan.

This brings us back to zinc. Of the multifarious alloys which were capable of looking very like gold and silver without having any of the precious metals in their composition at all, the most ubiquitous are the brasses and the bronzes. Some varieties of these can resemble gold and silver quite closely in appearance. So much is this the case that varieties of brass containing from 10 to 35 per cent Zn are, when comminuted to the form of very fine flakes, the principal constituents of gold paints at the present day. The characteristic golden colour persists strongly up to some 40 per cent Zn, after which the metal looks reddish, then white, especially if some nickel is added to make it a kind of cupro-nickel. Above 66 per cent Zn the brittleness becomes too great to give the alloys much usefulness.

In AD 1745 the ship *Gotheborg* was wrecked on a submerged rock near Gothenburg, her home port in Sweden, with the loss of a full cargo of porcelain, silk, tea and zinc, loaded at Canton eighteen months previously. About 1870 divers recovered most of the porcelain and some of the zinc ingots; these, upon analysis in 1912, proved to be of a purity corresponding to 98.99 per cent Zn, no copper,

Table 1 *Diluted or 'debased' golds (percentage compositions)*

	Au	Ag	Cu	Sn	Zn	Cd	Fe	Al	Pb	
'Dilutions'										
22-carat (coinage) gold	91.6	—	8.3	—	—	—	—	—	—	
hardened gold	91.6	—	—	—	8.3	—	—	—	—	must not go above 17 per cent Zn
'green' gold	75	12	9	—	—	4	—	—	—	a form of *electrum* or *asem*
v. pale yellow gold	33	66	—	—	—	—	—	—	—	above 50 per cent Ag tends to white
bright yellow gold	52	26	22	—	—	—	—	—	—	very like *Corp. Alchem. Gr.* I, xix, the *diplosis* of Eugenius
pale red gold	64	11	27	—	—	—	—	—	—	
bright red gold	50	—	50	—	—	—	—	—	—	
grey gold	80	10	—	—	—	—	10	—	—	
blue gold	75	—	—	—	—	—	25	—	—	
7-carat gold	29	33	38	—	—	—	—	—	—	lowest habitually used in jewellery
watch-bearings anti-friction metal	37.5	22.9	27.1	—	—	—	—	—	12.5	
Nuremberg gold	2.5	—	90	—	—	—	—	7.5	—	
scintillating purple gold	78	—	—	—	—	—	—	22	—	
Japanese 'black gold'										
shakudo	1–5	1–2	90–98	—	—	—	—	—	—	
shibu-ichi	0.1	40	59.4	—	—	—	0.5	—	—	
Talmi or Abyssinian gold	0.5–1.5	—	85–94	1	6–12	—	—	—	—	essentially a gold-containing brass
Leiden papyrus X, no. 31, *chrysocolla*	28.5	14.25	57.25	—	—	—	—	—	—	like gold solder

nickel, silver, arsenic or lead being present, only a little iron and antimony. 'The beautifully bright fracture and the purity of this zinc', wrote Hommel, 'would certainly be the delight of more than one manager of our own days, who has to resort to all kinds of impure ores with which to fill his retorts.' (Hommel 1912) And indeed under the name of tutenag (derived from *tūtiya*, but spelt in a hundred ways) zinc metal had been an important article of export commerce from China to Europe since about 1605. Though rightly identified with 'spelter', and used to make brass, its origin and preparation were not understood. On 29 May 1679 Sir Thomas Browne wrote to his son asking 'what *is* tooth-anage?'. In 1751 the industrial lexicographer Postlethwayt still did not know how it was made, but Staunton, as the result of his visit to China with the Macartney embassy, understood it well and explained it in his book of 1797. From 1699 onwards zinc was used for air-tight containers in the tea trade, especially in the form of an alloy with lead known as 'canister metal'. The encyclopaedists of East Asia were not always themselves much clearer in the mind about zinc, as one can see from the entry in the *Wakan Sanzai Zue*[8] of 1712, based on Wang Chi's[9] *San Tshai Thu Hui*[10] of 1609:

Aen (*ya chhien*[11]), also called *totamu*,[12] a word derived from some foreign language.

We really do not quite know what this (metal) is, but it belongs to the category (*lei*[13]) of lead, wherefore it is called 'inferior lead' (*ya chhien*[14]). It comes in plates over a foot long, five or six inches wide and less than an inch thick. It is obtained by smelting. There is also a kind called 'medicinal rubbings' (*yakuken*[15]), which may be in appearance like flower petals [probably flakes].

That which comes from Kuangtung province is the best, while that from Pa-niu in Tung-ching (Indo-china) is less good in quality. Nowadays in the making of vessels of brass (*kara kane*,[16] *thang chin*,[17] *shinchū-*,[18] *chen thou*[19]) it is indispensable to add *aen*, so this metal is very valuable. It is probably made by the transformation of calamine (*lu kan shih*) in furnaces.

3 Zinc smelting in the *Thien Kung Khai Wu*. The illustration in Thao Hsiang's edition of 1927, taken from a Japanese edition of 1771 and from the *Thu Shu Chi Chhêng* encyclopaedia of 1726. These sources reproduced drawings done about 1690, some of which were used in the *Kêng Chih Thu* (1696, 1739), the Chhing encyclopaedia (1726) and the *Shou Shih Thung Khao* (1742).

4 Zinc smelting in the *Thieu Kung Khai Wu*. The illustration in the original edition of 1637. *Ills. 3* and *4* both have the caption *Shêng lien wo chhien* (Distillation and magistery of mean lead).
The interpretation of this stack of crucibles in a pile of coal has caused difficulty. Sung Ying-Hsing's text says only that the smithsonite ore from Thai-hang Shan (the mountains between Shansi and Hopei) is filled into the crucibles, the lids of which are sealed on with mud slowly dried to prevent cracking and leakage, then they are piled in alternate layers with coal and charcoal briquettes, resting on a base of wood kindling. At red heat metallic zinc is formed within the crucibles.

This description has satisfied some writers, such as Li Chhiao-Phing and the Suns, yet it is clearly incomplete. St Julien & Champion suggested that CO and finely divided carbon from the pile passed in through the porous walls of the crucibles, thus reducing the ore, and believed that a second fusion was necessary to separate the metal from some kind of slag derived from impurities. This follows Sung's text but ignores the caption. Partington thought that the coal was put into the crucibles along with the zinc carbonate, and that the metal sublimed to the under surface of the lids. This contradicts the text though going some way to satisfy the caption.

It was W. Hommel (1912) who observed that the illustrations seem to show two kinds of crucibles; this is even clearer in the old Ill. 4 than in the later, more 'artistic' Ill. 3. He envisaged that one kind of crucible formed the retorts, while the other type served as receivers, each pair being connected by a short curved tube not noticed either by the draughtsman or in the very brief description. This interpretation gains in probability by the clear wording of the caption. And this would have been the procedure first adopted in the late ninth or early tenth century – a long time before the oldest European account of the metal by Libavius in 1606.

The pharmaceutical natural histories say that calamine ore was mixed with copper to make brass (*thou shih*[20]); there is no doubt of this, but we are not sure how it was done.

Other writers were more precise, and good statements can be found in the *Wu Li Hsiao Shih*[21] of 1664, while the classical account of zinc metal distillation occurs in 1637 in the *Thien Kung Khai Wu*.[22] In all these texts the term for zinc is *wo chhien*,[23] 'poor' or 'mean' lead, but Sung Ying-Hsing[24] was mistaken in saying, as he did, that this was a modern one, and implying that zinc had not long been known (*Ills. 3–4*).

Before giving the oldest occurrence of the name that we can find, a word must be said about the use of almost pure zinc coins in the Ming dynasty earlier than the time of Sung Ying-Hsing, a practice which continued into the Chhing (*Ill. 5*). The nature of this metal (from 97.6 to 99 per cent pure) was first realized by Sage, who in 1804 analyzed a coin

which may have been contemporary with him and cannot have been older than 1723. A careful study by Leeds (1955) long afterwards revealed that the minting of these matt grey coins could be demonstrated from 1402 onwards, through the Yung-Lo and Hsüan-Tê reign-periods, again in the middle of the sixteenth century, and for the first four decades of the seventeenth, then onwards from the beginning of the reign of the Khang-Hsi emperor in 1662. Chinese historical records of the Ming often mention brass coinage, but so far no textual reference has been found to the use of the *wo chhien* metal alone.

We are now in a position to look at the oldest occurrence of this term. It is in the *Pao Tsang Lun*[25] (Discourse on the Precious Treasury of the Earth), datable to AD 918, and it occurs in a discussion of lead and its relatives. Chhing Hsia Tzu[26] (whoever he was) said:

> Of lead there are several sorts. The lead from Persia, hard and white, is the best there is. 'Nodal' lead (*tshao chieh chhien*[27]) comes from Chien-wei[28] (modern Chia-ting in Szechuan); it is the essence of silver. 'Silver-restraining, or controlling' lead (*hsien yin chhien*[29]) is the lead from silver mines; it harbours within it the five colours, which is truly marvellous. Then there is the lead from Shang-jao[30] (in Chiangsi) and that from Lo-phing[31] (in Shansi), second only to that from Persia and Chien-wei. Fu-pan[32] lead is the precursor (*miao*[33]) of iron, and cannot be used. *Wo chhien*[34] ('poor' lead, i.e. zinc) can however be alloyed with other metals (*kho kou chin*[35]).

Wo chhien was probably not the only term for zinc metal at this period, for we sometimes meet with the expression *pai chhien*,[36] 'white lead', as in the *Tan Fang Chien Yuan*[37] (Mirror of Alchemical Processes and Reagents), written by Tuku Thao[38] just before the Sung, i.e. about AD 950. This is a term which has continued in use, along with *wo chhien*, down to the present time, contrasting with *hei chhien*,[39] 'black lead', which has always meant lead itself. The thing to remember then is that we can be sure of the existence and use of isolated zinc metal from AD 900 onwards.

We are now confronted with a group of ambiguous ancient words, *yin*,[40] *pai hsi*[41] (white tin), *hsi*[42] (tin), *hsi la*[43] or *hsi* and *la*,[44] *pai la*,[45] *lien*,[46,47] and *lien hsi* or *lien* and *hsi*, finally also *lien*.[48] Here it will be easier to reverse the method we have been using, and proceed from the most ancient mentions onwards. When the *Shan Hai Ching*[49] (Classic of the Mountains and Rivers, *c.* sixth to third century BC) speaks of *pai hsi*[50] produced at a mountain site, it has been thought to mean tin, yet Kuo Pho in his commentary, *c.* AD 300, says that *pai hsi* is the same as *pai la*.[51] In the *Erh Ya* dictionary (*c.* fourth century BC) *yin*[52] is given as a synonym for *hsi*[53] (tin), yet Kuo Pho comments again about AD 300 that this is the same as *pai la*.[54] The *Yü Phien* dictionary (AD 543) connects by saying that *yin*[55] is the same as *pai hsi*.[56] One might then write off *pai hsi*, *la* and *pai la*, as simply tin, were it not for the fact that in subsequent centuries they demonstrably meant something else. Consequently this something may have existed in Kuo Pho's time, and he (after all a layman) may have confused it with tin.

We must follow the fortunes of all these words and phrases independently, if not quite in chronological order. One of the interesting features of the economics chapters of the dynastic histories is that when speaking of coinage they sometimes give aggregate figures for the amounts of metal used yearly in the official mints, hence the composition of the prevailing alloy can be estimated, and this

5 Zinc coins of the Ming dynasty (AD 1368–1644): 1, Yung-Lo r.p.; 2, Hsüan-Tê r.p.; 3, Lung-Ching r.p.; 4, Thai-Chhang r.p.

can sometimes be confirmed by chemical analysis of extant coins. Thus in the *Sung Shih*,[57] relating to about the year AD 1092 and the premiership of the reformer Tshai Ching[58] (AD 1046–1126), we can read: 'He now advocated the use of "mixed tin money" (*chia hsi chhien*[59]). . . . For the making of every thousand coins, there were used eight catties of copper, four catties of black tin, and two catties of white tin.' Thus in a simple ratio there was 'black tin' and 'white tin' but not ordinary tin. From the *Yü Phien* dictionary we know that *hei hsi*[60] (black tin) was lead, so it would seem that the 'white tin' was zinc, and this is strikingly confirmed by modern analysis of coins from the Shao-Shêng reign-period (1094–1097), though those of neighbouring periods do not contain much zinc. The agreement is even quantitative, 14.5 per cent Zn being expected from the text, and 13.1 per cent obtained. Stepping back a little, *pai hsi chin*[61] occurs in the list of artificial golds given by the *Pao Tsang Lun*[62] (AD 918), where it may mean some form of 'debasement', probably using tin, zinc and lead; and *pai hsi yin*[63] similarly occurs in the parallel list of false and true silvers given in the *Jih Hua Chu Chia Pên Tshao*,[64] indicating an alloy based on a similar dilution of the precious metal. Since all these dates fall within the metallic zinc period we need not be hesitant in the identification, though perhaps *pai hsi* could also mean (especially in earlier times) an alloy of zinc with tin and lead. The term occurs sporadically later with the meaning of zinc (or its alloys), as in the *Chin Tan Ta Yao Thu*[65] of 1331, an important epitome of alchemy valid for its physiological as well as its laboratory form; and again in a travel book, the *Tao I Chih Lüeh*[66] of *c.* 1350, the author of which, Wang Ta-Yuan,[67] found plenty of it in the Malayan country Tan-Mei-Liu.[68] But then it seems to die out, presumably because *wo chhien* became the dominant term for metallic zinc.

Now for *la*, *hsi* and *la*, and *pai la*. While for Kuo Pho[69] in the Chin (*c.* AD 300) *pai la*[70] was simply a synonym of tin (*hsi*[71]), it was obviously something else, perhaps better known, in the Sui. The *Yü Phien*[72] (AD 543) defines *la* as 'the *la* that goes with *hsi* (tin)' or 'the *la* of tin' (*hsi la yeh*[73]). Referring to AD 585 the *Sui Shu*[74] says:

At that time (i.e. formerly) much coinage was used which was partly of tin and *la*. Now *hsi* and *la* were cheap, and many were anxious to make profit thereby. Private minting therefore could not be stopped, but now an edict forbade it, closing the tin and *la* refineries so that the casting (of such coins) by individuals among the people could not go on.

So *la* was not tin but something associated with tin. This is proved again by the *Hsin Thang Shu*[75] in several places. It says, for instance, that in the I-Fêng reign-period (AD 676–678) there was much private coining with copper, tin and *la*, as also in the Thien-Pao reign-period (AD 742–755). It then goes on:

In the 11th year of the Thien-Pao reign-period (AD 752) there were in the whole country ninety-nine mints, with thirty workers in each. Each mint manufactured annually 3,300 strings of cash, using for this purpose 21,000 catties of copper, 3,700 catties of *la* and 500 catties of tin.

The resulting composition, assuming that *la* was zinc, would be 83.5 per cent Cu, 2 per cent Sn and 14.5 per cent Zn, but coin analyses from a neighbouring period do not support that assumption. *La* could conceivably have been a brass, but more likely it was an alloy of tin and lead with some zinc; then the figures might well agree. Triple alloys of this kind may indeed give the clue to the solution of the whole problem even far back into antiquity.

The coinage techniques used in the Thang seem to have been continued during the Sung, perhaps even after the distillation of zinc from calamine had been discovered, judging at least from an interesting text relating how a metallurgical expert of the former Southern Thang dynasty was commissioned to report on the best methods for adoption. The *Sung Shih*[76] says:

There was a scarcity of copper, tin and lead, and doubt about the best alloy. After enquiry there was found among the Administrative Secretaries a man named Ting Chao,[77] who had been an official at the court of the Southern Thang dynasty (AD 937–958, in the Wu Tai period), and who knew Jao (-chou)[78] and Hsin (-chou)[79] and other regions where there were mountain valleys producing copper, tin and lead. This civil servant was accordingly given authority to investigate the former methods of casting and to call up men to mine the deposits of ores. The result was that the methods used at Yung-phing[80] were found to be the best, and these were the same as those which had been used in the Thang dynasty during the Khai-Yuan reign-period. In due course Ting Chao returned to the capital to make his report.

All this took place about the year AD 977. If it implies, as seemingly it does, that *la* continued in use during the Sung, the regularly high amounts of lead in the coins, together with the varying amounts of zinc, could be explained by an irregular composition of the product derived from mixed ores, metallic zinc perhaps being sometimes volatilized and lost more fully than at other times. Finally *la* appears again as part of the tribute of the Malayan country of Tan-Mei-Liu in AD 1000; this is clear evidence that there was an important source of zinc there, whence came brass itself as well as what may be suspected of being a variable-content Zn-Pb-Sn alloy. Once again, after the tenth or eleventh century the name of *la* dies out, presumably because the new availability of metallic zinc ruined the old production and import of the natural mixed product of zinc, lead and tin.

We have still not dealt with *lien*,[81,82,83] but it is rewarding in that it takes us back further than any of the terms in the preceding paragraphs. It occurs in the *Shih Chi*[84] (finished by 90 BC), which says that *lien*[85] and *hsi*[86] (tin) are produced near Chhangsha (in Hunan). Hsü Shen[87] (AD 121) gives it the metal radical and explains it as belonging to the class of copper (*thung shu yeh*[88]). No one has found the word in pre-Han writings so far, but there are several occurrences of it in the *Chhien Han Shu*,[89] e.g. in relation to government requisitioning in AD 10, and especially in connection with Wang Mang's[90] coinage. It says that 'when Wang Mang ascended the throne (in AD 9, as the first and only Hsin[91] emperor) he changed the rules of the Han and made coins of copper mixed with *lien* and *hsi* (*chieh yung thung, hsiao i lien hsi*[92])'. Modern analyses of Hsin coins show that they are mostly copper, with variable amounts of other metals, tin up to 7 per cent, zinc up to 7 per cent and lead up to 12 per cent. This would be consistent with the intentional addition of small amounts of tin, and of zinc-lead-tin alloys of variable composition; these other metals can certainly not have been impurities in the copper, especially as the literary evidence states that *lien* and *hsi* were added. What is also interesting is that the *Han Kuan I*,[93] a book about the Han bureaucracy written or published by Ying Shao[94] in AD 197, says that Wang Mang's coins were called Pai Shui Chen Jen,[95] i.e. 'White-Water Adepts', a distinct indication of the role of his Taoist alchemists in the 'adulteration' of the bronze. It only remains to add that in recent centuries the word *lien*[96] has been used for zinc in Yunnan province. This change of orthography may perhaps have been a local usage accompanying the change from the making of the old mixed metal to the preparation of pure metallic zinc.

To sum it up, the unravelling of these ancient words takes what was essentially zinc-capture back to the second century BC. What mineral complex could have yielded mixtures of zinc and lead that could have been combined with tin to make *lien* and *la*? There are, in fact, many, for example in Australia at Broken Hill in New South Wales a sulphide ore consisting of an extremely intimate mixture of zinc blende and galena occurring on a vast scale. It is very variable in composition, the crude material containing from 10 to 20 per cent zinc, 15 to 25 per cent lead and a small amount of silver, in a gangue of rhodonite, garnet, quartz and calcite. This has been a great source of the metals in question for many years, and smaller amounts of something similar may well have been worked in China in ancient times, as they are now. Indeed the chief production of zinc and lead in this century and the last has been at the Shui-khou Shan[97] mine in Hunan, south-west of Chhangsha – exactly the region where Ssuma Chhien said about 100 BC that the *lien* came from. Its ore gives about 28 per cent zinc and 29 per cent lead, so it is richer than Broken Hill. Another source is the Kung Shan mines in Yunnan, worked until recently by traditional methods, and smaller centres near Thêng-yüeh. We may thus not be far wrong if we visualize the regular production of alloys of zinc, lead and tin from the second or third century BC at least until the isolation of zinc in the ninth or the tenth century AD. Ssuma Chhien's *lien* and Ting Chao's *la* had a long run, and perhaps were little different from the 'canister metal' of the eighteenth-century China tea trade. And (to make contact again with the third rail of our exposition) by the same token *lien* and *la* (as well as calamine perhaps) were available to the alchemists, certainly by Li Shao-Chün's[98] time, conceivably by Tsou Yen's,[99] for the making of brass as artificial gold.

As now we leave this topic, it is worth while to look at a text which records something that happened in Ssuma Chhien's own life-time. Talking of the people who were occupying the tracts from Ta-Yuan (Ferghana) westwards to An-Hsi (Parthia) during the second half of the second century BC, Ssuma Chhien wrote:

> These countries produced no silk or lacquer, nor did they know the technique of casting (*chu*) iron for pots and pans and all kinds of useful implements. . . . When some deserters from the retinue of the Chinese embassy (*Han shih wang tsu*[100]) had settled there, however, they taught them to cast weapons (of iron) and many other useful things. And when (the people of these parts) got hold of Chinese yellow and white metal (*tê Han huang pai chin*[101]) they immediately used it for (casting) utensils and not for coining money.

The introduction of iron-casting into Central Asia at this time, *c.* 110 BC, remains a focal point of interest for that subject, but what matters for us here is the interpretation of the last sentence. One could suppose that the yellow metal (if not a much-debased low-carat gold) was a brass of some kind, or just possibly of course a medium-tin bronze. Similarly the white metal could have been a high-tin bronze like speculum metal, or, more interestingly, a cupro-nickel like the paktong already mentioned, or evidently a silver greatly diluted with tin or with the Zn-Pb-Sn alloy called *lien* and *la*. One thing at any rate is certain, namely that the Chinese were surprised that the Ferghanese-Parthians used it for vessels rather than for coinage; this suggests (*a*) that the metals were among those used for minting within China, and (*b*) that the Central Asians at that time lacked a money economy in which coins would have been useful. Hence the interest of some of the analyses which have been made of coins from the Former Han period. Coins of 186 BC have as much as 25 per cent lead, while those of 175 BC as much as 4 per cent zinc. The special interest of these lies in the fact that they date from the period preceding the 'anti-coining' edict of 144 BC which betrays the existence of so much deceptive alloying and aurifiction, indeed a whole tradition of it. But so far the analyses have been few, and it is greatly to be hoped that more will be made. The first half of the second century is a time of great importance for the history of metallurgical knowledge and practice in Chinese culture, and more light on it is urgently needed. In the meantime, one suspects that the 'yellow and white metals' which the Ferghanese-Parthians received from China were fairly complex alloys, certainly not purified gold and silver.

Having now come to the border of the brass country, one descries, on looking back, another of those curious parallelisms which have been met with before, situations where certain inventions or discoveries appear almost simultaneously at the two ends of the Old World. The inventions of the water-mill, and of rotary milling itself, are cases which spring to mind. Apart from the transient Homeric use of natural mixed ores of copper and zinc (if that was really what it was), brass seems to have become current during the third century BC both in the Greek and the Chinese culture-areas. This suggests an intermediate source from which the knowledge would have spread out in both directions. The later mentions of brass as a Persian export would point to the Iranian culture-area as the place where we ought to look, but unfortunately the early history of science and technology in that region is still so poorly documented that we know of no better evidence than in the other two, equally obscure, examples.

Notes: Chinese characters

1 爐甘石
2 白銅
3 宜興
4 周處
5 神農本草經
6 石膽
7 成金銀
8 和漢三才圖會
9 王圻
10 三才圖會
11 亞鉛
12 止多牟
13 類
14 亞鉛
15 藥研
16 唐金
17 唐金
18 真鍮
19 真鍮
20 鍮石
21 物理小識
22 天工開物
23 倭鉛
24 宋應星
25 寶藏論
26 青霞子
27 草節鉛
28 犍為
29 衡銀鉛
30 上饒
31 樂平
32 負版鉛
33 苗
34 倭鉛
35 可勾金
36 白鉛
37 丹方鑑源
38 獨孤滔
39 黑鉛
40 鈏
41 白錫
42 錫
43 錫鑞
44 錫, 鑞
45 白鑞
46 連
47 鏈
48 鎌
49 山海經
50 白錫
51 白鑞

52 鈏
53 錫
54 白鑞
55 鈏
56 白錫
57 宋史
58 蔡京
59 夾錫錢
60 黑錫
61 白錫金
62 寶藏論
63 白錫銀
64 日華諸家本草
65 金丹大要圖
66 島夷志略
67 王大淵
68 丹眉流
69 郭璞
70 白鑞
71 錫
72 玉篇
73 錫鑞也
74 隋書
75 新唐書
76 宋史
77 丁釗
78 饒州
79 信州
80 永平
81 連
82 鏈
83 鎌
84 史記
85 連
86 錫
87 許慎
88 銅屬也
89 前漢書
90 王莽
91 新
92 皆用銅殺以連錫
93 漢官儀
94 應劭
95 白水真人
96 鎌
97 水口山
98 李少君
99 騶衍
100 漢使亡卒
101 得漢黃白金

Bibliography

C/Han Chhien Han (Former Han dynasty)
H/Han Hou Han (Later Han dynasty)
S/Han Southern Han (dynasty)
H/Shu Hou Shu (Later Shu State)

A. Old Chinese References

Chhien Han Shu History of the Former Han Dynasty (206 BC – AD 24). H/Han (begun about AD 65) *c.* AD 100. Pan Ku.

Chin Tan Ya Yao Thu (Shang Yang Tzu Chin Tan Ta Yao Thu) Illustrations for the Main Essentials of the Metallous Enchymoma; the true Gold Elixir. Yuan, AD 1333; Chhen Chih-Hsü (Shang Yang Tzu) based on drawings and tables of the tenth century AD onwards by Phêng Hsiao, Chang Po-Tuan and Lin Shen-Fêng.

Erh Ya Literary Expositor (dictionary). Chou material, stabilized in Chhin or C/Han. Compiler unknown. Enlarged and commented on *c.* AD 300 by Kuo Pho.

Hsin Thang Shu New History of the Thang Dynasty (AD 618–906) Sung, AD 1061. Ouyang Hsiu and Sung Chhi.

Jih Hua Chu Chia Pên Tshao The Sun-Rays Master's Pharmaceutical Natural History, collected from Many Authorities. Wu Tai and Sung, *c.* AD 972. Often ascribed by later writers to the Thang, but the correct dating was recognized by Thao Tsung-I in his *Cho Kêng Lu* (AD 1366), ch. 24. Ta Ming (Jih Hua Tzu, the Sun-Rays Master) was perhaps Thien Ta-Ming.

Pao Tsang Lun (Hsien-Yuan Pao Tsang Chhang Wei Lun) (The Yellow Emperor's) Discourse on the (contents of the) Precious Treasury (of the Earth), (mineralogy and metallurgy). Perhaps in part Thang or pre-Thang; completed in Wu Tai (S/Han). Tsêng Yuan-Jung notes Chhao Kung-Wu's dating of it as AD 918 in his *Chhun Chai Tu Shu Chih*. Chang Tzu-Kao, p. 118, also considers it mainly a Wu Tai work. Attrib. Chhing Hsia Tzu; if Su Yuan-Ming and not another writer of the same pseudonym, the earliest parts may have been of the Chin time (third or fourth century AD); cf. Yang Lieh-Yü. Now only extant in quotations. Cf. *Lo-fou Shan Chih*, ch. 4, p. 13a.

San Tshai Thu Hui Universal Encyclopaedia; Ming AD 1609, Wang Chhi.

Shan Hai Ching Classic of the Mountains and Rivers. Chou and C/Han. Eighth to first century BC. Writers unknown.

Shen Nung Pên Tshao Ching Classical Pharmacopoeia of the Heavenly Husbandman. C/Han, based on Chou and Chhin material, but not reaching final form before the second century AD. Writers unknown. Lost as a separate work, but the basis of all subsequent compendia of pharmaceutical natural history, in which it is constantly quoted. Reconstituted and annotated by many scholars; best by Mori Tateyuki (1845), Liu Fu (1942).

Shih Chi Historical Records (or perhaps better: Memoirs of the (Royal) Historiographer) down to 99 BC, C/Han, *c.* 90 BC (first pr. *c.* AD 1000). Ssuma Chhien.

Sui Shu History of the Sui Dynasty (AD 581–671). Thang, AD 636 (annals and biographies); AD 656 (monographs and bibliography). Wei Chêng *et. al.*

Sung Shih History of the Sung Dynasty (AD 960–1279). Yuan, *c.* AD 1345. Tho-Tho (Toktaga) and Ouyang Hsüan.

Tan Fang Chien Yuan The Mirror of Alchemical Processes (and Reagents); a Source-book. Wu Tai (H/Shu) *c.* AD 938–965. Tuku Thao.

Tao I Chih Lüeh Records of the Barbarian Islands (in the Pacific and Indian Oceans, including the coasts of East Africa). Yuan, AD 1350, based on notes made during his travels from AD 1330 to AD 1349. Wang Ta-Yuan.

Thien Kung Khai Wu The Exploitation of the Works of Nature. Ming, AD 1637. Sung Ying-Hsing.

Wakan Sanzai Zue The Chinese and Japanese Universal Encyclopaedia (based on the *San Tshai Thu Hui*). Japan, AD 1712. Terashima Ryōan.

Wu Li Hsiao Shih Small Encyclopaedia of the Principles of Things. Ming and Chhing, finished by AD 1643, sent to his son Fang Chung-Thung in AD 1650, finally printed AD 1664. Fang I-Chih.

Yü Phien Jade Page Dictionary. Liang, AD 543. Ku Yeh-Wang. Extended and edited in the Thang (AD 674) by Sun Chhiang.

B. MODERN REFERENCES

CHANG TZU-KAO 1964 *Chung-Kuo Hua-Hsüeh Shih Kao* (*Ku-Tai chih Pu*) (A Draft History of Chemistry in China (Section on Antiquity)), Kho-Hsüeh, Peking.

HOMMEL, W. 1912 The Origin of Zinc Smelting, *Engineering and Mining Journal* XCIII, 1185.

LEEDS, E. T. 1955 Zinc Coins in Medieval China, *Numismatic Chronicle*, 6th Ser. XIV, 177.

LO TSUNG-CHEN 1957 *Chiangsu I-Hsing Chin Mu Fa-Chüeh Pao-Kao* (with a postscript by Hsia Nai). Report of an Excavation of a Chin Tomb at I-hsing in Chiangsu, that of Chou Chhu, d. AD 297, which yielded the belt-ornaments containing aluminium, *Chinese Journal of Archaeology* 18, 83.

1963 Rejoinder to Shen Shih-Ying, *Archaeological Correspondent* 3, 165.

POSTLETHWAYT, Malachy 1751–55 *The Universal Dictionary of Trade and Commerce; translated from the French of Mons. (Jacques) Savary (des Bruslons), with large additions*, 2 vols London.

SAGE, B. M. 1804 De l'Emploi du Zinc en Chine pour la Monnaie, *Journal de Physique* LIX, 216; Eng. tr. in Leeds (1955) from *Philos. Mag.* XXI (1805), 242.

SHEN SHIH-YING 1962 *Kuan-yü Chiangsu I-Hsing Hsi Chin Chou-Chhu Mu Chhu-Thu Tai-Shih Chhêng-Fên Wên-Thi* Notes on the Chemical Composition of the belt-ornaments from the Western Chin Period (AD 265 to 316) found in the Tomb of Chou Chhu at I-hsing in Chiangsu, *Archaeological Correspondent* 9, 503.

STAUNTON, Sir George Leonard 1797 *An Authentic Account of an Embassy from the King of Great Britain to the Emperor of China . . . taken chiefly from the Papers of H. E. the Earl of Macartney, K. B. etc . . .*, 2 vols London.

YANG KÊN 1959 *Chin-Tai Lü Thung ho-chin-ti Chien-Ting chi chhi Yeh-Lien Chi-Shu-ti Chhu-Pu Than-Thao*, An Aluminium-Copper Alloy of the Chin Dynasty (AD 265–420); its Determination and a Preliminary Study of the Metallurgical Technology (which it implies), *Chinese Journal of Archaeology* 26, 91.

Acknowledgments

The Editor and publishers are grateful to the Cambridge University Press for permission to reproduce material published in Joseph Needham and Lu Gwei-Djen, *Science and Civilisation in China*, Vol. V, part 2, 1974.

31

IGNACIO BERNAL

The Jaguar Façade Tomb at Dainzú

Of the many archaeological ruins in the Oaxaca Valley, Dainzú is one of the most recently excavated. Located east of Oaxaca City on Kilometre 24 of the highway to Tehuantepec, it is medium in size compared with other contemporary sites of the region. The part that has been studied is precisely the heart of the ancient city's ceremonial precinct. North, south, and west of this there still remain many unexplored mounds, and what was probably the residential zone extends at least to the left bank of the river that forms the city's western edge.

Among the many buildings found in the precinct we have made an almost exhaustive study of two, named A and B, and several others have been partially examined.

Mound A was the first to be excavated. The gallery of ballplayers found there has been the subject of various publications (Bernal 1968; 1973; Bernal and Seuffert, in press). Toward the west and on a lower level lies Mound B, a vast complex of rooms, temples, and patios that was evidently for public or ceremonial use. It has a series of superposed structures spanning a time range from Monte Albán Period I until the end of pre-Hispanic history. Although in very different measure, Periods II and IIIA are its most important, in spite of several late houses found on the surface.

The tomb that is dealt with in this article was found in this group. Explored in 1973–74, it is No. 7 of the Dainzú tombs. It was built entirely of stone, the roof formed of four large flat slabs and the floor lined with the same material. *Ill. 1* shows its architecture with both a ground plan and cross section. From this we can see that it is a typical Valley of Oaxaca tomb from Monte Albán Period II: spacious and well built with large stones that give it almost a megalithic appearance; the chamber has a flat roof and the open antechamber was filled with dirt after burial had taken place. Perhaps the only special detail is a small niche located very high up on the west wall of the antechamber, which contained only a fragment of clay tubing placed in a vertical position. Clay tubes such as these have been found in several tombs of this region. They did not serve for drainage nor did they connect one point with another. They were probably the 'soul duct' or passageway left so that the soul of the deceased person could leave the tomb and re-enter at will.

The most interesting features of the tomb are the lintel of the door and the supporting jambs (*Ill. 2*). In the centre is a jaguar's head worked in rather high relief, and on both sides appear the shoulders and upper part of the feline's front legs. On the front of the jambs and even continuing around the inner surface of the door are the rest of the animal's legs and claws. Thus the whole structure shows a complete jaguar in frontal view as though the spectator stood face to face with the animal and therefore could not see the rest of the body or the back feet. Since Olmec times the jaguar frequently appears in Mesoamerican art but I do not remember any portrayal quite like this one. Perhaps it is because Dainzú, while clearly forming part of the general Valley of Oaxaca culture, has certain idiosyncratic features that have not been found elsewhere up to now, and also because its sculptors were exceptional artists. On the other hand the style of the jaguar suggests a last Olmec reminiscence quite distant in time and remote in style from its original form; our jaguar, like some Olmec felines, has only three claws while other Oaxaca specimens have four. Even a large polychrome clay jaguar found in the West Platform at Monte Albán and pertaining to Period II has four claws (Caso and Bernal 1952, Fig. 82), and so does a later one (*ibid.* Fig. 84). The animal on the Dainzú tomb is naturalistic in its representation since it is not associated with a human figure nor does it wear a mask like the tigers of Mound A at Dainzú (Bernal and Seuffert, in press). Its position could indicate that it is guarding the tomb, and this might also be true of the clay tiger at Suchilquitongo (Caso and Bernal 1952, 62 and Fig. 98). In like manner it recalls the bat of Tomb 50 at Monte Albán (*ibid.* Fig. 122) or that of Cuilapa (Saville 1904, 52). The style of Dainzú Tomb 7 suggests Period II.

We found that the tomb had been opened, partially destroyed, and refilled with extraneous material.

This occurred at the end of Period IIIA, in about the third century AD. During this wanton destruction the jambs were not moved and we found them in place, but the lintel with the jaguar head had been turned around, perhaps in an act of *damnatio memoriae*, or as preparation for moving the stone to another site, an enterprise which luckily for us was not carried out. The fact is that the large hole through which the desecrators gained entrance remained open. They broke almost all the vessels, scattered the bones, and perhaps a short time later filled the tomb with material taken from a nearby structure.

Thus we have two lots of objects that with a little effort can be distinguished. The older one corresponds to the tomb's original interment, and the other consists of quite different fragments from a later period and structure. The first lot contained a small urn in widely scattered fragments, all of which were recovered and enabled the complete vessel to be reassembled (*Ill. 3*). It is quite interesting. The head, which we found first, is painted red with cinnabar and clearly represents Goddess 13 Serpent. Although we know that this deity first appeared in Oaxaca in the Transitional II-IIIA Period (Caso and Bernal 1952, Fig. 434), the one that most resembles the Dainzú specimen is the urn from Patio

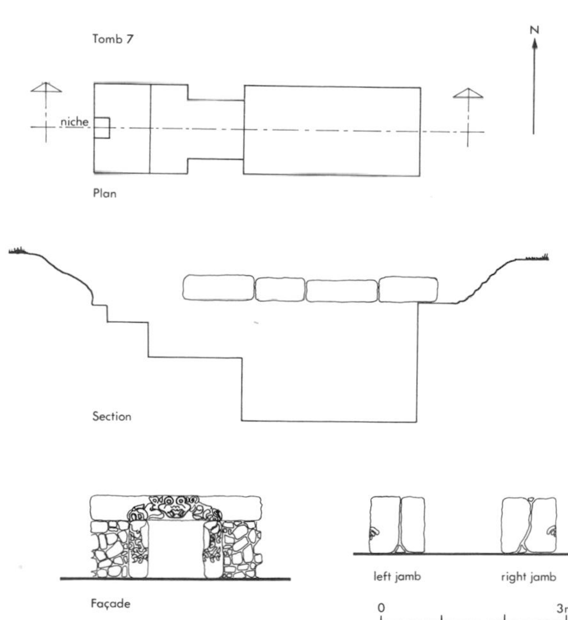

1 Ground plan and cross section of Tomb 7 at Dainzú.

2 Tomb 7 façade.

3 Urn with '1 Jaguar' hieroglyph.

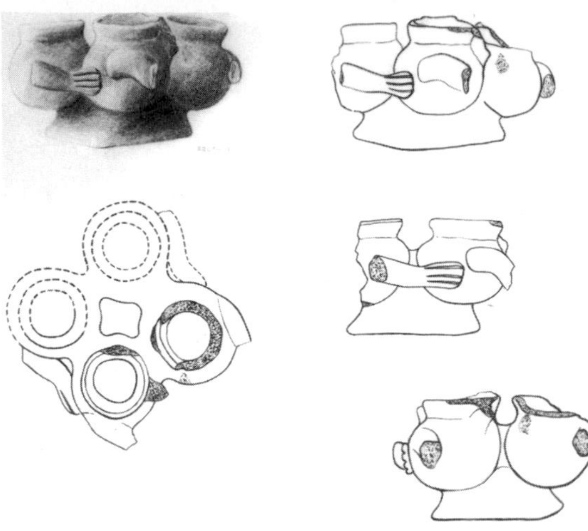

4 Drawing and partial reconstruction of a multiple jar.

I, Pit 2-R at Atzompa (*ibid.* Fig. 436). The head-dresses are identical in both cases. The hair protrudes under this as simple bands falling over the forehead and at the sides of the face. Both urns wear round ear-plugs and a necklace made of thick beads; their hands are on the chest. The braided head-dress must have been fashioned of a rather stiff material such as wicker or pliable twigs. This sort of crown was placed over the head and is the most distinctive feature of the goddess.

The body of the figure was also found in the tomb and shows that it is not a woman but a male personage since it does not wear a skirt. Although the form of the loincloth is not indicated, it can be assumed that the numeral one and the clearly portrayed jaguar head were embroidered on that garment. It is therefore a deity whose name is 1 Jaguar. We had already known of the god 1 Jaguar (*ibid.* 62–4), who is seldom seen but is represented in various forms. None of them is like the one of Tomb 7. This is undoubtedly a deity associated with the Goddess 13 Serpent and representing her male aspect. Such a duality is common, really characteristic among deities, and we know of many such cases not only in Oaxaca but also in other regions of Mesoamerica. We may recall for example the relation between the male bat and its companion goddess 2 J (*ibid.* 78–83).

The importance of dating the small urn is that it will give us the chronological locus of the tomb as a whole. The way the urn was found shows that it pertained to the original burial furniture; when the tomb was ravaged the urn was broken and its fragments scattered. We are not dealing with a single sherd like the many that were found and to which we will refer below. These cannot help to determine the period since they came both from the tomb itself and from the dirt that fell in later, and could even be recent since, as has been mentioned, part of the roof remained open and objects much later than the burial period may have fallen in through this gap. Judging from its small size and general style, the Dainzú urn pertains to the Transitional Period II-IIIA; but because of its similarity to the Atzompa urn, it could also date from the beginning of Period IIIA.

In addition to the urn, the tomb contained other objects including three hemispherical clay bowls, A 3, which must relate to the burial and not to its destruction. This type of vessel appears for the first time in Oaxaca in the Transitional Period although it becomes more common in Period IIIA, when it is made of thin orange clay characteristic of Classic Teotihuacan and also of Maya sites such as Kaminaljuyú. Another piece is formed of four small jars that are connected by human arms stretched between them. This is not characteristic of any period and is unique (*Ill. 4*). I believe it belonged to the original interment but cannot be sure since certain fragments are missing. An incised green stone, a fragment of obsidian blade, and a jade bead tell us nothing about the chronology nor are they representative pieces. The fragment of clay tubing (*Ill. 2*) from the antechamber does not suggest temporal placement either, since similar objects have been found in tombs of several periods. Finally, the bony remains were mere dust. They revealed nothing.

The second lot of objects belongs to the fill of the tomb that took place after its profanation. Three pieces are of stone. Two of these (*Ills. 5, 6*) are fragments of a bas relief which unfortunately we cannot interpret, but which suggest that it formed part of the decoration of a building. Their style appeared in Oaxaca at the beginning of Period IIIA and continued over several centuries. The third one is like a stone ball (*Ill. 7*) incised with a trilobate element also occurring frequently at Dainzú in Period IIIA. Several further fragments, when assembled, appear to represent half of a cylindrical stone column 19 cm in diameter, very well polished and finished. We know of none quite like this used on buildings in Oaxaca. A piece of another having the same diameter was found, but it was carved in a different stone and less polished. There were five highly decorated fragments of what must have been

5 Fragment of stone sculpture.

6 Fragment of stone sculpture.

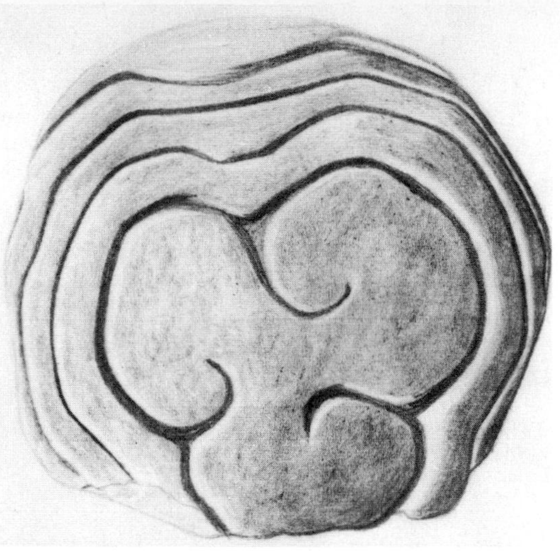

7 Stone ball-shaped object.

a clay frieze that was baked like a brick, stuccoed, and painted. Many other fragments of this same object were recovered from the area around the tomb but not enough to indicate what it represented (*Ills. 8–11*).

All these objects could belong to the end of Period IIIA, and this would mark the ultimate date for the destruction of the tomb. The sherds collected in the tomb may or may not pertain to the original burial, but they do not form complete or even partially complete objects; most of them correspond to Periods I and II. Only one of them – G 23 – is clearly from Period IIIA.

The floor of the antechamber was covered with a number of flagstones and a much larger slab in the middle. Believing that this might conceal something, we raised it. Only a figurine fragment undoubtedly older than Period IIIA and a Period I sherd were revealed.

From the above we see that evidence for dating the tomb is somewhat ambiguous. It appears to have been built during Period II, while the objects of the original interment could be from Transitional Period II–IIIA but more probably are from Period IIIA. The destruction occurred toward the end of the latter period. Thus I am inclined to suspect that the tomb dates from Transitional Period II–IIIA, when many traits of II were still in vogue but the Teotihuacan influences of the first part of IIIA were already being felt.

In view of several of the tomb's characteristics and some of its contents, it is unique among the many that have been excavated in the Valley of Oaxaca until now.

8–11 Fragments of stuccoed brick.

Bibliography

BERNAL, I. 1968 The ballplayers at Dainzú, *Archaeology* 21, 246–51.

1973 Stone reliefs in the Dainzú area, in *The Iconography of Middle American Sculpture*, The Metropolitan Museum of Art, 13–23, New York.

BERNAL, I. and SEUFFERT, A. in press *Los jugadores de pelota de Dainzú*, Graz.

CASO, A. and BERNAL, I. 1952 Las urnas de Oaxaca, *INAH Memorias* II, Mexico.

CASO, A., BERNAL, I. and ACOSTA, J. 1967 La cerámica de Monte Albán, *INAH Memorias* XIII, Mexico.

SAVILLE, M. H. 1904 Funeral urns from Oaxaca, *The American Museum Journal* IV, New York.

32

GORDON R. WILLEY

A Peruvian Pottery Collection in the Teatino Style[1]

[1] I am indebted to Professor J. H. Rowe and to Dr Duccio Bonavia for comments on the Teatino style and other matters in this paper. Mrs Elinor Reichlin, of the Peabody Museum Catalogue Department, helped me in assembling the collection; Mr Hillel Burger, Museum photographer, photographed the vessels.

THE TEATINO STYLE

In the development of Pre-Columbian Peruvian ceramics there is a time trend in decorative techniques which begins with incision-punctuation and other plastic surface treatments (Initial Period, *c.* 2000–1400 BC, and Early Horizon, *c.* 1400–400 BC), gradually shifts from these to combinations of incision and painting (the terminal Early Horizon and the early part of the Early Intermediate Period, 400 BC–AD 600), and finally moves on to the predominance of flat painting (latter half of the Early Intermediate Period and the Middle Horizon, *c.* AD 600–1000). I emphasize that this is a general trend and that there are exceptions. One of the most interesting of these exceptions is the Teatino Incised style which is the subject of this paper.

Pottery of the Teatino style was first discovered by Max Uhle (1913) in his excavations of 1904 at the famed Peruvian Central Coastal site of Ancon, not far north of Lima. The Teatino style had a distinctive incised, or incised and punctate, decoration, and in this it differed from the painted pottery of Tiahuanaco affiliation that Uhle found associated with it in the same graves. These associations, however, allowed Uhle to place the style chronologically into his period of Tiahuanaco influence or what has since been termed the Middle Horizon. This dating was confirmed a number of years later by W. D. Strong, who classified this particular incised pottery in his 'Middle Ancon I' period and provided the first brief descriptions of it (Strong 1925, 152, Fig. 6, Pl. 47a, b, e, j, l–o). The name Teatino was given to the style as the result of excavations carried out by J. C. Tello in the Quebrada de Teatino in the 1930s (Mejia Xesspe in Tello 1956, 322). The Quebrada de Teatino is located in the Lomas de Lachay, just to the north of the Chancay Valley. By way of further geographical orientation, Chancay is the first coastal valley to the north of Ancon. It was Tello's opinion that the incised pottery which he found in the Quebrada de Teatino, and which was very similar to that of Strong's Middle Ancon I incised, was a part of a very early stylistic horizon. He designated it 'Sub-Chavín', meaning by that Chavín-derived, and considered it a part of what is now called the Early Horizon. Other archaeologists (Kroeber 1944, 43–5; Willey 1951, 131–2) did not agree with Tello's assignment of the Teatino Incised pottery time, preferring the Middle Horizon assignment given it by Uhle and Strong.

Little more was added to the clarification of the Teatino Incised problem for a while. L. M. Stumer (1952; 1954) reported such pottery from locations in the Chillon (first valley to the south of Ancon) and Huaura Valleys (first valley to the north of Lachay), and a large collection of Teatino style vessels was made by E. E. Tabío at Lauri in the Chancay Valley. Then, in 1959, Jose Casafranca excavated a stratigraphic test pit in the Miramar section of Ancon, and this test produced Teatino Incised sherds in vertical sequence position. Utilizing the data from this test, and the large Tabío collection from the Chancay Valley, Duccio Bonavia wrote and published the first definitive article on the Teatino style in 1962.

Besides giving us the first detailed description of Teatino style pottery, Bonavia was able to summarize the known geographical distribution and to contribute substantially to its chronological definition. Teatino Incised pottery is found from the Huaura Valley on the north to the Chillon Valley on the south, with possible occurrences still farther south in the Rimac (the valley in which Lima is situated). The information from the Casafranca stratigraphic cut supports the Middle Horizon chronological position of the Teatino style rather than Tello's 'Sub-Chavín' or Early Horizon position. The earliest pottery from the lower levels of this cut, which was excavated to a depth of 4.00 m through bedded refuse, pertains to the Playa Grande-Maranga style. This style has also been referred to as 'Interlocking' (see Willey 1943, 149–52) and as the Lima style (see Patterson 1966, 34–6). Its chronological position is in the latter half of the Early Intermediate Period. In the test the Playa Grande-Maranga sherds were overlaid by Middle Horizon Tiahuanacoid-Epigonal materials;

but there was a considerable vertical overlap between these two stylistic groups. The Teatino Incised sherds were found largely with the Tiahuanacoid–Epigonal ones – confirming the Uhle-Strong grave lot findings – but Bonavia states that there was some overlap between the Teatino Incised and the earlier Playa Grande-Maranga sherd distribution (see Bonavia 1962, esp. Lams. I-A, I-B). However, I think it is difficult to appraise the significance of the vertical overlapping of pottery types in the stratitest; and the degree to which we are dealing with cultural contemporaneities or with simple mechanical mixture in the refuse must remain a question. The question also must remain, I believe, as to whether or not the Teatino style was present on the Central Coast before the arrival of Middle Horizon influences.

As to the long time gap between Chavínoid or Early Horizon pottery and that of the Teatino style, there can be no doubt. Accepting the present Peruvian chronology, as derived from radiocarbon dates, over a thousand years separates the two. Still one wonders, with Bonavia, if there is not some connection between the two. There is, of course, plenty of evidence for Early Horizon occupation on the Central Coast. Among other places, it occurs at Ancon (Willey and Corbett 1954); but no continuity between the Early Horizon incised and punctate wares and those of the Teatino style has yet been demonstrated. Perhaps, as Bonavia suggest, such a continuity exists elsewhere, as in the highland valleys back of the Central Coast. Another possibility is that the Teatino style is an archaism or revival, generated in imitation of the much older Early Horizon pottery. Recently, J. H. Rowe (1971) has pointed to several probable Chavín imitations in Early Intermediate, Middle Horizon, and even later styles. The cases which Rowe cites, however, involve design motifs and elements and, as such, are more definitive of archaistic imitation than the relatively simple technical idea of incision and punctation of vessel surfaces. Unfortunately, the designs on the Teatino style pottery are of such a rudimentary and reduced nature that they cannot be tied securely to Chavín motifs or iconography. Nevertheless, the possibility of the origins of the Teatino style through some mechanism of archaistic revival cannot be ruled out.

Meanwhile, we need to know more about the Teatino style. Distributional and chronological evidence needs further strengthening and clarification, and cultural context should be filled out. Among other things, the full typological range should be determined and the significance of typological variation understood. It is to this end of broadening our typological comprehension of the style that this brief paper is addressed. It is a description of a collection of vessels of the Teatino style, now in the possession of the Peabody Museum, Harvard University, that has not yet been reported upon.

THE PEABODY MUSEUM COLLECTION

The collection consists of 28 vessels. Of these 23 bear decorations in the unmistakable incised and punctate manner of the Teatino style. Five others are undecorated but closely resemble the decorated pieces in their ware characteristics.

The Question of Provenience. The provenience data, as recorded, are of doubtful reliability. The 28 vessels were part of a much larger collection acquired in Peru by the late S. K. Lothrop during the war years of 1941–45. In that period Lothrop made a number of coastal reconnaissance trips along the Peruvian coast, between La Chira in the north and Nazca in the south, although concentrating his attention to the valleys nearer Lima. He did very little actual excavating. Many of his collections were obtained by visiting the ancient cemetery sites which were being systematically looted by the 'huaqueros', or treasure hunters, and gathering up sherds and textile scraps which had been left behind by those illicit diggers. But most of the whole pottery vessels in his collection were pieces which he purchased from these grave-diggers, either in the field or in Lima. Consequently, he was dependent upon them for provenience information; and, as Lothrop himself was well aware, there was good reason to believe that some of this information could have been inaccurate. In 1945 the total Lothrop collections were shipped to the Peabody, and in the following year it was accessioned and catalogued under the series number 46–77–30/. In the cataloguing this accession coding is followed by an individual four-digit number for each specimen; and these last are the numbers cited below and in the illustration captions.

The Teatino style vessels here described were segregated from Lothrop's larger collection on a purely typological basis. After this segregation the limited provenience data for each specimen was checked, and these data were found to break down into two groups. According to Lothrop's information, 14 of the vessels were said to have come from various sites and regions in the Chicama Valley, North Coast; the other 14 are attributed

1 a, Subglobular olla (5131), ht. 13.7 cm, Humaya, Huaura; b, subglobular olla (5020), ht. 11.5 cm, Mocoyope, Chicama; c, subglobular olla (5132), ht. 9.2 cm, Humaya, Huaura; d, barrel-like olla (4903), ht. 13 cm, Sausal, Chicama; e, subglobular olla (5046), ht. 10 cm, Magdalena de Cao, Chicama; f, handled-pitcher (5042), ht. 9.3 cm, San Miguel, Chicama (?); g, tall flask-jar (5133), ht. 21.5 cm, Humaya, Huaura; h, tall flask-jar (4921), ht. 19.5 cm, Sausal, Chicama.

to some sites in the Huaura Valley of the Central Coast. From the distributional data on the Teatino style now available, as cited above, it is highly likely that all of the vessels in question came from the Huaura Valley and that there has been a confusion of Huaura and Chicama proveniences. Lothrop had in his total collection a number of vessels in other styles from the Chicama which supports this interpretation. Certainly pottery in the Teatino style has never been reported at any locality of the North Coast. As to the sites in the Huaura Valley which were listed in Lothrop's notes, all of them – Vilcoshuaura, Sayan, and Hacienda Humaya – lie east of the town of Huaura. Humaya, which is the location assigned to many of the vessels, is at a distance of about 25 kilometres from the town, on the right bank of the Rio Huaura. While long known to, and exploited by, 'huaqueros', there has been no scientific excavation at the site, nor is there any mention of it in the archaeological literature.[2] Finally, it is presumed that all of the vessels in the present collection, which are all intact or nearly so, came from graves; however, there are no grave associational data.

The Specimens. The vessels are of a uniform red colour. This results, in part, from the oxidization of both surfaces during firing although all vessels also have a red slip on one or both surfaces. This slip ranges from 'Weak Red' (10R-4/4) to 'Red' (10R-4/6) on the Munsell (1954 ed.) colour chart. In layman's terms it might be called a light brick red. Vessel surfaces diverge from this colour only on occasional spots where there are brown-to-black firing imperfections. Vessel walls are of a uniform thickness (4–7 mm) with little variation from base to rim. The paste cross-section is brown or grey-brown in colour with red-fired surfaces. Temper is sand or grit, which may have been natural to the clay. Occasional white flecks are seen in it, probably quartzite.

Vessel forms include: subglobular ollas (*Ill. 1a–c, e*), open bowls (*Ill. 2a–k*), kero beakers (*Ill. 3a–c*), tall flask-jars (*Ill. 1:g, h*), a tripod bowl (*Ill. 3h*), a handled pitcher (*Ill. 1f*), a ladle (*Ill. 3f*), a cornucopia shape (*Ill. 3i*), and some effigy jars (human face, animal face, shell (?)) (*Ill. 3g, e, d*). Vessels are medium-to-small in size. They could have served as dishes or small containers; however, it is possible that they were made for mortuary purposes alone. None shows evidence of use for cooking.

The characteristic decorative technique of the style is incision, combined with punctation. This was done after air-drying of the vessel but before firing. It is applied only to vessel exteriors. The incised lines are round-bottomed and have a distinct sheen (*Ill. 4b*). They average 2–3 mm wide and are usually quite shallow. Punctations are large dots or dash-like short marks. Relief-modelling is occasionally used as a decorative technique, as in the employment of slightly raised bands or in modelled-and-incised effigy faces.

[2] Some of this information is in Lothrop's letter of transmittal which accompanied the collection; but I am indebted to Dr Bonavia (letter of 18 June 1974) for the remainder.

2 a, bowl (5021), ht. 7.2 cm, Mocoyope, Chicama; b, bowl (5254), ht. 7.0 cm, Sayan, Huaura; c, bowl (5044), ht. 7.2 cm, Magdalena de Cao, Chicama; d, bowl (5022), ht. 7.7 cm, Mocoyope, Chicama; e, bowl (5045), ht. 6.7 cm, Magdalena de Cao, Chicama; f, bowl (5047), ht. 6.6 cm, Magdalena de Cao, Chicama; g, bowl (5137), ht. 6.5 cm, Humaya, Huaura; h, bowl (5018), ht. 6.3 cm, Mocoyope, Chicama; i, bowl (5136), ht. 3.8 cm, Humaya, Huaura; j, bowl (5093), ht. 6.8 cm, Humaya, Huaura; k, bowl (5019), ht. 7.2 cm, Mocoyope, Chicama.

3 a, kero beaker (4898), ht. 10.9 cm, Santa Clara, Chicama; b, kero beaker (4899), ht. 9.5 cm, Santa Clara, Chicama; c, kero beaker (5202), ht. 11.5 cm, Vilcoshuaura, Huaura; d, shell (?) effigy jar (5127), ht. 16 cm, Humaya, Huaura; e, animal head (llama?) effigy jar (5139), ht. 13.3 cm, Humaya, Huaura; f, ladle (5135), length 10.5 cm, Humaya, Huaura; g, human head effigy jar (5129), ht. 10.0 cm, Humaya, Huaura; h, tripod bowl (5124), ht. 11 cm, Humaya, Huara; i, cornucopia (5130), length 19.2 cm, Humaya, Huaura.

Design motifs are nearly always encircling bands, confined to a limited portion of vessel exteriors, such as small zones around ollas or bowls (*Ills. 1, 2*) or raised bands on beakers or bowls (*Ill. 3a–c, h*). The one exception in the present collection is the covering of most of the base of a bowl with a quatrefoil design (*Ill. 4a*). Motifs are geometric and predominantly rectilinear. They include: rows of pendant triangles (*Ill. 1b*) or, more commonly zigzag (*Ills. 1c; 2c; 3b*) or rectangular (*Ills. 1a, f; 2a b, d, e, j; 3a, c, i*) meanders. One vessel (*Ill. 1e*) has an encircling row of vertical 'shepherd's crook' elements, each outlined with dot punctations. Design layout is often poorly planned, as though the artist had begun his incised meander with no thought of spacing so that he ended up by making one indentation or panel much smaller or larger than the others. Execution is more often than not slovenly, with meander lines over-running their connections with each other.

In the accompanying illustrations (*Ills. 1–3*) all 28 of the vessels in the Peabody Museum collection are shown. The accompanying captions provide catalogue numbers and registered proveniences. As

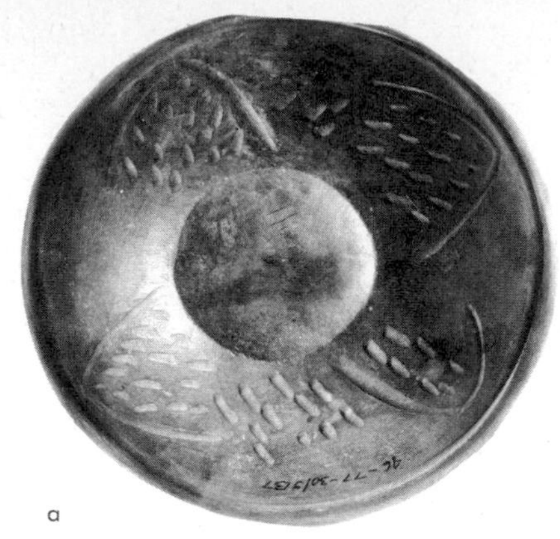

a

b

4 a, detail of *Ill. 2g*, base design; b, detail of *Ill. 2d*, wall design.

indicated, those proveniences for the Chicama Valley are very probably in error, and it is likely that all of the specimens came from the Huaura Valley.

Comparisons. There are numerous similarities between the Peabody Museum collection pieces and those that have been illustrated by Strong and Bonavia.

Strong (1925, Pl. 47a) shows a bowl form with straight or slightly incurved sides that can be matched with our *Ill. 2a, b*. This particular Ancon specimen has the characteristic double-line incised rectangular meander with punctate filler, as do the bowls of the present collection. The subglobular bowl from Ancon (Strong 1925, Pl. 47e) is like our *Ill. 1a-c, e*. Ancon forms which are not represented in the present collection are the collared subglobular ollas (*ibid.*, Pl. 47j, k) and the narrow-necked jars or bottles (*ibid.*, Pl. 47m-o). Strong's design layouts (*ibid.*, Fig. 6) include the rectangular meander with punctate fillers, the punctate-filled pendant triangles, and the zigzag meanders with no punctations, all of which are represented in the Peabody Museum collection.

The larger collection described by Bonavia (1962) has a number of collared jars and bottles which are like those of Ancon but which are not represented among our vessels. However, Bonavia (1962, Lam. II-B, f) illustrates a kero beaker with a centre band decoration, which is essentially the same type as *Ill. 3a-c*; his open bowls (*ibid.*, Lam. II-B, i, j, l) are like those shown on our *Ill. 2a, b, d, f, h* (note, especially, his II-B, l which has an encircling design at bowl base as in our *Ill. 2h*). There is a tripod bowl in the Bonavia collection (Lam. II-B, A-10) which recalls our *Ill. 3h*; however, the Bonavia tripod bowl has a collar feature which ours does not. His ladle (Lam. II-B, m) is almost identical with ours (*Ill. 3f*), including the double-line zigzag incised meander on the handle. Other form similarities between the Bonavia collection and that of the Peabody Museum include the handled pitcher (Lam. II-B, f.p.4 – see our *Ill. 1f*), the subglobular olla (Lam. II-B, A-13 – see our *Ill. 1e*), and a handled effigy (llama?) jar (Lam. II-B, A-ll – see our *Ill. 3e*).

In his design analyses Bonavia illustrates (Lams. II-B, III-B, IV-A) both the zigzag and rectangular meander patterns and the 'shepherd's crook' elements to which we have referred in the descriptions of the Peabody Museum collection of the Teatino style. On his Lam. VI-B he shows the pendant triangles with the dot or the dash-like punctate fillers, and his item 549 on that plate is an effigy face (probably human) with a modelled nose and incised eye much like our *Ill. 3g*. Another effigy jar on Bonavia's Lam. VII, 2, which may represent a jaguar, has an eye treatment identical to that of the animal of our *Ill. 3e*. In addition to these similarities, it should be noted that Bonavia's Lams. IV-B, V-A, V-B, VI-A depict either curvilinear meanders, which are not represented in our collection, or rather complex recti-curvilinear designs which we cannot match.

In addition to these specific form and design resemblances, it can also be said that the pottery which Bonavia illustrates has the same qualities of

[3] Professor Rowe has not examined the Peabody Museum collection; however, on the basis of his familiarity with the style he is of the opinion that its Middle Horizon occurrences belong to the 1B, 2A, 2B, and, possibly, 3 and 4 chronological subdivisions of that Horizon (personal communication of 15 May 1974).

incision-punctation techniques and slovenly execution which characterizes the specimens in the collection under consideration. To sum up:

1 Pottery of the Teatino style has been shown, through previous investigations, to pertain to the Peruvian Middle Horizon (*c.* AD 600–1000).[3] It is possible, although this has not been adequately demonstrated, that the style has its inception prior to the Middle Horizon. The known distribution of the style is in the Central Coastal valleys of the Chillon, Ancon, Chancay, and Huaura and their environs.

2 The incision-punctation decorative technique of the Teatino style is reminiscent of much earlier Peruvian Initial Period and Early Horizon styles. It is not known if this signifies: a) an as yet undisclosed continuity of decorative technique from these early times to the Middle Horizon; b) an archaistic revival of the technique; or c) a second and separate invention of the technique within the Peruvian area.

3 A Peabody Museum collection of 23 incised or incised-punctated vessels is definitely identified as belonging to the Teatino style. Five additional plain red ware vessels are also thought to pertain to the style. The typology of the Peabody Museum collection relates to a part, but not all, of the previously known morphological range of the style. Three (*Ill. 1d, g, h*) of the plain red ware vessels lie outside of this previously known range, and their inclusion within the style should be accepted with caution.

4 There are problems of provenience with the Peabody Museum Teatino style collection. According to the records, half of the collection comes from the Huaura Valley of the Central Coast, the other half from the Chicama Valley of the North Coast. On distributional information now available, it seems likely that the specimens attributed to the North Coast are incorrectly labelled and that the entire collection probably pertains to the Huaura Valley.

5 More formal, distributional, and chronological data are needed on this interesting Peruvian coastal style. This paper adds to the formal or typological corpus.

Bibliography

BONAVIA, Duccio 1962 Sobre El Estilo Teatino, *Revista del Museo Nacional* 31, Lima, Peru, 43–94.

KROEBER, A. L. 1944 *Peruvian Archaeology in 1942*, Viking Fund Publications in Anthropology, No. 4, New York.

MUNSELL (ed.) 1954 *Munsell Soil Color Charts*, Baltimore.

PATTERSON, T. C. 1966 *Pattern and Process in the Early Intermediate Period Pottery of the Central Coast of Peru*, University of California Publications in Anthropology 3, Berkeley and Los Angeles.

ROWE, J. H. 1971 The Influence of Chavín Art on Later Styles, *Dumbarton Oaks Conference on Chavín*, ed. E. P. Benson, Dumbarton Oaks, Washington, D.C., 101–24.

STRONG, W. D. 1925 *The Uhle Pottery Collections from Ancon*, University of California Publications in American Archaeology and Ethnology 21, No. 4, Berkeley.

STUMER, L. M. 1952 Investigaciones de Superficie en Caldera (Valle de Huaura), *Revista del Museo Nacional* 21, Lima, Peru, 38–67.

1954 The Chillón Valley of Peru. Excavations and Reconnaissance 1952–1953, *Archaeology* 7, 220–8.

TELLO, J. C. 1956 *Arqueologia del Valle de Casma*, Lima, Peru.

UHLE, M. 1913 Die Muschelhügel von Ancon, Peru, *Proceedings of the 18th International Congress of Americanists*, Part I, London, 22–45.

WILLEY, G. R. 1943 Excavations in the Chancay Valley, *Archaeological Studies in Peru, 1941–1942*, 123–96, Columbia Studies in Archaeology and Ethnology, 1, New York.

1951 The Chavin Problem: A Review and Critique, *South-western Journal of Anthropology* 7, 103–44.

WILLEY, G. R. and CORBETT, J. M. 1954 *Early Ancon and Early Supe Culture*, Columbia Studies in Archaeology and Ethnology 3, New York.

33

CHARLES THOMAS

The Archaeologist in Fiction

THE older lexicographers defined 'fiction' as the act of feigning or inventing. If we look into our hearts and minds, and admit (to ourselves) the degree to which we are obliged to feign and invent – with, of course, the highest possible motives – during the compilation of practically all archaeological literature, we can perceive a rough justice in the portrayal by novelists (for less lofty ends, naturally) of members of our calling down the years. That such depictions are, almost to a man or woman, inaccurate in detail, seems irrelevant. The archaeologist has evolved into a stock figure of literature, right down to the level of pulp novels and romantic weeklies. Unlike the Mad Scientist, or the Noble Young Doctor, he does not possess a built-in partner (boy assistant, dewy-eyed nurse), and indeed the nature of his profession, so commonly confused with that of the anthropologist, explorer, or paleontologist, requires him to operate solo. The lay writer frequently supposes that the archaeologist *excavates* solo, on very large sites, like a human bulldozer; but this is just one more facet of a certain unreality that tends to pervade the recital.

Would that my pen and my ability could encompass the whole vast topic of archaeology in fiction! Unfortunately one scarcely knows where to begin, or for that matter where to stop. There is the growing and fascinating genre of fictional treatment in the past, drawing upon published discoveries, with the writers avowedly seeking – if not always correctly regurgitating – specific guidance from archaeological friends and acquaintances. Robert Graves, Alfred Duggan, Henry Treece (whom I persuaded to excise some improbable Early Bronze Age rabbits from *The Golden Strangers*), and Rosemary Sutcliffe – the roll is an impressive one. To what extent are the works of the numerous *vulgarisateurs*, those vultures that scavenge around the fringes of our discipline, and wax fat on the leavings of undigested scholarship, fiction and fantasy rather than fact? One knows, moreover, of excavation reports and one might say whole books that . . . but enough; we shall tread upon firmer ground. This study, tribute to an old friend and notable antiquary who has rightly perceived us all as pismires crawling across the face of Eternity, will confine itself to the fictional portrayal of the archaeologist in English literature of all kinds, and will concentrate on material of the last seventy or eighty years.

Some points of interest rapidly emerge from such an enquiry. In the transformation to a paid, professional, archaeologist, the gentleman-antiquary has necessarily lost caste; what he did for love he now does for money, like a dentist or an ironmonger. Is the rather woolly popular image of the archaeologist to some extent moulded by literary treatment? Unflattering portraits have been given the world, a state of affairs not improved by the unmasking of non-archaeological forgeries, or by the publicity accorded to the more notorious archaeological quarrels. Excavations – at root, men and women living and working in the healthy outdoors on a high protein diet – are seen as potentially orgiastic, like some Primitive Methodist love-feast that has got out of hand; excavations are mainly distinguished from orgies through the cunning of archaeologists, who can usually get someone else to pay for them.

Works of the Victorian and early Edwardian era tended to reflect the antiquary of the day, a cultured gentleman like anyone else worthy of serious consideration. The very few professionals of that time, the museum men, attracted little notice, possibly because it was felt that their lives were quite ineffably dull. This is a pity. The full story of Sir Charles Hercules Read, F.B.A. (1857–1929), would by traditional accounts have made a rattling fine yarn. The nearest we get to professionalism is a vignette in one of Edith ('The Would-Be-Goods') Nesbit's books, a pale and kindly young man who is interested in Egyptology, works in a London museum, and represents (or so I have always understood) the youthful Flinders Petrie. And while we are on personalities, why no fictional treatment of Pitt Rivers, the recital of whose many marked idiosyncracies cries out too late for the pen of Charles Dickens?

The classic, the early nineteenth-century prototype, is Sir Walter Scott's own Antiquary, Jonathan Oldbuck, laird of Monkbarns. To Stuart Piggott we owe the demonstration (Piggott 1955; 1966; 1970) that this lovable figure is in part Scott's crabbed Gothic joke at himself, in part however the real-life Sir John Clerk, Baron Clerk of Penicuik (1676–1755). Both Scott and Clerk were no more than slightly less extravagant avatars of Monkbarns. The antiquarian theme is continued throughout the century, only occasionally reaching real distinction. It may be found, admixed with much sound learning, in John Meade Falkner's *The Nebuly Coat* (1903). Falkner, an authority in the realms of heraldry, ecclesiology, manuscripts and music – many of the ingredients of archaeology at the time of his birth (1858) – held in his time such quaintly assorted positions as the chairmanship of Armstrong Whitworth and the readership in palaeography at the Durham Colleges. His hero, Edward Westray, is primarily an architect; the milieu, a decaying coastal town of antiquity in what appears to be Dorset or Hampshire, gets far more sympathetic treatment than that of his other, Henry-Jamesian, novel *The Lost Stradivarius* (1895). Westray is cut from the cloth of R. K. Wright, Albert Way, and a whole generation of late Victorians.

The change-over to the fictional presentation that many of us know best – the archaeologist partly sinister, partly comic, and faintly a menace to the placidity of Society (if not to its morals) – started towards the end of the century. It entirely replaced a much lighter treatment. A scholarly lady of my acquaintance reminds me of a *Boy's Own Paper* serial, she thinks in the 1880s, called 'The Young Excavators'. It dealt with a brother-sister team, the sister in a riding-habit, with yards and yards of muslin floating from her topee, at work in the Near East. They find (and attack) a ziggurat, quoting Herodotus at each other the while; the paradise of good work is shattered by the entry of a third Young Excavator (male), who makes off with the sister. The concatenation is not unknown in much more recent excavations, at home as much as in the Levant, but hardly so delicately treated. A harmless tradition runs alongside this species, for instance in Charlotte M. Yonge's *The Daisy Chain* (1856), where we find kind-hearted children burying potsherds in the ground so that the funny, but nice, archaeologists shall not be entirely disappointed.

A large part of the transmogrification is bound up with the title 'Professor'. This alone merits a deep study. In the writings of early Dissent, it means one who professes (even Professes) his Christianity aloud, with needless ostentation; then one who teaches, outside a conventional school. The latter usage has survived in various nooks, for example music; and once I met a Professor who, it transpired, professed no more than the flute at the Royal Marines School of Music. Can it be that the awful assaults on established belief from the 1850s, spear-headed by that nicest of men, Charles Darwin, but consolidated by other and far less amiable scholars, drew something of a penumbra across the face of pure Professorship? Archaeology, its teachings far from immediately reconcilable with the Creation story in *Genesis*, and not at that time able to supply a candidate for Noah's Flood, is brought into conflict with religion in W. H. Mallock's *The Veil of the Temple* (*or, From Night to Twilight*), an extraordinary and still disturbing work, published in book form in 1904 – it was worked up from chapters that came out in the old *Monthly Review*. Using the device of a more or less continuous house-party, Mallock makes his characters examine the whole field of Christian dogmatics and Biblical exegesis in the harsh twin lamps of commonsense and contemporary knowledge. Strong amid the gentleman-rationalists is Rupert Glanville, archaeologist, excavator, and late President of the Board of Trade (!). Glanville wants to cut puny Man down to size, and does so through a guided tour of his private museum: 'my collection of antiquities in that building behind the fuchsias'. Though its foyer is conventional enough ('lined with shelves, supporting many dust-covered objects'), and Gallery No. 1 has a reconstruction of the Great Palace at Knossos ('flourishing before God created Adam'), worse is in store. The tour leads on to a linear gallery, one *thousand* feet in length, with a continuous shelf 'of which every foot represents a thousand years'; words like 'interglacial' are bandied about, and Christianity, a plaster Crucifix, stands twenty-two inches from the near wall.

From Rupert Glanville we move on to the Perilous Loner, the solitary archaeologist whose learning, because it involves the plucking of forbidden fruit, destroys him if not others. Arthur Machen (1863–1947) is not widely known, but those who know this master of the hidden worlds co-extant with our own will endorse my inclusion of his work.

In the late nineteenth century, interest in the darker sides of British pre- and protohistory had been aroused by such books as John Rhŷs's *Celtic Britain* (1884), G. L. Gomme's *The Village Community*, (1890), and by the formation of the Folklore Society.

Vestiges of Picts, Goidels, Turanians, and what-not, whose artifacts might be sought in remoter tracts of Britain beyond the railway network, were being adduced to explain fairy legends and surviving beliefs. In his *The Three Impostors* (1895), a jumble of linked stories in the manner of R. L. Stevenson, we encounter Professor Gregg, author (predictably?) of a *Textbook of Ethnology*, but not apparently overburdened with any teaching commitments. Over many years Gregg has amassed certain clues bearing upon the survival, in the wilds of the Welsh marches, of scarcely human autochthones. They are small, sinister, and identified by him with tribes noted by Solinus as inhabiting the inner parts of Libya; here surely we see a foreshadowing of Rhŷs and Brynmor Jones, *The Welsh People* (1900), whose notorious Appendix B ('Pre-Aryan Syntax in Insular Celtic') first sought to link aspects of the insular Celtic languages to the tongues of early North Africa. Professor Gregg's field-work in wild Wales leads him into strange paths, and then into oblivion; his posthumous testament ('The Statement of William Gregg, F.R.S., etc.') describes how he sought, and found, these gnarled fellow-countrymen.

Now precisely this theme occurs, though I fancy independently, in the writings of the first of three rollicking saga-men to whom we must address our attention – Buchan, Rider Haggard, and Conan Doyle. All three portrayed archaeologists after their fashion. John Buchan, Lord Tweedsmuir (1875–1940), though strong on plot and action, was frequently weak on detail. A friend of mine compiled a rich bouquet of purely architectural howlers from Buchan's books – notably the case of some typical Buchan aristocrat who, condescending to enter a cottage, contrived to trip over the *lintel* – and there are gross inconsistencies of dates and times in almost all the novels.

John Buchan, bemused as he was with the casually successful lives of lairds, Members of Parliament, brigadier-generals, and what the Germans call *Finanzkapitäne*, none the less had time to spare for those piddling ants that scurried about their feet, men of learning. His treatment was perhaps less than fortunate when he turned to archaeology. In one such novel (*John Macnab* (1925)), set in Scotland, a decaying laird, last of his hopelessly inbred line, permits a pushing American archaeologist to tackle what sounds like a chambered tomb within the policies. Our American does so, employing gillies, navvies, and so on but, impatient of these slow Old World procedures, he gets at the heart of the matter with a little-used aid to megalithic excavation, dynamite. This bold stroke pays off. The blasted tomb reveals not a sordid pile of bones and Beacharra-ware pots, but a veritable Holofernes-style treasury of bullion, laid there by some Viking bandit ancestor of Colonel Raden, the decadent laird.

In contrast, Buchan's native archaeologist is a timid creature. He can be found in a little-known work, *No Man's Land* (in a collection *The Watcher by the Threshold* (1915)). The hero is appropriately a Mr Graves, presumptively a Scot since he undertakes field-work in a kilt. His first book, 'a monograph on the probably Celtic elements in the Eddic songs', is said to have brought him 'the praise of scholars' (? T. F. O'Rahilly and R. A. S. Macalister), and 'the deputy-professor's chair of Northern Antiquities at Oxford'. We are aware that Oxford chairs are given for very curious reasons, but this seems unique. Mr Graves visits an area which those who know it can identify with a favoured Buchan stamping-ground, the Glentrool massif in Galloway. He goes climbing alone in the stark and wet hills, because (though he is too shy to tell fellow-scholars this) he believes that the Picts still live up there, in holes in the ground. They do indeed, and what is more, they drag him into one. These Picts keep themselves going, like early Highlanders, by stealing white girls from the Lowlands for breeding purposes. They use gold cups and barbed-and-tanged arrowheads, a firm indication of cultural time-lag; but in addition, they smell, and their habits leave much to be desired, so Mr Graves escapes. Later he returns, escapes again, and writes a book that none will believe; so the poor man falls into a decline and dies. 'His career', says *The Times*, 'is a sad instance of the fascination which the recondite and the quack can exercise even over men of proved quality.' There, but for God's grace, go many of us; but Mr Graves was at least linguistically sound, foreshadowing Professor Kenneth Jackson's mature conclusion by some decades, since his Picts speak a form of P-Celtic like 'an old book-tongue, commonly supposed to be an impure dialect once used in Brittany, which I had met in the course of my researches.'

Sir Arthur Conan Doyle (1859–1930) had plenty of time for men of learning. Most notable is that ebullient projection of his creator, Professor George Edward Challenger. Though his major field is supposed to be biology and zoology, he is also (as befits a polymath) equally at home in ethnology, and we must remind ourselves that – influenced by such powerful productions as Frazer's multibranched *The Golden Bough* (1890–1915) – people did not always make much of a clear distinction between ethnology and archaeology.

Conan Doyle did involve himself with 'straight' archaeology, in the Sherlockian canon. Among the long stories, there is the *Hound of the Baskervilles* (1902), replete in any event with *bon mots* (sample: 'Poor Sir Charles's head was of a very rare type, half Gaelic, half Ivernian in its characteristics'). Watson meets, on Dartmoor, a Mr Stapleton, naturalist and antiquary, who points out a prehistoric cluster of huts ('Neolithic man – no date'). Stapleton is quite sound for 1902. 'He (*scil.*, Neolithic man) grazed his cattle on these slopes, and he learned to dig for tin when the bronze sword began to supersede the stone axe. Look at the great trench on the opposite hill.' At least he has it in the right order. It is in this story that Watson finds Holmes camping out in a beehive hut, a corbelled stone structure of the kind investigated by R. Hansford Worth and Lady Fox – though, unlike either of these seekers after the past, Holmes manages to find one with the roof on.

Other Holmesian antiquarian touches occur in *The Devil's Foot* (from *His Last Bow* (1917), a tale which, as I hope to show in a forthcoming monograph, can be confidently located at Mullion, Cornwall, and in which Holmes decides (alas!) to investigate the Chaldean and Phoenician roots in the ancient Cornish language). Oriental archaeology, or Chinoiserie, is introduced into *The Illustrious Client* (*The Case-Book of Sherlock Holmes* (1927)). Watson is obliged to see the Australian murderer and collector, Baron Adelbert de Gruner, and for this purpose, posing as an antiquary, he attempts to cram up, in two days and in the London Library, the entire history of Chinese ceramics. He calls upon Gruner, bearing a nice specimen of a deep blue Ming eggshell saucer. 'Pray sit down, Doctor', the vicious Baron greets him. 'I was looking over my own treasures and wondering whether I could really afford to add to them. This little Tang specimen, which dates from the seventh century, would probably interest you.' But cunning Gruner has omitted the apostrophe in the dynastic name (*recte* T'ang, pronounced 'Dung') as a trap; Watson fails to spot this, as well as the fact that there *is* no 'deep blue' Ming, and he also fails to convince as to his knowledge of the Northern Wei dynasty and its place in ceramic history. Poor Watson! born too early to read the trenchant text-books of his later namesake William.

Sir Henry Rider Haggard (1856–1925) concerned himself with outdoor men of action, preferably involved with blood, noble Zulus, fair women, wild-life, and Africa. Not a few of his books dabble with antiquarianism, the most obvious example being *She* (1887), where we are given facsimiles of manuscripts, and meet Leo Vincey, the god-like young man with the tight fair curls and tiny mind. He has had a Classical upbringing, as befits the reincarnation of a Roman nobleman, and is engaged in the decipherment of something that might be demotic script (or then again might be meant to be Coptic). The allusion to Rome carries us back to Buchan, who was not very fond of the Romans, and described the shocking fate of an amateur dabbler in the lost Romano-Celtic cults of the north in *The Watcher by the Threshold* (1915), a theme also used by Arthur Machen on more than one occasion (e.g., *The Great God Pan* (1894)). The most compelling version, in which the *mores* of ancient Rome overseas are pictured as having developed over the centuries into those of a totalitarian regime, is also from a Celt. I know nothing of Joseph O'Neill, save that he was Secretary 'of a great Public Department in his country' (then the Irish Free State), but his *Land Under England* (1935) shows a Romano-British antiquary on Hadrian's Wall who goes underground, meets the surviving civilization of Rome in a Jules Verne world of awfulness and twilight, and achieves at some cost total identification with the object of his lifelong obsession.

The last flickerings of the Monkbarns tradition take us into the present century. Novels about Shetland are uncommon, but J. M. E. Saxby's *Viking Boys* (1892) has an antiquarian laird, his house crammed with lithic loot from the isles, of a sort that did actually exist in Scotland within the last few decades (and may still do so). Antiquarianism and archaeology with the correctly-detailed background had to await the published writings of M. R. James (from 1904 to 1925), conveniently in his *Collected Ghost Stories* (1931, and reprints). These elegant and delicious *contes*, the reading of which renders it quite impossible to visit (say) any isolated East Anglian rectory with complete equanimity; or to pass up a darkened drive with dripping laurels; or even to stay long in the back rooms of the Society of Antiquaries' Library on a winter afternoon on one's own, summarize most of the antiquarian world of Montague James's lifetime. The weak spot, not surprisingly, concerns excavation; for here again we meet the unlikely phenomenon of the sole excavator, unlikely because of the sheer physical accomplishment usually attributed to him by non-excavating authors. Thus, in *A Warning to the Curious* – set at 'Seaburgh' (Dunwich) – the unhappy Mr Paxton confesses that he has dug something out of a Saxon barrow, the original owner of which appears to want it back. 'I know something about digging in these barrows; I've opened many of them in the down country', says Paxton. In this present case, he actually *tunnels* into a 'light and sandy' mound ('I made my tunnel; I won't bore you with the details of how I supported it and filled it in when I'd done . . .') and what is more, does so by night.

The myth of the one-man dig dies hard. It fooled G. K. Chesterton; one of his Father Brown stories, *The Curse of the Golden Cross* (from *The Incredulity of Father Brown* (1926)) contains not one, but two such ventures. Professor Smaill, American, and 'an authority on certain archaeological studies touching the later Byzantine Empire', has conducted investigations in Crete and the Greek isles. 'I did a great deal of it practically single-handed,' he tells the ubiquitous Father – 'sometimes with the most rude and temporary help from the inhabitants of the place, and sometimes literally alone.' This includes work in 'a maze of subterranean passages', a dangerous locale for the solitary archaeologist, as Conan Doyle made quite clear in *The New Catacomb* (*The Conan Doyle Stories* (1929)). But Professor Smaill has his followers, and a second Byzantine pectoral cross is found in Sussex, by a Reverend Mr Walters. Mr Walters has excavated below his own parish church ('a very large hole') and has found the sarcophagus of a medieval noble, in a *terra subterranea* described in terms more appropriate to the Vatican excavations of 1953 onwards. Possibly the same miraculous power that directed the fossickings also disposed of the mass of displaced chalk.

My most recent example is to be found in Andrew Garve's *The Riddle of Samson* (1954) – Samson is one of the Isles of Scilly – where the hero sets out to engage in 'digging for old ruins' (his own phrase). To accomplish this laudable end, he has gathered together 'an entrenching tool, a galvanized wheelbarrow, a pick and shovel, and half-a-dozen big planks'. As no assistance materializes he excavates the site (unspecified, but either megalithic or monastic) all by himself. The most that one can say for him is that, after circumstances oblige him to flee to the mainland, he does at least send a telegram to a local supporter. This reads 'Detained in London; please fill in trench.'

Novels about archaeologists, or novels that include archaeologists among their *dramatis personae*, took on a new dimension after the Second World War. For archaeologists started to become *people*. Many served in Intelligence, some as colonels, some as sergeant-majors. One (Wheeler) became a real General, initiating a fashion that has been maintained by his admirers in modern Israel. The expansion of the profession; the fact that until about ten years ago the professional archaeologist in Britain knew most of his colleagues personally, and knew their backgrounds and private lives as well; and the brisk trade in marriage and remarriage which has long been current in the archaeological world; these all brought about a total loss of literary innocence. The process was completed when archaeologists themselves ventured into fiction. True, there had been Stanley Casson's inimitable (but imitated) *Murder by Burial* (1938), some relevant *œuvres* by the ever-versatile C. E. Vulliamy, and *Murder in Mesopotamia*, with other books, by Lady Mallowan (also known as Agatha Christie). Now, however, the fictional archaeologists started to become identifiable.

Angus Wilson's *Anglo-Saxon Attitudes* appeared in 1956. Despite its theme, the frantic attempts by a group of archaeologists and their followers to preserve (or to reveal) the secret that a find of Sutton Hoo proportions is in reality an elaborate Victorian fake, this has relatively little archaeology in it. But the knowledge that Mr Wilson worked for some years in the Library of the British Museum leads one to scrutinize the central figure for traces of a one-time colleague, later translated to Oxford. An eccentric old Lady who is portrayed as 'Dr Rose Lorimer' is clearly a conflation of the late Doctors Rose Graham and Margaret Murray, borrowing the disconcerting deafness and piercing grunts of the former, and the witchcraft theories of the latter.

Does Art in truth seek to imitate Nature? Archaeologists, as a genus, can be just as strange in life as in literature. C. P. Snow's acid exposition of Cambridge life, *The Masters* (1951), has another such portmanteau figure, 'Professor Gay', a blend in equal parts of the late Martin Charlesworth and the late H. M. Chadwick. Another of Sir Charles Snow's favourite characters – and I add, in parenthesis, my discovery that the names in the Lewis Eliot saga (Jago, Getliffe, Crawford, etc.) seem to be taken, doubtless subconsciously, from the facia-boards of back street shops in Sir Charles's native Leicester – is the manic-depressive linguist Roy Calvert. His twin pursuits are women, and Sogdian texts. It is alleged that a certain archaeologist forms a partial model for Calvert.

Under the transparent and quite unnecessary pseudonym of 'Dilwyn Rees' (*dilwyn* is a dubious Welsh verb, said by the dubious Owen Pughe to mean 'to cease keeping, to shed' – in this case, one's proper name?) Professor Glyn Daniel has given us two splendid detective stories, *The Cambridge Murders* (1945) and *Welcome Death* (1954). Both feature an auctorial self-projection, the bon-vivant Sir Richard Cherrington, archaeologist and Vice-President of his Cambridge college. *The Cambridge Murders* is larded with private academic jokes. Sir Richard's nephew, Giles Farnaby, is named after an obscure sixteenth-century Cornish composer; several other names are stolen from existing archaeologists, two of them (Piggott, Wheeler) being employed in decidedly menial rôles. Sir Richard signs his card as 'Ricky', and the murderer's home is said to be at Rockbourne. A visit to a roadhouse outside Cambridge introduces us to its chatelaine, 'Babs Chilcott', a name uncomfortably close to that of a former friend of the late Charles Seltman (author of *Women in Antiquity*, and several other bonhomous archaeological treatises).

Professor Daniel is eclipsed, as one who sails near the wind, by Lalage Pulvertaft (Mrs Peter Green), in her *No Great Magic* (1956), novel of an excavation, instantly recognizable as part of the Lough Gur campaign in Co. Limerick. Equally recognizable, too, are most of the protagonists. The story revolves around Professor Ashe, who hopes to find Mycenaean material in the Irish Bronze Age (thus anticipating by several seasons the discoveries at Tara); a lady archaeologist, Charlotte Darwin; minor digging characters, among them the author herself, I fancy; a 'Professor O'Sullivan' and his architectural assistant; and a crop of wealthy Anglo-Irish eccentrics. One must read the book in order to work out which characters are based on Christopher Hawkes, Liam de Paor, the late Sean P. Ó Ríordáin, Jacquetta Hawkes (of whom more below), *et alii* . . . and I understand that Stuart Piggott only escaped portrayal by a whisker.

In *No Great Magic*, sex rears its ugly head. There has long been, or there long was, a tacit agreement that romantic affairs on excavations, like those on long sea voyages as delineated by E. M. Forster and others, should be subsequently deemed not to have taken place; or, if they did occur, to have occurred in a space-time vacuum. The modern archaeological novel breaks this convention, thereby entirely justifying the pessimism of J. P. Droop (*Archaeological Excavation*, Cambridge (1915)). Droop, of whom I know nothing save that he taught at the University of Liverpool and was a student (in the British School of Archaeology) at Athens, that antique centre of pederasty, argued in a separate 'Epilogue' (pp. 63–4) against 'mixed digs'; women, he thought, would inhibit the healthy release of oaths and curses at moments of stress, and – comparing the constant lack of privacy on a dig to that of life in the Navy – he did not believe 'that such close and unavoidable companionship can ever be other than a source of irritation' when one has to share, with the ladies, 'a bond of closer daily intercourse'. Precisely such a theme occupied Dorothy Cowlin, author of *Rowanberry Wine* (1952), which describes the investigation of a Bronze Age (food-vessel?) barrow in Yorkshire with special stress on the private lives of the investigators. They are a singularly unappealing crowd, headed by Roger, who has sunk from the direction of major Middle East projects to headship of a red-brick Department of Archaeology. He has an affair with the District Nurse; his wife, in revenge, consoles herself with one of the students, a terrible young man who she thinks resembles 'an Egyptian god'. The dig itself opens with a burning-off of the whole area, thus confusing ancient and modern charcoal; not that this would have made much difference. The blurred message, if I read it aright, is that excavations will always be like this, and one must learn to forgive and forget when one returns to Civvy Street. Forget the peccadilloes, possibly; forgive such an excavation, never.

Symbolism, that scourge of post-war New Writing, did not leave archaeological fiction unscathed. In *Full Fathom Five* (1956), Hugh Sykes Davies, colleague of Glyn Daniel, and author of the quite terrifying *The Papers of Andrew Melmoth* (about a scientist who goes over to the rats), gives us a full-scale allegory about an excavation. A rich maniac is promoting the underwater exploration of some kind of stone row, or stone circle, set in either North Wales or western Scotland. The two archaeologists, who are antithetical, are called Self and Reason, and (though not too obviously) symbolize subjective and objective, wayward and controlled, approaches to the common goal. The boat from which they operate is named *Belphegor*. This, and only those versed in the byways of the Middle Ages can be expected to know it already, was the name of a demon, despatched by his companions from Hell to Earth so that he might test the truth of rumours concerning the happiness of married life among humans. After a short stay, he fled shrieking back to the Inferno. Dr Davies's book, beautifully constructed, with long lyrical passages, is none the less hard to understand. Its rather gloomy moral seems to be that devotion – in excess? – to any kind of intellectual pursuit, and archaeology itself is here such a pursuit, is incompatible with normal married life, if not with normal human relationships.

The unhappy *motif* of moral disintegration in the course of (and as the result of) an archaeological exploration – a process understood to be greatly accelerated in hot climates – attracted, in the same year (1956), Miss Storm Jameson. Her *The Intruders* is set in Provence, where a small Greek colony is under excavation. The atmosphere of dry heat, blinding light, apathy, and the hatred of the local peasantry for any stranger, is strongly conveyed. Under these nasty, and essentially un-British, conditions, the emotions which are normally kept on a tight rein as any excavation progresses – jealousy, greed, personal dislikes – escape, and are given full rein. The results include robbery, adultery, and murder; it says much for the bottom of our Anglo-Saxon archaeologists that they do not allow such petty trifles to deflect them from their work.

More, and more subtle, moral disintegration can be found in the shape of Roger Thurstan, the lecturer in archaeology at a Cornish university who commits the cardinal sin of salting his own medieval dig; Jessica Mann's *The Only Security* has also the – I think – unique distinction of introducing a woman professor of archaeology to the genre. In fact the reader of this latter-day series of Anglo-Saxon attitudes has the feeling that Thurstan's major crime lies not so much in that he murders in an attempt to hide his dread secret but that his entire publication record consists only of two interim reports of incompleted excavations.

One need not, of course, bind oneself to factual (or even to probable) archaeological sites and situations. Science fiction, and its nebulous cousin 'fantasy' writing, are worlds that welcomed the archaeologist, if only as a fresh face in a clapped-out soap opera. In the early days of the industry, many of the classic science-fiction magazines displayed a most lively interest in archaeology. *Astounding Science Fiction* (XI.4 (1955), 67ff.) has a perfectly sound resumé of our thinking about *Homo neanderthalensis* up to that date, with the provocative, well-argued concept that the genes which resulted in blond hair and fair skins among modern Caucasians may be a marked Neanderthaloid inheritance. In another issue, a first-class story posits the idea that the appearance of *H. sapiens*, and of the entire Upper Palaeolithic of the Old World, is a vast cosmic hoax; and that the whole cultural assemblage, complete with misleading fossils, fauna, stratigraphy, and the rest, was planted on us from Outer Space. We know this to be ridiculously untrue (or do we?) but, given acceptance of certain premisses, it is as impossible to refute this as it is to overthrow the *pensées* of St Thomas Aquinas.

A straight science-fiction novel by an Old Master, A. E. Van Vogt, is *The Voyage of the Space Beagle* (1951), in which a group of assorted scientists is engaged in a five-year voyage around outer space. The parallel (with Darwin's trip in a somewhat earlier *Beagle*) is well and wittily maintained. The scientific hierarchy includes an archaeologist, a Japanese (recognition, at last, of those campaigns in Iraq?), whose function is to advise, in the event of landings on inhabited or on formerly inhabited worlds, which stage in a Toynbee-type historical cycle appears to have been attained locally. On this basis, which is at once absolute and deterministic, useful predictions as to the reaction of the native population can be put forward. While deploring such a flirtation with the mad merry-go-round of cyclic history, we must recognize that Van Vogt makes a valid point here. I have in another context outlined (though I have never felt strong enough to publish) reasons why future expeditions into outer space should include archaeologists, since they alone are trained to analyze situations of human activity in the absence of humans, or to sift the evidence of artifacts abandoned by their makers. Take any standard work on the Palaeolithic, substitute the word 'Venusian' for the word 'Man', and by and large it makes sense. A. E. Van Vogt has produced a space archaeologist of merit.

More fantasy than science-fiction is Jacquetta Hawkes's purple novel, *Providence Island* (1959). This, too, is replete with partially recognizable colleagues. A curious and seedy professor of Classical archaeology is called 'Pennycuick', less a reminder of the Scots baronial home, perhaps, than of Mr Penniman, once a fixture in the Pitt Rivers Museum at Oxford. A young friend brings him a parcel of flints, a typically Upper Palaeolithic assemblage of Magdalenian character. These are all freshly chipped, as if by Flint Jack or some such gifted hand, and were found on a supposedly deserted (and unmapped) Pacific island. Pennycuick realizes all his assets to equip an expedition, recruits a few technicians, and enlists the aid of 'Dr Alice Cutter', whose emphatic portrayal, previous history (pp. 15 to 17), and professional interests, all suggest a projection of the author. The island is found, and proves to be inhabited by latter-day Magdalenians, who have developed certain psychic powers such as silent communication and effective invisibility. They are found, upon closer acquaintance, to speak *Basque* – for a recent comment on this hoary theme, see *Ulster Folklife*, 15/16 (1970), 142 – and at this point, some obvious symbolism creeps in. Alice Cutter goes native, partakes in an orgiastic festival and, in the embrace of an authentic Magdalenian, attains a psychic identification with her field of study that she has been unable to gain from more conventional field-work. In the end, however, it is the poor old Professor who stays behind with the anachronistic islanders, while Alice returns to Europe, raising the suggestion that only those who have nothing else left to live for can afford to become completely fused with their intellectual pursuits.

A literary excursion of this nature is bound to be as selective as it is personal; and of my numerous omissions from a catalogue of fictional archaeologists, as many result from my ignorance of their parent matrices as from any deliberate exclusion. A scarcely permissible excursion would be the examination, not of archaeologists in the twentieth-century novel, but of archaeological *sites* and their influences, baneful or otherwise, on human actions and human situations. Outstanding in this field are almost all the novels of that barely recognized genius, John Cowper Powys, especially his *Maiden Castle* (1937) and *A Glastonbury Romance* (1933); or, from that other great fount of English letters, the United States, the Gothic fantasies of H. P. Lovecraft in relation to antiquarian New England. If we must have a solitary instance, let us include *Priddy Barrows* (1944) by John Jarmain. An obsession with a small group of Mendip barrows that lies on his land slowly destroys a mad squire, Captain Hayes, who as a sideline runs the kind of preparatory school that the Department of Education and Science is still unable to prevent totally. The hero, an anticipatory kind of 'anti-hero' of no fixed roots (for it is 1944), goes to teach at this establishment, and finds his employer promoting the illegal excavation of barrow after barrow; not because he has any interest in them, but because he wants to punish the local antiquaries (the late H. St George Gray and others?) who are trying to stop him, as usual with little help from the appropriate state agency. Powerful, if cryptic, attachments to the bleak top-of-Mendip landscape lead our hero firstly to romantic attachments with daughters of the soil, and finally to the nocturnal seduction of an enormous girl, not only on one of Captain Hayes's barrows, but actually *in* the cutting. . . . Having thus, as it were, restored life to the wounded monument, he departs, the Office of Works stops the rot, the school burns down in an expiatory blaze, and the essential equipoise is restored.

The last book about imagined archaeologists, and to my mind the best, is *The Darkness Outside*, by the late George Johnston (1959), yet another Australian writer of distinction, with much the same ability to sketch a convincing setting as his compatriot Patrick White (and, like several of White's works, this book is dedicated to Sidney Nolan). George Johnston lived for a time in Cornwall, and I like to think that, during his continued questioning about the technicalities of excavation, I was able to help with a little of the bricks and mortar of this novel. A small party has returned to the huge, anonymous marshlands of southern Mesopotamia, an area described in a prose that suggests the quality of Nolan's Australian desertscapes. The leader, an American Orientalist, Elliot Purcell, has a private hypothesis about an undiscovered and very early civilization – in no way implausible, since it is implicitly the arrival-phase of the earliest Sumerians. He has a small staff. There is a monolithic Australian, ex-doctor and mental sheet-anchor, an unintentionally revealing portrait of George Johnston himself; a German called Steindorf, who has guilt-complexes (what fictional Teuton has not, after all?); a male ex-ballet dancer; and a young American girl, Grace, who has been taken on the team to learn the business as a favour to an influential friend.

The site adjoins one or other of the great rivers Tigris or Euphrates. As the work runs later into the season, there is a constant uncertainty as to whether to use the native labour force to build a massive levée, thus holding back the rising waters; or to deploy it on the most productive part of the site, and get to the heart of the matter as quickly as possible, before exposed levels are ruined by floods. Friction necessarily develops between the two men in charge of these complementary, but rival, projects. Those of us who have experienced, upon home territory, precisely this kind of conflict between equally essential tasks (either of which would absorb all available resources) can only admire the skill with which George Johnston handles the point.

Into this wholly isolated encampment, in contact with the world outside only when a passing caravan is seen across the river once every other month or so, a mysterious stranger erupts. He is an elderly and unhinged Englishman, dressed in tattered City-type clothing, who wanders in suddenly from the desert. His rambling tales, momentarily flickering into coherence, grip the party, who begin to believe that some cosmic disaster has gripped the distant civilized world – they have no means of checking that this is *not* the case – and the disaster is perceived to be a renaissance of that medieval terror, the Golden Horde. This time it is not the Huns, sweeping inexorably over Europe from the eastern steppes, but the Chinese.

The workmen, infected by the prevalent malaise, desert *en masse*. The elderly stranger dies. One of the excavators, escaping in their jeep, crashes it and kills himself. The others, having convinced themselves that they are living under a sentence of imminent death, find some consolation in an ideal of scientific duty. By heroic efforts they complete the bank that is to protect the opened cuttings from the floodwaters. At least, only the director, Purcell, and the young girl Grace, are left; they eventually succumb from starvation, but not before they have located, at a considerable depth, a sealed burial-chamber of proto-Sumerian date with fantastic and untouched material in it. The external calamity, which actually took place, is explained politically as one of the perennial Middle East revolutions, and physically, before the extinction of the party, it is manifested through an east-to-west dust storm of unusual severity.

Why is this such a good archaeological novel? It is most competently written – it avoids the stupid, supposedly archaeological, dialogues which mar virtually all the other works that I have mentioned, dialogues which could never, and I am certain do never, take place in the field between real archaeologists (even in front of television cameras). Page by page, Johnston deals, not so much with the improbable, but with what in that context would be both probable and likely. His book also illustrated – and in this respect it is rare indeed – a theme towards which many lesser writers blindly move: the awareness that on a long and exhausting excavation, where men and women are working under continuous stress on a task that is, by its nature, slightly unreal and artificial, personalities and relationships will undergo certain subtle changes, and at the time no one will realize this. A detailed portrayal of this process would, both psychologically and sociologically, be of much interest; one assumes that, in a condensed format, similar changes occur at (say) those ten-hour wrangles between politicians and trades union bosses. Alas, we must reconcile ourselves to the sorry fact that those who could, from the inside, write such a portrayal often have very good reasons for not doing so, or lack the literary talent to attempt the daunting task. Those who set out on the attempt, and there are fifty of them for each George Johnston that the world of letters produces, fail, from an insufficient knowledge of the *mise-en-scène*.

'Archaeology' is a term descriptive of a whole range of techniques for exploring the otherwise unrecorded past, but archaeologists are by definition *people*; and fictional archaeologists are no more than people in novels who happen to be taking part in some form of archaeology. More and more archaeologists – hundreds and hundreds of them – increase, collectively, the likelihood that a new George Eliot, Evelyn Waugh, or Iris Murdoch, will take time off to chronicle (we must hope, pseudonymously) the dark inner life of the laboratory, the excavation; the teaching department, the state agency. It is true that Doris Lessing (1971, esp. 163–9) has precisely caught the tone of the current methodological debate with her archaeologist who has 'doubts about its bases, premises, methods, and above all its unconscious biases'. Has Stuart Piggott himself yet been delineated (by the better class of novelist) in any work of literary pretensions? Has Sir Mortimer Wheeler? The intense, but grey, respectability that mantles such professional groups as the actuaries is scarcely conducive to fictional treatment, but archaeologists – much-travelled, much-praised, masters in their own courts, lords of a formidable realm of jargon and expertise – cry out for appropriate and dignified settings in the Great Archaeological Novel. Unless they provide at least one such by their own endeavours, who can guess what travesties may arise?

Bibliography

A. RELEVANT PAPERS BY STUART PIGGOTT

1955 The Ancestors of Jonathan Oldbuck, *Antiquity* XXIX, 150–6.

1966 The Roman Camp and Three Authors, *A Review of English Literature* VII, 21–8.

1970 Sir John Clerk and the 'Country Seat', in *The Country Seat: Studies in the History of the British Country House*, 110–16. London.

B. ARCHAEOLOGICAL FICTION MENTIONED IN THE TEXT

BUCHAN, John (Lord Tweedsmuir) 1915 *The Watcher by the Threshold, and Other Tales*, Edinburgh.

1925 *John Macnab*, London.

CASSON, Stanley 1943 *Murder by Burial*, London.

CHESTERTON, G. K. 1958 *The Incredulity of Father Brown*, Harmondsworth.

CHRISTIE, Agatha (Lady Mallowan) 1955 *Murder in Mesopotamia*, Harmondsworth.

CONAN DOYLE, Sir Arthur 1902 *The Hound of the Baskervilles*, London.

1917 *His Last Bow*, London.

1927 *The Case-Book of Sherlock Holmes*, London.

1929 *The Conan Doyle Stories* (collected edn), London.

1952 *The Professor Challenger Stories* (collected edn), London.

COWLIN, Dorothy 1952 *Rowanberry Wine*, London.

DANIEL, Glyn E. 1952 *The Cambridge Murders*, Harmondsworth.

1962 *Welcome Death*, Harmondsworth.

DAVIES, Hugh Sykes 1956 *Full Fathom Five*, London.

FALKNER, John Meade 1895 *The Lost Stradivarius*, Edinburgh.

1903 *The Nebuly Coat*, London.

GARVE, Andrew (pseudonym: Winterton, Paul) 1954 *The Riddle of Samson*, Glasgow.

HAGGARD, Sir Henry Rider 1887 *She*, London.

HAWKES, Jacquetta 1959 *Providence Island*, London.

JAMES, Montague Rhodes 1931 *Collected Ghost Stories*, London.

JAMESON, Storm 1956 *The Intruders*, London.

JARMAIN, (William) John (Fletcher) 1944 *Priddy Barrows*, Glasgow.

JOHNSTON, George 1959 *The Darkness Outside*, Glasgow.

LESSING, Doris 1971 *Briefing for a descent into Hell*, London.

MACHEN, Arthur (Llewellyn Jones) 1894 *The Great God Pan; and The Inmost Light*, London.

1895 *The Three Impostors; or, The Transmutations*, London.

MALLOCK, William Hurrell 1904 *The Veil of the Temple, or, From Night to Twilight*, London.

MANN, Jessica 1973 *The Only Security*, London.

O'NEILL, Joseph 1935 *Land Under England*, London.

POWYS, John Cowper 1933 *A Glastonbury Romance*, London.

1937 *Maiden Castle*, London.

PULVERTAFT, Lalage 1956 *No Great Magic*, London.

SAXBY, Jessie Margaret Edmonton n.d. (1892) *Viking Boys*, London.

SNOW, Charles P. (Lord Snow) 1956 *The Masters*, Harmondsworth.

TREECE, Henry 1956 *The Golden Strangers*, London.

VAN VOGT, A. E. 1951 *The Voyage of the Space Beagle*, London.

WILSON, Angus 1956 *Anglo-Saxon Attitudes*, London.

YONGE, Charlotte Mary 1856 *The Daisy Chain; or, Aspirations*.

34
Bibliography of Stuart Piggott's Publications

COMPILED BY MARJORIE ROBERTSON

THE terminal date for this list has been set at May 1975. Reviews (as opposed to review articles) have been omitted and journals have been listed under the year for which they were published. No systematic attempt has been made to include all direct reprints, although some important exceptions have been made.

1927

Early Iron Age rubbish pits at Knighton Hill, Berks., *Antiq. Journ.* VII, 517.

Fawler, as place-name, *Antiquity* I, 478–9.

A prehistoric village site at Knighton Hill, Compton Beauchamp, *Berks. Bucks. and Oxon. Archaeol. Journ.* XXXI, Part 1, 25–7.

1928

New camp on the Berkshire Downs, *Antiquity* II, 217–18.

Notes on the rediscovery of Berrygrove Roman villa and pottery on Blewburton Hill, Berks., *Antiquity* II, 359.

Bronze Age and late Celtic burials from Yateley, Hants., *Berks. Bucks. and Oxon. Archaeol. Journ.* XXXII, 69–73.

Berkshire mummers' plays and other folklore, *Folk-Lore* XXXIX, 271–81.

Excavation of an Early Iron Age site at Knighton Hill, near the White Horse Hill, Berks., *Man* XXVIII, 97–101.

Neolithic pottery and other remains from Pangbourne, Berks., and Caversham, Oxon., *Proc. Prehist. Soc. E. Anglia* VI, Part I, 30–9.

1929

Note about Alfred's castle, near Ashdown Park, Berks., *Antiquity* III, 352.

Mummers' plays from Berkshire, Derbyshire, Cumberland and Isle of Man, *Folk-Lore* XL, 262–77.

Letter: New light on Christopher Smart, *Times Lit. Supp.* (13 June), 474.

1930

Butser Hill, *Antiquity* IV, 187–200.

A primitive carving from Anglesey, *Man* XXX, 122–3.

1931

Ladle Hill – an unfinished hillfort, *Antiquity* V, 474–85.

The Uffington White Horse, *Antiquity* V, 37–46.

The Neolithic pottery of the British Isles, *Archaeol. Journ.* LXXXVIII, 67–158.

Letter: Book inscriptions, *Times Lit. Supp.* (23 July), 583.

1932

The Mull Hill Circle, Isle of Man, and its pottery, *Antiq. Journ.* XII, 146–57.

The name of the Giant of Cerne, *Antiquity* VI, 214–16.

Report on pottery from Kirk Maughold, *Journal of the Manx Museum* II, no. 32, 74.

Comparative notes on a series of Neolithic potsherds from Larne (with V. Gordon Childe), *Proc. Prehist. Soc. E. Anglia* VII, Part I, 62–6.

1933

Extract from a report in *Journ. of the Manx Museum* II (1932) (above), *Twenty-eighth annual report of the Manx Museum and Ancient Monuments Trustees*, 8.

The age of the British flint mines (with Grahame Clark), *Antiquity* VII, 166–83.

The pottery from the Lligwy burial chamber, Anglesey, *Archaeologia Cambrensis* LXXXVIII, 68–72.

1934

The relative chronology of the British long barrows, in *Proceedings of the First International Congress of Prehistoric and Protohistoric Sciences* (London, 1932), 143–4.

Neolithic and Early Bronze Age settlement at Broom Hill, Michelmersh, Hants. (with Rev. S. T. Percival), *Antiq. Journ.* XIV, 246–53.

Report on the pottery, in E. Cecil Curwen, Excavations in Whitehawk Neolithic camp, Brighton, 1932–3, *Antiq. Journ.* XIV, 112–21.

Note on Anna Stukeley's account of the Uffington White Horse, *Antiquity* VIII, 230.

The pottery from the Avebury excavations, in H. St George Gray, The Avebury excavations, 1908–1922, *Archaeologia* LXXXIV, 136–41.

The mutual relations of the British Neolithic ceramics, *Proc. Prehist. Soc. E. Anglia* VII, Part III, 373–81.

1935

The progress of early man (How-and-Why Series 18), London: A. and C. Black. (Illustrated by the author.)

Report on the pottery, in H. J. Cheney, An Aeneolithic occupation site at Playden, near Rye, *Antiq. Journ.* XV, 161–3.

Report on pottery, in J. G. D. Clark, *et al.*, Report on recent excavations at Peacock's Farm, Shippea Hill, Cambridgeshire, *Antiq. Journ.* XV, 284–319.

Handled beakers, *Antiquity* IX, 348.

Megalithic engravings, *Antiquity* IX, 342.

Stukeley, Avebury and the Druids, *Antiquity* IX, 22–32.

Neolithic pottery spoon from Kent, *Proc. Prehist. Soc.* I, 150–1.

A note on the relative chronology of the English long barrows, *Proc. Prehist. Soc.* I, 115–26.

A remarkable bowl from the Avebury megalithic avenue, *Proc. Prehist. Soc.* I, 147–8.

Two foreign stone axes from Hampshire, *Proc. Prehist. Soc.* I, 154.

Report on the pottery, in J. F. S. Stone, Some discoveries at Ratfyn, Amesbury and their bearing on the date of Woodhenge, *Wilts. Arch. Mag.* XLVII, 62–4.

1936

A potsherd from the Stonehenge ditch, *Antiquity* X, 221–2.

The recent excavations at Avebury (with Alexander Keiller), *Antiquity* X, 417–27.

Two Bronze Age barrows, excavated by Mr. Edward Cunnington (with C. D. Drew), *Proc. Dorset Nat. Hist. and Arch. Soc.* LVIII, 18–25.

Archaeology of the submerged land-surface of the Essex Coast (with S. Hazzledine Warren, J. G. D. Clark, *et al.*), *Proc. Prehist. Soc.* II, 178–210.

A beaker from the Skipsea peat, Yorkshire (with Nancy Newbigin), *Proc. Prehist. Soc.* II, 230–1.

The excavation of long barrow 163a on Thickthorn Down, Dorset (with C. D. Drew), *Proc. Prehist. Soc.* II, 77–96.

Handley Hill, Dorset – a Neolithic bowl and the date of the entrenchment, *Proc. Prehist. Soc.* II, 229–30.

A pottery spoon from the Mendips, *Proc. Prehist. Soc.* II, 143.

The pottery, in E. Cecil Curwen, Excavations in Whitehawk Camp, Brighton: third season, 1935, *Sussex Arch. Colls.* LXXVII, 75–80.

An early settlement at Theale, near Reading, Berks., *Trans. Newbury District Field Club* VII, no. 3, 146–9.

Excavations on Churn Plain, Blewbury, Berks. (with H. J. E. Peake, *et al.*), *Trans. Newbury District Field Club* VII, no. 3, 160–74.

A Saxon cross shaft fragment from Wantage, *Trans. Newbury District Field Club* VII, no. 3, 149–50.

1937
The long barrow in Brittany, *Antiquity* XI, 441–55.

Prehistory and the Romantic Movement, *Antiquity* XI, 31–8.

White quartz pebbles as funerary offerings, *Antiquity* XI, 354–5.

The excavation of a long barrow in Holdenhurst parish, near Christchurch, Hants., *Proc. Prehist. Soc.* III, 1–14.

Neolithic pottery from Hackpen, Avebury, *Wilts. Arch. Mag.* XLVIII, 90–1.

1938
The Hercules myth – beginnings and ends, *Antiquity* XII, 323–31.

Edited *Berkshire Archaeological Journal* XLII-XLIV (1938–40) (XLIV with P. S. Spokes).

A Neolithic 'A' habitation site at Corfe Mullen (with J. B. Calkin), *Proc. Dorset Nat. Hist. and Arch. Soc.* LX, 73–4.

The Early Bronze Age in Wessex, *Proc. Prehist. Soc.* IV, 52–106.

Excavation of an untouched chamber in the Lanhill long barrow (with Alexander Keiller), *Proc. Prehist. Soc.* IV, 122–50.

Appendix I: A note on the 'A' Beaker culture in the Bournemouth region, in C. M. Piggott, A Middle Bronze Age barrow and Deverel-Rimbury urnfield, at Latch Farm, Christchurch, Hampshire, *Proc. Prehist. Soc.* IV, 181–2.

Appendix V: The pottery from Nympsfield long barrow, in Elsie M. Clifford, The excavation of Nympsfield long barrow, Gloucestershire, *Proc. Prehist. Soc.* IV, 211.

1939
The Bagshot long barrow (with Alexander Keiller), in *Prehistory of the Farnham district*, Guildford: Surrey Archaeological Society, 133–49.

The Badbury barrow, Dorset, and its carved stone, *Antiq. Journ.* XIX, 291–9.

Decorated prehistoric pottery from the bed of the Ebbsfleet, Northfleet, Kent (with J. P. T. Burchell), *Antiq. Journ.* XIX, 405–20.

The flint axe from the barrow, in R. F. Jessup, Further excavations at Julliberrie's Grave, Chilham, *Antiq. Journ.* XIX, 267–9.

The chambered tomb in Beowulf (with Alexander Keiller), *Antiquity* XIII, 360–1.

Stone and earth circles in Dorset (with C. M. Piggott), *Antiquity* XIII, 138–58.

Timber circles: a re-examination, *Archaeol. Journ.* XCVI, 193–222.

Further Bronze Age 'dagger graves' in Brittany, *Proc. Prehist. Soc.* V, 193–5.

Excavation of a round barrow near Pewit Farm, Charlton Down, Berks., *Trans. Newbury District Field Club* VIII, no. 2, 109–16.

Trial excavation at Ram's Hill, *Trans. Newbury District Field Club* VIII, no. 2, 116–17.

1940
Excavations at Rams Hill, Uffington, Berks. (with C. M. Piggott), *Antiq. Journ.* XX, 465–80.

A trepanned skull of the Beaker period from Dorset and the practice of trepanning in prehistoric Europe, *Proc. Prehist. Soc.* VI, 112–32.

The excavations at Rams Hill, 1939 (with C. M. Piggott), *Trans. Newbury District Field Club* VIII, no. 3, 171–7.

1941

Grooved stone cists, Scotland and the Scillies, *Antiquity* XV, 81–3.

The sources of Geoffrey of Monmouth: I: The 'pre-Roman' King-List; II: The Stonehenge story, *Antiquity* XV, 269–86; 305–19.

An unrecorded Iron Age enclosure on Rockbourne Down, Hants., *Proc. Hants. Field Club* XV, Part I, 53–5.

First report of the Sub-Committee of the South-Western Group of Museums and Art Galleries on the Petrological Identification of Stone Axes (with Alexander Keiller and F. S. Wallis), *Proc. Prehist. Soc.* VII, 50–72.

1943

India's place in the prehistoric East, in *Longmans miscellany 1943*, Bombay, 235–49.

Dating the Hissar sequence – the Indian evidence, *Antiquity* XVII, 169–82.

The earliest Buddhist shrines, *Antiquity* XVII, 1–10.

Appendix I: The grave-structures in Beaulieu barrows II and IX, in C. M. Piggott, Excavation of fifteen barrows in the New Forest 1941–2, *Proc. Prehist. Soc.* IX, 24–5.

1944

A cylinder-seal from South India, *Antiquity* XVIII, 98–9.

Prehistoric copper hoards in the Ganges basin, *Antiquity* XVIII, 173–82.

Excavation of barrows on Crichel and Launceston Downs, Dorset (with C. M. Piggott), *Archaeologia* XC, 47–80.

Nomad house-sites in the western Himalayas, *Man* XLIV, 150–2.

1945

India's place in the prehistoric East, in *Longmans miscellany number one*, 235–49. (Reissue of *Longmans miscellany 1943*.)

Poems: 'Lahoul', 19–20, 'January in Delhi', 60–1, 'For Paul the Deacon – Monte Casino, A.D. 790', 79–80, 'Bohemond's Tomb', 88–93, in *Poems from India by members of the forces*, ed. R. N. Currey and R. V. Gibson, Bombay: Oxford University Press. London edition 1946.

Some ancient cities of India, Bombay: Oxford University Press.

Archaeological journalism in the 17th century, *Antiquity* XIX, 210–11.

Farmsteads in Central India, *Antiquity* XIX, 154–6.

The chambered cairn of 'The Grey Mare and Colts', *Proc. Dorset Nat. Hist. and Arch. Soc.* LXVII, 30–3.

Probable long barrow and stones near Eggardon, *Proc. Dorset Nat. Hist. and Arch. Soc.* LXVII, 29.

1946

The chronology of prehistoric North-West India, *Ancient India* I, 8–26.

The excavation of a barrow on Rockbourne Down (with C. M. Piggott), *Proc. Hants. Field Club* XVI, 156–62.

Field work in Colonsay and Islay, 1944–45 (with C. M. Piggott), *Proc. Soc. Ant. Scot.* LXXX, 83–103.

The destruction of 'The Sanctuary' on Overton Hill, *Wilts. Arch. Mag.* LI, 470–1.

An Early Bronze Age vessel from Ashley Hill, near Salisbury, *Wilts. Arch. Mag.* LI, 384–5.

1947

A new prehistoric ceramic from Baluchistan, *Ancient India* III, 131–42.

The Arreton Down Bronze Age hoard, *Antiq. Journ.* XXVII, 177–8.

Britons, Romans and Saxons round Salisbury and in Cranborne Chase: reviewing the excavations of General Pitt-Rivers, 1881–1897 (in collaboration with C. F. C. Hawkes), *Archaeol. Journ.* CIV, 27–81.

Knowlton Church, *Archaeol. Journ.* CIV, 163.

Stonehenge: a summary note, in the Report on the Royal Arch. Inst. Summer Meeting at Salisbury (1947), *Archaeol. Journ.* CIV, 4–6.

Notes on megalithic tombs in Sligo and Achill (with T. G. E. Powell), *Journ. Roy. Soc. Ant. Ireland* LXXVII, 136–46.

Roman burials at Middle Wallop, Hants., *Proc. Hants. Field Club* XVII, 60–3.

Notes on some North Wiltshire chambered tombs, *Wilts. Arch. Mag.* LII, 57–64.

1948

Fire among the ruins, 1942–1945 (poems), London: Oxford University Press.

Edited (with Christopher Hawkes) *A survey and policy of field research in the archaeology of Great Britain, I: the prehistoric and early historic ages to the seventh century A.D.*, London: Council for British Archaeology.

Notes on certain metal pins and a mace-head in the Harappā culture, *Ancient India* IV, 26–40.

Appendix: Throne-fragments from Pāṭaliputra, in R. E. M. Wheeler, Iran and India in pre-Islamic times: a lecture, *Ancient India* IV, 101–3.

An Early Bronze Age sanctuary site in the Scottish Lowlands, *Antiquity* XXII, 35–6.

Fire-dogs again, *Antiquity* XXII, 21–8.

Primitive house-types in Iberia, *Antiquity* XXII, 40–2.

Archaeology and the amateur, *Arch. News Letter* I, no. 1, 1–2.

Letter: Archaeology and the amateur, *Arch. News Letter* I, no. 4, 10.

Metal-work of the North British Iron Age. Resumé of a paper by S.P. given at C.B.A. Summer meeting at York, *Arch. News Letter* I, no. 6, 10–12.

The North British Iron Age – some comments. Resumé of a paper by S.P. given at a meeting of the Prehistoric Soc. and the Cumb. and Westm. Ant. and Arch. Soc., Carlisle (September 1948), *Arch. News Letter* I, no. 8, 9–10.

Prehistoric sculpture in the exhibition and a note on certain figurines. On the Indian Exhibition – sculpture and painting chiefly from the dominions of India and Pakistan exhibited at the Royal Academy of Arts, *Burlington Magazine* XC, 33–7.

A Bronze Age burial cist at Balbie Farm, Burntisland, *Proc. Soc. Ant. Scot.* LXXXII, 299–301.

The excavations at Cairnpapple Hill, West Lothian, 1947–48, *Proc. Soc. Ant. Scot.* LXXXII, 68–123.

Relações entre Portugal e as Ilhas Britânicas nos começos da Idade do Bronze, *Revista de Guimarães* LVII, 5–18.

The 'Black Warren' in Rockbourne, Hants., *Wilts. Arch. Mag.* LII, 398.

Destroyed megaliths in North Wiltshire, *Wilts. Arch. Mag.* LII, 390–2.

1949

British prehistory, London: Oxford University Press.

Sassanian motifs on painted pottery from North-West India, *Ancient India* V, 31–4.

The excavations at Cairnpapple Hill, West Lothian 1947–8, *Antiquity* XXIII, 32–9.

A Celtic exhibition in France, *Arch. News Letter* II, no. 3, 41.

British Council archaeological course in Wessex, *Arch. News Letter* II, no. 6, 93–5.

Excavations in three chambered tombs in Galloway, 1949, *Arch. News Letter* II, no. 7, 108–9.

Appendix: Grooved Ware from Honington, Cambridgeshire, in J. F. S. Stone, Some Grooved Ware pottery from the Woodhenge area, *Proc. Prehist. Soc.* XV, 127.

An Iron Age yoke from Northern Ireland, *Proc. Prehist. Soc.* XV, 192–3.

A wheel of Iron Age type from Co. Durham, *Proc. Prehist. Soc.* XV, 191.

The excavation of three Neolithic chambered tombs in Galloway, 1949 (with T. G. E. Powell), *Proc. Soc. Ant. Scot.* LXXXIII, 103–61.

1950

Articles in *Chambers's encyclopaedia* (New Edition), London: George Newnes. Vol. II: Avebury, 2–3, Bronze Age, 603–5; vol. V: Europe, Archaeology: Bronze Age, 457–61; vol. XIII: Stonehenge, 202–3, Stukeley, William, 233–4.

Prehistoric India to 1000 B.C., Harmondsworth: Penguin Books.

William Stukeley: an eighteenth century antiquary, Oxford: Clarendon Press.

Pestilences in sixth century Britain, *Antiquity* XXIV, 143–5.

The Zürich congress, *Antiquity* XXIV, 171–4.

Excavations at Stonehenge, 1950 (with R. J. C. Atkinson and J. F. S. Stone), *Arch. News Letter* III, no. 1, 3–4.

Swords and scabbards of the British Early Iron Age, *Proc. Prehist. Soc.* XVI, 1–28.

Comment on the pottery, in Reginald Musson, An excavation at Combe Hill Camp near Eastbourne, August 1949, *Sussex Arch. Colls.* LXXXIX, 110–14.

1951

Stonehenge reviewed, in *Aspects of archaeology in Britain and beyond: essays presented to O. G. S. Crawford*, ed. W. F. Grimes, London: H. W. Edwards, 274–92.

Cairnpapple Hill, West Lothian, Edinburgh: HMSO.

A picture book of ancient British art (with Glyn E. Daniel), Cambridge: University Press.

Prehistoric settlement, in *Scientific survey of South-Eastern Scotland*, Edinburgh: British Association Local Committee. (Prepared for the meeting of the British Association held in Edinburgh, 8–15 August 1951), 44–53.

The Society's lamp, *Antiq. Journ.* XXXI, 74.

Archaeology in Wessex: part I, *Arch. News Letter* IV, no. 3, 33–7.

Appendix: Report on the pottery from High Wheeldon Cave, in J. Wilfrid Jackson, Peterborough (Neolithic B) pottery from High Wheeldon Cave, Earl Sterndale, near Buxton, *Journ. Derbyshire Arch. and Nat. Hist. Soc.* LXXI, 74–7.

William Camden and the *Britannia* (Reckitt Archaeological Lecture), *Proc. Brit. Acad.* XXXVII, 199–217.

Excavations in the broch and hill-fort of Torwoodlee, Selkirkshire, 1950, *Proc. Soc. Ant. Scot.* LXXXV, 92–117.

1952

The excavation of two additional holes at Stonehenge, 1950, and new evidence for the date of the monument (with R. J. C. Atkinson and J. F. S. Stone), *Antiq. Journ.* XXXII, 14–20.

Celtic chariots on Roman coins, *Antiquity* XXVI, 87–8.

Archaeology in Wessex: parts II and III, *Arch. News Letter* IV, nos. 5 and 8, 65–9 and 113–17.

Note on pottery from the Charleton Higher Down – Little Piddle Down field system, in R. A. H. Farrar, Archaeological fieldwork in Dorset in 1952, *Proc. Dorset Nat. Hist. and Arch. Soc.* LXXIV, 90.

Excavations at Castle Law, Glencorse, and at Craig's Quarry, Dirleton, 1948–9 (with C. M. Piggott), *Proc. Soc. Ant. Scot.* LXXXVI, 191–6.

The Neolithic camp on Whitesheet Hill, Kilmington parish, *Wilts. Arch. Mag.* LIV, 404–10.

1953

The Wessex Early Bronze Age: a chronological re-assessment, in *Actes de la IIIe session Cong. Internat. des Sciences Préhist. et Protohist.* (Zurich, 1950), 225.

William Camden and the Britannia (Reckitt Archaeological Lecture, British Academy, 1951, reprinted from *Proc. Brit. Acad.* XXXVII), London: Oxford University Press.

Les relations entre l'Ouest de la France et les Iles Britanniques dans la préhistoire, *Annales du Midi* LXV, 5–20.

The tholos tomb in Iberia, *Antiquity* XXVII, 137–43.

A Bronze Age barrow on Turners Puddle Heath (with Geoffrey Dimbleby), *Proc. Dorset Nat. Hist. and Arch. Soc.* LXXV, 34–5.

Note on Bronze Age awls, in Aubrey L. Peake, The excavation of a bell-barrow, Oakley Down, Wimborne St. Giles, *Proc. Dorset Nat. Hist. and Arch. Soc.* LXXV, 40–1.

Bronze double-axes in the British Isles, *Proc. Prehist. Soc.* XIX, 224–6.

'Halberds' at Mycenae, *Proc. Prehist. Soc.* XIX, 231.

An iron object from Dunadd, *Proc. Soc. Ant. Scot.* LXXXVII, 193–4.

A Late Bronze Age hoard from Peeblesshire, *Proc. Soc. Ant. Scot.* LXXXVII, 175–86.

Three metal-work hoards of the Roman period from Southern Scotland, *Proc. Soc. Ant. Scot.* LXXXVII, 1–50.

1953–54

Le Néolithique occidental et le Chalcolithique en France: Esquisse préliminaire, *L'Anthropologie* LVII (1953), 401–43; LVIII (1954), 1–28.

1954

The Neolithic cultures of the British Isles, Cambridge: University Press.

The scabbard, in Sir Mortimer Wheeler *The Stanwick fortifications, North Riding of Yorkshire* (Rep. of the Research Com. Soc. Ant. London, no. XVII), 48–50.

Durrington Walls, Wiltshire: recent excavations at a ceremonial site of the early second millennium B.C. (with J. F. S. Stone and A. St. J. Booth), *Antiq. Journ.* XXXIV, 155–77.

Recent work at Stonehenge (reprinted from *The Times*, 4 August 1954), *Antiquity* XXVIII, 221–4.

Some primitive structures in Achill Island, *Antiquity* XXVIII, 19–24.

Magic island-sanctuaries of the Mediterranean, *Listener* LII (5 August), 205–7.

New light on the story of Stonehenge, *The Times* (4 August), 4.

1955

Poem: 'January in Delhi', in *A book of verse for young people*, ed. James A. Stone, Part II, London: Oxford University Press, 26–7.

The role of the city in ancient civilizations, in *The metropolis in modern life* (Columbia Univ. Bicent. Conf. Ser.), ed. R. M. Fisher, New York: Doubleday, 5–17. (In 1967 this volume was reissued in New York by Russell and Russell.)

Poem: 'The Tortoise', in *Modern verse 1900–1950*, ed. Phyllis M. Jones, London: Oxford University Press, 221–3.

The Druids and Stonehenge, in G. E. Daniel *et al.*, *Myth or legend?*, London: G. Bell, 97–104.

The archaeological background, in *The problem of the Picts*, ed. F. T. Wainwright, Edinburgh: Nelson, 54–65.

The ancestors of Johnathan Oldbuck (lecture to the Society of Antiquaries of Scotland, 10 January 1955), *Antiquity* XXIX, 150–6.

The Torrs chamfrein (with R. J. C. Atkinson), *Archaeologia* XCVI, 197–235.

Warriors and metalworkers. Report of a paper by by S.P. given at the Fourth Scottish Summer School in Archaeology, Edinburgh (July 1955), *Arch. News Letter* VI, no. 1, 15–16.

The thirteen tombs of Alaca Hüyük, *Listener* LIV (10 November), 790–2.

Windmill Hill – East or West?, *Proc. Prehist. Soc.* XXI, 96–101.

1956

Antiquarian thought in the sixteenth and seventeenth centuries, in *English historical scholarship in the sixteenth and seventeenth centuries*, ed. Levi Fox, Oxford University Press for the Dugdale Society, 93–114.

Architecture and ritual in megalithic monuments, *Journ. Roy. Inst. Brit. Archit.* LXIII, 175–81.

Architecture and ritual in megalithic monuments, *Monumental Journ.* XXIII, no. 10, 611–17; no. 11, 669–75.

Excavations in passage-graves and ring-cairns of the Clava group, 1952–3, *Proc. Soc. Ant. Scot.* LXXXVIII, 173–207.

Prefatory note, in F. P. Lisowski, The cremations from the Culdoich, Leys and Kinchyle sites, *Proc. Soc. Ant. Scot.* LXXXIX, 83.

Three Stonehenges, *The Times* (20 December), 9.

Report on excavations at Stonehenge, 1956, *Wilts. Arch. Mag.* LVI, 232–7.

1957

Articles in *Encyclopaedia Britannica*, London. Vol. II: Archaeology, XI: Indian subcontinent, 259E–H; vol. XIV: Malta, Archaeology, 739–40.

A tripartite disc wheel from Blair Drummond, Perthshire, *Proc. Soc. Ant. Scot.* XC, 238–41.

1958

Edited (with Margaret Stewart) *Inventaria Archaeologica GB 25–34*: Early and Middle Bronze Age grave-groups and hoards from Scotland, London: Garraway.

Native economies and the Roman occupation of North Britain, in *Roman and native in North Britain* (Studies in History and Archaeology), ed. I. A. Richmond, Edinburgh: Nelson, 1–27.

Translations of five epigrams of Martial, in *Roman readings*, ed. Michael Grant, Harmondsworth: Penguin Books, 349.

Scotland before history. An essay . . . with illustrations by Keith Henderson, London: Nelson.

The dawn: and an epilogue (review of V. G. Childe *The dawn of European civilization*, 6th ed., 1957 and *The prehistory of European society*, 1958), *Antiquity* XXXII, 75–9.

The excavation of the West Kennet long barrow: 1955–56, *Antiquity* XXXII, 235–42.

Vere Gordon Childe: 1892–1957, *Proc. Brit. Acad.* XLIV, 305–12.

Segmented bone beads and toggles in the British Early and Middle Bronze Age, *Proc. Prehist. Soc.* XXIV, 227–9.

Excavations at Braidwood fort, Midlothian and Craig's Quarry, Dirleton, East Lothian, *Proc. Soc. Ant. Scot.* XCI, 61–77.

1959

Approach to archaeology, London: A. and C. Black.

The *carnyx* in Early Iron Age Britain, *Antiq. Journ.* XXXIX, 19–32.

A Late Bronze Age wine trade?, *Antiquity* XXXIII, 122–3.

The radio-carbon date from Durrington Walls, *Antiquity* XXXIII, 289–90.

Stonehenge, science and archaeology, *New Scientist* VI, no. 141, 132–3.

1960

Appendix A: Excavations at Avebury, 4–9th July 1960, in *Anc. Mons. Boards 7th ann. reports*, 10.

Prehistory and evolutionary theory, in *Evolution after Darwin: The University of Chicago Centennial*, Vol. II: *The evolution of man*, ed. Sol Tax, University of Chicago Press, 85–97.

Neolithic and Bronze Age in East Europe, *Antiquity* XXXIV, 285–94.

Text of an address by S.P. at the opening of the Bronze Age Room at the Museum, Devizes, 21 May 1960, *Wilts. Arch. Mag.* LVII, 428–9.

1961

Edited *The dawn of civilization*, London: Thames and Hudson. To this S.P. contributed a foreword, 5; Introduction: the man-made world, 11–15; Epilogue: the heritage of Man, 387–8. S.P. thereafter General Editor of the series *Library of the Early Civilizations*, pub. by Thames and Hudson, based on contributions to this composite work.

The British Neolithic cultures in their continental setting, in *L'Europe à la fin de l'âge de la pierre* (Actes du Symposium consacré aux problèmes du Néolithique européen, Prague–Liblice–Brno, 5–12 octobre 1959), ed. J. Bohm and S. J. De Laet, Prague: Academia, Czechoslovak Academy of Sciences, 557–74.

The Badden cist slab (with Marion Campbell of Kilberry and J. G. Scott), *Proc. Soc. Ant. Scot.* XCIV, 46–61.

Filitosa, *Review of the Soc. for Hellenic Travel* I, 41–2.

1962

Prehistoric India to 1000 B.C. (The Belle Sauvage Library), London: Cassell.

Edited *The prehistoric peoples of Scotland* (Studies in Anc. Hist. and Arch.), London: Routledge and Kegan Paul. To the above S.P. contributed the chapter 'Traders and metalworkers', 73–103.

The West Kennet long barrow: excavations 1955–56 (Ministry of Works Archaeological Reports No. 4), London: HMSO.

Heads and hoofs, *Antiquity* XXXVI, 110–18.

Fourth report of the Sub-Committee of the South-Western Group of Museums and Art Galleries on the Petrological Identification of Stone Axes (with E. D. Evens, *et al.*), *Proc. Prehist. Soc.* XXVIII, 209–66.

The prehistoric origins of Europe: from the beginnings of agriculture to classical antiquity (Rhind Lectures 1962), six articles, *Scotsman* (15–17, 20–22 November).

From Salisbury Plain to South Siberia, *Wilts. Arch. Mag.* LVIII, 93–7.

1963

Les problèmes du Néolithique occidental, in *Les Civilisations Atlantiques du Néolithique à l'Âge du Fer* (Actes du Premier Colloque Atlantique, Brest, 11 Septembre 1961), ed. P.-R. Giot, Rennes: Travaux du Laboratoire d'Anthropologie préhistorique, 5–8; contributions by S.P. to discussion, 12–13, 21, 91.

Abercromby and after: the Beaker cultures of Britain re-examined, in *Culture and environment: essays in honour of Sir Cyril Fox*, ed. I. Ll. Foster and L. Alcock, London: Routledge and Kegan Paul, 53–91.

West Kennet long barrow: Wiltshire, London: HMSO.

The Bronze Age pit at Swanwick, Hants.: a post-script, *Antiq. Journ.* XLIII, 286–7.

A Romano-Celtic bronze head, *Antiq. Journ.* XLIII, 116–18.

Archaeology and prehistory (Presidential Address), *Proc. Prehist. Soc.* XXIX, 1–16.

1964

Preface and section 'Land transport', in *Advance: An account of prehistoric man's first steps in technology*, BBC Publications, 1–2 and 24–7.

Brazilian Indians on an Elizabethan monument, *Antiquity* XXXVIII, 134–6.

Iron, Cimmerians and Aeschylus, *Antiquity* XXXVIII, 300–3.

Cairnpapple, Castle Law hill-fort and souterrain, in Report of Roy. Arch. Inst. Summer Meeting, Edinburgh 1964, *Archaeol. Journ.* CXXI, 186–7.

The mystery of Stonehenge, *Life International* (13 July), 58–61.

Excavations at Avebury, 1960, *Wilts. Arch. Mag.* LIX, 28–9.

1965

Ancient Europe from the beginnings of agriculture to classical antiquity: a survey, Edinburgh: University Press.

Approach to archaeology, New York: McGraw-Hill Paperback/Harvard University Press.

Prehistoric societies (The History of Human Society, ed. J. M. Plumb) (with Grahame Clark), London: Hutchinson.

Alexander Keiller, 1889–1955, in *Windmill Hill and Avebury: excavations by Alexander Keiller 1925–1939*, ed. I. F. Smith, Oxford: Clarendon Press, xix-xxii.

Archaeological draughtsmanship: principles and practice: Part I: principles and retrospect, *Antiquity* XXXIX, 165–76.

Early Celtic weapons and parade gear in Scotland, *Scottish Art Review* X, 8–12.

The science of rubbish (review of *Prehistoric and early Wales*, ed. I. Ll. Foster and Glyn Daniel, 1965), *Spectator* (9 April), 482–3.

1966

Approach to archaeology, Harmondsworth: Penguin Books.

Arqueologia de la India prehistorica (Spanish translation), Mexico City: Fondo de Cultura Economica.

A scheme for the Scottish Iron Age, in *The Iron Age in Northern Britain*, ed. A. L. F. Rivet, Edinburgh: University Press, 1–15.

A new photographic technique at Croft Moraig (with Malcolm Murray), *Antiquity* XL, 304.

Ireland and Britain in prehistory: changing viewpoints and perspectives, *Journ. Cork Hist. and Arch. Soc.* LXXI, 5–18.

'Unchambered' long barrows in Neolithic Britain, *Palaeohistoria* XII (presented to A. E. Van Giffen for his 80th birthday), 381–93.

Appendix I: Note on the reconstructed drawing [of a cinerary urn], in Margaret E. C. Stewart, Excavation of a setting of standing stones at Lundin Farm near Aberfeldy, Perthshire, *Proc. Soc. Ant. Scot.* XCVIII, 138–40.

The Roman camp and three authors, *Review of English Literature* VII, 21–8.

Mycenae and barbarian Europe: an outline survey, *Sborník Národního Muzea v Praze A* XX (Neustupný festschrift), 117–25.

1967

Celts, Saxons and the early antiquaries (The O'Donnell Lecture, 1966), Edinburgh: University Press.

David Jones and the past of man, *Agenda* V (David Jones special issue), 76–9.

New perspectives in European prehistory – I: The new chronology; II: The Near East and eastern Europe, *Listener* XCVIII (16 and 23 March), 353–4 and 393–5.

Sir Cyril Fox, 1882–1967, *Proc. Brit. Acad.* LIII, 399–407.

1968

Ancient Europe from the beginnings of agriculture to classical antiquity: a survey, Chicago: Aldine Publishing Company.

The Druids, London: Thames and Hudson.

An ancient Briton in North Africa, *Antiquity* XLII, 128–30.

The earliest wheeled vehicles and the Caucasian evidence, *Proc. Prehist. Soc.* XXXIV, 266–318.

The beginnings of wheeled transport, *Scientific American* CCXIX (July), 82–90.

1969

Conclusion, in *The domestication and exploitation of plants and animals* (proceedings of a meeting of the Research Seminar in Archaeology and Related Subjects held at the Institute of Archaeology, London University), ed. P. J. Ucko and G. W. Dimbleby, London: G. Duckworth, 555–60.

Early Iron Age 'horn-caps' and yokes, *Antiq. Journ.* XLIX, 378–81.

Celtic art, *History of the English Speaking Peoples*, no. 2 (October), 72–5.

1970

The relative chronology of the British Early Bronze Age, in *Actes du VIIe Cong. Internat. des Sciences Préhist. et Protohist.* (Prague, 1966), 654–7.

Sir John Clerk and 'the Country Seat', in *The country seat: studies in the history of the British country house presented to Sir John Summerson on his 65th birthday*, ed. Howard Colvin and John Harris, London: Allen Lane, 110–16.

Early Celtic art (catalogue of an exhibition at the Royal Scottish Museum, Edinburgh and the Hayward Gallery, London, 1970) (with Derek Allen), Edinburgh: University Press for the Arts Council of Great Britain.

The Neolithic cultures of the British Isles (reissued in Cambridge University Press Library Edition).

Prehistoric societies (with Grahame Clark; reissued in paperback), Harmondsworth: Penguin Books.

British archaeology and the enemy (Presidential Address to the Council for British Archaeology), [C.B.A.] *Report no. 20*, 74–85.

Copper vehicle-models in the Indus civilization, *Journ. Roy. Asiatic Soc.* (Studies in honour of Sir Mortimer Wheeler), 200–2.

The Druids, *Man, Myth and Magic* no. 26, 719–21.

The prehistoric monuments, in *Illustrated guide to ancient monuments*: VI, *Scotland* (with W. Douglas Simpson), Edinburgh: HMSO (6th ed.), 9–33.

1971

Introduction: William Camden and the *Britannia* (reprinted from *Proc. Brit. Acad.* XXXVII), in *Camden's Britannia 1695* (facsimile of the 1695 edition), Newton Abbot: David and Charles, 5–13.

Firedogs in Iron Age Britain and beyond, in *The European community in later prehistory: studies in honour of C. F. C. Hawkes*, ed. John Boardman, M. A. Brown and T. G. E. Powell, London: Routledge and Kegan Paul, 243–70.

Introduction, to Inigo Jones (*et al.*) *The most notable antiquity of Great Britain vulgarly called Stone-Heng on Salisbury Plain, restored, by Inigo Jones.... To which are added the Chorea Gigantum, or, Stone-Heng restored to the Danes by Dr. Charleton; and Mr. Webb's Vindication of Stone-Heng restored ... London 1725* (facsimile reprint), Farnborough: Gregg.

The first peoples, in *Who are the Scots?*, ed. Gordon Menzies, London: BBC Publications, 11–21.

Excavation of a stone circle at Croft Moraig, Perthshire, Scotland, *Proc. Prehist. Soc.* XXXVII, Part I, 1–15.

Beaker bows: a suggestion, *Proc. Prehist. Soc.* XXXVII, Part II (Contributions to Prehistory Offered to Grahame Clark), 80–94.

An archaeological survey and policy for Wiltshire: Part III: Neolithic and Bronze Age, *Wilts. Arch. Mag.* LXVI, 47–57.

Note on the Neolithic cultural material from Green Howe, North Deighton, in Eric S. Wood, The excavation of a Bronze Age barrow: Green Howe, North Deighton, Yorkshire, *Yorks. Arch. Journ.* XLIII, 16–17.

1972

The beginning of the Neolithic in the British Isles, in *Die Anfänge des Neolithikums vom Orient bis Nordeuropa*, ed. H. Schwabedissen, (Fundamenta: Reihe A, Bd. 3): VII, *Westliches Mittelmeergebiet und Britische Inseln*, Cologne and Vienna: Böhlau Verlag, 217–32.

Conclusion, in *Man, settlement and urbanism* (proceedings of a meeting of the Research Seminar in

Archaeology and Related Subjects held at the Institute of Archaeology, London University), ed. P. J. Ucko, R. Tringham and G. W. Dimbleby, London: G. Duckworth, 947–53.

ඉන්දියාවේ පෙරඉතිහාසය (first Sinhalese edition of *Prehistoric India*), Department of Educational Publication of Ceylon.

Vorgeschichte Europas vom Nomadentum zur Hochkultur (first German edition of *Ancient Europe*), Munich: Kindler.

Dalladies, *Current Archaeology* 34, 295–7.

Excavation of the Dalladies long barrow, Fettercairn, Kincardineshire, *Proc. Soc. Ant. Scot.* CIV, 23–47.

A note on climatic deterioration in the first millennium B.C. in Britain, *Scottish Archaeol. Forum* 4, 109–13.

1973

Ancient Europe from the beginning of agriculture to classical antiquity: a survey (reissued in paperback), Edinburgh: University Press.

Contributed to the discussion on Grafton Elliot Smith: Egypt and diffusionism at the symposium *The concepts of evolution* (Symposia of the Zoological Society of London, no. 33), ed. S. Zuckerman, London, Academic Press for the Zoological Society of London, 439–41.

Section dealing with the periods from the Paleolithic and Mesolithic to the final phase of bronze technology, ending *c.* 500 BC, in *A history of Wiltshire* (The Victoria History of the Counties of England), vol. I, part 2, ed. Elizabeth Critall, Oxford University Press for the University of London Institute of Historical Research, 281–407.

Problems in the interpretation of chambered tombs, in *Megalithic graves and ritual: papers presented at the III Atlantic Colloquium Moesgård 1969* (Jutland Archaeological Society Publications XI), Copenhagen, ed. Glyn Daniel and Poul Kjærum, 9–15.

The Dalladies long barrow: N.E. Scotland, *Antiquity* XLVII, 32–6.

A saint in a stone circle, *Antiquity* XLVII, 292–3.

1974

Stuart Piggott was Consultant for Duncan Norton-Taylor, *The Celts* ('The Emergence of Man'), New York: Time – Life Books.

The Druids (reissued in paperback), Harmondsworth: Penguin Books.

Edited (with Glyn Daniel and Charles McBurney) *France before the Romans*, London: Thames and Hudson. To this S.P. and G.E.D. contributed preface, 8, and summary and conclusions, 220–3.

Preface (with D. G. Kendall) and concluding remarks of part II: Ancient astronomy: unwritten evidence, in *The place of astronomy in the ancient world* (Joint Symposium of the Royal Society and the British Academy, organized by D. G. Kendall, S. Piggott, D. G. King-Hele and I. E. S. Edwards), ed. F. R. Hodson, Oxford University Press for the British Academy, 3 and 275–6. Also published in paperback by the Royal Society in series *Philosophical Transactions A* CCLXXVI, no. 1257.

Edited and wrote introductions for *Sale catalogues of libraries of eminent persons. 10. Antiquaries* (gen. ed. A. N. L. Munby), London: Mansell with Sotheby Parke Bernet Pubs.

David Jones and the past of man, *Agenda* XI, no. 4-XII, no. 1 (Autumn–Winter 1973–4; David Jones special issue), 60–3.

Chariots in the Caucasus and in China, *Antiquity* XLVIII, 16–24.

William Stukeley: doctor, divine and antiquary, in *British Medical Journ.* 3, 725–7.

Innovation and tradition in British prehistory, *Trans. Archit. and Archaeol. Soc. Durham and Northumb.* NS III, 1–12 (The Birley Lectures).

The origins of the English county archaeological societies in *Trans. Birmingham and Warwicks. Archaeological Society* LXXXVI, 1–15.

1975

The Druids (new enlarged edition), London: Thames and Hudson.

Photographic Acknowledgments

LILI KAELAS	Antikvarisk-Topografiska Arkivet, 1 (photo Lars Bergström, by permission of the Swedish Defence Staff), 2 (photo M. Lagergren); Lars Bergström, 9; Geographical Survey Office, 8 (by permission of the Swedish Defence Staff); Gothenburg Archaeological Museum, 4, 5 (photo E. Lindälv), 6 (photo M. Djurfeldt), 7 (photo S. Hallgren); Kalmar County Museum, 10–13 (photos K. Pettersson); Regional Director, County of Västmanland, 3.
SETON LLOYD	Visual Publications, 2.
OLE KLINDT-JENSEN	Ulrik Møhl, 2; National Museum, Denmark, 1.
PAUL JOHNSTONE	Valerie Fenwick, 7; David Goddard, 9; Instituut voor Prae- en Protohistorie, Amsterdam, 6; Paul Johnstone, 10.
HERMANN BEHRENS	Landesmuseum für Vorgeschichte, Halle (Saale), 2–6.
MARIJA GIMBUTAS	Archaeological Museum, Plovdiv, 30 (photo K. Kónya); Archaeological Museum, Stara Zagora, 3 (photo K. Kónya); National Museum, Belgrade, 9 (photo M. Djordjević); Zemaljski Muzej, Sarajevo, 8 (photo K. Kónya).
P.J.R. MODDERMAN	P. Glazema, 1; Römisch-Germanisches Kommision, Frankfurt-am-Main (photo Dr F. Schubert), 3; Institut voor Prehistorie, Leiden (photo P.J. Boogerd), 2.
PIERRE-ROLAND GIOT	Laboratoire d'Anthropologie, Préhistoire, Protohistoire et Quaternaire Armoricains, University of Rennes, 1.
R.J.C. ATKINSON	Northamptonshire Libraries, Dryden Collection, 2,3.
MICHAEL J. O'KELLY	Michael J. O'Kelly, 1–3.
DAVID AND FRANCESCA RIDGWAY	Giorgio Buchner, 1b.
ANTONIO ARRIBAS	Department of Prehistory, University of Granada, 2,4.
OTTO-HERMAN FREY	Soprintendenza alle Antichità delle Venezie-Padova, Archivo Fotografico, 1,2.
S.J. DE LAET	ACL, Brussels, 5; Institut Belge d'Information et de Documentation, 4; M.E. Mariën, 2; Musée d'Histoire et d'Art, Luxembourg, 3 (photo J.E. Muller).
D.F. ALLEN	Bibliothèque Municipale, Grenoble, 2:3; Bibliothèque Nationale, Paris, 2:2; Musée des Antiquités Nationales, St-Germain-en-Laye, 2:1; Musée d'Avenches, Vaud, 2:5 (photo R. Bersier, Freiburg); Musée Historique Lorrain, Nancy (in E. Espérandieu, *Recueil général...*, Paris 1915), 1; National Museum of Archaeology, Sofia, 2:4.
KONRAD JAŻDŻEWSKI	Tadeusz Karpinski, 64; Stanisław Madajski, 63.
V.M. MASSON	Institute of Archaeology, Leningrad, 1–7, 10,11
K.R. MAXWELL-HYSLOP	P. Amiet, 3:1, 3:2, 5; British Museum, 2:1, 2:2, 4, 6; Hirmer Fotoarchiv, 8, 11, 12, 17; N.K. Sandars, 15.
JOSEPH NEEDHAM	Cambridge University Press, 1,2,5.
IGNACIO BERNAL	Lorenzío Gamio, 8–11; Andy Seuffert, 2–7.
GORDON R. WILLEY	Peabody Museum, Harvard University, 1–4.